SECOND EDITION

VICTIMOLOGY
Theories and Applications

ANN WOLBERT BURGESS

CHERYL REGEHR

ALBERT R. ROBERTS

JONES & BARTLETT
LEARNING

World Headquarters
Jones & Bartlett Learning
5 Wall Street
Burlington, MA 01803
978-443-5000
info@jblearning.com
www.jblearning.com

Jones & Bartlett Learning books and products are available through most bookstores and online booksellers. To contact Jones & Bartlett Learning directly, call 800-832-0034, fax 978-443-8000, or visit our website, www.jblearning.com.

Substantial discounts on bulk quantities of Jones & Bartlett Learning publications are available to corporations, professional associations, and other qualified organizations. For details and specific discount information, contact the special sales department at Jones & Bartlett Learning via the above contact information or send an email to specialsales@jblearning.com.

Victimology: Theories and Applications, Second Edition is an independent publication and has not been authorized, sponsored, or otherwise approved by the owners of the trademarks or service marks referenced in this product.

Some images in this book feature models. These models do not necessarily endorse, represent, or participate in the activities represented in the images.

This publication is designed to provide accurate and authoritative information in regard to the Subject Matter covered. It is sold with the understanding that the publisher is not engaged in rendering legal, accounting, or other professional service. If legal advice or other expert assistance is required, the service of a competent professional person should be sought.

Production Credits
Publisher: Cathleen Sether
Acquisitions Editor: Sean Connelly
Editorial Assistant: Caitlin Murphy
Production Manager: Tracey McCrea
Marketing Manager: Lindsay White
Manufacturing and Inventory Control Supervisor: Amy Bacus
Composition: DiacriTech
Cover Design: Kristin E. Parker
Rights & Photo Research Associate: Lauren Miller
Rights & Photo Research Assistant: Ashley Dos Santos
Cover Image: © photo-mania/ShutterStock, Inc.
Printing and Binding: Edwards Brothers Malloy
Cover Printing: Edwards Brothers Malloy

To order this product, use ISBN: 978-1-4496-8493-8

Library of Congress Cataloging-in-Publication Data
Burgess, Ann Wolbert.
 Victimology : theories and applications / Ann Wolbert Burgess, Cheryl Regehr, Albert R. Roberts.—2nd ed.
  p. cm.
 Includes bibliographical references and index.
 ISBN 978-1-4496-6533-3 (pbk.)
 1. Victims of crimes. I. Regehr, Cheryl. II. Roberts, Albert R. III. Title.
 HV6250.25.B87 2013
 362.88—dc23

                                                     2012011501

6048

Printed in the United States of America
17 16 15 14   10 9 8 7 6 5 4

Brief Contents

Contents

Preface

In the 19th century and early part of the 20th century, few scholars discussed or wrote about the victim's role in a criminal situation. It was not until the 1940s that interest in the victim developed. Von Hentig's paper titled "Remarks on the Interaction of Perpetrator and his Victim" (1941) and his book *The Criminal and his Victim* (1948); Mendelsohn's paper "New Bio-Psycho-Social Horizons: Victimology" (1947); and Ellenberger's study on the psychological relationship between the criminal and his victim (1954) brought clear scholarly focus to the plight of the victim.

The last quarter of the 20th century brought even more focus to the victim. The First International Symposium on Victimology held in Jerusalem in 1973 gave the discipline of victimology international recognition as a distinct focus separate from the discipline of criminology. The scholarly papers presented at the symposium were divided

into five volumes that aimed to provide new data, theoretical inputs, and analyses to encourage the building of ideas and the development of intellectual dialogues in the field of victimology. In particular, the volumes sought to contribute to a discourse within the international community of scholars and to bring together scholars whose paths might not easily cross, despite their common interest.

At the opening ceremony of the symposium, Professor Israel Drapkin, chairman of the Organizing Committee, identified five purposes of the meeting:

To reach agreement on the scope of victimology.

- To establish a valid typology of victims as an indispensable tool for future developments.
- To analyze the role of the victim, both in juridical and judicial settings, to improve the current situation.

- To analyze the offender–victim relationship, particularly with regard to the main categories of criminal offense.
- To develop strategies to improve society's reaction toward victims, be it by means of compensation, insurance, prevention, or treatment.

Although the science of victimology has expanded over the decades, it is upon this early scholarly and research foundation that this textbook on victimology has been conceptualized. This textbook provides an overview of issues related to people who become victims of a wide variety of crimes. At times, these crimes are specific to particular populations, such as children, the elderly, women, or individuals and groups of a specific race or religion. At times, these crimes are more general in who is targeted, such as in the case of Internet crime. We have focused on the incidence of each type of victimization, the impact of the crime on victims, the motivation of the perpetrator, strategies for intervention, laws that define the nature of the crime, and legal attempts to punish offenders and protect victims and society at large.

The second edition of the text includes chapter cases for discussion and expands the traditional academic concepts and theories of victimology to include an applied component for those students who will assess and/or treat victims or offenders. The text emphasizes data from North America regarding the scope of the problem, measurement of victimization, the typologies of victims and offenders, victim impact statements, policies, services, and future research areas. This text is written for students whose work or careers will bring them into contact with victims, offenders, and/or the justice system.

Acknowledgments

The authors would like to thank Stefan Treffers for his research additions to the second edition and the following for their contributions to the 1st edition of *Victimology: Theories and Applications*:

Paul Thomas Clements
Drexel University

Dr. Clements is an associate clinical professor at the College of Nursing and Health Sciences at Drexel University, where one of his online courses for Drexel's forensic health certificate is Victimology for Health Professionals. Dr. Clements has been a psychiatric forensic specialist for more than 15 years, specializing in intrapsychic sequela and behavioral manifestations following exposure to interpersonal violence, crime, and sudden traumatic death.

Kathleen P. Brown
University of Pennsylvania

Dr. Brown is a practice associate professor and nurse practitioner in women's health at the School of Nursing at the University of Pennsylvania. She is director of the Sexual Assault Nurse Examiner Program and coordinates the forensic science courses. Educated at the University of Pennsylvania, Dr. Brown's clinical work and research focus on victims of sexual assault. She has published her research on domestic violence, forensic interview, and evidence collection.

Mary Ellen O'Toole
Supervisory Special Agent, FBI (retired)
Behavioral Analysis Unit

Dr. O'Toole was a special agent for the FBI for 27 years, with the last 13 as one of the FBI's senior behavioral profilers, assigned to the Behavioral Analysis Serial Killer Unit at the FBI Academy.

She consults internationally on a wide range of cases and specializes in the interpretation of violent crime scenes and offender behavior through the lens of the Psychopathic Personality Construct. She has multiple publications on crime scene analysis, psychopathy, and stalking. She was the FBI's primary researcher and author of *The School Shooter: A Threat Assessment Perspective.*

In addition, the authors would like to thank the following for their review of *Victimology: Theories and Applications:*

Ashley G. Blackburn, University of Houston-Downtown
Audrelee Dallam-Murphy, Westfield State College
Kathleen A. Fox, Sam Houston State University
Ray Greenwood, Retired Virginia Beach Police Captain, and Old Dominion University
J. Greg Gullion, Texas Wesleyan University
Susan C. Herrick, West Liberty University
Philip D. Holley, Southwestern Oklahoma State University
Liz Marie Marciniak, University of Pittsburgh at Greensburg
Raisa Martinez, Miami Dade College
Nancy J. Merritt, Front Range Community College Larimer Campus

About the Authors

Ann Wolbert Burgess, RN, DNSc, FAAN, is professor of Psychiatric Mental Health Nursing at Boston College Connell School of Nursing. She received her bachelors and doctoral degrees from Boston University and her masters degree from the University of Maryland. She teaches five forensic courses: Victimology, Forensic Mental Health, Forensic Science, Forensic Science Lab, and Case Studies in Forensics. She, with Lynda Lytle Holmstrom (Boston College), cofounded one of the first hospital-based crisis intervention programs for rape victims at Boston City Hospital. She is licensed as an advanced practice nurse in Pennsylvania and Massachusetts, where she also maintains prescriptive authority. Dr. Burgess has testified as an expert witness in 29 states and has received grants and published articles on the topics of rape trauma, child sexual abuse, child pornography, serial offenders, crime classification, posttraumatic stress, elder abuse, and mental disorders.

Dr. Burgess served as chair of the first Advisory Council to the National Center for the Prevention and Control of Rape of the National Institute of Mental Health, was a member of the 1984 US Attorney General's Task Force on Family Violence, served on the planning committee for the 1985 Surgeon General's Symposium on Violence, and served on the National Institute of Health National Advisory Council for the Center for Nursing Research from 1986 to 1988. She was a member of the 1990 Adolescent Health Advisory Panel to the Congress of the United States Office of Technology Assessment and Chair of the National Institutes of Health AIDS and Related Research Study Section (ARRR 6) from 1992 to 1994. She was elected to the National Academy of Sciences Institute of Medicine in October 1994 and chaired the 1996 National Research Council's Task Force on Violence Against Women. She was inducted into the Sigma Theta Tau Her current research is on patterns of murder-suicide and fetal abduction by cesarean section.

Cheryl Regehr, MSW, PhD, is the Vice-Provost of Academic Programs for the University of Toronto. Former Dean of the Factor-Inwentash Faculty of Social Work, she is a Professor in the Faculty of Social Work, and has cross-appointments to the Faculty of Law and the Institute for Medical Sciences at University of Toronto.

Dr. Regehr's practice background includes over 20 years of direct service in forensic social work and emergency mental health and in the administration of mental health programs, specializing in civil litigation and criminal court assessments of trauma victims and violent offenders, and organizationally based trauma interventions. She was the director of the Crisis Response Team at Pearson International Airport, served on the mental health advisory for the Department of National Defence and Veteran's Affairs Canada, and currently is a member of the Board of Trustees for the University Health Network. In 2004, she was awarded the Amicus Award by the American Academy of Psychiatry and the Law for her contributions to forensic mental health.

Dr. Regehr's program of research has the following two intersecting components: 1) competency in professional practice; and 2) examining aspects of recovery from trauma in such diverse populations as victims of rape, firefighters, police and paramedics witnessing traumatic events, and child welfare workers. Her current funded research includes examining the factors influencing clinical decision making in social workers and professional competency. Her publications address measurement of competency, trauma, and the interface between the law and mental health.

Albert R. Roberts, PhD, DACFE, was professor of Criminal Justice (former chairperson) and director of Faculty and Curriculum Development, Administration of Justice and Interdisciplinary Criminal Justice Programs in the Faculty of Arts and Sciences, Livingston College Campus at Rutgers, New Jersey in Piscataway. He has been a tenured professor at Rutgers since 1989, prior to which he taught at Indiana University, Seton Hall University, Brooklyn College of City University of New York, and the University of New Haven. Professor Roberts had approximately 30 years of full-time university teaching experience, including 15 years of administrative experience. He received an MA degree in sociology from the Graduate Faculty of Long Island University in 1967 and a DSW in 1978 (which became a PhD in 1981) from the School of Social Work and Community Planning at the University of Maryland in Baltimore. Professor Roberts was a member of the Board of Scientific and Professional Advisors and a board certified expert in traumatic stress for the American Academy of Experts in Traumatic Stress. He was also a diplomat of the American College of Forensic Examiners and a lifetime member of the Academy of Criminal Justice Sciences.

Tribute

I t is with deep regret and profound admiration that we remember Professor Albert R. Roberts, who died in his home in June 2008 during the writing of the 1st edition of this text. Professor Roberts was an academic of tremendous breadth who had a profound influence on the fields of social work, criminal justice, and mental health. Al Roberts was a prolific scholar as the author of dozens of books and hundreds of journal articles. Through his editorial leadership in books and journals, Al Roberts fostered interactions and intellectual exchange among academics, policy makers, and practitioners across different fields of study—pushing each to consider the intersections between scholarship and practice in their work. As a revered scholar, Professor Roberts' influence will continue long into the future. His energy, enthusiasm, and excitement in all scholarly activities will be greatly missed.

Crime and Victimology

CHAPTER 1

■ Objectives

- To define victimology and criminology
- To describe victims of violence and trends in crime
- To outline the costs and consequences of criminal victimization
- To describe the advances in forensics in solving crimes

■ Key Terms

Cold case
Costs of victimization
Crime victim
Crime victims' rights
Criminology
Forensic victimology
National Crime Victimization Survey (NCVS)
Victimology

CASE

The November 2, 2007, murder of British exchange student Meredith Kercher in Perugia, Italy, set into motion an investigation that resulted in the arrest, trial, and conviction of her roommate, Amanda Knox, an exchange student from Seattle, Washington. Knox's boyfriend, university student Raffaele Sollecito, and a neighbor of Kercher, Rudy Guede, described as a drifter, were also convicted for the murder. The prosecution's theory was that the victim was forced to participate in a sex game, fueled by drugs, which spiraled out of control. Testimony focused on telephone records, text messages, DNA evidence, bloody fingerprints, and shoe prints. However, 23-year-old Knox, who served 4 years of a 26-year prison sentence, consistently denied any participation in the murder. An appeal of Knox's conviction began in 2010. Independent experts claimed that the collection of evidence fell below international standards and that because of the errors made by police during the original investigation, the evidence against Knox and Sollecito should not be admissible (Vargas & Natanson, 2011).

This case raises four important points with respect to the field of victimology. First, who are the victims? Clearly, Meredith Kercher was a rape-murder victim. But what about the status of Knox and Sollecito, who denied the prosecution's theory and have steadfastly maintained their innocence? Second, forensic evidence, if present, is critical to link a person to the crime. Does the strength of this evidence justify conviction? Third, this case involves the trial of an American citizen in a foreign jurisdiction. How might differences in international justice procedures and American law procedures influence the case? Fourth, in addition to Kercher as the primary victim in this case, were Knox and Sollecito also victims of the system?

The lack of physical evidence, specifically DNA, to implicate Knox and Sollecito in the murder was not the only problem with this case. There were complaints of incompetent police work and investigators not familiar with working homicide cases. Knox and Sollecito both asked for attorneys but were denied counsel. There was a failure to establish motive or intent for the rape and murder. Knox could barely speak or read Italian. She was interrogated 41 hours over 4 days, did not realize that she was a suspect in the case, was pressured into signing a confession that wrongly accused her employer, and held a naive belief in the Italian justice system.

Both she and Sollecito continued to plead their innocence despite serving 4 years in prison. The appeal process for both Knox and Sollecito was favorable, and they were acquitted of the murder charges. The defense said the evidence unequivocally pointed to a single attacker, Guede, a drug dealer who fled to Germany after the murder. He was arrested there, brought back to Italy, and tried and convicted of the killing. His conviction was upheld on appeal, and he remains in prison.

After the acquittal Amanda Knox returned to her home in Seattle, Washington. The case, one of the most-watched trials in Italy, tapped into an intense debate over Italy's justice system ("As Amanda Knox Heads Home," 2011). See **Figure 1-1**.

■ Introduction

The unsettling reality regarding crime in the world today is that it is widespread, very often violent in nature, and completely disregards all boundaries. There is no home, no community, and no region in North America that can consider itself "safe" from the risk of criminal assault. With recent estimates of the number of crime victims, including violent, personal, and property crime, in the United States reaching as high as 22 million, it behooves all of us, both individually and collectively, to support emerging

FIGURE 1-1 The Amanda Knox Case
© ANTONIO CALANNI/AP Photos

efforts aimed at two distinct but related areas: crime prevention and crime victim assistance. To be sure, averting criminal behavior altogether is the more preferable of the two. Given the improbability of accomplishing this in the immediate future, however, it becomes all the more urgent to be prepared to assist those who are victimized. **Table 1-1** illustrates the numbers of victims of violent crime for the years 2008 and 2009.

Unprecedented numbers of victims are turning to victim assistance programs, mental health centers, domestic violence shelters, and victim compensation programs. Research, as well as experience, has shown

TABLE 1-1 Victims of Violent Crime in the United States, 2008 and 2009

	2008	% of total population	% of violent crime	2009	% of total population	% of violent crime	% change 2009 from 2008
Total population	304,374,846			307,006,550			0.86%
Violent crime	1,392,629	0.46%	100.00%	1,318,398	0.43%	100.00%	−5.33%
Murder and nonnegligent manslaughter	16,442	0.01%	1.18%	15,241	0.00%	1.16%	−7.30%
Forcible rape	90,479	0.03%	6.50%	88,097	0.03%	6.68%	−2.63%
Robbery	443,574	0.15%	31.85%	408,217	0.13%	30.96%	−7.97%
Aggravated assault	842,134	0.28%	60.47%	806,843	0.26%	61.20%	−4.19%

Data from Federal Bureau of Investigation (FBI), 2011. Victim Rights. Retrieved from http://www.fbi.gov/stats-services/victim_assistance/victim_rights.

that these individuals frequently suffer from significant emotional pain and trauma, physical injuries, and/or financial loss, whereas "secondary victims"—relatives and close friends of victims—also endure both mental anguish and economic hardship. Emergency medical care, mental health counseling, social services, financial aid, victim compensation, and law enforcement protection must be readily available for those injured as a result of either violent or property-related offenses. Unfortunately, despite remarkable advances made in terms of our understanding of the nature of crime victimization and our awareness of the need for victim support, to date most victim assistance policies and programs need to be expanded and updated. This chapter describes the victims of crime, the cost of victimization, trends in crime, and the application of forensic victimology in solving cases.

■ Discipline of Victimology

Criminology, defined as the scientific study of non-legal aspects of crime, arose in the 18th century out of concerns about the use of what was perceived to be cruel and arbitrary means of justice. Through the use of scientific methods, criminologists sought to refocus approaches to crime on prevention of criminal activity and reformation of offenders. Edwin H. Sutherland (1947) defined the objectives of criminology as the development of general and verified principles and knowledge regarding the process of law, crime, and treatment of prevention. The etiology of crime and the characteristics of the criminal became the focus of criminological study. Drawing on diverse fields such as sociology, psychology, economics, human geography and statistics, present day criminologists use a variety of research and analysis methods to better understand crime and criminal activity (DeFlem, 2006, Merriam-Websiter Dictionary, 2012).

In contrast, victimology is the study of the victim, including the offender and society. Victimology is a social-structural way of viewing crime and the law and the criminal and the victim. Victimology, characterized by Fattah (2000) as a young and promising discipline and old as humanity itself, did not emerge as a scientific subject for study until after World War II. In the 1940s and 1950s, based on the research of Benjamin Mendelsohn and Hans Von Hentig (1948), victimology began to emerge as a distinct and viable field of study. Historically, victimology was a branch of criminology, and as such the early criminologists and victimologists focused their analyses and writings on typologies of crime victims, assessing the ways in which a victim may contribute, knowingly or unknowingly, to his or her own victimization. Von Hentig's work (1946) identified categories of individuals who were to be prone to becoming crime victims. Marvin Wolfgang's doctoral dissertation at the University of Pennsylvania in the 1950s built on Von Hentig's theories and led to Dr. Wolfgang's research conclusions that the majority of criminal homicides in the city of Philadelphia were victim precipitated because the victim either provoked the perpetrator or the victim was motivated by an unconscious desire to commit suicide (Wolfgang, 1958). As one might expect, such findings inevitably resulted in a gross misunderstanding of the plight of crime victims and categorical dismissal of the validity of their rights and needs.

Because the victim component of crime represented a serious theoretical void, a struggle developed as to the independence of this new discipline in relationship to the established field of criminology. Many, including Fattah, continue to view victimology as an integral part of criminology, whereas others, especially those who work directly with victims, see the field as separate and independent. Fattah (2000) argues that the study of crime victims and of criminal victimization has the potential of reshaping criminology and that it may be the paradigm shift that criminology needs. Recent developments in victimology have undergone a transformation through major achievements in the applied field. This remarkable phase in the evolution of victimology, continues Fattah, was one of consolidation, data gathering, theory formulation, victim legislation, and sustained efforts to improve victims' lot and alleviate their plight.

Advances in the various theoretical victimology models explain the variations in victimization risks, the clustering of victimization in certain areas and certain groups, and the phenomenon of repeat victimization. Many countries have passed victim bill of rights legislation, including the adoption of the UN Declaration of Basic Principles of Justice for Victims of Crime and Abuse of Power by the General Assembly of the United Nations (1985). There has been the creation of state compensation to victims of violent crime, the reemergence of restitution by offender, and the establishment and proliferation of victim–offender mediation programs. Victim therapy has become an acknowledged way of dealing with the traumatic aftereffects of victimization.

Fattah predicts the future developments in victimology will include an emphasis on scientific research, particularly qualitative research, and that the need for advocacy, partisanship, and therapy will decline. In its place will rise the restorative justice paradigm with victimology developing into a truly scientific discipline with a truly humanistic practice (Fattah, 2000).

■ Victims of Violence

People are fascinated by crime. Crimes, and the legal proceedings that surround them, excite the public's interest for a variety of reasons: some, according to Fletcher (1988), because they involve celebrities, some because they are gruesome, some because they raise important social or legal issues, some because of their racial character, some because of the bizarre behavior of the parties, and some because of the plight of the victim. Cases that have received wide media attention for specific reasons include murdered children, professionals as victims, and victims of workplace violence.

Murdered Children

In 1996 almost 2,000 children were murdered in the United States, but none of those murders fascinated the American public and attracted the mass media like that of JonBenét Ramsey, a child beauty pageant contestant. Although the spotlight has dimmed over the years, the case has been reopened, and public bias regarding the parents as suspects, similar to the Caylee Anthony case, remains.

In the early morning of December 26, 1996, in Boulder, Colorado, Patsy Ramsey reportedly found a ransom note on the family's back staircase demanding $118,000 for her 6-year-old daughter, JonBenét. The Ramseys quickly realized that JonBenét was missing from her bedroom and called 911. Later that day John Ramsey discovered JonBenét's body covered in her special white blanket in the wine cellar. She had been strangled with a garrote made from a piece of cord and the broken handle of a paintbrush; to add to the horror there was evidence of sexual assault. The official cause of death was asphyxiation due to strangulation associated with blunt force head trauma.

The early investigation focused on the three-page ransom note, and police took hair and blood samples from members of the Ramsey family. The district attorney's office strongly supported a family member theory to the murder, whereas a private investigator, Lou Smit, and Federal Bureau of Investigation (FBI) profiler, John Douglas, supported an intruder theory. A Boulder County grand jury was convened on September 16, 1998, and for a year heard testimony, forensic evidence, analysis of handwriting, DNA evidence, and hair and fiber evidence. No indictment was returned by the grand jury because of conflicting testimonies and theories.

In 2002 the Ramseys filed and defended a series of libel lawsuits against media outlets who tried to implicate them in their daughter's murder.

In 2003 an Atlanta federal judge dismissed a civil lawsuit against John and Patsy Ramsey, stating there was no evidence showing the parents killed JonBenét and abundant evidence that an intruder killed the child. The judge criticized the police and the FBI for creating a media campaign designed to make the family look guilty. That same year, Mary Keenan, recently elected district attorney, agreed to look at all the evidence in the case, including foreign, male DNA that was found in JonBenét's underwear that had never been tested. In 2006 Patsy Ramsey died of a recurrence of ovarian cancer. Nevertheless, in February 2010 the Boulder Police Department took the case back from the district attorney to reopen the investigation

Over the years several theories have been raised regarding the death of JonBenét. One theory suggests Patsy Ramsey injured her child in a burst of anger over bedwetting, proceeded to kill her either in rage or to cover up the original injury and wrote the ransom note. Another speculated that John Ramsey had been sexually assaulting his daughter and murdered her as a cover. Third, the brother of JonBenét was suspected of being jealous of his sister and murdered her. A final theory suggested that an intruder sexually assaulted and murdered the child. To complicate the family murder theory, DNA evidence did not match the mother, father, or brother and failed to find a match in the FBI CODIS database. This cold case remains focused on a forensic evidence match to JonBenét Ramsey or the crime scene and/or confession from the offender. See **Figure 1-2**.

FIGURE 1-2 JonBenét Ramsey
© ZUMA Wire Service/Alamy Images

Professionals as Victims

Dr. George Tiller, 67, was one of the few doctors who performed late-term abortions, raising concerns among citizens in Wichita, Kansas, that Dr. Tiller was contravening state law, public morality, and religious values. For two decades groups petitioned outside the offices of George Tiller, people signed petitions, and individuals made death threats against him. On May 31, 2009, Tiller was shot in the head at point-blank range (despite wearing a bulletproof vest) by Scott Roeder, an antiabortion activist. Tiller was killed during a Sunday morning service at the Reformation Lutheran Church in Wichita, where he was serving as an usher. Tiller's killing has been labeled an act of domestic terrorism and an assassination.

Scott Roeder took the stand in his own defense on January 28, 2010. He admitted to killing Dr. Tiller, described his views on abortion, and defended his act as an attempt to save unborn children. On January 29, 2010, the jury returned a verdict of guilty on all three charges (one count of first-degree murder and two counts of aggravated assault) after less than 40 minutes of deliberation. On April 1, 2010, in Wichita, Kansas, Sedgwick County District Judge Warren Wilbert sentenced Roeder to the maximum time allowed in Kansas, known as a "hard 50," meaning he has no possibility of parole for 50 years.

Assassinations have been part of human history from early times. Victims who are killed for political reasons are sometimes aware of their danger, as in the case of Dr. Tiller, or sometimes totally unaware, as in the case of President Abraham Lincoln. In either case, such murders trigger great public outcry for the victims, their families, and their communities.

Victims of Revenge

On Christmas Eve 2008 Bruce Jeffrey Pardo, the newly divorced husband of their daughter, arrived at the home of Joseph and Alicia Ortega dressed in a Santa Claus suit. He opened fire and killed nine people inside the house, including the elder Ortegas, his ex-wife Sylvia, three of their (Bruce and Sylvia) children, two daughters-in-law, and a teenager working at a computer. Pardo held no criminal record and had no history of violence. Police speculate the motive of the attack was related to marital problems. Pardo's wife of 1 year had settled for divorce in the prior week. He had also lost his job in July. Pardo owed her $10,000 as part of the divorce settlement, according to court documents, which detailed a bitter split. He also lost a dog he doted on and did not get back a valuable wedding ring.

Pardo complained in a court declaration that Sylvia Pardo was living with her parents, not paying rent, and had spent lavishly on a luxury car, gambling trips to Las Vegas, meals at fine restaurants, massages, and golf lessons. There is some speculation that the divorce may have been caused by Pardo concealing a child from a previous relationship. This child had been severely injured and disabled in a swimming pool accident. It was also revealed that Pardo planned to kill his own mother because she apparently displayed sympathy for Sylvia Pardo during the divorce.

Although there was no history of domestic conflict in divorce papers, this mass murder might have had some warning signs, such as the rage and anger toward the in-laws and resentment of financial expenditures and revenge toward the distribution of marital property. Clearly, the victims were taken by surprise in a blitz attack and had no time to defend themselves.

Victims of Workplace Violence

"We're now just trying to figure out who's shot, who's not accounted for," said Brett Hollander, the director of marketing at Hartford Distributors (CBSNews, 2010). This chilling statement was quoted in one of the initial press reports from the summer of 2010 shooting in a beer distribution company in Manchester, Connecticut. Approximately 60 people were in the warehouse at the 7 a.m. shift change when Omar Thornton fatally shot eight fellow employees and then himself. The shooting occurred minutes after Thornton was confronted by management with video evidence that he was stealing beer. He was given the option of quitting the job or being fired. Thornton did not deny the allegations, signed the release papers, and then withdrew a gun from his lunch box. Witnesses on the scene described Thornton as cool and calm as he proceeded to shoot those around him in the head.

During the past decade newspapers rarely have missed an opportunity to report the latest murder, robbery, physical or sexual assault, or stalking incident occurring in the workplace. Of these incidents, the ones that receive the most attention are, not surprisingly, workplace shootings. Frequently, violent episodes in the workplace can be prevented. With this in mind, some companies have begun to provide employee assistance programs, stress management and anger control workshops, and fitness and exercise facilities. In addition, corporate security and human resource personnel often receive training in crisis intervention, psychological risk assessments, and critical incident debriefing. No office, business, or institution is immune to the threat of violence, and careful planning and program development are crucial to handling threats appropriately and containing and preventing future violent incidents.

■ Who Is a Victim?

The word "victim" is derived from the Latin *victima* and originally contained the concept of sacrifice. The sense of an offering to the temple is implied in the Bible (Leviticus 1.2, 1.14, 2.1, etc). The word "victim" is not found in the Bible, but the concept of a person suffering from acts committed by an aggressor is.

A case of murder is found in the Bible involving Adam and Eve's first-born and second-born sons, Cain and Abel. Cain was described as "a tiller of the soil," and Abel was described as "a keeper of sheep." According to Judaic translations, both prepared a thanksgiving sacrifice, but God showed a preference for Abel's offering, whereupon, in a fit of jealousy, Cain slew his brother and became the first murderer in history. When confronted by God, Cain first lies by saying he does not know. He then says, "Am I my brother's keeper?," and to this God replies, "Your brother's blood cries out to Me from the ground!" (Genesis 4:9–10). Cain is banished from civilization, but first a sign is placed on him—not as a felon's brand ("the mark of Cain") but to protect him from roving hunters. The rabbis, while condemning Cain's sin, also saw him as a genuine penitent who was therefore not punished by death (Wigoder, 2002).

This biblical reference reflects several points. First, rivalry, envy, and anger provoked a violent attack. Second, the suffering of the victim (brother's blood cries out) is acknowledged. Third, Cain's denial of the act is countered by the forensic facts, and the heinous nature of the act (murder) is punished by exile.

In more contemporary times the term "victim" has been greatly expanded to imply a wide range of unfortunate circumstances, such as victims of war, or accidents, or financial scams, or identity theft. Each of these various meanings of the term "victim" reflects general use of language. Within scientific inquiry Mendelsohn (1976) suggests that the concept of victim may be viewed as containing four fundamental criteria:

1. *The nature of the determinant that causes the suffering.* The suffering may be physical, psychological, or both depending on the type of injurious act.

2. *The social character of the suffering.* This suffering originates in the victim and others' reaction to the event.

3. *The importance of the social factor.* The social implications of the injurious act can have a greater impact, sometimes, than the physical or psychological impact has.

4. *The origin of the inferiority complex.* This term, suggested by Mendelsohn, manifests itself as a feeling of submission that may be followed by a feeling of revolt. The victim generally attributes his or her injury to the culpability of another person.

A victim of a violent crime can be operationally defined as an individual who has been confronted, attacked, assaulted, or violated by a perceived predator, resulting in serious short-term, as well as long-term, physical and/or mental injuries to the crime victim. Crime victims suffer from illegal criminal acts and usually struggle with a number of medical, psychological, and financial problems caused by burglary, rape, theft, domestic violence, robbery, pickpocketing, carjacking, purse snatching, stalking, or attempted murder. In sharp contrast, victims of accidents; natural disasters such as hurricanes, tornadoes, or earthquakes; and diseases such as cancer, AIDS, or other social and public health problems are *not* harmed by illegal criminal acts. The **National Crime Victimization Survey (NCVS)** provides definitions of crimes resulting in victimization for the purposes of data collection and reporting. This information includes the specific type of crime experienced, the location of the incident, whether the incident was reported to police or other officials, the type and value of the property involved, and the identity and personal characteristics of the victim. **Table 1-2** provides a summary of crimes resulting in victimization.

There is no characteristic profile of a crime victim. Persons of all ages, races, ethnicities, and socioeconomic ranges are subject to criminal assault of one form or another. However, victimization statistics from the U.S. Bureau of Justice Statistics (2009) reveal that not all groups have an equal likelihood or probability of becoming a crime victim. Research indicates that young black males, 16 to 24 years of age and living in high-crime, urban areas, are the most likely to fall victim to crime due largely to factors such as lack of adequate housing, education, or employment. In sharp contrast, elderly white females who live in low-crime areas and generally do not venture out at night are the least likely to become victimized. Lifestyle, location, and race appear to be the primary predictors of who is most likely to become a victim of crime. Specifically, based on a review of the FBI's Uniform Crime Reports (2010a), African Americans and Latinos are much more likely than Whites to be assaulted, raped, or robbed.

Federal law both defines the term "victim" and outlines crime victims' rights. A **crime victim** refers to a person, organization, or business that has been directly harmed (physically, emotionally, or financially) as a result of the commission of an offense. In general, victims' rights apply after charges have been filed by a U.S. Attorney's office. Some individuals are viewed to not have the capacity to exercise their own rights. Such individuals include victims of crime who are under 18 years of age, incompetent, incapacitated, or deceased. In these cases the legal guardians of the crime victim or the representatives of the crime victim's estate, family members, or any other persons appointed as suitable by the court may assume the crime victim's rights. A person who is a defendant in the crime being investigated or prosecuted cannot act as a proxy for a victim.

TABLE 1-2 Crimes Resulting in Victimization

Type of Crime	Definition
Burglary	The unlawful or forcible entry or attempted entry of a structure with the intent to commit an offense therein. This crime usually, but not always, involves theft. It is a property crime.
Larceny	The theft or attempted theft of property or cash without using force or illegal entry. An alternate label for this crime is "theft." It is a property crime.
Personal crime	A criminal act affecting a specific person. Crimes against persons, as defined by NCVS, include rape, sexual assault, robbery, assault, and purse snatching/pocket picking. The victimization is personal either through the direct experience of force or threat of force or by theft directly from one's person.
Personal larceny	Purse snatching and pocket picking. Personal larceny involves the theft or attempted theft of property or cash directly from the victim by stealth but without force or threat of force. It is both a property crime and a personal crime.
Property crime	The illegal taking or damaging of property, including cash and personal belongings. Examples include burglary, theft, robbery, and vandalism. In many instances, the offender acts furtively, and the victim is often not present when the crime occurs.
Robbery	The taking of property or cash directly from a person by force or threat of force. Robbery is both a property crime and a violent crime.
Vandalism	The willful or malicious destroying, defacing, or damaging of property without the consent of the owner. It is a property crime.
Violent crime	Rape, sexual assault, robbery, and assault, including both attempted and completed crimes. The defining element is the use of force or threat of force. Violent crimes involve contact between the victim and the offender.

Data from National Crime Victimization Survey (NCVS) and the National Incident-Based Reporting System (NIBRS).

In the United States crime victims' rights (2004) refer to the eight rights included in Justice for All Act, Section 3771 of Title 18 of the U.S. Code, Crimes and Criminal Procedure:

- The right to be reasonably protected from the accused.
- The right to reasonable, accurate, and timely notice of any public court proceeding, or any parole proceeding, involving the crime or any release or escape of the accused.
- The right not to be excluded from any such public court proceeding, unless the court, after receiving clear and convincing evidence, determines that testimony by the victim would be materially altered if the victim heard other testimony at the proceeding.
- The right to be reasonably heard at any public proceeding in the district court involving release, plea, [or] sentencing, or any parole proceeding.

- The reasonable right to confer with the attorney for the government in the case.
- The right to full and timely restitution as provided in law.
- The right to proceedings free from unreasonable delay.
- The right to be treated with fairness and with respect for the victim's dignity and privacy.

For purposes of these rights and services victims are defined in specific ways in the federal law (FBI, 2011).

■ Trends in Crime

Among news reporters, historians, and criminologists who review and interpret these findings, there are predictable reactionary stances, including the alarmists, the skeptics, and the realists. Frequently, members of the press tend toward alarmism, singling out and sensationalizing specific instances within a 50-year span. Such instances include cases like that of Lorena Bobbit, who in 1993 cut off half of her husband's penis while he lay sleeping; or of Lyle and Erik Menendez, who in 1993 murdered their parents, or the 2006 arrest of three Duke lacrosse players for rape. Some historians fall into the skeptic category, where a 5- or 20-year cyclical decline (mostly down, with some brief spurts in specific years) in most crime categories is viewed as temporary because history sometimes repeats itself. The realists are many of the academic scholars and criminologists who can examine a 10- or 25-year trend analysis and with reasonable certainty predict that 10, 20, or 25 years of overall declines in crime rates are not temporary.

Common perceptions are that U.S. society is more violent than most societies, that it is more violent today than ever before, and that violence is increasing. The facts are more complex, however, and simple generalizations can be misleading (Reiss & Roth, 1993). Crime in the United States is a significant criminal justice and public health problem, and despite a declining crime rate during the past two decades, the serious nature of homicide, forcible rape, robbery, aggravated assault, domestic violence, burglary, larceny-theft, carjacking, and motor vehicle theft impacts millions of victims and their families each year. Despite this, using Uniform Crime Reporting data (FBI, 2010a), the United States experienced a 5.33% decrease in the number of violent crimes and a 2.8% decline in the number of property crimes in 2010 when compared to data from 2009. The report is based on information the FBI gathered from 13,007 law enforcement agencies that submitted 6 to 12 comparable months of data for both 2008 and 2009 (FBI, 2010b).

In another survey, the NCVS, violent and property crime rates in 2008 were at or near their lowest levels in over three decades (Rand, Lynch, & Cantor, 1997; Rand, 2009). The violent crime rate in 2008—19.3 victimizations per 1,000 persons age 12 or over—was statistically unchanged from the previous year's estimate of 20.7 per 1,000 persons. The property crime rate of 135 victimizations per 1,000 households was lower than the rate of 147 per 1,000 households in 2007. There was no statistical difference between the 2007 and 2008 crime rates for any crime of violence. Overall in 2008, U.S. residents experienced 1.3 million violent crimes (forcible rape, robbery, and aggravated assault) and 16.3 million property crimes (household burglary, theft, and motor vehicle theft) (Rand, 2009).

The FBI preliminary crime statistics for the year 2010 saw a decrease in the crime rate (FBI, 2010a, 2010c). **Figure 1-3** illustrates the drop in violent crime from 2006 to 2010, with overall violent crime figures, especially robbery and forcible rape, showing the most decrease.

Adults and young people alike are most commonly the victims of property crime. Eighty-two percent of all crimes against adults involve property. Among young people, 68% of all victimizations relate to property and 36% relate to violent crime (including robbery). The lower rate of property crime among young people does not reflect the fact that they

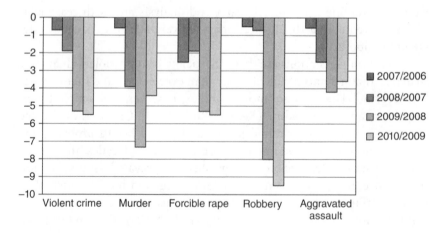

FIGURE 1-3 Percent Change in Violent Crimes for Consecutive Years—2006 to 2010

Data from Federal Bureau of Investigation (FBI). 2011. Victim Rights. http://www.fbi.gov/about-us/cjis/ucr/crime-in-the-u.s/2010/preliminary-annual-ucr-jan-dec-2010.

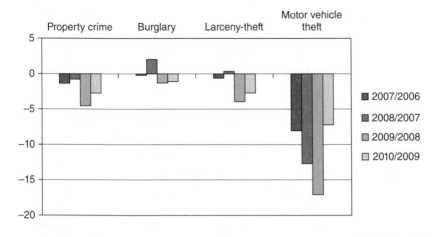

FIGURE 1-4 Percent Change in Property Crimes for Consecutive Years—2006 to 2010
Data from Federal Bureau of Investigation (FBI). 2011. Victim Rights. http://www.fbi.gov/about-us/cjis/ucr/crime-in-the-u.s/2010/preliminary-annual-ucr-jan-dec-2010.

are less likely to have something stolen but rather the fact that they are more likely to experience violent victimization (Hashima & Finkelhor, 1999). **Figure 1-4** illustrates the drop in property crime from 2006 to 2010, with the 2008/2009 showing the greatest decrease in motor vehicle theft, property crime, larceny-theft, and burglary.

Statistics Canada is Canada's central statistical office. In addition to conducting a census every 5 years, there are about 350 active surveys on other topics related to the population, economy, society, and culture. Similar to U.S. statistics, Statistics Canada, using data provided by police forces across the country, reported 2.1 million crimes in 2008, a drop of 5% from 2009. The Crime Severity Index, which tracks violent crime, also dropped to its lowest level since that index was created in 1998 (Statistics Canada, 2011).

■ Costs and Consequences of Crime

A 2-year multidisciplinary research effort, funded by the National Institute of Justice and published in 1996, estimated the costs and consequences of personal crime for Americans (Miller, Cohen, & Wiersema, 1996). Their report estimated annual direct tangible costs to crime victims of $105 billion in medical expenses, lost earnings, and public programs related to victim assistance. Pain, suffering, and reduced quality of life increased the cost to $450 billion annually (Miller et al., 1996). Anderson (1999) estimated the total annual cost of criminal behavior in the United States, arguing that past research typically focused on particular costs, regions, or crime categories. Anderson estimated the direct and indirect costs that extend over the expenses of the legal system to consider ancillary costs that had not yet been included into an overall formula for the cost of crime. These costs included victims', criminals', and prisoners' time; the fear of being victimized; and the cost of private deterrence. Anderson estimated the net annual burden of crime to exceed $1 trillion.

Canada has approximately one-tenth the population of the United States (Government of Canada, 2006). Zhang (2008) estimated the total (tangible) social and economic costs of *Criminal Code* offenses in Canada were approximately $31.4 billion. This amounted to a per capita cost of $943 per year. However, Zhang pointed out that this was likely to be a conservative estimate due to the unavailability of data in many areas. Despite best efforts to account for all the financial impacts of crime, only a partial picture of the true range of costs is ever available. The costs identified are borne by the criminal justice system, victims of crimes, and third parties in general (Zhang, 2008). For instance, it is estimated that the Canadian criminal justice system cost about $15.0 billion in 2008. This includes policing, courts, prosecution, legal aid, correctional services, and mental health review boards. Individual victims, however, paid an estimated $14.3 billion for crimes committed against them that same year. Their costs included medical attention, hospitalizations, lost wages, missed school days, and stolen/damaged property. Of the total costs, 47.0% represented lost wages and productivity and 42.9% lost or stolen property (Zhang, 2008). Indirect victims also bear costs due to grieving the loss of a loved one or caring for a victim. When all costs were taken into account, Zhang (2008) estimated total costs of crime for a 1-year period in Canada to be $99.6 billion.

A breakdown of the costs can be reviewed in three areas: health and medical costs, economic costs, and criminal justice costs.

Health Costs

Tangible losses consist of direct costs for damages, and injuries resulting from victimization include medical and mental health expenses. Physical means of violence to a victim include a person's body (hands, fists, feet), instruments such as firearms and knives, flammable liquids and explosives, poisons, and animals (such as attack dogs). Although insurance often covers partial or full restitution for such costs, victims can still be required to pay insurance deductibles and face higher premiums when renewing their insurance (Macmillan, 2002).

Physical injury can range from minor harm, such as bruises and lacerations, to serious harm, such as broken bones and need for hospitalization, to lethal injury and death. Some violent crimes leave no visible sign of injury. This is true in some rape cases where, contrary to popular opinion, there are no general body injuries or any pelvic or genital injuries.

Wallace and Roberson (2011) list four general classifications of physical injuries to victims. First, *immediate injuries* include cuts, contusions, and/or broken bones that generally heal fairly quickly and are not viewed as serious by the victim. Immediate injuries can take longer to heal in persons who are elderly, have existing disabilities, are taking certain medications, or have an immune disorder. For example, Larry was hit over the head and robbed of his wallet by four men in a restaurant parking lot. At the hospital emergency room the physician stitching his head remarked that Larry was lucky—that the last man who was attacked in that parking lot did not survive. Larry filed a civil law suit and received a jury verdict of $200,000 because the restaurant was on notice that their parking lot was not secure, as there were no security surveillance system or security officers patrolling the lot.

Second, *some injuries leave visible scars*, such as facial scaring, loss of teeth or fingers, or loss of mobility. Victims who have been shot will have permanent scars that remind them daily of the crime. Child abuse victims or victims of domestic violence may have lasting scars from physical beatings. As an illustration, Lin was exiting her car at her apartment complex when at gunpoint she was forced back in to the passenger side and carjacked. After forcing her to withdraw money from an ATM, Lin was ordered out of the car and instructed to keep on walking and not to look back. Despite her following instructions she was shot three times in the back. She managed to crawl to a porch and call for help. The three men were found and prosecuted. Lin won a jury award of $1.3 million. Scars from the shootings have continued to remind Lin of her ordeal.

Third, *unknown long-term physical injuries* can cause a change in life activities. Rape victims may be exposed to a permanent sexually transmitted disease such as herpes virus or HIV and AIDS. For example, Jaylee was working in a convenience store when a man forced her into a back room at gunpoint and raped her orally. Later she developed gonorrhea of the throat and had significant voice changes due to scarring of her vocal cords.

Fourth, *long-term catastrophic injuries* can restrict a victim's mobility. In one rape case the perpetrator intentionally broke a victim's neck, resulting in a paraplegic outcome. These severe injuries result in great stress on victims' families, who also need to alter their lifestyle to care for the victim. Such injuries may reduce the life span of the victim and alter the quality of life.

Injuries from violent crime are a major concern for hospital staff. In 2008, 21 million crimes were committed in the United States; of these, 5 million were violent, including 14,299 homicides, and 16 million were property crimes (Rand, 2009). Of these crimes, 47% of violent crimes and 40% of property crimes were reported to the police. This high rate of violence is of great significance to area hospitals, as these victims are often brought to emergency departments with traumatic injuries for immediate treatment and interventions. Within the health care industry there is increasing concern regarding the physical injuries associated with violent crime as well as the emotional impact it has on its victims. Complications from injuries can cause functional, cognitive, and emotional disability as well as the presence of significant comorbid conditions and potential death.

There are no national data on psychological consequences of crime victims. However, the less direct consequences of violence may be delayed or cumulative. The stress induced by violent acts, especially when repeated within a partner relationship, may culminate in severe emotional trauma or physical illness. The cost of rehabilitation is also part of health costs (Reiss & Roth, 1993).

Financial Losses

Financial costs for health-related injuries of crime victims are staggering. In 2007, for crimes both reported and not reported in the United States, the total economic loss to victims was $2 billion for violent crime and $16 billion for property crime (Bureau of Justice Statistics, 2008). Economists have used a variety of measures to place monetary values on tangible and intangible losses resulting from crime victimization. Tangible economic costs include loss of productivity in terms of wages and salary and days lost from school, work, and other activities. An impaired capacity to work, to continue in school, or to maintain one's quality of life is less often recognized, but consequential, costs of violent victimization. There can be loss of property or possessions during burglaries and robberies. In 2000, 36% of rape and sexual assault victims lost more than 10 days of work after their victimization, and property crimes cost victims more than $11.8 billion (Bureau of Justice Statistics, 2002). State compensation programs paid crime victims and their families $370 million in benefits in the federal fiscal year 2001, which represents an increase of $52 million from 2000 and an increase of $120 million from 1998 (National Association of Crime

Victim Compensation Boards [NACVCB], 2002). Vandalism costs totaled 1.7 billion in damages to households in the United States in 2000 (Bureau of Justice Statistics, 2000).

The NACVCB reports that 28% of adults receiving crime victim compensation benefits in 2001 were victims of intimate partner violence, and child victims of physical and sexual abuse received another 23% of all claims paid (NACVCB, 2002). The cost of domestic violence to the U.S. economy is more than $8.3 billion. This cost includes medical care, mental health services, and lost productivity (e.g., time away from work) (Rice, Finkelstein, Bardwell, & Leadbetter, 2004).

The use of weapons, namely guns and knives, in incidents of inter-personal violence is considered an insidious public health danger. This violence causes strain to its victims, their families, community members, health care practitioners, and law enforcement officials. Gunshot wounds, sometimes called ballistic trauma, refer to the physical trauma caused by the discharge of a gun during a conflict. In terms of public health, it is estimated that over 500,000 injuries are sustained annually from the use of firearms. In terms of economic cost, estimates are that the expenditures of shootings and stabbings in the United States are greater than $20 billion each year. In the state of Massachusetts expenditures related to stabbings and shootings are estimated to be greater than $18 million each year (Hume, McKenna, & McKeown, 2007). Despite the reported costs of these incidents, they do not account for the emotional impact of these events on victims and their families.

Economic Costs of Crime-related Drug Abuse

The crime-related cost of drug abuse increased from $60.8 billion in 1992 to 88.9 billion in 1998 and was projected to reach $100 billion in 2000 (Office of National Drug Control Policy, 2001). The estimated number of arrests for drug abuse violations for adults has been increasing, whereas the number for juveniles, persons under age 18, has stabilized (**Figure 1-5**). Drug abuse violations are defined as state or local offenses relating to the unlawful possession, sale, use, growing, manufacturing, and making of narcotic drugs, including opium or cocaine and its derivatives, marijuana, synthetic narcotics, and dangerous nonnarcotic drugs such as barbiturates.

The mission of the Substance Abuse and Mental Health Services Administration (SAMHSA) is to reduce the impact of substance abuse and mental illness of U.S. communities. SAMHSA identified eight strategic initiatives to focus its resources on areas of urgency and opportunity. One initiative, trauma and justice, aims to reduce the pervasive, harmful, and costly health impact of violence and trauma by integrating

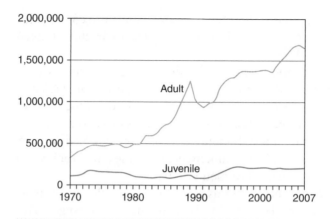

FIGURE 1-5 Drug Arrests by Age
Data from the Federal Bureau of Investigation (FBI) the Uniform Crime Reports (UCR) 2008. http://bjs.ojp.usdoj.gov/content
/glance/drug.cfm.

trauma-informed approaches throughout health, behavioral health, and
related systems and by addressing the behavioral health needs of people
involved in or at risk of involvement in the criminal and juvenile justice systems (SAMHSA, 2010). According to SAMHSA, in 2009 an estimated 21.8
million Americans, or 8.7% of those aged 12 or older, were current (past
month) illicit drug users. Illicit drugs include marijuana/hashish, cocaine
(including crack), heroin, hallucinogens, inhalants, or prescription-
type psychotherapeutics used nonmedically. The SAMHSA survey also
reported that over the past decade use for prescription opioids other
than for medical purposes grew more than 330%. It was estimated that
4.4 million people misused opioid pain relievers in the year of the study
and that nearly 1.6 million of these individuals met criteria for opioid
dependence by the American Psychiatric Association's *Diagnostic and
Statistical Manual of Mental Disorders*, 4th edition, revised (SAMHSA,
2003). This form of abuse results in increased workloads on emergency
departments and mental health clinicians and an increase in law enforcement time spent dealing with crime-related drug abuse.

Substance abuse, in particular opioid dependence, is a potentially
lethal and costly disorder that affects over 4 million individuals every year
in the United States. The consequences of insufficient treatment for these
individuals are decreased ability to care for themselves as well as increased
risk for criminal activity, which can place the individual, the family, and
society in harm's way. In addition to the enormous cost of treatment,
criminal proceedings, and housing of persons in prison secondary to

drug charges, the effects of criminal activity from lack of involvement in treatment place many of these individuals in the path of violence.

Criminal Justice Costs

Additional costs to society arise from the discretionary collective response to violent victimization. Law enforcement, adjudication, victim services, and correctional expenditures add thousands of dollars of cost to each criminal event. The phenomenon of double victimization is described as follows: The first victimization is where the victim suffered at the hands of the criminal. The victim can then be revictimized by the criminal justice system. This second victimization by the system includes time lost in interviews and completing paperwork, waiting in corridors for hearings and trials, and delays and postponements of the case.

Forensic Advances

The television show *CSI* is one of the most popular dramatic series internationally. As a result of this high-profile focus on forensic evidence, juries have come to unrealistically expect quick forensic results at a level of certainty that is not possible in light of modern scientific ability. Nevertheless, over the past two decades forensic sciences have played an important role for victimology and the criminal justice system by providing law enforcement and investigators with scientifically based information through the analysis of physical evidence. The Amanda Knox trial illustrates the importance of forensic evidence.

Forensic evidence is collected at a crime scene, analyzed in a laboratory, and often presented in court. Complex cases may involve many forensic experts with backgrounds in biology, chemistry, physics, computer science, and other disciplines. The discipline of forensic technology has grown significantly as the biological sciences and technical fields have been able to successfully use new technologies to solve crime. Forensic technology includes a wide range of sciences, including DNA testing, ballistics, fingerprinting, and toxicology. Forensic analysts and technologists collect evidence at crime scenes, analyze the evidence in laboratories, and provide testimony at court proceedings (Cohen, 2011).

Forensic science and technology is more important than ever in solving criminal cases, and learning to use this advanced technology facilitates the work of law enforcement. One of the most significant recent advances has been in the area of DNA testing. DNA testing involves identification of the genetic makeup of an individual through the analysis of repeating nucleotides known as short tandem repeats.

Sequencing patterns are compared in two or more samples, and the probability that the samples are from the same individual are calculated. Since the mid-1980s this technology has significantly increased the ability to solve cold cases and locate suspects as well as free those individuals who have been wrongfully imprisoned. Further, computerized collections of information, such as the Automated Fingerprint Identification System and the National Integrated Ballistic Imaging Network, represent a significant advance over former systems. The Automated Fingerprint Identification System has copies of hundreds of thousands of fingerprints and bullets and bullet casings, allowing for computerized matching. Before this, fingerprint cards were stored in cabinets at police headquarters, rendering it nearly impossible to match a fingerprint from a crime scene to those previously collected.

The Henry C. Lee Institute of Forensic Science at the University of New Haven is one example of an institute that provides advanced forensic evidence collection training, access to state-of-the-art forensic technology, and the expertise of specially trained forensic consultants to state police at no cost to the departments. **Table 1-3** illustrates some of the technology available through the Lee Institute for training of law enforcement.

TABLE 1-3 **Advanced Technology for Law Enforcement**

SICAR	coding technique to characterize shoe prints and tire treads that form the basis for the database search and match operations, which allow police to identify the make and model of footwear or tires using tracks left at the scene of a crime.
Ground-penetrating radar	useful for locating buried bodies, coffins, or other evidence such as a cache of weapons or disturbed soil.
Portable Raman Spectrometer	allows for rapid, accurate identification of chemicals found at a crime scene. The quick identification of unknown materials can provide investigative leads and eliminate unnecessary delay while determining if a sample is safe or if it is potentially a significant item of evidence.
Infrared still and high-definition digital video cameras	help detect patterns such as gunshot residue patterns on skin and clothing that may be overlooked without specialized equipment.
Portable video detector with fiber optics	allows police on scene to search areas inaccessible to standard cameras. The extended, flexible optic tube can reach into pipes where evidence may be hidden or extend the search capabilities at a disaster or explosion scene.
Specialized crime scene materials and tools	help eliminate collection and storage issues and help with shooting and crime scene reconstructions.

Courtesy of The Henry C. Lee Institute of Forensic Science and the University of New Haven.

Forensic Victimology and Investigative Profiling

The scientific study of the victim has been especially useful to criminal profilers in analyzing crime scenes for the purpose of identifying offender profile characteristics. In turn, profile characteristics provide police with data on which to classify a crime and identify suspects in unsolved cases. The work of investigative analysts at the FBI Academy in Quantico, Virginia, led to an expansion of traditional crime categories. The result of this work was the publication of a book, *The Crime Classification Manual* (Douglas, Burgess, Burgess, & Ressler, 2006). To classify a crime using *The Crime Classification Manual*, questions about the defining characteristics of the crime need to be answered. These characteristics include information about the victim, the crime scene, and the nature of the victim–offender exchange. Victimology is the complete history of the victim and is a crucial part of the anatomy of a crime. The critical question is to evaluate why a particular person was targeted for a violent crime; the answer will lead to motive.

Forensic victimology is defined by Turvey and Petherick (2008) as the scientific study of victims for the purposes of addressing investigative and forensic issues. Turvey and Petherick (2008) explained that the forensic victimologist is best conceived as an objective, dispassionate scientific examiner. These examiners are critical and skeptical as they thoroughly investigate the facts. To that end, they take nothing for granted, look for corroboration of any alleged victims' statements, seek out collateral sources of information, and investigate alternate or contributing motives for victim behavior. Most importantly, the forensic victimologist is barred from assuming that alleged victims must have been victimized. Verification that someone is indeed a victim must be established unequivocally and may not be asserted simply for ideological purposes. According to Turvey and Petherick, forensic victimologists investigate as scientists, report as educators, and understand the gravity of their eventual courtroom testimony.

Investigative Criminal Profiling

Investigative profiling is best viewed as a strategy that enables law enforcement to narrow the field of options and generate educated guesses about the perpetrator. It has been described as a collection of leads (Rossi, 1982), as an informed attempt to provide detailed information about a certain type of criminal (Geberth, 1981), and as a biological sketch of behavioral patterns, trends, and tendencies (Vorpagel, 1982). Geberth (1981) noted the investigative profile is particularly useful when the criminal has demonstrated some clearly identifiable form of psychopathology. In such a case the crime scene is presumed to reflect the murderer's behavior and personality in much the same way as furnishings reveal a homeowner's character.

Investigative or criminal profiling is, in fact, a form of retroclassification, or classification that works backward. Typically, we classify a known entity into a discrete category based on presenting characteristics that translate into criteria for assignment to that category. In the case of homicide investigation, investigators have neither the entity (for example, the offender) nor the victim. It is thus necessary to rely on the only source of information that typically is available: the crime scene. This information is used to profile, or classify, an individual. An important part of profiling is using the concepts of victimology and crime scene investigation. The assessment areas are described followed by an analysis of a cold case.

Crime Scene Analysis

Victimology is critical to a crime investigation as a first step in determining motive. Victims are assessed as to their risk level in terms of lifestyle and situation. Lifestyle risk level is a function of age, physical size, race, marital status, living situation, location of residence, and occupation. Situational risk assesses the victim's location and activities at the time of the crime and interacts with lifestyle risk. For example, the situational risk of a person remains the same inside a residence unless the doors are unlocked. Traveling to a social site, workplace, or residence may increase a person's situational risk level. Situational risk level varies from day to day depending on a person's routine.

An example of an individual with a high lifestyle risk who increased his situational risk is a 15-year-old White male runaway from a youth residential shelter. He had been removed from his residence for truancy and being incorrigible. The victim was found on a little traveled rural road, dead of massive thermal burns, in the ashes of a cardboard barrel, the metal rings of which were in the debris. Paint thinner was used as the accelerant, and the victim was identified through dental records. Victimology noted the victim to be a troublemaker, streetwise, and involved in all types of street activity.

The very young and the elderly may be high-risk victims under certain situations. Children walking home from school or alone at home may be targeted or stalked. Elderly living alone may be targeted because of their situation and fragility. On New Years Eve several offenders entered the home of a 73-year-old White widow and beat her with fists about the head and face. There were no signs of forced entry. The victim was tied at the wrists using her nylon hose. She was found the next day in her backyard covered with a piece of sheet metal and boards. She had been hit with a blunt instrument, possibly a brick found at the scene. The victim's skull was struck many more times than necessary to kill her. Some watches and coins were known to be taken from the home. It was not known why the victim was taken outside because she had been beaten while in the house. Victimology noted the widow lived alone in a small town residential area, and it was rumored that she had money in the house.

The crime scene assessment is divided into four distinct scenes. The initial contact scene is where the victim has the first contact with the offender. The assault scene is where the assault, physical or sexual, occurs. The death scene is where the death of the victim takes place. The body location scene is where the body is discovered. These four scenes can be the same physical location, multiple locations within a single building, physically separated locations, or any combinations of the above. For each crime scene location an assessment is made of the risk level of the victim and the offender. The initial contact scene risk is a function of location, time of day, number of people at the location, and the routine of the victim as to the location. The risk level of location for offender is a function of the offender's risk at being at the crime scene.

Cold Case Analysis

The National Institute of Justice defines a cold case as any case where all investigative leads have been exhausted or, alternately, a case that has not been solved for (generally) at least 1 year and so has been closed from further regular investigations. A cold case may be closed for various reasons: previously available technology was not able to adequately analyze the evidence in order to form a conclusion, witnesses were hostile and uncooperative, various time constraints hindered the investigation, the originally assigned detectives had a heavy workload, or a lack of worthwhile leads stalled the case. Heurich (2008) suggested that investigations regularly slow or stop completely, resulting in cold cases, often due to police agencies lack of manpower, equipment, and funding to support units dedicated to investigating and analyzing these cold cases. As homicide and sexual assault units are backlogged with active cases, cold cases rarely get attention, leaving survivors angry and society at risk.

In response to concerns about unsolved cases, the National Institute of Justice instituted a grant program aimed at solving cold cases with DNA. The program was designed to assist states and local governments to identify, review, investigate, and analyze violent crime cold cases, such as homicides and rapes, that had the potential to be solved through DNA analysis. In 2005 the National Institute of Justice awarded a total of $14.2 million to 38 state and local agencies; in 2007 the Institute awarded more than $8 million to 21 state and local agencies. As a result of the program, agencies have been able to focus resources on solving serious crimes such as homicides, sexual assaults, and other violent offenses using new technologies that may have been unavailable at the time. As noted by Heurich (2008), the ability to reopen and solve previously unsolved cases assists families and victims to find some form of resolution.

■ Summary

The definition of "victim" dates back to early religious practice and sacrifices. Victimology, as a new discipline, was fully launched in the mid-1070s. The costs of victimization are staggering when including costs to the victims and their families, costs to the systems who care for victims, and costs to society through the criminal justice system and the fear it engenders in the public. Victimology is a critical component of investigating violent crime and of analyzing a crime scene with the goal of identifying profile characteristics. Forensic victimology is the key to crime analysis, crime motivation, and suspect identification in homicide cases. The dynamics of victimization tell important information about the impact to the victim. Investigative or forensic victimology is a new and rapidly developing subdivision of victimology in general. It is one of the applied aspects of understanding crime with the goal of prevention.

■ Key Terms

Cold case: A criminal investigation that has not been solved for (generally) at least 1 year and, as a result, has been closed from further regular investigations.

Costs of victimization: Health and medical costs, economic costs, and criminal justice costs.

Crime victim: A person who has been directly and proximately harmed (physically, emotionally, or financially) as a result of the commission of an offense.

Crime victims' rights: Eight rights included in Section 3771 of Title 18 of the U.S. Code, Crimes and Criminal Procedure.

Criminology: The study of the etiology of crime and the characteristics of the criminal.

Forensic victimology: An important tool for investigating and solving cold cases.

National Crime Victimization Survey (NCVS): A series of surveys, previously called the National Crime Survey, that collect data on personal and household victimization since 1973.

Victimology: The study of the victim from a social-structural way of viewing crime and the law and the criminal and the victim.

■ Discussion Questions

1. How is the victimization experience different or similar for a crime victim versus a victim of a social and public health problem?
2. Compare and contrast victimology and criminology.
3. Why might there be a disconnect between public and media perceptions of victimization and statistics that suggest crime has declined?
4. How does the subdivision of forensic victimology contribute to suspect apprehension?
5. How do you believe the JonBenét Ramsey murder will be solved?
6. Are Amanda Knox and Raffaele Sollecito victims of the justice system?
7. How important is DNA evidence in the Meredith Kercher murder?

■ Resources

American Statistical Association Committee on Law and Justice Statistics
http://www.amstat.org/comm/index.cfm?fuseaction=commdetails&txtComm=CA02

Bureau of Justice Statistics
http://www.ojp.usdoj.gov/bjs/

Centers for Disease Control and Prevention Division of Violence Prevention
http://www.cdc.gov/ncipc/dvp/dvp.htm

Crimes Against Children Research Center
http://www.unh.edu/ccrc/

National Center for Juvenile Justice
http://www.ncjj.org/

National Institute of Justice's Data Resource Program
http://www.nij.gov/funding/data-resources-program/welcome.htm

Office for Victims of Crime
http://www.ojp.usdoj.gov/ovc/

Office of Justice Programs: Violence Against Women and Family Violence
Program
http://www.nij.gov/topics/crime/violence-against-women/welcome.htm

WISQARS™ (Web-based Injury Statistics Query and Reporting System)

WISQARS™ is an interactive, online database that provides fatal and nonfatal injury, violent death, and cost of injury data from a variety of trusted sources. Retrieved August 14, 2011 from http://www.cdc.gov/injury/wisqars/index.html

■ References

Anderson, D. (1999). The aggregate burden of crime. Retrieved from http://ssrn.com/abstract=147911

As Amanda Knox Heads Home, the Debate Is Just Getting Started. (2011, October 4). *New York Times*, A18.

Bureau of Justice Statistics. (2000). *Crime and the nation's households, 2000*. Washington, DC: U.S. Department of Justice.

Bureau of Justice Statistics. (2002). *National crime victimization survey: Personal and property crimes, 2000*. Washington, DC: U.S. Department of Justice.

Bureau of Justice Statistics. (2008). Criminal victimization in the United States, 2008, Criminal victimization. Retrieved from http://bjs.ojp.usdoj.gov/content/pub/pdf/cv08.pdf

Bureau of Justice Statistics. (2009). Criminal victimization in the United States, 2007: Statistical table 81. Retrieved from http://www.ncvc.org/ncvc/main.aspx?dbName=DocumentViewer&DocumentID=38710

CBS News. (2010, August 3). Hartford Distributors shooting: Angry employee allegedly kills multiple people. Retrieved from http://www.cbsnews.com/8301-504083_162-20012503-504083.html

Cohen, S. (2011). About forensic technology. Retrieved from http://www.ehow.com/about_4759973_forensic-technology.html#ixzz1Tc30b5kx

DeFlem, M. (2006). *Sociological theory and criminological research: Views from Europe and the United States*. New York: Elsevier/JAI Press.

Douglas, J.E., Burgess, A.W., Burgess, A.G., & Ressler, R.K. (2006). *The crime classification manual*. San Francisco: Jossey-Bass.

Fattah, E. (2000). Victimology, past, present and future. *Criminologie, 33*(1), 17–46.

Federal Bureau of Investigation (FBI). (2010a). *FBI 2009 murder statistics by type of weapon*. Washington, DC: U.S. Department of Justice, U.S. Government Printing Office.

Federal Bureau of Investigation (FBI). (2010b). FBI releases 2010 crime statistics. Retrieved from http://militarygear.com/asp/2010/12/22/fbi-releases-2010-crime-stats/

Federal Bureau of Investigation (FBI). (2010c). Retrieved from http://www.fbi.gov/about-us/cjis/ucr/crime-in-the-u.s/2010/preliminary-annual-ucr-jan-dec-2010

Federal Bureau of Investigation (FBI). (2011). Victim rights. Retrieved from http://www.fbi.gov/stats-services/victim_assistance/victim_rights

Fletcher, G.P. (1988). A crime of self-defense: Bernhard Goetz and the law on trial. *The Free Press,* pp. xi, 253.

Geberth, V. (1981). Psychological profiling. *Law and Order, 56,* 46–49.

Government of Canada. (2006). Costs of crime in Canada. Retrieved from http://www.victimsweek.gc.ca/archive2006/fact-sheets/p2.html

Hashima, P., & Finkelhor, D. (1999). Violent victimization of youth versus adults in the National Crime Victimization Survey. *Journal of Interpersonal Violence, 14*(8), 799–820.

Heurich, C. (2008). Cold cases: Resources for agencies, resolution for families. *NIJ Journal, 260,* 1–4.

Hume, B., McKenna, M., & McKeown, L. (2007). *Injuries to Massachusetts residents 2004.* Boston: Department of Public Health.

Justice for All Act. (2004). Office of Victims of Crime, DOJ, Washington, DC.

Macmillan, R. (2002). Statistics: Costs of crime. Retrieved from http://www.encyclopedia.com/doc/1G2-3403000253.html

Mendelsohn, B. (1976). Pioneers in victimology. *Victimology: An International Journal, 1*(2), 189–228.

Miller, T.R., Cohen, M.A., & Wiersema, B. (1996). *Victim costs and consequences: A new look.* Washington, DC: National Institute of Justice.

Merriam-Webster Dictionary. (2012). Retrieved from http://www.merriam-webster.com/concise/criminology

National Association of Crime Victim Compensation Boards (NACVCB). (2002). Compensation at record highs. *Victim Compensation Quarterly*, 3.

Office of National Drug Control Policy (ONDCP). (2001). *The economic costs of drug abuse in the United States, 1992–1998.* Washington, DC: Executive Office of the President.

Rand, M. (2009). Criminal victimization, 2008. Retrieved from http://www.ojp.usdoj.gov/bjs/pub/pdf/cv08.pdf

Rand, M.R., Lynch, J.P., & Cantor, D. (1997). *Criminal victimization, 1973–1995.*

Reiss, A.J., & Roth, J.A. (Eds.). (1993). *Understanding and preventing violence.* Washington, DC: National Academy Press.

Rice, M., Finkelstein, D.P., Bardwell, R.A., & Leadbetter, S. (2004). The economic toll of intimate partner violence against women in the United States. *Violence and Victims, 19*(3), 259–272.

Rossi, D. (1982). Crime scene behavioral analysis: Another tool for the law enforcement investigator. *Police Chief, 57,* 152–155.

Statistics Canada. (2011). Crime Statistics Severity. The Daily. http://www .statcan.gc.ca/daily-quotidien/110721/dq110721b-eng.htm

Substance Abuse and Mental Health Services Administration (SAMHSA). (2003). *Cost of prescription opioid.* Washington, DC: U.S. Department of Justice.

Substance Abuse and Mental Health Services Administration (SAMHSA). (2010). Eight strategic initiatives. Retrieved from http://www.samhsa.gov /traumaJustice/

Turvey, B., & Petherick, W. (2008). *Forensic victimology.* San Diego: Elsevier Science.

United Nations. (1985). *Declaration of basic principles of justice for victims of crime and abuse of power.* G.A. 40/34, annex, 40 U.N. GAOR Supp. (No. 53) at 214, U.N. Doc. A/40/53.

Vargas, E., & Natanson, P. (2011). Amanda Knox "shocked" when Rudy Guede implicates her in murder. Retrieved from http://abcnews.go.com /International/amanda-knox-shocked-rudy-guede-implicates-murder /story?id=13936041

Von Hentig, H. (1948). *The criminal and his victim: Studies in the sociobiology of crime.* New Haven, CT: Yale University Press.

Vorpagel, R.E. (1982). Painting psychological profiles: Charlatanism, charisma, or a new science? *Police Chief, 49,* 156–159.

Wallace, H., & Roberson, H. (2011). *Victimology: Legal, psychological and social perspectives.* Upper Saddle River, NJ: Pearson Education.

Wigoder, G.G. (Ed.). (2002). *The new encyclopedia of Judaism.* New York: The New York University Press.

Wolfgang, M. (1958). *Criminal homicide.* New York: Harper & Row.

Zhang, T. (2008). The costs of crime in Canada. Retrieved from http://www .justice.gc.ca/eng/pi/rs/rep-rap/2011/rr10_5/index.html

Measurement of Crime and Victimization

CHAPTER

2

■ Objectives

- To present various sources of data regarding crime and victimization
- To identify means of collecting data on crime and victimization
- To discuss strengths and limitations of various data sources

■ Key Terms

Cleared by exceptional means
Dark figure of crime
Hierarchy rule
Incidence
National Crime Victimization Survey (NCVS)
National Incident-Based Reporting System (NIBRS)
Prevalence
Uniform Crime Reports (UCR)

CASE

On July 23, 2011, a 32-year-old Norwegian, Anders Behring Breivik, gave himself up to police after admitting to massacring 69 people, mostly teenagers, attending a summer camp of the youth wing of Norway's ruling Labour Party. Breivik was also charged in the crime of bombing Oslo's government district and killing seven people hours earlier. A video posted on YouTube showed several pictures of Breivik, including one of him in a Navy Seal–type scuba diving outfit, pointing an automatic weapon. "Before we can start our crusade we must do our duty by decimating cultural marxism," said a caption under the video called "Knights Templar 2083," which also provided a link to a 1,500-page electronic manifesto stating Breivik was the author.

Terrified survivors of the shooting rampage said bullets came from at least two sides. "I heard shots, screams and people begging for their lives. He just blew them away," a Labour Party youth member said. "I was certain I was going to die." "People ran everywhere. They panicked and climbed into trees. People got trampled." "We are all in sorrow. Everybody is scared," said another Norwegian. Police took almost 1½ hours to stop the massacre, the worst by a single gunman in modern times. Witnesses said the gunman, wearing a police uniform, was able to shoot unchallenged for a prolonged period, forcing youngsters to scatter in panic or to jump into the lake to swim for the mainland (Beaumont, 2011).

This type of antigovernment carnage is not unique. Timothy McVeigh, then 33, killed 168 people between the ages of 4 months and 73 years with a truck bomb in Oklahoma City on April 19, 1995. On November 8, 2009, a U.S. Army psychiatrist, Major Nidal Malik Hasan, then 39, opened fire inside Fort Hood in Texas. Thirteen people were killed and 30 people were injured. Fort Hood, located near Killeen, Texas, was the site of another mass shooting on October 16, 1991, when George Hennard, then 35, drove his pickup truck through the windows of Luby Cafeteria's restaurant and shot and killed 23 people and wounded 23 before turning the gun on himself. See **Figure 2-1A** and **Figure 2-1B**.

FIGURE 2-1B
Anders Behring Breivik's Victims
© WOLFGANG RATTAY/Reuters/Landov

◼ Introduction

Mass murders of strangers, as illustrated in these opening cases, shatter a sense of safety and security for individuals, their families, their communities, and society as a whole. The levels of crime victimization in the community, as well as people's perceptions of their safety, is an issue that impacts directly or indirectly the quality of people's lives. While those experiencing direct victimization in particular may suffer financially, physically, or emotionally, fear of crime has widespread impact, restricting community engagement, reducing levels of trust, and affecting on social cohesion (Fattah, 1997). Yet, public perceptions regarding the incidence of crime and risk of victimization are not necessarily congruent with actual rates. Although the public often expresses fear that crime and victimization is increasing, empirical data suggest the incidence of violent crime is in fact on the decline.

Measuring crime offenses and its victims is critical to identifying the short- and long-term effects of crime, to increase knowledge regarding victims' needs, to direct funds toward the development and enhancement of victim service programs, and to add to the scientific base of victimology. The results of continued study and research efforts assist in policy development in areas of the criminal justice system and in outlining emerging issues or trends in the area of crime victimization.

Individuals, the community, and governments gather information about crime and victimization in a number of ways. Statistical data are a key component of information about crime and are critical to decision making, research, and policy development. In some instances, results from different data sources may provide a different picture of crime in the community, with administrative data indicating a trend in one direction and survey responses indicating the opposite. Different data sources collected via different methods can produce equally valid but quite varied sets of crime victimization rates. All sampling methods can be criticized; nevertheless, most advance the measurement of crime beyond anecdotal evidence or media reports alone. The challenge for data users is to understand the bases of these different data sets and then subsequently identify statistics that are most relevant for their needs.

The purpose of this chapter is to provide the major crime and victimization data sources and discuss the comparability of various crime measurement instruments and databases. **Table 2-1** identifies major data sources in crime and victimization.

TABLE 2-1 Crime and Victimization Databases

Database	Source of data	Type of data	Aims
Measurement of Crime			
Uniform Crime Reports (UCR) • United States • Canada	Compiled from law enforcement agency data across the country	Crimes reported to police based on standardized definitions	Allow for cross jurisdictional comparisons
National Incident-Based Reporting System (NIBRS) • United States	Compiled from law enforcement agency data across the US	Crimes, offender characteristics and victim characteristics	Expands the URC data set to accurately reflect crime rates
National Prisoner Statistics Program (NPS) • United States	Census and survey data collected from prisons and correctional facilities	Prison characteristics, staff characteristics, prisoner characteristics	Identifies trends in crime and incarceration, improves planning of prison resources
Adult Criminal Court Survey (ACCS) • Canada	Data reported by court systems	Offender characteristics, nature of crime, sentencing and disposition	Identifies trends in crime and sentencing, improves court procedures
Measurement of Victimization			
National Crime Victimization Survey (NCVS) • United States	General population survey - nationally representative sample of U.S. population	Victims' experiences of crime victimization	Determines the incidence of both reported and unreported crime. To understand the nature and impact of crime.
General Social Survey – Victimization (GSS) • Canada • United States	General population survey	Self-report data on victimization, perceptions of crime, and attitudes toward the justice system	To better understand how Canadians perceive crime and the justice system and their experiences of victimization
British Crime Survey (BCS) • England and Wales	General population survey	Criminal victimization and attitudes toward crime, police, and the justice system	To understand the incidence of victimization and public attitudes
International Crime Victims Survey (ICVS) • Over 70 countries	Survey of households using a standardized questionnaire	Incidence of particular crimes, victim satisfaction with justice and services, attitudes toward crime	To provide international comparative data on crime and longitudinal trends
Interpol • 190 member countries	World's largest international police organization	Helps police on the ground understand crime trends, analyze information	Conduct operations and arrest as many criminals as possible.

Data from Australian Bureau of Statistics. 2004. Information Paper: Measuring Crime Victimisation. Australia: The Impact of Different Collection Methodologies, 2002, cat. no. 4522.0.55.001, ABS, Canberra. Retrieved from http://www.abs.gov.au/ausstats/abs@.nsf/Lookup/5BF3A030F523595BCA2578B00011A06B?opendocument.

■ Uniform Crime Reports

In 1929 the U.S. Wickersham Commission, appointed by president Herbert Hoover and named after former attorney general chairman, George W. Wickersham, was composed of 11 committees and convened for 2 years (National Commission on Law Observance and Enforcement, 1931). It was established to address the issue of crime in general but also as a way to resolve the debate over the continuing problem of prohibition and organized crime. The Commission conducted the first comprehensive national study of crime and law enforcement in U.S. history and published its findings in 14 volumes covering every aspect of the criminal justice system, including the causes of crime, police and prosecutorial procedures, and the importance of probation and parole (National Commission on Law Observance and Enforcement, 1931).

The Commission proposed a comprehensive national criminal justice statistics program under an independent central statistical agency. Although this plan did not achieve fruition, it later led to a cooperative system for statistical crime reporting, called the Uniform Crime Reporting (UCR) program, aimed at meeting a need for reliable, uniform crime statistics for the nation (National Commission on Law Observance and Enforcement, 1931). The UCR program was conceived and designed in 1929 for the law enforcement community throughout the United States. The task for implementing the directive went to the Federal Bureau of Investigation (FBI). Initially, whether the FBI should be responsible for data collection was questioned because of concern about the use of information as a basis for appropriation requests or expansion of powers and equipment by the agency; however, it has remained under FBI control as a major database for law enforcement (Kempf, 1990).

The following are some of the advantages of the UCR program:

- Data are compiled annually from jurisdictions all over the United States, which allows comparisons by location and analysis of trends over time.
- Crime definitions are standardized. For instance, serious crime is divided into two groups: personal offenses, such as murder, forcible rape, robbery, and aggravated assault, and property offenses, including burglary, larceny-theft, motor vehicle theft, and arson.
- Information gathered provides data for patterns of crime and criminals.

UCR Data Collection

The Uniform Crime Report collects offense information for murder, nonnegligent manslaughter, forcible rape, robbery, aggravated assault, burglary, larceny-theft, motor vehicle theft, and arson. These reports are compiled monthly by police departments and submitted to the FBI or state-level UCR programs. Crimes selected for inclusion in the Uniform Crime Reports are those most likely to be reported and those that occur with sufficient frequency to allow for comparisons. Thus, serious but infrequent crimes such as kidnapping are not included. Further, the report does not gather data on offenses in violation of federal law, many white collar crimes, commerce and industry violations, or drug offenses such as arrests and drug seizures (MacKenzie, Baunach, & Roberg, 1990).

In addition to offense and arrest data, supplemental data are recorded (FBI, 2011a, 2011b). For instance, in the case of robbery these include property stolen and recovered, and in the case of homicide age, sex, and race of the murder victims and offenders, weapons used, and the victim–offender are recorded. The FBI also collects data on hate crimes and on cases where enforcement officers are killed or assaulted (James & Rishard, 2008).

During the early years of the Uniform Crime Report the database relied largely on the cooperation of local police departments for the collection of information; however, it has become increasingly mandatory. In 2009 over 17,000 law enforcement agencies submitted data to the Uniform Crime Report (98% of the nation). Forty-six states submit data every month through a state UCR program, and 4 states submit data directly to the FBI. The FBI requires the following from each state UCR program (James & Rishard, 2008, p. 6):

- Conform to national standards, definitions, and information reported
- Acceptable quality control procedures
- Cover a percentage of the state's population equal to that covered by the national UCR program
- Adequate field staff for audits and support
- Provide the FBI with duplicates of all data collected
- Proven capability to supply data in time to meet deadlines

An aspect of the Uniform Crime Report is the clearance of cases. Law enforcement agencies can clear or close offenses in one of two ways: by arrest or by exceptional means (FBI, 2011b). An offense is cleared by arrest or solved for crime reporting purposes when at least one person has been arrested, charged with the commission of the offense, and turned over to the court for prosecution (whether following arrest, court summons, or police notice). In its clearance calculations, the UCR program counts the number of offenses cleared, not the number of persons arrested. The arrest of one person may clear several crimes, and the arrest of many persons may clear only one offense. In addition, some clearances that an agency records in a particular calendar year may pertain to offenses that occurred in previous years.

Case clearances can be classified as exceptional in certain situations where elements beyond law enforcement's control prevent the agency from arresting and formally charging the offender. According to the FBI, an offense can be **cleared by exceptional means** if (1) there is an identified offender; (2) sufficient evidence has been collected to support an arrest, make a charge, and turn over the offender to the court for prosecution; (3) the offender's exact location has been identified so he or she can be taken into custody immediately; and (4) law enforcement agencies have encountered a circumstance outside their control that prohibits arrest and prosecution. Such cases can include situations where the offender has died, the victim refuses to cooperate with the prosecution after the offender is identified, or extradition is denied because the offender committed a crime in another jurisdiction and is being prosecuted for that offense (FBI, 2009a).

UCR statistics for 2009 (FBI, 2011b) indicate 47.1% of violent crimes and 18.6% of property crimes were cleared by arrest or exceptional means. Of the violent crimes of murder and nonnegligent manslaughter, forcible rape, robbery, and aggravated assault, murder had the highest percentage, with 66.6% of offenses cleared. When examining the property crimes of burglary, larceny-theft, and motor vehicle theft, larceny-theft was the offense most often cleared, with 21.5% cleared by arrest or exceptional means (**Figure 2-2**).

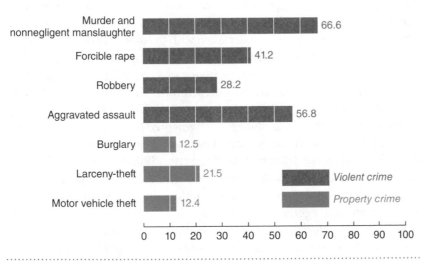

FIGURE 2-2 Percent of Crimes Cleared by Arrest or Exceptional Means

Data from FBI. Offense Cleared. 2009. Crime in the United States. http://www2.fbi.gov/ucr/cius2009/offenses/clearances /index.html.

In December 2010 the FBI released a new UCR data tool, developed by the Bureau of Justice Statistics (BJS, 2010; FBI, 2011a), as part of ongoing collaboration between the Department of Justice and FBI to improve accessibility of crime data for researchers and the public. The online UCR data tool facilitates the search for crime data going back to 1960 and lets users perform queries on custom variables such as year, agency, and type of offense. Until now, making comparisons of the UCR data required searching the annual reports and then manually calculating trends. The new tool aims to make it easier for users—especially law enforcement partners who supply the data—to make use of the raw numbers.

■ National Incident-Based Reporting System

For 60 years data collection and dissemination through the UCR program remained virtually unchanged. However, increasingly criticisms focused on the following limitations:

- Statistics were maintained only on reported crimes and ignored unreported cases.
- Data could be incomplete and manipulated as a way for a city to boost its image.
- Data were lacking regarding victims and offenders.
- Data were only reported on those who were arrested.

Consequently, critics suggested the Uniform Crime Report underreported the true level of crime. Thus, in the late 1970s a thorough evaluation of the Uniform Crime Report was undertaken with the objective of recommending an expanded and enhanced data collection program that would better meet the needs of law enforcement, policy makers, and program developers. The multiyear examination of the Uniform Crime Report resulted in a report titled the *Blueprint for the Future of the Uniform Crime Reporting Program* (FBI, 1985). This Blueprint, augmented by a process of consultation with law enforcement agencies, became the basis for the development of the National Incident-Based Reporting System (NIBRS) (FBI, 2009b).

Similar to the Uniform Crime Report, the NIBRS collects data on crimes known to the police. However, unlike the Uniform Crime Report the data are not aggregated. Data for each criminal incident are collected on 53 different dimensions, including the specific offenses in the incident, victim and offender characteristics, characteristics of the person(s) arrested, and types of property lost or recovered. Further, the range of offenses on which data are collected was expanded to include

TABLE 2-2 **Advantages of NIBRS**

- Data collection is not restricted to a limited number of offense categories (i.e., Part I offenses).
- Offense definitions can meet state, local, and national reporting needs.
- Details on individual crime incidents (offenses, offenders, victims, property, and arrests) can be collected and analyzed.
- Arrests and clearances can be linked to specific incidents and offenses.
- Distinctions can be made between attempted and completed crimes.
- Linkages can be established between variables for examining interrelationships between offenses, offenders, victims, property, and arrestees.
- Detailed crime analyses can be made within and across law enforcement jurisdictions.
- Strategic and tactical crime analyses can be made at the local and regional levels.

Data from James, N., & Rishard, L. 2008. How Crime in the United States Is Measured. Document RL34309. Washington, DC: Congressional Research Service. P. 17.

two categories of offenses (designated A and B) containing a total of 33 different offenses. Each state must be certified to submit data to the FBI (James & Rishard, 2008). **Table 2-2** outlines the advantages of NIBRS.

The NIBRS website (http://www.icpsr.umich.edu/icpsrweb/NACJD/NIBRS) states that databases are available for online data analysis. Users are advised they should be able to perform certain statistical procedures on the data, create custom subsets, or browse the codebook on the Web, without downloading the entire collection and importing the data into a statistical package. The options of NIBRS are as follows:

- Search for variables of interest in a data set
- Review frequencies or summary statistics of key variables to determine what further analyses are appropriate
- Review frequencies or summary statistics for missing data
- Produce simple summary statistics for reports
- Create statistical tables from raw data
- Create a subset of cases or variables from a large collection to save time and storage space downloading to a personal computer

Despite the advantages of the NIBRS over the Uniform Crime Report, there continues to be concern about its representativeness and effectiveness as a crime measurement tool. Addington (2008) stated that, unlike the Uniform Crime Report, the NIBRS is voluntary and requires a lengthy certification process for each law enforcement agency. This has resulted in a gradual conversion from UCR to NIBRS reporting. In 2007 31 states had been NIBRS certified and 6,444 law enforcement agencies contributed NIBRS data to the UCR Program (FBI, 2009a). Further, those jurisdictions reporting NIBRS data had smaller populations, and none were in communities of over 1 million people (Addington, 2008).

■ UCR Canada

Established in 1962, the Canadian UCR survey was designed to measure the incidence of crime in Canadian society. Substantiated crime data reported by all police departments across the country are collected and collated by the Canadian Centre for Justice Statistics. Data include the number of criminal incidents, the clearance status of those incidents, and persons-charged information. The original survey (referred to as UCR1.0) consisted solely of aggregate summary data for 100 criminal offenses. In 1988 this was modified to include an incident-based survey (referred to as UCR2.0) that records micro-data on victims, offenders, and offense characteristics for each criminal incident. Subsequent modifications in 1998 and 2004 simplified the data collection and reporting methods. In both surveys police agencies act as respondents, and response rate and compliance is nearly 100%. These data are used for crime analysis, planning regarding distribution of policing resources, and program development (Statistics Canada, 2011c).

■ Challenges in the Measurement of Crime

Attempts to uniformly report and measure crime across a wide variety of jurisdictions are fraught with challenges (Akiyama & Nolan, 1999; Caspi et al., 2002; Chilton & Jarvis, 1999). One issue relates to biases inherent in decisions as to which crimes will be included and which will not. For instance, James and Rishard (2008) identified that neither the Uniform Crime Report nor NIBRS collects data on political crime, price-fixing, or illegal environmental pollution and suggest that both sources undercount corporate and occupational crimes. Political pressure to lower crime rates, the extent to which agencies follow FBI definitions of crime, the efficiency of agencies at detecting crime, the willingness of citizens to report crime, and the effectiveness of record-keeping systems may all affect UCR data (James & Rishard, 2008). Specific challenges addressed in this section include definitional challenges, reporting challenges, and challenges related to policing practices.

Definitional Challenges

UCR classification methods have been criticized for being vague, imprecise, and subject to varying interpretation. Definitions may vary subtly from the jurisdictions' legal definition of crimes, and each offense definition requires factors to provide sufficient basis for classification. In attempting to deal with definitional challenges in UCR, a number of rules have been established, including the hierarchy rule, hotel rule, and a definition of case clearance.

The hierarchy rule in the UCR definitions requires that when multiple offenses occur in a single incident, only the most serious offense is scored. An example of the hierarchy rule is the Petit triple family murders that occurred in Cheshire, Connecticut, in July 2007. Two men, Steven Hayes and Joshua Komisarjevsky, followed Jennifer Hawke-Petit and her 11-year-old daughter Michaela home from a grocery store and targeted the family as wealthy. According to Hayes's confession, the two men planned to rob the house and flee the scene with the family bound and unharmed. However, upon their early morning arrival they found William Petit sleeping on a couch on the porch. With a bat Komisarjevsky had found in the yard, he bludgeoned Petit and then restrained him in the basement at gun point. The children and their mother were each bound and locked in their respective rooms. Hayes says he and Komisarjevsky were not satisfied with the small amount of cash found but that a bankbook revealed an available balance. Hayes thus coerced Jennifer Hawke-Petit to withdraw $15,000 from her line of credit. The bank surveillance cameras captured the transaction showing Hawke-Petit the morning of July 23 informing the teller of her situation. The teller then called 911 and reported the details to police. The Cheshire police response to the bank teller's "urgent bid" began with assessing the situation and setting up a vehicle perimeter that took more than half an hour and provided the time used by the assailants to conclude their modified plan.

Upon returning to the house, Komisarjevsky sexually assaulted Michaela and photographed her on his cell phone and provoked Hayes to rape and strangle Hawke-Petit. A fire was then ignited, and Hayes and Komisarjevsky fled the scene in the Petit family car. William Petit had been able to free himself, escape, and call to a neighbor for help. The car was pursued by police, and the suspects were apprehended and arrested one block away. The whole invasion lasted 7 hours. Two daughters died of smoke inhalation (ABC News, 2010).

The eight multiple crimes included home invasion, kidnapping, assault, hostage taking, burglary, rape, murder, and arson. Using the hierarchy rule, the crime with the highest priority was premeditated murder, based on the fact the two men took time to buy gasoline for the cover-up. None of the other crimes would appear in statistics.

The hotel rule states that when multiple dwelling units under a single manager are burglarized and the offenses are more likely to be reported by the manager rather than individual occupants, the burglaries are scored as one offense. The separation of time and space rule states that when there is a difference in the time interval and distance between different offenses, each incident must be handled separately (hierarchy and hotel rules cannot apply) (James & Rishard, 2008).

Reporting Challenges

The production of data for the crime databases relies on the participation of victims, witnesses, and police. Thus, a number of factors influence whether a particular crime occurrence will be reported in such databases. First, there must be an awareness that the crime has occurred. Sometimes crimes such as theft or larceny may go undetected for prolonged periods of time. Second, citizens must define the crime as worthy of police intervention. Individual citizens may fail to report crimes to police because they are unaware of the procedures of reporting crime, are doubtful that the police can do anything about the crime, believe the police are incompetent or uninterested, or believe the offense was not important enough to warrant police attention. Business owners may not report crimes to police because the property is insured, may believe there is no personal gain in reporting, or fear rate increases in their policies. Third, police must decide whether a crime has occurred. Police may fail to report crimes by overlooking certain violations (e.g., minor drug violations) or succumb to pressure to reduce crime by downgrading offenses. In dealing with youth, police may defer the incident to responsible adults and avoid making formal reports. Finally, when all the preceding decisions have been made, the information must go to the appropriate authorities for inclusion in the Uniform Crime Report (Kempf, 1990; MacKenzie et al., 1990). Thus, data depend highly on a series of decisions made by a variety of individuals.

Challenges Related to Policing Practices

Jurisdictional variations in police practices can affect reported crime rates. For example, police officers who have more discretion to settle disputes on the streets may prevent crimes from developing. Reporting of rape and sexual assault crimes may vary because of the attitudes of police services toward those who are victimized, the creation of victim–witness assistance programs in police departments, and improved treatment of complainants by the criminal justice system. Other police-related factors are as follows:

- *Response time to a call:* In both the case of the Norway massacre and the Petit triple homicide, police were criticized in their delay in responding to the call, resulting in higher numbers of victims. Police departments that have tried to study the issue, however, identify challenges with collecting accurate data. In 2008 the Arizona police department attempted to collect data on response time for police incidents dating between 2007 and 2008; however, they had difficulty interpreting the data because there was no standard way for officers to report on scene. For example, while the assigned officer responds to a call a second officer arrives on scene, but the response time clock continues to tick for the incident until the first officer logs on scene (Leung, 2011).

- *Level of professionalism:* Citizens expect police to be knowledgeable and professional in their response to victimization. If they are not, people become increasingly reluctant to report crime. Carter and Wilson (2006) analyzed 19 studies that investigated the relationship between education level and police officer performance and found performance measures used most frequently were disciplinary actions, citizen complaints, and commendations, followed closely by volume of arrests or summons and sick time used. These measures, while easily available, do not necessarily address public concerns about professionalism in police interactions with the community.

- *Policing styles* (reactive vs. proactive): There is great variation in policing styles. In one Milwaukee study, even though the overall number of incidents dispatched to police officers had declined over the past 6 years, response times to almost every incident category increased. The police department explained the longer response times as the result of a focus on proactive policing policy (Dispatch Magazine, 2011).

- *Arrest practices:* The arrest process can vary among jurisdictions and may also be influenced by a variety of factors. Kempf (1990) argued that few offenses are a result of direct police observation and therefore police rely on the report of the victim in making a decision to arrest a defendant, offense seriousness, the relationship between victim and offender, situational evidence, and other factors.

■ National Prisoner Statistics Program

Crime can also be measured by collecting data on prisoners. One of the earliest databases in the United States is the National Prisoner Statistics Program (NPS), which first began in 1926. Its aim is to provide national and state-level data on the numbers of prisoners in state and federal prison systems. These data include prisoner characteristics (e.g., race, gender, and age), type of offenses, and time in prison. Neither census nor survey information on inmates in state and local correctional facilities attempts to measure crime rates or trends but both collect information on demographic, social, and criminal characteristics of inmates, movement of inmates within and between facilities, and the prison facilities that house them.

As particular challenges arise, additional data are collected to determine the extent and risk associated. For instance, the Summary of Sentenced Population Movement (West, Sabol, & Greenman, 2010) includes number of prisoners who are HIV positive. Since 1972 the program has been run under the auspices of the BJS. In 1983 the NPS and the Uniform Parole Reports were combined into the National Corrections Reporting Program.

MacKenzie and colleagues (1990) identified the following objectives and outcomes of the NPS data collection:

- To determine the physical capacity, staffing, and programming needs of prison facilities through an analysis of characteristics of offenders and the crimes they have committed
- To identify and analyze major issues and trends in corrections related to facilities such as the influence of sentencing patterns on occupancy rates, trends in population growth, expenditures, staffing patterns, and program availability
- To obtain information on special issues, such as the number of inmate deaths related to HIV infection or the number of inmates that are illegal aliens

NPS Data Collection

Two aspects of the NPS data collection are the census and the survey. The census requires the participation of every prison and correctional facility in the United States. The survey includes a representative sample of facilities and a random sample of inmates drawn from those sample facilities. **Table 2-3** shows data included in the NPS census and survey.

■ Adult Criminal Court Survey

The goal of the Canadian Adult Criminal Court Survey is to develop and maintain a database of statistical information on appearances, charges, and cases in adult criminal courts (Statistics Canada, 2011a). Information is collected on age and gender of the accused, case decision patterns, sentencing information, amount of fine, and case elapsed time. These statistics are collected by the Canadian Centre for Justice Statistics in collaboration

TABLE 2-3 Data Collected in the National Prison Statistics Census and Survey

Facility and Inmate Characteristics	• Community access: ability of inmates to leave the facility to attend work or study release
	• Security level of the institution: maximum, medium, minimum
	• Programs and resources: for example, medical units, general work release or prerelease programs
	• Inmate capacity
	• Age of facility
	• Health and safety conditions: for instance, whether inmates are on medication, the number of assaults on inmates
	• Operating and capital expenditures
	• Staffing: including race, gender, and work assignments
Inmate Characteristics	• Number of inmates
	• Program involvement: the number and sex of inmates enrolled in academic, counseling, and work release programs on the reference date
	• Work assignments: the number and sex of inmates enrolled in industries, maintenance jobs, and vocational training on the reference date, and the average hourly wage paid to each inmate
	• Special inmate counts: for instance, the number of illegal aliens and persons younger than age 18
Criminal Characteristics	• Prior criminal involvement
	• Current offense
	• Victim–offender relationships
Non-Criminal Characteristics	• Demographic and socioeconomic characteristics
	• Military service
	• History of drug and alcohol abuse

Data from MacKenzie, D.L., Baunach, P.J., & Roberg, R.R. (1990). Measuring Crime: Large-Scale, Long-Range Efforts. New York: State University of New York.

with provincial and territorial departments and is a census for provincial and superior criminal courts in Canada.

Information is collected every fiscal year (April 1 to March 31) and includes persons 18 years or older at the time of offense, companies, and youths who have been transferred to adult criminal court. No sampling is required because the census includes all populations who come into contact with criminal courts (Statistics Canada, 2011a).

■ Challenges in Measuring Crime with Offender Data

There are several limitations to surveys that collect offender data. First, the NPS does not allow for generalizability of findings to all offenders because the survey is limited to those inmates who serve time in facilities. Similarly, the Adult Criminal Court Survey reports data only on those who appear in court. Thus, as discussed in the issues related to measurement of crime above, the data are skewed to reflect those offenders for whom their crime was reported, the police chose to arrest, the prosecutor chose to proceed with charges, and, in the case of the NPS, the jury chose to convict and the judge chose to sentence.

The second limitation is the lack of sufficient data to make conclusions about the causes of crime because only a select sample of offenders is represented in the data. Data collection in census methods relies on the interpretation of questionnaires by administrators who work in jurisdictions with different policies and practices. Further, the definitions of each data item are often not sufficiently clear and may change from year to year because societal mores and political pressures influence what factors are of interest and importance.

Third, there is a lack of a consistent sample. For example, in the case of the NPS, youthful offenders were included in the 1974 consensus and excluded in the 1979 and 1984 censuses (MacKenzie et al., 1990).

■ Victimization Surveys

Two important factors converged to catapult victim surveys into the criminal justice and victimology arena. First, by the 1960s, 30 years after its creation, the UCR program was increasingly being called into question by official and journalistic investigations of police offense statistics and by critical social science analyses regarding its ability to provide a full picture of crime and its consequences. Second, the crime victim movement was exerting pressure on criminologists to provide crime statistics that included victims. Some social scientists were already promoting adapting self-report national household surveys to describe the nature of and changes in the crime problem that would be less vulnerable to the limitations of UCR.

The development of the crime victimization survey was initiated by two commissions appointed in 1965 by President Lyndon B. Johnson and headed by Nicholas Katzenbach, the U.S. Attorney General: the President's Commission on Crime in the District of Columbia and the President's Commission on Law Enforcement and Administration of Justice, precursor of the National Institute of Justice. The surveys intended to capture individuals' experiences with crime and with justice agencies. A goal of both commissions was to reduce the amount of crime that eluded the attention of the police.

The results of the first victimization survey pilot showed that, depending on the type of crime, there were 3 to 10 times as many crimes reported by victims than were recorded by UCR. Since those early surveys, self-report measures of criminal victimization have become widely used social indicators and research tools in criminology and criminal justice. A great deal has been learned about the strengths and weakness of this methodology. Victim surveys substantially improved the information available on the volume of crime and indicated that household surveys could help estimate the extent of the full picture of crime as well as estimate the number of victimizations at a national level. Victim surveys also provided more detailed information on crime events than did national data systems based on police records. These surveys asked respondents to provide information on themselves, the offenders, the nature of the crime, and the context in which it occurred. Although this type of information may have been available in local police files, it was not assembled nationally by agencies like the FBI in a form that allowed easy access. Moreover, the detail available in police files varied substantially, depending on the willingness of police officers to ask victims systematically for the specifics of crime events (Cantor & Lynch, 2000).

Victimization surveys are interview reports with a random sample of people to ask whether they have ever been a victim of a crime. Community surveys provide a way of asking people directly about their experiences of crime and are designed specifically for statistical purposes. The primary reason for conducting a survey is that many victims of crime do not report their experiences to police and so are not counted in administrative data. **Table 2-4** shows the advantages of victim surveys for measuring crime.

A wide variety of information is required to effectively describe people's experiences as victims and answer research and policy questions about crime and victimization. For example, data may be required to

- Estimate the overall risk of becoming a victim
- Monitor trends in crime victimization over time and across different geographic locations
- Identify risk factors in becoming a victim to assist in establishing priorities for service providers, such as police and victim support groups
- Contribute to understanding long-term outcomes for victims of crime

TABLE 2-4 **Advantages of Victim Surveys for Measuring Crime**

Issue	Advantage
Crime causation	Availability of disaggregate data on crime events not known to police
Theory development	New way to view crime regarding theories of routine activity, opportunity theory, rational choice theory, etc.
Consequences of crime	Identify the aftermath of crime as it affects the victims, families, and communities
New areas of study	Data on why victims call (or do not call) the police
Response to victims	Mobilization of resources other than police
Building victimology theory	Occurrence of crime events and risk of criminal victimization
Control sample	Surveys include victim and nonvictim sample to test theories
Offender populations	Composition and profiles of offenders not arrested
Repeat victimization	Effect on data collection and crime statistics

Victim Survey Methods

Surveys collect data about different aspects of crime victimization, and some concepts and data items are common across all surveys. The differences are found in the survey methodology used to collect information. **Table 2-5** provides considerations for victim survey design. Given the factors described in relation to survey design and operations, each survey data set needs to be considered a unique, stand-alone data set, and data items, even when appearing to measure similar concepts, should not be compared across the different survey data sources (Australian Bureau of Statistics, 2004).

Generations of Victim Surveys

Hindelang (1976) described the development of community surveys as falling into "stages" or "generations." Each stage sought to improve the methodology by identifying problems in an earlier stage.

FIRST-GENERATION VICTIM SURVEYS The first generation of victim surveys included two stages. Stage 1 was the President's Commission convened in the mid-1960s. This survey served as pilot work to test the feasibility of counting crime victims. The report contrasts results of its 10,000-household National Survey of Criminal Victims (conducted by the National Opinion Research Center) as well as city-level victim surveys for Washington, Chicago, and Boston (conducted by the Bureau of Social Science Research

TABLE 2-5 Considerations for Victim Survey Design

Sample design	• Selection of a sample is dependent on a number of considerations including: - aims and content of the survey - level of accuracy at which the survey estimates are required - costs and operational constraints of conducting the survey
Scope of design	• Scope and coverage for the survey may vary - for instance rural vs. urban areas vs. remote geographical areas
Questionnaire format	• Study results are dependent on the nature of questions asked including: - target information to be collected - the manner in which questions are phrased
Data collection procedure	• Mode of the data collection - for example, short telephone interview, longer face-to-face interviews • Each method has advantages and disadvantages that can impact on the survey results
Response rate	• Provides an indication of the influence of nonresponse bias on the data collected in the survey • Will vary across the surveys • The influence of nonresponse bias must be addressed
Interpretation of data	• The goal to interpreting crime victimization data accurately is (1) to understand the data source (2) to make informed decisions about which data source meets the particular data requirements under interpretation

and the University of Michigan Survey Research Center) with the FBI's Uniform Crime Reports. Concluding that lack of information on offenses not reported to police makes it difficult to develop useful crime policy, the commission recommended the development of a nationwide crime victimization survey (President's Commission on Law Enforcement and Administration of Justice, 1967).

Stage 2 was a survey by the National Opinion Research Center that targeted 10,000 households and asked persons to report on incidents in the past year. The interviewer then focused on the two most recent and more serious crimes. The results of this survey claimed UCR underreported crime by about 50%. The National Opinion Research Center reported four times as many rapes and over three times as many burglaries. Of note was the lone exception of motor vehicle theft. This lack of discrepancy was most likely due to insurance company policy requiring a police report for a reimbursement check. The victimization surveys quickly pointed out unreported crimes (Biderman & Reiss, 1967).

SECOND-GENERATION VICTIM SURVEYS Second-generation surveys sought to correct the problems identified in first-generation surveys and involved several methods:

- *Record checks:* This method sought to compare information from police records to victimization survey data.
- *Reverse record check:* This was done by locating crime victim names in police files and contacting them and administering a victim survey. The responses were checked against police records. Analysis of these data revealed memory decay increased over time and the best recall was within 3 months. Also, the wording of questions and order of presentation affected responses (Hindelang, 1976).
- *Forward record check:* People in a victim survey were asked whether they had contacted police about the incident. Researchers then checked police records for a written case. Police reports for about one-third of cases could not be found. However, when records were found, the record and victim account showed a great deal of similarity (Schneider et al., 1978; BJS, 2010).

THIRD-GENERATION VICTIM SURVEYS In the early 1970s the Census Bureau conducted the first National Crime Survey (NCS) with a probability sample of 72,000 households. Each member of the household was interviewed every 6 months for a total of seven interviews over a 3½-year period. Many concerns identified in the first- and second-generation surveys were addressed and corrected in this stage (James & Rishard, 2008).

FOURTH-GENERATION VICTIM SURVEYS Concerns were again addressed over wording, bounding, memory decay, and telescoping of third-generation surveys, leading to a fourth generation. Redesign efforts were made to address the questionnaire and the data collection procedures. Fourth-generation victim surveys include the widely used National Crime Victimization Survey.

■ National Crime Victimization Survey

The National Crime Victimization Survey (NCVS) was designed with four primary objectives: (1) to develop detailed information about the victims and consequences of crime, (2) to estimate the number and types of crimes not reported to the police, (3) to provide uniform measures of selected types of crimes, and (4) to permit comparisons over time and types of areas. The survey categorizes crimes as "personal" or "property." Personal crimes cover rape and sexual attack, robbery, aggravated and simple assault, and purse snatching/pocket picking, whereas property crimes cover burglary, theft, motor vehicle theft, and vandalism. For each incident the NCVS acquires information on the month, time, and location of the crime; the relationship between the victim and offender; characteristics of the offender; self-protective actions taken by the victim during the incident and results of those actions; consequences of victimization; whether the crime was reported to police and the reason for reporting or not reporting; and offender use of weapons, drugs, or alcohol (James & Rishard, 2008). Data from the NCVS survey are particularly useful for calculating crime rates, both aggregated and disaggregated, and for determining changes in crime rates from year to year. **Table 2-6** indicates the major steps taken in the development of the NCVS.

TABLE 2-6 Development of the National Crime Victimization Survey

1967	• President's Commission on Law Enforcement and Administration of Justice
1968	• Establishment of the Law Enforcement Assistance Administration in the U.S. Department of Justice
1970	• Pretesting involving reverse record checks • Small scale samples
1971	• Initial implementation – questions are added to the Census Bureau's Quarterly Household Survey • Sample of 15,000 households are asked to recall events in past 12 months
1972	• New National Crime Surveys of 72,000 households
1986–1990	• Redesign and testing 　- more thorough descriptions 　- questions added to stimulate participant recall 　- computer-assisted interview introduced 　- sexual assault questions added 　- intimate partner violence questions improved
1990–1992	• Phase in of new questionnaire
Mid-90s	• Context variables on public housing, college or university housing, and attendance or employment at colleges or universities are added to the screening questions
2001	• Questions on cybercrime are added
2004	• Identity theft questions are added
2006	• The Supplemental Victimization Survey (SVS), focusing on stalking

Data from National Academies of Science. 2008. James, N., & Rishard, L. 2008. How Crime in the United States Is Measured. Document RL34309. Washington, DC: Congressional Research Service.

Data Collection for the NCVS

NCVS uses a representative sample of households stratified proportionally to represent the larger population. All members of the household over the age of 12 are interviewed, including persons living in group quarters such as dormitories, rooming houses, and religious dwellings but excluding correctional quarters such as prisons (James & Rishard, 2008). Interviews are conducted every 6 months for 3 years; the first and fifth interviews are conducted in person, and the others are held by telephone whenever possible. The sample includes 49,000 households comprising about 100,000 persons and obtains an average annual response rate of over 96%.

Crime analysts measure crime rates in several different ways, and the distinction between these various forms of reporting is vital to understanding crime studies. Prevalence measures how many people experience a particular crime during their lifetimes. Incidence gives a snapshot of how many crimes take place during a particular period of time, often a year. The rate of occurrence is calculated by dividing the actual number of occurrences by the number of possible times the outcome could have occurred. Every year the BJS publishes national crime rates, or the incidence of crime in various jurisdictions per 1,000 persons or households.

Personal crime rate = number of person crimes / (*N* persons / 1,000)
Household crime rate = number of household crimes / (*N* households / 1,000)

NCVS Summary Findings for 2009

Available data demonstrate differential rates of various crimes, indicating not everyone has the same chance of being victimized. Groups of people have differing rates of victimization, and UCR regional, state, and college data illustrate not all geographic areas have the same rates. The BJS reports yearly findings from the NCVS. For example, some of the summary findings from BJS for 2009 are as follows (BJS, 2010):

- *Gender:* In 2009 men were slightly more likely than women to be victims of violent crime. Women were more likely than men to be victimized by someone they knew. Seventy percent of all violent crimes against women were committed by a known offender (an intimate, family member, or friend/acquaintance), compared to 45% of violence against men. Twenty-six percent of the nonfatal violence against women was committed by an intimate (current or former spouse, boyfriend, or girlfriend), compared to 5% of the violence against men.

- *Reporting:* Nearly half of all violent crimes and about 40% of all property crimes were reported to police in 2009. Of the violent crimes, robbery (68%) and aggravated assault (58%) were most reported. Fifty-five percent of rape/sexual assaults and 42% of simple assaults were reported to the police. A higher percentage of motor vehicle thefts (85%) than burglaries (57%) and thefts (32%) were reported to police (Rand, 2009).
- *Race:* In 2009 the rate of violent victimization against Blacks was 27 per 1,000 persons aged 12 or older, for Whites 16 per 1,000, and for persons of other races 10 per 1,000. Blacks were victims of rape/sexual assault, robbery, and aggravated assault at rates higher than those for Whites. Hispanic persons were victims of about 640,000 crimes of violence, rape/sexual assault, robbery, or aggravated or simple assault. Violent crime rates have declined for both males and females since 1994.
- *Time of occurrence:* Fifty-five percent of incidents of violent crime occurred during the day between 6 a.m. and 6 p.m. More than half (55%) of rape/sexual assaults occurred at night from 6 p.m. to 6 a.m. Almost half (46%) of household burglaries occurred during the daytime hours.
- *Place of occurrence:* Almost 33% of violent crimes occurred in or near the victim's home. About 9% of purse snatching/pocket pickings occurred inside a restaurant, bar, or nightclub; 13% occurred in other commercial buildings; and 6% occurred in parking lots or garages. Of victims of violent crime, 22% were involved in some form of leisure activity away from home at the time of their victimization, 31% were at home, and another 16% were at work or traveling to or from work when the crime occurred.
- *Distance from home:* In 2009, 58% of violent crimes occurred within a mile of the victim's home, including 21% that occurred in the home and 18% that occurred near the home. Only 3% of violent crimes occurred more than 50 miles from home.
- *Injury and medical care:* About 28% of victims of robbery and assault were injured. About 549,810 victims of violent crime received some type of medical care. Of these victims, about 21% were treated in an emergency department or clinic and about 4% were hospitalized.
- *Time lost from work:* About 7% of victims of violent crime lost some time from work, and household members who were victimized by property crimes also lost time from work in about 6% of victimizations.

- *Amount of economic loss:* In 2009 the total economic loss from crimes measured by the NCVS was $16,327 million. These losses included costs for medical care, time lost from work, property loss and damage, costs to repair or replace property, and time spent dealing with the criminal justice system. These costs do not include additional costs incurred by the victim after the time of interview or other costs not measured by the survey.
- *Recovery of losses:* The median dollar loss for crimes involving loss was $200. Only 7% of victims of violent or property crime recovered some of their losses. Motor vehicle theft was the crime most likely to result in some or all recovery of property. Thirty-five percent of households experiencing motor vehicle theft recovered all of their losses.
- *Weapon use:* An offender was armed with a gun, knife, or other object used as a weapon in an estimated 22% of all incidents of violent crime. Offenders used firearms to commit 8% of violent crime incidents in 2009. Robberies (47%) were the most likely to involve an armed offender.

■ National Family Violence Survey

In 1976 the National Family Violence Survey (NFVS) was conducted; in 1985 it used the Conflict Tactics Scale (CTS) as a means of determining rates of aggression in marital relationships. The CTS is the most widely used measure of spousal violence, focusing on three types of aggression: physical assault, psychological aggression, and negotiation (Straus, 2007). Physical violence by the CTS index is often subdivided into two categories: minor violence and severe violence. Minor violence includes throwing an object, pushing, grabbing, shoving, and slapping. Severe violence includes kicking, biting, hitting, beating up, choking, or using a weapon.

The 1985 NFVS resulted in a rate of violence of 116 per 1,000 couples, that is, almost 12% of husbands in the United States perpetrated violence against their wives that year; in 3% of cases this violence was severe. However, unlike previous studies, it suggested that women perpetrated even more violence toward husbands. The rate of violence by women against their husbands was 124 per 1,000 couples, just over 12%, and in 4% of cases the violence was severe.

Bachman (1998) identified discrepancies between the NFVS and other surveys of crime and violence. For instance, estimates of violence against women using the CTS screening instrument in the NFVS almost doubled the rates of intimate partner violence against women estimated by the NCVS. Further, the NCVS finds that women are much more likely to experience an act of intimate partner violence than are men (9.3 per 1,000 vs. 1.4 per 1,000). Bachman (1998) suggested that this discrepancy is in part because the CTS measures acts of violence in isolation from the circumstances under which the acts were committed, ignoring who initiates the violence, the relative size and strength of the persons involved, and the nature of the participant's relationship. In addition, the NCVS uses a sampling strategy different from the NFVS in that, in addition to heterosexual people in traditional marital relationships, it also includes others, such as single, divorced, and never married women. This is critical, because rates of intimate partner violence are eight times higher in separated women than in married women (Bachman & Saltzman, 1995). Other factors identified by Bachman (1998) include the nature of questions asked (general questions about crime vs. questions about conflict tactics in the home), which results in different definitions of violence, and the multiple time periods over which the NCVS is conducted, which allows for comparisons. **Table 2-7** compares factors that may contribute to differences in incidence rates of violence.

Rand and Rennison (2005) discuss the apparent differences between violence against women estimates from NCVS and NVAWS stating that contrary to some literature findings, the NVAWS did not produce

TABLE 2-7 Factors That May Contribute to Different Incidence Rates of Violence Against Women

Methodology	National Family Violence Survey	National Crime Victimization Survey
Sample population	Married or cohabiting heterosexual couples over age 18 may result in higher estimates	Including all individuals over age 12 in sample may result in lower estimates because of decreased violence against women between 12 and 18 and over 65 years
Number of times interviewed	Interviewed respondents once, which may produce higher victimization rates	Interviewed respondents multiple times to eliminate duplicate reports
Context of the survey	Violence is considered "marital conflict"	Violence is considered a crime; some respondents may not view assaults by intimates a crime
Number of household members interviewed	Interviewed one member of the married or cohabiting couple	Interviewed all family members; may prevent some respondents from disclosing incidents of violence
Context of violence	Does not distinguish acts of self-defense	Asks questions to distinguish acts of self-defense

Bachman, R. (1998). Incidence Rates of Violence Against Women: A Comparison of the Redesigned National Crime Victimization Survey and the 1985 National Family Violence Survey. Harrisburg, PA: VAWnet, a project of the National Resource Center on Domestic Violence/Pennsylvania Coalition Against Domestic Violence. Retrieved 12/18/11, from: http://www.vawnet.org

statistically significant estimates of violence against women greater than NCVS findings. The researchers suggest incident counting protocols used in NVAWS and the recalibrated NCVS increased the error and decreased the reliability of the estimates (Rand & Rennison, 2005). Challenges in determining rates of victimization from surveys are discussed in more detail below.

■ Canadian General Social Survey

The General Social Survey (GSS) began collecting information in 1985 on how Canadians perceive their health and social supports. The survey is administered through telephone interviews across all Canadian provinces. A stratified sample of households is selected through random digit dialing. Until 1998 the sample size for the survey was 10,000 persons. In 1999 it was increased to 25,000 persons and covered social topics such as health, time use, victimization, education, work and retirement, family, and social support. Addition of new modules and creation of new surveys allows data to be gathered from different topics related to important policy areas (Dryburgh, 2009). One such module is the GSS-Victimization.

According to Statistics Canada (2011b), the purpose of the GSS-Victimization module is to better understand how Canadians perceive crime and the justice system. Each survey contains a standard set of demographic questions. The survey then asks respondents about reported and unreported experiences of crime, violence, physical assaults, emotional abuse, and financial abuse. Each cycle includes new information on victimization, such as Internet victimization and cyber-bullying, added in 2009 (Dryburgh, 2009). The goal is to determine the extent of both reported and unreported crimes and to better understand why people may or may not choose to report a crime. The results of the survey inform public policy and the development of services. Reports from the GSS-Victimization module are as follows:

- Aboriginal people as victims and offenders
- Crime prevention measures taken by Canadians
- Family violence in Canada
- Hate-motivated crime
- Seniors as victims of crime
- Visible minorities as victims of crime
- Criminal victimization in the workplace
- Sexual orientation and victimization
- Violence against women

British Crime Survey

The British Crime Survey, administered to a national representative sample of citizens, produced its first report in 1982. One of the largest social surveys conducted in Britain, it was originally administered every 4 years, and then every 2 years; however, from 2001 onward the survey has been conducted annually. In 2001 the sample included 40,000 respondents as well as "boost" samples of 3,000 non-White respondents and 1,500 respondents aged 16 to 24 years to increase their representation (Jones, 2006).

The British Crime Survey is a face-to-face survey of people in England and Wales in which respondents are asked if they have been a victim of a crime in the past 12 months. The crimes are divided up into personal offenses (assaults, robberies, thefts from a person, other personal thefts, and sexual offenses) and household offenses (car thefts, bicycle thefts, other thefts, vandalism of household property, and domestic burglary). Until recently the British Crime Survey did not cover crimes against those younger than age 16 years, but since January 2009 children aged 10 to 15 have been included for interview. However, these remain experimental statistics and are not currently included in routine British Crime Survey publications. The British Crime Survey also collects data regarding public attitudes toward police, the criminal justice system, crime, and antisocial behavior (Economic and Social Data Service, 2001).

International Crime Victims Survey

In 1980 a group of European criminologists initiated an international victimization study for the purposes of generating international comparative crime and victimization data. The project is now known as the International Crime Victims Survey (Van Dijk, van Kesteren, & Smit, 2008). After the first round in 1989, the surveys were repeated in 1992, 1996, 2000, and 2004/2005. The United Nations became involved in the project in 1992 to organize the surveys in developing countries; respondents come from industrial countries in Europe, North and South America, Asia, Southern Africa, Australia, and New Zealand (Nieuwbeerta, 2002). In 15 years of operation more than 300,000 people were interviewed about their experiences of victimization in 78 different countries (Van Dijk et al., 2008).

In the International Crime Victims Survey, respondents over the age of 16 are asked whether they have been victims of a crime in the previous year. The survey covers 10 conventional crimes (theft of a car, theft from a car, theft of a motorcycle or moped, theft of a bicycle), burglary, attempted burglary, theft of personal property, and contact crimes (robbery, sexual offences, and assault and threat). In several countries questions have been added about street-level corruption, consumer fraud (including Internet fraud), drug-related crime, and hate crime (Van Dijk et al., 2008). Respondents are first asked about their crime experiences within the past 5 years, such as when they occurred, what happened, and whether police were notified (Nieuwbeerta, 2002). Other data collected involve concern about crime, attitudes toward police, and recommendations for fair sentencing.

■ Challenges in Measuring Victimization

The task of describing the national pattern of violence from the various reporting systems is complicated because they differ in terms of (1) the domain of events they attempt to capture, (2) the unit of count on which their statistics are based, (3) the timing of the counting and tabulation, (4) the sources of discretion and error in recording the counting events, and (5) not counting neglected victims. Victimization surveys are also subject to problems mainly involving ensuring representative samples, dependence on respondents' memories, willingness of victims to talk about their experiences, and failure to realize an incident is relevant to the survey. This section describes three main types of challenges for measuring victimization through national surveys: challenges related to sampling, challenges related to victim responses, and challenges related to interpretation of data.

Challenge Related to Sampling

Victimization surveys use a sample of the population to represent the experiences and perceptions of the entire population. Thus, the representativeness of the sample is key for population-based estimates and generalizations to be accurate. Survey designers go to great lengths to ensure that samples are stratified in such as way as to reflect the general population on a number of demographic, economic, and cultural variables. Nevertheless, the representativeness of the sample is challenged by a number of factors.

Telephone-based surveys are limited to individuals that own phones and have numbers listed in telephone directories. Thus, people from lower socioeconomic groups that do not own a phone and young people who use cell phones rather than home phones are eliminated from the sample. However, the expense of in-person samples means that telephone interviews are the most common method of administration.

Some individuals refuse to participate in surveys, and it is not always clear whether these people represent a particular subsample of the population. For instance, Schwartz, Steffenmeier, Zhong, and Ackerman (2009) focused on gender biases inherent in crime victimization surveys.

They suggested an underestimation of rates of victimization against males due to nonresponse (Schwartz et al., 2009). Other populations that may not respond are those who are fearful of authorities, such as undocumented immigrants, or are more generally fearful, such as elderly or other vulnerable individuals.

Challenges Related to Victim Responses

The accuracy of victimization surveys relies on the sincerity of participants, their goodwill, and their ability to understand the questions and provide the required answers. Accuracy can be compromised when participants may not want to reveal incidents where they were a victim or may not provide important details about their victimization. In addition, one may exaggerate the frequency, extent, or seriousness of the incidents, or the reverse. Specific challenges include recall, telescoping, repeated victimizations, and victim knowledge.

RECALL Victim surveys tend to use either 6-month or 1-year reference points, for instance, asking "over the past year have you experienced any of the following?" Generally, respondents are able to recall more accurately an event that occurred within 3 months of the interview rather than one that occurred within 6 months; they can recall events over a 6-month period more accurately than those over a 12-month period. However, a shorter reference period requires more field interviews per year, increasing the data collection costs significantly. These increased costs would have to be balanced by cost reductions elsewhere, such as sample size. Reducing sample size, however, reduces the precision of estimates of relatively rare crimes.

TELESCOPING Another concern of researchers using reference periods in retrospective surveys is telescoping. Telescoping refers to a respondent's misspecification of when an incident occurred in relation to the reference period. For example, telescoping occurs if a respondent is asked about victimizations within the past 6 months and the respondent erroneously includes a victimization that occurred 8 months ago. Telescoped events, which actually occurred before the reference period, can be minimized at the time of the first interview by a technique known as bounding.

Bounding compares incidents reported in an interview with incidents reported in a previous interview and deletes duplicate incidents that were reported in the current reference period. In the NCS and NCVS designs each household visit is used to bind the next one by comparing reports in the current interview to those given 6 months prior. When there is a duplicate report, the respondent is reminded of the earlier report and asked if the new report represents the incident previously mentioned or if it is different. The first interview at a household entering the sample is unbounded, and data collected at these interviews are not included in NCS and NCVS estimates. However, if a household in a sample moves and another household moves into that address, the first interview with the replacement household is unbounded but is included in NCS and NCVS estimates (NCVS, 2011).

REPEATED VICTIMIZATIONS Individuals who have been repeatedly victimized, particularly by family members, may not remember individual incidents or may remember only the most recent event. Thus, information provided on specific incidents may in fact be blended recollections of several incidents. For instance, a person who experiences repeated assaults at the hands of an intimate partner may not be able to fully differentiate one episode from another. Alternatively, a person in a high-risk profession or neighborhood may have experienced multiple victimizations from different people and cannot recall when each occurred, what happened in one incident versus another, or which one involved the police.

In the NCVS, when a respondent experiences six or more similar but separate victimizations with limited recall, the interviewer is instructed to record these as a series of incidents. When calculating annual victimization rates, series victimizations are not included. Further, the incident report may record only the most recent incident.

VICTIM KNOWLEDGE Victimization surveys do not provide information of crimes for which the victim is not aware. For example, young children may not understand the nature of sexual acts and may not be aware they have been sexually victimized. A new immigrant woman may not define assault by her husband as a crime because it may not be defined as such in her country of origin.

Challenges Related to Interpretation of Data

Some of the shortcomings and limitations of victim surveys relate to the collecting, coding, and processing of statistical data. Face-to-face and telephone interviews depend on the accuracy and training of the interviewers who classify and code responses. Inaccurate coding or classification may introduce bias. Addington (2008) assesses the extent of nonresponse bias on the National Incident-Based Reporting System (NIBRS) estimates of violent crime.

Artificial fluctuations may occur in the interpretation of data. Upward crime trends may be due to careful reporting of offenses, and downward trends may indicate lower reporting or relaxed enforcement rather than changes in the commission of offenses. Thus, heightened public awareness about a particular type of crime may prompt overreporting or, alternatively, reduce underreporting. Similarly, increased police presence in a community or community confidence in the police may affect reporting of victimization not only to police (thereby affecting crime statistics) but also to survey administrators (thereby affecting victimization statistics).

Finally, changes in legislation may also affect the reporting of crimes. For example, the legalization of pornography in Denmark and the liberalization of sexual attitudes were followed by a decline in reported adult sexual offenses but an increase in child pornography cases.

■ Summary

The search for methods to provide reliable data on the number of crimes occurring in the country has involved a wide variety of approaches, including data collection by police and courts on crimes committed, data collection on offenders, and, more recently, victimization surveys. Victimization surveys have been described as a means to tap the "dark figure" of crime (Coleman & Moynihan, 1996), referring to the volume of incidents that are not officially recorded. Such data are believed to provide a more accurate representation of the "true" figure of crime.

No single data source is able to provide all the information required to build a full picture of crime and victimization. Rather, multiple sources of information provide data on different aspects of victimization. At times, the results from different sources vary widely, such as in the case of estimates of family violence between the NCVS and the NFVS. Nevertheless, each reporting system provides critical insights into the rate and nature of crime from a particular lens. It remains the responsibility of those analyzing, reporting, and using the data to determine what these various perspectives do and do not tell us about crime and its victims.

■ Key Terms

Cleared by exceptional means: Occurs when the police are unable to place formal charges against an alleged offender, for example, because the offender is dead, a victim refuses to cooperate, or extradition is denied.

Dark figure of crime: Describes the amount of unreported or undiscovered crime.

Hierarchy rule: This rule requires counting only the highest offense and ignoring all others; it applies only to the crime reporting process and does not affect the number of charges for which the defendant may be prosecuted in the courts.

Incidence: Crimes that take place during a particular period of time.

National Crime Victimization Survey (NCVS): A series of surveys, previously called the National Crime Survey (NCS), that has been collecting data on personal and household victimization since 1973.

National Incident-Based Reporting System (NIBRS): A more detailed version of the Uniform Crime Reporting program.

Prevalence: How many people experience a particular crime during their lifetime.

Uniform Crime Reporting (UCR): Provides some of the most commonly cited crime statistics in the United States and is concerned with index crimes that include attempted or completed murder and nonnegligent manslaughter, forcible rape, robbery, aggravated assault, burglary, larceny-theft, and motor vehicle theft.

Discussion Questions

1. How would you measure both the victim count and the crime offense count for the Anders Behring Breivik mass murders?
2. Discuss the hierarchy rule and the Petit triple murder.
3. Compare and contrast measurement of crime and offenders and measurement of victims in terms of sample, methodology, data collection, analysis, interpretation, and outcomes.
4. How would you measure risk of being a victim?
5. What suggestions do you have for measuring and establishing a useful international database for victimization?
6. What actions and attitudes assist law enforcement in measuring crime victimization?

Resources

American Statistical Association Committee on Law and Justice Statistics
http://www.amstat.org/comm/index.cfm?fuseaction=commdetails&txtComm=CA02

Bureau of Justice Statistics
   http://www.ojp.usdoj.gov/bjs/
Centers for Disease Control and Prevention Division of Violence Prevention
   http://www.cdc.gov/ncipc/dvp/dvp.htm
Crimes Against Children Research Center
   http://www.unh.edu/ccrc/
National Center for Juvenile Justice
   http://www.ncjj.org/
National Institute of Justice's Data Resource Program
   http://www.nij.gov/funding/data-resources-program/welcome.htm
Office for Victims of Crime
   http://www.ojp.usdoj.gov/ovc/
Office of Justice Programs: Violence Against Women and Family Violence
   Program
   http://www.nij.gov/topics/crime/violence-against-women/welcome.htm
National Archive of Criminal Justice Data lists the following data resource
   guides:
National Crime Victimization Survey Resource Guide. http://www.icpsr.umich
   .edu/icpsrweb/NACJD/NCVS/

- Capital Punishment in the United States
- Chicago Women's Health Risk Study
- Expenditure and Employment for the Criminal Justice System
- Federal Justice Statistics Program
- Geographical Information Systems
- Homicide
- Homicides in Chicago
- Law Enforcement Management and Administrative Statistics
- National Corrections Reporting Program
- National Crime Victimization Survey
- National Incident-Based Reporting System
- National Juvenile Corrections Data
- Project on Human Development in Chicago Neighborhoods
- Survey of Inmates in State and Federal Correctional Facilities
- Terrorism and Preparedness Data Resource Center
- Uniform Crime Reporting Program
- Violence Against Women

■ References

ABC News. (2010). Accused Petit murderer Joshua Komisarjevsky: "I lost control" and "enjoyed it." Retrieved from http://abcnews.go.com/US /petit-murder-trial-steven-hayes-diary-joshua-komisarjevsky/story?id =11916557

Addington, L. (2008). Assessing the extent of nonresponse bias on the NIBRS estimates of violent crime. *Journal of Contemporary Criminal Justice, 24*(1), 32–49.

Akiyama, Y., & Nolan, J. (1999). Methods for understanding and analyzing NIBRS data. *Journal of Quantitative Criminology, 15*(2), 225–238.

Australian Bureau of Statistics. (2004). Information paper: Measuring crime victimisation, Australia: The impact of different collection methodologies, 2002. Retrieved from http://www.abs.gov.au/ausstats/abs@.nsf/Lookup /5BF3A030F523595BCA2578B00011A06B?opendocument

Bachman, R. (1998). Incidence rates of violence against women: A comparison of the redesigned National Crime Victimization Survey and the 1985 National Family Violence Survey. Retrieved from http://www.vawnet.org

Bachman, R., & Saltzman, L.E. (1995). Violence against women: Estimates from the redesigned National Crime Victimization Survey (NCJ-154348). Bureau of Justice Statistics, U.S. Department of Justice.

Beaumont, P. (2011). Anders Behring Breivik: Portrait of a mass murderer. Guardian.co.uk. Retrieved from http://www.guardian.co.uk/world/2011 /jul/23/anders-behring-breivik-norway-attacks

Biderman, A.D., & Reiss, A.J. (1967). On exploring the "dark figure" of crime. *Annals of the American Academy of Political and Social Science, 374* (November): 1–15.

Bureau of Justice Statistics. (2010). UCR data tool. Retrieved from http://bjs .ojp.usdoj.gov/

Cantor, D., & Lynch, J.P. (2000). Self-report surveys as a measure of crime and criminal victimization. In D. Duffee (Ed.), *Measurement and analysis of crime and justice* (pp. 85–138). Washington, DC: National Institute of Justice. Retrieved from https://www.ncjrs.gov/criminal_justice2000 /vol_4/04c.pdf

Carter, L., & Wilson, M. (2006). Measuring professionalism in police officers. *Police Chief, 73*(8).

Caspi, A., McClay, J., Moffitt, T., Mill, J., Martin, J., Craig, I., Taylor, A., & Poulton, R. (2002). Role of genotype in the cycle of violence in maltreated children. *Science, 297*(5582), 851–854.

Chilton, R., & Jarvis, J. (1999). Victims and offenders in two crime statistics programs: A comparison of the National Incident-Based Reporting System (NIBRS) and the National Crime Victimization Survey (NCVS). *Journal of Quantitative Criminology, 15*(2), 193–205.

Coleman, C., & Moynihan, J. (1996). Haunted by the dark figure: Criminologists as ghostbusters? In M. Maguire (Ed.), *Understanding crime data: Haunted by the dark figure.* Buckingham, UK: Open University Press.

Dispatch Magazine Online. (2011). Newspaper studies Milwaukee police response times. Retrieved from http://www.911dispatch.com/page/2/

Dryburgh, H. (2009). Introduction to the General Social Survey. *Canadian Review of Sociology, 46*(4), 273–285.

Economic and Social Data Service. (2011). British Crime Survey. Retrieved from http://www.esds.ac.uk/government/bcs/datasets/

Fattah, E.A. (1997). *Criminology: Past, present and future. A critical overview.* Basingstoke, UK: Macmillan.

Federal Bureau of Investigation (FBI). (1985). Blueprint for the future of the Uniform Crime Reporting Program (Blueprint). Retrieved from http://www.ucrdatatool.gov/abouttheucr.cfm

Federal Bureau of Investigation (FBI). (2009a). Percent of crimes cleared by arrest of exceptional means. Retrieved from http://www2.fbi.gov/ucr/cius2009/offenses/clearances/index.html

Federal Bureau of Investigation (FBI). (2009b). National Incident-Based Reporting System (NIBRS). Retrieved from http://www.fbi.gov/about-us/cjis/ucr/ucr

Federal Bureau of Investigation (FBI). (2010). Cybercrime statistics. Retrieved from http://scamfraudalert.wordpress.com/2010/03/13/fbi-2009-cybercrime-statistics/

Federal Bureau of Investigation (FBI). (2011a). Crime statistics: New online tool makes research easier. Retrieved from http://www.fbi.gov/news/stories/2010/november/ucrtool_112910/ucrtool_112910

Federal Bureau of Investigation (FBI). (2011b). Preliminary annual Uniform Crime Report for 2010. Retrieved from http://www.fbi.gov/about-us/cjis/ucr/crime-in-the-u.s/2010/preliminary-annual-ucr-jan-dec-2010/.

Hindelang, M. (1976). *Criminal victimization in eight American cities: An analysis of common theft and assault.* Cambridge, MA: Ballinger.

James, N., & Rishard, L. (2008). *How crime in the United States is measured.* Document RL34309. Washington, DC: Congressional Research Service.

Jones, S. (2006). *Criminology* (3rd ed.). New York: Oxford.

Kempf, K.L. (1990). *Measurement issues in criminology*. New York: Springer-Verlag.

Leung, L. (2011). Surprise wants better data on police response times. Retrieved from http://www.azcentral.com/community/westvalley/articles/2008/11/27/20081127gl-nwvresponse1128.html#ixzz1Vy8eYbZ0

MacKenzie, D.L., Baunach, P.J., & Roberg, R.R. (1990). *Measuring crime: Large-scale, long-range efforts*. New York: State University of New York.

National Commission on Law Observance and Enforcement. (1931). Guide to federal records in the National Archives of the United States. Retrieved from http://www.archives.gov/research/guide-fed-records/groups/010.html

National Crime Victim Survey (NCVS). (2011). Methodological issues in the measurement of crime. Retrieved from http://www.icpsr.umich.edu/icpsrweb/NACJD/NCVS/

National Prisoner Statistics Summary of Sentenced Populations. (2009). Retrieved from http://bjs.ojp.usdoj.gov/content/pub/pdf/nps1b_09.pdf

Nieuwbeerta, P. (2002). *Crime victimization in comparative perspective: Results from the International Crime Victims Survey, 1989–2000*. Boom Juridische Uitgevers. The Federation Press, Australia.

President's Commission on Law Enforcement and Administration of Justice. (1967). *Task force report: Crime and its impact—an assessment* (p. v). Washington, DC: U.S. Government Printing Office.

Rand, M.R. (2009). National Crime Victimization Survey, Criminal Victimization, 2008. Bureau of Justice Statistics Bulletin, NCJ 227777, 1–7.

Rand, M.R., & Rennison, M. (2005). Bigger is not necessarily better: An analysis of violence against women estimates from the National Crime Victimization Survey and the National Violence Against Women Survey. *Journal of Quantitative Criminology, 21*(3), 267–291.

Schneider, A.L., Griffith, W.R., Sumi, D.H., & Burcart, J.M. (1978). *Portland forward records check of crime victims*. Washington, DC: National Institute of Law Enforcement and Criminal Justice.

Schwartz, J., Steffenmeier, D., Zhong, H., & Ackerman, J. (2009). Trends in the gender gap in violence: Reevaluating NCVS and other evidence. *Criminology, 47*(2), 401–425.

Statistics Canada. (2011a). Adult Criminal Court Survey (ACCS). Retrieved from http://www.statcan.gc.ca/cgi-bin/imdb/p2SV.pl?Function=getSurvey&SDDS=3312&lang=en&db=imdb&adm=8&dis=2

Statistics Canada. (2011b). General Social Survey-Victimization. Retrieved from http://www.statcan.gc.ca/cgi-bin/imdb/p2SV.pl?Function=getSurvey&SDDS=4504&lang=en&db=imdb&adm=8&dis=2

Statistics Canada. (2011c). Uniform Crime Reporting survey (UCR). Retrieved from http://www.statcan.gc.ca/cgi-bin/imdb/p2SV.pl?Function=getSurvey&SDDS=3302&lang=en&db=imdb&adm=8&dis=2

Straus, M. (2007). Conflict tactics scales. In N.A. Jackson (Ed.), *Encyclopedia of domestic violence* (pp. 190–197). New York: Routledge.

Van Dijk, J.J.M., van Kesteren, J.N., & Smit, P. (2008). *Criminal victimisation in international perspective: Key findings from the 2004–2005 ICVS and EU ICS*. The Hague: Boom Legal Publishers.

West, H.C., Sabol, W. J., & Greenman, S.J. (2010). Prisoners, 2009. U.S. Department of Justice, Office of Justice Programs. Bureau of Justice Statistics. Washington, DC: NCJ 231675. Retrieved from http://bjs.ojp.usdoj.gov/content/pub/ascii/p09.txt

Theories of Victimization

CHAPTER

3

◾ Objectives

- To describe the history of victimology theories
- To identify and discuss victim-based theories
- To identify and discuss interactional theories of victimization
- To identify and discuss societal theories of victimization
- To introduce ecological theory
- To apply theories to a case

◾ Key Terms

Classical criminology
Critical criminology
Just world theory
Lifestyle routine activities theory
Positivistic
Spiritualistic theories
Stockholm syndrome

CASE

On July 2, 2003, NBA professional basketball star Kobe Bryant was charged with sexual assault of a 19-year-old employee of a Colorado hotel. Prosecutors stated Bryant flirted with the woman, a front desk employee, and after a tour of the resort, the two ended up in his room and began to kiss. While acknowledging that the kissing was consensual, the victim said that "at some point Bryant's voice became deeper and he became rougher. She asked him to stop, but Bryant allegedly blocked her exit, grabbed her, and forced her over a chair to rape her." The attorneys argued "that Bryant's hands were around the woman's neck, equating a perceived threat of potential strangulation if she resisted his advances." (CBS News, 2009) Testimony from the victim included that she cried during the act and said no at least twice. The bellman told investigators that as the woman left work that night, she was upset and crying, her clothes and hair were disheveled, and she reported that Bryant had choked her and forced sex on her. Evidence included a T-shirt of Bryant's stained with the victim's blood and a small bruise on her jaw.

During his interview with detectives Bryant initially denied having sex with the woman, then changed his account after the investigators told him they had physical evidence to support a sexual encounter, saying she initiated consensual sex. He continued to say the woman never cried, and she gave him a kiss goodbye before she left his room. Defense counsel challenged the victim's initial inconsistent statements to detectives, forensic evidence, and her past emotional and mental health stability (CBS News, 2009). District Judge Terry Ruckriegle ruled "that the woman's sex life in the 3 days surrounding her encounter with Bryant could be admitted as evidence, which may have bolstered the defense's contention that she had sex with someone else after leaving Bryant and before she went to a hospital exam—a potentially key blow to her credibility." (ESPN, 2004)

FIGURE 3-1 Kobe Bryant
© Domenic Gareri/ShutterStock, Inc.

Although victim names are not to be published in the media, blunders by the court made this victim's name, address, telephone number, and photographs available on the Internet. With her identity revealed, the victim received at least two death threats and relentless media attention. As a result the victim chose to no longer participate in the trial, and the criminal case was dropped by prosecutors in the midst of jury selection. A civil lawsuit filed against Bryant was settled with specific terms of the settlement not being disclosed to the public. As part of an agreement with the accuser to dismiss the sexual assault charge, Bryant issued an apology to the victim, her family, his family, and community citizens (ESPN, 2004). See **Figure 3-1**.

■ Introduction

From the beginning of time, people have attempted to understand and explain why some individuals become victims of natural disasters, disease, attack by wild animals, and violence by the hand of other humans. The thought that such events are random is intolerable, and thus explanations help create order and dispel generalized fear and anxiety. Theories regarding victimization are shaped by the scientific knowledge, religious beliefs, and social structures of the time in which they originate. However, theories also shape public attitudes and social policy regarding legal responses and justice approaches. If victimization is caused by God as punishment for evil within the person, the person is to be shunned or killed. If victimization is caused by the offender and the victim is innocent, it is the offender who should be punished. If the victim somehow precipitated the crime, culpability is shared. If societal structures are the causes of crime and victimization, then social change is necessary. This chapter traces the development of theories for understanding victimization to present-day constructions. It also examines the impact of theory on social policy and justice.

■ History of Victimology and Theory Development

The concept of victim, one of the most ancient of humanity, emerges from the attempt of people and the societies in which they lived to both explain the reasons for victimization and determine appropriate redress. In his ground breaking work in *Theoretical Criminology* published in 1958, Vold provided a framework for categorizing theories that relate to victimology beginning with early spiritual explanations, followed by classical and positivist explanations, and biological, social and economic explanations.

Spiritual Explanations began in early times as people attempted to make sense of unexplained events. Natural disasters such as floods, earthquakes and draught were explained by attributing them to the interference of the spirit world. Thus, human suffering was viewed as a form of universal justice, taking vengeance for an evil committed by the individual or a member of their family. The gods could be appeased through the use of sacred rites, such as offering animals or humans as sacrifices (Vold & Bernard, 1986).

When suffering was caused by another human being, justice was primarily accomplished through individual acts of revenge, with victims or families of victims taking the law into their own hands and, in effect, donning the role of judge, jury, and executioner. Nevertheless, the gods could intervene. Babylonian law as articulated in The Code of Hammurabi (1786 BC), for example, represented a system of restitution based on revenge and cruelty and required a victim's family and community to assume responsibility for aiding the victim if the offender was unable to be brought to justice (see Chapter 5 for additional information about this code). The code regulated the organization of the Babylonian society and ensured the accountability of those in positions of responsibility and authority, primarily through death. For example, a craftsman whose shoddy workmanship resulted in the collapse of a house and the death of its owner was to be slain; if the owner's son was killed, then the builder's son was slain. Additionally, however, death was the punishment for providing false testimony in court, trading with a minor or slave, or stealing a pig (Van De Mieroop, 2005). Mosaic law, as described in the Torah and the Bible, tempered earlier forms of punishment outlined in the Code of Hammurabi and moved to a concept whereby the punishment was determined by the severity of the crime. "An eye for an eye, a tooth for a tooth . . . ," for instance, is a familiar biblical reference that highlights views regarding crime and punishment (Mathew 5:38). The first reference to this theme is found in the Old Testament book Exodus (21:23–25) and reads as follows:

> Thou shalt give life for life,
> Eye for eye, tooth for tooth, hand for hand, foot for foot,
> Burning for burning, wound for wound, stripe for stripe.

During the middle ages in England, there was a shift in viewing crime as an offense against a victim to an offense against God and the king. Henry II produced a common law in which the debt for crime was owed not to the victim but to society and the state. In this system the victim's needs became subjugated to the more immediate needs of the state. As such, an informal system of extrajudicial activity flourished, including payment of compensation, retribution, and vigilantism (Kearon & Godfrey, 2007). Similarly, in the early 1700s aboriginal communities responded collectively to criminal offenses, with tribal law tending to view any transgression against an individual as a transgression against the entire community. The community, in essence, appropriated a victim's concerns, and whether the communal response included a long-standing blood feud, vendetta, or even monetary reparation, the core purpose was not the restoration of any moral order but rather the reestablishment of authority and the securing of optimal conditions for survival of the community as a whole.

Under the Code of Hammurabi, grim retaliatory punishments took no note of excuses or explanations with one striking exception, spiritual intervention. Specifically, an accused person could cast himself into the river Euphrates and if the current safely returned him to shore, he was declared innocent (Van De Mieroop, 2005). Similarly, in the 1200s trial by ordeal was a method of determining if a woman was a witch. By this method, a woman would be tied up and thrown into blessed water. If she sank she was determined to be innocent, but if she floated her status as a witch was confirmed. Running the gauntlet or walking on fire were other examples or ordeals that if passed could determine innocence. Trial by ordeal was condemned by the Pope in 1215. Nevertheless, a more recent example of spiritualistic theories in action was the famous witches trials in Salem Massachusetts in 1692 in which 24 suspected witches were put to death for allegedly causing unexplained illnesses in children (Bernard, Snipes & Gerould, 2010).

Classical criminology emerged from the philosophy of the Enlightenment, and the concept that the rights of man needed to be protected from the oppression and corruption of existing institutions. Most oppressive of these institutions was thought to be the justice system which was characterized by arbitrary and harsh punishments and an absence of due process (Taylor, Walton & Young, 1973). A key contributor to this new ideology was Cesare Bonesana Marchese de Beccaria whose essay *On Crimes and Punishments* (1764/1963) was based on the concepts of social contract theory or utilitarianism as elucidated by such philosophers as Hobbes, Locke, Montesquieu and Rousseau. Beccaria proposed the following: all men are self-seeking and capable of committing crime; society has an interest to maintain social order and humans accept that anti-social behavior must be controlled; punishment must be used to deter crime but this punishment must be proportional to the crime (Taylor, Walton & Young, 1973; Vold & Bernard, 1986). Beccaria's ideas were so revolutionary at the time that he published his essay anonymously and in 1766 it was condemned by the Catholic Church and placed on the Index of Forbidden books. Nevertheless, in 1791 following the French Revolution, his principles formed the basis of the French legal code (Bernard, Snipes and Gerould, 2010).

The classical criminological theory that arose from Beccaria's work had considerable appeal due to the notion of rational choice. That is, individuals will freely determine whether to engage in crime based on an analysis of the relative costs and benefits. The means of deterring crime are therefore straightforward, and simply rely on ensuring that the pain or cost of committing crime is higher than the pleasure or benefits accrued from the crime. This notion of deterrence remains a central feature of sentencing decision-making today (Regehr & Kanani, 2010). Rasche (1996) identifies that the popularity of the classical school was the degree to which it placed responsibility for crime on the rational decision-making of the individual criminal. However, the focus on the criminal act as the means for determining punishment ignored individual differences between those who committed crime. The rise of science, medicine and other social research during the 18th and 19th centuries revealed increasing numbers of ways in which people were not self-determining. This included both external factors, such as the physical, social and economic environment, and internal factors such as mental capacity and maturity, mental and physical health, and psychopathology. Thus, **positivistic** explanations for crime grew in popularity. These explanations were premised on the assumption that human behavior was influenced, at least in part, by predetermined biological, psychological and social factors. These models brought with them the appeal of "objectivity" (Taylor, Walton & Young, 1973).

Biological theories focused on hereditary and defectiveness and presumed that criminality could be either inherited genetically or produced by biological or physical defects. Early biological approaches included Phillipe Pinel's *Nosographie philosophique ou methode de l'analyse appliquee a la medecine* (1798) and Henry Maudsley's The Physiology and Pathology of the Mind (1867). Both these authors now have large forensic mental health facilities named in their honor in Montreal Canada and London England respectively. While some early biological models were later refuted such as those that focused on physical attributes including phrenology (the shape of the skull as an indicator of criminal intents) or the analysis of facial features, others continue to hold promise. For instance, recent research has focused on neurotransmitters, hormones and both the central nervous system and the autonomic nervous systems (Bernard, Snipes & Gerould, 2010). Vold and Bernard (1986) caution that biological factors must be seen solely as a contributor to criminal activity and not a cause. These factors may increase the likelihood of criminal behavior but only in interaction with psychological and social forces.

Psychological theories focus on the notions of personality or mental disorder, beginning with Sigmund Freud's pioneering work in psychoanalytic theory and the unconscious, whereby behavior is driven by the urges and impulses of the ID and moderated or controlled by the superego. More recent models such as those of Albert Bandura focused on behaviorial approaches and the individual's cognitive appraisal of the rewards associated with deviant behavior. Such theories differ widely in their assumptions about how the human mind works, but they have in common an attempt to explain human behavior in terms of psychological functioning. Hans Eysenck (1947), for instance, described extraversion and neurosis as leading to criminal behavior. Later, Robert Hare described psychopathic traits and developed the Psychopathy Checklist (Hare, 1991). As noted above with respect to biological factors however, psychological factors may create a predisposition to criminal behavior, but are unlikely to act in isolation to social factors.

Social structural theories began with the work of Durkheim (1964) who introduced the science of political economy. In order to maintain a society, all members must give up freedoms and make sacrifices; what is in the interests of society is not consistently in the interests of individual citizens. The law plays the role of maintaining order by repressing deviation and enforcing conformity. However, resources and sacrifices are not equally distributed in society and crime results from the dissatisfaction caused by social inequality. This work gave rise to a large body of theory related to the intersection between crime and poverty. Merton (1938) argued that it is the social structure and culture of American society that gives rise to crime. That is, the assumption that accumulated wealth is associated with higher social value and worth degrades those who do not possess such resources. This produces strain in all members of society, but particularly those in the less privileged classes. This strain eventually results in criminal behavior (Vold & Bernard, 1986). Rasche (1996) suggests that the conclusion of social structural theories is that a society creates its own problems with crime and the solution to crime is changing of social structures.

Related to social structural theories are social control theories. Rather than assuming that biological, psychological or social factors cause people who would normally be law abiding to commit crime, control theories assume that all people would naturally commit crime but are controlled by forces in society to refrain from doing so (Bernard, Snipes & Gerould, 2010). One theorist in this area, Hirschi (1969), suggests that control is exerted by social bonds such as those with family, peer groups, or within important organizations such as school. Subsequently Hirschi added the concept of self-control, whereby the early social bonds with parents and others lead to the formation of internal mechanisms for control. Policy implications of these theories focus on two aspects. First, programs aimed at parenting to increase the likelihood of instilling values that will result in internal control. Secondly opportunities for social engagement of older youth such as school-based or community-based programs that enhance social bonds (Bernard, Snipes & Gerould, 2010).

Another form of control is labeling (Becker, 1963). Labeling theory suggests that society attempt to control behavior through social stigma but attaching negative labels to it. This stigma has two possible negative outcomes for society. First, it may create further social disengagement, thereby limiting opportunities and increasing the risk of criminal activity. However, such labeling behaviors may also become self-fulfilling as those to whom the labels are attached embrace it as their identity and then behave according. In this instance, the label paradoxically becomes a badge of honor in certain social groups.

Social structural and social control theories gave rise in turn to critical criminology. This model arose as a revolt against traditional theories for crime and deviance. These new emerging models which included Marxist, feminist and conflict models, suggested that deviant action must be examined from the perspective of the deviant actor. That is, how do they describe their intentions? Further, these models include a denial of absolutism, that is, definitions of social order are not consensual or monolithic (Taylor, Walton and Young, 1975). A present day example of this concept is the Occupy Wall Street movement and subsequent riots that have at times emerged from the movement. It is a matter of perception whether individuals in these movements who engage in violent activity are social activists using legitimate means of protest or terrorists committing punishable crimes.

A wide range of theories continues to attempt to understand crime and victimization. However, they tend to fall into three broad categories: theories that focus on the role of the victim in his or her own victimization, theories that focus on the interaction between the victim and the offender that result in crime, and theories that focus more broadly on societal influences that lead to victimization.

■ Victim-Based Theories

By the mid-20th century, in an effort to better understand the phenomenon of victimization, criminologists began to develop methods for categorizing different types of victims, referred to as victim typologies. These typologies were based on a variety of factors, including biological, sociological, psychological, demographic, and psychiatric. Benjamin Mendelsohn (1940) coined the term "victimology," proposing that this be an entirely new field of study, not merely a branch of criminology but a separate and distinct discipline that would be the "reverse of criminology" (Schafer, 1968, p. 42). In 1937 Mendelsohn interviewed victims and, from his analysis, concluded that most victims at least unconsciously participated in their own victimization. Mendelsohn's (1940, 1974) original formulation classified victims according to their relative degree of responsibility and power to control or affect situations. These categories, further described by Zur (1994), also judged the degree of guilt or responsibility, ranging from total innocence/no guilt to 100% responsibility/total guilt (**Table 3-1**).

Fattah (1967) similarly sought to classify victims according to their level of participation in the crime. His five major classes parallel those of Mendelsohn: the nonparticipating victim, the latent or predisposed victim, the provocative victim, the precipitating victim, and the false victim.

In 1965 Hermann Mannheim suggested that the distinction between criminal and victim actually often becomes vague and blurred in individual cases. He continued that the deeper and longer one scrutinized the actions of persons involved in a crime, the more doubtful it is who is to blame for the tragic outcome (Mannheim, 1965a, 1965b). Henri Ellenberger (1954), a prominent psychoanalyst of the same era, concentrated his research on the psychological dynamic between offender

TABLE 3-1 Mendelsohn's Six Victim Types

Victim who is completely innocent.

- Does not share any responsibility of the offense with the perpetrator

- The ideal victim
- Includes children, those of random or rampage shooting, of unexpected natural disasters, and who suffer a crime while they are unconscious

Victim with minor guilt and responsibility due to his or her own ignorance.

- With some thought, planning, awareness, information, or consciousness, he or she could have expected danger and avoided or minimized the harm to himself or herself

- Adults who were victimized due to being in the wrong place at the wrong time
- Includes person attacked walking on a dark street

Victim who is as guilty as the offender (voluntary victim) and shares equally in responsibility.

- Chose to be part of the interaction. He or she is not caught by surprise, and common sense could have anticipated the damage that occurred.

- People victimized while engaging in risky behavior
- Includes contracting a sexually transmitted disease from a prostitute; or seeking, challenging, or enticing the perpetrator; or being a willing participant in a chicken game, gun dual, or double suicide

Victim who is slightly guiltier than the offender (provoker).

- An active participant in an interaction where he or she likely to get hurt
- Seeks the damaging contact, while the offender can easily withdraw from the situation

- Someone who provokes or induces someone to commit a crime
- Includes an abusive husband who is killed by his battered wife, cult members who chose to enter the cult as adults and then were brainwashed and harmed (e.g., Jonestown, Waco)

Victim who is exclusively responsible for his or her victimization.

- initiates the contact and commits an act that is likely to lead to injury

- Someone injured while committing a crime
- Includes a violent perpetrator who is killed by another person in self-defense or a mentally healthy and competent individual who commits a rationally planned suicide

The imaginary victim.

- Has suffered nothing at all but accuses another falsely

- The false accusation may be volitional or involitional
- Includes false allegations of assault and a delusional individual

Data from Mendelsohn, B. (1940). Rape in criminology. Giustizia Penale; Zur, O. (1994). Rethinking "Don't Blame the Victim": Psychology of Victimhood.

and victim. Ellenberger stressed the importance of focusing particular attention on what he refers to as "victimogenesis" rather than "crimino-genesis," and he urged criminologists to study dangers to which victims could be vulnerable due specifically to their occupation, social class, or physical condition.

Zur (1994) cautioned that these descriptive categories, in their attempt to differentiate among many situations of victimhood, are controversial, inconclusive, and incomplete, particularly with respect to guilt and responsibility. Cultural, demographic, and personal variables, although not accounted for in the above categories, are nevertheless critical for any assessment of guilt and responsibility. It is also important when evaluating the degree of responsibility in a given situation that the following parameters be assessed: ethnicity (minorities are at greater risk of victimization than those in the majority), gender (women are at greater risk than men are in certain personal crimes, such as rape), socioeconomic status, physical attributes (such as strength and ability), mental status, familial background, and cultural values (cultures that promote violence vs. those that promote harmony) (Zur, 1994).

Hans von Hentig, in his classic book, *The Criminal and His Victim* (1948), offered another victim typology that explored the relationship between the offender and the sufferer. A section of his book, titled "The Victim's Contribution to the Genesis of Crime," concluded that many victims may actually contribute to their victimization by inciting or provoking the offender or by fostering a situation in which they are likely to be victimized. Von Hentig's 13 Category Typology is based on psychological, social, and biological factors, in contrast to Mendelsohn's categories based on guilt and responsibility (**Table 3-2**). A read of von Hentig's categories quickly highlights the influence of dominant societal beliefs on the development of theory.

Another criminologist scholar, Stephen Schafer, reviewed both Mendelsohn's and von Hentig's work and devised his own concept, termed "functional responsibility." Titling his book, *The Victim and His Criminal*, in direct opposition to von Hentig's title and work, he asserted that victimization occurs as a result of the functional interplay of causative elements. He believed that a typology of criminal–victim relationships, along with the pattern of social situations in which they appear, might be more useful, and he emphasized that victim–risks evaluation was the most promising (Schafer, 1968) (**Table 3-3**).

The concept of victim precipitation has a long history in the victimology literature. It implies that the victim has something to do with his or her own victimization. This concept needs a context for definition. In a small town it may be quite normal to leave a car or house unlocked. However, in a large urban area this act could be seen as precipitation. The person who left keys in a car did not mean for it to be a temptation–opportunity situation, but it can be. Is the husband who has chronically ridiculed and abused his wife only to be shot by her after an assault partially responsible for his own victimization? Studying victim culpability, according to Galaway and Hudson (1981), involves efforts to measure the extent to which culpability may occur for selected types of victimization.

This concept of victim culpability was introduced by Wolfgang as victim precipitation with regard to homicide cases in which he believed

TABLE 3-2 Hans von Hentig's 13 Category Typology

The young	• Viewed by criminals as weak or inexperienced and vulnerable to attack. • Not usually victims of crimes for profit. • May be kidnapped for profit or used by criminals to commit crimes against property.
The female	• Described by von Hentig as another form of weakness because they have less strength against an attacker.
The old	• Likely to be victims of property crimes because they have accumulated wealth and have wealth-giving power. • Can be viewed as weaker due to less physical strength than a younger person.
The mentally defective	• Von Hentig identified the mentally ill, mentally retarded, and substance abusers as handicapped in any struggle against crime.
Immigrants	• Von Hentig described immigrants as vulnerable while adjusting to a new culture in that they can suffer poverty, emotional difficulties, and rejection by groups in the new country. • Criminals often understand the immigrant's disturbed situation and take advantage of it.
Minorities	• The minorities' position is similar to the immigrants'. • The lack of equality increases their chances of victimization. • Racial prejudices can lead to violent criminal–victim relationships.
Dull normals	• Von Hentig said that "dull normals" are born victims in that the criminal or swindler can exploit their vulnerability.
The depressed	• Von Hentig believed that a depressed person's attitude is apathetic and submissive, and thus the person is unable to have any fighting qualities. • The depressed person's mental resistance is reduced, and he or she is open to victimization.
The acquisitive	• Von Hentig described how criminal syndicates, racketeers, gamblers, confidence men, and others exploit the victim's need for money.
The wanton	• Von Hentig describes this person as dimmed by the generalization of laws and obscured by social conventions.
The lonesome and heartbroken	• Von Hentig cites mass murders as preying on this type of victim and gives the examples of Henri Desire Landru, Fritz Haarmann, and Jack the Ripper. • These murderers took advantage of the loneliness of their victims.
Tormentors	• Von Hentig describes tormentors as being in family tragedies. • Examples include an alcoholic or psychotic father who tortured his family over time and who is finally killed by his son. • This type of victim was said to strain a situation to such a degree that he becomes a victim of the stressful atmosphere he himself creates.
The blocked	• Von Hentig defines the blocked victim as a person who has been so enmeshed in a losing situation that defensive moves become impossible. • He gives the example of someone being blackmailed and then unable to seek the assistance of the police.

Data from von Hentig, H. 1948. The criminal and his victim: Studies in the sociobiology of crime. New Haven, CT: Yale University Press.

TABLE 3-3 Schafer's Victim Precipitation Typologies

Unrelated victims	No responsibility; the victim was an unfortunate target of the perpetrator
Provocative victims	The victim shares responsibility, and the offender is reacting to something in the victim's behavior
Precipitative victims	Victims who leave themselves open for victimization by placing themselves in dangerous settings
Biologically weak victims	Age or deficit places these victims at risk for victimization
Socially weak victims	For example, minorities or immigrants are victimized because they have not adjusted to the culture
Self-victimizing victims	Persons who are involved in crimes, such as drug use, prostitution, or gambling, whereby the victim and offender act in concert
Political victims	Persons who oppose those in power and are victimized to be kept under control

Data from Schafer, S. 1968. The victim and his criminal: A study in functional responsibility. New York: Random House.

the victim to be suicide oriented. He viewed a victim's will to live to be a mitigating factor in the offender's guilt. As Wolfgang stated, "In many cases the victim has most of the major characteristics of an offender; in some cases two potential offenders come together in a homicide situation and it is probably only chance which results in one becoming a victim and the other an offender" (Wolfgang, 1958, p. 265). Wolfgang (1958, 1959) viewed the victim and offender as separate, distinct entities that simultaneously act as equal participants in the homicide. He conducted a study focused exclusively on criminal homicides committed in the city of Philadelphia (as recorded by the Philadelphia Homicide Squad) from January 1948 to December 1952, during which time there were 588 homicide victims, with 621 suspects taken into custody. Wolfgang's conceptualization of the victim-precipitated homicide was derived from the cases in which the victim had been found to be the direct and primary precipitator of the crime, that is, the first to use physical force immediately before the homicide. Wolfgang's Philadelphia study concluded that just over one-fourth of the 588 homicides (150 homicides, or 26%) were victim precipitated.

Recent homicide typologies can be useful in facilitating our understanding of the dynamics of homicide and victim involvement. One evidence-based homicide typology was developed based on a longitudinal study of 336 homicide offenders in New Jersey (Roberts, Zgoba, & Shahidullah, 2007). A fourfold typology was developed: (1) homicide precipitated by a general altercation or argument, (2) homicide during the commission of a felony, (3) domestic violence–related homicide, and (4) homicide as a result of an alcohol-related accident. An in-depth analysis revealed that most homicides precipitated by an argument involved a perpetrator who easily went into a rage and/or did not value human life (Roberts et al., 2007).

Menachem Amir, a student of Marvin Wolfgang's, analyzed Philadelphia police records on rape incidents between 1958 and 1960. He concluded that 19% of the forcible rape cases were victim precipitated (Amir, 1971). One of the risk factors he identified was that of alcohol use, especially if both victim and perpetrator had been drinking. Amir's book was published at the time the women's movement began to focus on the issue of rape, resulting in considerable criticism by feminist activists and researchers. In particular, Weiss and Borges (1973) faulted his study on the basis of relying on police accounts, methodological and procedural errors, and a faulty theoretical framework. For example, Amir suggested that victims might desire the rape as a rebellious behavior.

Galaway and Hudson (1981) argued that the concept of victim culpability raises interesting problems. Although there is evidence that some victims may be partially responsible for their victimization, there is also the danger of fueling a widespread phenomenon of blaming the victim. The Lebanese American artist, poet, writer, philosopher, and theologian Kahlil Gibran expressed the victim culpability concept poetically in his 1920 book, *The Forerunner*, through a poem titled "Critics" (**Box 3-1**).

Blaming the victim is a phenomenon common to both people hearing of a crime and to victims themselves. Of the many factors that contribute to victim blaming is a belief in a just world. **Just world theory** is based on the concept that in an effort to retain the belief that the world is predictable and essentially safe, people who become aware that another is victimized will search for an explanation and rationalize that the victim must in some way have deserved his or her plight (Learner, 1980). This is a common theme in rape crisis work, where not only society often blames the victim for her own assault, but victims themselves internalize the sense of culpability and begin to self-blame (Koss, 2000). In the mid-1970s the women's movement launched a formidable campaign to address this deep-seated myth that female victims of forcible rape and attempted rape had, in some way, provoked the assault. The goal of this national effort was to exorcise the automatic and generally accepted response of blaming the victim and to raise awareness about where the sole responsibility for such violent crimes truly lay: with the perpetrators themselves. In an effort to assist women in crisis, many grassroots community organizations began to develop women's support groups, counseling centers,

> **Box 3-1   Critics**
>
> One nightfall, a man traveling on horseback towards the sea reached an inn by the roadside. He dismounted and, confident in man and night like all riders towards the sea, he tied his horse to a tree beside the door and entered into the inn.
>
> At midnight, when all were asleep, a thief came and stole the traveler's horse.
>
> In the morning the man awoke, and discovered that his horse was stolen. And he grieved for his horse, and that a man had found it in his heart to steal.
>
> Then his fellow lodgers came and stood around him and began to talk.
>
> And the first man said, "How foolish of you to tie your horse outside the stable."
>
> And the second said, "Still more foolish, without even hobbling the horse!"
>
> And the third man said, "It is stupid at best to travel to the sea on horseback."
>
> And the fourth said, "Only the indolent and the slow of foot own horses."
>
> Then the traveler was much astonished. At last he cried, "My friends, because my horse was stolen, you have hastened one and all to tell me my faults and my short-comings. But strange, not one word of reproach have you uttered about the man who stole my horse."
>
> *Source:* Gibran (1920/1963, pp. 33–34)

and rape crisis centers both locally and at major universities and medical centers across North America. As a result of this nationwide initiative law enforcement officials, prosecutors, hospital emergency department staff, nurses, and social workers began to implement rape crisis intervention programs, distributing a variety of materials aimed at encouraging women to report rape to police and to seek medical attention and crisis counseling. The work of the women's movement extended to victims of domestic violence, and battered women's shelters as well as services were established to help these women.

The challenge in the victimology field is to continue engaging in both conceptual and empirical work regarding victim culpability but to discover ways to be sure this work is appropriately used and to avoid widespread victim blaming (Galaway & Hudson, 1981). Vulnerability refers to the susceptibility of a person to being victimized through no fault of his or her own based on demographics or other characteristics as described in von Hentig's typology. For example, does age matter in victimization, such as the very young or the very old? Are women more susceptible than men to certain types of victimization? Is race a factor for some groups?

Galaway and Hudson (1981) suggested the analysis of victim vulnerability serves at least two useful functions. First, identification of a population group that may be susceptible to victimization may assist in crime prevention efforts for this group. Second, such an analysis may help to dispel common beliefs or myths and direct a more precise focus on the nature of the crime victimization problem. Galaway and Hudson gave the example of evidence that most crimes are intraracial, which helps dispel the myth that Black offenders victimize White citizens. In the age category, victimization surveys indicate that the elderly are less victimized than younger population groups; however, as a group they are more fearful of crime. Thus, victim programs might direct attention toward the elders' fear of crime and recommend strategies to decrease that fear.

■ Interactional Theories

Interactional theories consider that intersection between the victim and the offender and their environment. One of the most commonly used interactional theories of victimization is the **lifestyle routine activities theory** (Cohen & Felson, 1979; Hindelang, Gottfredson, & Garafalo, 1978). This theory proposes that certain personal characteristics and lifestyle activities increase or decrease an individual's risk of victimization. These can include age, gender, employment status, and marital status. With this in mind, certain groups can be expected to have a higher risk for both property and violent victimization. Due to variations in lifestyle, vulnerable groups, which include individuals who are young, male, unemployed, and unmarried, experience greater risks due to increased exposure. Indeed, research suggests that people with risky lifestyles are more prone to victimization (Schreck & Fisher, 2004). Such risky lifestyle activities include substance abuse, indiscriminate socializing, engaging in criminal activities, types of employment, and prior experience with direct or vicarious victimization (Fisher, Sloan, Cullen, & Lu, 1998; Lasley, 1989; Mustaine, 1997; Mustaine & Tewksbury, 1998).

Lifestyle, however, is not purely a personal choice. Hindelang and colleagues (1978) proposed that an individual is constrained by role expectations and structural characteristics based on factors such as age and race. Their adaptations to these constraints are reflected in routine daily activities, both vocational (e.g., school and work) and leisure activities, that may expose an individual to high-risk victimization situations (Walklate, 1989). For instance, a single mother on welfare may have no option but to live in a high crime neighborhood. Both she and her children are thus exposed to opportunities for victimization that a child born to a professional couple in the suburbs is not. Hindelang and colleagues

TABLE 3-4 Eight Propositions Regarding Lifestyle and Victimization

- The probability of suffering a personal victimization is directly related to the amount of time that a person spends in public places (e.g., on the street, in parks, etc.) and particularly in public places at night.
- The probability of being in public places, particularly at night, varies as a function of lifestyle.
- Social contacts and interactions occur disproportionately among individuals who share similar lifestyles.
- An individual's chances of personal victimization are dependent on the extent to which the individual shares demographic characteristics with offenders.
- The proportion of time an individual spends among nonfamily members varies as a function of lifestyle.
- The probability of personal victimization, particularly personal theft, increases as a proportion of time that an individual spends among nonfamily members.
- Variations in lifestyle are associated with variations in the ability of individuals to isolate themselves from persons with offender characteristics.
- Variations in lifestyle are associated with variations in the convenience, the desirability, and the vincibility of a person as a target for personal victimizations.

Data from Walklate, S. 1989. *Victimology: The Victim and the Criminal Justice Process.* London. Unwin Hyman Ltd.

suggested that personal victimization is related to a number of interrelated factors, such as those found in **Table 3-4.**

Lifestyle can also be influenced by other social factors. Indeed, a major assumption of routine activities theory is that social changes affect criminal opportunities. For instance, increased demand of expensive goods increases the risk they will be stolen. Further, increases in safety precautions taken by the public may decrease the availability of victims and displace criminals to another location (Meier & Miethe, 1993). Cohen and Felson (1979) proposed a routine activities theory of crime to explain the rising crime rates in the United States after World War II. They suggested that after World War II, Americans began spending more time outside of their homes, either working or engaging in leisure activities; these changes in lifestyle and behaviors put them at a greater risk for victimization. More suitable targets became available because homes were left unattended for extended periods of time, and individuals often found themselves in unfamiliar places. Fattah (2000), in an attempt to develop a comprehensive system for understanding victimization from an interactive model approach, grouped relevant factors into 10 categories (**Table 3-5**). This model incorporates victim characteristics, victim beliefs and behaviors, offender motivations, interactions between victims and offenders, the environment, and social attitudes.

Fattah (1979) identified fear of crime as a factor that influences victimization. Studies suggest that individual characteristics are related to

TABLE 3-5 Factors Affecting Victimization

Opportunities	• Linked to the characteristics and activities of potential targets
Risk factors	• Sociodemographic (age, gender, area of residence) • Lifestyle (alcohol use)
Motivated offenders	• Criteria by which offenders choose victims
Exposure	• Degree to which lifestyle and environment precipitate exposure to offenders
Associations	• Degree of homogeneity with offender populations • Contacts through personal, social or professional life
Dangerous times, dangerous places	• Times with higher risk including nights and weekends • Places with higher risk including bars and clubs
Dangerous behaviors	• Negligence and carelessness for property crimes (not locking) • Behavior where ability to defend oneself is reduced (hitchhiking)
High-risk activities	• Illegal activities in the pursuit of fun • Dangerous occupations (such as prostitution)
Defensive / avoidance behaviors	• Fear of crime and prevention are important in reducing victimization • Elderly people for instance curtail activities
Structural / cultural proneness	• Powelessness and deprivation are associated with increased victimization • Cultural marginalization and stigmatization increase risk for instance of hate crimes

Data from Fattah, E. 2000. Victimology, past, present and future. *Criminologie. 33*(1) 17-46.

fear of crime, including an individual's gender, age, race, income, and urban residence. This research has generally found that women, the elderly, non-Whites, the poor, and those who live in urban areas are more fearful of crime than are other groups in the population (Clemente & Kleiman, 1977; Kennedy & Silverman, 1985). Not surprisingly perhaps, these groups were identified in von Hentig's categories of victims in 1940. As such, members of these groups often engage in avoidance behaviors that limit their activities and freedom of movement.

Another defensive behavior is victim resistance. Resistance extends the idea of victim responsibility, a concept proposed by Schafer (1968), to include responsibility for thwarting the act. Resistance is defined by Claster and David (1981) as action by a potential victim during a confrontation that is designed to interfere in any way with completion of the criminal act or escape. Resistance may comprise active conduct, like physical retaliation or calling for help, but it can also include a refusal to meet the demands of an offender, similar to the passive or nonviolent resistance made famous by Mahatma Gandhi and his followers. A crucial factor that impinges on the potential victim, affecting his or her behavior with a criminal adversary, is that of social power, as noted by Schafer (1968). Comparing physical size, occupation, sex, age, or number of participants for both parties may reflect the actual power relationship, for example. The practical question that victim resistance raises is this: How should I act if I perceive myself as a potential victim? The issue of resistance—its presence or absence—remains a current concept in victimology research.

An interactional factor that incorporates earlier formulations of victim responsibility (Mendelsohn, 1940) is mutual violence or role reversals. These concepts describe the movement from victim to offender and/or offender to victim over time. Other terms to describe this concept include the cycle of violence, reciprocal violence, or the transgenerational transmission of violence. An example is intimate partner violence where police officers attending an emergency call determine that both parties have been engaged in the violence and they are unable to assess who started the violence. This has led to a major challenge with respect to mandatory reporting laws and an increase in victims being arrested and charged in domestic violence calls (McDermott & Garofalo, 2004). It has further led to the acceptance of "battered woman syndrome" as a defense for murder (Regehr & Glancy, 1995). The link between childhood victimization and juvenile or adult offending has methodological concerns, not the least of which include the lack of uniformity of behaviors, self-report, and baseline data from control groups. However, there is the public perception that in a culture of violence, victims become offenders and vice versa.

Perhaps the most interesting example of the interaction between the victim and the offender is the **Stockholm syndrome**, a term coined after a Swedish incident in 1973. At 10:15 a.m. on Thursday, August 23, 1973, Jan-Erik Olsson, who was on leave from prison, entered the Sveriges Kreditbank in central Stockholm with a submachine gun. "The party has just begun," he announced, taking four of the bank's employees hostage in an 11 by 47 foot vault until late in the evening of August 28. In answer to his demands, another criminal was brought to the bank and joined Olsson in the siege. Over the 5.5 days of captivity a relationship developed between the hostage takers and their victims. Indeed, the victims later identified they were more frightened of the police than the captors. Further, after their release the victims asked that mercy be shown toward the offenders.

Stockholm syndrome is the dramatic and unexpected realignment of affections to the positive bond between hostage and captor and to the feelings of distrust and hostility on the part of the victim toward authority.

Ochberg and Soskis (1982) contended that positive bonds do not form immediately but are usually established by the third day. They identified four factors that promote the Stockholm syndrome: intensity of the experience, duration, dependence of the hostage on the captor for survival, and distance of the hostage psychologically from authority. Based on their research, Grahm and Rawlings (1991) suggested that bonding with an abuser may be a *universal survival strategy for victims of interpersonal abuse*. Studies of other hostage-like groups suggest this concept can be applied to hostages, concentration camp prisoners, cult members, prisoners of war, civilians in Chinese Communist prisons, procured prostitutes, incest victims, physically and/or emotionally abused children, and battered women. In the most famous U.S. case of the Stockholm syndrome, Patty Hearst, the granddaughter of publishing baron William Randolph Hearst, was kidnapped by the leftist Symbionese Liberation Army in 1974 and robbed a San Francisco bank together with her captors.

■ Societal-Based Theories of Victimology

Societal-based theories of victimology see the basis of crime and victimization in social structures that precipitate and perpetuate unequal relationships, unrest, anger, and need. In this way violence is politically, economically, and socially induced. These authors frequently look at the impact of crime on the poorest, most vulnerable, and most marginalized members of society and interclass conflicts caused by inequalities in wealth, power, and authority (Wolhuter, Olley, & Denham, 2009). Theoretical approaches that fall into the category include critical criminology and feminist criminology.

Within critical criminology it is possible to see distinct but related subschools of thought. Conflict theory, first suggested by Sellin (1938) in the early 20th century, essentially sees crime as the product of whoever wins the power struggle over the labeling apparatus. Thus, when one nation conquers another and imposes its law over the conquered land, behaviors that might have been acceptable yesterday may become criminalized today. Therefore, it is more important to understand the actions of norm creators, norm interpreters, and norm enforcers than it is to understand norm breakers. The social implications of this approach are somewhat fatalistic: We will always have crime because someone will always be the loser in the power struggles in society, so the only real question is how to minimize it.

By comparison, Marxist theory, a second subschool of critical criminology, takes this line of reasoning much further but ends up with a potential for cure. Based on the work of Karl Marx (1904/1959), Marxist theory asserts that crime is primarily the product of capitalist political economies, which tend to make everyone involved in them greedy and self-centered. Although there is little hope to eliminate crime while capitalistic political economies survive, there is the theoretical possibility of a systemwide cure for crime if capitalism can be overthrown. The cure for crime is revolution, which is either a happy or a horrendous prospect depending on your point of view. Short of revolution, the best we can hope for is to understand the functioning of criminal justice agencies to try to mitigate their oppression.

An aspect of critical criminology is the concept of social capital, which can be understood as the value of social interactions. These connections or social networks can result in collective action (Coleman, 1988). Early writings on the roots of social capital can be noted in the founding documents of American government, such as James Madison's contributions to the Federalist Papers and the commentary of Alexis de Tocqueville in *Democracy in America*, that encourage pluralist and participatory democracy. The concept of social capital has increased in visibility over the past decade because of its intuitive appeal. For example, if the social ties that bind communities together are strengthened, community members will be healthier, happier, and productive. Crime and its negative effects will have significantly lowered opportunities to hurt the community (Schafft & Brown, 2003). Grootaert (1998) suggested that social capital is the missing link that differentiates healthy and prosperous communities from those torn by poverty, conflict, and strife. Inner city racial riots of the 1960s and 1970s could be viewed as the result of systemic inequality or victimization. Gangs arising from inequitable societies can result in serious victimization in a community. A resurgence of gangs in the 21st century has caused considerable tragedy in drive-by shootings, some of which have injured or killed innocent bystanders.

Feminist criminology arose during the 1980s as a result of concern over the inadequacy of existing criminological theories to explain the relationship between women and crime. Traditional models were not seen to adequately consider issues of power and vulnerability. Feminist researchers consistently pointed to the lack of attention to issues such as rape and sexual assault in academic, legal, and legislative forums (Walklate, 1989). Crime surveys ignored crimes committed largely against women, suggesting they were less important or resulted in lower levels of suffering. Thus, crimes against women, such as intimate partner violence, were not only hidden but were indeed seen as tacitly sanctioned by the state. Dubinsky (1992), for instance, in reviewing historical legal and societal treatment of rape victims, asserted that whether a raped woman is a "designing woman" or a "virtuous maiden" has always been determined by the morals and social values of the time in which she lived. Further, concerns arose over the dominance of victim-based models for understanding victimization and the tendency of these models to assign blame to the victim for his or her own suffering (Wolhuter et al., 2009). Feminist criminology addresses these issues by placing a gender-based lens on power relationships and legally ascribed rights of women.

■ Ecological Theory

Although not strictly a theory of victimology, ecological theory is increasingly used as an integrative framework for understanding victimization. Ecological theory seeks to understand human experience and behavior within a "person-in-environment" framework (Bronfenbrenner, 1979; Germain & Gitterman, 1996). Ecological theory sees individuals as influenced by intersecting levels of ecological systems: the individual (or ontogenic), which includes factors internal to the individual such as personal characteristics and formative history; the micro-system, which considers interactions between the individual and the person's context such as family, peers, and cultural affiliations; the exosystem, which is the environment in which the person resides, his or her neighborhood and community including their limitations and resources; and the macro-system, which includes those factors that are economic, social, and political in nature (Belsky, 1980; Bogo, 2006; Bronfenbrenner, 1979; Germain & Gitterman, 1996). Of significance is that each of these ecological subsystems is viewed to influence the range of choices and options available to victims and ultimately their decisions and behaviors (Bogo, 2006; Bronfenbrenner, 1979). **Figure 3-2** presents this model.

Alaggia, Regehr, and Jenny (2011) use ecological theory to understand the factors that impede women's disclosure of intimate partner violence. In their analysis of the responses of 118 participants in a mixed-methods study, they identified intrapersonal factors, including levels of posttraumatic stress symptoms, internalized views of love, and the desire to keep their family together and make things work, that interacted in complex ways to inhibit disclosure. At the micro-system level, familial and cultural beliefs about marriage and family and cultural norms regarding the acceptability of abuse impacted women's decisions to disclose. These were often reinforced by mezzo-system or community attitudes. For example, fear of losing family support and potential cultural rejection were given as examples of undesirable outcomes of disclosing abuse. Finally, at the macro-system level, the very policies that were developed and occasionally

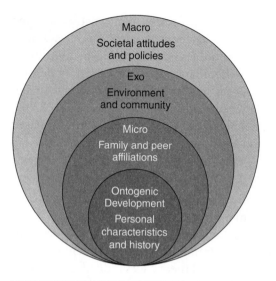

FIGURE 3-2 Four Systems of the Ecological Framework

Data from Bronfenbrenner, U. 1979. *The ecology of human development.* Cambridge, MA: Harvard University Press.

amended to support women to disclose intimate partner violence have had adverse effects as reported by the participants in the current studies. For instance, mandatory charging policies by police that were designed to protect and increase safety for women were actually perceived to take control away from women, further disempowering them.

■ Case Analysis Using Victimology Theories

In the case of *Commonwealth of Virginia v. Turman* (2007), Myron Turman was convicted of rape and sexual battery. Turman appealed the conviction on the grounds that an America Online Instant Messenger conversation between Turman and the victim was inadmissible evidence. The court of appeals found that the Commonwealth of Virginia had sufficiently identified Turman as the individual who sent the instant messages. The conviction was upheld. The victim (we will call her "Ms. S") had known Turman since 1999, and they were considered to be friends. A month before the attack, in September 2002, Turman and Ms. S had consensual sex. On the night of October 5, 2002, she was at a dance club where Turman contacted her to ask when she was planning to leave. When she returned home in the early morning of October 6, Turman was waiting for her in the parking lot of her residence. After allowing Turman into her residence, Ms. S became uncomfortable with his behavior and asked him to leave. Ms. S had lain down on her bed and denied Turman's request to lie down on the bed with her. She then went into another room of her residence and asked Turman to leave. Turman responded by "grabbing [the victim in a bear hug . . . and carrying] her into the bedroom." Turman began performing oral sodomy on the victim and then engaged in sexual intercourse with the victim despite her requests that he stop. Turman then said he wanted to perform anal sodomy and did so despite the victim's denial of the request. After the victim had succeeded in freeing herself of Turman, she insisted that he leave and threatened to call the police. She did not initially call the police because Turman seemed to agree to leave. When the victim restated her intention to call the police, Turman "lunged and took the telephone from her." She then ran to another phone and called the police just before she heard the front door slam. Ms. S was taken to a hospital and examined by a sexual assault nurse examiner; the injuries were consistent with the described sexual assault. She had bruises on her right thigh and left arm and a tear to her anus.

Turman admitted to police officers that he had sex with Ms. S on October 6 but contended that the encounter was consensual. He claimed that he left her residence after she began talking about her boyfriend and that she threatened to call the police and claim that he raped her if he told anyone about the encounter. A key piece of evidence was an America Online Instant Messenger conversation between Turman and the victim several months after the attack. In the conversation, Turman indirectly confessed to the assault, apologizing and claiming he was high on ecstasy. The conversation was presented to the jury during the testimony of the victim; although she did not print or save a copy of the conversation, she recalled the conversation from memory. Turman argued that the instant messages were not admissible because they were hearsay and that he could not be definitely identified as the sender of the messages because two of his friends and his estranged wife had access to his account. The court found that the instant message conversation was admissible in its presentation to the jury in the testimony of the victim. The jury was instructed to consider the flight of Turman from the scene after the victim called the police. While she was on the line with the authorities, she heard the door slam, an indication that Turman had left.

Analysis

This attack was premeditated. Turman had called Ms. S to find out when she would be going home, and when she arrived Turman was waiting for her. Turman made indirect advances that were clearly rejected before he carried Ms. S against her will into the bedroom; he asked if he could lie down on the bed with her, and she said no. He had gained access to the victim's residence because of his friendship with the victim. The attack can be classified as an acquaintance rape, where the perpetrator abuses the trust of the victim. Acquaintance rape provides a perfect example of the tension or conflict between different theoretical formulations. What is the responsibility of the victim relative to the responsibility of the offender and society? This tension is played out in media accounts of date rape trials and in the courtroom.

Victim-based theories of victimology would place Ms. S in von Hentig's victim category of "the female." From this perspective her physical strength relative to that of the offender was a significant factor leading to the assault. Mendelsohn's classifications consider the concept of victim responsibility. Someone using this classification may argue that either Ms. S. has "minor guilt" in that she could have anticipated the danger and minimized the risk. Finally, Schafer's victim precipitation typologies may focus on the facts that Ms. S let Turman into her home and had previously had sex with him. Using these facts they may argue that her behavior could be misinterpreted by Turman as an invitation. Looking at the four phases of a sexual assault, the victim had an early awareness of danger before the attack. She rejected his advances from the very beginning and asked him to leave without a major unwanted advance from Turman. The threat of attack in this case was so sudden that the victim had no time to stall, bargain, or to perform any sort of evasive tactic. Turman responded violently to the victim's request that he leave, grabbing her and carrying her to the bedroom. The victim repeatedly expressed verbal resistance throughout the attack. She was also struggling with the realization that she was being raped: "[I was] trying to figure out what in the world was going on, why was this gentleman acting like this." Considering each fact, victim responsibility and victim precipitation were found by the court to be outweighed by offender responsibility.

Interactive theories would consider Ms. S's lifestyle and the manner in which her activities (such as attending bars) put her at higher risk of victimization. Fattah's (2000) factors affecting victimization would consider the danger associated with her relationships with others, the places she frequents, and her behaviors, including engaging in high risk behaviors and defensive/avoidance behaviors. As with victim-basing theories, application of these theories can lead to victim-blaming and excusing of offender culpability. Further, from a just world perspective, people can focus on the behavior of the victim and not that of the offender to ease fears that they themselves are at risk of harm.

From a feminist criminology perspective, the motive for all sexual violence is clearly the need for power and control. Brownmiller (1975), for instance, suggested that rape was traditionally defined by men rather than women and that men use and all men benefit from the use of rape as a means of perpetuating male dominance by keeping all women in a state of fear. In this case, Ms. S was initially going to call the police in response to the attack, but she stopped when Turman began to put his clothing on. There is a high frequency of nonreporting among rape victims. Reasons for this include secondary victimization in the courtroom and during police investigations, self-blame, and avoidance of reexperiencing traumatic stimuli.

Ecological theory would integrate each of these perspectives into a comprehensive understanding. From the court's perspective, this was a clear case of acquaintance rape. Her injuries were consistent with her description of the assault. The combination of the injuries and the Instant Messenger conversation gives credence to the victim's story. If Turman's testimony was true—that he became uncomfortable when the victim began to talk about her boyfriend and that she subsequently threatened to falsely accuse him of rape if he told anyone about the sexual encounter—then the victim would have likely never followed through on her threat to call the police after he left. Turman also claimed there was no definitive way to prove he was the individual who sent the instant message; however, what was said in the conversation was specific to the case and would most likely not have come from one of the other individuals with access to his account.

■ Summary

Victimology draws on both traditional concepts of the victim–offender relationship, victim resistance, cultural and community factors, prevention and rehabilitation, victim vulnerability, and victim precipitation that have been the foundation of the discipline. Modern theories of victimization can be divided into three main categories: victim-based theories, interactive theories, and societal-based theories. Victim-based theories of victimology consider characteristics of individuals that make them vulnerable to victimization, including biological, sociological, psychological, demographic, and psychiatric. Interactional theories consider that intersection between the victim and the offender and their environment. Societal theories include both critical criminology and feminist criminology. These theories in large part turn the focus away from attempting to explain just criminal behavior and toward understanding social responses to crime. Ecological theory attempts to integrate aspects of all other theories. This theory seeks to understand human experience and behavior within a "person-in-environment" framework. As such, it considers the individual, his or her associations, the community in which he or she resides, and social and political influences on choice.

■ Key Terms

Classical criminology: A view that people have free will and the appropriate and timely punishment will deter crime.

Critical criminology: Combines an analysis of the state with the lived experience of victims. This model includes radical, Marxist, and feminist approaches.

Just world theory: Tendency of people to attribute blame to victims of crime to retain a sense that the world is safe.

Lifestyle routine activities theory: Certain personal characteristics and lifestyle activities increase or decrease an individual's risk of victimization.

Positivistic: Derives knowledge from the scientific method.

Spiritualistic theories: Attribute victimization to the acts of gods, demons, cosmic forces, and other supernatural forces.

Stockholm syndrome: Dramatic and unexpected realignment of affections to the positive bond between hostage and captor and to the feelings of distrust and hostility on the part of the victim toward authority.

■ Discussion Questions

1. What are two examples of victim blame?
2. How does victim precipitation differ (if at all) from victim vulnerability?
3. What type of prevention program would you recommend for a change in college students' lifestyle routine?
4. Discuss the following case in terms of theories of victimization.

Two suspects arrived in town 2 days before a shooting. The suspects began dealing drugs out of different units in a housing project and hired residents, including the victim, as drug runners to deliver drugs to prospective buyers. These runners were alleged to have planned to rob the suspects, and at one point all the runners went to the unit where the suspects were staying but were unsuccessful in their robbery attempt. The suspects then stopped dealing and left the area. During the early morning hours the victim and two others were seen talking in the housing project when the suspects pulled up in a car without lights. The suspects got out and ran up to the victim, ordered the others out of the way, and then began to fire point blank eight times into the 21-year-old's body. He was transported unconscious to the hospital, where he died 16 days later. During the autopsy, five .22-caliber bullets were removed from his body. No casings were found at the scene. Victimology noted that the victim lived in a high drug, low income, high unemployment, single parent area. The victim was described as a drug dealer, user, and enforcer who was known to be combative and argumentative.

■ References

Alaggia, R., Regehr, C., & Jenny, A. (2011). Risky business: An ecological analysis of intimate partner violence disclosure. *Research on Social Work Practice.* doi:10.1177/1049731511425503

Amir, M. (1971). *Patterns in forcible rape.* Chicago: University of Chicago Press.

Beccaria, C. (1963). *On crimes and punishments* (H. Paolucci, Trans.). Indianapolis, IN: Bobbs-Merrill (original work published 1764).

Becker, H. (1963). *The outsiders.* New York: New York Free Press.

Belsky, J. (1980). Child maltreatment: An ecological integration. *American Psychologist, 35*(4), 320–335.

Bernard, T., Snipes, J., & Gerould, A. *Vold's Theoretical Criminology.* Sixth Edition. New York: Oxford University Press.

Bogo, M. (2006). *Social work practice: Concepts, processes, & interviewing.* New York: Columbia University Press.

Bronfenbrenner, U. (1979). *The ecology of human development.* Cambridge, MA: Harvard University Press.

Brownmiller, S. (1975). *Against our will: Men, women and rape.* New York: Simon and Schuster.

CBS News. (2009, May 7). *Kobe records released.* Retrieved from http://www.cbsnews.com/stories/2004/08/16/national/main636205.shtml

Claster, D.S., & David, D.S. (1981). The resisting victim. In B. Galaway & J. Hudson (Eds.), *Perspectives on crime victims* (pp. 183–188). St. Louis, MO: Mosby.

Clemente, F., & Kleiman, M.B. (1977). Fear of crime in the United States: A multivariate analysis. *Social Forces, 56,* 519–531.

Cohen, L.E., & Felson, M. (1979). Social change and crime rates: A routine activity approach. *American Sociological Review, 44,* 588–608.

Coleman, J.S. (1988). Social capital and the creation of human capital. *American Journal of Sociology, 94*(Suppl.), S95–S120.

Commonwealth of Virginia v. Turman. (2007). 39 Va. App. at 337 n. 4.

Dubinsky, K. (1992). Maiden girls or designing women? The crime of seduction in turn-of-the-century Ontario. In F. Iacovetta & M. Valverde (Eds.), *Gender conflicts: New essays in women's history.* Toronto, Ontario, Canada: University of Toronto Press.

Ellenberger, H. (1954). Psychological relationships between the criminal and his victim. *Revue Internationale de Criminologie et de Police Technique, 2,* 103–121.

ESPN. (2004, Sept. 2). Kobe Bryant's apology. Retrieved from http://sports.espn .go.com/nba/news/story?id=1872928

Eysenck, H. (1947). *Dimensions of personality.* London: Routledge.

Fattah, E. (1967). Towards a criminological classification of victims. *International Criminal Police Review, 209,* 162–169.

Fattah, E. (1979). Recent theoretical developments. *Victimology: An International Journal, 4*(2), 199–213.

Fattah, E. (2000). Victimology, past, present and future. *Criminologie, 33*(1), 17–46.

Fisher, B.S., Sloan, J.J., Cullen, F.T., & Lu, C. (1998). Crime in the ivory tower: The level and sources of student victimization. *Criminology, 36,* 671–710.

Galaway, B., & Hudson, J. (1981). *Perspectives on crime victims.* St. Louis, MO: Mosby.

Germain, C., & Gitterman, A. (1996). *The life model of social work practice: Advances in theory and practice* (2nd ed.). New York: Columbia University Press.

Gibran, K. (1963). *The forerunner: His parables and poems* (Trans.). London: Heinemann (original work published 1920).

Grahm, D., & Rawlings, E. (1991). Bonding with abusive dating partners: Dynamics of Stockholm syndrome. In B. Levy (Ed.), *Dating violence, women in danger.* Seattle, WA: Seal Press.

Grootaert, C. (1998). Social capital: The missing link? Social Capital Initiative Working Paper No. 3. Washington, DC: World Bank.

Hare, R. (1991). *Manual for the revised psychopathy checklist.* Toronto, Ontario, Canada: Multihealth Systems.

Hindelang, M.J., Gottfredson, M.R., & Garafalo, J. (1978). *Victims of personal crime: An empirical foundation for a theory of personal victimization.* Cambridge, MA: Ballinger.

Hirschi, T. (1969). *Causes of delinquency.* Los Angeles: University of California Press.

Kearon, T., & Godfrey, B. (2007). Setting the scene: A question of history. In S. Walklate (Ed.), *Handbook of victims and victimology* (pp. 17–36). Portland, OR: Willan Publishing.

Kennedy, L.W., & Silverman, R.A. (1985). Significant others and fear of crime among the elderly. *International Journal of Aging and Human Development, 20*, 241–256.

Koss, M.P. (2000). Blame, shame, and community: Justice responses to violence against women. *American Psychologist, 55*(11), 1332–1343.

Lasley, J.R. (1989). Drinking routines/lifestyles and predatory victimization: A causal analysis. *Justice Quarterly, 6*, 529–542.

Lerner, M. (1980). *Belief in a just world.* New York: Plenum Press.

Mannheim, H. (1965a). *Ideologie und Utopie* (3rd enlarged ed.). Frankfurt: Schulte-Bulmke (original published in 1929).

Mannheim, H. (1965b). *Comparative criminology.* London: Routledge & Paul.

Marx, K. (1959). *Critique of political economy* (Trans.). New York: International Library (original work published 1904).

Maudsley, H. (1867). *The Physiology and Pathology of Mind.* London: Macmillan

McDermott, J.M., & Garofalo, J. (2004). When advocacy for domestic violence victims backfires. *Violence Against Women, 10*(11), 1245–1266.

Meier, R., & Miethe, T. (1993). Understanding theories of criminal victimization. *Crime and Justice: A Review of Research, 7*, 459–499.

Mendelsohn, B. (1940). *Rape in criminology.* Giustizia Penale.

Mendelsohn, B. (1974). The origin of the doctrine of victimology. In L. Drapkin & E. Viano (Eds.), *Victimology.* Lexington, VA: Lexington Books.

Merton, R. (1938). Social structure and anomie. *American Sociological Review, 3*, 672–682.

Mustaine, E.E. (1997). Victimization risks and routine activities: A theoretical examination using a gender-specific and domain-specific model. *American Journal of Criminal Justice, 22*, 41–70.

Mustaine, E.E., & Tewksbury, R. (1998). Predicting risks of larceny theft victimization: A routine activity analysis using refined lifestyle measures. *Criminology, 36*, 829–857.

Pinel, P. (798). *Nosographie philosophique ou methode de l'analyse appliquee a la medecine* (Paris, an VII).

Ochberg, F.M., & Soskis, D.A. (Eds.). (1982). *Victims of terrorism.* Boulder, CO: Westview Press.

Regehr, C., & Glancy, G. (1995). Battered woman syndrome defense in the Canadian courts. *Canadian Journal of Psychiatry, 40*(3) 130–135.

Regehr, C., & Kanani, K. (2010). *Essential Law for Social Work Practice in Canada*. Toronto: Oxford University Press.

Roberts, A., Zgoba, K., & Shahidullah, S. (2007). Recidivism among four types of homicide offenders: An exploratory analysis of 336 homicide offenders in New Jersey. *Aggression and Violent Behavior, 12*(5), 493–507.

Schafer, S. (1968). *The victim and his criminal: A study in functional responsibility*. New York: Random House.

Schafft, K.A., & Brown, D.L. (2003). Social capital, social networks, and social power. *Social Epistemology, 17*(4), 329–342.

Schreck, C.J., & Fisher, B.S. (2004). Specifying the influence of family and peers on violent victimization: Extending routine activities and lifestyle theories. *Journal of Interpersonal Violence, 19*, 1021–1041.

Sellin, T. (1938). *Culture, conflict and crime* (Bulletin No. 41). New York: Social Science Research Council.

Taylor, I., Watson, P., & Young, J. (1973). *The New Criminology: for a social theory of deviance*. London: Routledge & Kegan Paul.

Van De Mieroop, M. (2005). *King Hammurabi of Babylon: A biography*. Malden, MA: Blackwell.

Vold, G. (1958). *Theoretical Criminology*. New York: Oxford Press

Vold, G., & Bernard, T. (1986). *Theoretical Criminology*. New York: Oxford University Press.

von Hentig, H. (1948). *The criminal and his victim: Studies in the sociobiology of crime*. New Haven, CT: Yale University Press.

Walklate, S. (1989). *Victimology: The victim and the criminal justice process*. London: Unwin Hyman.

Weiss, K., & Borges, S.S. (1973). Victimology and rape: The case of the legitimate victim. *Issues in Criminology, 8*, 71–115.

Wolfgang, M. (1958). *Patterns of criminal homicide*. Philadelphia: University of Pennsylvania Press.

Wolfgang, M.E. (1959). Suicide by means of victim precipitated homicide. *Journal of Clinical and Experimental Psychopathology and Quarterly Review of Psychiatry and Neurology, 20*, 335–349.

Wolhuter, L., Olley, N., & Denham, D. (2009). *Victimology: Victimization and victims' rights*. London: Routledge-Cavendish.

Zur, O. (1994). Rethinking "don't blame the victim": Psychology of victimhood. *Journal of Couple Therapy, 4*(3/4), 15–36.

Victim Rights and Services CHAPTER 4

■ **Objectives**

- To describe the basis and rise of the victims' rights movement
- To describe victim compensation and restitution
- To describe the psychological impact of victimization
- To outline assessment and treatment options for crime victims

■ **Key Terms**

Primary victimization
National Organization for Victim Assistance (NOVA)
Secondary victimization
Tertiary victimization
Victim Information and Notification Everyday (VINE) program
Victims of Crime Act (VOCA)

CASE

On the morning of September 11, 2001, nineteen al-Qaeda terrorists hijacked four commercial passenger jet airliners and intentionally crashed two of the airliners into the Twin Towers of the World Trade Center in New York City, killing over 2,000 people (**Figure 4-1**). Both towers collapsed within two hours, destroying nearby buildings and damaging others. A third airliner crashed into the Pentagon (**Figure 4-2**). Hijackers had redirected the fourth plane toward Washington, DC, targeting either the Capitol Building or the White House, but crashed it in a field near Shanksville in Stony Creek Township,

FIGURE 4-1 American Airlines Flight 11 hit the north tower at 8:46 a.m. and United Flight 175 hit the south tower at 9:03 a.m.
© Str Old/Thomson Reuters

Pennsylvania, after passengers attempted to retake control of the airliner (**Figure 4-3**). There were no survivors from any of the flights. Al-Qaeda leader Osama Bin Laden claimed responsibility (CBC News, 2004).

The most expansive Federal Bureau of Investigation (FBI) inquiry in history was launched, given the code name "PENTTBOM." At the peak of the case more than half of the agents employed by the agency worked with other agencies to identify the hijackers and their sponsors and to head off any possible future attacks. They followed more than half a million investigative leads, including several hundred thousand tips from the public (FBI, 2011).

Among the 2,753 victims who died in the attacks on the World Trade Center were 343 firefighters and 60 police officers and 8 paramedics. Another 184 people were killed in

FIGURE 4-2 American Airlines Flight 77 crashed into the Pentagon at 9:03 a.m.
© Hyungwon Kang/Thomson Reuters

FIGURE 4-3 Shanksville crash site of United Airlines Flight 93 at 10:03 a.m.
© DANIEL LOVERING/Reuters/Landov

the attack on the Pentagon. The Shanksville crash killed all 44 people aboard, including the 4 hijackers. In the immediate aftermath of the attack, emergency victim services were established for victims and their families, and psychological first aid services were made available to the thousands of rescue and recovery workers who were sifting through the wreckage to look for survivors and remains of humans for identification and burial. Longer term counseling services reached out to victims and survivors who were experiencing symptoms of posttraumatic stress and loss. The U.S. government instituted a no-fault compensation program targeted at the 3,000 families that lost someone in the attacks. Over 97% of those eligible applied for the compensation, with an average award of $2 million for surviving families (Feinberg, 2004).

■ Introduction

The unpredictable nature of crime results in a major impact on the victim, on his or her family, and on the community in which he or she lives. Sellin and Wolfgang (1964) identified three levels of victim impact:

- **Primary victimization**, which affects the targeted or personalized victim
- **Secondary victimization**, which involves impersonal victims, such as commercial establishments, churches, schools, and public transportation. More recently the definition of secondary victimization has been modified to include those assisting victims such as emergency responders and therapists (Figley, 1995; Stamm, 1995).
- **Tertiary victimization**, which is diffuse and extends to the community at large

The consequences of crime vary depending on the nature of the crime and the level of victimization. As a result, victim services must comprise a range of legal, psychological, medical, and financial supports and interventions that address the varying needs of those affected.

Four case examples of single victimization are depicted below that elucidate the variable nature of crime and the services available to those victimized.

- *Robbery case.* Sam, a 21-year-old auto parts salesman, was robbed at gunpoint upon returning to his apartment in Yonkers, New York. Sam's most vivid recollection of his encounter was staring into the barrel of a 9-millimeter, semiautomatic gun. The perpetrator got away with $169.00 in cash, several credit cards, and Sam's coat, watch, glasses, and shoes. For a month after the attack Sam was plagued by nightmares several nights a week, and finally he went for counseling at the local mental health center. In addition, the victim advocate at the local victim assistance agency in Westchester County helped Sam complete a victim compensation application so that he could be compensated for his monetary and property losses. He was also eventually reimbursed for 6 weeks of mental health counseling.

- *Rape case.* Julie, a 28-year-old advertising executive, was raped at knifepoint when at midnight she returned from work to her apartment in Brooklyn, New York. She noticed the lock on the front door of her building was broken, which concerned her, but nevertheless she proceeded to the tenant mailboxes. Suddenly, someone grabbed her from behind, put a knife to her throat, and ordered her to remove her clothes suggesting he would stab her in the throat if she refused. In terror, she complied and was raped. The rapist told her she had a great body just like his sister and that he might be back in a week or 2. Julie told the female detective in the sex crimes unit she feared the rapist might have AIDS or another sexually transmitted disease and that he would return. She was tested for the HIV virus during her rape examination and returned every 6 months for routine testing.

- *Domestic violence case.* Dani, age 36, was stabbed to death by her ex-husband, Mustapha Sandi, in October 2007. Dani's two sons, ages 9 and 3, witnessed the fatal stabbing of their mother. The first police officer to arrive at the scene indicated that the 9-year-old child said: "My daddy stabbed my mommy, don't let my mommy die. Take care of my mom." There was a history of domestic violence complaints; a temporary restraining order against Mustapha Sandi had recently expired. Mustapha was a recently retired professor from a mathematics and physics department at a community college and the head of a construction-management company. The victim, Dani Sandi, was the director of a licensed practical nurse program in New Jersey at the time of her murder. Social services placed the children with relatives of the mother and arranged for grief counseling.

- *Felony murder case.* James Stevenson owned a liquor store with his brother-in-law. A man brandishing a gun robbed him on Christmas Eve, and in the ensuing struggle James Stevenson was shot to death. The California State Victim Compensation Board reimbursed Mr. Stevenson's wife for funeral expenses, and she now attends a homicide survivors' support group in Los Angeles.

Pervasive media attention that tends to focus on high-profile crime cases sometimes serves to confuse the general public with respect to who is most likely to be a victim of crime. For example, Ronald Goldman and Nicole Brown Simpson were certainly victims of a violent crime, but their case is in no way typical or representative. They were White, they resided in two of the wealthiest areas in the United States (Beverly Hills and Brentwood, California), and Ms. Brown Simpson was a spouse in an interracial marriage—all conditions that would make her statistically less likely to become a homicide victim (studies have shown that in most cases of domestic homicide where the spouse or former spouse is the perpetrator, interracial marriage was not a factor). On the contrary, although anyone can be a victim of crime, those that are at highest risk of crime are young people living in low income neighborhoods.

Regardless of their demographic or social situation, victims of crime are physically or emotionally injured by the intentional, premeditated act of a fellow human being. Whether the victim was robbed, raped, assaulted, or murdered, the resulting trauma usually consists of psychological pain and torment, physical injuries, and intense fear of being victimized again.

■ Victims' Rights Movement

The development of American law with respect to victims' rights is built on a 4,000-year history that includes Babylonian, Roman, Mosaic, and English laws. American law combined common law, written statutes enacted by a legislative body, and constitutionally enshrined rights. From the 16th century until early in the 19th century victims were largely responsible for pursuing justice themselves. In many cases the victim arranged for a posse to capture the thief, paid an attorney to prosecute the case, and may have even paid the expenses for a circuit judge to come to that jurisdiction. A major shift from this perspective was the advent of public prosecutors, first established in 1704 in Connecticut. While other states similarly adopted legislation enshrining public prosecutors' offices, private models continued to be widespread until the late 1800s (Derene, Walker, & Stein, 2007).

This shift to a public prosecution model coincided with two other factors that reduced the centrality of victims in the process of justice. First, the focus of crime turned to the general welfare of the community, emphasizing traditional English theory that crime was primarily a wrong against the public and only secondarily against the individual. Secondly, stemming from this focus, restitution was seen as being owed to society, not to the victim. Thus, punishment no longer focused on fines paid to the victims in compensation, rather incarceration had become the primary model of punishment by the early 19th century. Restitution to the victim became an afterthought that along with victims' rights was relegated to the civil court system for almost 125 years (Derene et al., 2007). Not until the mid-20th century did societal views of criminals' and victims' rights begin to change.

The crime victims' movement that began in the 1970s ushered in an array of positive changes to the social, economic, and political forces that caused harsh and neglectful treatment of crime victims, directly confronting damaging notions of victim blaming. This movement also led to landmark federal legislation that resulted in major funding initiatives throughout the nation for prosecutor-based victim/witness assistance programs, state crime victim compensation programs, police victim assistance programs, shelters for battered women, restitution programs, and sexual abuse treatment and prevention programs (Young and Stein, 2004).

In 1973 a dedicated group of victim advocates and scholars from around the globe assembled in Jerusalem, Israel, for the first International Symposium on Victimology (Drapkin & Viano, 1974). This pivotal event further demonstrated an international awareness of and interest in the victim experience and revitalized advocacy for victims' rights. A broad cross-section of concerned citizens, victim advocates, and feminist leaders began to merge their efforts, forming a number of effective advocacy coalitions. As international pressures grew with respect to concerns about victims and their rights, the United Nations (1985) brought into effect the Declaration of the Basic Principles of Justice for Victims of Crime and Abuse of Power, which identified the need for state action in protecting the rights of victims (**Table 4-1**).

In recognition of the UN Declaration, various provincial governments in Canada agreed to the basic principles of justice for victims of crime by enacting victims' rights legislation, beginning with Manitoba's

TABLE 4-1 **United Nations Declaration of the Basic Principles of Justice for Victims of Crime and Abuse of Power**

Access to Justice and Fair Treatment

- Victims should be treated with compassion and respect
- Judicial systems should be established that enable victims to seek redress
- Victims should be informed
- Victims' views should be presented and considered
- Victims should be assisted in the process
- Privacy and safety should be ensured
- Informal mechanisms for dispute resolution should be available

Restitution

- Offenders should be responsible for their behavior and make restitution
- Governments should consider restitution
- Where public officials acting in an official capacity violated national laws, victims should receive restitution from the state

Compensation

- Where compensation is not fully available from the offender, the state should endeavor to provide financial compensation

Assistance

- Victims should receive material, medical, psychological, and social assistance
- Police, justice, health, and social service personnel should receive training to sensitize them to the needs of victims

Data from United Nations. 1985. Declaration of Basic Principles of Justice for Victims of Crime and Abuse of Power. G.A. 40/34, annex, 40 U.N. GAOR Supp. (No. 53) at 214, U.N. Doc. A/40/53.

Justice for Victims of Crime Act (1986). The Manitoba legislation included provisions such as crime prevention, mediation, conciliation, and reconciliation procedures as means of assisting victims. By contrast, 10 years later in 1995 Ontario enacted the Victims' Bill of Rights that focused entirely on crime control. Although such differences and others exist, victims' bills of rights throughout Canada generally contain the following rights (Young, 2001):

- To be informed of the final disposition of the case
- To be notified if any court proceeding for which they have received a subpoena will not occur as scheduled
- To receive protection from intimidation
- To be informed of the procedure for receiving witness fees
- To be provided with a secure waiting area (when practical)

- To have personal property in the possession of law enforcement agencies returned as soon as possible
- To be provided with appropriate employer intercessions to minimize loss of pay due to court appearances.

Although victims' rights legislation in Canada is viewed as a positive step, critics have expressed concern that despite the best intentions, these bills of rights fail to meet the needs of victims for several reasons. First, there exists no remedy for lack of compliance by law enforcement and the courts with notification requirements. For instance, the Ontario Victims' Bill of Rights (1995) states as follows: "No new cause of action, right of appeal, claim or other remedy exists in law because of this section or anything done or omitted to be done under this section." This was upheld in an Ontario case in which the judge stated, "I conclude that the legislature did not intend for section 2(1) of the Victims' Bill of Rights to provide rights to the victims of crime … they have no claim before the courts because of it" (*Vanscoy and Even v. Her Majesty the Queen in Right of Ontario*, 1999).

Similarly, during the 1980s and 1990s important legislation was enacted in the United States that expanded victims' rights and allocated critical funding for victim/witness assistance programs, battered women's shelters, sexual assault treatment and prevention programs, and victim compensation programs. Society's fear of crime, fueled by advances in the women's movement, the report of the President's Task Force on Victims of Crime (1982), the passage of the Federal Victim and Witness Protection Act in 1982, and the Victims of Crime Act (VOCA) in 1984, resulted in federal subsidies to state and local victim service, victim compensation, victim/witness assistance, domestic violence, and sexual assault prevention programs. The VOCA legislation created a substantial federal fund within the U.S. treasury accumulated from federal criminal fines, penalties, and asset forfeitures. In 1988 amendments to VOCA required that victim compensation eligibility in all states be extended to include domestic violence victims and victims of drunk-driving accidents, as well as nonresident commuters and visitors.

During the 1990s the U.S. federal government and a growing number of states adopted victims' rights legislation. In April 2004 the U.S. Congress enacted the Crime Victims' Rights Act, which identifies the following rights:

- To be reasonably protected from the accused
- To reasonable, accurate, and timely notice of proceedings
- To not be excluded from any such public proceeding

- To be reasonably heard
- To confer with an attorney for the government in the case
- To full and timely restitution as provided by law
- To be free from unreasonable delay

This federal act formed a basis on which many state legislatures moved to expand rights and services for victims of crime with measures that address such things as victim notice, participation, restitution, and compensation. In addition, many states have instituted additional protections for victims of violence. Wisconsin, for instance, prohibits district attorneys and police officers from insisting or suggesting that a victim of sexual violence should submit to a lie detector test. Colorado allows victims to use pseudonyms and issues orders to protect identity. As of 2007 there were approximately 12,000 victim/witness assistance and service programs, including sexual assault treatment programs, battered women's shelters, self-help and support groups for families of homicide victims, support groups for battered women, and community coalitions and task forces on sexual assault and battered women.

■ Restitution

Restitution is the money a judge orders an offender to pay to the victim. It is part of the offender's sentence and is based on the victim's expenses resulting from the crime and the offender's ability to pay. The expenses might include medical/dental expenses, lost wages due to the crime, and stolen or damaged property. Courts in every state have the statutory authority to order restitution, and in more than one-third of all states they are required to do so unless there are compelling or extraordinary circumstances that make this unjust or impossible (Office for Victims of Crimes [OVC], 2002). Nationally, restitution is imposed in about 13% of violent offenses (Ruback & Bergstrom, 2006). Many problems exist with this system however. For instance, research indicates that poor offenders are less likely to be ordered to pay restitution than nonpoor offenders, resulting in an inequity among victims depending on the wealth of their offender. Further, there is ambiguity in many jurisdictions about who is responsible for enforcing restitution orders. Although the U.S. Department of Justice does not oversee the collection of restitution, most Department of Justice crime victims compensation programs do have a collections unit that works to recapture claim costs back from offenders and liable third parties. This unit also monitors and collects punitive damage award judgments, which helps fund Department of Justice crime victims programs. To determine the amount of restitution ordered, a copy of the sentencing order includes the time frame in which the defendant is expected to begin making payments.

■ Victims' Compensation

Although restitution refers to money paid by an offender for the losses and damages incurred by a victim, victims' compensation refers to funds paid by the state to ameliorate the personal costs of crime. Crime victim compensation does not depend on whether the case is charged or if the offender is found guilty. Internationally, the unrelenting advocacy work of Marjory Fry, a Quaker and magistrate, is credited with spearheading the notion of state-funded compensation for victims. Fry succeeded in focusing attention on the inadequacy of court-ordered restitution, where offenders are often either not apprehended or not convicted and, when convicted, historically do not have the financial resources available to reasonably compensate a victim (Fry, 1957). This resulted in the first legislation of its kind, the New Zealand Criminal Compensation Act of 1963, followed 1 year later by similar legislation in England.

In 1965 California led the way for crime victim compensation in the United States by becoming the first state to establish a statewide victim compensation program, with a number of other states quickly following suit with similar legislation: New York in 1966, Hawaii in 1967, and Massachusetts in 1968. The principal objective of these early programs was to establish a system that would enable victims to receive financial compensation for injuries sustained, including ongoing, crime-related medical expenses.

At present victim compensation in the United States is handled in one of four ways: (1) as a component of victim witness programs, (2) through victim–offender reconciliation programs, (3) in conjunction with parole or probation supervision, or (4) through court-based employment programs (Ruback & Bergstrom, 2006). In most states victim compensation or restitution programs give victims an opportunity to claim all relevant losses, and usually this is limited to economic losses.

The Crime Victims Fund in the United States was established through the VOCA in 1984. This fund is supported by money collected through criminal fines, forfeited bail bonds, penalties, and special assessments. These funds come entirely from offenders and not from taxpayers. Victims can apply to this fund to cover crime-related medical costs, funeral costs, mental health counseling, or lost wages, which are beyond the costs covered by insurance programs. Maximum awards generally range from $10,000 to $25,000, although some states have different maximums, which may be higher or lower. Generally, victims are required to report the crime within 3 days of the offense and file the claim within 2 years. Despite good intentions, McCormack's study (1989) of the New Jersey Violent Crime Compensation Board revealed that in 1987 as few as 8% of the reported 45,000 violent crime victims had actually filed a compensation claim, leading researchers to conclude there was a need for more claims offices, particularly in high crime neighborhoods.

In Canada, Alberta developed the first legislation in 1969 that led to the development of a victim compensation program (Young, 2001). However, in 1992 the Canadian federal government discontinued transfer payments for victim compensation and as a result Newfoundland, the Yukon, and the Northwest Territories abandoned their compensation programs (Roach, 1999). Although in Canada, as in the United States, an award for compensation does not depend on a criminal conviction, in some jurisdictions (Alberta, Ontario, Prince Edward Island [PEI], and Nova Scotia) a claim may be denied or reduced if the victim failed to report the offense within a reasonable time or refused reasonable cooperation with a law enforcement agency. Where eligibility is determined, entitlement is not automatic and falls within the discretionary power of the board. For instance, in determining whether to make an order for compensation, all provinces except Saskatchewan allow the board to consider the behavior of the victim that may have contributed to his or her injury (Regehr and Kanani, 2010). Some circumstances, consideration may also be given to the character of the applicant. Awards can include compensation for expenses actually and reasonably incurred, loss due to disability and inability to work, maintenance of a child born due to sexual assault, and pain and suffering (Regehr and Kanani, 2010).

It should be noted that awards made under victim compensation programs are generally perceived to be quite low. However, studies of victims receiving this compensation suggest they view the compensation not as financial assistance or compensation but rather as a public acknowledgment of the harms committed against them (Regehr et al., 2008).

Eligibility for Compensation

Requests for compensation have different categories and payment limits. Despite imposed limits there have been successful challenges to policy as evidenced by the following case reported in the Crime Victim Compensation Quarterly (2011). In this reported case, an 11-year-old girl sought compensation as a secondary victim to crime. The girl was on a school bus when a fellow student was stabbed and then collapsed, bleeding, on the claimant's lap. The state compensation program provided funding for up to $1,000 for counseling to people "exposed" to crimes who were not the subject of an attack themselves. However, the girl remained in counseling for 5 years at the expense of $20,000. Her lawyer argued that the girl should be treated as a "primary victim," eligible for the program's full maximum of $35,000.

Discussion surrounding this case focused on whether the girl should be treated as "primary" or "secondary" under her own state laws. A group of advisors approached by the Crime Victim Compensation Quarterly believed that the primary consideration should be whether the girl was in a "zone of danger," in reasonable fear for her own safety because of the proximity of the attack. Elements of the case considered were that the girl was trapped on the bus, had no route of escape, and thus faced possible harm herself. Most programs' laws did not have a special category for witnesses, so the choice for program administrators consulted was either to deny the claim because the girl was not the direct victim or to find a way to consider her a primary victim. Most of the program directors consulted believed that given these facts, she should be considered a primary victim (Crime Victim Compensation Quarterly, 2011).

Costs of Victim Compensation

U.S. compensation programs spent a record combined total of $499.9 million in state and federal funds in federal fiscal year 2010. The amount was 16% more than was spent in 2005 and almost 72% more than in 2000, when spending was under $300 million. Over the same period the number of violent crimes went down 12.5%, as measured by the FBI's Uniform Crime Reports, from 1,425,486 in 2000 to 1,390,745 in 2005 and an estimated preliminary figure of around 1,250,000 violent crimes in 2010 (a remarkable 5% drop from 2009's 1,318,398). Thus, a 12.5% drop in the number of violent crimes corresponded with a 67% increase in compensation claims. This increase reflects larger numbers of compensation claims, inflation in medical costs, and new eligible benefits, including forensic exam payments and domestic violence relocation (Crime Victim Compensation Quarterly, 2011).

Innovative Compensation Laws

As society encounters new types of crimes, legislation is written to deal legally with the offender. One such example is dealing with pimps of teenage prostitutes. A bill drafted in December 2008 by Assemblyman John Hambrick of Las Vegas directed proceeds from convicted pimps to fund a shelter for underage prostitutes. Data indicated that every Wednesday morning for 28 months, 385 teenage prostitutes between the ages of 12 and 15 appeared in District Judge William Voy's court where they received minor sentences. Voy called the teenagers a unique kind of victim in that they did not realize they were victims but rather developed a form of Stockholm syndrome whereby they believed the pimp was their friend. In the Hambrick bill 60% of funds raised by the forfeitures would go to the district attorney's office to help prosecute pimps and 40% would go toward a secure facility to provide safe housing and psychological services for the teens. This bill was modeled after laws used to confiscate assets of drug dealers (Hambrick, 2011).

9/11 U.S. Compensation Fund

In response to the overwhelming needs of those who lost family members and victims who survived the 9/11 attacks, the September 11th Victim Compensation Fund was created by an Act of Congress, the Air Transportation Safety and System Stabilization Act (49 USC 40101). The Act sought to compensate the victims of the attack (or their families) in exchange for their agreement not to sue the airline corporations involved. Kenneth Feinberg was appointed by Attorney General John Ashcroft to be Special Master of the fund. He worked for 33 months pro bono and developed the regulations governing the administration of the fund and also administered all aspects of the program. After an application for compensation, an offer was made to each family who lost someone in the 9/11 attacks and each victim based on an estimate of how much each victim would have earned in a full lifetime (on average this was $1.8 million). If a family accepted the offer, it was not possible to appeal. Families unhappy with the offer were able to appeal in a nonadversarial, informal hearing to present their case however they wanted. In the end, 7,300 claims for death and injury were received representing 98% of families who experienced loss and totaling $7 billion (U.S. Government Benefits Help, 2011).

In addition to the 9/11 fund, the U.S. government developed a support program for all victims involved in terrorism cases. Kathryn Turman, director of the FBI Office of Victim Assistance Program, described the program's work (Turman, 2004). The 56 FBI field offices have a total of 122 full-time victim specialist positions, in addition to 20 staff at the main office at FBI Headquarters that oversee all programs and positions and provide support and assistance to them. Other cases where services were provided include bank robberies, kidnappings, aviation accidents, and the shootings at Virginia Tech and at Red Lake reservation in Minnesota. They have also assisted with Katrina, providing support not only for federal employees but also working side by side with

TABLE 4-2 FBI Victim Assistance Programs for Terrorism Cases

Task	Action
Notification of death or injury of U.S. citizens within the first few hours	Victim assistants will reach out to the family, offer condolences, and provide information on what will happen next and why and what help they can expect from the FBI.
Many of the events have occurred overseas	Are responsible for transporting the victim's remains back to the United States, coordinating the autopsy (which is necessary for the investigation), collecting dental records and DNA from family members, and making arrangements for the final journey home.
Personal effects and death certificates	Provide comfort and support. One letter from the 7-year-old son of a terrorism victim: "Thank you for bringing my Daddy home," he wrote. "Thank you for sending Ms. B_____ to give me my Daddy's jewelry. I didn't get to say goodbye to him on the phone but I got to say goodbye at the church."
Survivors need information provided from an official source	The FBI will continue to keep survivors informed no matter how many years an investigation may last.
9/11 terrorist attack had strong assistance from the PENTTBOM team of investigators	Worked with over 10,000 victims and family members of the 9/11 attacks, created a special informational web page for families as well as a toll-free number and Internet address where they can directly reach FBI victim assistance program.
Lessons learned	Rights and needs of victims must be built into our response to terrorism from the beginning.
Systems in place	Need to provide ongoing information and answer difficult questions, and help survivors find assistance resources regardless of how many victims there are and where they live.
Terrorism is now a part of our daily reality	Must never forget that the impact on individuals and families lasts long after the crime scenes have been cleared; memorials, erected; and perpetrators, tried and sentenced.

Data from Turman, K. 2004. Helping terrorism victims and their families. FBI Headline News, March 26, 2004. Retrieved from http://www2.fbi.gov/page2/march04/turman032604.htm.

the Red Cross assisting with shelters. **Table 4-2** shows the services provided for federal bombing cases.

■ Victims' Rights and the Courts

Victim Impact Statements

Courts have traditionally not allowed victims to participate in the sentencing process. In 1982, for instance, in Canada, Justice McLachlin, in denying a victim's request to have input into the sentencing of an offender, concluded that crime victims have no standing under the Criminal Code. Similarly, considerable concern has existed in the United States that victim presence will interfere with the process of justice. Nevertheless, victim impact statements were first introduced in the United States in the mid-1970s, and by the end of the 1990s they were admissible in 49 states. Some states provided additional measures regarding victim impact statements. Illinois requires that any written statement submitted to the state attorney be considered by the courts. Virginia ensures that victim impact statements are heard by the courts after any guilty finding or plea bargain that accepts guilt. Mississippi has enshrined a right that allows victims to make oral and written statements to the presiding judge.

Case law in the United States has similarly underlined the important role of victim impact statements. The *R. v. Jacob* case involved a horrific crime of home invasion in the middle of the night, whereby the victim's hands, feet, and face were bound, her hair cut by use of a knife, and multiple physical and sexual assaults were perpetrated (*R. v. Jacob*, 2002). The victim impact statement was read in court. Sentencing judge Stuart Barry in his judgment emphasized four contributions of victim impact statements:

1. *Fostering experience of justice:* Victims must be able to participate in the decision-making process of sentencing in a manner that is meaningful to and needed by them. Although necessary to leave the ultimate responsibility for the decision with the court and retain the primacy of the state voice in sentencing, the victim must be afforded a meaningful opportunity to participate if justice, as well as law, is to be served.

2. *Making offenders aware:* Offenders are rarely exposed to the tragedies they cause. If offenders can avoid exposure to the pain they cause, they can cling to their rationalizations for crime. Offenders immersed in the game-like nature of the adversarial system need to confront the human dimensions of their actions.

3. *Measuring the severity of crime:* In addressing many of the sentencing principles, the court must be acutely aware of the specific impacts of the crime on victims and on the community. After hearing the legal facts surrounding numerous crimes; after reading numerous presentence reports and psychological assessments, victim impact statements, and various supporting documents; and after listening to countless submissions from counsel, judges may not fully appreciate the uniqueness of each case if the victim's voice is left out.

4. *Community awareness:* The community must hear from the victim. Crime, in many ways, isolates a victim from the community. Communities need to hear from the victim to be fully cognizant of what needs to be done in the community to prevent similar acts and to know what is needed to support this survivor and other victims and survivors.

Although victim impact statements have been around for a considerable period of time, their use remains limited. For instance, the government of Canada introduced victim impact statements as part of the revisions to the Criminal Code of Canada in 1988, yet a British Columbia study published in 1992 determined that victim impact statements were obtained in only 2% to 6% of cases and filed into court in only 1% to 2% of cases. It has been suggested that this, in part, is due to the reluctance of victims to expose their suffering to adversarial challenge (Roach, 1999). Another study found that between 14% and 18% of victims expressed concerns about participating in preparing impact statements, fearing retribution from the offender and/or his friends (Giliberti, 1991). Similarly, in a U.S. study conducted before the 2004 legislation, it was found that less than 18% of victims or families attended sentencing, only 15% prepared written statements, and only 9% were permitted oral submissions (Finn-DeLuca, 1994).

It is not yet clear how relatively new legislation may increase participation. Thus, although victim impact statements may be enshrined in law, in the end it may be that very few statements are used in court. Reasons given by prosecutors for not using them included the belief that they contained no new information, that they were too vague or irrelevant, and that they were of doubtful accuracy.

Victim impact statements are generally prepared statements detailing physical, psychological, financial, and social harms the victim suffered as a result of a crime committed against them. These statements, either in oral or written form, are presented to the sentencing judge after the defendant has been proven guilty in the sentencing phase of the trial (Garkawe, 2007). A family member or other individual may deliver the statement if the victim, such as children or homicide victims, is incapable of doing so (Englebrecht, 2011). Impact statements may also be subject to varying degrees of regulation regarding who may testify to the impact of the crime, the content of the impact statement, the number of individuals allowed to speak, the degree of opinionated narratives, and the nature of the discussion in which the statement is shared (Englebrecht, 2011).

Victim support groups have argued that victim impact statements benefit victims by increasing their recognition in the criminal justice system, increasing their satisfaction with the sentencing process, and increasing their cooperation with the system (Garkawe, 2007). In addition, these statements may reveal harms suffered by the victim that were not otherwise apparent to the judge, especially in cases where a guilty plea has been issued, resulting in a limited amount of evidence. According to Trueblood (2011), "victim impact statements provide a way for victims of crime to participate in the criminal justice system process and allow the victims to help focus the court on the human costs of crime" (p. 616).

However, there have been conflicting views on whether victim impact statements should be accepted as evidence and whether they should have any influence on sentencing decisions. According to section 718.1 of the Criminal Code of Canada, "a sentence must be proportionate to the gravity of the offense and the degree of responsibility of the offender" (Criminal Code, 1985). It is clear that the impact of a crime on the victim is relevant to the seriousness of the crime. However, among many other sentencing factors that are considered during the sentencing process, harms identified in the victim impact statement may play a relatively small role in determining the offender's punishment (Garkawe, 2007). Some empirical research has shown that "in a vast majority of cases the use of VIS [victim impact statement] had no effect on the final result" of sentencing decisions (Garkawe, 2007, p. 107). In their study of impact statements in 500 felony cases, Erez and Tontodonato concluded that victim impact statements do not have an impact on the length of sentences; nevertheless, they do have some impact on the nature of the sentence. That is, whether an offender is sentenced to incarceration or probation is to some degree influenced by the victim impact statement. However, they conclude that the nature of the crime and the character of the offender continue to be the primary considerations (Erez & Tontodonato, 1990).

A cited reason for using victim impact statements is so victims have the opportunity to have their voices heard. Research conducted by Regehr, Alaggia, Lambert, and Saini (2008) found that those victims who were able to present their victim impact statement in court felt empowered and positive about the experience. However, those who were not able to read their statement for such reasons as the offender pled guilty or there was a plea bargain felt cheated by the process. Researchers concluded that completing a victim impact statement neither necessarily leads to victim satisfaction nor increases a victim's willingness to cooperate with systems in the future (Young, 2001). Rather, satisfaction depends on whether the statement is considered and acknowledged by the judge and the degree to which the victims continued to be informed of the process.

National Victim Information and Notification Everyday Program

The Victim Information and Notification Everyday (VINE) program is a national initiative that enables victims of domestic violence or other indictable crimes to access reliable information about criminal cases and custody status of offenders 24 hours a day—via phone, Internet, or e-mail. Through VINE, victims can register to be notified immediately in the event of their offender's release, escape, transfer, or court appearance. Currently available in over 2,100 communities across the nation, including most large metropolitan areas, the VINE program has been able to successfully provide a certain degree of comfort and peace of mind to crime victims and their families.

■ Services for Victims

Victim services have risen exponentially over the past three decades. For instance, in the United States, the National Organization for Victim Assistance (NOVA) was established in 1975 as a national umbrella organization dedicated to expanding current victim services, developing new programs, and supporting passage of victims' rights legislation. In addition to this vital work, NOVA also serves as a conduit of information and technical assistance for local and regional victim assistance programs (NOVA, 1983).

In 1988 through an amendment to the 1984 VOCA, the federal Office for Victims of Crimes (OVC) was formally established. An official agency of the U.S. Department of Justice, the OVC is an important resource for crime victims and the service organizations charged with assisting. Its mission, according to the OVC website (www.ovc.gov) is "to oversee diverse programs that benefit victims of crime. OVC provides substantial funding to state victim assistance and compensation programs and supports training designed to educate criminal justice and allied professionals regarding the rights and needs of crime victims" (Office for Victims of Crimes, 1988). The OVC offers a vast array of tools and resources for service providers, including funding, research, training and technical assistance, maintenance of an extensive list of relevant publications, and coordination of the National Calendar of Crime Victim Assistance–Related Events, a leading resource for locating and promoting events that address crime victims' rights and services, where users can search or submit events for free. In addition to NOVA and OVC, which offer a broad range of services to victims of many types of crime, other services exist that target people who have encountered specific types of victimization such as rape and intimate partner violence.

Women's Movement and Services for Rape Victims

In the early 1970s, when police departments and rape crisis centers first began to address the crime of rape, little was known about rape victims or sex offenders. Feminist groups had just begun to raise the issue of rape, and in 1971 the New York Speak-Out on Rape event was held, drawing widespread attention to sexual violence. Contemporary feminists who raised the issue early were Susan Griffin (1971) in her now classic article on rape as the "all-American" crime, and Germaine Greer (1973) in her essay on "grand rapes" (legalistically defined) and "petty rapes" (everyday sexual rip-offs). Susan Brownmiller (1975) wrote about the history of rape and urged people to deny its future.

The general public was not particularly concerned about rape victims; very few academic publications or special services existed; funding agencies did not see the topic as important; and health policy was almost nonexistent. But by 1972 the antirape movement began to attract women from all walks of life and political persuasions. Various strategies began to emerge, particularly the self-help program now widely known as the "rape crisis center." One of the first such centers was founded in Berkeley in early 1972, known as Bay Area Women Against Rape. Within months of the opening of the Berkeley center, similar centers were established in Ann Arbor, Michigan; Washington, DC; and Philadelphia, Pennsylvania. Concurrently, hospital-based rape counseling services began in Boston and in Minneapolis. Soon, centers replicated and services flourished. Although volunteer ranks tended to include a large number of university students and instructors, they also included homemakers and working women. The volunteer makeup usually reflected every age, race, socioeconomic class, sexual preference, and level of political consciousness. Volunteers were, however, exclusively women. Among the women, the most common denominators were a commitment to aiding victims and to bringing about social change (Largen, 1985).

THE "SECOND ASSAULT": EARLY RESPONSE BY THE SYSTEM TO RAPE VICTIMS The rape crisis centers provided victims with the support and counseling that enabled them to move through the traumatizing experience of rape both mentally and emotionally. However, rape survivors would often experience victim-blaming treatment from system personnel that would often worsen the victim's physical and mental distress. Additionally, the physical ordeal of the medical exam and subsequent investigation could often be a humiliating and dehumanizing experience for the victim. These postassault experiences, which became known as the "second assault," consisted of a series of uncomfortable experiences after their victimization. First, rape victims were traditionally seen in the emergency department by male physicians and generalist nurses, who often lacked the time and experience to do a thorough examination of the victim that would assist law enforcement and prosecutors. Rape victims were not a high priority for emergency care, and even when medical needs were satisfied, their emotional needs were not. Before the sexual assault nurse examiner (SANE) programs, medical staffs had an image of the "real" rape victim and much energy went into determining the "legitimacy" of the rape case (i.e., was the victim really raped?). Rape victims often felt depersonalized, lost, and neglected.

Second, the environment of the emergency department and needs of the victim were often at odds. Many victims complained about the long wait, having to wait alone, a lack of privacy, and not being informed of exam results. Rape victims were not a priority with emergency department physicians. Physicians were reluctant to do the rape examination because they lacked experience and training in forensic evidence collection and because they were vulnerable to being subpoenaed and required to testify. Physicians were able to examine the victim's body for bruises and prepare slides to look for sperm and other biological evidence; however, they were often unaware of the procedures for collecting biological evidence. There was a lack of knowledge around how to preserve evidence on clothing and other biological evidence such as hair samples and fingernail scrapings that may have been left by an assailant. There was also a lack of continuity of care. Medical providers did not communicate with each other, so victims returning for follow-up care found it difficult to be asked again by new people why they needed medical attention.

Finally, documentation collected on the victim would often include damning information such as prior sexual experience or phrases that included judgmental statements about the victim. Medical records were also found to be illegible. Ultimately, victims were left on their own to cope financially, legally, and emotionally with the aftermath of the crime (Holmstrom & Burgess, 1983).

SANE-SART: PAST AND PRESENT   It was against this backdrop of problems that prompted communities throughout the United States to involve nurses in the care of the sexual assault victim. Nurses, medical professionals, counselors, and advocates working with rape victims agreed that services provided to sexual assault victims in the emergency department were inadequate when compared to the standard of care given to other patients

(Ledray, 1999). Thus, SANE programs and sexual assault response teams (SARTs) emerged in the 1970s, with the first SANE program in Tennessee. SANE programs were created whereby specially trained forensic nurses provide 24-hour coverage as first-response care to adult and adolescent sexual assault victims in emergency departments and nonhospital settings (Campbell, Townsend, Long, & Kinnison, 2005).

Nurses have always cared for patients who were victims of violence. However, forensic nursing has only recently been recognized as an emerging specialty area of contemporary nursing practice. Forensic nursing history has been traced to the 18th century when midwives were called into court to testify on issues pertaining to virginity, pregnancy, and rape. Clinical forensic nursing practice focuses on the collection of evidence from living patients who have been victims of crimes or traumatic injuries. The forensic and clinical training SANEs receive prepare them to care for victims of crime who have needs for crisis intervention and physical and emotional care often within an emergency department. Today, SANE programs have grown in number, and many are still reaching maturity. Ciancone, Wilson, Collette, and Gerson (2000) conducted a survey of SANE programs in the United States. Of the 58 programs that responded, 55% had been in existence for fewer than 5 years and 16% had been in existence for more than 10 years. Campbell and colleagues (2005) surveyed SANE programs and reported on the rapid growth of programs; 58% had emerged within the past 5 years. Trends noted included newer programs created through a joint task force or through collaboration with other community groups, more diverse funding available as opposed to using hospital funds, and significantly larger programs with more staff and serving more patients, which reflected organizational growth.

SANE programs soon became an integral part of a team of primary and secondary responders known as a SART, which included law enforcement, detectives, victim advocates, and health care providers. The main goal of a SART is to assist the sexual assault victim through the criminal justice process. The second goal is to increase the odds of successful prosecution by enhancing evidence collection and facilitating communication among all parties in the process. The third goal is to help victims recover and cope from their experience through counseling and support (Girardin, 2005; Wilson & Klein, 2005).

Domestic Violence and Intimate Partner Violence Services

A distinct victim classification is found among women who are physically and/or emotionally abused by their spouse or intimate partner, abuse that is often long term and sometimes fatal. Estimates indicate that approximately 8.7 million women are battered by their current or former intimate partners each year (Roberts, 2007; Roberts & Roberts, 2005), and an extensive survey conducted in 2005 focused specifically on programs for battered women and their children (Roberts, Robertiello, & Bender, 2007). The notion of tailoring victim services specifically for women experiencing intimate partner abuse took hold in the late 1970s, in the wake of wide-ranging legislation. In the beginning battered women's shelters served primarily as temporary "safe havens" for women and children in the throes of violent domestic crisis, but by the mid-1990s a substantial number of shelters had gone beyond simply providing emergency shelter to implementing more comprehensive services, including counseling, legal advocacy, and job placement. With regard to program administration, the domestic abuse movement has matured from a grassroots movement of paraprofessionals and former abused women to one of trained professional social workers and counselors, many of whom have bachelor's and/or master's degrees (Roche & Sadoski, 1996).

By 1989, 48 states had provisions for the funding of domestic violence intervention programs, 34 states had funding mechanisms in place for general victim service and witness assistance programs at the local level, and 25 states had provided funding for local sexual assault crisis services. Money for such services was garnered through a variety of sources, including alcohol taxes, notoriety-for-profit laws, bail forfeiture, state income tax checkoffs, surcharges on criminal fines, variable penalty assessments levied by judges on convicted felons, and fixed penalty assessments on convicted offenders of criminal offenses and/or traffic offenses.

By the end of the 20th century the battered women's movement had become well established in terms of funding and staffing, with approximately 1,250 battered women's shelters in operation throughout the United States and Canada (Roberts, 1990). By the early 21st century police departments throughout the United States had made major progress in implementing mandatory and pro-arrest intimate partner violence policies and procedures (Roberts & Kurst-Swanger, 2002). With the passage of civil and criminal statutes to protect abused women in all 50 states, police administrators, police officers, and policy makers have become more sensitive and responsive to victims of intimate partner violence. All 50 states and most highly populated cities and counties throughout the United States have implemented mandatory and warrantless arrest laws, in which either some evidence of probable cause or a copy of a temporary or permanent restraining/protective order is all that is needed. In addition, police dispatchers, police officers, and investigators are responding quickly and efficiently to intimate partner violence calls (Roberts & Kurst-Swanger, 2002).

The latest developments within law enforcement agencies are specialized intimate partner violence and crisis intervention units. These include police social worker teams as well as police-crisis worker teams. Such teams can be found in Arizona, California, Florida, Georgia, Illinois, Maryland, Massachusetts, Michigan, Missouri, New Jersey, New York, North Carolina, Ohio, Pennsylvania, South Carolina, Tennessee, Texas, Virginia, Washington, and Wisconsin.

Although the intimate partner violence movement has made, and continues to make, great strides, a number of categories of women remain underserved in many of the states surveyed. The most frequently noted categories included non–English-speaking (and/or undocumented), rurally based, those with mental health issues, gay/lesbian/bisexual/transgender, those with cultural/racial issues, the elderly, children, and the disabled.

Comprehensive Continuum of Services for Crime Victims

Arlene Bower Andrews (1992), building on the victim assistance program guides outlined by NOVA and OVC, developed a step-by-step description of victim services. Her continuum focused on the specific role and functions of victim advocates and social workers, including crime prevention, early intervention and risk reduction, crisis intervention, recovery assistance, collaboration, and advocacy. Prevention is proactive and focuses on competence building and empowerment of individuals, including promoting basic life skills such as communication, problem-solving, and stress reduction. Community prevention activities include neighborhood crime watch programs, graffiti and trash removal, and school–police liaison programs. Risk reduction strategies include considerable increase in street lighting, video surveillance cameras, alarms, fences, and/or open building designs in high crime areas. Recovery assistance includes medical assistance, mental health treatment, and social services ranging from court transportation assistance, case management, home care and emergency food assistance, and services for disabled crime victims with special needs.

CRIMINAL JUSTICE ADVOCACY Criminal justice assistance for crime victims may well be comprehensive and include police investigation, victim/witness notification of court hearings, witness preparation, help completing and expediting restitution and compensation claims, and so on. Collaboration involves interagency assessment and treatment planning, weekly interagency case analysis, joint staff training, and interagency purchase agreements. Advocacy includes individual case advocacy, group advocacy, community advocacy, and legislative advocacy. More specifically, victim advocates may be involved in advocating for housing rental assistance or emergency food assistance one day and lobbying with legislative aides and legislators the next day for new legislation to provide increased funding and resources to vulnerable victims of violent crimes.

The National Coalition Against Domestic Violence (NCADV), established in 1978 as an alliance of state coalitions and emergency shelters, consists of a representative from each state (Roche & Sadoski, 1996). The NCADV and the 50 statewide domestic violence coalitions lobby and advocate for improved social services and legal rights for battered women and their children. The NCADV is a nationwide organization of intimate partner violence advocates; self-identified formerly battered women; professional social workers, nurses, and attorneys; and service providers and lobbyists. Its mission includes coalition building on the local, state, and national levels; its board of directors represents local and state coalitions as well as diverse groups of women affected by intimate partner violence (Brownell & Roberts, 2002). The coalition not only serves as a national toll-free information and referral center but also has an active public policy office in Washington, DC, that lobbies Congress, monitors state and federal legislative developments, and advises grassroots organizations on legislative developments (http://www.ncadv.org).

The National Network to End Domestic Violence (NNEDV), established in 1990, is another membership and advocacy organization of state domestic violence coalitions. As of 2002 it provided services to over 2,500 local member programs. Similar to its sister organization the NCADV, the NNEDV provides assistance with coalition building and advocacy to strengthen the responsiveness of federal public policies that concern vulnerable battered women and their children. "The NNEDV developed domestic violence policy that was instrumental in the drafting of the VAWA 1994 legislation. The national network has been successful in having the federal funding appropriation for intimate partner violence coalitions and programs raised from $20 million to almost $90 million between 1995 and 2000" (Brownell & Roberts, 2002, pp. 86–87). The network views itself as the voice of domestic violence advocates before Congress, the executive branch, state legislative bodies and committees, and the courts (Brownell & Roberts, 2002).

VICTIM SERVICES AND WITNESS ASSISTANCE In the mid-1970s victim/witness programs began to emerge. By the end of the decade Viano (1979) counted 265 such programs. Victim/witness assistance programs are usually located either within the local county prosecutor's offices, the county court house, or adjacent to the court building. These programs are designed to encourage witness cooperation in the filing of criminal charges as well as testifying in court. In general, these programs include a witness notification and case monitoring system in which staff keep witnesses advised of indictment, continuances, and postponements; specific trial and hearing dates; negotiated pleas; and trial outcomes. In addition, many of these programs provide secure and comfortable reception rooms for witnesses waiting to testify, transportation services, and an escort to accompany the witness to court and to remain with that individual to explain and interpret the court proceedings. Typically, these programs also prepare and distribute court-orientation pamphlets about the adjudication process, with titles such as "Crime Victims' Bill of Rights," "Witness Guidelines for Courtroom Testimony," "What You Should Know About Your Criminal Court and the Court Process," and "Information Guide for Crime Victims."

According to a national organizational survey of victim service and witness assistance programs (Roberts, 1990), slightly under one-third of these programs reported having childcare available for the children of victims and witnesses while parents testified in court. Providing responsible and structured child care for a parent while he or she is testifying in court provides an invaluable service (Roberts, 1990); unfortunately, criminal justice agencies often remain unaware of the impact of victimization on the children of victims and witnesses, in particular a victim/parent's emotional reactions, losses, physical injuries, and disruptions. Victim/witness assistance programs need to be concerned with the special needs of children not only because many parent witnesses will not be able to testify if they cannot find adequate child care during a traumatizing court ordeal, but, more importantly, because it is the humane thing to do. An added benefit is that some children may have witnessed the crime and can provide additional identifying characteristics of the perpetrator (Roberts, 1990).

The overriding purpose of victim/witness assistance programs and units is to assist witnesses in overcoming the anxiety and trauma associated with testifying in court while encouraging witness cooperation in the prosecution of criminal cases. The primary objectives of such programs are identified as follows (Roberts, 1990):

- Providing victims and witnesses with the message that their cooperation is essential to crime control efforts and successful criminal prosecution
- Informing victims and witnesses of their rights to receive dignified and compassionate treatment by criminal justice authorities

- Providing information to witnesses regarding the court process, the scheduling of the case, the trial, and the disposition
- Providing orientation to court and tips on how best to testify and accurately recall the crime scene

Victim service or crisis intervention programs for crime victims do not seem to be as common as victim/witness assistance programs. This type of program is usually lodged in a police department, sheriff's office, hospital, probation department, or not-for-profit social service agency. As a rule, such programs attempt to intervene within the first 24 hours after the victimization. They provide a comprehensive range of essential services for crime victims, such as mobile crime scene response; crisis counseling; help in completing victim compensation applications; emergency financial assistance and food vouchers to local supermarkets; transportation to court; the local battered women's shelter, the hospital, or the victim assistance program office; repairing or replacing of broken locks and windows; assistance in replacing lost documents (e.g., birth certificates, marriage licenses, wills); and referrals to the prosecutor's intimate partner violence or sexual assault intake unit and to community mental health centers and social service agencies for both short-term and extended treatment.

Providing victim assistance and support services that will facilitate the crime victim's recovery is difficult and complex. Several research studies indicated that the two most effective methods of lessening psychological consequences, including fear and distress, are restoring tarnished beliefs and correcting negative cognitions and irrational beliefs and building on inner strengths and positive coping skills (Roberts, 2007; Roberts & Roberts, 2005).

In 1981 the first national survey of victim service and witness assistance programs was published by Albert Roberts, examining patterns of program development and the state of the art in victim services, based on 184 responding programs. Survey results indicated availability of a broad range of services, identified in **Table 4-3**. In addition to these core services, approximately three-fourths of survey respondents were able to provide legal advocacy for clients, two-thirds offered services for the disabled, and one-third had bilingual counselors available. Forms of assistance less likely to be available included batterer intervention, crime scene advocacy, and transitional housing, whereas important services such as medical advocacy, employment or financial aid, elder abuse assistance, and youth education and mentoring were, proportionately speaking, almost nonexistent.

TABLE 4-3 Services Offered by Victim Service and Witness Assistance Programs

Crisis intervention	This service is offered in the immediate days or weeks following a victimizing experience. The goal is to reduce the acute trauma symptoms.
24-hour hotline	This service is available to anyone telephoning in to report or require assistance as a victim or the witnessing of a crime.
Assistance with the court process	Trained staff focus on the victim to explain the various aspects of the court process and provide a bridge between the victim and court.
Assistance with completing victim compensation forms	Trained staff explain the various victim compensation forms and can help with filling out of the forms especially if the victim has any type of disability.
Court advocacy	A member of a victim crisis center acts as an advocate to the victim by explaining the court process and accompanying the victim to court
Shelter	Crisis centers have lists of shelters where victims of violence and their children may live safely for a short time.
Referral to a mental health agency	Crisis intervention staff have a list of therapists for victims who need more than crisis care.
Transportation to court	Advocacy staff will transport victims to court.
Public education	An important part of crisis services is to educate the public on crime and victimization. The education is conducted in schools, community groups, and to health care and law enforcement groups.

Data from Roberts, A. R. 1990. *Helping Crime Victims: Research, Policy, and Practice.* Thousand Oaks, CA: Sage Publications.

Nearly all programs examined identified themselves as nonprofit, with funding usually accomplished by combining two or more revenue sources. In general, most programs received well over half of their funding from state and/or federal (VOCA) subsidization. Supplemental funding was frequently provided through a variety of channels, from general county revenue to fundraising and private-party donations, although there was no discernable consistency between surveyed programs as far as access to these types of additional resources.

The number of battered women served overall by these programs (including hotline contact) ranged from as low as 28, at a shelter in Arkansas, to almost 36,000 in Nevada, with an average usually reported somewhere between 500 and 1,500 (Roberts, 1981). These clients frequently had the benefit of receiving critical services from full-time staff—on average, between 8 and 10 per agency—equipped with advanced training and education, although part-time workers (usually between two and six), student interns, and volunteers still made up a large percentage of shelter staff. Typically, the point of first contact was via the crisis hotline or "walk-in," but it was also common for women to be referred to a program by the police or by a crisis response team at a hospital or community mental health center. Among survey participants, most indicated their initial plan of response included one or more of the following: intake interview, risk and/or needs assessment, establishment of a safety plan, and referral of the victim to a shelter and/or other appropriate agencies (Roberts, 1981). A solid, standard crisis intervention procedure was succinctly outlined by Catherine Olde, director of Brighter Tomorrows in Grande Prairie, Texas:

> Once the client contacts us, usually by referral or police, other service program or medical facility, needs are assessed and type of services needed is determined or safety plan is reviewed. If shelter is needed, then client is directed to pick-up location.

By and large this well-rounded plan paralleled those in other states.

When asked to identify their program strengths and weaknesses, many program directors had similar and not altogether unexpected responses. Most believed the success of their services was directly related to hiring and retaining a knowledgeable, dedicated, compassionate staff that could implement and manage a variety of programs and support groups. Beyond this, networking and collaboration with other agencies, assisting clients through the legal process, and soliciting community support were viewed as primary strengths. In terms of program weaknesses, a lack of sufficient funding topped the list of nearly half of the survey respondents, whereas lack of staffing, transportation, and adequate housing were the next most frequently identified areas of difficulty (Roberts, 1981).

■ Code of Ethics for Victim Services

Concerns have been raised at times about the oversight of victim services and the degree to which they adhere to a common set of ethical principles and professional standards. As a result the Canadian Department of Justice undertook a project to identify what jurisdictions have codes of ethics for their victim services providers and to identify and compare the common elements present in these codes, as well as in the development of these codes (McGibbon, 2011). The study identified great variations in practice across western nations but nevertheless identified some common themes and issues across jurisdictions:

- *Striking a balance between respecting the voice of victims and protecting clients:* That is, clients have the right to choose services that meet their needs and to refuse service, even if such refusal may increase the risk of danger. For instance, a battered woman may refuse to enter a shelter and may instead decide to return home.

- *Providing information to clients:* This includes not only information about the rights of victims and services available but also information about the limits of confidentiality. That is, when might their statements be subpoenaed into court.
- *Providing safe space:* Including both physically and psychologically safe space, and including safeguarding their identity from the public and media as necessary.
- *Ensuring the safety of children:* Despite concerns for confidentiality, service providers must report child abuse and neglect to appropriate authorities.
- *Maintaining professional boundaries:* Service providers must ensure they do not establish personal or sexual relationships with clients.
- *Providing advocacy:* Victim service providers see their responsibility not only to the individual victim but also to provide advocacy to improve the services for all victims.

▮ Psychological Response to Victimization

The traumatic memories that haunt people after experiencing overwhelming terror has been a theme in literature from Homer to Shakespeare's Macbeth Act V, iii. By the late 1850s Briquet suggested a link between the symptoms of hysteria and childhood histories of trauma (Mei & Merksey, 1980). During this time a small Anglo-Saxon literature emerged documenting responses to accidents (e.g., "railway spine" after train accidents) and war trauma ("soldier's heart").

The relationship between trauma and psychiatric illness, however, began to be explored only in the last two decades of the 19th century when neurologist Charcot lectured on the functional effects of trauma on behavior (see a review by van der Kolk, 1994). Charcot's student, Pierre Janet, undertook one of the first systematic studies of the relationship between trauma and psychiatric symptoms and delivered a major paper at the Harvard Medical School in 1906 (van der Kolk, Brown, & van der Hart, 1989). Janet realized that different temperaments predisposed people to deal with trauma with different coping styles. He coined the term "subconscious" to describe the collection of memories that form the mental schemes that include the person's interaction with the environment. He suggested it was the interplay of memory systems and temperament that made each person unique and complex (van der Kolk et al., 1989).

Similarly, Freud, in one of his earliest published works, *Studies in Hysteria*, suggested the concept of "anxiety neurosis" or "hysteria" in which a horrific psychological event leads to physical consequences (Breuer & Freud, 1895). He later shifted from a trauma-related paradigm of neurosis to a paradigm that centered on intrapsychic fantasy. In a later work, *Beyond the Pleasure Principle*, he once again addressed the issue of traumatic neurosis and looked at trauma as disequilibrium (Freud, 1961).

Posttraumatic Stress Disorder

The history of the development of trauma theory was intensified around war and combat stress during both the first and second world wars. However, despite such recognition systematic inquiry into the phenomenon of posttraumatic stress was remarkably late in coming. Indeed, it was not until the mid-1970s that the concept of posttraumatic stress disorder (PTSD) emerged due to two social factors: the return of soldiers from the Vietnam War and the emergence of "rape trauma syndrome" (Burgess & Holmstrom, 1974). In 1980 PTSD was determined to be a separate and distinct diagnostic category by the American Psychiatric Association, with three revisions to diagnosis since then.

Using current criteria (APA, 2000), to qualify for a diagnosis of PTSD an individual must be exposed to a traumatic event in which he or she experienced, witnessed, or was confronted with actual or threatened death or serious injury and his or her response involved intense fear, helplessness, or horror. Symptoms fall into three clusters. *Reexperiencing symptoms* include intrusive thoughts, nightmares, feelings as if the event were recurring, and intense psychological and/or physiological distress at exposure to cues that retrigger the event. *Avoidance symptoms* include efforts to avoid thoughts or stimuli that are reminiscent of the event, avoiding people and places that cause distress, inability to recall important aspects of the event, restricted affect, and feelings of detachment. *Arousal symptoms* include difficulty falling or staying asleep, emotional outbursts, difficulty concentrating, hypervigilance, and exaggerated startle response. Biological correlates of these reactions include increased heart rate, skin conductance, and blood pressure.

TRAUMA AND THE LIMBIC SYSTEM   One way to explain the long-term effects of trauma is to understand the neurobiology of trauma and its effect on the limbic system. The limbic system is the alarm system for the body that protects the individual in the face of danger. It is the place where all sensory information enters the human system and is encoded. When trauma is experienced the neurohormonal system releases and is regulated by epinephrine, which helps mobilize resources during dangerous states. However, when individuals are trapped and cannot remove themselves either through fleeing or fighting, a particular type of learning, termed "trauma learning," occurs that does not allow a reduction of stress through adaptive means of the fight-or-flight response. Due to excesses and depletion of hormones in the brain structures responsible for interpreting and storing incoming stimuli, alterations occur in memory systems. The individual becomes immobilized, and as the level of autonomic arousal increases, there is a move into a numbing state through the release of opiates in the brain. This numbing state accounts for disconnection of the processing and encoding of information. In a sense, when the trauma is over the alarm system remains somewhat stuck between the accelerated fight-or-flight response and the numbing state, resulting in an alteration in an adaptive capacity. This alteration is a cellular change that becomes fixed in its patterning and is difficult to change or extinguish. Of particular importance are various theories of modulating effects in the brain. We can all appreciate this fight-or-flight and numbing in the face of danger; what we are now understanding is that trauma can have a lasting effect on basic processes of adaptation and growth.

Because these neurosystems of arousal and numbing are intricately related to information processing and memory, there is a distinctive type of memory in which experiences are recalled as if they were happening (e.g., a flashback). Thus, when external events trigger an association to the abuse itself, the person is thrown into this panic memory and feels subjected to a hostile exploited environment even though nothing like that is going on. Internal events can also trigger trauma-specific reactions, for example, night terrors. These experiences are not like typical dreams. Rather, they are vivid, visceral responses as if the trauma is occurring.

ASSESSMENT MEASURES AND PROTOCOLS FOR PTSD Clinicians have the responsibility of assessing trauma in a victim, making a diagnosis, and devising a treatment plan. Ron Acierno at the National Violence Against Women Prevention Research Center at the Medical College of South Carolina has outlined the assessment measures and protocols commonly used to measure the mental health impact of violence against women. These protocols are divided into interviews and questionnaires and are briefly described in **Table 4-4**.

TABLE 4-4 **Assessment Measures for PTSD and Other Symptomotology**

Structured Clinical Interview for DSM-IV Axis I Disorders (SCID-IV-PTSD) **Instrument is designed to be administered by a clinician or trained mental health professional.**	Semistuctured interview for making the major DSM-IV Axis I diagnoses. Specific inquiries, read verbatim to respondents, assess presence or absence of each DSM-IV PTSD symptom. Symptom presence is rated on a three-point confidence scale based on the interviewer's interpretation of victim's responses to prompts.
Clinician Administered PTSD Scale-1 (CAPS-1)	Structured interview designed to make a categorical PTSD diagnosis, as well as to provide a measure of PTSD symptom severity
PTSD Symptom Scale-Self-Report version (PSS-SR)	A 17-item self-reported questionnaire to assess symptoms of posttraumatic stress disorder
Impact of Event Scale (IES)	A 22-item self-report measure constructed to assesses intrusion, avoidance, and hyperarousal symptoms of PTSD experienced over the past week
Beck Depression Inventory-2	A 21-item scale contains four statements reflecting current manifestations of depression in increasing intensity, from neutral to severe
Beck Anxiety Inventory (BAI)	A 21-item self-rating scale of anxiety symptomatology
Trauma Symptom Inventory (TSI)	The TSI assesses acute and chronic posttraumatic symptomatology, including the effects of rape, spouse abuse, physical assault, combat experiences, major accidents, and natural disasters, as well as the lasting sequelae of childhood abuse and other early traumatic events.
Symptom Checklist-90-R (SCL-90-R)	A 90-item self-rating scale of general symptoms, computerized scored in 9 subscales

Data from Acierno at the National Violence Against Women Prevention Research Center at the Medical College of South Carolina.

■ Treatment Interventions

Robert's Crisis Intervention Model

In terms of crisis resolution, Roberts's seven-stage crisis intervention model (Roberts, 2005) provides a structured and targeted framework that can lay the foundation for more comprehensive, long-term service plans. **Table 4-5** shows the stages of crisis intervention.

The goal of Roberts's crisis intervention model is to ensure a victim's immediate safety and stabilization, followed by problem solving and the exploration of alternative options that hopefully will culminate in a meaningful action plan. The use of standardized test measurements is highly recommended in making a comprehensive assessment, and several are available that can enable crisis workers to retrieve specific and relevant information: the Expanded Conflict Tactics Scales of

TABLE 4-5 Roberts's Seven-Stage Crisis Intervention Model

Stage 1: Assessing Safety	Evaluate (1) the severity of the crisis, (2) the client's current emotional state, (3) immediate psychosocial and safety needs, and (4) level of client's current coping skills and resources
Stage 2: Establishing Rapport and Communication	Goals are assessment and identification of critical areas of intervention, recognition of the duration and severity of violence, and acknowledgment of what has happened
Stage 3: Identifying the Major Problems	Prioritize the problems or impacts by identifying them in terms of how they affect the survivor's current status
Stage 4: Dealing with Feelings and Providing Support	Demonstrate empathy and an anchored understanding of the survivor's experience so symptoms and reactions are normalized and can be viewed as functional strategies for survival
Stage 5: Exploring Possible Alternatives	Explore alternatives of (1) situational supports or social agencies to help resolve crisis-related problems; (2) coping skills and strategies to help the client reach a precrisis level of functioning; and (3) positive and rational thinking patterns, to lessen the client's levels of anxiety, stress, and crisis
Stage 6: Formulating an Action Plan	Help the client achieve a level of functioning and maintain coping skills and resources and have a manageable treatment plan, allowing the client to follow through and be successful
Stage 7: Follow-Up Measures	Crisis resolution addressed: (1) Physical Safety and Survival, (2) Ventilation and Expression of Feelings, (3) Cognitive Mastery, and (4) Interpersonal Adjustments and Adapting to a new environment

Data from Roberts, A. R. 2005. Bridging the past and present to the future of crisis intervention and crisis management. In A. R. Roberts (Ed.), *Crisis Intervention Handbook: Assessment, treatment and research* (3rd ed., pp. 3–33). New York: Oxford University Press.

Aggression—both verbal and physical (Straus, Hamby, Boney-McCoy, & Sugarman, 1996); the Beck Depression Inventory (Beck & Steer, 1984); the Derogatis Symptom Checklist-90-Revised (Derogatis, 1992); and the Trauma Symptom Checklist-40 (Briere & Runtz, 1989). These are intended to elicit responses that can provide clinicians with a multifaceted snapshot of a victim's trauma history and current psychological state, including varying degrees of depression, anxiety, sexual problems, dissociation, sleep disturbances, and post–sexual abuse trauma.

Although the seven-stage model can be viewed as a stand-alone protocol for initial crisis intervention, it is imperative that it be functionally viewed as the first step on a continuum of established strategies and supports designed to facilitate long-term treatment, cognitive reorientation and empowerment of the victim, and freedom from the abusive environment.

Treatment Models

Once preliminary assessment and stabilization have been accomplished, the more chronic difficulties must be addressed to progress toward significant and lasting emotional, behavioral, and environmental change. **Table 4-6** outlines some of the treatment models.

COGNITIVE-BEHAVIORAL THERAPY   A number of reviews of the effectiveness of cognitive-behavioral approaches for PTSD have been conducted and conclude that cognitive-behavioral therapy is effective in reducing the severity of posttraumatic stress symptoms in individuals who have experienced a wide range of traumatic events and in individuals who suffer from both acute and chronic symptoms (Regehr & Glancy, 2010). The basis of cognitive therapeutic methods is that behavior is a learned rather than an innate process. Operant conditioning, described by B. F. Skinner in his 1938 book, *The Behavior of Organisms: An Experimental Analysis*, postulates that a response that is reinforcing (rewarded) will reoccur, whereas the premise of social learning theory proposed by Bandura in 1977 is that learning takes place by modeling (observing and imitating others) as well as through self-reinforcement and self-evaluations. Treatment strategies include systematic desensitization, aversion therapy, shaping behaviors by rewarding successive approximations of the desired result, positive and negative reinforcement, and role modeling of adaptive behaviors. Cognitive restructuring, identifying dysfunctional core beliefs, role plays and rehearsals, relaxation and stress management training, self-monitored homework assignments, and problem solving are used to reinforce the goals of positive learning and change.

The general approach for cognitive-behavioral therapy, a widely accepted, evidence-based, cost-effective psychotherapy for many

TABLE 4-6 **Treatment Models**

Cognitive Behavioral Therapy (CBT)	Psychotherapy based on modifying everyday thoughts and behaviors, with the aim of positively influencing emotions
Problem Identification and Problem Solving	Redirection of the client's emotions and skills *away from* fear, powerlessness, and subjugation, and *toward* self-confidence, self-reliance, and competent decision making
Psychotherapy	A range of techniques based on experiential relationship building, dialogue, communication, and behavior change
Eye Movement Desensitization and Reprocessing (EMDR)	Client attends to past and present experiences in brief sequential doses while simultaneously focusing on an external stimulus

disorders, developed out of behavior modification and cognitive therapy. The particular therapeutic techniques commonly include relaxation and distraction techniques; keeping a diary of significant events and associated feelings, thoughts, and behaviors; questioning and testing assumptions or habits of thoughts that might be unhelpful and unrealistic; gradually facing activities that may have been avoided; and trying out new ways of behaving and reacting.

ADDITIONAL TREATMENT INTERVENTIONS Psychotherapy is an interpersonal, relational intervention used by trained psychotherapists to aid victims in problems of living. This usually includes increasing individual sense of well-being and reducing subjective discomforting experience. These include psychodynamic, cognitive-behavioral, interpersonal, experiential, and body-centered therapies. Eye movement desensitization and reprocessing integrates elements of many effective psychotherapies in structured protocols that are designed to maximize treatment effects. Eye movement desensitization and reprocessing is an information processing therapy and uses an eight-phase approach.

TERMINATION, REFERRALS, AND EVALUATION Primary treatment effectively ends when a client has stabilized enough to pursue his or her own goals of independent living with appropriate supports and resources. Referrals for legal, financial, and educational assistance should be made, and regular follow-up contact should be part of any treatment plan. Clinicians must also stress the importance of seeking help immediately for any crisis situation or safety concerns, ensuring the client of the availability of prompt intervention and assistance.

Ideally, evaluation of strategies and interventions conducted will be an ongoing practice at each stage along the recovery continuum, not just with regard to a specific client but also to the future implementation of intervention and therapeutic models vis-à-vis broader program policies and procedures.

■ Summary

As individuals and communities worldwide have risen up in an effort to be more compassionate to the suffering of their fellow citizens, so too has society as a whole evolved from barbarianism to humanitarianism vis-à-vis our vast and complex criminal justice systems. Clearly, governments and citizens have made tremendous strides with regard to their understanding and treatment of crime victims. Advocacy, legislation, and education have provided the cornerstones for advancing the belief that crime victims deserve compassion and assistance rather than blame. We still remain, however, on the precipice of a successful, fully realized legacy of programs and services for victims of crime and are therefore charged with vigorously continuing the work.

■ Key Terms

Primary victimization: Affects the targeted or personalized victim.

National Organization for Victim Assistance (NOVA): Established in 1975 as a national umbrella organization and is dedicated to expanding current victim services, developing new programs, and supporting passage of victims' rights legislation.

Secondary victimization: Affects impersonal victims, such as commercial establishments, churches, schools, and public transportation.

Tertiary victimization: Diffuse and extends to the community at large.

Victim Information and Notification Everyday (VINE) program: Enables victims of intimate partner violence to access court information.

Victims of Crime Act (VOCA): The VOCA Act established the Crime Victim's Fund that is supported by fines collected from persons who have been convicted of criminal offenses.

■ Discussion Questions

1. Consider the rights of the victim delineated by the United Nations. Select one that requires greater focus and attention in our country and discuss means for improvement.

2. Considering different models of victim compensation, what do you believe victims should be compensated for and who should pay?

3. Should victim witness statements be admissible in court? Why?

4. How have rights movements contributed to the development of services for victims? What has been neglected by this advocacy approach to legislative change?

■ Resources

American Probation and Parole Association
   http://www.appa-net.org/

American Prosecutors Research Institute
  http://www.ndaa.org/
Canadian Resource Centre for Victims of Crime
  http://www.crcvc.ca/en/compensation.php
Criminal Injuries Compensation Board
  http://www.cicb.gov.on.ca/en/index.htm
National Institute on Mental Health, Post-traumatic Stress Disorder
  http://www.nimh.nih.gov/health/publications/post-traumatic-stress-
  disorder-easy-to-read/index.shtml
Office for Victims of Crime
  http://www.ojp.usdoj.gov/ovc/about/index.html

References

Andrews, A.B. (1992). *Victimization and survivor services*. New York: Springer.

American Psychiatric Association (APA). (2000). *Diagnostic and Statistical Manual of Mental Disorders* (4th edition). Washington, DC: APA Press.

Bandura, A. (1977). *Social learning theory*. New York: General Learning Press.

Beck, A.T., & Steer, R.A. (1984). Internal consistencies of the original and revised Beck Depression Inventory. *Journal of Clinical Psychology, 40*(6), 1365–1367.

Breuer, J., & Freud, S. (1895). *Studies in hysteria*. Boston: Beacon Press.

Briere, J., & Runtz, M. (1989). The Trauma Symptom Checklist (TSC-33): Early data on a new scale. *Journal of Interpersonal Violence, 4*, 151–163.

Brownell, P., & Roberts, A.R. (2002). National organizational survey of domestic violence coalitions. In A.R. Roberts (Ed.), *Handbook of domestic violence intervention strategies* (pp. 80–98). New York: Oxford University Press.

Brownmiller, S. (1975). *Against our will: Men, women, and rape*. New York: Simon & Schuster.

Burgess, A.W., & Holmstrom, L.L. (1974). Rape trauma syndrome. *Am J Psychiatry, 131*(9): 981–986.

Campbell, R., Townsend, S.M., Long, S.M., & Kinnison, K.E. (2005). Organizational characteristics of sexual assault nurse examiner programs: Results from the national survey project. *Journal of Forensic Nursing, 1*(2), 57–64.

CBC News. (2004, October 29). Bin Laden claims responsibility for the 2001 attacks against the United States. Retrieved from http://www.cbc.ca/world/story/2004/10/29/binladen_message041029.html

Ciancone, A.C., Wilson, C., Collette, R., & Gerson, L.W. (2000). Sexual assault nurse examiner programs in the United States. *Annals of Emergency Medicine, 35*(4), 353–357.

Criminal Code of Canada. RSC, 1985, c C-46

Crime Victim Compensation Quarterly. (2011). 2012 VOCA cap may remain level as budget issues grow. Retrieved from http://www.nacvcb.org/NACVCB/files/ccLibraryFiles/Filename/000000000114/newsletter.2011-2final.pdf

Derene, S., Walker, S., & Stein, J. (2007). History of the Crime Victim's Movement in the United States. *Senator Tommy Burks Victim Assistance Academy Participant Manual.* Tennessee: The Tennessee Coalition Against Domestic Violence and Sexual Assault.

Derogatis, L.R. (1992). *SCL-90-R: Administration, scoring and procedures manual. II.* Baltimore, MD: Clinical Psychometric Research.

Drapkin, I., & Viano, E., eds. (1974). *Victimology: a new focus.* Lexington, MA: Lexington Books. From International Symposium on Victimology, 1st, Jerusalem, 1973. 5 volumes.

Englebrecht, C. (2011). The struggle for "ownership of conflict": An exploration of victim participation and voice in the criminal justice system. *Criminal Justice Review, 36*(2) 129–151.

Erez, E., & Tontodonato, P. (1990). The effect of victim participation in sentencing on sentence outcome. *Criminology, 28*, 451–474.

FBI. (2011). 9/11 Investigation. Famous cases. Retrieved from http://www.fbi.gov/about-us/history/famous-cases/9-11-investigation/9-11-investigation

Feinberg, K. (2004). What have we learned about compensating victims of terrorism? Retrieved from http://www.rand.org/publications/randreview/issues/summer2004/33.html

Figley, C. (1995). *Compassion Fatigue: Coping with Secondary Traumatic Stress Disorder in Those who Treat the Traumatized.* New York: Brunner/Mazel.

Finn-DeLuca, V. (1994). Victim participation at sentencing. *Criminal Law Bulletin, 30*, 403–428.

Freud, S. (1961). *Beyond the Pleasure Principle (The Standard Edition).* Trans. James Strachey. New York: Liveright Publishing Corporation.

Fry, M. (1957, July 7). Justice for victims. *Observer* (London, England), p. 8.

Garkawe, S. (2007). Victim impact statements and sentencing. *Monash University Law Review.* 33, 90–114.

Giliberti, C. (1991). Evaluation of victim impact statement projects in Canada: A summary of findings. In G. Kaiser, H. Kury, & J. Albrecht (Eds.), *Victims and criminal justice.* Freiburg, Germany: Max-Planch Institute.

Girardin, B. (2005). The sexual assault nurse examiner: A win-win solution. *Topics in Emergency Medicine*, 27(2), 124–131.

Greer, G. (1973, January). Seduction is a four-letter word. *Playboy*, 80–82, 164, 178, 224–228.

Griffin, S. (1971). Rape: The all-American crime. *Ramparts*, 10(3) 26–35.

Hambrick, B. (2011). Sex Trafficking Bill Passes Senate. Retrieved from http://hambrick4assembly.com/2011/05/17/press-release-sex-trafficking-bill-passes-senate-to-be-signed-by-governor/

Holmstrom, L.L., & Burgess, A.W. (1983). *The victim of rape: Institutional reactions*. New Brunswick, NJ: Transactions.

Largen, M.A. (1985). The anti-rape movement: Past and present. In A.W. Burgess (Ed.), *Rape and sexual assault* (pp. 1–13). New York: Garland Press.

Ledray, L. (1999). Sexual assault nurse examiner (SANE) development & operation guide. Washington: U.S. Department of Justice, Office of Victims of Crime.

Mai, F.M., & Merskey, H. (1980). Briquet's Treatise on Hysteria. A synopsis and commentary. *Archives of General Psychiatry 37*, 1401–1405.

Manitoba Victims' Bill of Rights. (1986). Retrieved http://www.canlii.org/mb/laws/sta/v-55/20050110/whole.html

McCormack, R.J. (1989, April). A perspective on United States crime victim compensation. Paper presented at the annual meetings of the Academy of Criminal Justice Sciences, Washington, DC.

McGibbon, A. (2011). Codes of ethics for victim services. Retrieved from http://www.justice.gc.ca/eng/pi/rs/rep-rap/rd-rr/rr07_vic4/p2.html

National Organization for Victim Assistance. (1983). *The victim service system: A guide to action*. Washington, DC: Author.

Office for Victims of Crime (OVC). (1988). Restitution: Making it work. Retrieved from http://www.aardvarc.org/victim/restitution.shtml

Office for Victims of Crime (OVC). (2002). Restitution-Making it work. Department of Justice, Office of Justice Programs. Retrieved from http://www.ovc.gov/archive/index.html

Ontario Victims' Bill of Rights, 1995, S.O. 1995, c. 6 http://www.e-laws.gov.on.ca/DBLaws/Source/Statutes/English/2000/S00032_e.htm

President's Task Force on Victims of Crime. (1982). *Final report*. Washington, DC: U.S. Government Printing Office.

R. v. Jacob. (2002). YKTC 15.

Regehr, C., Alaggia, R., Lambert, L., & Saini, M. (2008). Victims of sexual violence in the Canadian criminal courts. *Victims and Offenders*, 3(1), 1–15.

Regehr, C., & Glancy, G. (2010). *Mental health social work in Canada.* Toronto, Ontario, Canada: Oxford University Press.

Regehr, C., & Kanani, K. (2010). *Essential law for social work practice in Canada.* Toronto, Ontario, Canada: Oxford University Press.

Roach, K. (1999). *Due process and victim's rights: The new law and politics of criminal justice.* Toronto, Ontario, Canada: University of Toronto Press.

Roberts, A.R. (1981). *Sheltering battered women: A national study and service guide.* New York: Springer.

Roberts, A.R. (1990). *Helping crime victims: Research, policy, and practice.* Thousand Oaks, CA: Sage.

Roberts, A.R. (2005). Bridging the past and present to the future of crisis intervention and crisis management. In A.R. Roberts (Ed.), *Crisis intervention handbook: Assessment, treatment and research* (3rd ed., pp. 3–33). New York: Oxford University Press.

Roberts, A.R. (2007). Overview and new directions for intervening on behalf of battered women. In A.R. Roberts (Ed.), *Battered women and their families: Intervention strategies and treatment programs* (3rd ed., pp. 3–32). New York: Springer.

Roberts, A.R., & Kurst-Swanger, K. (2002). Police responses to battered women: Past, present and future. In A.R. Roberts (Ed.), *Handbook of domestic violence intervention strategies* (pp. 101–126). New York: Oxford University Press.

Roberts, A.R., Robertiello, G., & Bender, K. (2007). National survey of 107 shelters for battered women and their children. In A.R. Roberts (Ed.), *Battered women and their families: Intervention strategies and treatment programs* (3rd ed., pp. 109–132). New York: Springer.

Roberts, A.R., & Roberts, B.S. (2005). *Ending intimate abuse: Practical guidance and survival strategies.* New York: Oxford University Press.

Roche, S.E., & Sadoski, P.J. (1996). Social action for battered women. In A.R. Roberts (Ed.), *Helping battered women: New perspectives and remedies* (pp. 13–30). New York: Oxford University Press.

Ruback, R., & Bergstrom, M. (2006). Economic sanctions in criminal justice: Purposes, effects and implications. *Criminal Justice and Behavior, 33*(2), 242–273.

Sellin, T., & Wolfgang, M.E. (1964). *The measurement of delinquency.* New York: Wiley.

Skinner, B.F. (1938). *The behavior of organisms: An experimental analysis.* New York: Appleton-Century.

Stamm, B. (1995). *Secondary traumatic stress: Self-care issues for clinicians, researchers, and educators.* Lutherville, MD: The Sidran Press.

Straus, M.A., Hamby, S.L., Boney-McCoy, S., & Sugarman, D.B. (1996). The revised Conflict Tactics Scales (CTS2): Development and preliminary psychometric data. *Journal of Family Issues, 17*(3), 283–316.

Trueblood, C. (2011). Victim impact statements: A balance between victim and defendant rights. *Phoenix Law Review, 3*(2), 605–640.

Turman, K. (2004, March 26). Helping terrorism victims and their families. Retrieved from http://www2.fbi.gov/page2/march04/turman032604.htm

United Nations. (1985). *Declaration of basic principles of justice for victims of crime and abuse of power.* G.A. 40/34, annex, 40 U.N. GAOR Supp. (No.53) at 214, U.N. Doc. A/40/53.

U.S. Government Benefits Help. (2011). Victims compensation fund. Retrieved from http://www.usgovernmentbenefits.org/hd/index.php?t=victims+compensation+fund

Van der Kolk, B.A. (1994). The body keeps score: Memory and the evolving psychobiology of post-traumatic stress. *Harvard Review of Psychology, 1*(5), 253–265.

Van der Kolk, B.A., Brown, P., & van der Hart, O. (1989). Pierre Janet on post-traumatic stress. *Journal of Traumatic Stress, 2,* 365–378.

Vanscoy and Even v. Her Majesty the Queen in Right of Ontario. (1999). O.J. No.1661 (Ont. Sup. Ct. Jus.).

Viano, E. (1979). *Victim/witness services: a review of the literature.* Washington, DC: US Department of Justice.

Wilson, D., & Klein, A. (2005). *An evaluation of the Rhode Island sexual assault response team (SART).* National Criminal Justice Research Service. Washington: U.S. Department of Justice.

Young, A. (2001). *The role of the victim in the criminal justice process: A literature review 1989–1999.* Ottawa, Ontario, Canada: Policy Centre for Victims' Issues, Department of Justice, Research and Statistics Division.

Young, M., & Stein, J. (2004). *The History of the Crime Victims Movement in the United States.* Office of the Victims of Crime. Retrieved from https://www.ncjrs.gov/ovc_archives/ncvrw/2005/pg4c.html#d

Justice Systems

CHAPTER
5

■ Objectives

- To outline the history of the evolution of laws
- To describe the victim process in the criminal justice system
- To describe the civil court system

■ Key Terms

Adjudication
Civil justice system
Criminal charges
Criminal law
Defendant
English common law
Grand jury
Laws
Pretrial
Third-party liability
Victim impact statement

CASE

The Anthony case riveted the public for 3 years. Caylee Marie Anthony, 2 years old, went missing on Monday, June 9, 2008, in Orlando, Florida. Five weeks later her mother reported her missing, and a nationwide search ensued for the missing child. Over time,

FIGURE 5-1 Casey Anthony
© JOE BURBANK/MCT/Landov

evidence accumulated that Casey Anthony, Caylee's mother, had lied to police, the strong odor of decomposition was discovered in her car trunk, and questions were raised about her inappropriate behavior for a mother of a supposed missing child. Anthony was charged with child neglect, was jailed, and was believed guilty by public vote.

Meanwhile, her parents made an appeal to the media to help in the search for their missing grandchild. In December 2008 a meter reader reported a grisly finding: a bag with bones and duct tape hanging from a child's skull in swampy woods near the Anthony home. DNA identified the skeletal remains of Caylee. Her mother, Casey Anthony, was charged with first-degree murder, a capital death penalty case. In June 2011, however, she was acquitted of three murder charges and convicted of four counts of lying to the police. She was released on July 13, 2011, for time served but was required to complete 1-year probation on check fraud charges she admitted to in 2010. See **Figure 5-1**.

■ Introduction

Victims of crime may come into contact with one of two aspects of the justice system, the criminal justice system and the civil justice system. If the crime is reported to the police, the victim enters the criminal justice system. A police investigation may involve interviewing of the witness and gathering evidence, arresting and charging a suspect, prosecution and sentencing of the accused, and perhaps ultimately incarceration of the offender. In the criminal justice system a crime has been committed against the state and the victim is a witness in the service of justice. The prosecuting attorney represents the interests of the state against the accused offender; he or she does not represent the interests of the victim. Further, the decision to pursue criminal charges and proceed to court rests with the prosecution, not the victim. Although programs that assist victims in the criminal justice system may be available, the criminal justice process is designed to judge the guilt or innocence of accused offenders and, if found guilty, to punish and/or rehabilitate them for the greater good of society.

The civil justice system, by contrast, is designed to ensure the rights of individual citizens who suffered the direct impact of the crime. Regardless of whether there was a prosecution, victims can bring their claims before the court and ask to have the responsible parties held accountable. Control over initiating a legal process rests with the citizen, not the state.

This chapter focuses on the importance of the development of laws over time and the victim process and role in the criminal and civil justice systems. Cases, including that of Casey Anthony, who was charged with the murder of her child; Jaycee Dugard, a victim of kidnapping; and the Petit triple murders, are used to illustrate various components of the justice systems. The chapter provides information on crime in North America, noting that the justice systems of the United States and Canada are governed by local, state, or federal laws.

In addition to the civil and criminal justice systems, victims may encounter two other justice systems not covered here. First, the family law system considers issues related to family disputes and obligations. These include legal relationships surrounding divorce, child custody, and child support. From the perspective of victims of crime, family law may be relevant in cases of spousal violence, child abuse, and child abduction (*West's Encyclopedia of American Law*, 1998a). Second, the juvenile justice system is responsible for handling cases involving young offenders. The first juvenile court in the United States was established in 1899 with the goal of controlling serious juvenile offending. Similarly, Canada created an Act Respecting the Arrest, Trial and Imprisonment of Youthful Offenders in 1894 followed by the Juvenile Delinquents Act in 1908. These acts saw offenses of youth as conditions of delinquency and offenders in need of guidance and supervision (Regehr & Kanani, 2010). In 1974 the United States Juvenile Justice and Delinquency Prevention Act created the Office of Juvenile Justice and Delinquency Prevention. The establishment of this office was an acknowledgment that young people in crisis, whether they are serious, violent, and chronic offenders or victims of abuse and neglect, pose a challenge to the nation (Office of Juvenile Justice and Delinquency Prevention, 2011). Individuals who are victims of youthful offenders may access information from the Office of Juvenile Justice and Delinquency Prevention to better understand the process they will encounter in the justice system.

■ Evolution of Laws

English writer and historian Colin Wilson refers to the "warrior tradition" that typified much of life in the early centuries, stating it is not exactly known when piracy and banditry became common in Europe but it was probably toward the end of the third millennium BC (Wilson, 1984). Wilson quotes the Greek historian Thucydides, writing in the fifth century BC, that in times ancient to him, the world was commanded by leaders of powerful bands of raiders who plundered towns and villages with such intensity that all Greeks were required to carry weapons in defense of their homes and persons (Wilson, 1984). The "warrior mentality" was both myth and a very current dangerous reality to the people of those times. These ancient civilizations attempted to deal with their reality by developing criminal justice systems (Wilson, 1984).

A crime is an act prohibited by criminal law that involves a victim and a perpetrator. The justice system is based on law, that is, a set of rules usually enforced through a legal institution. The purpose of law is to provide an objective set of rules for governing conduct and maintaining order in a society. This justice system can be confusing and frustrating to victims who must navigate it. However, a review of the history of laws helps to explain the various aspects and steps involved in the criminal and civil justice systems.

■ Historical Perspective

Greek Mythology

Greek mythology involves stories of gods and goddesses for the purposes of describing and enforcing moral standards and to explain the world and events that befell people. For example, thunder and lightning were believed to be caused by Zeus hurling his thunderbolt. The list of chief writers through whom the myths have been told is not lengthy. Homer heads the list with his two most famous poems, *The Iliad* and *The Odyssey*, written sometime around 1000 BC. Homer's Zeus is a person living in a world where civilization has made an entry and where he has established a standard of right and wrong. Zeus punishes men who lie and break their oaths; he is angered by an ill treatment of the dead; he pities and helps others; and he intervenes in disputes, beseeching others to show mercy. In *The Odyssey*, Homer describes a concept familiar to many today, writing that those who fail to help the needy and strangers are in fact sinning against the god Zeus.

Hesiod also wrote about mythology and may be of interest to victimology students. Writing in approximately 750 BC, Hesiod addresses the concept of evil and suggests that a man who inflicts evil on vulnerable people invokes the wrath of Zeus (Hamilton, 1942). As a peasant who lived among the poor, Hesiod believed the poor must have a just god. He wrote, "Fishes and beasts and fowls of the air devour one another. But to man, Zeus has given justice. Besides Zeus on his throne Justice has her seat" (Hamilton, 1942, p. 20). These passages introduce a victim concept and show the great and bitter needs of the helpless were reaching up to heaven and changing the god of the strong into protector of the weak (Hamilton, 1942).

Urukagina

The concept of law is as old as civilization itself. Urukagina was a ruler of the city-state Lagash in Mesopotamia from 2380 to 2360 BC. His reform to fight corruption has been cited as a key example of a legal code. He exempted widows and orphans from taxes, compelled the city to pay funeral expenses (including the ritual food and drink for the journey of the dead into the lower world), and decreed that the rich must use silver when purchasing from the poor. He also said that powerful rich men could not force poor people to sell if they did not wish to.

Code of Ur-Namm

The Code of Ur-Namm (*ca.* 2112–2095 BC) is reported to be the oldest known tablet containing a law code surviving today and was established during the Sumarian dynasty in Mesopotamia. In contrast to the lex talionis principle of Babylonian law of an "eye for an eye," the code was viewed as advanced because of the monetary fines it set. The capital crimes of murder, rape, robbery, and adultery were offenses punishable by death.

Code of Hammurabi

The Code of Hammurabi was established circa 1786 BC again in ancient Mesopotamia, at the time Hammurabi established Babylon, the world's first metropolis. As the first ruler of the Babylonian empire, he holds the claim of restoring order and justice to Mesopotamia. Although Hammurabi did conquer other city-states to expand his empire, he let the rulers of the cities-states live and justly rule the people with fair laws. He wrote 282 laws governing family, criminal punishment, civil law, ethics, business, prices, trade, and every other aspect of ancient life known as "the Code of Hammurabi." His stated purpose was to promote the welfare of the people and cause justice to prevail in the land by destroying the wicked and the evil, that the strong might not oppress the weak (Stearns, Adas, Schwartz, & Gilbert, 2003). These laws were carved on an 8-foot high stone monument in public view so that all people could read and know what was required of them. Putting the laws into writing was important in itself because it suggested the laws were immutable and above the power of any earthly king to change.

In the prologue to his code Hammurabi declared his desire to "establish justice," and at the end he declared that through his enactments that the strong person shall not injure the weak person, and that there be justice for widows and orphans. Although Hammurabi had the right motives for producing these laws that he believed Marduk, the chief god of Babylon, had given him the commission to write, many of the laws seemed strict, harsh, and cruel. Two examples of the severity and harshness of some of the punishments for lawbreaking included cutting off the hand of the son if he strikes his father and putting to death someone who steals the minor son of another man (Stearns et al., 2003). The punishment varied depending on the class of offenders and victims, with upper classes, who were expected to be more responsible, receiving harsher punishments. Nevertheless, the code was also one of the earliest examples of the idea of presumption of innocence, and it further suggested that the accused and accuser had the opportunity to provide evidence in a dispute or conflict.

Mosaic Law

Moses (between 1300 and 1150 BC in Egypt) was a most important figure in Judaism. According to the Old Testament, through Moses, God gave to the Israelites the Ten Commandments on stone tablets. The Mosaic Law begins with these Ten Commandments and includes a variety of rules of religious observance. In Judaism the first five books are called the Torah, or "the Law." These commandments become the basis of Judeo-Christian morality and for many of the criminal laws in our modern society (e.g., the prohibition against murder, theft, and perjury).

Roman Law

The development of Roman law covers more than 1,000 years from the Law of Twelve Tables (from 449 BC) to the Corpus Juris Civilis (Corps of Civil Law) of Emperor Justinian I (around 530). A critical feature of Roman law was the Law of Twelve Tables, the earliest Roman code of laws, written by a special commission of 10 men in approximately 451 BC. The tables were supposedly written in response to the plebeians' protest that the patrician judges were able to discriminate against them with impunity because the principles governing legal disputes were known only orally. No complete text of the code survives, and it is known only from quotations and references. The Twelve Tables served as the foundation of Roman law and embraced all spheres of law: private, criminal, public, and sacred. They were never abolished, but later enactments made them obsolete. The Twelve Tables made law less mystical and not derived from revelation but more the product of the Roman citizenry itself. It was a publicly stated and accessible guide for the average citizen's course of conduct.

Code of Justinian

Justinian I was one of the more famous of all the emperors of the Byzantine, or Eastern Roman, Empire and was the originator of the Code of Justinian. Born a barbarian, he became a powerful ruler and law reformer. He is known today chiefly for his codification of law. After taking rule Justinian found the laws of the empire in great confusion. Many were out of date; some contradicted others; nowhere did a complete collection of them exist. Justinian appointed a commission to study the problem. The work of the commissioners resulted in the publication of the *Code of Justinian*. The result was a three-book collection that encompassed the decrees of emperors, the opinions of the lawyers and judges who had interpreted these decrees, and a description of the legal principles in simple terms. A fourth book, *Novella Constitutions*, included the ordinances of Justinian after the codification. These four together constituted the *Code of Justinian*, or Civil Law (*Corpus Juris Civilis*), and mark the beginning of recording case law.

Feudalism

Feudalism had its roots in the eighth century in France. This manner of law established fiefs or the granting of labor and law, which were the rewards for contributing to military service. In England in 1066 William the Conqueror established feudalism after the defeat of the Anglo-Saxons as a reward to those who were loyal to him. By the middle ages, feudalism became a system of duties and rights that bound nobility or an upper class in loyalty and responsibility to a king or lord. This loyalty to the king was in exchange for land (fiefs) that was worked by lower class labor (serfs). In return for their servitude the serf received the protection of the landowner. This type of system clearly benefited the monarchy and the upper class. The king or monarchy held public power privately, and the nobles were bound to the monarch in both military and civil capacities.

In colonial America the principles of feudalism continued as an extension of the English nobility system. Feudal domains were established by the early colonists to secure property and wealth. Colonies were established by the Puritans and the Protestants in New England; proprietary colonies were established by the Anglicans in Maryland, the Carolinas, and Delaware; and similar systems were established by the Dutch in New Amsterdam (later New York) and New Jersey.

English Common Law

English common law has its foundations in the traditional unwritten law of England, based on custom and usage. Centuries before the Norman Conquest, decisions regarding legal issues were made by councils of the king and passed down to village meetings. Each community then developed its own set of customs and expectations. It was not until the ninth century that King Alfred moved to unify the various kingdoms into a single kingdom of England and similarly attempted to create a more unified approach to legal decision making. His wife, Queen Martia, is credited with writing down the pre-Saxon compendiums of the common law, known as Alfred's Code. With his invasion of England in 1066, William the Conqueror combined the Anglo-Saxon law with Norman law to form what we now know as English common law. This particular form of law is thus based on custom and precedent rather than statutory laws, in that the recorded legal decisions of one court shape future decisions (Baker, 2002).

The common law of the United States is based on Sir William Blackstone's Commentaries on the Laws of England, completed in 1769 and based on a course of study he undertook at Oxford University. The commentaries can be found online at http://www.lonang.com/exlibris/blackstone/. Over time, English common-law precedents were enacted into the legislation of various states with the exception of Louisiana, which is still influenced by the Napoleonic Code. Similarly, in Canada all provinces use common law, with the exception of Quebec, which also follows a system based on Napoleonic Code.

■ Contemporary Codes and Laws

Early English common law forms the basis for much of our contemporary legal system. The Magna Carta of England and the U.S. Constitution both stand as great documents and great moments in the history of American law. The Magna Carta grants basic liberties for all British citizens. The U.S. Constitution, adopted in 1787, established certain individual rights, defined the powers of the federal government, and limited punishment for violation of laws.

Constitutional law is another form of American criminal law. It does not define crimes but rather sets limits on laws as it applies to individuals (Wallace & Roberson, 2010). Similarly, the Constitution Act, part of the Canada Act of 1982, declared the Constitution of Canada to be the supreme law of Canada. The Canadian Constitution sets out the basic principles of democratic government and defines the three branches of government: (1) the executive, which includes the prime minister and other ministers, which is responsible for administering and enforcing laws and which answers to the legislature; (2) the legislature, which has the power to make, alter, and appeal laws; and (3) the judiciary, which interprets and applies the law (Regehr & Kanani, 2010).

■ Concepts Related to Justice and Alternative Forms of Justice

The concept of justice is one of the key features of a society. Justice, according to Rawls (1971), is the concept of moral rightness based on ethics, rationality, law, natural law, fairness, and equity. Theories of justice vary greatly, but Rawls argues there is evidence that everyday views of justice can be reconciled with patterned moral preferences (Rawls, 1971). Justice concerns the proper ordering of things and persons within a society. As a concept it has been subject to philosophical, legal, and religious reflection and debate throughout history. According to most theories of justice, it is overwhelmingly important. Rawls, for instance, claims that "[j]ustice is the first virtue of social institutions, as truth is of systems of thought" (Rawls, 1971, p. 3).

There are several types of justice. However, those that concern the issue of crime victims and the offenders are retributive justice, utilitarian justice, distributive justice, and restorative justice, as shown in **Table 5-1**.

Retributive Justice

Retributive justice is based on the principles that guilt of an accused must be proven, and once established, punishments of the offender must be proportional to the crime committed. As is noted in ancient codes of law, such as the Code of Hammurabi, law has a role in maintaining social order, and retributive justice models work to restore equilibrium by enforcing action against the offender. The theory is often associated with harsh punishment and societal vengeance. One example of the enactment of such a legal theory is the practice of imposing differential prison sentences on first-time offenders and repeated offenders. For example, in the 19th century, New York State introduced the act *Persistent Felony Offender* that established longer sentences for repeat offenders. Despite the legislation, however, judges had considerable discretion regarding the term of

TABLE 5-1 **Types of Justice**

Type	Definition
Retributive justice	A theory of justice that dictates a proportionate response to crime proven by lawful evidence so that punishment is justly imposed and considered as morally correct and fully deserved. For retributionists, punishment is backward looking and strictly for punishing crimes according to their severity.
Utilitarian justice	For utilitarians, punishment is forward looking, justified by a purported ability to achieve future social benefits, such as crime reduction.
Distributive justice	This concept of justice is directed at the proper allocation of things—wealth, power, reward, respect—between different people. A number of important questions surrounding justice have been fiercely debated over the course of Western history. What is justice? What does it demand of individuals and societies? What is the proper distribution of wealth and resources in society: equal, meritocratic, according to status or some other arrangement?
Restorative justice	The focus is on the needs of victims and offenders in contrast to a focus on punishing the offender. Victims are active participants in the process, whereas offenders are encouraged to take responsibility for their actions.

incarceration imposed, allowing them to take into consideration other factors in addition to number of previous offenses (Zimring, Hawkins, & Kamin, 2001). Several states enacted habitual offender laws in the 1990s that impose mandatory prison sentences for criminals convicted on three or more occasions (known as "three strikes" laws).

Utilitarian Justice

Utilitarianism, a term proposed by John Stewart Mill in 1863, is a principle of justice based on the greatest good for the greatest number. Moral worth of an action is judged by its overall utility. Thus, punishment for crime is not retribution against the offender but rather an attempt to prevent future harms. Future harm may be prevented by keeping a dangerous person safely incarcerated; however, punishment of offenders can also serve as a deterrent to others. This concept is differentiated from deontology, which is based on a form of absolutism or irrefutable moral laws. Certain acts are wrong and others are right, independent of the goodness or badness of their outcomes (Craig, 1998).

Distributive Justice

Distributive justice is concerned with the fair allocation of resources among diverse members of a community. Different distributions advance various social goals. For example, John Rawls (1971) writes that one's place of birth, social status, and family influences are matters of luck and that a goal of distributive justice is to limit the influence of luck so that goods might be distributed more fairly and to everyone's advantage. Robert Nozick (1977), on the other hand, believes that a goal of distributive justice is setting down rules that individuals should follow in acquiring and transferring resources and benefits to ensure a fair process of exchange. Others believe distributive justice must be a matter of both process and outcome (Maiese, 2003).

Restorative Justice

The term "restorative justice" refers to informal and nonadjudicative forms of dispute resolution, such as losses suffered by a victim (Cheon & Regehr, 2006). This concept also includes offender mediation, family conferences, neighborhood accountability boards, and peacemaking circles that promote joint decision-making power (Bazemore & Schiff, 2001; Roach, 2000). A central concept of restorative justice is that it can repair the harms of crime and restore what has been lost (Zehr, 1995). In this model it is believed that victims and offenders when put together in the right circumstances can negotiate a mutually agreeable plan for easing the burden on the victim both psychologically and materially (Umbreit, 1995). Restorative justice is not about determining guilt or innocence; it is rather a means for negotiating ways to mediate the effects of crime. This model attempts to move from punishment to repairing the harms caused by the crime by balancing the needs of the victims, citizens, and offenders (Cheon & Regehr, 2006).

Restorative justice models have a number of elements. First, restorative justice generally involves not only the victim and the offender but also the members of the community, because the community is viewed to have a stake in the outcome. Community members are expected to have an ongoing role in supporting victims in the healing process, enforcing agreements, and influencing the offender's behavior to prevent further offending (Dodd, 2002; Presser & Gaarder, 2000). The involvement of community members has another purpose, however: to bring the crime out of the closet and into the open light. This exposure has been described as shaming by people important to the offender, including family and community members (Braithwaite, 2000). This shaming is then followed by gestures of reintegration and support, which are seen to deter antisocial behavior and enable more prosocial behavior in the future.

A second key element is the role of the victim. The model generally involves a meeting or series of meetings that community members, the offender, and the victim attend. The victim describes the impact of the offense and what might be needed to assist him or her in healing.

During the process of restoration, victims of crime are provided with opportunities to discuss how the crime affected them, get information about the offender's motivation, and have input into sanctions and restitution (Bazemore, 2001). This is a significant departure from the retributive model, in which the needs of the victim are considered secondary to the needs of police, judges, and prosecutors and in which resources to assist victims are scarce. In the end, victims are expected to benefit from reparative words such as an apology by the offender or statements of support by others and actions offered by the offender and/or community. This can be augmented by the provision of financial compensation by the offender or material assistance by the community.

Finally, the role of the offender is key to the success of the model. The offender is expected to accept responsibility for his or her harmful actions and to make amends (Dodd, 2002). As stated above, an important part of this process often includes apologies to the victim and some type of restoration. For instance, if the offender is a juvenile that has committed a property crime against a member of the community, the juvenile might be expected to pay for the repair of the damage or offer his or her physical labor to restore the damage. The goal is to return offenders to a law-abiding life and reintegrate them into the community (Presser & Van Voorhis, 2002).

■ Criminal Law

Criminal law is concerned with actions that are dangerous or harmful to society as a whole, in which prosecution is pursued not by an individual but rather by the state. The purpose of criminal law is to define what constitutes a crime and to prescribe punishments for committing such a crime. Criminal law must include both factors. Criminal justice is concerned with the enforcement of criminal law.

The U.S. and Canadian court systems are based on the principles of federalism. Federalism is a system of government in which a constitution separates out the power and authority between a central governing authority and units called states or provinces. Federalism is a system in which sovereignty is shared between the national and state governments. Proponents of this federation system are often called federalists.

The U.S. Constitution established the rules under which the federal government could operate. The Federalist Papers, one of the most important documents in American political history, is a compilation of 85 essays. They were written for the people of the State of New York to support and vote for ratification of the new constitution. These articles, written by Alexander Hamilton, James Madison, and John Jay, analyzed the deficiencies of the Articles of Confederation and the benefits of the new, proposed Constitution and argued the political theory and function behind the various articles of the Constitution.

In Canada, a common federal Criminal Code applies in all jurisdictions. The Canadian Constitution defines the powers of government; the Canadian Charter of Rights and Freedoms protects the fundamental rights of Canadians; the legislatures make, alter, and repeal laws; and the judiciary and administrative bodies interpret and apply the law.

Wallace and Roberson (2010) describe the main characteristics of the court system. The first congress established a federal court system and permitted individual states to continue their own judicial structure, thus maintaining a dual system of state and federal courts. Thus, a victim may be a witness in a state or federal (or both) court. The 1991 Rodney King case, where an African American taxi driver was stopped, beaten, and arrested by four Los Angeles policemen, is one example. The four officers were tried in a state court for using excessive force but were acquitted. The news of acquittal triggered the Los Angeles riots of 1992. By the time the police, the U.S. Army, the Marines, and the National Guard restored order, the casualties included 55 deaths, 2,383 injuries, more than 7,000 fires, damages to 3,100 businesses, and nearly $1 billion in financial losses. On May 1, 1992, the third day of the L.A. riots, King appeared in public before television news cameras to appeal for calm. After the riots the Department of Justice reinstated investigation and obtained an indictment of violations of federal civil rights against the four officers. The federal trial focused more on the evidence as to the training of officers instead of just relying on the videotape of the incident. The jury found two officers guilty, who were subsequently sentenced to 30 months of prison, and two officers were acquitted of all charges.

A second characteristic of the American court system is the lack of oversight or supervision it has as it carries out its duties. However, the U.S. Supreme Court and the various state supreme courts do review appellate cases from lower courts; in that sense there is supervision of the district or first level of the court system. A third feature of the U.S. court system is one of specialization that occurs primarily at the state and local levels. For example, special courts are designated to hear juvenile cases or family law cases. At the federal level, there are courts that hear specific cases such as for bankruptcy (Wallace & Roberson, 2010).

Levels of the U.S. Court System

In the early days of the federation, each of the 13 original states had their own court system. However, over time, several reform movements have assisted in streamlining and modernizing this system. The reforms have resulted in many states adopting a three-tier judicial system of trial courts, appellate courts, and state supreme courts. Victims of violence appear at the trial court level because this level is where criminal cases start and finish.

The flowchart in **Figure 5-2** shows the steps in the criminal justice system; this chart updates the original chart prepared by the President's Commission on Law Enforcement and the Administration of Justice in 1967 (President's Commission on Law Enforcement and Administration of Justice, 1967). The chart summarizes the most common events in the criminal and juvenile justice systems, including entry into the criminal justice system, prosecution and pretrial services, adjudication, sentencing and sanctions, and corrections. A discussion of the events in the criminal justice system follows.

DISTRICT COURT LEVEL Courts of general jurisdiction are granted the authority to hear and decide issues brought before them. These courts generally hear all major civil or criminal cases. They may be known by various names, including superior courts, circuit courts, or district courts. A case may have its verdict appealed by either the prosecution or the defense. The intermediate level is called the courts of appeals. These courts hear and decide issues of law. There is no jury to decide factual disputes. The appellate level has the authority to uphold the decision or to reverse the decision of the lower courts and to send the case back with instructions. Again, in either situation the party who loses the appeal at this level may file an appeal to the next higher appellate court (Wallace & Roberson, 2010).

The final appellate courts are the highest level of appeal in a state and are known as the supreme courts or courts of last resort. There may be a number of justices sitting on this court depending on the state. This court rules on state constitutional or statutory issues. Once this court has decided an issue, the only appeal left is to file in the federal court system.

FEDERAL COURT SYSTEM In contrast to state courts, whose origins are traced to historical accident and custom, federal courts were created by the U.S. Constitution. From this point Congress enacted various legislation that resulted in the contemporary federal court system. The Judiciary Act of 1789 created the U.S. Supreme Court and established district courts and the circuit of appeals. There are three levels to this system: federal district courts, federal circuit courts, and the U.S. Supreme Court (Wallace & Roberson, 2010). The federal district courts are the first level of the federal court system. These courts have jurisdiction over all cases having a violation of federal statutes. Examples of cases heard in federal district court

What is the sequence of events in the criminal justice system?

FIGURE 5-2 Steps in the Criminal Justice System

Data from Bureau of Justice Statistics. http://bjs.ojp.usdoj.gov/content/justsys.cfm.

are infant and child abductions, domestic violence or rape cases where the victim has been taken across state lines, certain homicide cases, and child pornography cases. The federal circuit courts are the intermediate level of appeal within the federal system. The federal system is divided into 11 circuits. An appeal is heard by three appellate court judges.

The U.S. Supreme Court is the highest court in the United States. It can provide judicial review for all lower state and federal court decisions. The court meets on the first Monday in October and usually remains in session until June. It hears very few cases. The justices' caseload has increased steadily to a current total of over 10,000 per term. Plenary review, with oral arguments by attorneys, is granted in about 100 cases per term. Formal written opinions are given in 80 to 90 cases. About 50 to 60 additional cases are disposed of without granting plenary review.

Canadian Court System

In Canada there are four levels of court (Department of Justice, 2003; Regehr & Kanani, 2010):

1. *Provincial courts:* These courts handle criminal offenses, family law matters (except divorce), and young offender cases. In addition, some provinces and territories have established provincial courts dedicated to particular offences or offenders, such as small claims courts, drug treatment courts, youth courts, and domestic violence courts.

2. *Provincial/territorial superior courts:* These courts deal with the most serious criminal and civil cases. In addition, most superior courts have family law divisions to deal with particularly difficult divorce and property claims.

3. *Provincial and federal courts of appeal:* These courts deal with appeals from the lower courts and with constitutional questions.

4. *Supreme Court of Canada:* This is the highest court of appeal. This court also decides questions on the Constitution and other controversial questions.

Generally, a decision made in a lower court can be appealed to the next level of court until the case reaches the Supreme Court of Canada. Lower courts must follow precedents set by higher courts, and thus decisions made by the Supreme Court of Canada direct decisions at all other levels. When new legislation is passed, however, the courts must include these directives in the decision-making process. Furthermore, as stated earlier, the Canadian Charter of Rights and Freedoms must ultimately govern judiciary decisions in that the courts must ensure legislation does not violate individual rights and freedoms (Regehr & Kanani, 2010).

■ Entering the Criminal Justice System

The act of reporting a crime starts a complicated process. A number of institutions immediately swing into motion. Victims find themselves caught up in protocols that are routine to authorities but new and not completely understood by them. At the very least, victims will be questioned by authorities and their statements recorded in official files. These things may not be done against a victim's will, but more may be done than he or she bargained for. It thus becomes especially important that victims understand the process, which is one reason that victim services have been established.

Reporting the Crime: Interactions with the Police

The police are generally the first official a victim encounters. The questions police ask tend to focus on what happened, who is involved, where it happened, and why it happened. The style of questioning used in the interview of a victim by law enforcement depends on the officers, their training, and the nature of the crime. The opening statement made by an officer is crucial in setting the tone of the interview. Officers who want to put a victim at ease will give a brief explanation by saying, "I will need some information about what happened. And I have to ask some questions." Other officers are blunt and simply begin by asking questions without any introductory comments, such as "Tell me what happened."

In most interviews the officers will ask about the incident, the relationship (if any) of the victim to the assailant, and the victim's background. The tone and demeanor of the officers make a difference in the reaction of the victim to the interview. Officers who are empathetic will end an interview with a supportive question, such as "Is there anything else you can tell me that would help me?" Officers who are less sympathetic may ask more confrontational questions, perhaps about a victim's past behavior that sounds abrasive. This style of officer may also end the interview with a statement about the consequences possible for the assailant, such as "It can be a life sentence for this." This officer may seem intent to test the strength of a victim's motivation to follow through in the court process.

Once the crime is reported, the next step is making a decision about pressing charges. Victims quickly learn that the state has an interest in what happens in a case. Legally, the crime is committed against the state and the victim is a witness. One rape victim, laughing at the irony, said, "What kills me is that the Commonwealth got raped and I'm only a witness" (Holmstrom & Burgess, 1983, p. 55).

Police officers differ in the degree of enthusiasm they express for pursuing some cases legally. Crimes committed by strangers are responded to more enthusiastically than are interpersonal violence cases. For example, police officers do not see all claims of rape as being equal. Instead, they have in their minds an image of what constitutes an ideal victim case. Such cases are often described as being "strong" or "weak." Holmstrom and Burgess (1983) identified four types of criteria police officers use in making this distinction in rape cases. First, police looked at the quality and consistency of the information they received. To be strong, the case cannot rest on the victim's statement alone but must have corroborating evidence. Police like to have forensic findings, injuries, and/or a witness. Conversely, in describing a weak case, officers are skeptical of a victim who changes his or her story. Police prefer a consistent and unchanging statement. Second, police officers look to characteristics of the victim, especially his or her behavior and moral character. A case is strong if the victim was forced to accompany the offender and weak if he or she accompanied the offender willingly. Characteristics of a strong case include the victim not exposing him- or herself to risk, being sober, being upset, and being emotionally stable. Characteristics of weak cases include being drunk or on drugs, having a psychiatric history, having a history of attempted suicide, taking chances, or being unconcerned (in demeanor) about the incident.

Third, police look at the relationship between victim and offender. It is a strong case if the offender is a stranger, if the victim is a teenager, or if the offender in his or her twenties or thirties. Police are less enthusiastic about cases where both parties are teenagers with only a year or so difference in ages or are known to each other. Fourth, police look at the characteristics of the offender. They are very enthusiastic if they find the offender has other charges against him or her or a prison record. In one case the offender had both a prior rape charge and a charge of armed robbery on a male victim who was severely injured during the crime. In the burglary incident, a knife penetrated the victim's back, breaking two ribs and puncturing a lung. The victim was taken to the hospital where a team of surgeons worked on him. Complications occurred, and he was a month in the hospital. The robbery victim and the rape victim both made a positive identification of the assailant. The police were anxious to see the assailant "off the streets" and kept saying, "He's a goner" (Holmstrom & Burgess, 1983, p. 43).

Fifth, the police officer has the serious task of writing the police report. Although there are various training methods for report writing, the first rule of thumb in police report writing is to describe what happened in chronological order. The first line is almost always the same.

On [date] while working with [name of officer] we received a call from 911 dispatcher [name] to 123 Anywhere St. for a Man with a Gun. Police officers are questioned in court as to whom they were working with, who gave them the call, the time of the call, and/or what the call was about. The remaining report describes the action taken by the officer. The report is viewed as highly credible, and thus accuracy is essential and the report is necessary for the prosecution of a case.

POLICE AND THE VICTIM   Considerable publicity is given to the emotional difficulties victims face in dealing with police. But the difficulties police face in dealing with crime victims has received less attention. Holmstrom and Burgess (1983) identified several reasons police take crime victims seriously. They are often the first professional group to arrive on the scene, occasionally even arriving while the crime is in progress. They observe victims who are distraught, screaming, bleeding, injured, and crying. Furthermore, police stay with the victims as they go through the criminal justice system. Other professionals such as physicians, nurses, forensic examiners, and prosecutors are with the victims for a relatively short time period. However, the same teams of police officers usually follow victims through the system. They take victims to the hospital, talk to them during the investigation, sit with them during waiting time at the hospital or courthouse, and attend court sessions. Thus, they come to know certain individual victims better than other groups do and also observe firsthand much of the aftermath of the crime (Holmstrom & Burgess, 1983).

Police officers, like health professionals and court officials, are asked to engage in work that can be emotionally disturbing. They see victims who have been robbed, injured, beaten, raped, and murdered. They must deal with violence of rape, arson, and death. They see the suffering of victims. They need access to information about injury to bodies. They must ask for information about the private lives of victims. They need this information for investigative purposes and also to prepare for court. Their work is in the realm of uncertainty: What really happened and who is telling the truth?

Thus, one would expect to find institutionalized roles and social control mechanisms in place for police to carry out their work. Professional protocol is one example of this control mechanism. For example, police are never present during the physical examination of a victim. They wait in a designated area for a staff member to provide information. It is appropriate for police officers to develop what might be called "professional armor" to protect themselves against the emotional aspects of their work to remain "affectively neutral" (Parsons, 1951).

Media reports have portrayed both positive and negative police treatment of crime victims. Positive reactions focus on victims feeling they were treated well and that the police officer made them feel better. Negative reactions include victims feeling as though people stared at them, that they had no privacy when talking, or that they felt pressured into pressing charges.

Pressing Charges

The criminal justice system does put pressure on victims to participate in the court process. Once victims talk with police, the police must decide whether or not to press charges. In large part this depends on whether the victim is willing to participate in the justice system. Victims may get entangled in the legal process before they can get their own thoughts straight. Victims may be ambivalent about involving the full weight of the justice system, especially in cases where they know the perpetrator or the perpetrator is a family member, as in domestic violence. Victims may not want to participate in the judicial system to avoid the ordeal of court, because they are afraid of the perpetrator taking revenge, to avoid sending a person to jail, because they feel sorry for the perpetrator, because they just want to forget the whole thing, and because they are afraid of identifying the wrong person (Holmstrom & Burgess, 1983).

The government through the criminal justice system brings criminal cases to court. The American and Canadian systems of justice have evolved from English common law into a complex series of procedures and decisions. Founded on the concept that crimes against an individual are crimes against the State, the justice system prosecutes individuals as though they victimized all of society. However, crime victims are involved throughout the process, and many justice agencies have programs that focus on helping victims.

Once a law enforcement agency has established that a crime has been committed, a suspect must be identified and apprehended for the case to proceed through the system. Sometimes, a suspect is apprehended at the scene; however, identification of a suspect sometimes requires an extensive investigation. Often, no one is identified or apprehended. In such situations the case remains open. Statutes exist in every jurisdiction for how long a case may remain open. Currently, there is no statutory time period for a murder case. In such cases the file is classified in the cold case division of a police department.

In some instances a suspect is arrested and later the police determine that no crime was committed, charges are dropped, and the suspect is released. In other instances the assailant, his or her social network, and the defense counsel may pressure the victim to drop charges. Holmstrom and Burgess (1983) found 24 of the 115 rape victims were so pressured. In addition, seven victims reported "mysterious happenings," such as unexplained phone calls, they interpreted as efforts at intimidation. Assailants and their networks used three main approaches: threats (14 cases), sympathy appeals (5 cases), and bribes (2 cases). In addition, there was harassment from the defense counsel before court in 11 cases.

Pretrial

After an arrest, law enforcement agencies present information about the case and about the accused to the prosecutor, who will decide if formal charges will be filed with the court. Victims usually have knowledge of the police officer's role but are less certain of the role of the prosecutor or district attorney. Victims need to understand that the prosecutor represents the state's interests, is supposed to be on their side, and that they do not need their own lawyer. As in the police interview, the prosecutor will interview the victim and style will matter. Some prosecutors try to put the victim at ease with introductory phrases and explain why they need to know the answers to certain questions.

Prosecutors, like police and hospital staff, have their image of what constitutes an ideal case. Police talk of strong and weak cases. Hospital staff talk of whether a rape case is "legitimate," and prosecutors talk about whether or not the victim will make a "good witness." Prosecutors want witnesses to be explicit and consistent in their testimony. It is important that victims work with the prosecutor and his or her team on the preparation of the case. The victim's appearance and demeanor are important also. Court is a stressful and controlling environment. Victims need to be able to hold up under the pressure of cross-examination. In one case a victim became so upset she walked out in the middle of her testimony. Most prosecutors' offices have victim witness staff that assist in working with witnesses to prepare them for their testimony.

If no charges are filed, the accused must be released. The prosecutor can also drop charges after making efforts to prosecute (nolle prosequi). A suspect charged with a crime must be taken before a judge or magistrate without unnecessary delay. At the initial appearance the judge or magistrate informs the accused of the charges and decides whether there is probable cause to detain the accused person. If the offense is not very serious, the determination of guilt and assessment of a penalty may also occur at this stage.

The defense attorney represents the rights and interests of the suspect. Often, the defense counsel is assigned at the initial appearance. All suspects prosecuted for serious crimes have a right to be represented by an attorney. If the court determines the suspect is indigent and cannot afford such representation, the court will assign counsel at the public's expense. Four types of defense attorneys are public defenders, contract defense services, assigned defense counsel, and private defense counsel.

PRETRIAL RELEASE A pretrial-release decision may be made at the initial appearance but may occur at other hearings or may be changed at another time during the process. Pretrial release and bail were traditionally intended to ensure appearance at trial. However, many jurisdictions permit pretrial detention of **defendants** accused of serious offenses and deemed to be dangerous to prevent them from committing crimes before trial. The court often bases its **pretrial** decision on information about the defendant's drug use, as well as residence, employment, and family ties. The court may decide to release the accused on his or her own recognizance or into the custody of a third party after the posting of a financial bond or on the promise of satisfying certain conditions such as taking periodic drug tests to ensure drug abstinence.

Preliminary Hearing

In many jurisdictions a preliminary hearing may follow the initial appearance. The main function of this hearing is to discover if there is probable cause to believe the accused committed a known crime within the jurisdiction of the court. If the judge does not find probable cause, the case is dismissed; however, if the judge or magistrate finds probable cause for such a belief or the accused waives his or her right to a preliminary hearing, the case may be bound over to a grand jury.

Grand Jury

A **grand jury** hears evidence against the accused presented by the prosecutor and decides if there is sufficient evidence to cause the accused to be brought to trial. If the grand jury finds sufficient evidence, it submits to the court an indictment, which is a written statement of the essential facts of the offense charged against the accused. In some jurisdictions defendants, often those without prior criminal records, may be eligible for diversion from prosecution subject to the completion of specific conditions such as drug treatment. Successful completion of the conditions may result in the dropping of charges or the expunging of the criminal record where the defendant is required to plead guilty before the diversion.

Given the time and effort put into an investigation and arrest of a suspect, police and prosecutor sometimes pressure the victim to persevere in the court process. They may be firm ("Be at court") or try to appeal to the victim's sympathies ("You can't back out on me after all the work I did to arrest him"), or they may appeal to the victim's sense of civic duty or a duty to protect other potential victims. The pressure to testify may also be placed on other witnesses that know of the crime or the victim or the defendant.

Plea Bargain

A plea bargain is an agreement in which a defendant pleads guilty to a lesser charge and the prosecutor in return drops more serious charges. The plea bargain is then presented to the judge who may or may not accept it. For example, Joanne Thompson faced five counts of felony embezzlement after she and another employee, Mike Nemeyer, were arrested in separate cases in June 2010. Both were accused of stealing money from her former employer, New York City–based billionaire Edgar Bronfman, and his property, Georgetown Farms. Bronfman's family once owned the Seagram's liquor empire, and Bronfman has an estimated net worth of $2.6 billion. Nemeyer was found not guilty on all counts after a 3-day jury trial in October. Thompson testified against Nemeyer in his trial in hopes of lightening her own sentence. Defense attorney Scott Goodman and Commonwealth's Attorney Elliott J. Casey reached an agreement that would have spared Thompson any jail time. The prosecutor argued that it would be unfair for Thompson to endure any incarceration whatsoever while the other walks free. His conclusion was based on Thompson's willingness to cooperate during the Nemeyer trial. However, Judge Cheryl Higgins did not accept the agreement, stating she was uncomfortable agreeing to this particular sentence, adding that the proposed punishment was a deviation from guidelines (Koon, 2011).

Suppression Hearings and Change of Plea Hearings

A victim is generally entitled to be present at a suppression hearing or a change of plea hearing, which both occur in open court. At a suppression hearing the defense challenges the prosecution's evidence and whether or not law enforcement complied with legal rules in collecting evidence. A victim, along with a victim advocate, may be present in court during the hearing, which ordinarily involves testimony of witnesses, including police officers. If the motion to suppress is granted, evidence may be excluded from the county prosecutor's case, which may impact whether the case can be proven at trial. If the motion is overruled, the evidence may be presented at trial to assist in proving the case. In the Anthony case in March 2011, there were several days of testimony in a suppression hearing to determine if statements made by Casey Anthony to detectives after being placed in custody, in jail, through video visitations with family, and letters to another inmate should be suppressed.

A change of plea hearing is when the accused, upon consulting with his or her criminal defense attorney, decides to change the plea from not guilty ordinarily to a plea of guilty as part of an agreed sentence recommendation to resolve the case short of trial. The accused agrees to waive his or her constitutional rights, including the right to a jury trial in adult cases, which result in a criminal conviction. The court is required to inform the accused of the rights being waived and ensure that the change of plea is voluntary. In the Garrido case, at the last minute Phillip Garrido decided against pleading guilty—as expected—to Jaycee Dugard's kidnapping, with his lawyer citing problems with the grand jury. However, they subsequently made a surprise change of plea after prosecutors agreed to drop some charges against Nancy Garrido if Phillip pleaded guilty to almost the full indictment. Their change in pleas meant Jaycee Dugard and her children would not have to testify at a trial.

Many cases of conviction result from guilty pleas rather than guilty verdicts in trials. Victims may believe they have no say in plea bargaining; this can have a negative effect on victims, who may believe the criminal justice system has let them down. To avoid this situation a victim should be present in court for this hearing, along with a victim advocate. The court may ask whether the victim has been consulted about the change of plea and the sentence recommendation agreed upon between the parties to the case. A presentence investigative report may be ordered, which provides the court with background information about the accused and the crime committed for purposes of the court considering the appropriate sentence to be ordered in the case. A sentencing hearing may take place at a change of plea hearing if prison is jointly recommended between the parties in the case. Therefore, it is important that a victim be present to speak to the court if a sentencing takes place immediately after the defendant's change of plea.

Criminal Justice Trials

There are two types of trials in the criminal justice system: a bench trial, which is before a judge, and a jury trial, which is before a group of citizens. It is the jury trial that is written into every document significant to the notion of American independence and justice. It finds voice in the Magna Carta, Declaration of Independence, all the state constitutions enacted between 1776 and 1786, and in the body of the U.S. Constitution and three of the Bill of Rights. Even before the enactment of the Constitution, the jury trial had become an important protection from false accusations of crime for colonial Americans (Antkowiak, 2006).

Consistent with the overall philosophy of the criminal justice system, the government faces the hurdle of having to prove the guilt of an accused to a nongovernmental body (a jury) to the highest standard known to the law: proof beyond a reasonable doubt. That is, the government must prove each element of the offense to convince a jury of the guilt of a defendant. To prove its case, the government needs evidence. Besides the testimony of witnesses, the government seeks to offer a wide variety of physical evidence it has obtained during its investigation. Evidence includes the collection of such items as body fluids, fingerprints, and fibers that then can be subjected for forensic testing for a match to the crime scene, to the defendant, and to the victim.

Victims are often confronted with repeated postponements or continuances in court proceedings. Postponements may be due to the request of the defense because the defendant has defaulted or changed lawyers or the lawyer has not had time to prepare the case. Sometimes a trial is postponed due to the prosecution because a witness is not available or the victim does not appear. The data between the date of the crime and the final verdict may easily be over a year.

Each time the case is scheduled at the district court level or the superior court level, witnesses, including the victim, are to appear. For victims, witnesses, and the defendant there is a lot of waiting. Victim services were implemented in prosecutor offices because of delays in the system as a way to ease the waiting and to reduce the cost, both financial and emotional, on victims and their families.

IN THE COURTROOM   The victim enters the courtroom to a formal, authoritative, solemn atmosphere. The placement of furniture indicates who has the authority. The judge's bench is on a raised platform, and behind the judge's chair are the seal of the jurisdiction and the flags of the appropriate federal and state governments symbolizing the power and authority of the state. Court personnel wear special uniforms. The judge usually wears a black robe and enters the courtroom through a special door.

Adjacent to the judge's bench are the witness stand and the desks where the court clerk and the court reporter sit. The courtroom is divided into two parts by a barrier known as the bar. On one side is the judge's bench, the tables for the plaintiff, the defendant and his or her respective counsel, and a separate group of seats known as the jury box where the jury sits. Apart from the parties to the case and any witnesses, only the lawyers can literally pass the bar (court personnel and jury members usually enter through separate doors), which is how the term "the bar" has come to refer to the legal profession as a whole. The bailiff stands against one wall and keeps order in the courtroom.

The ideology of both the American and Canadian legal systems is the adversarial system of law. There are many rules to the system, including the presumption of innocence of the defendant, the defendant's right to counsel, the right of the defendant not to testify, placing the burden of proof on the state, and the standard of proof beyond a reasonable doubt. Three rules that can create difficulties for victims include the defendant's right to a public trial, to see his or her accuser, and to cross-examine the state's witnesses.

Although many people in a courtroom have specific reasons for being present, there are also spectators who sit in the courtroom during a trial. These spectators may be family and friends of either the prosecution side or the defense side. There may be lawyers waiting for their turn in court, members of the general public, and court watchers who regularly pass the time of day watching cases. Victims are questioned in front of these strangers. They may be asked identifying information, such as where they live and work as well as minute details on the crime itself. In rape cases, detailing the sexual aspects of the incident can be embarrassing and difficult.

The right of the defendant to see his or her accuser means that both victim and defendant are present in the courtroom. Thus, victims come face to face again with the person who has injured them and must testify in his or her presence. Prosecution and defense have the right to question each other's witnesses. The cross-examination recapitulates, on a psychological and verbal level, the original crime.

JURY TRIAL   Once the legislative body has defined the crime, the final determination of whether the crime was committed is turned over not to a body of governmental officials but to a committee of the governed: the jury. The jury trial became an important protection from false accusations of crime for colonial Americans. A great deal of faith was placed in the common law jury as providing this important protection of liberty (Antkowiak, 2006). The right to trial by jury can be found in every document relevant to the notion of American independence and justice. As stated above, writings can be found in the Magna Carta, Declaration of Independence, all state constitutions enacted between 1776 and 1786, the body of the Constitution of the United States, where it is found in Article III, and three of the Bill of Rights (Antkowiak, 2006).

Members of a jury are drawn from a group of citizens who sit in judgment of the defendant. The number of jury members varies by jurisdiction and depends on the state constitution. The jury listens to the evidence and testimony presented. Both prosecution and defense give opening and closing statements. After closing arguments the judge provides instructions to the jury as to the meaning of the law. The jury deliberates and tells the bailiff when they have reached a verdict. The verdict is then taken into court and presented to the judge. The judge then asks the foreperson of the jury to read the verdict.

VICTIM'S RIGHT TO HEAR TESTIMONY Victims have the right to be present at a trial and likely will be called as a witness in the state's presentation of evidence. A separation of witnesses order, however, may prevent a victim from being in the courtroom during testimony heard before the victim testifies. This separation order prevents a possible claim that the victim tailored his or her testimony by hearing the testimony of other witnesses first. Once a victim has testified, a victim ordinarily can be present in court to hear the testimony of other witnesses and closing arguments, as long as the victim does not disrupt the proceedings in some way.

A judicial release hearing is when a defendant who has been convicted of a felony and sentenced to prison requests that the court release him or her from prison on a term of community control. If the court is considering granting early release, a hearing in open court must be held and the victim is entitled to be present and provide input to the court on whether or not the court should grant early release from prison on community control. The decision to grant or deny judicial release is made by the court, upon reviewing legal guidelines and evaluating factors present in a specific case, including any agreed upon sentence recommendation (Seneca County Prosecutor's Office, 2009).

Civil Commitments for Sex Offenders

Some states have used civil commitment proceedings to remove habitual sex offenders from society for extended periods of time. The U.S. Supreme Court ruled in *Kansas v. Hendricks* (1997) that such laws do not violate the Constitution's double jeopardy or ex post facto clauses. The commitment is intended to reduce the risk of future dangerous sexual behavior. It is not meant to serve as punishment for past crimes. Civilly committed sex offenders may be held for an indeterminate amount of time. In other words, they may be held as long as warranted to successfully treat them and to satisfy public safety concerns (Denner & Pellegrino, 2011).

Other Postconviction Hearings

Postconviction hearings include a direct appeal of a conviction, a judicial release hearing, and other possible hearings, including community control violation hearings. If a convicted criminal files a direct appeal upon being found guilty at trial, a victim has a right to be notified and present at the oral arguments on the appeal and to be informed of the outcome of the appeal. An appeal that results in a judgment of conviction being affirmed upholds the trial court's proceedings and its sentencing order. An appeal that results in a reversal of the conviction means there was a significant error in the lower court proceedings, which may allow for a retrial.

There are cases in which the victim should have been told of a postconviction hearing or of a parole hearing and is not aware that an offender has been released. Even with the Victims' Bill of Rights, there is not always accountability on the part of the correctional system that the victim is notified when the offender is released. In such cases, the Victim Advocacy office or Attorney General's office should be notified for correction.

Other postconviction hearings may involve notice to a victim of an upcoming parole hearing. Communication to the parole board is given through the county prosecutor's office or victim assistance program for serious felony offenses. A community control violation may involve victim notification, particularly if the nature of the alleged violation relates to the victim. A victim may receive a subpoena to testify at a revocation hearing.

Casey Anthony's Trial and Acquittal

Both the prosecutor and defense attorney make opening and closing statements about the evidence in the case. In the opening statements the attorneys state what they plan to present, such as "you will hear 'X' and 'Y'," contrasted with the closing argument when the prosecutor can state that "X and Y" together prove guilt because of their conclusion. The defense attorney, in contrast, usually argues that the case has ample reasonable doubt.

The Casey Anthony case was an example of "reasonable doubt" and citizen reaction to the justice system. On July 5, 2011, people outside the courthouse in Orange County Florida and across the country were outraged by the acquittal verdict in the trial for the murder of her toddler daughter, Caylee. The verdict surprised many legal analysts and commentators and spared the 25-year-old from a possible death penalty, which prosecutors planned to seek if Anthony had been found guilty as charged of first-degree murder. The prosecution's case argued that Casey Anthony used chloroform on her daughter before leaving her in the trunk of a car and duct taping her mouth and nose. The prosecutor's rationale was that Casey Anthony was a party girl who wanted to enjoy her personal life and free herself from parental responsibility. The defense's theory was that the death was accidental, and attorney Baez contended that there were holes in the prosecution's forensic evidence, saying it was based on a "fantasy."

A *not guilty verdict* generally implies that a jury did not have adequate evidence and testimony to connect a defendant to the crime. In the Casey Anthony case, the following key points suggest some of the issues with the testimony the jury considered that resulted in the failure of the State of Florida's case:

I. *The car:* Casey Anthony's car became the first piece of evidence. The maternal grandmother, Cindy Anthony, called 911 on July 15, 2008, told the emergency dispatcher she had not seen the child for 31 days, and that Casey's car smelled as though there had been a dead body inside it. Prosecutors immediately took Casey into custody, interrogated her, and began to analyze contents of the car in an attempt to prove that she was responsible for Caylee's body being in the trunk of her car based on the following:

A. Trunk odor. Testimony was given on two odors found in the car trunk: the smell of human decomposition and chloroform. Trunk odor of decomposition (dead body, dead fish, maggots) was discussed by Cindy, George, and Casey Anthony as well as tow yard employees and a dog handler. Testimony was given on unusual levels of chloroform found in the trunk, the chemical believed to be used to kill Caylee. Tests conducted on the air in the trunk by the U.S. Federal Bureau of Investigation laboratory and by Dr. Vass's odor-analysis technique long after Caylee's disappearance indicated high levels of chloroform. At trial, defense argued that chloroform was a volatile liquid that would dissipate quickly into the surrounding air, that Dr. Vass's odor-analysis technique was unreliable and untested for proving decomposition of a body, and blamed the stench on garbage found in the trunk.

B. Hairs. Investigators testified that the hairs found in the trunk contained no roots or tissue and the only test could be for mitochondrial DNA, which is passed down through female ancestors. That meant the hairs could belong to as many as five people: Casey, her mother, grandmother, brother, and Caylee. Two experts examining the same hair could have two opinions: that the darkening was caused by either decomposition or air pockets. Identifying human hairs is not an exact science.

C. Insects. Insects are common in murder cases where a body is found outside, but without a body in the trunk forensic entomologist experts could not prove it was a human body in the trunk.

II. *Caylee Anthony's body:* The child's body was not found until Roy Kronk, a meter reader, again called law enforcement on December 11, 2008. Four months before, in August 2008, Kronk had called law enforcement three times when he saw a partially submerged bag in the same area the remains were found in December 2008. Deputy sheriffs claimed to have searched the area without success. By December 2008, six months after the child was last seen, her body had decomposed in a wooded area 20 feet off the road and less than a mile from her grandparents' home. There were 350 pieces of evidence found at the crime scene, including a handful of bones, a blanket that matched the bedding at her grandparents' home, laundry bags, and a relatively rare brand of duct tape.

A. Plastic bag. Lorie Gottesman, a 20-year forensic specialist at the U.S. Federal Bureau of Investigation, testified that she found no match between black plastic bags containing a portion of Caylee's skeletal remains and similar black plastic bags collected from the Anthony home.

B. Skull. Some crime scene photos showed the skull with a piece of duct tape around the lower facial region. In others it appeared to be lying alongside the skull. Kronk claims in December that he placed a stick in the right eye socket of the skull and "pivoted" it back and forth, thus indicating evidence interference.

C. Duct tape. Prosecutors contended that Anthony placed the duct tape over Caylee's nose and mouth. To support that theory, they used a video demonstration of an image of Caylee's decomposing duct-taped skull superimposed over a photograph of the toddler cheek-to-cheek with her mother as they both smiled.

III. *Cause of death:* Juries usually need to hear how the child died and by what means. Medical examiners were unable to pinpoint the cause of Caylee's death or the manner of death, although a medical examiner, Dr. Jan Garavaglia, testified that she determined Caylee's manner of death to be homicide but listed it as "death by undetermined means." Forensic pathologist Dr. Werner Spitz said he could not determine Caylee Anthony's manner of death but said there was no indication to him that she was murdered. Additionally, Spitz testified that he believed the duct tape found on Caylee's skull was placed there after the body decomposed, opining that if tape was placed on the skin, there should have been DNA left on it, and suggested that someone may have staged some of the crime scene photos.

IV.   *The computer:* Cyber-evidence is believed to be reliable. To try to prove their assertion that Anthony searched the Internet for home-made chloroform recipes, prosecutors called on digital forensics experts who recovered searches from Anthony's laptop, even after they had been erased. However, investigators could not place a person at the computer. Prosecutors emphasized that the Internet searches occurred on Anthony's computer, whereas defense lawyers stressed that many people other than Anthony had access to the computer.

A jury generally needs three issues answered for a guilty verdict: motive, opportunity, and intent. Despite the claim by the state that Casey wanted to live the life of a party girl, there was no evidence Casey wanted Caylee dead for any reason. The fact that Casey had neither car nor child at various times on the 16th and 17th means there is much doubt about whether Casey had the opportunity to kill Caylee. In light of Lee's testimony, the only way Casey could get Caylee back was to stay quiet and *not* talk to the police. There was no evidence of intent to harm Caylee (Murphy, 2011).

Wendy J. Murphy, a former child abuse prosecutor, was not surprised at the verdict and called for full disclosure of the sealed evidence of photographs. It is true, writes Murphy, that Casey Anthony's failure to report Caylee missing for more than a month is powerful evidence of her consciousness of guilt. The question is guilt about what? It's just as possible Casey did not kill her child, that she was afraid to call the police, and that her fear was related to some unknown evidence such as those sealed photographs of Caylee. As Casey's brother Lee testified at trial, Casey was told Caylee was taken from her to "teach her a lesson." If Casey knew the people who had Caylee and stayed quiet in the hope they would give her child back, her failure to report Caylee missing makes sense (Murphy, 2011).

Sentencing

If a defendant is acquitted, the judge thanks the jury for their work and releases the defendant. If the defendant is found guilty, the trial moves into the sentencing phase. The court considers principles of sentencing in its deliberations, including punishment of the offender, denunciation of the crime, general (the public) and specific (the offender) deterrence from committing crimes of this nature, and protection of the public. In arriving at an appropriate sentence, a sentencing hearing may be held at which evidence of aggravating or mitigating circumstances is considered. In assessing the circumstances surrounding a convicted person's criminal behavior, courts often rely on presentence investigations by probation agencies or other designated authorities. Although sentencing is proportional to the crime, not the harms caused by it, courts may also consider victim impact statements.

A restitution order ordinarily is included in the sentencing order. All documented economic loss such as loss of income due to lost time at work because of any injury caused to the victim, and any property loss, medical cost, or funeral expense incurred as a result of the commission of the offense may be submitted to the court to determine restitution.

VICTIM IMPACT STATEMENT   The 1991 case of *Payne v. Tennessee* (501 U.S. 808) was believed to be the first case to recognize the rights of crime victims to make a **victim impact statement** in the sentencing phase of a criminal trial. On June 27, 1987, Pervis Tyrone Payne took cocaine and drank malt liquor and, after viewing pornography, attempted to rape and then murdered an acquaintance of his, Charisse Christopher, and her 2-year-old daughter. Police were called by neighbors who witnessed a bloody Payne exiting the apartment building.

Forensic evidence noted 42 stab wounds to Charisse's body. Payne had also made multiple stab wounds to Charisse's 3-year-old son, who was rushed to the hospital. The evidence of fingerprints, the victim's blood-soaked clothes, and Payne's property left at the scene was sufficient to cause a jury to convict Payne of two counts of first-degree murder, two counts of attempted murder, and a related charge. During sentencing the prosecutor introduced victim impact statements to show the effect of the murders on the friends and family of the neighbor.

Payne appealed the sentence, claiming it was an unconstitutional violation of his Eighth Amendment right against cruel and unusual punishment and argued that the victim impact statements emotionally influenced the jury to recommend the death penalty. Payne pointed to the U.S. Supreme Court decisions that held that victim impact statements were *not* admissible during the sentencing phases of capital murder trials.

The case was appealed, and the Tennessee Supreme Court upheld the sentence. Payne appealed again, and the Tennessee Supreme Court found that the victim impact statements did not create a constitutionally unacceptable risk of an arbitrary imposition of the death penalty. The U.S. Supreme Court upheld the sentence finding that the introduction of victim impact statements was not an unconstitutional violation of the

Eighth Amendment, overruling two prior cases of *Booth v. Maryland* (1987) and *South Carolina v. Gathers* (1989). That ruling left it up to the states to allow or disallow victim impact statements (*Payne v. Tennessee*, (90-5721), 501 U.S. 808 (1991)).

Impact of Trials on Juries

Some cases can have tremendous impact emotionally on a jury. Such was the case in the trial of the two defendants of the Petit family murders (*New York Times*, 2010). To address the secondary trauma of that case, the Connecticut state judicial branch, for the first time in state history, offered posttraumatic stress assistance to jurors who served in the Petit family triple-murder trial. Because the jurors were required to look at disturbing images and hear grisly testimony during the 2-month trial, their service necessitated these actions. A spokesperson confirmed that such posttraumatic assistance has never been done before by the state's judicial branch. The trial of Casey Anthony is another example of a case that took a toll on the jurors. Because of public outrage and death threats, the judge refused initially to release the names of the jurors in the Anthony trial, and most did not respond to any media interviews.

Restitution

Courts in seventeenth century England were believed to be the first courts to develop the concept of restitution as a contractual remedy. This concept of giving back to an injured party migrated to courts in the United States, and has become an integral part of the criminal justice system. The basic principle is to achieve fairness and prevent unjust enrichment of a party.

The criminal is generally perceived as the appropriate source of benefits for the victim of crime. Yet those remedies that involve the criminal—self-help, civil actions, and restitution ordered by a criminal court—are inadequate for most victims of crime because in theory, victims of crimes have, for centuries, had the option of bringing tort (civil) actions against individuals who have wronged them. All too often, however, offenders remain unidentified, rendering it impossible to file any sort of claim. Further, even when the perpetrator is known, victims frequently cannot afford to bring suit, or if a successful suit is accomplished, offenders are often poor, making actual financial compensation highly unlikely. Civil actions are also commonly subject to delays of several months or even years, which can discourage such actions at the outset and certainly diminish a victim's hope for any tangible satisfaction.

Restitution may take the classic form of return or repair of stolen or damaged property. It most often involves monetary payments, either lump sum or periodic, for property loss or damage. It may also involve payments for personal injuries. The increased use of restitution in contemporary times started at the Minnesota Restitution Center in the 1970s. It has since spread throughout the United States, with restitution experiments at various stages in the criminal justice process funded by the Law Enforcement Assistance Administration (LEAA/OJP Retrospective, 1996).

A second, less formal method of achieving restitution in the mid-1970s, the neighborhood justice center, was the forerunner of the current restorative justice concept. Many communities in the United States established programs, with the cooperation of police departments and prosecutors, in which victims of minor crimes were brought together with offenders to resolve original or resulting disputes. The supposed advantage to the victim of mediation or arbitration is restitution rather than merely the satisfaction that the offender has been prosecuted.

■ Capital Punishment and Death Penalty Cases

Early Roots of Capital Punishment

Early laws that encouraged individuals to seek retribution by killing their offenders began the tradition of defining and listing the crimes that would deserve a death penalty and set a precedent for Western legal codes. For example, the Babylonian Code of Hammurabi, written around 1700 BC, arbitrarily made selling beer and revealing the location of sacred burial places crimes punishable by death (Henderson, 2000). Around the seventh century AD government leaders concluded that crimes harmed society's collective interests and so became more involved in controlling and punishing crimes. To protect society, leaders passed laws that devised a list of different punishments specific to the crime. Laws focused more on keeping peace in society than serving justice, with the Justinian Code of AD 529 standing as an example. In the ancient Greco-Roman state the prime reason for execution was to punish those who attacked the state. The use of capital punishment for two specific offenses were Socrates's execution for heresy, circa 399 BC, and the crucifixion of Jesus Christ, circa AD 33, whose formal charge was sedition against the state (Henderson, 2000). Throughout this era punishment was violent and often a means of inflicting torture along with death.

During the Middle Ages the methods of finding criminals guilty included a fight between the offender and the victim (or family member), the torture of the accused to see if he or she would survive, and testimony as to the truthfulness of the accused. This latter method of determining innocence or guilt was reserved for the members of the higher classes of society (Banks, 2005). These three methods slowly lost popularity as the government realized they were ineffective, and trial by jury became the accepted and effective way of establishing guilt and was widely used by the mid-13th century. As civil and criminal law developed, torture was phased out, but very slowly. Some commonly used methods of torture were chopping off the hands and feet, impaling the body on a large stake, stripping off the skin, boiling the body alive in oil, drawing and quartering, burning at the stake, and crucifying. The centuries between 1400 and 1800 were marked by enough executions that the laws on capital punishment were later dubbed the "Bloody Code" (Levinson, 2002). The 18th-century European Enlightenment focused on ideas that emphasized the value of humankind and individual potential. Reformists began thinking about how the government could serve the common good, and the use of incarceration and taking away liberty as punishment grew in favor (Banks, 2005).

Capital Punishment in America

The American system of capital punishment, based on British law, grew out of the Western basis of capital punishment: personal retribution. The colonies began to define American legal codes, and patterns of punishment surfaced. The Bill of Rights, ratified in 1791, controlled the use of capital punishment by prohibiting "cruel and unusual punishment" in the Eighth Amendment. In the first half of the 19th century prisons began to provide tailored punishment to convicts, offering probation and other rehabilitative programs. Hanging was criticized as too brutal, the product of a more barbaric society, and a growing faith in science as the means of ameliorating aspects of the human condition led to the advent of the electric chair. The first chair was built in New York in 1888 and used in 1890 to execute William Kemmler. On the morning of March 29, 1889, William Kemmler, 30, was drinking beer when John Debella, one of his employees, arrived to take him to work. Kemmler became angry when his common-law wife, Tillie Ziegler, talked to Debella. He accused her of deceiving him, stealing money from him, and planning to leave him. Tillie admitted that it was all true. Kemmler became quiet, left the house, returned with a hatchet, and struck Tillie in the head over 20 times. When he was finished he went to a neighbor's house and said "I killed her. I had to do it. I meant to. I'll take the rope for it." Kemmler was tried, convicted, and executed August 6, 1890 (MacLead, 2011).

Capital punishment was on the decline around the turn of the 20th century. Crime continued to be seen as the result of a criminal's environment, and science was suggesting it was also the result of inborn genetic traits. As the criminal was viewed as a victim of outside forces, the death penalty became less and less just. The shift away from capital punishment changed when America entered World War I. Because of the fear generated by the Russian Revolution and class conflicts, many states that had abolished the death penalty reinstated it, and no states abolished capital punishment until the 1950s. In fact, there was significant growth in the support for and use of capital punishment from 1920 to 1935.

In the mid-1950s the death penalty debate resurfaced. Caryl Chessman, 27, convicted of kidnapping, robbery, sexual mistreatment, and attempted rape, was sentenced to death because kidnapping carried a mandatory death sentence in California, based on the passage of the 1933 Lindbergh federal law. Chessman appealed his sentence 42 times and remained on death row for 12 years before being executed in 1960 (*West's Encyclopedia of American Law*, 2011). Chessman wrote several books while in prison, one of which was an autobiography, titled *Cell 2455, Death Row*. Chessman's case brought the death penalty question back to the forefront of issues facing society.

Simultaneously, support for capital punishment was waning as many nations around the world abolished the death penalty (Death Penalty Information Center, 2009). The main points of the worldwide debate currently surrounding the death penalty are not new but seem to accumulate and converge as societies progress. All these questions have been asked throughout history and continue to be weighed as society tries to determine whether capital punishment itself will ultimately live or die.

Death Penalty Case

Legal experts have dubbed the Petit triple family murders in Cheshire, Connecticut, as a "poster child" for the debate on capital punishment (*New York Times*, 2010). Defendant Hayes's own defense attorney alluded to the difficulty of producing a jury who would not be so outraged as to incline toward the death penalty. He acknowledged that even someone opposed to the death penalty in general would have difficulty not recommending it in this case. The notoriety of this crime extends well beyond Cheshire and even the state; indeed, it has national implications and genuine human interest.

To illustrate the influence of this case, in 2009 the Connecticut General Assembly sent legislation to abolish the state's death penalty to Governor Rell ostensibly to be signed into law. However, on June 5, 2009, Rell vetoed the bill instead and cited the Cheshire murders as an exemplary reason for doing so (Governor Rell Vetoes HB 6578, 2009). On November 8, 2010 Governor Rell issued the following statement regarding the jury's recommendation of a sentence of death for Hayes (Governor Rell, 2009):

> The crimes that were committed on that brutal July night were so far out of the range of normal understanding that now, more than three years later, we still find it difficult to accept that they

happened in one of our communities. I have long believed that there are certain crimes so heinous, so depraved, that society is best served by imposing the ultimate sanction on the criminal. Steven Hayes stands convicted of such crimes—and today the jury has recommended that he should be subjected to the death penalty. I agree.

Correctional System

After a conviction the sentence is imposed. In most cases the judge decides on the sentence, but in some jurisdictions the jury, particularly for capital offenses, decides the sentence. Offenders sentenced to incarceration usually serve time in a local jail or a prison. Offenders sentenced to less than 1 year generally go to jail (2 years in Canada); those sentenced for longer periods of time go to prison. Persons admitted to the prison system may be held in prisons with varying levels of custody or in a community correctional facility. A prisoner may become eligible for parole after serving a specific part of his or her sentence. Parole is the conditional release of a prisoner before the prisoner's full sentence has been served. The decision to grant parole is made by an authority such as a parole board, which has power to grant or revoke parole or to discharge a parolee altogether. The way parole decisions are made varies widely among jurisdictions.

Offenders may also be required to serve out their full sentences before release (expiration of term). Those sentenced under determinate sentencing laws can be released only after they have served their full sentence (mandatory release) less any "goodtime" received while in prison. Inmates get goodtime credits against their sentences automatically or by earning them through participation in programs. If released by a parole board decision or by mandatory release, the release will be under the supervision of a parole officer in the community for the balance of his or her unexpired sentence. This supervision is governed by specific conditions of release, and the release may be returned to prison for violations of such conditions.

■ Civil Justice System[1]

Civil laws are rules and regulations that govern transactions and grievances between individual citizens. The civil justice system is really a system of private justice. In the legal system of continental Europe, the civil justice

[1]This section on the Civil Justice System, Copyright © 2000 by the National Center for Victims of Crime has been adapted, with permission. This information may be freely distributed, provided that it is distributed free of charge, in its entirety, and includes this copyright notice.

system is referred to as "private law." This is in contrast to "public law," such as in criminal law where the government or the public is always a party (Cafardi, 2006). In the civil justice system parties are private individuals or corporations or companies who are either suing or being sued. The parties involved are the plaintiff and the defendant, and it is the plaintiff's burden to prove the elements of a civil claim against a defendant. If the elements of the claim are proven, the defendant will have to pay the plaintiff. Criminal justice deals with alleged crimes and can lead to fines or prison. A civil justice case deals with civil claims and can lead to money damages and injunctions (Cafardi, 2006). Crime victims seek civil justice by filing lawsuits against criminal perpetrators or other responsible parties to be compensated for the damages incurred as a result of the criminal act.

More than 35 million Americans are victimized by crime each year. The consequences of crime frequently extend far beyond the criminal act. All too often victims are left with expenses for medical procedures, physical rehabilitation, counseling, and lost wages. It is estimated that crime costs victims $345 billion annually. Although many crime victims and their families have some knowledge about the legal system, they are often unaware that two systems of justice are available in which to hold the offender accountable: the criminal justice system and the civil justice system.

The criminal courts can provide crime victims with a sense of justice and can sometimes provide victims compensation through restitution orders. Unfortunately, even when restitution is ordered, it is rarely enforced. This lack of enforcement combined with statutory restrictions on the type of damages that may be included in a restitution order often result in restitution falling far short of meeting victims' needs. Compensation may also be available from the state's crime victims' compensation board; however, these programs are often subject to restrictions and limitations that may prevent crime victims from being fully compensated.

Civil Procedures

The civil justice system, unlike the criminal justice process, does not attempt to determine the innocence or guilt of an offender and does not seek to incarcerate the offender. Rather, the civil courts attempt to ascertain whether an offender or a third party is civilly liable for the injuries sustained as a result of the crime. In civil cases the "crime" is referred to as a tort. For most criminal offenses there is a corresponding tort for which a crime victim may bring a civil suit. **Table 5-2** provides examples of causes of civil action.

Most often, a civil court's finding of liability means the defendant must pay the victim and/or the victim's family monetary damages. In

TABLE 5-2 **Causes of Civil Action**

Causes	Definitions
Assault	Putting the victim in fear of being injured while the perpetrator has the present and immediate capacity to inflict that injury.
Battery	Any intentional physical contact that offends the victim. Battery includes but is not limited to the crimes of sexual battery, rape, molestation, fondling, forcible sodomy, malicious wounding, and attempted murder.
Wrongful death	A death caused by another person that occurs without justification or excuse, including murder, manslaughter, and vehicular homicide.
False imprisonment	Holding a victim against his or her will for any amount of time, no matter how brief. This often occurs in rape and kidnapping situations.
Intentional or reckless infliction of emotional distress	Causing a victim emotional distress or anxiety through extreme, outrageous, and offensive conduct. Emotional distress is usually claimed in conjunction with another tort rather than standing alone. Emotional distress is frequently seen in stalking cases.
Fraud	An intentional misrepresentation of facts made to deceive the victim, resulting in damages. This is often seen in white collar or economic crimes such as criminal fraud, telemarketing schemes, racketeering, etc.
Conversion	The theft or destruction of personal property, other belongings, or money. This includes larceny, concealment, embezzlement, etc.

this respect the civil justice system can provide victims with more of the monetary resources needed to help rebuild their lives. Furthermore, the civil justice system often provides victims and their families with a sense of justice the criminal courts cannot. Rather than holding a defendant accountable for his or her "crime against the state," the civil justice system holds a defendant who is found liable directly accountable to the victim for the harms he or she has suffered.

Process for a Civil Claim

The first step in the civil process is to file the claim or complaint. The victim and the victim's attorney have control over the causes of action against the third party or offender, in contrast to the criminal justice process whereby the prosecutor controls the filing of charges. The claim or complaint is a written document usually called a pleading. There are three components to a claim: (1) it establishes the subject matter jurisdiction, (2) it sets for the facts constituting the cause of action, and (3) it asks for certain types of relief (Wallace & Roberson, 2010). The causes of action, or legal theories, need to be proven for the victim, called the plaintiff, to receive compensation for injuries.

Two types of monetary awards are available. *Compensatory damages* in the form of monetary amounts are awarded to plaintiffs for the injuries they suffered. *Punitive damages* are monetary amounts awarded to the plaintiff to punish the defendant and to send a message to other similarly situated persons, usually third parties such as a corporation for failing to provide adequate security. The complaint lists the issues and parties involved in the law suit. The complaint also asks for relief. This relief is known as the *prayer* and generally cites a specific amount of money or, if unknown at the time, states "damages according to proof."

Once the complaint is filed in the proper jurisdiction, the defendant(s) is served with a copy. A response is generally required in 30 days or a default judgment may be entered for the plaintiff.

PRETRIAL ACTIVITIES   A number of pretrial activities may occur before either mediation or a trial. These legal maneuvers often account for the delays in the process. The most important motion that can be filed by the defense is a *summary judgment*. This motion is used to dismiss the entire case or to strike portions of the complaint. *Discovery* allows each side to learn the facts and theories each side is claiming. The tools of discovery include depositions, interrogatories, and requests for production of documents. The chart in **Figure 5-3** flows from top to bottom unless indicated otherwise by arrows and is a useful schematic for both U.S. and Canadian civil justice processes.

BURDEN OF PROOF   In the civil justice system liability must be proven by a preponderance of the evidence, which simply means that one side's evidence is more persuasive than the other. This standard is far less than the proof beyond a reasonable doubt required for a conviction in the criminal justice system. Therefore, it is sometimes possible to find the defendant liable in a civil case even though a verdict of "not guilty" was rendered in the criminal case—or even if the offender was never prosecuted. A good example of this principle is the O.J. Simpson case. Simpson, a former professional football player and well-known sports commentator, was prosecuted for the murder of his former wife, Nicole Brown, and her friend, Ron Goldman. In 1995 the jury found Simpson not guilty of the murders. Despite Simpson's acquittal in the criminal justice system, the families of Nicole Brown and Ron Goldman filed a wrongful death lawsuit against Simpson. A civil trial was held in 1997 and Simpson was found liable for the deaths of Brown and Goldman. The jury in the civil case awarded the victims' families $33.5 million in damages. Although a criminal conviction may increase the chances of a perpetrator being held civilly liable, it is by no means a requirement for bringing a civil action.

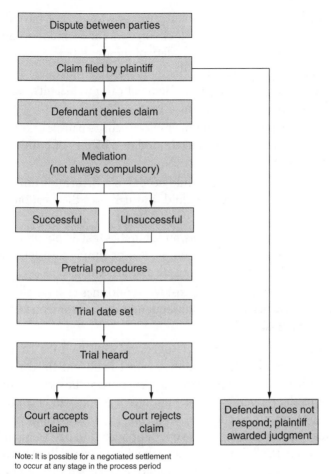

Note: It is possible for a negotiated settlement to occur at any stage in the process period

FIGURE 5-3 Civil Justice Process Flowchart

Data from Alberta Justice. 2008. Justice Process. (Civil Claims) http://www.justice.gov.ab.ca/civil/process.aspx.

Third-Party Liability

There has been increasing success over the years in the civil courts to obtain reparations for the victim from third parties instead of the offender. The courts view that those who could have prevented the commission of a crime through the exercise of due care are civilly liable to the victim for his or her injuries. Such **third-party liability** extends to those having a duty to have interfered with the offender on behalf of the victim. Third-party defendants are not the persons who actually commit the acts but instead are those parties who may have contributed to or facilitated them. The following are a few examples of possible third-party defendants in a victim's case:

- Hotel, motel, and apartment owners who do not have adequate security measures, such as locks on doors and windows, and proper lighting to provide for the safety of their guests.
- Colleges and universities that fail to provide adequate security for students or fail to notify students of campus assaults, leaving students vulnerable to victimizations.
- Shopping malls that do not employ security patrols or other necessary measures despite a likelihood or a history of criminal attacks on customers.
- A person who allows a child access to a firearm or other dangerous instrument and the child, in turn, uses the weapon to injure another person.
- Child-care centers, schools, and churches that do not properly check the backgrounds of their employees or simply transfer employees to other locations following allegations of abuse.
- A tavern owner or social host who continues to serve alcohol to an inebriated person who subsequently injures someone in a drunk driving crash.

It should also be noted that successful civil lawsuits could have a significant deterrent effect. Actions against negligent third parties can promote enhanced safety practices and encourage the exercise of greater caution, thereby reducing the likelihood that others will become victims of crime. For example, in a 1998 case, *Fough v. Texas Health Enterprises, Inc.*, Texas's largest nursing home operator agreed to pay $4.65 million to the estate of a partially paralyzed woman who was sexually abused repeatedly by a male nurse's aide. Trial evidence established that the defendant nursing home was negligent in hiring the nurse's aide by (1) failing to check job references, (2) ignoring a 2-year gap in his employment history, (3) failing to verify his nurse's aide certification status with the State of Texas and the State of Kansas, and (4) failing to submit the criminal history checks required under law. It was undisputed that the nurse's aide had previously served time in the penitentiary for felony crimes, which made him ineligible for employment in a nursing home.

Jaycee Dugard was abducted at the age of 11 in 1991 by convicted sex offender Phillip Craig Garrido. It was not until 18 years later that she was discovered and freed by law enforcement officials. In July 2010 the State of California approved a $20 million settlement with Jaycee Dugard to compensate her for lapses in supervision of Garrido by the Corrections Department that prolonged Dugard's continued captivity, ongoing sexual assault and mental abuses (La Ganga & Goldmacher, 2010). The settlement, part of AB1714, was approved by the California State Assembly by a 70 to 2 vote and by the California State Senate by a 30 to 1 vote. San Francisco County Superior Court Judge Daniel Weinstein, who mediated the settlement, stated that the settlement was reached to avoid a lawsuit that would be an added invasion of privacy and publicity for California (La Ganga & Goldmacher, 2010).

Considerations for Pursuing Civil Justice

A significant difference between the criminal and civil court systems is that in a civil case, the victim, usually through the advocacy of a privately retained attorney, controls essential decisions shaping the case. It is the victim who ultimately decides, usually on the advice of his or her attorney, whether to sue, accept a settlement offer, or go to trial.

Through civil litigation more and more victims are obtaining payment for medical expenses, psychological counseling, lost wages, earning ability, and property loss. In addition, they are more frequently recovering damages for "pain and suffering," a remedy traditionally unavailable through restitution ordered by criminal courts. However, a victim contemplating a civil lawsuit should bear in mind that obtaining a civil judgment is only half the battle. In many cases in which the victim wins a judgment, it may be difficult to collect the money awarded by the court. Victims, their lawyers, and advocates recognize that justice demands that such judgments be satisfied. Unfortunately, many defendants do not pay these judgments, and the victim and his or her attorney before filing a civil lawsuit should consider this possibility seriously. Nevertheless, there are numerous sources of assets with which perpetrators can satisfy civil judgments. Many of those sources fall into three broad categories:

- *Current and expected assets:* These include cash, securities, wages, and both real and personal property as well as expected assets such as inheritances, interests in estates, pensions, and annuities.
- *Insurance:* Many perpetrators will have some kind of insurance coverage: homeowners, automobile, professional, general liability, etc. Although most insurance policies exclude intentional acts from coverage, there are some circumstances that allow perpetrators to use insurance coverage to satisfy civil judgments.
- *Windfalls:* Perpetrators sometimes come into sums of money that no one could have anticipated such as unexpected inheritances or proceeds from lawsuits. Some prisoners have even won lotteries.

Statutes of Limitations

There are time limits for filing civil suits set by statute. These statutes of limitation vary from state to state but usually are from 1 to 3 years. Any suit filed after the expiration of the statute of limitations is time barred and cannot proceed. There are certain circumstances, such as those involving child victims and victims with repressed memories, where the time in which victims can file suit has been extended. Although there is a limited time in which to file a suit, once a judgment is obtained, it is valid for a minimum of 20 years and can often be extended. In other words, even if a perpetrator has no assets today, filing suit and securing a judgment may allow the victim to seize assets the perpetrator may obtain many years in the future.

■ Summary

Throughout the Middle Ages laws were often created or abolished according to the ruling nobility, and law could be established by philosophers or religion. In contemporary societies laws are typically created and enforced by governments. These laws may coexist with or contradict other forms of social control, such as religious proscriptions, professional rules and ethics, or the cultural mores and customs of a society.

Under the U.S. form of government, each state and the federal government has its own criminal justice system. In Canada a federal criminal code covers all jurisdictions. All systems must respect the rights of individuals set forth in court interpretation of the constitutional rights of individuals and defined in case law.

Although money awarded in civil lawsuits can never fully compensate a victim for the trauma of his or her victimization or the loss of a loved one, it can provide valuable resources for crime victims to help rebuild their lives. Furthermore, the exposure to civil liability is a powerful incentive for landlords, businessmen, and other proprietors to enact the security measures necessary to prevent future victimizations.

■ Key Terms

Adjudication: Includes all formal and informal steps within the criminal process.

Civil justice system: A network of courts and legal processes that enforce, restore, or protect private and personal rights.

Criminal charges: A formal accusation of having committed a criminal offense.

Criminal law: Concerned with actions that are harmful to society in which prosecution is pursued by the state, not the individual.

Defendant: A person or institution against whom an action is brought in a court of law; the person being sued or accused.

English common law: The traditional, unwritten law of England that forms the basis of modern statutes.

Grand jury: A jury convened to inquire into accusations of crime and to evaluate the grounds for indictments.

Laws: Define the criminal justice system within each jurisdiction and delegate the authority and responsibility for criminal justice to various jurisdictions, officials, and institutions.

Pretrial: A conference held before the trial begins to bring the parties together to outline discovery proceedings and to define the issues.

Third-party liability: Responsibility held by a person or organization that did not commit the offense but may have contributed to or facilitated the offense.

Victim impact statement: A statement given by the victim(s) that details how the crime has affected him or her.

■ Discussion Questions

1. How does mythology contribute to the laws of society?

2. Give examples of the contributions of primitive laws under various rulers in Egypt.

3. Identify the key documents that contribute to early American and Canadian law.

4. Why do you believe criminal justice professionals failed to recognize that victims deserve to have their legal and constitutional rights protected before the late 1980s?

5. How is the victimization experience different or similar for a crime victim versus a victim of a social and public health problem?

6. Questions for debate on the death penalty:
   - Does the death penalty protect society by ridding it of evil and actually deterring people from committing crimes?
   - Does it exact retribution from criminals appropriately, in fair proportion to the crime committed?
   - Is the punishment used fairly in terms of the race and class of its victims?

- Is capital punishment barbaric, or does it have a place in civilized society?
- Is the death penalty justified in the vast monies saved by not having to support such criminals with incarceration for their lifetimes, or is its cost to society's humanity even dearer?

■ Resources

National Center for Victims of Crime
http://www.ncvc.org/ncvc/Main.aspx
Office of Juvenile Justice and Prevention Programs
http://www.ojjdp.gov/

■ References

Antkowiak, B. A. (2006). Criminal law and procedure. In C. H. Wecht & J. T. Rago (Eds.), *Forensic science and the law*. Boca Raton, FL: Taylor and Francis.

Baker, J. (2002). *An introduction to English legal history.* London: Butterworths.

Banks, C. (2005). *Punishment in America.* Contemporary World Issues. Santa Barbara, CA: ABC-CLIO.

Bazemore, G. (2001). Young people, trouble and crime: Restorative justice as a normative theory of informal social control and social support. *Youth & Society, 33*(2), 199–226.

Bazemore, G., & Schiff, M. (2001). *Restorative justice: Repairing harm and transforming communities.* Cincinnati, OH: Anderson Press.

Braithwaite, J. (2000). Shame and criminal justice. *Canadian Journal of Criminology, 42*(3), 281–298.

Cafardi, N. P. (2006). The civil justice system. In C. H. Wecht & J. T. Rago (Eds.), *Forensic science and the law*. Boca Raton, FL: Taylor and Francis.

Cheon, A., & Regehr, C. (2006). Restorative justice in cases of intimate partner violence: Reviewing the evidence. *Victims and Offenders, 1*(4), 369–394.

Craig, E. (1998). *Encyclopedia of philosophy.* London and New York: Routledge.

Death penalty for Hayes for Petit murders. (2011). Gov. Rell's statement.

Death Penalty Information Center. (2009). Introduction to the death penalty. Retrieved from http://www.deathpenaltyinfo.org/part-i-history-death-penalty

Denner, J., & Pellegrino, R. (2011). Civil commitment. Retrieved from http://criminal.findlaw.com/crimes/more-criminal-topics/sex-offenders/civil-commitment.html

Department of Justice. (2003). Canada's court system. Retrieved from http://www.justice.gc.ca/en/dept/pub/trib/page1.html

Dodd, J. D. (2002). Justice Options for Women Project. Dialogue on restorative justice and women who are victims of violence: A discussion paper in preparation for the restorative justice and violence against women workshop. Retrieved from www.isn.net/~tha/justiceoptions /4pagediscussionpaper.pdf

Governor M.J. Rell. (2009). *An Act Concerning the Penalty for a Capital Felony*, HB 6578. Hartford, CT. Executive Chambers. Retrieved from http://www.ct.gov/governorrell/cwp/view.asp?A=3675&Q=441204

Hamilton, E. (1942). *Mythology*. New York: Mentor Books.

Henderson, H. (2000). *Capital punishment* (rev. ed.). New York: Facts on File.

Holmstrom, L.L., & Burgess, A.W. (1983). *The victim of rape*. New Brunswick, NJ: Transaction Books.

Koon, S. (2011). Judge rejects plea bargain from woman accused of stealing from Brofman. Retrieved from http://www2.dailyprogress.com/news/2011 /dec/06/judge-rejects-plea-bargain-woman-accused-stealing--ar-1525299/

La Ganga, M.L., & Goldmacher , S. (2010, July 2). Jaycee Lee Dugard's family will receive $20 million from California. Los Angeles Times. Retrieved from http://articles.latimes.com/2010/jul/02/local/la-me-0702-dugard-settlement–20100702

LEAA/OJP Retrospective. (1996). 30 Years of federal support to state and local criminal justice. U.S. Department of Justice, Washington, D.C. Retrieved from https://www.ncjrs.gov/pdffiles1/nij/164509.pdf

Levinson, D. (2002). Capital crimes. In *Encyclopedia of crime and punishment* (Vol. 4). Thousand Oaks, CA: Sage.

MacLead, M. (2011). The electric chair. Retrieved from http://www.trutv.com /library/crime/notorious_murders/not_guilty/chair/5.html

Maiese, M. (2003). Distributive justice. Retrieved from http://www.beyondintractability.org/bi-essay/distributive_justice/

Manitoba Victims' Bill of Rights, C.C.S.M. c. V55. Retrieved from http://www.canlii.org/mb/laws/sta/v-55/20050110/whole.html

Mill, J. S. (1863). *Utilitarianism*. London: Parker, Son, and Bourn.

Murphy, W.J. (2011). Not guilty verdict was the right result but we're not done yet. Retrieved from http://www.patriotledger.com/opinions/x1498054785 /WENDY-MURPHY-Anthony-verdict-was-right-but-we-re-not-done

New York Times. (2010, November 8). Petit family killings. Retrieved from http://topics.nytimes.com/top/reference/timestopics/people/p /petit_family/index.html

Nozick, R. (1977). *Anarchy, state, and utopia.* New York: Basic Books.

O'Brien, V. (1993, December). *Civil legal remedies for crime victims.* Washington, DC: U.S. Department of Justice, Office for Victims of Crime.

Office of Juvenile Justice and Delinquency Prevention. (2011). About OJJDP. Retrieved from http://www.ojjdp.gov/about/about.html

Parsons, T. (1951). *The social system.* Glencoe, IL: Free Press.

Payne v. Tennessee (90-5721), 501 U.S. 808 (1991).

President's Commission on Law Enforcement and Administration of Justice. (1967). *The Challenge of Crime in a Free Society.* U.S. Government Printing Office.

Presser, L., & Gaarder, E. (2000). Can restorative justice reduce battering? Some preliminary considerations. *Social Justice, 27*(1), 175–195.

Presser, L., & Van Voorhis, P. (2002). Values and evaluation: Assessing processes and outcomes. *Crime and Delinquency, 48*(1), 162–188.

Rawls, J. (1971). *A theory of justice.* Harvard, MA: Harvard University Press.

Regehr, C., & Kanani, K. (2010). *Essential law for social work practice in Canada.* Toronto: Oxford University Press.

Roach, K. (2000). Changing punishment at the turn of the century: Restorative justice on the rise. *Canadian Journal of Criminology, 42*(3), 249–280.

Seneca County Prosecutor's Office. (2009). Seneca County victim rights. Retrieved from http://www.senecapros.org/victims_rights.html

Stearns, P., Adas, M., Schwartz, S., & Gilbert, M. (2003). *World civilizations: The global experience* (AP edition). New York: Pearson Education, Inc.

Umbreit, M. (1995). The development and impact of victim–offender mediation in the United States. *Mediation Quarterly, 12*(3), 263–276.

Wallace, H., & Roberson, C. (2010). *Victimology: Legal, psychological and social perspectives* (3rd ed.). Boston: Allyn and Bacon.

West's Encyclopedia of American Law. (1998). Family law. Retrieved from http://www.answers.com/topic/family-law#ixzz1fy4yedCi

West's Encyclopedia of American Law. (1998). Feudalism. Retrieved from http://www.answers.com/topic/feudalism

West's Encyclopedia of American Law. (2011). Caryl Chessman. Retrieved from http://www.answers.com/topic/caryl-chessman#ixzz1WQjXf896

Wilson, C. (1984). *A criminal history of mankind.* New York: G.P. Putnam's Sons.

Zehr, H. (1995). Justice paradigm shift? Values and visions in the reform process. *Mediation Quarterly, 12*(3), 207–216.

Zimring, F.E., Hawkins, G., & Kamin, S. (2001). *Punishment and democracy: Three strikes and you're out in California.* New York: Oxford University Press.

Child Abuse and Neglect

CHAPTER 6

■ **Objectives**

- To define and describe the various forms of child maltreatment and their dynamics
- To outline the short- and long-term consequences of child maltreatment
- To describe a typology of child predators
- To describe resources for intervening in child maltreatment

■ **Key Terms**

Child maltreatment
Developmental disability
Developmental traumatology
Disclosure
Fetal homicide
Fetal rights
Incest
Statutory rape

Acknowledgment ▬▬▬▬▬▬▬

We thank Paul Clements for his contributions to sections of this chapter in the first edition of *Victimology*.

CASES

Scott Brown, the junior senator from Massachusetts, stunned the public by disclosing both physical abuse and sexual abuse as a child in his book, *Against All Odds* (2011). He revealed that his stepfather repeatedly beat both him and his mother and that he was sexually abused by a counselor at a summer camp when he was 10 years old. Senator Brown kept this secret for over 40 years due to shame, embarrassment, the threat that he would be hurt badly if he ever told, and the belief that boys don't tell. Brown wrote that the incident showed him there were no safe havens and no one he could truly trust. He continued to disclose that, as a teen, he engaged in numerous incidents of shoplifting, including stealing a three-piece suit from a

department store and steaks and hamburger from the supermarket. When he was caught shoplifting albums by Black Sabbath and other rock artists, he was admonished by a judge to straighten up. He did. He went to college, attended law school, ran for political office as a Republican in an overwhelmingly Democratic state, and was elected in 2009 to fill the senate seat vacated by Senator Edward Kennedy, a Democrat, who had died. See **Figure 6-1**.

Brown isn't the only public figure whose sexual abuse has become public knowledge. At 9 years old and living in Milwaukee, Oprah Winfrey and her siblings were left alone with their 19-year-old cousin. It was this cousin who sexually abused Oprah for the first time: She was raped and then taken out for ice cream and told to keep it a secret—which she did. She was again abused by a family friend and an uncle years later, ongoing abuse that she kept silent. Without receiving much direction from her mother and unable to discuss her sexual

abuse, Oprah resorted to acting out: skipping school, dating, stealing money from her mother, and running away. She was sent back to live with her father in Nashville. At 14 Oprah discovered she was pregnant, although she hid this news from her parents until she was in her 7th month. The day she told her father the news of her pregnancy, she went into early labor and delivered her baby that day, a boy, who died within 2 weeks of his birth (Fry, 2011; Oprah.com, 2006). See **Figure 6-2**.

The message from these public figures is that childhood victimization occurs across gender, race, and socioeconomic factors, that nondisclosure is not uncommon, that resiliency is possible, and that the abuse is never forgotten.

■ Introduction

Childhood is supposed to be a happy, conflict-free time of life; however, negative life events can converge on a child to create victimization and trauma. As the case examples above illustrate, many children remain silent about their abuse for years, may have episodes of acting out, or may become pregnant; when there is disclosure, they risk the public reaction from their family, the abuser, and the community.

The Centers for Disease Control and Prevention defines child maltreatment as any act or series of acts of commission or omission by a parent or other caregiver that results in harm, potential for harm, or threat of harm to a child (Leeb, Paulozzi, Melanson, Simon, & Arias, 2008). Child abuse can occur in a child's home or in organizations, schools, or communities in which the child interacts. The types of maltreatment that involve acts of commission include physical abuse, sexual abuse, and psychological abuse. The following types of maltreatment involve acts of omission (Leeb et al., 2008):

- Failure to provide
  - Physical neglect
  - Emotional neglect
  - Medical/dental neglect
  - Educational neglect
- Failure to supervise
  - Inadequate supervision
  - Exposure to violent environments

Child abuse has existed across time and has even been traced to the prehistoric period. Children have been maltreated and exploited throughout history as they were long considered family property. Fathers in ancient times could sell, mutilate, or kill their children. Many religions used child sacrifice to please and appease gods. Infanticide was common. Children born with infirmities, retardation, or deformity were killed to maintain and strengthen society. In most cultures severe punishment and harsh treatment were deemed necessary for rearing and educating children (Volpe, 2011).

In the past several decades, childhood victimization has been formally categorized as a pervasive public health problem and at pandemic levels globally. This formal recognition resulted from media campaigns, increased reporting, enhanced comprehensive and sensitive assessment of childhood victims, and by giving them a "voice" as well as recognizing their human rights (American Public Health Association, 1975, 1986; deMause, 1998; National Association of Counsel for Children, n.d.a.; World Health Organization, 2004, 2006).

deMause (1998) described the history of childhood as a nightmare we have only recently begun to address. He suggested the further back in history one goes, the lower the level of child care and the more likely children are to be killed, abandoned, beaten, terrorized, and abused. Congruent with these thoughts, Hopper (2007) offered a similar yet contemporary statement. Hopper (2007) agreed that children have been abused throughout human history but emphasized its acknowledgment as a main cause of many people's suffering and personal problems is recent. Some believe we are beginning to face the true prevalence and significance of child abuse, whereas others worry that many people have become obsessed with child abuse and deny any personal responsibility for their problems while "blaming" them on abuse and bad parenting.

On any given day people can pick up a newspaper or turn on a television and hear yet another report of a missing, abused or neglected, or, even worse, murdered child (Mugavin, 2005). The seeming significant increase in the frequency of child abuse is not necessarily a reflection of elevated occurrence or prevalence but rather that society, over time, has come to terms with the reality of the large numbers of children who experience or witness violence, abuse, or neglect; consequently, we have become more aware and understanding of the importance of reporting to child protective agencies, forensic nurses, and law enforcement (National Association of Counsel for Children, n.d.b; Pleck, 2003). Further expanding and enhancing such reporting, all 50 states, as well as all major health care–related associations and professional licensing and credentialing bodies, have passed some form of a mandatory child abuse and neglect reporting law to provide assessment, protection, and intervention for all children with suspected or documented abuse or neglect (National District Attorneys Association, n.d.).

One of the greatest challenges for child survivors of abuse, their families, and their health care providers is grappling with the perception of the abused child as "damaged goods" (Clements & Benasutti, 2003). By expanding awareness and understanding of the risk and plight of children relative to abuse, while simultaneously enhancing assessment, therapeutic intervention, and medicolegal interface with law enforcement and the judicial system, interventions can promote adaptive mental health and on-time emotional growth and development with survivors of abuse, neglect, and other forms of interpersonal violence (Clements & DeRanieri, 2006; LaSala & Lynch, 2006; World Health Organization, 2006).

■ Scope of the Problem

The National Child Abuse and Neglect Data System, a reporting system for all cases that come to the attention of child protection services, provides a primary approach for obtaining statistics related to child abuse and neglect. Four other approaches are used to examine the occurrences of child maltreatment (Levanthal, 2005):

1. Prospective data collection in selected communities to identify cases of child maltreatment even if not reported to Child Protective Service (CPS). This approach has been used in four national studies. In each study the number of identified victims of child maltreatment has been substantially higher than the number of cases substantiated by CPS over the comparable time period.

2. Asking adults about the details of how they have treated their children over a specific period, such as the previous month or a year (Straus, Hamby, Finkelhor, Moore, & Runyon, 1998).

3. Asking children about their experiences of violence, including their experiences of maltreatment (Finkelhor & Dziuba-Leatherman, 1994).

4. Asking adults how they were treated during childhood (Finkelhor & Dziuba-Leatherman, 1994).

This last approach has helped in gaining an understanding of how many adults have experienced different types of maltreatment during childhood. For example, many studies have asked adult men and women about their experiences of sexual abuse in childhood and adolescence. A review of studies of community samples in the United States and Canada found the prevalence of sexual abuse reported by women was 2% to 62% and by men, 3% to 16% (Finkelhor & Jones, 2006). Finkelhor and Dziuba-Leatherman (1994) suggested that a reasonable summary statistic for women would be 20% and for men, 5% to 10%.

National Child Abuse and Neglect Data System

The National Child Abuse and Neglect Data System is a voluntary reporting system in the United States developed by the Children's Bureau of the U.S. Department of Health and Human Services to collect and analyze annual statistics on child maltreatment from state child protection agencies. The data from Child Protective Services (CPS) is based on cases reported to child protective agencies. **Table 6-1** summarizes the findings of this report.

National Incidence Study

The National Incidence Study (NIS) is a congressionally mandated, periodic effort of the U.S. Department of Health and Human Services. In 1974 Public Law 93-247 mandated the first NIS (NIS-1), which collected data in

TABLE 6-1 **United States Child Protective Services Report**

Incident	Findings
Reporters of child maltreatment	58.3% were education personnel
	16.5% legal personnel
	16.4% law enforcement personnel
	11.4% social services staff
	Other reporters were nonprofessionals, including friends, neighbors, sports coaches, and relatives.
Confirmed child victims to Child Protective Services	Birth to 1 year had the highest rate of victimization at 20.6 per 1,000 children.
	51.1% of victims were girls.
	22.3% were African American.
	20.7% were Hispanic.
	44% were White.
Types of child maltreatment	78.3% of victims suffered neglect.
	17.8% of victims suffered physical abuse.
	9.5% of victims suffered sexual abuse.
	7.6% suffered psychological maltreatment.
Child fatalities	An estimated 1,770 children died due to abuse or neglect.
	The overall rate of child fatalities was 2.34 deaths per 100,000 children.
	35.8% of child fatalities were attributed to neglect.
	23.2% died exclusively from physical abuse.
	80.8% of the children who died due to child abuse and neglect were younger than 4 years old.
Perpetrators of child maltreatment	80.9% of duplicate perpetrators of child maltreatment were parents.
	Women comprised 53.8% of perpetrators.
Services for the child and family	59.9% of victims received postresponse services.
	20.8% of victims were removed from their homes.

Data from Child Welfare Information Gateway. 2011. Child Maltreatment 2009: Summary of key findings. Washington, DC: U.S. Department of Health and Human Services, Children's Bureau. Child Welfare Information Gateway. Available online at www.childwelfare.gov/pubs/factsheets/canstats.cfm.

1979 and 1980. Three additional cycles of data were collected in 1986–87, 1993–94, and 2005–06. The NIS serves as the nation's needs assessment on child abuse and neglect. It offers a unique perspective on the scope of the problem beyond the children that child protective service agencies investigate. Although the NIS includes children investigated by child protective service agencies, it also obtains data on other children who were not reported to CPS or who were screened out by CPS without investigation. These additional children were recognized as maltreated by community professionals. Thus, the NIS estimates include both abused and neglected children who are in the official CPS statistics and those who are not.

The NIS follows a nationally representative design, so the estimates reflect the numbers of abused and neglected children in the United States who come to the attention of community professionals. Because the three previous cycles used comparable methods and definitions, one can compare NIS-4 estimates with those earlier studies to identify changes over time in the incidence and distribution of abused and neglected children. Using the Harm Standard, which includes only children who have already experienced harm from abuse or neglect, more than 1.25 million U.S. children, or 1 child in every 58, experienced maltreatment during the year 2005–2006. Of this total, 44% were abused and 61% were neglected. Rates of reported abuse in each abuse category were as follows (Sedlak et al., 2010):

- 58% (323,000 children) experienced physical abuse
- 24% experienced sexual abuse
- 27% experienced emotional abuse
- 47% experienced educational neglect
- 38% experienced physical neglect
- 25% experienced emotional neglect

There was a 19% decrease in the total number of maltreated children between wave 3 and 4 of the survey. When the increase in the number of children in the United States over the interval is considered, this change is equivalent to a 26% decrease in reported child maltreatment. It is hoped that improved societal conditions and better supports for families are reflected in this decline and not a decrease in reporting.

Canadian Incidence Child Abuse Statistics

The Canadian Incidence Study of Reported Child Abuse and Neglect (CIS) is a national initiative to collect data on children who come to the attention of a child welfare authority due to alleged or suspected abuse and/or neglect in the year the study is conducted. The objectives of the CIS are to provide reliable estimates of the incidence of reported child abuse and neglect and to compare findings over time as data collection for the CIS is completed in 5-year cycles. The third cycle of the study, CIS-2008, tracked 15,980 child maltreatment investigations conducted in a representative sample of 112 Child Welfare Service organizations in all provinces and territories in Canada (Trocme, Fallon, MacLaurin, Sinha, & Black, 2008). In this study the largest proportion of substantiated cases was for neglect (34%) or for exposure to domestic violence (34%), whereas 20% of children

TABLE 6-2 **Canadian Child Abuse Major Findings**

- Police-reported data for 2009 indicated that children and youth under the age of 18 were most likely to be sexually victimized or physically assaulted by someone they knew (85% of incidents).
- Nearly 55,000 children and youth were the victims of a sexual offense or physical assault in 2009, about 3 in 10 of which were perpetrated by a family member.
- Six in 10 children and youth victims of family violence were assaulted by their parents. The youngest child victims (under the age of 3 years) were most vulnerable to violence by a parent.
- In 2009 the rate of family-related sexual offenses was more than four times higher for girls than for boys. The rate of physical assault was similar for girls and boys.

Data from Statistics Canada. 2010. Family violence in Canada, A Statistical Profile. Retrieved from http://dsp-psd.pwgsc.gc.ca/Collection/Statcan/85-224-X/85-224-XIE.html.

were physically abused, 9% were emotionally abused, and 3% were sexually abused (Trocme et al., 2008). In addition, Statistics Canada collects population-based data, the findings of which can be found in **Table 6-2**.

■ Legislative Framework

The protection of children is a primary responsibility of any society, and, as such, child protection (or child welfare) legislation has a long history in North America and Europe. According to UNICEF (2011), child protection is the response to violence, exploitation, and abuse of children by both governments and citizens. This protection is inclusive of the commercial sexual exploitation, trafficking, child labor, and harmful traditional practice. In 1989 the United Nations brought leaders together to establish the first internationally binding legislation to protect children. The UN Convention on the Rights of the Child spells out basic human rights for children: the right to survival; to develop to the fullest; to protection from harmful influences, abuse, and exploitation; and to participate fully in family, cultural, and social life (United Nations, 2009). The Convention protects children's rights by setting standards in health care; education; and legal, civil, and social services. Each nation that signed the agreement is responsible for establishing legislation that ensures the protection of children.

In both Canada and the United States children who were not cared for by their parents often were taken into mandated servitude. In Ontario, for instance, the Orphan's Act of 1799 empowered town wardens to bind orphaned children to apprentices. This legislation and similar legislation throughout North America viewed children as small adults and perpetrated the belief that hard work was the solution to social ills (Regehr & Kanani, 2010). By the 1800s charitable and religious organizations began to establish children's homes to care for orphan, abandoned, and neglected children. However, concerns were raised about the treatment of children in these homes, and in 1909 the first White House Conference on the Care of Dependent Children was convened with the aim of preventing the removal of children from homes. State laws followed that for the first time addressed the protection of children. However, it was not until some time later that the state took responsibility for the care of children.

The 1935 Social Security Act authorized the first federal grants for child welfare services in the United States. The first Children's Aid Society in America opened in New York City in 1953. In 1954 in Canada the first legislation, the Child Welfare Act, was enacted that placed accountability for child protection on the state. In 1974 the U.S. Congress enacted the Child Abuse Prevention and Treatment Act that required each state to establish policies and procedures for the reporting and investigation of child abuse and neglect. Today, the U.S. government is a major funder of child protection services that are provided by state and local authorities and by nonprofit social service organizations.

Mandated Reporting

In general, child welfare legislation throughout North America mandates the reporting of suspected child abuse to child welfare authorities. The types of professionals mandated to report child maltreatment has expanded over the years to include almost anyone who comes in contact with children, such as physicians, dentists, nurses, teachers, mental health professionals, social workers, police, and clergy. Mandated reporters are expected to report both by telephone to a central hotline and in writing. Most state laws indicate that mandated reporters must report if there is a reasonable suspicion of abuse or neglect; they do not have to be 100% certain. State statutes protect the reporter for reporting in good faith. The failure to report a suspected case can place the child at risk of a more serious episode of maltreatment, and this inaction can result in prosecution by the state.

Role of Child Protective Services

CPS have advanced in major ways. They investigate cases of suspected child maltreatment and place children in foster care. There has also been expansion into attempting to help families receive additional services such as with nurse practitioners and substance abuse referral. There have been major changes in how child maltreatment cases are investigated. Investigations can include CPS and the police, and many states have passed legislation for the development of regional multidisciplinary investigative teams. Over the past three decades increasing attention has been paid to research on children as reporters of their experiences, in particular children reporting suspected sexual abuse. Research has assisted in studying the short- and long-term memories of children, how they describe events, and factors that affect reporting. Guidelines have been published, and forensic interviewers have been specially trained in asking children nonleading questions about their experiences.

Child Fatality Review Boards

State laws define child fatality review panels or boards. The rationale for such panels is based on the fact that child deaths are often regarded as an indicator of the health of a community. The ultimate purpose of review boards is to reduce the incidence of preventable child deaths, with the following goals:

- To promote cooperation, collaboration, and communication between all groups that serve families and children
- To maintain a database of all child deaths to develop an understanding of the causes and incidence of those deaths
- To recommend and develop plans for implementing local service and program changes, and to advise the department of health of aggregate data, trends, and patterns found in child deaths.

■ Typology of Child Maltreatment

The term "child abuse" has been broadened into an all-encompassing term of child maltreatment. Maltreatment of children includes neglect, physical abuse, sexual abuse, and emotional maltreatment. Physical abuse against children was first recognized in the 1960s with the advent of both the women's movement and its concern for vulnerable members of society and with the advent of improvements in medical technology (such as the x-ray). This was then followed by recognition of child sexual abuse in the 1970s and 1980s. The importance of the emotional aspects of child maltreatment has been particularly important for understanding both short- and long-term outcomes of child abuse. It has been increasingly clear that children reported for one type of maltreatment have often suffered from other types as well.

Neglect

Child neglect is generally characterized by omissions in care resulting in significant harm or risk of significant harm. Neglect is frequently defined in terms of a failure to provide for the child's basic needs, such as of adequate food, clothing, shelter, supervision, or medical care. It may include abandonment of the child and failure to see that the child receives adequate education and nutrition. Although neglect can be a one-time incident, such as leaving a child unsupervised in an unsafe setting, it is usually a pattern of unsafe care caused by a serious mental health problem or substance abuse on the part of the parent or caregiver (**Table 6-3**).

Physical Abuse

Joel Steinberg, a former New York criminal defense attorney, was convicted of manslaughter in the November 2, 1987, death of a 6-year-old girl, Lisa, whom he had "adopted." Court records indicated Steinberg ate dinner and freebased cocaine as Lisa lay unconscious for hours in the bathroom of a Greenwich Village apartment after being felled by a "staggering blow" to her head. When Lisa died in a hospital, she weighed 43 pounds and her little body was covered in bruises. Hedda Nussbaum, Steinberg's partner, was found to have suffered extensive and permanent injuries at Steinberg's hands and became a figure of pity and revulsion as the history of her dysfunctional relationship with Steinberg was revealed.

Child physical abuse is the intentional act of injury to a child. Such acts may cause harm to the child or they may intend to harm. It includes examples such as punishing a child severely, such as when a parent loses control and shakes a crying infant. Injuries for abuse or neglect must be distinguished from accidental or unintentional injuries. The two most

TABLE 6-3 **Possible Signs of Child Neglect**

Consider the possibility of neglect when the *child*

- Is frequently absent from school
- Begs or steals food or money
- Lacks needed medical or dental care, immunizations, or glasses
- Is consistently dirty and has severe body odor
- Lacks sufficient clothing for the weather/is dressed inappropriately
- Abuses alcohol or other drugs
- States that there is no one at home to provide care

Consider the possibility of neglect when the *parent or other adult caregiver*

- Appears to be indifferent to the child
- Seems apathetic or depressed
- Behaves irrationally or in a bizarre manner
- Is abusing alcohol or other drugs

Data from Recognize Child Abuse, www.preventchildabuse.org.publications/parents/downloads/recognizing-abuse.pdf

common instruments used in child abuse, other than the hand, are belts and electric cords. Burn injuries make up about 50% of child abuse cases. Most deliberate burns are from very hot tap water. Contact burns are usually of the branding type and will mirror the object used to cause the injury. The most common type of instrument used to inflict contact burns in child abuse cases is a cigarette. Clinicians are taught to distinguish intentional signs of injury from accidental. For example, in deliberate immersion burns, the depth of the burn is uniform. The wound borders are very distinct, sharply defined "water lines" with little tapering of depth at edges. There is little evidence that the child thrashed about during the immersion, indicating the child was held in place. On occasion there may be bruising of soft tissue to indicate that this happened.

Shaken baby syndrome is a term developed to explain those instances in which severe intracranial trauma occurred in the absence of signs of external head trauma. The mechanisms of injury in shaken baby syndrome historically result from a combination of physical factors, including the proportionately large cranial size of infants, the laxity of their neck muscles, and the vulnerability of their intracranial bridging veins, due to the subarachnoid space (the space between the arachnoid membrane and the pia matter, which are the inner two of the three membranes that cover the brain) being somewhat larger in infants. However, the primary factor is the proportionately large size of the adult relative to the child. Shaking by admitted perpetrators has produced remarkably similar injury patterns.

Munchausen's syndrome by proxy is a form of child abuse in which the abuser fabricates an illness in a child for the purposes of obtaining attention by medical professionals. The child is taken for medical care with fabricated symptoms or feigned illness knowing this will most likely result in hospitalization of the child victim for tests or observation. As a consequence the parent obtains attention and sympathy. The syndrome was first identified in 1977 by Professor Roy Meadow, a pediatrician at the University of Leeds, England. He described two initial cases, the first in which a mother poisoned her toddler with excessive salt and second in which the mother put her own blood in the baby's urine.

Roesler and Jenny (2009) suggested retiring the name Munchausen's syndrome by proxy and replacing it with a more fitting name to appreciate that children can be abused by their parents in the medical environment, such as pediatric condition falsification (Ayoub & Alexander, 1998). This term clearly labels the problem as the caretaker, who provides a false history to the medical community but is sometimes a difficult diagnosis for nonmedical personnel from child services, law enforcement, and the judicial system to associate with child abuse. Munchausen's syndrome by proxy is listed as a factitious disorder by proxy in the *Diagnostic and Statistical Manual of Mental Disorders*, 4th edition, revised (American Psychiatric Association, 2002). This may change in the next edition of the manual when it is reviewed and released.

Caution must be taken regarding different cultural norms. Some cultural practices are generally not defined as physical abuse but may result in physically hurting children. For example, "coining," or *cao gio*, is a practice used to treat illness by rubbing the body forcefully with a coin or other hard object, and *Moxabustion* is an Asian folkloric remedy that burns the skin. The rule of thumb for practitioners is the injury may be due to cultural practices, which are generally respected. However, if the injury or harm is significant, professionals typically work with parents to discourage harmful behavior and suggest preferable alternatives.

Child Sexual Abuse

Infants, preadolescent children, and teenage boys and girls may be targets of sexual abuse. In adult relationships sexual encounters occur in three ways: through negotiation and consent, through pressure and exploitation, or through force and assault. The first method is regarded as a healthy and mature manner of relating sexually to another person. In the second method one adult takes sexual advantage of another, usually through a position of dominance, and the subordinate person agrees to the sexual activity to achieve some nonsexual goal. Depending on the nature of the power imbalance in the relationship, this can result in criminal prosecution and/or civil liability. The third method, legally termed rape, involves the threat of harm or injury and/or actual physical assault to establish sexual contact and is a criminal activity.

Only through negotiation and consent can sexual relations properly be achieved. However, negotiation and consent are precluded between an adult and a preadolescent or underage person because such a person has not developed sufficient knowledge or wisdom to be able to negotiate such an encounter on an equal basis with an adult. Although the youngster may be sexually mature, she or he is not psychologically equipped to deal with sexual situations on an equal basis with an adult and can therefore be easily manipulated. By definition, children are immature; thus, adults can capitalize in self-serving ways on this immaturity and can exploit the child in a variety of ways: physical, social, psychological, and emotional (Groth, 1979).

Sexual abuse includes physical contact, including the touching or exposing of sexual or other intimate parts of a person for the purpose of arousing or gratifying sexual desire in either the perpetrator or the subject child.

Statutory rape is defined as the crime of engaging in sexual activity with a person who has not yet reached the age of consent. Even if the activities are consensual, the adult can still be charged with statutory rape if the other party is younger than the age of consent. Minors and physically and mentally incapacitated persons are deemed incapable of consenting to sex under rape statutes in the United States and Canada (*West's Encyclopedia of American Law*, 1998). An age of consent statute is believed to have first appeared in 1275 in England as part of the rape law. The statute was considered a misdemeanor to "ravish" a "maiden within age." The phrase "within age" was interpreted by jurist Sir Edward Coke as meaning the age of marriage, which at the time was 12 years of age (Robertson, n.d.).

Child pornography, another form of child sexual abuse, can be behaviorally defined as a sexually explicit reproduction of a child's image, including sexually explicit photographs, negatives, slides, magazines, movies, videotapes, and computer disks. In essence, it is the permanent record of sexual abuse or exploitation of a child. To legally be child pornography, it must be a visual depiction (not the written word) of a minor (as defined by statute) that is sexually explicit (not necessarily obscene, unless required by state law). Child pornography by itself represents an act of sexual abuse or exploitation of a child and by itself does harm to the child.

Psychological Maltreatment

Psychological maltreatment—also known as emotional abuse and neglect—refers to a repeated pattern of caregiver behavior or extreme incident(s) that conveys to children that they are worthless, flawed, unloved, unwanted, endangered, or only of value in meeting another's needs. Psychological maltreatment is the most difficult form of child maltreatment to identify. In part, the difficulty in detection occurs because the effects of psychological maltreatment, such as lags in development, learning problems, and speech disorders, are often evident in both children who have experienced and those who have *not* experienced maltreatment. Additionally, the effects of psychological maltreatment may become evident only in later developmental stages of the child's life (Hart & Brassard, 1987) (**Table 6-4**).

TABLE 6-4 **Forms of Psychological Maltreatment**

Form of Maltreatment	Definition
Terrorizing	Threatening violence against a child, placing a child in a recognizably dangerous situation, terrorizing a significant other of the child
Spurning	Belittling, hostile rejecting, ridiculing
Isolating	Confining the child, placing unreasonable limitations on the child's freedom of movement, restricting the child from social interactions
Exploiting or corrupting	Modeling antisocial behavior such as criminal activities, encouraging prostitution, permitting substance abuse
Denying emotional responsiveness	Ignoring the child's attempts to interact, failing to express affection
Mental health, medical, and educational neglect	Refusing to allow or failing to provide treatment for serious mental health or medical problems, ignoring the need for services for serious educational needs

Data from Hart, S. N. & Brassard, M. R. 1987. A major threat to children's mental health: psychological maltreatment. *American Psychologist, 42,* 161–165.

Fetal Death

In 1969 Teresa Keeler, 8 months pregnant, was beaten unconscious by her jealous ex-husband, Robert Keeler, who told her during the attack he was going to "stomp it out of her." Later, at the hospital, Keeler delivered a stillborn baby girl who suffered a fractured skull. Prosecutors attempted to charge Robert Keeler with the beating of his wife and for the murder of the fetus, but the California Supreme Court dismissed the charges, stating that only someone born alive could be killed and the fetus was not a human being (Montaldo, 2011).

Fetal death refers to the spontaneous intrauterine death of a fetus at any time during pregnancy. Fetal deaths later in pregnancy (at 20 weeks of gestation or more, or 28 weeks or more, for example) are also sometimes referred to as stillbirths. In the United States state laws require the reporting of fetal deaths, and federal law mandates national collection and publication of fetal death data. Most states report fetal deaths of 20 weeks of gestation or more and/or 350 grams birth weight. However, a few states report fetal deaths for all periods of gestation. Fetal death data are published annually by the National Center for Health Statistics, in reports and as individual-record data files. Historically, under both English common law and U.S. law, the fetus has not been recognized as a person with full rights. Instead, legal rights have centered on the mother, with the fetus treated as a part of her. Nevertheless, U.S. law has in certain instances granted the fetus limited rights, particularly as medical science has made it increasingly possible to directly view, monitor, diagnose, and treat the fetus as a patient.

Due to public pressure the debate over fetal rights intensified and legislation began to define the fetus as a person under fetal homicide or "feticide" laws. Such legislation is debated under names such as the Fetal Protection Act, the Preborn Victims of Violence Act, and the Unborn Victim of Violence Act. On April 1, 2004, President Bush signed into federal law the Unborn Victims of Violence Act, also known as "Laci and Conner's Law." This law states that any "child in utero" is considered to be a legal victim if injured or killed during the commission of a federal crime of violence. The Bill defined "child in utero" as "a member of the species homo sapiens, at any stage of development, who is carried in the womb" (p. 1).

The fetal homicide law was used to prosecute Scott Peterson with two counts of murder of Laci Peterson, his wife, and their 7-month unborn son, Conner. Peterson, 36, was sentenced to death by lethal injection in March 2005 after being convicted of both homicides and disposing of his pregnant wife in the San Francisco Bay on Christmas Eve day of 2002. His case is currently on appeal (Scott Peterson, 2005). Further, former pro football player for the Carolina Panthers, Rae Carruth, was convicted of conspiracy to commit the murder of Cherica Adams, who was 7 months pregnant with his child. He was also found guilty of shooting into an occupied vehicle and of using an instrument to kill a fetus. Adams died as a result of the gunshot wounds, but her son was born 10 weeks premature in an emergency department before Cherica died. Carruth received close to the maximum sentence of 19 to 24 years in prison. Co-defendant Michael Kennedy, 35, testified against Carruth and spent 14 years and 9 months behind bars for second-degree murder at the Central Prison in Raleigh. He was released July 2011. Carruth is set to be released in October 2018, and the shooter, co-defendant Van Brett Watkins, is expected to be released in March 2048 (*Charlotte Observer*, 2011).

■ Theories of Child Maltreatment

Theories of child maltreatment drive an understanding of how abuse and neglect occur and underscore the need for an understanding of etiology to focus intervention efforts where they will be most effective. Theoretical frameworks that explain the complex causes of child maltreatment are helpful to the measurement, study, and treatment of the child victim. Several frameworks have been proposed over the years, such as the intergenerational transmission of violence, social learning theory, and environmental circumstances.

Intergenerational Transmission of Violence

Punitive child-rearing practice was the focus of early longitudinal studies of the etiology of antisocial and criminal behavior (Glueck & Glueck, 1950; Robins, 1966). Paternal discipline (corporal punishment, authoritarian attitudes, strict discipline), maternal supervision (laxness), parental affection toward the child (rejection), family disruption (divorce), and deviant parental characteristics (substance abuse, mental problems, criminality) were core elements in the Glueck model of criminality prediction. Later studies included factors such as lack of interaction between parents and the child, parental conflicts and disagreement on child-rearing methods, socioeconomic difficulties, parental criminality, alcoholism, and mental health problems (Eron, Huesmann, & Zelli, 1991).

The longitudinal findings that show both child abuse and child neglect may lead to antisocial and criminal behavior and/or abuse of one's own children have been called the intergenerational transmission of violence, the cycle of violence, the abused to abuser theory, and the victim to offender approach. Even before Kempe, Silverman, Steele, Droegemuller, and Silver (1962) reported prevalence of parental violence directed at their children and described the "battered child syndrome," psychiatric case studies suggested that cruel punishment, severe discipline, and other kinds of physical abuse could produce later violent behavior (Satten, Menninger, Rosen, & Mayman, 1960; Silver, Dublin, & Lourie, 1969).

One important issue concerns "abuse-resistant" or resilient children who were maltreated but who managed to survive without later antisocial or aggressive behaviors. Most reviews of the cycle of violence hypothesis suggest that the severity, frequency, and perpetrator of abuse; the absence or presence of compensatory or protective factors; and the intrinsic vulnerabilities or strengths of the child may play an important role in determining the consequences (Haapasalo & Pokela, 1999).

Social Learning Theory

Social learning theory argues that abusive parents provide aggressive models for their children (Huesmann & Eron, 1986). McCord (1988) proposed that parental aggressiveness may be transmitted to children in the cycle of aggression by two processes: (1) by teaching them that expressive behavior, including injurious actions, is normal and justified and (2) by teaching that egocentrism is both normal and desired and aggression is permissible in getting others to do what one wishes.

Ecological Theory

Initially, the focus was on parental psychopathology; however, a more useful approach focuses on the abnormalities in the parent–child relationship (Bavolek, 2000) in the context of an ecological model of parenting (Belsky, 1985). Bavolek (2000) noted the following four abnormalities in the parent–child relationship that can lead to abuse or neglect:

- Inappropriate parental expectations of the child
- Lack of empathy toward the child's needs
- Parent's belief in physical punishment
- Parental role reversal

According to Belsky (1985), these parental thoughts, feelings, and behaviors need to be considered in an ecological model in which the parent–child relationship is viewed as existing in layers of systems, including the family, the extended family, the social setting, and the cultural context. How parents feel about and behave toward their child are influenced by characteristics of the child (e.g., unwanted), parent (abused during childhood), family (domestic violence), social setting (poor housing), and cultural contact (violence in the neighborhood). This more complex approach to understanding parenting behaviors in general also can be used in targeting interventions to support the parent–child relationship, such as helping families by linking them to services for depressed parents, housing, treatment facilities, and so on.

Part of the ecological theory includes environmental circumstances that can elicit stressful behaviors. Gil (1979) termed the social setting in which life experiences aggravate the "triggering context" for abusive parents. Several stressors include family structure such as the single parent, lack of family support, and extreme levels of economic deprivation.

Attention to Prevention

A major focus has been on prevention over the past decades. A major strategy has been the use of regular and frequent home visiting for socially high-risk, first-time mothers, beginning during pregnancy or shortly after the child's birth and through the first several years of life. The home visitors have been nurses and focus on the following:

- To provide advice about and model effective parenting

- To help mothers develop parenting skills and good relationships with their infants
- To help mothers make good decisions about returning to school, choice of day care, and relationship with baby's father
- To recognize early problems related to family violence and maltreatment in the home
- To help ensure the child receives appropriate medical care
- To help families link to community-based services, such as mental health services for the mother or developmental services for the child

■ Dynamics of Disclosure in Child Abuse

Disclosure, or telling someone of the abuse, varies by type of child maltreatment. Usually, visible signs of physical abuse, such as cuts, bruises, burns, or broken bones, are present. In neglect, there will be poor hygiene, weight loss, or withdrawn behavior. Sexual abuse symptoms include stomachaches, headaches, and development of fears, anxiety, or sexualized behaviors. However, in sexual abuse typically children do not immediately or directly tell someone they have been abused. Disclosures are more likely to arise after an extended period of time when the perpetrator is no longer in the environment or after some type of emotional upheaval.

Several factors influence a child's ability and willingness to disclose sensitive information, especially around the identity of an abuser. One influence is the response of the caregiver, professional, or police officer to the child's disclosure of abuse. If the person reacts with shock or negativity or disbelieves the child, there may be no further information given. There may be denial or even a recantation. The dynamics of child sexual abuse are pressure, sex, and secrecy in cases in which there is a known relationship between victim and abuser. First, the abuser must pressure the child by developing a relationship and then groom the child for the sexual relationship. This grooming can take weeks and months before a sexual intent is started. Second, the abuser then engages the child in sexual activities that can range from fondling to penetration. Third, for an abuser to be successful with a child victim, he or she must try to conceal the deviant behavior from others. More likely than not, he or she will try to pledge the child to secrecy in several ways. The dynamics are the setting for the various causes of delayed disclosure. The psychological factors that can lead a victim to disclose after a delay usually depend on who is a trusted person in the victim's support network. Delay can be

TABLE 6-5 **Causes of Delayed Disclosure of Abuse**

	Definition
Relationship of victim and offender	When the relationship involves family, it is less likely a victim will disclose due to the issue of family loyalty.
Age difference	The younger the victim, the more likely it is the victim will not disclose.
Pressure by the offender	The offender may use various strategies to ensure secrecy or merely direct the victim not to tell, e.g., "this is our special secret."
Threats	The offender may threaten the victim with some consequence or harm if he or she tells. The victim may fear punishment if he or she tells.
Repercussions	The victim may believe he or she will not be taken seriously or that there will be negative repercussions from telling.
Communication	The victim may not know what or how to tell about the sexual abuse. He or she may not know the words to use.
Fears	The victim may fear abandonment or rejection if he or she tells.
Emotions	The victim may have a wide range of emotions such as fear, guilt, shame, and embarrassment. If the abuser has authority over the victim, it will be difficult for the victim to disclose, as he or she may fear betrayal of the relationship.

days, weeks, months, or years. Victims may give a subtle message to see a person's reaction, may become symptomatic and an alert adult picks up the cues and helps the victim disclose, or victims learn more about sexual abuse and are able to report themselves (**Table 6-5**).

■ Effect of Traumatic Events on Children

The research in the field of child maltreatment has increased markedly. This research has had an impact on practice, understanding the scope of the problem, and the short- and long-term consequences of child maltreatment. These studies have made clear that child maltreatment is just not a childhood problem but can leave lasting problems. Research has also contributed to describing the phenomenon of child maltreatment and the range of clinical presentations and findings.

A traumatic event may be a sudden and unexpected occurrence that causes intense fear and may involve a threat of physical harm or actual physical harm. Or, a traumatic event may occur over time and include multiple types of abuses. A traumatic experience, whether sudden or chronic in nature, can have a profound effect on the physical health, mental health, and development of the child.

Children exhibit a wide range of symptoms depending on the type of maltreatment. Common general symptoms include withdrawn behavior, depression, sleeping and eating changes, development of fears and phobias, and psychosomatic symptoms (stomachaches, headaches). School problems may begin, such as absences or drops in grades. Children can begin to ignore health habits and develop poor hygiene or, in contrast, excessive bathing. Children may become highly anxious or feel guilty. Children can feel stigmatized and develop symptoms such as feelings of guilt/responsibility for the abuse. Children can develop feelings around betrayal that include lack of trust, especially of those who were supposed to be protective and nurturing. Children also feel powerlessness.

Children who are victims of sexual abuse may develop aversive feelings about sex, overvaluing sex, sexual identity problems, and hypersexual or sexual avoidance. There is no standard or typical symptom that can identify an individual as having survived incest. Individual reactions and symptoms depend on age at time of abuse, age at time of disclosure, support (or lack of support) from other caregivers, length of abuse, sex of the victim, and perpetrator.

Developmental Traumatology

Developmental traumatology is a key way to understand child trauma. That is, how children process trauma depends on their age and level of development. By understanding how children experience traumatic events and how they express their lingering distress over the experience, parents, clinicians, and school personnel can better respond and help them through this challenging time.

In general, for children a traumatic experience may cause ongoing feelings of concern for their own safety and the safety of others. These children may become preoccupied with thoughts about their actions during the event, often times experiencing guilt or shame over what they did or did not do at the time. They might engage in constant retelling of the traumatic event or may describe being overwhelmed by their feelings of fear or sadness.

Preschool children may lose recently acquired developmental milestones and may increase behaviors such as bedwetting and thumb sucking, and regress to simpler speech. They may become clingy to their parents and worry about their parent's safety and return. These young children may also become more irritable with more temper tantrums and more difficulty calming down. A few children may show the reverse behavior and become very withdrawn, subdued, or even mute after a traumatic event. These children may have difficulties falling or staying asleep or have nightmares about the event or other bad dreams. Typically, these children will process the event through posttraumatic play. For example, one child bitten by a dog would, months later, go under a dinner table and bite the legs of people. This is an example of repetition of the traumatic event and will continue until the child's anxiety is reduced.

Children exposed to a traumatic event feel self-conscious about their emotional responses to the event. They often experience feelings of shame and guilt about the traumatic event and may express fantasies about revenge and retribution. A traumatic event for adolescents may foster a radical shift in the way these students think about the world. Some of these adolescents may begin to engage in self-destructive or accident-prone and reckless behaviors. There may be a shift in their interpersonal relationships with family members, teachers, and classmates. These adolescents may show a change in their school performance, attendance, and behavior.

Children with Developmental Disabilities

Children with developmental disability or other physical challenges are exposed to abuse at a significantly high rate (National Child Traumatic Stress Network, 2004). These situations continue to be fraught with issues relative to lack of reporting and accurate assessment, often due to impaired communication or the perception by others that these cases cannot be successfully prosecuted or treated.

Although violence is widespread in the United States, the rate of this problem related to those with a developmental disability is misunderstood, and, at times, the survivors are virtually "invisible." Of interest to the interdisciplinary team including family, psychiatric nurses, and other community health practitioners are the mental health consequences for those persons with developmental disabilities. In the flurry of activity after traumatic events, the loss and related bereavement process, along with long-term effects, may be misinterpreted and overlooked in "translation" as the team endeavors to assess and understand the impact. What may be different in comparison with other survivors are the ways they think about themselves as victims, react to the violent event, and express their fears and ongoing concerns (Focht-New, Clements, Barol, Service, & Faulkner, 2008).

Violence and abuse against children with developmental disability often results in intense and confusing feelings and can activate fears and concerns regarding their own vulnerability (including the awareness they may be unable to protect themselves). They may also become fearful of the potential for future violence. Children with developmental disability, however, can have responses that are uniquely difficult because they are not always adequately prepared to decipher and manage what they are feeling. Numerous feelings may arise simultaneously and be difficult for the individual to articulate and the caregiver to understand. They may experience multidirectional anger at the offender, those they perceive did not protect them, or toward themselves for feeling they could have done something to prevent the violence. Feelings of abandonment by their caregivers may surface or great physical and emotional pain and sorrow that may have accompanied the violence. The child may express their anger, pain, and trauma by becoming withdrawn or depressed or developing physical symptoms (Burgess, Hartman, & Clements, 1995; Sunderland, 1995).

Consequences of Child Abuse Extend into Adult Life

There have been major efforts to understand the consequences of maltreatment. The following three epidemiological approaches have been used to investigate this problem:

- Use of longitudinal cohorts to follow maltreated children over time to look at developmental problems, juvenile or adult violence, mental health problems, and substance abuse.
- Use of case-control design in which cases are adults with a specific problem, such as depression, and controls are adults who do not have the problem. The subjects are then asked about childhood experiences with maltreatment.
- A third approach identifies a sample of adults from a specific population or geographic areas and asks about physical and sexual abuse. Rates of the outcomes are then compared to groups with and without certain past experiences.

In addition to epidemiologic studies concerning the consequences of child maltreatment, there is new interest in how early experiences affect the development of the brain and the neuroendocrine system.

■ Complex Child Trauma

Complex trauma outcomes refer to the range of clinical symptomatology that appears after such exposures. Exposure to traumatic stress in early life is associated with enduring sequelae that not only incorporate, but also extend beyond, posttraumatic stress disorder (PTSD). These sequelae span multiple domains of impairment and include (1) self-regulatory, attachment, anxiety, and affective disorders in infancy and childhood; (2) addictions, aggression, social helplessness, and eating disorders; (3) dissociative, somataform, cardiovascular, metabolic, and immunological disorders; (4) sexual disorders in adolescence and adulthood; and (5) revictimization (Dube et al., 2001).

Cause of Complex Trauma

The growing field of developmental traumatology is providing us with insights as to how the mechanisms of abuse and neglect can influence behavior. Early sustained abuse can produce physiological changes in the developing brain resulting in difficulty modulating emotional responses (including anger and depression), difficulty interpreting social situations, and difficulty in thinking that contributes to impulsivity, antisocial behavior, and sexual misconduct (Schwartz, Prentky, Pimental, & Cavanaugh, 2006). Essentially, early life attachments (also called bonding) translate into a blueprint of how the child will perceive situations outside the family. Positive attachment based on warmth, affection, caring, protective behaviors, and accountability leads to basic trust. It is at the core of building a social human being. Through attachment, the person gets feedback for the emerging of self. Around 18 months of age, there is consolidation of a sense of self. Early development of the ability to self-soothe provides an inner core of calmness and the ability to avoid being overwhelmed by stimuli and results in an integrated sense of self.

Social bonding can fail or become narrow and selective. Caretakers can ignore, rationalize, or normalize various behaviors in the developing child or, through their own problems (such as violent behavior), support the child's developing distortions and projections. An ineffective social environment can occur through aggressive or sexual behavior being ignored or by failing to intervene to correct behavior.

The child who lacks protection by a caretaker experiences tremendous anxiety, is overwhelmed, and may survive through dissociating him- or herself from the trauma. This dissociation also inhibits a sense of feeling connected to the outside world. Children become isolated and disconnected from others.

Case of Complex Trauma

One of the most powerful forces impacting a child's development is the caregiver history. Homes in which a parent abuses drugs or alcohol, is sexually indiscriminate, has long prison confinement, is absent from the home, or has serious psychiatric history affect a child negatively. The lack of consistent caregiving that occurs when a child is born into an abusive or neglectful family and/or has inconsistent care or institutional placement can lead to deficits in social and interpersonal skills. Appropriate caregiving during early childhood facilitates neurological development so that impulses arising from the primitive parts of the brain are integrated with the reasoning capacities in the higher levels of the brain. However, lack of consistent caregiving is known to disrupt normal development in a variety of ways.

Reactive attachment disorder is one condition that may develop because the child's basic needs for comfort, affection, and nurturing are ignored and positive, caring attachments with others are never established. This may permanently change the child's growing brain, hurting the ability to establish future relationships (Mayo Clinic staff, n.d.).

This reactive attachment disorder may take many paths depending on the child's abusive upbringing. Children who are subjected to changes in caregivers never learn to develop secure attachments of any sort and often develop highly ambivalent attachment styles. These children have problems empathizing with others and may act out in aggressive and sexually inappropriate ways.

Jane was a low-birth-weight infant (2 pounds); her mother was addicted to and took drugs during pregnancy. There were also high amounts of lead in the house. Jane developed a learning problem stated to be caused by the high lead and that required her to be placed in special schools and learning programs.

Jane, a twin, was one of eight children all from different fathers. Two brothers (one died at birth) and a sister were deceased. Her father, now deceased, was absent from her life. Jane was a child of inconsistent caregiving. She lived with an aunt and uncle when her mother could not care for her children; she was returned to the mother when she was 6. Her mother served a significant amount of time in prison for theft, burglary, and drug use. The uncle, although not a blood relative, also lived with the family for over 40 years. A man named Ralph also lived at the house around the mid-1990s; the mother had planned to marry him but he started using drugs. The mother states she stopped using drugs. A female friend of her mother's also lived at the house on occasion, as she and the mother were romantically involved. Jane reported sibling incest when she was 6 or 7 with her brother who was 4 years older. He offered her to some of his friends for sex. Jane began taking money for sex as a young adolescent.

Jane was already having major conflicts with family, school, and peers in her early teens. She had run away from home, was using drugs, and was homeless. She was hospitalized for fighting her brothers. They teased her and called her a whore; she argued with them and stated she felt like punching them in the face. She claimed her mother cursed at her, hit her with a stick, and threatened to kick her out of the house before a suicide attempt. She also had a case pending for retail theft.

DIAGNOSTIC CONSIDERATIONS Exposure to complex trauma in children carries an enormous cost to society, both in lives impacted and dollars spent. Although in many ways the costs are inestimable, the repercussions of childhood trauma may be measured in medical costs, mental health utilization, societal cost, and the psychological toll on its victims.

The current psychiatric diagnostic classification system does not have an adequate category to capture the full range of difficulties that traumatized children experience. Although the narrowly defined PTSD diagnosis is often used, it rarely captures the extent of the developmental impact of multiple and chronic trauma exposure. Other diagnoses common in abused and neglected children include depression, attention deficit hyperactivity disorder, oppositional defiant disorder, conduct disorder, generalized anxiety disorder, separation anxiety disorder, and reactive attachment disorder. Each of these diagnoses captures an aspect of the traumatized child's experience but frequently does not represent the whole picture. As a result treatment often focuses on the particular behavior identified rather than on the core deficits that underlie the presentation of complexly traumatized children.

Suicidal Impulses and Violence Against Others

The adult world's capacity to assess adolescent behavior is often compromised by the resistance and inability to recollect and relate to one's own adolescent development. Consequently, there is a split in terms of the adult's view of the adolescent. Some adults are constantly critical and negative in their appraisals and consideration of adolescents, whereas others are indulgent beyond reasonableness and accept all types of deviant and disturbed behavior as simply "a phase of growing up." Somewhere in between there is an area of understanding that is necessary both to be tolerant of adolescent behavior and to be cognizant of patterns of behavior that indicate a young person is in trouble.

Childhood physical and sexual abuse are related to numerous problems for victims later in life, including attempted suicide (Joiner et al., 2007) and repeated suicidal behavior (Ystgaard, Hestetun, Loeb, & Mehlum, 2004). A powerful graded relationship exists between adverse childhood experiences and risk of attempted suicide throughout the life span (Dube et al., 2001). Childhood physical and sexual abuse, abuse-related injuries, and traumatic brain injuries were found to be prevalent in populations of female prison inmates who have engaged in high rates of suicidal behaviors (Brewer-Smyth, Burgess, & Shults, 2004). Sexual abuse by a family member has been related to a decreased diurnal variation of the stress hormone cortisol and increased homicidal behavior in females (Brewer-Smyth & Burgess, 2008). Yet little is understood about risk factors for violent, homicidal, and suicidal behaviors of females. In particular, relationships between these behaviors and physiological associations with previous abuse-related injuries and neurological impairment need to be defined.

Suicide attempts, also described as parasuicidal behavior or nonfatal suicide-related behavior, are failed attempts to kill oneself (Hauenstein, 2001). Self-directed violence is a significant cause of morbidity and mortality in the United States. Each year there are 30,000 deaths from suicide, compared to 17,000 homicides (Centers for Disease Control and Prevention, 2004). Suicide continues to be the third leading cause of death among teenagers and young adults (Centers for Disease Control and Prevention, 2004). The majority of youth who engage in suicidal behavior, however, do not die. An estimate of 8 to 25 attempted suicides occur per every suicide death (Moscicki, 2001). Risk factors for attempted suicide by youth include depression, physical or sexual abuse, and disruptive behavior (Petronis, Samuels, Moscicki, & Anthony, 1990; U.S. Public Health Service, 2001).

Violence that is related to abuse is not only directed toward the self. In a study of school shootings in 37 communities across the United States, Vossekuil, Fein, Reddy, Borum, and Modzeleski (2002) found that in 78% of cases perpetrators exhibited some form of suicidal behavior or ideation before or during the attack. Even among teenagers who engage in less violent forms of violence, studies suggest they also are more likely to struggle with suicidal thoughts and behaviors than their nonviolent peers (Borowsky, Hogan, & Ireland, 1997; Coker et al., 2000; Swahn, Lubell, & Simon, 2004). Lubell and Vetter (2006) suggested that it should not be terribly surprising that suicidality and interpersonal violence are correlated.

However, despite this expanding research, efforts to develop and implement effective suicide and violence prevention strategies continue to occur in relative isolation from one another. Lubell and Vetter (2006) argued that this bifurcation between researchers and practitioners does not take advantage of opportunities to integrate knowledge and maximize the impact of prevention programs. The purpose of their study was to reevaluate existing data of incarcerated females in the context of youthful suicide ideation and behaviors and criminal behaviors toward others.

Not only are suicide and interpersonal violence leading health problems in the United States, but these two problems have also been linked in the psychiatric literature for over a century. Early psychological for-mulations by Freud (1963) and Menninger (1933) suggested that hostile and aggressive impulses underlying suicidal and violent behavior develop from similar frustrations within the individual (Lubell & Vetter, 2006). Expanding on these theories, Plutchik and colleagues developed a two-stage model of the relationship between "outward and inward directed aggressiveness" (Plutchik, 1995; Plutchik, van Praag, & Conte, 1989).

Case of Matricide

A 16-year-old youth was convicted of stabbing and beating his 48-year-old mother after a dispute over a letter from the school regarding his nonat-tendance. The argument continued into the following day; the juvenile threw bleach at this mother and picked up a kitchen knife. She followed him into the bathroom; he stabbed her numerous times and then struck her over the head with a baseball bat. He ransacked the bureaus and threw his blood-stained clothes and bat into a nearby marsh. The juvenile later returned to the house with a friend and found the body. After intensive investigation, the son confessed. The crime is cause-specific, family vio-lence. There was information that the mother had physically and sexually abused the youth as a small child.

■ Treatment for Child Victims

The immediate and long-term consequences of child abuse and neglect point to the fact that many child victims will need treatment interven-tion. Such intervention can occur on a crisis basis or may address more longstanding issues.

Crisis Intervention

The immediate concern in crisis situations involving children is safety and security. Child protection services focus on assessing immediate risk and ensuring the child is safe from further harm in the immediate future. Once safety is established, crisis intervention focuses on helping the child and whatever supportive adults may be in his or her life. This is a highly supportive intervention that builds on client strengths, helps identify short-term goals, and helps clients identify how they will go about attaining them. When addressing the needs of children and families in crisis, close cooperation between community services ensures the maximum benefit from utilization of resources. Poor communication and lack of coordi-nated efforts between health, legal, social service, education, volunteer, and church-related resources can create extreme frustration for families who are in crisis. For instance, many clients have grown to distrust agencies that promise cooperation from other organizations. Often, they have been told that an agency would help, only to learn they are ineligible, must go on a waiting list, must subscribe to the helper's value system, or must accept a substitute service. Even worse, some clients have been criticized and humiliated for not understanding agency eligibility requirements.

To provide stability and consistent support for families, crisis workers can guide them to appropriate organizations and services, but it helps when crisis workers give the name of a specific person rather than simply a telephone number. During the initial crisis, crisis workers may even need to accompany the clients to appointments. As the family begins to stabilize, members can be expected to take more individual initiative. As a support system the crisis worker should always be available by phone or beeper. Advocacy for clients, in helping them access and use resources, dramatically enhances the therapeutic relationship.

As identified by the U.S. Department of Health and Human Services (1994), abusive families' diverse needs require services from many different organizations. Presently, services are fragmented into various aspects, including investigation, crisis intervention, concrete services, and long-term treatment, and health, social, legal, housing, education, employment, mental health, spiritual, and financial all fall under the mandates of different governmental and community organizations. So-called wrap-around services provide whatever the family thinks it needs to stabilize. Obviously, this requires strong, collaborative efforts among community resources (U.S. Department of Health and Human Services, 1994).

Trauma-Focused Cognitive-Behavioral Therapy

Evidence is growing that trauma-focused cognitive-behavioral therapy (TF-CBT) is an effective treatment for sexually abused children, including those who have experienced multiple other traumatic events. Most studies that have evaluated TF-CBT have been well designed (Cohen, Deblinger, Mannarino, & Steer, 2004; Cohen, Mannarino, & Knudsen, 2005). This treatment model represents a synthesis of trauma-sensitive interventions and well-established CBT principles (Beck, 1993).

TF-CBT takes a child and parent psychotherapy approach for children and adolescents who are experiencing major emotional and behavioral difficulties related to traumatic life events. It is a components-based treatment model that incorporates trauma-sensitive interventions with cognitive behavioral, family, and humanistic principles and techniques (Cohen, Mannarino, & Deblinger, 2006).

The therapy was developed to resolve PTSD and depressive and anxiety symptoms, as well as to address underlying distortions about self-blame, safety, the trustworthiness of others, and the world (Cohen, Mannarino, & Deblinger, 2006). The treatment also fits traumatic experiences into a broader context of children's lives so their primary identity is not that of a victim.

Core components of TF-CBT are psychoeducation about child trauma and PTSD, affective modulation skills, individualized stress-management skills, an introduction to the cognitive triad (relationships between thoughts, feeling, and behaviors), creating a trauma narrative, cognitive processing, safety skills, and a parental treatment component. Parents are seen separately from their children for most of the treatment and receive interventions that parallel those provided to the child, along with parenting skills. Several joint parent–child sessions are also included to enhance family communication. Most TF-CBT treatment studies have consisted of 12 treatment sessions (Cohen, Mannarino, & Deblinger, 2006).

ATTACHMENT TRAUMA THERAPY Traditional therapy techniques are usually unproductive with attachment-impaired children, because they rely on the child's ability to form trusting relationships, which an attachment-impaired child is unable to do. Attachment therapy is a multidimensional intervention with the primary goal of creating or restoring a secure bond of trust between a parent and child, not between the therapist and child. Attachment therapy involves the parents and the child working together rather than the therapist working with the child alone. Attachment therapy is directive, experiential, and confrontational, in that it deals with the drama, trauma, and truth of the child's life.

Consequently, one needs to examine the nature of their framework for not only assessing the individual child but for assessing the social and family contexts of a child. For those children whose sense of other and self is compromised by abuse and there is withdrawal from the world of people and personal achievement and satisfaction, we often find an array of avoidant behaviors. Sometimes the pressure of unhappiness and unchanging family patterns often find these children and youth pressed to a singular alternative: that is, to eliminate the people who are abusing them. This is where we have the tragic outcome of isolated youths killing a parent or parents or people who have been subjecting them to continuous harmful situations. At times, in the context of running away from home, these same youths can find themselves in a peer relationship following someone in aggressive acts toward strangers.

■ Summary

The challenges to providing intervention and treatment to victimized children and their families are clear. Early recognition of child maltreatment provides an opportunity to reduce the pain of the child and help families to change their behaviors to assist their children. Neutralizing the impact of trauma on the development of the child may prevent victim to offender role reversal and also decrease any suicidal thoughts. Intervention programs for children need to be part of every mental health center.

■ Key Terms

Child maltreatment: Describes the four types of child mistreatment: physical abuse, sexual abuse, emotional abuse, and neglect. In many cases children are the victims of more than one type of abuse. The abusers can be parents or other family members, caretakers such as teachers and babysitters, acquaintances (including other children), and (in rare instances) strangers.

Developmental disability: A cognitive, emotional, or physical impairment, especially one related to abnormal sensory or motor development, that appears in infancy or childhood and involves a failure or delay in progressing through the normal developmental stages of childhood.

Developmental traumatology: The systemic investigation of the psychiatric and psychobiological impact of overwhelming and chronic interpersonal violence on the developing child. This relatively new area of study synthesizes knowledge from an array of scientific fields, including developmental psychopathology, developmental neuroscience, and stress and trauma research.

Disclosure: A child telling that someone has abused or hurt him or her. This can be very difficult, and how the professional/investigator responds can be critical for all facets of subsequent intrapsychic and interpersonal recovery.

Fetal homicide: Also called feticide, it is an act that causes the death of a fetus.

Fetal rights: The rights of any unborn human fetus, which is generally a developing human from roughly 8 weeks after conception to birth.

Incest: Sexual intercourse with a descendent by blood or adoption.

Statutory rape: Sexual intercourse with a person under the age of consent and by an adult age 18 years or older.

■ Discussion Questions

1. Do you believe there were more instances of child abuse 100 years ago? Why or why not?
2. Why might the rates of reported child abuse be decreasing in recent surveys?
3. Is it actually possible for a 10-year-old to be at risk for suicide? Explain your answer.
4. Should fetal death be included as child abuse?
5. Why is the age of the child when the violence occurred an important part of assessment and planning?

■ Resources

American Academy of Pediatrics: Violence Prevention
    http://www.aap.org/healthtopics/violprev.cfm

American Bar Association. Invisible Victims: Violence Against Persons with Developmental Disabilities
    http://www.abanet.org/irr/hr/winter00humanrights/petersilia.htm

ARC: The ARC's Questions and Answers about People with Mental Retardation and Sexual Abuse
    http://www.wsf.org/behavior/guidelines/sexualabuse.htm

Centers for Disease Control and Prevention: FACT SHEET – Understanding suicide
    http://www.cdc.gov/ncipc/pub-res/suicide_factsheet2008.pdf

Centers for Disease Control and Prevention: Violence Prevention
    http://www.cdc.gov/ncipc/dvp/dvp.htm

Disability, Abuse & Personal Rights Project
    http://www.disability-abuse.com/

Kid-Safe Network
    http://www.kidsafenetwork.com/

National Center for Missing and Exploited Children (NCMEC) – CYBERTIPLINE: Reporting categories
    http://www.missingkids.com/missingkids/servlet /PageServlet?LanguageCountry=en_US&PageId=2447

Police Notebook: Kid Safety on the Internet
    http://www.ou.edu/oupd/kidsafe/start.htm

References

American Psychiatric Association. (2002). *Diagnostic and statistical manual of mental disorders* (4th ed.). Washington, DC: American Psychiatric Association.

American Public Health Association. (1975). Policy statement database. Child abuse. Policy Date: 1/1/1975. Policy Number: 7512. Retrieved from http://www.apha.org/advocacy/policy/policysearch/default.htm?id=790

American Public Health Association. (1986). Policy statement database. Prevention of child abuse. Policy Date: 1/1/1986. Policy Number: 8614(PP). Retrieved from http://www.apha.org/advocacy/policy/policysearch/default.htm?id=1129

Ayoub, C., & Alexander, R. (1998). Definitional issues in Munchausen by proxy. *American Professional Society on the Abuse of Children Advisor 11*(1), 7–10.

Bavolek, S.J. (2000). *The nurturing parenting programs.* Washington, DC: Office of Juvenile Justice and Delinquency Prevention, U.S. Department of Justice.

Beck, A. (1993). *Cognitive therapy and the emotional disorders.* New York: Penguin.

Belsky, J. (1985). The determinants of parenting: A process model. *Child Development, 55*(1), 83–96.

Borowsky, I.W., Hogan, M., & Ireland, M. (1997). Adolescent sexual aggression: Risk and protective factors. *Pediatrics, 100*(6), E7.

Brewer-Smyth, K., & Burgess, A.W. (2008). Childhood sexual abuse by a family member, salivary cortisol, and homicidal behavior of female prison inmates. *Nursing Research, 57*(3), 166–174.

Brewer-Smyth, K., Burgess, A.W., & Shults, J. (2004). Physical and sexual abuse, salivary cortisol, and neurological correlates of violent criminal behavior in female prison inmates. *Biological Psychiatry, 55*(1), 30–40.

Brown, S. (2011). *Against all odds.* New York: Harper.

Burgess, A.W., Hartman, C.R., & Clements, P.T. (1995). The biology of memory in childhood trauma. *Journal of Psychosocial Nursing, 33*(3), 16–26.

Centers for Disease Control and Prevention. (2004). Web-based Injury Statistics Query and Reporting System (WISQARS). Retrieved from www.cdc.gov/ncipc/wisqars

Charlotte Observer. (2011). Driver in Carruth murder case released from prison. Retrieved from http://www.charlotteobserver.com/2011/07/20/2469034/driver-in-carruth-murder-case.html#ixzz1T2bwfqT2

Clements, P.T., & Benasutti, K.M. (2003). Mental health aspects of child survivors of abuse and neglect. In E.R. Giardino & A.P. Giardino (Eds.), *Nursing approach to the evaluation of child maltreatment* (pp. 306–329). St. Louis, MO: G. W. Medical.

Clements, P.T., & DeRanieri, J.T. (2006). Youth exposure to violence, terrorism and sudden traumatic death. In R.M. Hammer, B. Moynihan, & E.M. Pagliaro (Eds.), *Forensic nursing: A handbook for practice* (pp. 305–320). Sudbury, MA: Jones & Bartlett.

Cohen, J.A., Deblinger, E., Mannarino, A.P., & Steer, R.A. (2004). A multisite, randomized controlled trial for children with sexual abuse-related PTSD symptoms. *Journal of the American Academy of Child and Adolescent Psychiatry, 43*, 393–403.

Cohen, J.A., Mannarino, A.P., & Deblinger, E. (2006). *Treating trauma and traumatic grief in children and adolescents.* New York: The Guilford Press.

Cohen, J.A., Mannarino, A.P., & Knudsen, K. (2005). Treating sexually abused children: 1 year follow-up of a randomized controlled trial. *Child Abuse & Neglect, 29*, 135–145.

Coker, A.L., McKeown, R.E., Sanderson, M., Davis, K.E., Valois, R.F., & Huebner, E.S. (2000). Severe dating violence and quality of life among South Carolina high school students. *American Journal of Preventive Medicine, 19*(4), 220–227.

deMause, L. (1998). The history of child abuse. *Journal of Psychohistory, 25*(3), 216–236.

Dube, S.R., Anda, R.F., Felitti, V.J., Chapman, D.P., Williamson, D.F., & Giles, W.H. (2001). Childhood abuse, household dysfunction, and the risk of attempted suicide throughout the life span: Findings from the Adverse Childhood Experiences Study. *Journal of the American Medical Association, 286*(24), 3089–3096.

Eron, L.D., Huesmann, L.R., & Zelli, A. (1991). The role of parental variables in the learning of aggression. In D.J. Pepler & K.H. Rubin (Eds.), *The development and treatment of childhood aggression* (pp. 169–188). Hillsdale, NJ: Erlbaum.

Finkelhor, D., & Dziuba-Leatherman, J. (1994). Children as victims of violence: A national survey. *Pediatrics, 94,* 413–420.

Finkelhor, D., & Jones, L. (2006). Why have child maltreatment and child victimization declined? *Journal of Social Issues, 62*, 685–716.

Focht-New, G., Clements, P.T., Barol, E., Service, K., & Faulkner, M. (2008). Persons with developmental disabilities exposed to interpersonal violence and crime: The impact of intrapsychic trauma. *Perspectives in Psychiatric Care: The Journal for Advanced Practice Psychiatric Nurses, 44*(1), 3–13.

Freud, S. (1963). In J. Strachey (Ed.), *The standard edition of the complete psychological works of Sigmund Freud* (Vol. 14). London: Hogarth Press.

Fry, E. (2011). A childhood biography of Oprah Winfrey. Retrieved from http://oprah.about.com/od/oprahbiography/p/oprahchildhood.htm

Gil, D.G. (1979). *Child abuse and violence*. New York: AMS Press.

Glueck, S., & Glueck, E.T. (1950). *Unraveling juvenile delinquency*. Cambridge, MA: Harvard University Press.

Groth, A.N. (1979). *Men who rape*. New York: Plenum.

Haapasalo, J., & Pokela, E. (1999). Child-rearing and criminality. *Aggression and Violent Behavior, 4*(1), 107–128.

Hart, S.N., & Brassard, M.R. (1987). A major threat to children's mental health: Psychological maltreatment. *American Psychologist, 42*, 161–165.

Hauenstein, E.J. (2001). Case finding and care in suicide: Children, adolescents, and adults. In M.A. Boyd (Ed.), *Psychiatric nursing: Contemporary practice*. Philadelphia: Lippincott Williams & Wilkins.

Hopper, J. (2007). Unavoidable controversies & biases, in historical contexts. Retrieved from http://www.jimhopper.com/abstats/#s-intro

Huesmann, L.R., & Eron, L.D. (1986). *Television and the aggressive child: A cross-national comparison*. Lawrence Erlbaum.

Joiner, T.E., Sachs-Ericsson, N.J., Wingate, L.R., Brown, J.S., Anestis, M.D., & Selby, E.A. (2007). Childhood physical and sexual abuse and lifetime number of suicide attempts: A persistent and theoretically important relationship. *Behaviour Research and Therapy, 45*(3), 539–547.

Kempe, C.H., Silverman, F.N., Steele, B.F., Droegemuller, W., & Silver, H.K. (1962). The battered-child syndrome. *Journal of the American Medical Association, 181*, 17–24.

Laci and Conner's Law. (2004). Unborn Victims of Violence Act. Legislative Report of 2004, Washington, DC.

LaSala, K.B., & Lynch, V.A. (2006). Child abuse and neglect. In V.A. Lynch & J.B. Duval (Eds.), *Forensic nursing* (pp. 249–259). St. Louis, MO: Mosby.

Leeb, R.T., Paulozzi, L., Melanson, C., Simon, T., & Arias, I. (2008). Child maltreatment surveillance: Uniform definitions for public health and recommended data elements, Version 1.0. Retrieved from http://www.cdc.gov/ViolencePrevention/pub/CMP-Surveillance.html

Leventhal, J.M. (2005). Overview of child maltreatment. In A.P. Giardino & R. Alexander (Eds.), *Child maltreatment*. St. Louis, MO: G. W. Medical Publishing.

Lubell, K.M., & Vetter, J.B. (2006). Suicide and youth violence presentation: The promise of an integrated approach. *Aggression and Violent Behavior, 11*(2), 167–175.

Mayo Clinic Staff. (2011). Reactive attachment disorder. Retrieved from http://www.mayoclinic.com/health/reactive-attachment-disorder/DS00988

McCord, J. (1988). Parental behavior in the cycle of aggression. *Psychiatry, 51*(1), 14–23.

Menninger, K.A. (1933). Psychoanalytic aspects of suicide. *International Journal of Psychoanalysis, 14,* 376–390.

Montaldo, C. (2011). Retrieved from http://www.Charles Montaldo.About.com

Moscicki, E.K. (2001). Epidemiology of completed and attempted suicide: Toward a framework for prevention. *Clinical Neuroscience Research, 1,* 310–323.

Mugavin, M.E. (2005). A meta-synthesis of filicide classification systems: Psychosocial and psychodynamic issues in women who kill their children. *Journal of Forensic Nursing, 1*(2), 65–72.

National Association of Counsel for Children. (n.d.a). Child maltreatment. Retrieved from http://www.naccchildlaw.org/childrenlaw /childmaltreatment.html

National Association of Counsel for Children. (n.d.b). Children and the law: Reporting child abuse. Retrieved from http://www.naccchildlaw.org /childrenlaw/reportingchildabuse.html

National Child Traumatic Stress Network. (2004). Facts on traumatic stress and children with developmental disabilities. Retrieved from http://www .nctsnet.org/nctsn_assets/pdfs/reports/traumatic_stress_developmen- tal_disabilities_final.pdf

National District Attorneys Association. (n.d.). Mandatory reporting of child abuse and neglect: State statutes and professional ethics. Retrieved from http://ndaa.org/pdf/mandatory_reporting_state_statutes.pdf

Petronis, K.R., Samuels, J.F., Moscicki, E.K., & Anthony, J.C. (1990). An epide- miologic investigation of potential risk factors for suicide attempts. *Social Psychiatry and Psychiatric Epidemiology, 25*(4), 193–199.

Pleck, E. (2003). Criminal approaches to family violence: 1640–1980. In M. Silberman (Ed.), *Violence and society: A reader* (pp. 161–173). Upper Saddle River, NJ: Prentice Hall.

Plutchik, R. (1995). Outward and inward directed aggressiveness: The interac- tion between violence and suicidality. *Pharmacopsychiatric, 28*(Suppl 2), 47–57.

Plutchik, R., van Praag, H.M., & Conte, H.R. (1989). Correlates of suicide and violence risk III: A two-stage model of countervailing forces. *Psychiatric Research, 28*(2), 215–225.

Regehr, C., & Kanani, K. (2010). *Essential law for social work practice in Canada* (2nd ed.). Toronto, Ontario, Canada: Oxford University Press.

Robertson, S. Age of consent laws, in children and youth in history, item #230, Retrieved from http://chnm.gmu.edu/cyh/teaching-modules/230

Robins, L. (1966). *Deviant children grown up.* Baltimore, MD: Williams & Wilkins.

Roesler, T., & Jenny, C. (2009). *Medical child abuse: Beyond Munchausen syndrome by proxy.* Washington, DC: American Academy of Pediatrics.

Satten, J., Menninger, K., Rosen, I., & Mayman, M. (1960). Murder without apparent motive: A study in personality disorganization. *American Journal of Psychiatry, 117,* 48–53.

Schwartz, D., Prentky, R.A., Pimental, A., & Cavanaugh, D. (2006). Descriptive study of precursors to sex offending among 813 boys and girls: Antecedent life experiences. *Victims & Offenders, 1*(4), 61–77.

"Scott Peterson sent to San Quentin". (2005). MSNBC. Retrieved from http://www.msnbc.msn.com/id/7217582/

Sedlak, A.J., Mettenburg, J., Basena, M., Petta, I., McPherson, K., Greene, A., & Li, S. (2010). Fourth National Incidence Study of Child Abuse and Neglect (NIS-4): Report to Congress, Executive Summary. Washington, DC: U.S. Department of Health and Human Services, Administration for Children and Families.

Silver, L.B., Dublin, C.C., & Lourie, R.S. (1969). Does violence breed violence? Contributions from a study of the child abuse syndrome. *American Journal of Psychiatry, 126,* 404–407.

Straus, M.A., Hamby, S.L., Finkelhor, D., Moore, D.W., & Runyon, D. (1998). Identification of child maltreatment with the Parent-Child Conflict Tactics Scales: Development and psychometric data for a national sample of American parents. *Child Abuse & Neglect, 22,* 249–270.

Sunderland, R. (1995). *Helping children cope with grief: A teacher's guide. Picking up the pieces* (2nd ed.). Fort Collins, CO: Services Corporation International.

Swahn, M., Lubell, K., & Simon, T. (2004). Suicide attempts and physical fighting among high school students—United States, 2001. *Journal of the American Medical Association, 292,* 428–429.

The Oprah Winfrey Show. (2006). Why 15-Year-Old Jessica Coleman Killed Her Baby. Retrieved from http://www.oprah.com/oprahshow/All-American-Tragedy

Trocme, N., Fallon, B., MacLaurin, B., Sinha, V., & Black, T. (2008). *Canadian incidence study on child abuse and neglect.* Ottawa: Public Health Agency Canada.

UNICEF. (2011). Child protection from violence, exploitation and abuse. Retrieved from http://www.unicef.org/protection/index_3717.html

United Nations. (2009). The Convention on the Rights of the Child. Retrieved from http://www2.ohchr.org/english/law/crc.htm

U.S. Department of Health and Human Services. (1994). Crisis intervention in child abuse and neglect user manual series. *Child Welfare Information Gateway.* Retrieved from http://www.childwelfare.gov/pubs/usermanuals /crisis/crisisj.cfm

U.S. Public Health Service. (2001). Suicide in the U.S.: Statistics and prevention. Retrieved from http://www.nimh.nih.gov/health/publications/suicide-in-the-us-statistics-and-prevention/index.shtml

Volpe, R. (2011). The Canadian encyclopedia, historica-dominion. Retrieved from http://thecanadianencyclopedia.com/index.cfm?PgNm=TCE& Params=A1ARTA0001576

Vossekuil, B., Fein, R.A., Reddy, M., Borum, R., & Modzeleski, W. (2002). *The final report and findings of the safe school initiative: Implications for the prevention of school attacks in the United States.* Washington, DC: U.S. Secret Service and the U.S. Department of Education.

West's Encyclopedia of American Law. (1998). Statutory rape. Farmington Hills, MI: The Gale Group.

World Health Organization. (2004). Guidelines for medico-legal care for victims of sexual violence. Retrieved from http://whqlibdoc.who.int /publications/2004/924154628X.pdf

World Health Organization. (2006). Prevention of child maltreatment—WHO scales up child maltreatment prevention activities. Retrieved from http:// www.who.int/violence_injury_prevention/violence/activities/child_ maltreatment/en/index.html

Ystgaard, M., Hestetun, I., Loeb, M., & Mehlum, L. (2004). Is there a specific relationship between childhood sexual and physical abuse and repeated suicidal behaviour? *Child Abuse and Neglect, 28,* 863–875.

Child Abduction and Exploitation

CHAPTER
7

Objectives

- To describe fetal, infant, and child abduction
- To define the types of missing children
- To identify vulnerable groups of children for abuse
- To describe international child labor laws and child trafficking

Key Terms

Alien
Child pornography
Child prostitution
Child trafficking
Fetal abduction
Infant abduction
Missing children
Thrownaways

Acknowledgment

We thank Paul Clements for his contributions to sections of this chapter written in the first edition of *Victimology*.

CASES

Child Prostitution

The Downtown Eastside, known as "Low Track" because of the incidence of drug abuse, drug-related crime, and prostitution, is a notorious neighborhood in Vancouver, British Columbia, Canada, a beautiful city bordered by the Pacific Ocean and the Rocky Mountains. Well known as Canada's poorest postal code, the area has been described as "a world of misery crammed into 10 blocks" (Matas & Peritz, 2008, p. 1). Drugs of choice are heroin and crack cocaine, supplied by motorcycle gangs or Asian cartels that stake out choice blocks and use brute force in defending their territory. In 1998 this area averaged one death per day from drug overdoses, the highest rate in Canadian history (Newton, n.d.).

Most of Vancouver's Eastside female addicts support their habits via prostitution, trolling the streets night and day, feeding on crack cocaine. Safe sex is an illusion in this neighborhood, which includes the highest HIV infection rate in North America (Newton, n.d.).

Even more disturbing about the Eastside is its "kiddy stroll," where child prostitutes as young as 11 (average age 14) offer sex for money. In 2001 an estimated 500 child prostitutes worked the area; however, true estimates are difficult because many young prostitutes are kept behind closed doors by pimps who solicit customers for them (Canadian Broadcasting Corporation, 2001). As one indicator, a 1995 survey of prostitutes in the Eastside revealed that 73% reported entering the sex trade as children. See **Figure 7-1**.

Child Kidnapping

On June 10, 1991, at age 11, Jaycee Dugard was kidnapped on her way to the school bus stop. She was abducted by a couple in a gray sedan as her stepfather watched from his driveway two blocks away. Eighteen years later she was discovered at the age of 29. Jaycee Dugard had been kept in a small concealed area behind the home of Phillip and Nancy Garrido in Antioch,

FIGURE 7-1 Missing persons from Vancouver's East Side.
© Andy Clark/Thomson Reuters

California, for 18 years. On August 26, 2009, she was discovered by serendipity in the course of another investigation. The day earlier, convicted sex offender Phillip Craig Garrido visited the campus of UC Berkeley accompanied by two young girls. Their unusual behavior sparked a police investigation. It was later revealed the girls were the children of the long-missing Jaycee Dugard.

Phillip and Nancy Garrido were charged with abduction, rape, and forcible confinement. At the trial Jaycee testified that she was forced to have sex with Garrido and was threatened with a stun gun if she did not comply. It was further revealed that Nancy Garrido was fully involved with the kidnapping and confinement of Jaycee. Jaycee's testimony stated that she and Nancy would watch television and have dinner together and that Nancy would at times offer to have sex with Garrido to spare Jaycee. During her time in captivity Jaycee Dugard bore two daughters, ages 11 and 15 at the time of her reappearance in 2009. She testified that she never tried to escape because she feared what would happen to her. On June 2, 2011, Phillip Garrido was sentenced to 431 years; his wife received 36 years to life in prison. See **Figure 7-2**.

Victims have the opportunity to read or to have read a victim impact statement at the time of a criminal trial against their victimizer. The following is the victim impact statement made by Jaycee Dugard at the April 28, 2011, sentencing hearing, where Phillip and Nancy Garrido pled guilty to kidnapping and rape. Dugard, who did not attend the sentencing, had sent a written statement that was read in court (Dugard, 2011):

> I chose not to be here today because I refuse to waste another second of my life in your presence. I've chosen to have my mom read this for me. Phillip Garrido, you are wrong. I could never say that to you before, but I have the freedom now and I am saying you are a liar and all of your so-called theories are wrong. Everything you have ever done to me has been wrong and someday I hope you can see that. What you and Nancy did was reprehensible. You always justified everything to suit yourself but the reality is and always has been that to make someone else suffer for your inability to control yourself and for you, Nancy, to facilitate his behavior and trick young girls for his pleasure is evil. There is no God in the universe that would condone your actions. To you, Phillip, I say that I have always been a thing for your own amusement. I hated every second of every day of 18 years because of you and the sexual perversion you forced on me. To you, Nancy, I have nothing to say. Both of you can save your apologies and empty words. For all the crimes you have both committed I hope you have as many sleepless nights as I did. Yes, as I think of all of those years I am angry because you stole my life and that of my family. Thankfully I am doing well now and no longer live in a nightmare. I have wonderful friends and family around me. Something you can never take from me again. You do not matter anymore.

■ Introduction

Children suffer abuse and neglect at the hands of their parents, guardians, and other family members. Such forms of abuse are by far the most common forms of victimization children experience at the hands of adults in North America. However, public awareness and fear are often focused on other forms of victimization of children, most commonly that perpetrated by a stranger. These include the abduction of children and the exploitation of children, particularly sexual exploitation. Indeed, for certain groups of children, such forms of victimization are all too common. UNICEF summarized these concerns as follows: "All children have the right to be protected from violence, exploitation and abuse. Yet, millions of children worldwide from all socio-economic backgrounds, across all ages, religions and cultures suffer violence, exploitation and abuse every day. Millions more are at risk" (UNICEF, 2010, p. 1).

■ Scope of the Problem

The 2002 World Health Organization study on violence against children provides a wealth of international data on the abduction and exploitation of children. This study estimated that 150 million girls and 73 million boys under the age of 18 experience forced sexual intercourse or other forms of physical sexual violence (World Health Organization, 2002). This abuse comes in many forms, one of which is children forced to work in the sex trade. UNICEF in its publication, *State of the World's Children* (2010), concluded that in the United States alone at least 100,000 children are involved in commercial sexual exploitation. Similarly, the U.S. Department of Labor publication, "Forced Labor: The Prostitution of Children" (1996), reported approximately 100,000 child prostitutes work in the United States. An estimated 14,500 to 17,500 foreign nationals are trafficked into the United States each year. The number of U.S. citizens trafficked within the country is even higher, with an estimated 200,000 American children at risk for trafficking into the sex industry. UNICEF estimates that 1.2 million children are trafficked worldwide (UNICEF, 2010).

The FBI reports the average age of a child targeted for prostitution is between 12 to 14 for girls and 11 to 13 for boys. These youth are dependent on their pimps for everything and should they try to escape, they are often subject to brutal beatings or even killed. The FBI in conjunction with the National Center for Missing & Exploited Children launched the Innocence Lost National Initiative to address the growing problem of children recruited for prostitution (FBI, 2003). There are 38

Innocence Lost task forces and working groups in cities throughout the United States. As of 2010, the initiative has located and recovered more than 1,100 children. And prosecutors have earned nearly 600 convictions as a result (Harrington, 2010).

Child abduction and exploitation are remarkably common occurrences not only in far-away countries characterized by political corruption, tyranny, and severe poverty but also in North America. In the United States statistics are collected by the National Incidence Studies of Missing, Abducted, Runaway, and Thrownaway Children (NISMART). Studies and data collection by NISMART are undertaken in response to the Missing Children Act of 1982 and the subsequent Missing Children Assistance Act of 1984, which requires the Office of Juvenile Justice and Delinquency Prevention to conduct periodic studies to determine the number of U.S. children reported missing and the number of children recovered during a given year. According to NISMART-2 the following statistics were reported (Sedlak, Finkelhor, Hammer, & Schultz, 2002, p. 5):

- **797,500** children (younger than 18) were reported missing in a one-year period of time studied resulting in an average of 2,185 children being reported missing each day.
- **203,900** children were the victims of family abductions.
- **58,200** children were the victims of nonfamily abductions.
- **115** children were the victims of "stereotypical" kidnapping. (These crimes involve someone the child does not know or someone of slight acquaintance, who holds the child overnight, transports the child 50 miles or more, kills the child, demands ransom, or intends to keep the child permanently.)

The Canadian missing children program website is a partnership between the Royal Canadian Mounted Police (RCMP), Canada Border Services Agency, Department of Foreign Affairs and International Trade, and the Department of Justice.

The Royal Mounted Canadian Police operates the Our Missing Children as a national initiative under the umbrella of the National Missing Children Services and the National Child Exploitation Coordination Centre in Ottawa. As part of the Our Missing Children program, the RCMP assists all law enforcement agencies in their efforts to find and return missing children. This program also coordinates investigations on missing children nationally and internationally. As well, when an Amber alert is activated, Our Missing Children is responsible for disseminating an emergency alert to the various North American

TABLE 7-1 **Canadian Missing Children Reports Summary for a 10-Year Period**

	Profile							
	Kidnap	PA	Run	Unknown	Acc	Wander	Other	Total
2007	56	285	46,189	11,216	33	576	2,227	60,582
2006	46	326	46,728	10,761	24	567	2,009	60,461
2005	30	349	51,280	12,079	45	704	2,061	66,548
2004	31	332	52,280	11,373	27	671	2,552	67,266
2003	39	358	53,459	10,922	21	805	2,205	67,809
2002	35	429	52,390	10,994	38	594	2,052	66,532
2001	48	387	53,434	10,364	49	742	1,970	66,994
2000	42	416	50,633	10,031	35	597	1,958	63,712
1999	52	358	47,585	9,884	38	496	1,947	60,360
1998	42	426	48,388	10,254	28	623	2,326	62,087
1997	60	426	45,527	9,404	37	506	2,138	58,098

Kidnap: Kidnapping/Stranger Abduction, PA: Parental Abduction, Run: Runaways, Acc: Accident, Wander: Wandered.

Appendix 1 Canadian Missing Children Reports Summary CPIC Year-end Transaction Reports for 2007 Frequency by Category and by Year Reported Missing http://www .rcmp-grc.gc.ca/pubs/omc-ned/an-ra/annrep-rappann-07-eng.htm RCMP. Reproduced with the permission of the Minister of Public Works and Government Services Canada, 2012.

partners. The Our Missing Children program is managed by a member of the Federal Investigation Section (RCMP, 2011).

The National Missing Children Services (NMCS) reports that from December 1988 to December 31, 2009, 11,144 cases were opened and 8,410 cases closed. As of 2009, 2,734 cases were active (RCMP, 2011). The Canadian statistics indicate a significant decrease in children missing since 2005 (**Table 7-1**).

■ Legal Framework

The 1948 Universal Declaration of Human Rights was the first international statement addressing issues of slavery, justice, and the status of refugees and minority groups. This declaration clearly articulated that children are entitled to the rights and procedures in international law. This was further enshrined in 1959 by the Declaration of the Rights of the Child and in 1989 by the Convention on the Rights of the Child.

Child Abduction and Murder

Child abduction and murder that is not associated with child abuse and neglect is a relatively rare occurrence in our society, and consequently legislation has largely been reactive to high profile cases that capture the public attention, beginning in 1932 with the Lindbergh kidnapping. Charles Augustus Lindbergh, Jr., 20-month-old son of the famous aviator and Anne Morrow Lindbergh, was kidnapped at about 9:00 p.m. on March 1, 1932, from the nursery on the second floor of the Lindbergh home near Hopewell, New Jersey. A ransom note demanding $50,000 was found on the nursery windowsill. After the Hopewell police were notified, the report was telephoned to the New Jersey State Police, who assumed charge of the investigation, with the Bureau of Investigation soon to join. The toddler's body was found on May 12, 1932, in a wooded area; cause of death was determined to be a severe blow to the skull. Bruno Hauptmann was eventually charged, found guilty, and executed, although he continued to proclaim his innocence. The crime inspired the "Lindbergh Law," which made kidnapping a federal offense.

Adam John Walsh was abducted from a Sears store in Hollywood, Florida, on July 27, 1981, and later found murdered. This crime prompted Adam's father to become an advocate for victim's rights and to assist in the formation of the National Center for Missing & Exploited Children. John Walsh continued his work in the victim's area by hosting the television program, "America's Most Wanted." The "Code Adam" program, named for Adam Walsh, established a protocol to find missing children in department stores.

On October 22, 1989, Jacob E. Wetterling, age 11, was riding his bicycle with his brother and a friend when a masked gunman ordered the boys to stop. The man asked the boys their ages and then grabbed Jacob. He has never been found. The "Jacob Wetterling Crimes Against Children and Sexually Violent Offender Registration Act" was passed as part of the Federal Violent Crime Control and Law Enforcement Act of 1994. This law requires states to implement a sex offender and crimes against children registry.

Megan Kanka, age 7, was abducted, raped, and murdered by Jesse Timmendequas, who lived across the street. Timmendequas was a repeat child sexual offender. He was found guilty and is serving life without parole in a New Jersey prison. Megan's parents, Richard and Maureen Kanka, began the Megan Nicole Kanka Foundation with the belief that parents should have the right to know if a dangerous sexual predator moves into their neighborhood. The Kankas circulated a petition demanding immediate legislative action. The petition garnered over 400,000 signatures, and the law was passed in an unprecedented 89 days. Megan's home state of New Jersey passed the first so-called Megan's Law in 1994.

Child Trafficking and Child Prostitution

The UN Convention Against Transnational Organized Crime came into force in 2003 and was supplemented with a protocol titled "The Protocol to Prevent, Suppress and Punish Trafficking in Persons, Especially Women and Children." Under this protocol all signatory countries must criminalize trafficking in persons and undertake other initiatives to combat trafficking, including education campaigns and social and economic programs. An additional protocol under the Convention on the Rights of the Child addresses the sale of children, child prostitution, and child pornography. It specifically requires states to criminalize such acts as transferring a child's organs for profit or engaging in forced child labor (United Nations, 2002a). This protocol requires the following:

- Recognize the vulnerability of child victims and adapt procedures to meet their needs
- Inform child victims of their rights
- Provide supports for child victims
- Protect the privacy and identity of child victims
- Ensure child victims and their families are free from intimidation and retaliation
- Avoid unnecessary court delays or delays in granting of compensation

The trafficking of women and children has a long history in the United States. In response to the concern about national trafficking rings, the Mann Act (or the White Slave Traffic Act) was passed into law in 1910 making interstate transportation of women for the purposes of prostitution, debauchery, or "immoral purposes" a felony offense (PBS, 2005). The law, however, differentiated between foreign-born "alien" and American-born children and women. Immigration officials were to maintain information on foreign-born women and children and brothel owners. Specifically, the law designated the Commissioner-General of Immigration to keep records concerning the "procuration of alien women and girls with a view to their debauchery, and to provide supervision over them" (PBS, 2005). The law continues that persons who control or harbor females for the work of prostitution within 3 years after her entry to the United States and party to the suppression of White slave traffic need to file with the Commissioner-General of Immigration information as to the alien girl's or woman's name, her age, nationality, parentage, address, facts as to the date and port of entry to the United States, and her "procuration to come to this country within the knowledge of such person" (PBS, 2005).

Over the years there have been multiple changes to the Mann Act, and additional legislation has addressed many of the concerns of the original Act. These concerns include making the Act gender neutral, increasing the focus on juveniles, limiting the focus to prostitution, adding a problem of child pornography, and addressing international trafficking. More recently, the 2000 Trafficking Victims Protection Act (TVPA; 22 U.S.C. § 7101 et seq.) was enacted to prosecute traffickers as a better way to protect victims in the United States. The TVPA has been reauthorized in 2003, 2005, and 2008, each time enhancing and strengthening the law. The TVPA promotes a victim-centered prevention and assistance approach and increases measures to prosecute and punish offenders. Since 2000, the U.S. government has provided hundreds of millions of dollars in foreign assistance to combat human trafficking internationally (USA TVPA, 2008).

As in the United States, mid-1800s prostitution laws in Canada did not differentiate between children and adults. Children were seen as little adults who were responsible for their own behavior and were not afforded the protection of the state. By the late-1800s, however, the law began to recognize the emergence of "White slavery" and the trafficking of women and children. Thus, in 1892 the Canadian government made a number of amendments to the Criminal Code of Canada aimed at protecting children and young women from sexual predators. Additional legislation in the early 1900s focused on rehabilitation approaches for young prostitutes but largely ignored the actions of male customers and conditions that led to prostitution. Beginning in the 1970s there was renewed interest in child sexual exploitation, and the government convened at the Committee on Sexual Offences Against Children and Youth, which resulted in a report in 1984 (known as the Badgley Report). The Committee found that (1) most young prostitutes were girls, (2) 27.6% of girls and 13.1% of boys in prostitution were under the age of 16, and (3) many of the youth in prostitution had run away from intolerable home situations, often including child sexual abuse (Committee on Sexual Offences Against Children and Youth, 1984). One recommendation of this report was the suggestion that criminalization of youth prostitution would aid in protecting these young people. This recommendation was highly criticized for ignoring structural issues and blaming victims who became child prostitutes and was not enacted.

In 1988 the federal government introduced a bill to protect child victims of sexual abuse that increased the severity of sentences, improved conditions for child witnesses, and criminalized the sexual procurement of youth. This made it easier for police to target pimps and customers of child prostitutes. Nevertheless, in the early days this law was rarely enforced, in large part due to the attitudes of police and others toward child prostitutes. For instance, in the first 6 years of the new law, only six charges were laid in Vancouver despite awareness of a severe problem in that city. By the mid-1990s, however, the belief grew that youth in the sex trade are victims, and the focus shifted to services and policies to help those who wanted to leave prostitution to do so (Justice Canada, 2011).

In addition, Canada has provisions in the Criminal Code regarding trafficking; however, 2002 amendments to the Immigrant and Refugee Protection Act provide that "persons shall knowingly organize the coming into Canada of one or more persons by means of abduction, fraud, deception or use or threat of force or coercion" (Raaflaub, 2006, p. 1). The maximum penalty for this offense is a fine of $1 million life imprisonment, or both (Parliament of Canada, 2011).

■ Fetal and Infant Abduction

The taking of a fetus or infant under 6 months of age by nonfamily members is not a crime of epidemic proportion; nevertheless, 280 cases have been reported to the National Center for Missing & Exploited Children (NCMEC) between the years 1983 and 2011, resulting in considerable anguish for those involved (NCMEC, 2011). Of these cases, 46% of the children were abducted from a hospital, 40% were abducted from homes, and 14% were abducted in other places (NCMEC, 2011). Violence toward the mother was reported in 29% of cases where the child was abducted in a location other than a hospital (NCMEC, 2011). The increase in cases in fetal and infant abductions may be due to identification and recognition of the problem, better reporting procedures, and/or a greater willingness by health care facility administrators to report abductions (NCMEC, 2011).

Fetal Abduction

A fetal abduction is a kidnapping before a fetus is born by the criminal removal of the fetus from the uterus of the pregnant mother. In the first case of fetal abduction by cesarean section reported in the literature (Yutzy, Wolfson, & Resnick, 1993), in 1987 Darci Pierce, age 19 and married, approached a pregnant woman as she left a prenatal clinic at Kirtland Air Force Base in Albuquerque, New Mexico. Using a gun (replica), the abductor forced the mother into her car and initially drove to her own home, where she had surgical instruments and medical books. When Pierce discovered her husband was at home, she drove to an isolated desert area, strangled the mother to unconsciousness, and then, using a set of car keys, performed a cesarean section and delivered a live baby girl. She then hid the body of the mother under some bushes. Needing a birth certificate, Pierce drove to a local car dealership where she told a friend she had just delivered a baby. She was taken to the local hospital where the on-call physician performed a gynecological examination that revealed she had not recently given birth to a baby. The authorities were notified and Pierce was taken into custody (Yutzy et al., 1993). She was found guilty but mentally ill and received a 30-year prison sentence.

A 2002 study by Burgess, Baker, Nahirny, and Rabun concluded cesarean section murder is a new category of personal cause homicide. In this study it was evident that considerable planning had occurred before the crime was committed. In many cases the abductor first befriends the pregnant victim to gain access to the eventual goal of extracting the baby by cesarean section. The motivations for such a gruesome crime include the desire to solidify a relationship with a romantic partner and to fulfill a fantasy of bearing a child (Burgess et al., 2002).

Infant Abduction

An **infant abduction** is a kidnapping where the infant has been born, is less than 6 months of age, and is then abducted from a hospital, clinic, home, or other location. The abduction of infants by nonfamily members is a subject of concern to health care staff in all specialty fields because a primary agency standard is patient safety. Some hospitals use video surveillance to monitor the movements of infants. Other hospitals now use an electronic security system for infants by which a security tag is placed around the infant's wrist or ankle. The security system is alerted when the child is removed from a specified area. However, the RCMP report that these security tags have been removed by infant abductors and are not a fail-safe method (RCMP, 2011). Hospital-based staff in maternity centers, neonatal centers, and pediatric units need to know the red flags for infant abduction. Also, staff in emergency centers, home nursing, and community-based facilities need to be alert to this type of criminal behavior in females seeking to kidnap infants.

In July 2007 Shameka Pittman, dressed in purple hospital scrubs and posing as a nurse, took an infant from his mother in the maternity ward. Hospital staff sounded an alarm, causing the elevators to shut down and doors to lock. The infant was found in a diaper bag hidden behind a couch. In court, the prosecutor noted that in the 13 months preceding the kidnapping Pittman had repeatedly gone to doctors, claiming to be pregnant but testing negative. In June 2007 Pittman went to an emergency department claiming she was 38 weeks pregnant and her water had broken. The doctor asked Pittman's visitors to leave the room and then told her she was not pregnant. Pittman replied, "OK. I'm glad you didn't say it in front of my visitors." The prosecutor argued that had the hospital's alert system failed to work, Pittman's family would never have known she had not given birth to the child herself. The defense attorney argued that Pittman's repeated doctor visits showed mental health issues that were compounded by her drug and alcohol abuse. He said, "What she needs is an order for mental health treatment." The judge sentenced Pittman to 5 years in prison, far longer than the probationary term suggested by her sentencing guidelines. In addition to the prison sentence, the judge ordered Pittman never to visit a maternity ward unless admitted there as a patient. She also must seek mental health and substance abuse counseling.

In a study conducted by Burgess, Carr, Nahirny, and Rabun (2008) based on data from 248 NCMEC cases from 1983 through 2007, significant differences were noted in abduction patterns from earlier to later time periods. Specifically, the abductions of Hispanic infants went from 17% to 32% with a corresponding decrease in the proportion of White children abducted, whereas African American infants remained more or less constant at 40% and 43%. Similarly, the proportion of Hispanic abductors nearly doubled from 14% to 25%, whereas the proportion of White abductors decreased from 46% to 32%. The percentage of unmarried suspects increased from 32% to 52%. The total number of parental injuries went from 11 (9%) in the earlier period to 21 (17%) in the later period. The number of lethal injuries doubled, from 7 (6%) to 15 (12%). The proportion of abductions involving the use of a weapon nearly doubled, from 11% in the earlier period to 20% in the later one. The number of suspects arrested increased from 90 (88%) to 101 (94%); the number indicted increased from 82 (87%) to 99 (93%). **Table 7-2** shows the profile of infant abductors according to this study.

Family responses in cases where the infant is returned unharmed and no violence was used against the victim include severe stress and anxiety during the period when the infant is missing. Despite relief when the baby is returned, however, parental distress does not end. The family members have to rebond with the infant and testify in a criminal case. In cases with violence, family members experience feelings of fear, terror, distress, and anger. Some report having little appetite, difficulty sleeping, and feelings of irritability and numbness.

In cases of child abduction where the mother of the infant or fetus had been killed, joy of the infant's return is mixed with grief. In the study

TABLE 7-2 **Profile of Infant Abductors**

- A woman between the ages of 12 and 50 years who is often overweight
- Is compulsive and often uses manipulation and deceit to gain access
- Often indicates she has either lost or cannot have a baby
- Lives in, or is familiar with, the community where the abduction occurs
- Can provide good care for the baby once the abduction occurs
- Is often married or living with a man
- Visits nursery and maternity units before the abduction and asks detailed questions about procedures and unit layout; the abductor may also try to abduct from the home setting
- Usually plans the abduction but does not necessarily target a specific infant; often seizes any opportunity that presents
- Frequently impersonates a nurse or other allied health care personnel
- The typical abductor who doesn't target a health care setting has these characteristics:
  - Significantly more likely to be single while claiming to have a partner
  - Often targets a mother, whom she may find by visiting hospitals, and tries to meet the target family
  - Often both plans the abduction and brings a weapon, although the weapon might not be used
  - Often impersonates a health care or social services professional when visiting the home

Data from Burgess, A.W., Carr, K.E., Nahirny, C., & Rabun, J.B. Non-Family Infant Abductors: 1983-2006, 2008. *American Journal of Nursing. 108*(9), 32-38.

by Burgess and colleagues (2008) a maternal grandmother described how difficult it was to have to produce her daughter's dental records (because a fire had been set to hide her murder). The grandmother's distress led to psychiatric hospitalization as she reported repeatedly hearing auditory memories of her daughter's voice crying out to her. Time, sometimes thought to assist in healing wounds, did not help in many of the infant and fetal abduction cases involving violence. A maternal grandmother who had been shot at the time of the incident in which her daughter was killed said, "Although it had been fourteen years, the situation still hits me." She vividly remembered her daughter's last words to the perpetrator, "Don't kill my mother!" This woman was particularly dismayed 5 years later when the perpetrator blamed her for the violence inflicted on her daughter (Burgess et al., 2008).

■ Missing Children

The term "missing children" refers to children whose whereabouts are unknown to their parent, guardian, or legal custodian. This includes two categories of children: those who are taken in either familial or nonfamilial abductions and those who are runaways, thrownaways, or otherwise missing.

In the United States, resources are provided for missing children, their families, and the professionals who serve them through clearinghouses. The NCMEC maintains a liaison with each missing-child clearinghouse and helps ensure they are familiar with the many resources available through NCMEC. NCMEC provides state-level clearinghouses with training, technical assistance, and vital information to better assist them in handling missing-child cases. The missing-child clearinghouses are diverse in their delivery of services because of state and territorial mandates and the variety of agencies in which they exist. The primary areas of focus for missing-child clearinghouses are networking, information dissemination, training development and delivery, data collection, and provision of technical assistance in cases of missing and sexually exploited children.

Family Abductions

Although the abduction of children by strangers is the greatest fear of all parents, in fact the abduction of children by a member of the family is the most common occurrence. Family abductions typically involve the violation of a custody agreement or decree, such as the failure to return a child at the end of a legal or agreed on visit. For such a violation to be considered an abduction, the child must be away at least overnight and attempts made to conceal the child's location and prevent contact with the child. Further, the abductor must have the intent to keep the child indefinitely or to permanently alter the custody arrangements. The exact number of parental abductions is unknown, but estimates suggest several hundred such abductions per year occur in Canada and the United States (Kiedrowski & Dalley, 2008). In a review of the existing literature in the area, Kiedrowski and Dalley (2008) provide a profile of parental abductions of children, depicted in **Table 7-3**.

The aftereffects of such abductions are seen in both children and parents. The parenting relationship is obviously severely affected, permeated by distrust and fear. Funds available to support and raise the child are redirected to extensive legal costs, travel, accommodation, and search and recover fees, which are compounded by income loss. Emotional harm to the child is another outcome. For instance, children are forced to hide their identity (and, in some cases, to cross-dress to hide their identity), may be told the other parent died or does not love them anymore, may lose all family contact with other and friends, and are forced to live like fugitives. Less frequently, the child may be subject to physical or sexual abuse. After returning home children experience nightmares, sleeplessness, and emotional distance from others (Dalley, 2007).

TABLE 7-3 Profile of Parental Abductions of Children

- Either parent may abduct his or her own child; male and female children are equally likely to be abducted.
- Mothers are more likely to abduct after a court order, whereas fathers are more likely to abduct before a court order.
- Fathers who abduct are more likely to be employed, whereas mothers who abduct are more likely to be unemployed.
- Most children taken are between 3 and 7 years of age.
- Communication usually occurs between the abducting parent and the searching parent.
- Accomplices are used in half the cases, usually family members or current partners.
- Most cases are resolved within 1 week.

Data from Kiedrowski, J & Dalley, M. 2008. Parental Abduction of Children: An Overview and Profile of the Abductor. Royal Canadian Mounted Police. Retrieved from http://www.rcmp-grc.gc.ca/pubs/omc-ned/parent-eng.htm.

The Missing Children Society of Canada (n.d.) offers a fact sheet to assist parents in these circumstances, with the following suggestions:

- File a missing persons report with police and provide identifying data, such as birth certificates, fingerprints, pictures, and so on.
- Flag the child's birth certificate, school records, and medical records in case requests for information or transfer of records are made.
- Inquire about change of address of the abductor in records pertaining to employment, professional licensing bodies, motor vehicle registration, pension, tax records, and so on.
- Keep a notebook and record any forms of contact.

Nonfamily Abduction

According to U.S. law, nonfamily abductions are defined as the coerced and unauthorized taking of a child into a building, a vehicle, or a distance of more than 20 feet and/or the detention of a child for a period of more than 1 hour. Attempted abductions include luring of a child for the purposes of committing another crime. This definition includes abductions conducted by friends and acquaintances as well as strangers, and most of these abductions occur within a quarter mile of the child's home. More than 65% of children abducted by nonfamily members are girls; of these 46% are sexually abused and 31% are physically abused. In 75% of cases the perpetrator is a male, 67% of them are below 29 years of age, and most target children within their own ethnic group (Sedlak et al., 2002).

There are four categories of nonfamilial child abductors identified by the FBI (Wilson, 2010):

- *Pedophiles* are the largest single category of child abductors. These individuals are able to connect easily with children and obtain their confidence, which then makes the child vulnerable to abduction. The child often initially has confidence in the person and then becomes aware the person is exploitative.
- *Serial killers* are methodical and ritual in their approaches, using power, dominance, and control as tactics. Such abductors are more likely to use a blitz attack method in which the offender suddenly approaches and overwhelms the child.
- *Profiteers* abduct children for the purpose of criminal exploitation, for instance, in prostitution, pornography, or illegal adoption rings.
- *Childless psychotics* tend to abduct children in a delusional state, attempting to correct the reality that they are unable to have children or have lost their own children, for instance, to child protection services.

Thrownaways/Runaways

Runaways make up the majority of missing children. They are often described by family and others in their social network as delinquents or troublemakers; in actual fact, however, they are often not running to something but away from something. Thrownaways is a term used by NISMART to describe children who have experienced any of the following situations: the child was told to leave the household, the child was away from home and the parent/guardian refused to allow the child back, the child ran away but the parent/guardian made no effort to recover the child or did not care whether or not the child returned, or the child was abandoned or deserted. Thus, the distinction between runaways and thrownaways is not entirely clear. NISMART-2 (2003) estimated in 1999 that 1,682,900 children in the United States had a runaway/thrownaway episode. Twenty-one percent of these situations were reported to the police for the purposes of relocating them. Youths aged 15 to 17 made up two-thirds of children in this category.

Children and youth in the thrownaway category are at highest risk of exploitation by child traffickers. The child is usually homeless and in need of food and shelter. The trafficker plays the role of parent or romantic friend, offering care, understanding, and attention. Offering free drugs is often a part of this package. In the end the child is manipulated into survival sex, frequently in exchange for drugs. A series of FBI sting operations in 2009 resulted in 2,300 arrests and the recovery of 170 children in this circumstance (McLaughlin, 2009).

Lost, Injured, or Otherwise Missing Children

This category includes children missing for varying periods of time that do not fit into any other category. Nearly half of the children in this category are below age 5. Often, they suffer from some sort of disability or challenge that puts them at risk for becoming lost or injured. It is important to note that this group of children suffer the most physical harm compared to every other category, except those children abducted by strangers.

AMBER Alert

AMBER, America's Missing: Broadcast Emergency Response, was created in 1996 in Texas after the abduction of 9-year-old Amber Hagerman. The purpose of AMBER was to develop an early warning system, with collaboration between law-enforcement agencies, broadcasters, and transportation agencies to activate an urgent bulletin in the most serious child-abduction cases. Since its inception the program has gained national attention, and now all 50 states have implemented the system. As of 2012, there have been 564 successful recoveries as a result of these alerts (NCMEC, 2012).

When a child goes missing, law enforcement is contacted. An AMBER alert is issued after certain criteria have been met. Although there are no national guidelines, most states have similar stipulations for issuing an alert. First, the abduction must be confirmed: the child cannot just be a runaway. Second, the child must be at risk of injury or death. Third, law enforcement needs information about the child and the captor and his or her vehicle. Finally, the child must be younger than 17 years of age. It is recommended that all missing child data be entered into the National Crime Information Center (NCIC) run by the FBI (FBI, 2008). The success of AMBER alert is due in large part to the efforts of the media, law enforcement, and observant citizens.

■ Child Labor

Forms of child labor, including indentured servitude and child slavery, have existed throughout history. Children's role in the family was often to help earn money for their families' survival. In the 21st century, in sections of Peru, many working children are active in the country's informal economy, which accounts for nearly 50% of the country's economic output (U.S. Department of Labor, n.d.). Child labor is prevalent in the brick-making sector of Huachipa. Working children in this sector help their parents to meet daily quotas starting as young as 3 years old. Children carry heavy loads of brick or sand throughout the day, and, as a result, many children suffer from spinal and bone deformities (U.S. Department of Labor, 1999).

In Canada children were considered cheap farm labor until the end of the 19th century. As an economic asset they were counted and treated as such along with cows, chickens, and horses. The residue of this history remains in current Canadian attitudes toward the use of corporal punishment and in the legal sanction of physical punishment by parents provided by current provisions of the Criminal Code of Canada (Volpe, 2011).

In America, as industrialization moved workers from farms and home workshops into urban areas and factory work, children were often viewed as able to conform to work requirements, were cheaper, and were less likely to strike. Child labor began to decline as the labor and reform movements grew and labor standards in general began improving, increasing the political power of working people and other social reformers to demand legislation regulating child labor. Women-led organizations, such as state Consumers' Leagues and Working Women's Societies, helped to generate the National Consumers' League in 1899 and the National Child Labor Committee in 1904, which shared goals of challenging child labor. Efforts were successful to provide free, compulsory education for all children and culminated in the passage of the Fair Labor Standards Act in 1938, which set federal standards for child labor (Child Labor Education Project, 2004).

■ Child Trafficking

In 2000 the United Nations General Assembly adopted the *Protocol to Prevent, Suppress and Punish Trafficking in Persons, Especially Women and Children.* This act marked a significant milestone in international efforts to stop the trade in people. As the guardian of the Protocol, United Nations Office of Drugs and Crime (UNODC) addresses human trafficking issues through its Global Programme against Trafficking in Persons. While over 147 States have signed and ratified the Protocol, translating the protocol into reality has been problematic. Very few criminals have been convicted and most victims are probably never identified or assisted (UNODC, 2006).

The United Nations (2002b, p. 1) defines trafficking as follows:

> [T]he recruitment, transportation, transfer, harbouring, or receipt of persons, by means of threat or use of force or other forms of coercion, of abduction, of fraud, of deception, of the abuse of power or of a position of vulnerability or of the giving

or receiving of payments and benefits to achieve the consent of a person having control over another person for the purposes of exploitation. Exploitation shall include, at a minimum, the exploitation or the prostitution of others or other forms of sexual exploitation, forced labour or services, slavery or practices similar to slavery, servitude or the removal of organs.

Although the transport of slaves on British ships was abolished in 1807 and slavery is illegal today in virtually every country, human trafficking, the modern-day equivalent to slavery, remains rampant throughout the world. In 1865 the Thirteenth Amendment to the Constitution was ratified abolishing slavery in the United States. The U.S. Department of State initiated monitoring human trafficking in 1994, when the issue began to be covered in the Department's "Annual Country Reports on Human Rights Practices." Originally, coverage focused on trafficking of women and girls for sexual purposes. The report coverage has broadened over the years, and U.S. embassies worldwide now routinely monitor and report on cases of trafficking in men, women, and children for all forms of forced labor, including agriculture, domestic service, construction work, and sweatshops as well as trafficking for commercial sexual exploitation (U.S. Department of State, 2008).

Trafficking is a transnational criminal enterprise that recognizes neither boundaries nor borders. Profits from trafficking feed the coffers of organized crime. A 2002 study by UNICEF estimated that profits from human trafficking are $7 billion per year worldwide. Trafficking is linked to other criminal activities, such as document fraud, money laundering, and migrant smuggling. Moreover, as a matter of policy, the U.S. government opposes prostitution and any related activities as contributing to the phenomenon of trafficking in persons. These activities are inherently harmful and dehumanizing (Ashcroft, 2004).

In describing the types of human trafficking in the Mekong Sub-Region, which includes Laos, Thailand, Vietnam, and Cambodia, the United Nations Inter-Agency Project (UNIAP) indicates it takes many forms. For instance, children are taken from Cambodia to beg or sell flowers on the streets of Thailand, Chinese boys are stolen and sold to those who want a son, Cambodian babies are stolen and then adopted by well-meaning parents in the United States, young Vietnamese brides go to meet their new husbands in Taiwan only to discover that he is a pimp, and adults are taken and then held to work in factories, brothels, houses, or fishing boats (United Nations Inter-Agency Project 2001–2005).

World Vision's Child Sex Tourism Prevention Project aims to deter potential child sex tourists before they harm children and provides assistance to U.S. and other law enforcement agencies in their work to identify and prosecute offenders (World Vision International, 2008). An estimated 2 million children are enslaved in the global sex trade market. Children in countries such as Cambodia, Thailand, Costa Rica, Mexico, and Brazil are coerced, abducted, or sold by their parents to work in brothels catering to wealthy Western customers (World Vision International, 2008). These children not surprisingly suffer from physical, emotional, and social harms, including HIV infection, rejection by families and society, shame, fear, and despair. As another example, in Eastern Europe, Romanian women are deceived and taken to Germany and other parts of the world, including North America, to work as exotic dancers or prostitutes, unable to free themselves due to torture, extortion, and their illegal status in the country in which they now reside (UNODC, 2006). In child trafficking, children are recruited and trafficked to earn money by begging or selling goods. Child beggars are sometimes maimed by their captors to generate sympathy and generosity from potential buyers.

Over the past 15 years "trafficking in persons" and "human trafficking" have been used as umbrella terms to describe activities in which one person obtains or holds another person in compelled service. The TVPA, mentioned above, describes this compelled service using a number of different terms: involuntary servitude, slavery, debt bondage, and forced labor. The 11th Trafficking in Persons report ranks 184 countries as to their level of accomplishment in combating human trafficking (UNODC, 2006) (**Table 7-4**).

■ Child Prostitution

Child and juvenile pornography and prostitution are difficult topics to study for several reasons. First, it is hard to determine the numbers of children being exploited due to the clandestine nature of the activity. Second, law enforcement is often handicapped in investigating cases because of the child's attachment to the caregiver. Third, estimates of the number of child prostitutes and children who are trapped into pornography, both nationally and internationally, are exceptionally variable and impressionistic. Child pornography has increasingly moved to the Internet and is thus covered in reviews on cybercrime as well.

Although there are barriers to our understanding the origins of child prostitution, law enforcement recognizes it is a problem of considerable magnitude. Most of our knowledge of child prostitution comes from children and juveniles who have run away from home and are existing

TABLE 7-4 **Types of Child Trafficking**

Type of Child Trafficking	Example	Reference
Baby adoption	Guatemalan babies trafficked for adoption by couples in North America and Europe	UNICEF (2010) estimates that 1,000 to 1,500 are trafficked each year.
Mail-order brides as young as age 13	Mainly from Asia and Eastern Europe	UNICEF (2010) states these girls and women are powerless, isolated, and at great risk of violence.
Domestic work and sexual exploitation	Large numbers of children are trafficked in West and Central Africa	UNICEF (2010) estimates 90% of the domestic workers are girls.
Child sex workers	Mekong subregion of Southeast Asia	Surveys indicate that 30–35% of all sex workers are between 12 and 17 years of age. The global market of child trafficking is over $12 billion a year, with over 1.2 million child victims (UNODC, 2006).
Child prostitution and child pornography	Lithuania Mexico's social service agency reports tourist destinations are among those areas with the highest number.	20–50% of prostitutes are believed to be minors. There are reportedly more than 16,000 children engaged in prostitution (Patt, 2011).
Forced child labor	Child performs work that financially benefits someone outside the child's family and does not offer the child the option of leaving	U.S. Department of Labor identifies examples including cocoa production in Ghana, cotton in Uzbekistan, and soccer balls in India (USDOL, 2012a).
Child soldiers	Involves the unlawful recruitment or use of children—through force, fraud, or coercion—as combatants or for labor or sexual exploitation by armed forces	U.S. Department of Labor addresses issues in Burundi, the Congo, and Rwanda (USDOL, 2012b).

on the street or who are institutionalized. These runaways, often around the ages of 14 and 15, have told their histories of prostituting to police and mental health staff. Although these estimates are, at best, crude and vary widely, they appear to reflect a problem of considerable magnitude. For the most part, these young runaway prostitutes are escaping from chaotic and abusive home environments and are subsisting on the streets by prostituting themselves. Children that have been initiated into a life of prostitution, often at a very young age, constitute a population that remains largely invisible. Their invisibility stems, in part, because they are living with families in the community and are often being prostituted by caregivers, relatives, and acquaintances. Unless they come to the attention of the child welfare system, they do not become "known" until after they run away, get into trouble, and eventually fall into the category of teenage prostitutes struggling to survive on the street. It is at that point that law enforcement becomes aware of them because of committing delinquent acts.

There can be three parties involved in prostitution: the pimp (who receives the goods or money), the prostitute (who provides the sex), and the john (or client). The principle-defining characteristic of prostitution is a barter of sexual services in exchange for goods or money. Typically, the exchange goes from the adult clients, or "johns," to the adults who are sexually exploiting the children. The exploitative adults typically receive drugs and/or money from the clients in payment for sex with the children. When the child receives something in exchange for sex, it is invariably "goods" (e.g., clothing, video games, records, toys, and books). Prostituting a child is an extreme form of sexual abuse.

Making of Teenage Prostitutes

Generally, there are several entrances into youth prostitution (**Table 7-5**). The first group comprises children who run away from their abusive, dysfunctional families and are prostituted by professional pimps who run stables of sexually exploited children. The second group comprises children who are reared in environments in which sexual exploitation and sexual barter are simply one feature of the overall pattern of abuse to which they are exposed. Frequently, their caretakers were either prostitutes themselves or were involved with other sexually abusive adults.

The typical pattern of sexual exploitation involves initial abuse of the child by either a pedophile or incestuous caretaker. The sexual abuse evolves into sexual exploitation when the caretakers discover a market for the sexual services their children could provide. These "caretaker pimps" begin by bringing in known like-minded friends and acquaintances, who provide money and drugs in exchange for sex with the children. Eventually, the "business" might branch out to include strangers. To ensure some degree of compliance, the children are given material goods but rarely money. Eventually, these children can strike out on their own unless the social welfare system or law enforcement becomes aware of their plight and intervene.

TABLE 7-5 **Avenues into Child Prostitution**

Avenue	Definition
Parent as role model	Some children are exposed to the world of prostitution from birth by their parents, for example, a mother as a professional prostitute brings her daughter with her from motel to motel as she engages in her illicit activities or a child whose father was her mother's pimp.
Parental incest	Some children are initiated into sexual activity through parental sexual abuse. The parent begins the incest, then videotapes and photographs the child, and then brings adults in for sex.
Chaotic and abusive, sexualized home environments	Some children live in multiple abusive and sexualized homes. The child learns that it is both acceptable and appropriate to trade sexual favors for shelter, love, and money.
Child sex rings	Child sex rings include adults who sexually exploit multiple children.
Sibling incest	Older siblings can sexually exploit younger siblings and use threats to provide sexual services promised to peers.
Incest and prostitution normalized	Some children grow up in a home in which there is physical, psychological, and sexual abuse; gross neglect; and extensive drug use. The eventual exchange of sex for drugs outside the home is a logical and inevitable outgrowth of such upbringing.
Unclear origin	Not all cases of child prostitution can be traced to early life events. In general, however, child prostitutes are clearly a product of a highly sexualized home environment.

■ Typologies of Sex Offenders of Children

An overriding feature of descriptions of the many victimizations of children described in this chapter is sexual exploitation. This section thus focuses on sexual offenders that victimize children—the underlying factor that fuels many of these crimes. There are two basic ways an offender gains sexual access to the child: by pressuring the child into sexual activity through enticement, encouragement, or instruction and by forcing the child into the sexual activity through threat, intimidation, or physical duress.

Coerced Versus Forced

In the *coerced* situation the offender initially establishes a nonsexual relationship with the child so that the child comes to trust and feel comfortable with the offender. Then, the offender influences the child to engage in sexual activity through the offer of some type of reward (such as candy or money), by misrepresenting moral standards (such as telling the child that all boys and girls do this), or through trickery and deception (e.g., "This is going to be a game, and we're going to wrestle"). The most commonly used technique of luring the child into this coerced sexual activity is by capitalizing on the child's need for attention, approval, and human contact. In such situations the offender spends considerable time with the child, gives the child a lot of attention, and makes the child out to be special or a favorite. Children respond to attention and are taught to be obedient, so the intended victim cooperates and goes along with the sexual demands of the offender. The child does this to secure the promised reward because of confusion and lack of understanding or to get approval and recognition. As one offender said, "I can look at kids in a school yard and tell you who is an easy mark. It will be the child alone and off by himself, the one who appears lonely and has no friends. The quiet kid—the one no one is paying any attention to—that's the one who will respond to some attention" (Groth, 1979, p. 142).

In coerced sex encounters the offender does appear to have a high emotional investment in his or her victim and uses the child to gratify the unmet needs for approval, recognition, and affiliation in his or her own life. The child makes the offender feel good. This type of offender does not find satisfaction in his or her adult relationships but in his or her encounters with children; the sexual activity serves to validate his or her worth as a person. When this is the dominant motive, the offense is characterized by a relative lack of physical force in the commission of the offense. Such offenders describe their victims in positive terms, such as innocent, clean, loving, open, warm, affectionate, attractive, and undemanding. They feel safe and secure with children. They are usually dissuaded if the child resists or refuses them. They do not resort to force but instead seek out another, more cooperative or accommodating victim.

In the *forced* situation the offender gains access to the child through intimidation in the form of verbal threats (e.g., "Do what I say and you won't get hurt) or physical actions, such as grabbing hold of the child or through the use of a weapon. Or the offender resorts to physical force to overcome the child's resistance and, in some cases, derives pleasure from hurting and sexually abusing the child.

These situations are comparable to rape. In these assaults sexuality becomes an expression of power and anger. Such offenders describe the victim as small, weak, helpless, unable to resist, easily controlled, and vulnerable. They feel stronger and more dominant in regard to a child. Any resistance on the part of the child may result in increased aggression on the part of the offender. The offender does not take no for an answer and will enforce his or her sexual demands. In most of these cases whatever force is used is directed toward having control over the child (Burgess, Groth, Holmstrom, & Sgroi, 1978).

The selection of a child as the target of a sexual assault is multidetermined. An adult is physically superior to a child, and the offender may feel stronger and more powerful in regard to a child victim compared to an adult victim. The child does not pose as much of a physical or psychological threat. The child is sexually immature and inexperienced, and the offender may believe there is less risk his or her sexual performance will be compared to others'. The offender may not feel as sexually inadequate with a child as he or she would with an adult. The child may represent everything negative the offender believes about him- or herself and the abuse, in part, serves as a punishment for the offender's self-hatred. Or the child may be a means by which the offender attempts to control or retaliate against another adult. These represent some of the dynamics suggested by clinicians who have worked with the child molester (Groth, 1979). In addition, two types of child molesters are described by whether the sexual abuse is a situational event or whether it is a preferential choice.

Situational Predators Versus Preferential Predators

In the situational offense there is evidence of impulsive, opportunistic, predatory behavior, such as the victim being present or a spur-of-the-moment decision to offend. Situational child molesters do not have a true sexual preference for children but engage in sex with children for varied and sometimes complex reasons, ranging from child availability to offender inadequacy (e.g., raping a child because she is available and vulnerable). For such a child molester, sex with children may range from a one-time episode to a long-term pattern of behavior. The more long-term the pattern, the harder it is to distinguish it from preferential molesting. The situational child molester usually has fewer numbers of different child victims. Vulnerable individuals such as the elderly, sick, or disabled may also be at risk of sexual victimization. For example, the situational child molester who sexually abuses children in a daycare center might leave the job and begin to abuse elderly people in a nursing home.

Preferentially motivated sexual offenses usually involve strong patterns of behavior or sexual rituals that are difficult for the offender to change. Sexual ritual involves repeatedly engaging in an act or series of acts in a certain manner because of a sexual need. In other words, for a person to become sexually aroused and/or gratified, he or she must engage in the act in a certain way. This sexual ritualism can include such things as the physical characteristics, age, or gender of the victim; the particular sequence of acts; the bringing or taking of specific objects; or the use of certain words or phrases.

Sexual ritual is more than the concept of method of operation or modus operandi, (MO). MO is something done by an offender because it works. Sexual ritual is something done by an offender because of a psychological need. Therefore, it is much harder for an offender to change, vary, or adjust the ritual than his or her MO. Both preferential and situational sex offenders may have an MO, but the preferential offender is more likely to have a sexual ritual.

The preferential offense often has clear evidence that the offender thought, planned, and went searching for a particular victim. Preferential child molesters have a definite sexual preference for children. Their sexual fantasies and erotic imagery focus on children. Preferential child molesters almost always have access to children, molest multiple victims, and collect child pornography or child erotica.

A preferential child molester (pedophile) might have other psychosexual disorders, personality disorders, or psychosis or may be involved in other types of criminal activity. A pedophile's sexual interest in children might be combined with other sexual deviations (paraphilias), which include indecent exposure (exhibitionism), obscene phone calls (scatophilia), exploitation of animals (zoophilia), urination (urophilia), defecation (coprophilia), binding (bondage), baby role playing (infantilism), infliction of pain (sadism, masochism), real or simulated death (necrophilia), and others. The preferential child molester must have (1) high amount of victim contact and (2) high level of fixation or pedophilic interest (Prentky & Burgess, 2000).

High Contact Versus Low Contact Offenders

A preemptory distinction is made between those offenders who have spent a substantial amount of their time in close proximity to victims (high contact) and those offenders who have spent little or no time with victims outside of rape and sexual assaults (low contact). Amount of contact is a behavioral measure of the time spent with victims. It includes both sexual and nonsexual situations but excludes the contact that results from parental responsibilities. The contact distinction must be distinguished from the fixation decision, which attempts to assess the strength of an individual's pedophilic interest.

Evidence for high contact includes structured and nonstructured involvement with a victim through an occupation or through recreation (e.g., schoolteacher, bus driver, carnival worker, riding stable attendant, newspaper delivery person, scout leader, sports coach, youth group volunteer, babysitter). These occupational criteria are only intended to help identify the level of contact for those already determined to be child molesters. Other evidence for high contact may include regular visits by the victim to the offender's home or the offender acting as an adopted father or big brother. In addition, we assume that repeated sexual (non-incestuous) encounters with a victim imply the development of a relationship that goes beyond sexual involvement. For that reason, when there are three or more sexual encounters with the same victim, the offender is coded as having high contact (Prentky & Burgess, 2000).

Case of a Preferential Child Molester/Spree Crime and Multiple Victims

The following case provides examples of multiple factors and complexity of dynamics that can occur in crimes of abuse committed against children. These examples provide insight into the multilevel and multidimensional facets of assessment that will enhance comprehensive assessment and intervention with child victims.

- On August 28, around 10 p.m., Elizabeth, age 15, was walking with her girlfriend, Kate. A man on a bicycle kept riding by them, asking if they wanted to buy any weed. They said no. He then asked if they wanted a joint and asked their names. Elizabeth said she did not have a name. The girls walked faster; however, the man rode by and grabbed Elizabeth's backside. The girls were stunned and then ran and called 911.

- Two days later, on August 30, around 6:40 p.m., Kathleen, age 13, was rollerblading at a school with friends and noticed someone following them. A man asked Kathleen if she liked Bones, Thugs and Harmony (a music group). She said no. Then he asked her if she wanted to "get it on." She again said nothing but felt nervous and scared. Then he put his bike in front of her and grabbed her backside and sped away on his bike. Kathleen told people at the apartment who called 911 and the police came.

- On August 30, around 7 p.m., Amanda, age 9, was riding her bicycle and a man came up to her, put his hand on the brake handle and his other hand around her, and asked if she wanted to go bike riding with him. He asked her name and address. She said nothing. He tried to grab her backside, but she pushed his hand away. He left and she told her mother, who then called the police.

- On August 30, around 8:20 p.m., Morris, age 76, had bought food at Wendy's, and as he approached his car a large figure said hello and then said "Let me help you Pop." Morris was trying to open the door with keys. The man began struggling; the door flung open. The man asked for his keys and wallet, threatening he was going to kill him with a gun. He tried to get in the car, but Morris fought him. Suddenly the man left, and Morris reported the incident to the police.

- On August 30, around 9:20 p.m., Robert, age 15, was approached by a man on a bicycle and asked if he and his friend had any money. They said no. The man threatened to kill them if they reported him. The boys told their parents and the police were called.

- About 9:35 p.m., Chris, age 17, was with his friend Robert playing "Manhunt." The boys saw a man biking in and out of people's driveways checking to see if anybody was home. The man then "cut the boys off" with his bike and asked if they had any money. Then he said they should be sure to forget they saw his face.

- On August 30, around 10 p.m., Mrs. Peck and her husband were watching TV when they heard a noise in their back room and thought it was the cat. The wife walked back and noticed the screen had been pushed in. She checked outside and noticed a lawn chair had been moved from the pool, pulled up underneath the window, and the toys for her two daughters, ages 4 and 9, were strewn around. She called the police.

- On August 30, around 10:15 p.m., Mrs. Fried heard a noise downstairs and asked her husband to check the back door. He found it open with the handle forced. Mrs. Fried discovered her purse was missing (from the dining room table), which held her money and credit cards. She later found her 6-year-old daughter's black glove to her Nerf football missing from the outside sandbox.

- On August 30, about 10:55 p.m., Laura, age 8, was lying in her bed on the second floor listening to her CD tape. She saw someone walk into the room. First she thought it was her dad, and then thought it was the exterminator "that kills bugs," but then realized it was a stranger. She asked, "Who are you and what are you doing?" He said to "be quiet" and "be calm." He said he had a knife. He picked her up, put his hands around her neck and over her mouth, and told her not to scream. He dragged her down the stairs when her dog, Rocky, a Rhodesian ridgeback, suddenly came down the stairs from the third floor and leapt at the man. He loosened his hand and Laura was able to scream. The man dropped her on the stairs. The dog bit the man on the wrist and he ran out of the house. Laura's mother came out of her room and called the police. The backyard had a trampoline, a rope, a shed with toys, and a garage with basketballs and bikes and scooters.

- An investigating officer was dispatched to the scene and observed a blue mountain bike, a woman's handbag containing a CD player and headphones, and numerous items bearing the name "Lisa." The officer saw the defendant at the softball field park, tackled him, and took him into custody. Upon searching him the officer found a set of GM car keys, a GE keypad, as well as a rabies tag in his right front pants pocket. The officer also found a CD for Bones, Thugs, and Harmony and solar sunglasses. The defendant had blood on his shirt (which was turned inside out) and puncture marks on his wrist. He admitted to the burglaries. In reference to the girl, he said he just knocked her down the steps, did not take her, and was using her as a shield against the dog. No weapon was found. He claimed he was just burglarizing the house and that he needed a car to "get out of town."

CASE ANALYSIS This was a spree crime, that is, one continuous event that started on August 28 and continued through August 30 with multiple locations and no cooling off period. The offender was consistently looking for victims. He was mission oriented, and the crimes accelerated with the buildup of emotion. He first talked to the children, then touched them, and then attempted to abduct one. He targeted homes that had children's toys present outside.

Burton was a preferential child molester with a sexual preference for children. He had a long history of indecent exposure to children, for example, calling them over to his car to ask directions, staring at them, using obscene language, and exposing himself. In many ways he fit the old stereotype of the man hanging around playgrounds with a bag of candy. He liked to watch children or engage in brief sexual encounters; however, he lacked interpersonal skills for grooming the child. This type of offender is more likely to abduct because he or she cannot seduce the child because of poor social skills.

There were phases of buildup to the abduction. He had a fantasy about sex with a child that led to a need to carry out the plan. His mission was to obtain a child, but he needed money and mobility or a vehicle for escape. He selected a child who was a stranger so as not to be caught. Fantasy driven, he took increased risks to get a child. Part of the pleasure was the complete control over the child. He usually rehearsed before the abduction.

In summary, Burton had a crime spree pattern with a classic escalation of intent. He targeted vulnerable victims (children, older man with hands occupied, people in bed sleeping). His nonsexual crimes had sexual and aggressive language. He sought out homes with toys in yards and probably had them under surveillance. The child victims in this case were referred to victim counseling programs through the prosecutor's office. The child most traumatized due to the offender's direct contact with her was Laura. Her therapy required individual as well as family work. Laura was unable to sleep in her own room for months, sleeping instead with her parents. Her parents redecorated and rearranged furniture before her return to her room.

■ Summary

This chapter focused on multiple forms of exploitation and abduction of children. Although not a crime of large number, the stealing of a fetus through cesarean section is addressed, as is the infant abductions reported to the NCMEC. Older children who are missing due to abduction, running away, or being "thrown away" is a far greater issue. The Jaycee Dugard case revealed problems with California's system for monitoring convicted sex offenders after it was determined that parole agents had missed numerous clues and chances (over 18 years) to find her. At an international level, the 10th anniversary reauthorization TVPA law was ground-breaking legislation because it was the first comprehensive federal law that addressed child trafficking in the modern era. One of its most important contributions was the formulation of a victim-centered paradigm for addressing the crime and a three-pronged approach for prevention of trafficking, protection of victims, and prosecution of perpetrators. Issues of impact for child victims and their families who survive exploitation illustrate the resiliency as well as long-term memories. Jaycee Dugard tells us she had no choice but to endure and the sounds of her imprisonment continue to haunt her.

■ Key Terms

Alien: Term used in the Mann Act to denote foreign-born persons.

Child pornography: Obscene photographing, filming, or depiction of children for commercial purposes or for arousal of self, subject child, or viewing audience.

Child prostitution: Inducing or encouraging a child to engage in sex for financial or other gain.

Child trafficking: Abduction and sale of children.

Fetal abduction: Kidnapping before a fetus is born by the criminal removal of the fetus from the uterus of the pregnant mother.

Infant abduction: Kidnapping after the infant is born and is less than 6 months old, usually from a hospital, clinic, home, or other location.

Missing children: Children whose whereabouts are unknown to their parent, guardian, or legal custodian.

Thrownaways: Children who have been told to leave the household, are refused reentry into their home after running away, are not sought by parents or others when they run away, or are abandoned or deserted.

■ Discussion Questions

1. What is the role of international law and law enforcement in child trafficking?
2. What challenges are presented to law enforcement and service providers with respect to child prostitution?
3. If you were to design an educational campaign with respect to child abduction, what would be the focus?
4. What services would you request for a 14-year-old found by police on "Low Track" in Vancouver, British Columbia?
5. Debate the pros and cons of youth prostitution as a victimless crime.

■ Resources

Canadian Missing Children Program: a partnership between the Royal Canadian Mounted Police (RCMP), Canada Border Services Agency, Department of Foreign Affairs and International Trade, and the Department of Justice

http://www.rcmp-grc.gc.ca/omc-ned/index-accueil-eng.htm

Child Labor Public Education Project

http://www.continuetolearn.uiowa.edu/laborctr/child_labor/

Missing Children Society of Canada

http://www.mcsc.ca/

National Center for Missing & Exploited Children

http://www.missingkids.com/missingkids/servlet/PublicHomeServlet?LanguageCountry=en_US

National Incidence Studies of Missing, Abducted, Runaway, and Thrownaway Children (NISMÀRT)

https://www.ncjrs.gov/html/ojjdp/nismart/04/

References

Ashcroft, J. (2004). *U.S. Department of Justice Report to Congress from Attorney General John Ashcroft on U.S. Government efforts to combat trafficking in persons.* Washington, DC: U.S. Printing Office.

Burgess, A., Baker, T., Nahirny, C., & Rabun, J. (2002). Newborn kidnappings by Cesarean section. *Journal of Forensic Science, 47*(4), 827–830.

Burgess, A.W., Carr, K.E., Nahirny, C., & Rabun, J.B. (2008). Non-family infant abductors: 1983–2006. *American Journal of Nursing, 108*(9), 32–38.

Burgess, A.W., Groth, A.N., Holmstrom, L.L., & Sgroi, S. (1978). *Sexual assault of children and adolescents.* Lexington, MA: Lexington Books.

Canadian Broadcasting Corporation. (2001). Child prostitution widespread: Experts. Retrieved from http://www.cbc.ca/news/canada/story/2001/02/27/hooker_folo010227.html

Child Labor Education Project. (2004). University of Iowa Labor Center. Retrieved from http://www.continuetolearn.uiowa.edu/laborctr/child_labor/about/us_history.html

Committee on Sexual Offences Against Children and Youth. (1984). *Sexual offences against children.* Ottawa: Department of Supply and Services.

Dalley, M. (2007). The left-behind parents' view of the parental abduction experience. National Missing Children Services. National Police Services Publ. Ottawa: Royal Canadian Mounted Police.

Dugard, J. (2011). Victim impact statement. *ABC News.* Retrieved from http://abcnews.go.com/GMA/jaycee-dugards-victim-impact-statement/story?id=13745897

Federal Bureau of Investigation. (2003). Innocence Lost National Initiative. Retrieved from http://www.missingkids.com/missingkids/servlet/PageServlet?LanguageCountry=en_US&PageId=4166

Federal Bureau of Investigation. (2008). National Crime Information Center (NCIC). Retrieved from http://www.fas.org/irp/agency/doj/fbi/is/ncic.htm

Groth, A.N. (1979). *Men who rape.* New York: Plenum.

Harrington, T. (2010). FBI—Fighting child exploitation. Retrieved from http://www.fbi.gov/news/speeches/fighting-child-exploitation

Justice Canada. (2011). Youth involvement in prostitution: A literature review and annotated bibliography. Retrieved from http://canada.justice.gc.ca/eng/pi/rs/rep-rap/2001/rr01_13/a12.html

Kiedrowski, J., & Dalley, M. (2008). Parental abduction of children: An overview and profile of the abductor. Retrieved from http://www.rcmp-grc.gc.ca/pubs/omc-ned/parent-eng.htm

Matas, R., & Peritz, I. (2008). Canada's poorest postal code in for an Olympic clean-up? Retrieved http://www.theglobeandmail.com/news/national/canadas-poorest-postal-code-in-for-an-olympic-clean-up/article704374/page2/

McLaughlin, E. (2009). Expert: Child trafficker target runaways, "throwaways." Retrieved from http://edition.cnn.com/2009/CRIME/11/18/domestic.child.trafficking/index.html?eref=edition

Missing Children Society of Canada. (n.d.). What do I do? Parental abductions. Retrieved from http://www.mcsc.ca/my-child-is-missing

Newton, M. (n.d.). Robert Pickton: The Missing Vancouver Women. Ch. 2, Tru/Crime Library. Retrieved from http://www.missingpeople.net/robert_pickton.htm

National Center for Missing & Exploited Children. (2011). Missing Kids. Retrieved from http://www.missingkids.com/missingkids/servlet/PublicHomeServlet?LanguageCountry=en_US

National Center for Missing & Exploited Children. (2012). Amber alert program. Retrieved from http://www.ncmec.org/missingkids/servlet/PageServlet?LanguageCountry=en_US&PageId=4319

Parliament of Canada. (2011). Human trafficking. Retrieved from http://www.parl.gc.ca/Content/LOP/ResearchPublications/prb0425-e.htm#intllaw

Patt, M. (2011). Child Prostitution—Lithuania. Retrieve from http://gvnet.com/childprostitution/Lithuania.htm

PBS. (2005). The Mann Act—Full text. Retrieved from http://www.pbs.org/unforgivableblackness/knockout/mannact_text.html

Prentky, R.A., & Burgess, A.W. (2000). *Forensic management of the sex offender*. New York: Plenum.

Raaflaub, T. (2006). Human trafficking in Canada. Retrieved from http://www.parl.gc.ca/Content/LOP/ResearchPublications/prb0425-e.htm

Royal Canadian Mounted Police (RCMP). (2011). Assistance to Federal Agencies and Joint Project: Our missing children. Retrieved from http://www.rcmp-grc.gc.ca/pubs/index-eng.htm#r6.5

Sedlak, A.J., Finkelhor, D., Hammer, H., & Schultz, D.J. (2002). National estimates of missing children: An overview. In *National incidence studies of missing, abducted, runaway, and thrownaway children*. Washington, DC: Office of Juvenile Justice and Delinquency Prevention, Office of Justice Programs, U.S. Department of Justice. Washington, DC: Government Printing.

UNICEF. (2010). UNICEF releases startling report on child protection from http://www.fouryearsgo.org/2010/08/19/world-news/child-protection-from-violence-exploitation-and-abuse/violence, exploitation and abuse

United Nations Inter-Agency Project. (2001–2005). Human Trafficking in the Greater Mekong Sub-Region. Academy for Educational Development. Retrieved from http://www.humantrafficking.org/organizations/36

United Nations Office on Drugs and Crime. (2006). Trafficking in persons report. Retrieved from http://css.unodc.org/pdf/brazil/Trafficking%20in%20Persons%20Report%202006_US%20gov.pdf

USA Trafficking Victims Protection Act (TVPA). (2008). 50 key provisions. Retrieved from http://www.wunrn.com/news/2008/12_08/12_15_08/121508_usa2.htm

United Nations. (2002a). Rights of the Child. Retrieved from http://www.amnesty.ca/themes/children_un_convention.php

United Nations. (2002b). Trafficking in Women and Girls. Retrieved from http://www.un.org/womenwatch/daw/egm/trafficking2002/reports/WP-DAW.PDF

U.S. Department of Labor. (1999). Child Labor Report Press Conference. Retrieved from https:///www.dol.gov/oasam/programs/history/herman/speeches/990325ah.htm

U.S. Department of Labor. (2012a). Office of Child Labor, Forced Labor, and Human Trafficking. Retrieved from http://www.dol.gov/ilab/programs/ocft/

U.S. Department of Labor. (2012b). Fact Sheet. Retrieved from http://www.dol.gov/ilab/programs/iclp/childsoldiers/factsheet.htm

U.S. Department of State. (1999). Human rights report, Section 6d. Retrieved from www.state.gov/www/global/uman_rights/1999_hrp_report

U. S. Department of State. (2008). 2007 Country Report. Released by Bureau of Democracy, Human Rights and Labor. Retrieved from http://www.state.gov/j/drl/rls/hrrpt/2007/

Volpe, R. (2011). The Canadian encyclopedia , historica-dominion. Retrieved from http://thecanadianencyclopedia.com/index.cfm?PgNm=TCE&Params=A1ARTA0001576

Wilson, S. (2010). Child abduction, abductors, and warning signs. Kidproof. Retrieved from http://kidproofblog.com/2010/05/01/child-abduction-abductors-and-warning-signs/

World Health Organization. (2002). *World Health Report. Reducing risks: Promoting health life.* Retrieved from http://www.who.int/whr/2002/en/

World Vision International. (2008). Child sex tourism prevention project partners. Retrieved from http://www.worldvision.org/content.nsf/learn/globalissues-stp-partners

Yutzy, S., Wolfson, J., & Resnick, P. (1993). Child stealing by cesarean section. *Journal of Forensic Science, 38*(1), 192–196.

School Violence

CHAPTER
8

Acknowledgment

We thank Mary Ellen O'Toole and Paul Clements for their contributions to sections of this chapter in the first edition of *Victimology*.

CASE

Lawrence (Larry) King was different from most kids who attended E.O. Green Junior High School in Oxnard, California. After being taken from the home of his adoptive parents, he lived in a youth center called Casa Pacifica that provided foster care for children. He wore mascara, jewelry, lipstick, and stiletto shoes to school. He interacted primarily with girls and openly spoke about his attraction to boys. At one point he asked his teachers to call him Leticia and indicated that he wanted a sex change. It was for these reasons that his eighth grade classmate Marissa Moreno said others taunted him and called him gay. In response to the taunting, Larry would suggest that the other boys were sexually interested in him and would flirt with them. Larry became a central focus of discussion in the school, mainly surrounding whether he should be allowed to dress differently or should conform to school dress code policies. Memos were circulated to teachers about tolerating difference. As a preventative measure Larry was removed from gym class due to issues in the changing room.

Larry then took a particular interest in a fellow student, 14-year-old Brandon McInerney. Brandon was also a troubled boy; both his parents were drug addicts with criminal records, and he seemed to have an unusual interest in World War II Nazism. One day in February Larry initiated a game with the girls, asking who they wished would be their special love on Valentine's Day. Larry then walked up to Brandon, who was playing basketball nearby with friends. Interrupting the game, he asked Brandon to be his valentine. Friends responded with taunts that the two were going to make gay babies. Rumors flew through the school that Brandon would seek revenge. The next day, February 2, 2008, Brandon followed through on his threats. While students sat together in the school's computer lab, Brandon pulled out a concealed handgun and shot Larry in front of his stunned classmates. Two days later Larry died in the hospital (Cathcart, 2008; Setoodeh, 2008).

■ Introduction

In the past certain amounts of violence within schools were tolerated or condoned. Physical discipline of children within the school system continues to exist in many parts of the world, and indeed it was only in 1992 that the Society for Adolescent Medicine wrote a position paper as follows (p. 245):

> The Society for Adolescent Medicine concludes that corporal punishment in schools is an ineffective, dangerous, and unacceptable method of discipline. The use of corporal punishment in the school reinforces the notion that physical aggression is an acceptable and effective means of eliminating unwanted behavior in our society. We join many other national organizations recommending that it be banned and urge that nonviolent methods of classroom control be utilized in our school systems. We must abandon such a technique which overtly promotes more violence on our children.

Similarly, bullying among peers was viewed to be part of the maturation process and generally not a cause for adult intervention. Thus, schools have not traditionally been seen as places where children and adolescents can be safe from violence. Now, however, there is widespread concern about physical abuse that students may suffer at the hands of adults or other children. In light of high profile cases of violence in schools, there is also considerable concern regarding gang violence and school shootings.

■ Scope of the Problem

In the United States statistics on the incidence of school violence are compiled by the National Center for Education Statistics using data from the U.S. Department of Education, the Centers for Disease Control and Prevention (CDC), the Bureau of Justice Statistics, and the National Crime Victimization Survey. Annual National Center for Education Statistics reports present a comprehensive picture on the incidence of school violence in the United States (Robers, Zhang, & Truman, 2010); **Table 8-1** provides summary statistics. In the most recently reported school year (2008–2009), 38 violent deaths of students, teachers, staff, or parents occurred on school property, including 24 homicides and 14 suicides (Robers et al., 2010). Nevertheless, these figures are only a small percentage of homicides and suicides of youth aged 5 to 18 years. It is sobering to note that 50 times more homicides and 150 times more suicides occurred in this population off school property during that same period. Nonfatal crimes show a different picture, however. Young people were more likely to experience both theft and violent crimes at school (1.2 million reports) than away from school

TABLE 8-1 School Violence in the United States

- 8% of students in grades 9–12 reported being threatened or injured with a weapon on school property, including threats with guns, knives, and clubs.
- 31% of students in grades 9–12 reported they had been in a physical fight at least one time during the previous 12 months anywhere.
- 11% of students said they had been in a fight on school property during the previous 12 months.
- Students ages 12–18 were victims of about 1.2 million nonfatal crimes (theft plus violent crime) at school (2008).
- 85% of public schools recorded that one or more incidents of crime had taken place at school, amounting to an estimated 2.0 million crimes.
- Of the 38 student, staff, and nonstudent violent deaths on school property occurring during the 2008–2009 school year, 24 were homicides and 14 were suicides.
- In 2007, approximately 5% of students ages 12–18 reported they were afraid of attack or harm at school.

Data from Robers, S., Zhang, J., and Truman, J. 2010. Indicators of School Crime and Safety: 2010 (NCES 2011-002/NCJ 230812). National Center for Education Statistics, U.S. Department of Education, and Bureau of Justice Statistics, Office of Justice Programs, U.S. Department of Justice. Washington, DC.

(1 million reports). However, this pattern differs according to age, with younger adolescents (aged 12–14) more likely to be victimized at school and older students (aged 15–18) more likely to be victimized away from school. Of all types of school violence, bullying is the most prevalent in middle schools, with 44% of middle schools in the United States reporting this problem. Gang violence is the most prevalent form of violence in high schools; indeed, 43% of high schools in the United States report gangs as a problem (Robers et al., 2010).

Teachers are also victims of crime at school. Survey results from 2007–2008 reported by Robers and colleagues (2010) indicate that 7% of teachers are threatened and 4% are physically attacked on the job. This rate is higher for teachers in inner city schools, 10% of whom report being threatened and 7% of whom report being attacked. Rates are also comparatively higher for high school teachers than for junior school teachers and for male teachers than for female teachers.

■ Legislation Addressing School Violence

Addressing school violence through legislation is complex given the diverse nature of this issue. At the federal level in the United States, the Gun-Free Schools Act was introduced in 1994 as an amendment to the 1964 Elementary and Secondary Schools Education Act. It requires that "each State receiving Federal funds under this Act shall have in effect a State law requiring local educational agencies to expel from school for a period of not less than one year a student who is determined to have brought a weapon to a school" (Section 14601 (b) 1). Individual states were required to enact legislation in compliance with this Act by October 1995. Florida, for instance, has the following legislation (Section 790.115):

> A person who exhibits a sword, sword cane, firearm, electric weapon or device, destructive device, or other weapon, including a razor blade, box cutter, or knife … at any school-sponsored event or on the grounds of facilities of any school, school bus, or school bus stop, or within 1,000 feet of the real property that comprises a public or private elementary school, middle school, or secondary school, during school hours or during the time of a sanctioned school activity, commits a felony of the third degree.

Under the Gun-Free Schools Act, education agencies must also have a policy that refers any student with a weapon to the criminal or juvenile justice system.

Individual states have attempted to address school violence beyond weapons use. For instance, the New York legislature passed the Safe Schools Against Violence in Education (SAVE) legislation in 1990. This legislation is broad based and has requirements for violence prevention training for teachers, school safety plans, building emergency response plans, codes of conduct, reporting requirements, and procedures for dealing with violent students. Penalties for assaults on teachers were increased in the SAVE legislation, changing them from misdemeanors to felony offenses. Colorado has introduced the Safe Schools Bullying Policy that defines bullying and requires each school district to develop policies and committees that address bullying.

Gang violence is a serious problem in North American schools, and yet law enforcement has been largely unable to effectively address the issue. In large part this is due to difficulties in obtaining convictions through criminal justice processes. In the United States some states attempted to address the problem through civil means. At present, most states have legislation addressing various aspects of gang activity such as gang participation or wearing gang clothing. For instance, the California Education Code does not allow wearing of gang clothing in schools. Arizona law allows for extended sentences if a felony is committed in a school safety zone. Illinois law makes it a felony to recruit for a gang on school property. Nevada directs boards of trustees of school districts to adopt antigang policies.

Police departments across the United States are developing specialized gang units. Three hundred sixty-five gang units employing 4,300 officers were found in the United States in 2007 (Langton, 2010). In 2009 Canada introduced specific legislation to address gang violence (Bill C-14, 2009). Changes to the Criminal Code of Canada included the following:

- Murders connected to organized crime activity are automatically classified as first-degree and are subject to a mandatory sentence of life imprisonment without eligibility for parole for 25 years.
- A new offense for drive-by and other reckless shootings was added. The minimum sentence for this offense is longer if the offense was committed for a criminal organization or with a prohibited or restricted firearm.
- Two new offenses of aggravated assault against a peace or public officer and assault with a weapon on a peace or public officer were added with maximum penalties of 14 and 10 years, respectively.

■ Bullying

Bullying is an insidious problem, with the potential for devastating emotional and physical effects, which has existed probably since the beginning of time. According to the Stopbullying.gov website, "Bullying is unwanted, aggressive behavior among school aged children that involves a real or perceived power imbalance. The behavior is repeated, or has the potential to be repeated, over time" (U.S. Department of Health and Human Services, 2012). In a large national survey in the United States, over 15,000 students reported on their bullying experiences. Thirty percent reported moderate to frequent involvement with bullying, 13% indicated they were bullies, 10.6% indicated they were victims, and 6.3% indicated they were both (Nansel et al., 2001). In 2007 the National Center for Education Statistics reported that 32% of students aged 12 to 18 identified they were bullied in the past year: 21% were ridiculed, 18% were the subject of rumors; 11% were physically bullied, and 6% were threatened (Robers et al., 2010). Twenty-one percent of primary schools and 44% of middle schools reported during the 2007–2008 school year that bullying occurred between students on a daily or weekly basis (Robers et al., 2010).

Types of Bullying

Bullying can occur in many forms; the broad categories are physical, emotional, and social bullying. Bullying can occur through direct contact or indirectly through rumors and social exclusion. Increasingly, bullying is occurring via electronic means, called cyberbullying.

Physical bullying can include pushing, hitting, tripping, spitting at, or, more rarely, physical beating. This type of bullying peaks during grades 6 through 8 and is reported about twice as often by boys than by girls. Verbal bullying includes taunts, threats, name calling, and derogatory comments. Approximately twice as many students indicate they are victims of verbal bullying than those who admit to perpetrating it. Social bullying involves rumors and behaviors aimed at deliberate social exclusion. This is more commonly reported by girls than by boys.

Factors Contributing to Bullying

Inevitably, when researchers attempt to determine factors that contribute to bullying they reach the conclusion that it is caused by multiple factors. These factors can include individual factors of both the victim and the bully, family of origin factors, the peer group, and the school setting.

A study of 185 grade 9 students in Sweden revealed that students were most likely to attribute the causes of bullying to individual characteristics of the bully (69%) and secondarily to characteristics of the victim (42%) (Thornberg & Knutsen, 2011). In this study students were most likely to believe that others were bullies because of personal flaws, such as low self-esteem, psychological problems, issues with hostility, or coming from a problematic family with poor parenting. Students also believed that the bullying behavior was motivated by a desire for social positioning and attempting to protect oneself from social exclusion. The most common victim characteristic thought by students to result in bullying was that the victim was deviant, irritating, or weak. Only 13% of this sample thought bullying was caused by peer group pressure. A mere 7% attributed it to school factors, such as boredom or poor antibullying policies, and, similarly, 7% thought it was due to societal or human nature factors (Thornberg & Knutsen, 2011).

Many studies have confirmed that students who are victims of bullying do have distinguishing characteristics. They are more likely to report being physically hurt by a family member (23.2% of bullied students compared to 6.2% of nonbullied students), and 22.8% report witnessing violence in their families (compared to 6.6% of nonbullied students) (CDC, 2011). The rate of family violence among bullied students is also higher than among students who admit to being bullies (CDC, 2011). Other studies have demonstrated that it is the interaction between these individual variables and other variables that lead to bullying behavior. For instance, Lee (2011) demonstrated that although individual factors of both the victim and the bully were important, these were mediated by parenting factors (including authoritarian parenting and domestic violence), teacher interventions, and peer group interactions. Another study demonstrated that students with high self-esteem were *less* likely to bully in a positive school environment where students did not believe violence was normal. However, high self-esteem students were *more* likely to bully in negative school environments where violence was the norm (Gendron, Williams, & Guerra, 2011).

A particularly confusing aspect of bullying, however, is that bullying is often perpetrated by someone the victim believes to be a friend. Mishna, Wiener, and Pepler (2008) conducted qualitative interviews with a subsample of children who identified being bullied in a citywide survey. Of those interviewed, 89% indicated they had been bullied by a friend. In this study parents and teachers were also interviewed, and, interestingly, for the most part they had not identified the child as being bullied by friends. Thus, this type of bullying is more insidious and less recognizable. Parents may unwittingly place the child in difficult situations by encouraging interactions with the bullies and questioning the child when they do not wish to participate in activities. For children, this type of bullying resulted in high levels of distress, and due to the sense of betrayal and isolation, these children experienced self-blame for the bullying and difficulty in disclosing the bullying to others for fear of losing the friendship and expectations that adults will not intervene (Mishna & Alaggia, 2005).

Effects of Bullying

Outcomes for both bullies and those who are bullied are serious. Those who bully experience academic problems, poor psychological adjustment, and later, delinquency (Nansel et al., 2001). Bullies have higher rates of alcohol and drug abuse, are more likely to engage in early sexual activity, are more likely to have criminal convictions later in life, and are more likely to be perpetrators of intimate partner violence. Those who are bullied experience psychological distress and adjustment problems, heightened anxiety, and low self-esteem. Bullied students can exhibit avoidant and withdrawal behaviors, such as refusing to attend school, or self-protective behaviors, such as carrying a weapon or joining a gang (Wynne & Joo, 2011). From a mental health perspective, bullying has been associated with depression, anxiety, eating disorders, and a wide range of somatic symptoms (CDC, 2011; Ttofi & Farrington, 2008). Those who have been bullied are considerably more likely to have seriously considered suicide (24.9%) than students who have not been bullied (4.5%) and have much higher rates of intentional self-injury (40.9% vs. 8.4%) (CDC, 2011).

On January 2, 2002, J. Daniel Scruggs, a 12-year-old boy, was found dead, hanging by a tie in his closet. The fact that such a young child would commit suicide baffled many. As it turns out, Scruggs was the victim of relentless bullying at the middle school he attended. Daniel was a small boy, weighing only 63 pounds, and, although he had a high IQ, suffered from a learning disability. As a result, he was a lonely outcast who was severely tormented by the peers at his school. His classmates would push him around and call him names because he wore mismatched clothes, acted strangely, and smelled like he rarely bathed. He was hit, kicked, spit on, laughed at, thrown down a flight of stairs, and sometimes made to eat his lunch off the cafeteria floor. Classmates report that Daniel was bullied every day he was in school and teachers rarely did anything to stop the behaviors or hold the bullies accountable. His gym teacher stated that he had witnessed Daniel being physically picked up by a peer and spun in the air. The incident had been reported to school administrators, but no disciplinary action had been taken (Stowe, 2003). By the seventh grade Daniel often refused to bathe and even soiled himself so he would not have to go to school. He had been moved to a trailer behind the school designated for children who had trouble fitting in with other students. School officials had also recommended to Daniel's mother that she seek counseling for him. As a result of Daniel's chronic truancy, the Department of Children and Families became involved. The appointed caseworker suggested that Daniel change schools but nevertheless failed to see how serious the case really was. In fact, the case was closed 6 days before Daniel's death despite the fact that he had missed 74 of the 78 preceding schools days (Santora, 2003).

Daniel's mother was a single mother who worked two jobs and raised Daniel and his sister all on her own. Their father had physically abused his wife and abandoned his family when Daniel was only 3 months old. Daniel's mother worked at Daniel's school as a teacher's aide and said that she complained to school officials about the bullying but stated she had no idea how severe the abuse really was until it was too late. After Daniel's death his mother had planned to sue the school for ignoring how badly he had been mistreated and not intervening or providing the help he needed. However, the mother was arrested and charged with three counts of risk of injury to a minor and one count of cruelty to persons. The police alleged that Ms. Scruggs had raised Daniel in an unhealthy home environment and failed to provide him with the proper medical and psychological care he needed. Their home was filled with piles of debris, clothing, dirty dishes, garbage, and other clutter (Santora, 2003).

Ms. Scruggs went on trial and was found guilty on one count of risk of injury to a minor for an unhealthy home environment. Jurors report the decision was based on the fact that every night Daniel slept surrounded by steak knives out of fear. The judge spared Ms. Scruggs from having to serve a prison sentence and instead placed her on probation for 5 years with 100 hours of community service. The judge also ordered her to undergo mandatory counseling. This was the first case in Connecticut in which a parent was held criminally accountable for a child's suicide (Salzman, 2004). After pronouncing the sentence the judge affirmed that "the law requires parents and caregivers to protect their children, to keep them safe, and to make sure they're not subjected to risks to their health" (Salzman, 2004, p. 4). He further admonished Ms. Scruggs for the lack of remorse she displayed regarding her son's death and the horrible circumstances in which he was forced to live (Salzman, 2004).

An investigation conducted by the state's child advocate and chief state's attorney found that school officials, the state's child protection system, and Ms. Scruggs had all failed Daniel in one way or another. Not one of these parties acted in a way to ensure Daniel received the care he so desperately needed. Instead, his frantic cries for help were ignored and left unanswered. Daniel's experience of relentless bullying and subsequent suicide led to a new law in Connecticut that now requires schools to report bullying to the authorities (Santora, 2003).

Managing and Preventing Bullying

Given the nature of bullying, approaches to managing and preventing it are necessarily broad based. Successful programs to address bullying use a whole-school approach that involves strong teacher leadership; clear behaviors and norms; adult awareness, supervision, and monitoring; student involvement in program development and delivery; and age- and gender-appropriate social skills training (Public Safety Canada, 2008). In 1994 the Cherry School District in Colorado developed a program titled Bully-Proofing Your School that serves as a model to other communities. In this program members of the school community work together to identify and alter the factors that allow bullying to occur. The program focuses on "the caring majority" of students and involves teaching students strategies for developing and maintaining a caring environment. Similarly, the Olweus Bullying Prevention Program (also from Colorado) has now been implemented in over a dozen countries and involves individual, classroom, and school level interventions. Farrington and Ttofi (2009) conducted a systematic review of 30 studies examining the efficacy of school-based intervention programs in reducing bullying. They concluded that such programs reduce bullying by 20% to 23%. In their meta-analysis the most important factors associated with decreased bullying were consistent disciplinary methods, parent meetings, playground supervision, and cooperative peer group work.

In response to the troubling results of a national survey on bullying published in 2001 (Nansel et al., 2001), U.S. Department of Health and Human Services Health Resources and Services Administration launched the Stop Bullying Now! campaign. This national media campaign focused on youth aged 9 to 13 and the adults in their lives. It sought to raise awareness about bullying, to shape attitudes and behaviors, and to identify strategies for intervention. An accompanying interactive website (http://stopbullyingnow.hrsa.gov/) features webisodes that help kids, teens, and teachers recognize and stop bullying. This website also identifies that parents have a role to play in preventing and/or stopping bullying and recommends that parents watch for the signs identified in **Table 8-2**. However, although the information in **Table 8-2** can be helpful, relying on signs of bullying does have risks. One study found that parents and teachers frequently did not identify a child who was being bullied or questioned the veracity of a child's disclosure of bulling

TABLE 8-2 Signs of Bullying

Signs a Child May Be a Victim of Bullying
• Comes home with damaged clothing or belongings
• Frequently loses books and/or personal belongings
• Has unexplained injuries
• Attempts to avoid school because of headaches, stomachaches, feeling sick
• Does not want to visit with friends or has fewer friends
• Changes in eating habits
• Feels helpless, bad about themselves, moody, anxious, or angry
• Afraid of going to school, doing activities with friends

Signs a Child May Be a Bully
• Becomes violent or gets into fights with others
• Gets sent to the principal's office or has frequent detentions
• Has extra money or belongings
• Blames others
• Has friends who are bullies

Adapted from www.stopbullying.gov.

because the child did not "fit" expectations about how a victimized child presents, for instance, grades had not dropped, they appeared to have friends, they remained calm and focused (Mishna, Pepler, & Weiner, 2006). It is thus important for parents and teachers to not only watch for warning signs but also to be open to disclosures from children and youth who do not fit the model.

■ Gang Violence in Schools

Gangs began in the United States in the 1820s in New York in response to large-scale immigration. These early gangs were populated by White Europeans who faced extreme economic and social conditions (Howell, Egley, Tita, & Griffiths, 2011). The next documented wave of gang activity occurred in the 1920s, when 1,313 gangs were reported in Chicago. Sociologist Frederick Thrasher (1927) described the manner in which European-born and first-generation youth joined gangs in response to societal conditions in which they found themselves. These youth, he observed, were struggling with the clash between cultural customs from the homeland and the expectations of their new country. Their lives lacked the organizing and stabilizing structures experienced by peers with longer family histories in America, and thus they were prey to the organization offered by gangs (Thrasher, 1927). Gang problems in many cities began to emerge again in the 1970s and expanded throughout the 1980s and 1990s. At that time most gang members were African American or Latino youth. Conditions believed to contribute to this rise were the losses of hundreds of thousands of factory jobs leading to poverty, economic marginalization, and social disorganization in some U.S. cities. An informal economy involving illegal activity grew and flourished. By 2000, however, the membership of gangs had again shifted in response to large-scale immigration from Latin America and Asia (Moore & Hagedorn, 2001).

A **youth gang** is a self-formed association of peers who have the following characteristics: three or more members, generally aged 12 to 24 years; a name and some sense of identity, generally indicated by such symbols as style of clothing, graffiti, and hand signs; some degree of permanence and organization; and an elevated level of involvement in delinquent or criminal activity (National Youth Gang Center, 2008). They control their territories through violence and intimidation. They increase their size through recruiting members, often from single-parent, low-income households. As of September 2005 Los Angeles County had over 1,400 gangs, with a total membership exceeding 160,000. Estimates based on law enforcement reports in 2009 suggested there were 28,100 gangs and 731,000 gang members in the United States (Egley & Howell, 2011) (**Figure 8-1**).

Gang Participation

Gangs frequently are formed in response to an awareness that other gangs are forming. Members are drawn together because of a perceived need for protection. Rivalries exist over neighborhood dominance, drug turf, and symbolic ascendance or power. In general, these gangs are not well organized and have weak control over their members. The response to perceived threat from others outside the gang is violence. One attraction to gangs is the loyalty that members have to one another. Gangs provide a family system that is often very alluring to youth. According to the National Youth Gang Center (2008), several factors contribute to the development of youth gangs:

- Conventional socializing agents, such as families and schools, are largely ineffective and alienating and adult supervision is absent.
- Adolescents have a great deal of free time that is not consumed by other prosocial roles.
- Members have limited access to appealing careers or jobs.
- Young people have a place to congregate—usually a well-defined neighborhood.

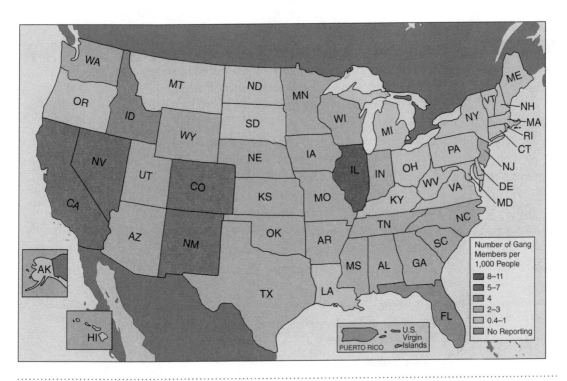

FIGURE 8-1 Gang Membership per Capita by State

Data from National Gang Intelligence Center. 2009. Gang Proliferation. Retrieved from http://www.justice.gov/ndic/pubs32/32146/gangs.htm.

Sharkey, Shekhtmeyster, Chavez-Lopez, Norris, and Sass (2011) provided a summary of theories to explain youth attraction to gangs, found in **Table 8-3**.

Nevertheless, gangs are not a safe haven for members. As a result of the weak organizational structure and lack of control over members, violence is used as a threat if members are not compliant (Decker & Curry, 2002). When joining a gang, an initiate must prove his or her worthiness. In some gangs initiation involves committing a crime, or new members might have to be "beaten in," where members punch and kick them for a period of several minutes while they cannot fight back (Carlie, 2002). Female gang members are either "beaten in" or "sexed in," which includes sex with numerous members and may result in violent sexual assault (Walker, 2008). Without question, initiations are generally very brutal; however, when this initial step is complete the seemingly unlimited benefits of love, belonging, and protection are quite alluring.

TABLE 8-3 **Theories for Understanding Gang Participation**

Theory	Characteristics
Strain theory	Multiple strains, including poverty and social disintegration, challenge youth
	Unable to achieve success in socially defined manner
	Look to achieve success through gang activities
Social learning theory	Family disorganization
	Family structures do not model healthy development
	Gang provides normative model for behavior
Systems theory	Family disorganization and inability to meet need
	Other systems (school, church) do not fill the gap
	Gang provides a protective, structured environment
Social control theory	Lack of clear community expectations of behavior
	Gang provides clear rules and expectations
Self-control theory	Inability to control own impulses
	Fits with gang activities

Data from Sharkey, J., Shekhtmeyster, Z., Chavez-Lopez, L., Norris, E. & Sass, L. 2011. The protective influence of gangs: Can schools compensate? *Aggression and Violent Behavior. 16*, 45-54.

Gang Violence

Gang members account for a disproportionate amount of violence in our society. In large part this is because gangs play an important role in facilitating drug sales, resulting in a concomitant need for protection. As more guns were drawn into the urban drug markets in the early 1990s, they eventually became diffused throughout the youth population and contributed to a sudden spike in homicides in the United States between 1990 and 1994. Between 1998 and 2003 gang members were believed to commit 6% of violent crime in the United States (Harrell, 2005). Not surprisingly perhaps, gang violence is most likely to occur in large cities and least likely to occur in rural areas as demonstrated in **Figure 8-2** (National Youth Gang Center, 2011). Individuals between the ages of 12 and 19 were 4 times more likely to be victims of gang violence than those aged 20 to 49 and 10 times more likely than those people over the age of 50. Young males were at highest risk (Harrell, 2005). Of those young people who are victims of gang crime, it is gang members themselves who are at highest risk (Delisi, Barnes, Beaver, & Gibson, 2009).

In Chicago, gang-motivated homicides represented approximately one-fourth of all homicides between 1993 and 1995, and 45% of homicides in Los Angeles between 1994 and 1995 were gang related (Decker & Curry, 2002). Gang homicides are more likely to occur between members of the same ethnic group and involve younger offenders and victims than nongang homicides. The peak risk ages to be killed in a gang homicide

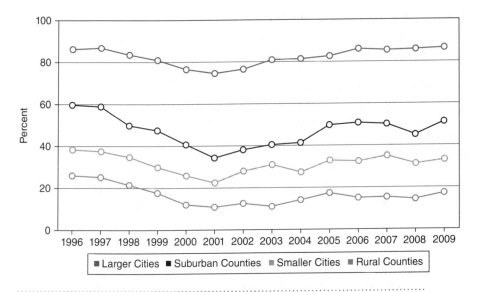

FIGURE 8-2 Prevalence of Gang Violence by Area Type

Data from National Youth Gang Center. 2011. http://www.nationalgangcenter.gov//.

are between 15 and 19 years. The homicides are more likely to have multiple participants, occur in the street, and involve the use of automobiles. They are significantly more likely to involve firearms (Decker & Curry, 2002). The issue of perceived threat from a rival gang is key to understanding gang homicide. Further, many of the killings are retaliatory in nature. Gang violence escalates rapidly as one event triggers another.

Victims of Gang Violence

A special report from the Office for Victims of Crime (Seymour & Ray, 1996) identified several characteristics unique to victims of gang violence. First, victims and witnesses generally live among the perpetrators of their crimes. They frequently face the entire gang, as opposed to a sole perpetrator, even at the funeral of their murdered family member. Victims and witnesses are often intimidated into not cooperating with the criminal justice system and are fearful of retaliation if they do. Second, victims and survivors are often seen as contributing in some way to the crime. This is particularly true for surviving family members of murdered children, some of whom were members of gangs. Third, victims are frequently afraid or unable to exercise victims' rights. As a result of intimidation, fear of retaliation, or due to poverty or culture, many victims of gang violence do not exercise their rights, which often include the right to be notified of, attend, and be heard at court proceedings; to be informed when the defendant

TABLE 8-4 Characteristics of Victims of Gang Violence

- Victims and witnesses generally live with and/or among the perpetrators of their crimes, similar to domestic violence victims.
- Victims and survivors are often seen as contributors to the crime.
- Victims are frequently afraid or unable to exercise victims' rights.
- Victims may be fearful of seeking or receiving restitution for fear of intimidation or retaliation.
- Despite legislation that allows for relocation, prosecutors lack funding for relocating victims and witnesses of gang violence.
- Lack of English language skills often prohibits engagement in the judicial process.
- Victims may be affected by cultural norms and mores that include a general distrust of government, and hence they may not access, or even be aware of, available services or participate in any way within the criminal justice system.

Data from Office for Victims of Crime. 1996.

is released or escapes; and to receive restitution. Safety and protection issues for victims are a serious concern. See **Table 8-4** for characteristics of victims of gang violence.

Addressing Gang Violence in Schools

Gangs are a significant problem in schools. A U.S. national survey released in August 2010 revealed that 45% of high school students and 35% of middle school students say there are gangs or gang members in their schools (Arciaga, Sakamoto, & Jones, 2010). Further, an earlier study revealed that 7.6% of secondary school boys and 3.8% of girls reported belonging to a gang (Gottfredson & Gottfredson, 2001). Although earlier views considered girls in gangs to be largely "possessions," it is increasingly clear they are intricately involved in criminal activity and violence (Moore & Hagedorn, 2001). Despite this, only 5% of principals surveyed indicated gang activity in their schools (Arciaga et al., 2010). Nevertheless, gangs can be identified in schools through gang attire (clothing, jewelry, belt buckles, customized T-shirts), hand signs, behaviors, and graffiti. These identifying characteristics serve several purposes: scaring off enemies, getting victims to comply, discouraging bystanders from interfering, and discouraging witnesses from coming forward. Considering the factors that attract youth to gangs discussed in **Table 8-3**, school-based interventions are vital and should include the following:

- Programs to strengthen families and parenting skills
- Programs that promote and strengthen social and academic competencies

- Programs that enhance a sense of community among students, teachers, and academic leaders
- Engagement of community groups and community leaders
- Provision of social and instrumental supports for youth at risk

■ Teachers as Victims of School Violence

Violence against teachers is an area that has received surprisingly little attention considering the rates at which teachers are victims of aggression and assault. A study by the U.S. Bureau of Labor Statistics, for instance, reported that schools have the highest percentage of compensation claims for nonfatal violent events. In California, this is a rate 3.5 times higher than the average in the workforce (Casteel, Peek-Asa, & Limbos, 2007). During the 2007–2008 school year, 8% of U.S. secondary school teachers and 7% of elementary school teachers reported being threatened with injury by a student; 6% of elementary school teachers and 2% of high school teachers reported being assaulted (Robers et al., 2010).

Reports from other countries indicate shocking rates of violence against teachers. For instance, 49% of teachers in Slovakia reported experiencing violence in the past 30 days (Dzuka & Dalbert, 2007). Other studies focus on student reports of violence toward teachers. A study conducted in Taiwan, for instance, found that over 30% of students in grades 4 through 12 reported being involved in at least one aggressive behavior toward teachers in the past 12 months (Chen & Astor, 2008). Students reported mocking, cursing, insulting, teasing, or playing harmful tricks on teachers. A much smaller number (2.4%) reported actual acts of physical violence. Reported reasons for violence, in order of frequency, were what were perceived to be unreasonable requirements (55.7%), unfair treatment (48.6%), disagreements (41.6%), in response to punishment (23.2%), being upset (16.1%), and perceived provocation (11.5%) (Chen & Astor, 2008). A small number of students indicated that teachers were simply easy targets (5.9%) (Chen & Astor, 2008).

A national survey of students in Israel revealed lower yet still significant rates of violence (Khoury-Kassabri, Astor, & Benbenishty, 2009). In this survey 14% of students reported verbal aggression against a teacher, almost 7% reported destroying personal belongings of a teacher, and slightly less than 4% of students reported physical violence against a teacher. Factors associated with higher reported rates of violence and aggression included male gender, lower family income, and lower educational attainment of parents. Further, violence against teachers is higher in areas with greater amounts of community violence.

■ School Shootings

School shootings are a sad part of our crime culture in the 20th and 21st centuries. Although rare events, when they occur school shootings shock the conscience of society and generate demands for such actions as tighter gun controls, stronger mental health intervention, and faster, more efficient law enforcement responses. The issues facing educators, law enforcement agencies, and the mental health community are how to identify students at risk of lethal violence, how to assess the degree of threat, and, tragically, how to manage the aftermath of these horrifying events.

Columbine

The name "Columbine" has become synonymous with school shootings. The Columbine High School massacre occurred on Tuesday, April 29, 1999 when two students, Eric Harris and Dylan Klebold, shot and killed 12 students and a teacher, as well as wounding 24 others, before committing suicide. It remains the third-deadliest school shooting in U.S. history, after the 1966 University of Texas mass shooting and the 2007 Virginia Tech shootings.

The massacre began with Eric and Dylan hauling two bombs hidden in duffle bags into the school cafeteria each consisting of a propane tank, a gasoline tank, a detonator, and a timer. The bombs, set to explode at 11:17 a.m., were placed within close range of the table occupied by the "jocks," that were among the 480 students eating lunch. Dylan and Eric left the cafeteria and strategically positioned themselves outside the building, ready to shoot students as they fled the bombs. Their weapons, a semi-automatic handgun and a 12-gauge, sawed-off shotgun, were hidden under black trench coats. They carried duffle bags with back-up weapons including explosive devices, ammunition, and knives. Their cars were fixed with bombs timed to explode while emergency response personnel were on scene. The plan was to kill 500 people. Mercifully however, the bombs did not explode and the young men therefore changed plans, ran into the school and began their shooting spree (Larkin, 2007).

Time Magazine (Gibbs & Roche, 1999) describes the content of videos taped by Dylan and Eric prior the attacks. In the tapes they itemize their hatred towards all "niggers, spics, Jews, gays, f____ing whites," students who abused them, and others who did not defend them. They brag with anticipation that "It's going to be like F___ing Doom." Eric and Dylan prepared extensively for the massacre, trying on their coats with weapons concealed, carrying weapons in their duffle bags, concealing equipment in their bedrooms. It has been identified that in hindsight, there were clues that these students were dangerous (Achenbach & Russakoff, 1999). In a composition for class, as a young child Eric created a story in which he and his brother were Rambo-like heroes armed with M-16s and fighting off an army. In the year before the Columbine shooting, he kept a journal in which he detailed year-long plans for killing others which he hoped would result in 500 dead and he and Dylan hijacking a plane and crashing into New York City. In creative writing class in high school, neither young man attempted to conceal their dark interests, consistently turning in violent stories that they shared with the class. In the fall, they made a video for a government and economics class in which they pretended to be hit men who could be hired to bring justice to jocks who picked on other students, ending it with a violent scene in which they bludgeoned the head of a dummy covered in fake blood (Achenback & Russakoff, 1999). Added to this were violent blogs and a violent website that hosted the first-person shooting game DOOM. Further videos documented their shooting practice, and a final one contained a goodbye and apology to friends and family. Despite all of this and an arrest in January 1998 for stealing a computer, the true danger was tragically never noted.

Indications and Threats of Violence

After a violent incident has taken place, retracing an offender's past and identifying clues that in retrospect could have been signs of danger can yield significant, useful information. However, even clues that appear to help interpret past events cannot be taken as predictors of similar events in the future. At this time no research has identified traits and characteristics that can reliably distinguish school shooters from other students, including other students who may threaten but never carry out their threats. Many students appear to have traits and characteristics similar to those observed in students who were involved in school shootings. They dress a similar way, they have similar tastes in music, they are loners, many even have felt bullied, yet the vast majority of these students have never acted out in a violent way. Simply put, there is no "profile" of a school shooter. However, lessons are learned from every school shooting incident and every school shooter. In 1999, following the mass shooting at Columbine High School, the U.S. Federal Bureau of Investigation's (FBI) National Center for the Analysis of Violent Crime hosted the first of its kind conference on school shootings. Based on the data generated from this conference combined with their extensive experience in the area of threat assessment, in 2000 the FBI published a monograph titled, "The School Shooter: A Threat Assessment Perspective" (O'Toole, 1999).

Threat is defined by *Webster's* dictionary as an expression of intention to inflict evil, injury, or damage. A threat can be spoken, written, or symbolic, for example, motioning with one's hands as though shooting at another person. Threats also carry varying levels of intensity, and, fortunately, most people who threaten are unlikely to carry out their threat. However, as in the case example at the beginning of this chapter, a relatively common threat of one student toward another can at times result in tragic consequences. Thus, all threats must be taken seriously and evaluated. A comprehensive threat assessment program should include not only procedures to assess a threat but also to assess a student's behavior and other communications that could indicate future violence. Threats can be classified into four types: **direct threat**, **indirect threat**, **veiled threat**, and **conditional threat** (**Table 8-5**).

The assessment of threat requires specialized training and generally contains four elements: personality dynamics of the individual issuing the threat, family dynamics, school dynamics, and social dynamics. Hong, Cho, Allen-Meares, and Espelage (2011) provide an ecological assessment of the Columbine tragedy using this multiple element analysis. *Personality dynamics* considered include means of managing stress

TABLE 8-5 Types of Threats

Type of Threat	Definition
Direct threat	Identifies a specific act against a specific target
	Delivered in a straightforward, clear, and explicit manner: "I am going to place a bomb in the school's gym."
Indirect threat	Tends to be vague, unclear, and ambiguous
	Plan, intended victim, motivation, and other aspects of the threat are masked or equivocal
	Suggests that a violent act *could* occur, not that it *will* occur: "If I wanted to, I could kill everyone at this school!"
Veiled threat	Strongly implies but does not explicitly threaten violence
	Clearly hints at a possible violent act but leaves it to the potential victim to interpret the message: "We would all be better off without you around anymore."
Conditional threat	Often seen in extortion cases
	Warns that a violent act will happen unless certain demands or terms are met: "If you don't pay me 1 million dollars, I will place a bomb in the school."

Data from O'Toole, M.E. 1999. The School Shooter: A Threat Assessment Perspective. FBI Critical Incident Response Group, National Center for the Analysis of Violent Crime, Quantico, VA.

and conflicts, expression of anger, resiliency, response to authority, need for control, and ability to empathize with others. From this perspective both Eric and Dylan had undergone counseling for depression, impulsivity, and antisocial behavior. Eric had paranoid traits and unconstrained aggression, and Dylan was described as overly sensitive to shame and humiliation. Thus, consistent with literature on risk factors, the perpetrators were primarily male, had histories of mental and emotional distress, and had histories of aggression and antisocial behavior (Hong, Cho, & Lee, 2010). *Family dynamics* consider both role modeling in the family and the ability of family to provide a supportive environment. Questions have been raised about the family environments of Dylan and Eric and the fact that parents did not see the evidence reported in the youth's journals, the accumulation of weapons, and the concerns reported by friends and neighbors (Hong et al., 2011). Strong parent–child relationships and positive parental modeling are protective factors against violence. School dynamics include the culture, rules, and roles of people within the school. Dylan and Eric did not fit into the school culture and were frequently taunted by kids. Peer victimization and poor peer relationships are common themes in postmortem examinations of school shootings (Hong et al., 2010). Finally, *social dynamics* involve issues related to larger society. Dylan and Eric were obsessed by violent video games and attended gun shows, both of which are common features of American society. Lack of access to mental health services and availability of weapons are risk factors for violence of all types (Hong et al., 2010). For most individuals this does not result in violence, but when personality and other factors interact, it can support unhealthy beliefs and provide access to means of violence. The FBI divides risk into the categories listed in **Table 8-6.**

Effects of School Shooting

The tragic events of Virginia Tech, Northern Illinois University, and Columbine have had a wide range of impacts on campuses. One impact is the increase of security systems, including emergency communication systems through text, e-mail, and phone alerts; increased security staff; and allowing security staff and others to carry concealed weapons on campus (Kaminsky, Koons-Witt, Thompson, & Weiss, 2010). A second impact is on students who were present at schools where shootings occur. Such exposure not surprisingly can result in symptoms of posttraumatic stress. Factors that are protective and are associated with fewer posttraumatic stress symptoms include having a strong social support network, family support, and a sense of self-worth (Grills-Taquechel, Littleton, & Axsom, 2011). Interestingly, student exposure to media attention of the event has not been found to be

TABLE 8-6 Levels of Threat Risk

Level	Characteristics
Low level: Poses a minimal risk to the victim and public safety.	Vague and indirect
	Information is inconsistent, implausible, or lacks detail
	Lacks realism
	Content suggests person is unlikely to carry it out
Medium level: Could be carried out, although it may not appear to be entirely realistic	More direct and concrete
	Wording suggests some thought as to how the act will be carried out
	May be a general indication of a possible place and time that still falls well short of a detailed plan
	No strong indication of preparatory steps, although there may be some veiled reference or ambiguous or inconclusive evidence pointing to that possibility
	May contain an allusion to a book or movie that shows the planning of a violent act or a vague, general statement about the availability of weapons
	May be a specific statement seeking to convey that the threat is not empty: "I'm serious!" or "I really mean this!"
High level: Appears to pose an imminent and serious danger to the safety of others	Direct, specific, and plausible
	Suggests concrete steps have been taken toward carrying it out, for example, has acquired or practiced with a weapon or has had the victim under surveillance
	Example: "At 8 o'clock tomorrow morning, I intend to shoot the principal. That's when he is in the office by himself. I have a 9mm. Believe me, I know what I am doing. I am sick and tired of the way he runs this school."
	Direct, specific as to the victim, motivation, weapon, place, and time, and indicates the threatener knows his or her target's schedule and has made preparations to act on the threat

Data from O'Toole, M.E. 1999. The School Shooter: A Threat Assessment Perspective. FBI Critical Incident Response Group, National Center for the Analysis of Violent Crime, Quantico, VA.

associated with higher posttraumatic stress among those at the school, but being interviewed by the media was associated with higher levels of post-traumatic stress when compared to those who refused to be interviewed or those who were not approached by reporters (Haravuori, Suomalainen, Berg, Kiviruusu, & Marttunen, 2011). Another impact is generalized fear. In one of the few studies examining fear in college students on other campuses after the Virginia Tech and Northern Illinois University shootings, researchers found that students had significantly higher fears of being attacked with a weapon or murdered on campus. The authors concluded that this is largely due to media coverage of mass shootings that highlight and magnify this relatively rare yet devastating form of school violence (Kaminsky et al., 2010).

■ Summary

Violence is a tragic yet all too common aspect of children's and youths' experience in North American schools. The most common form of violence involves bullying, where one child or young person experiences physical, verbal, or social violence caused by peers. Increasingly, we are aware that not only students but also teachers can be victims of such behaviors. Although some may argue this has always been a reality of school life, the consequences can be devastating, leading to mental health problems and further violence directed at self (in the form of suicide) or others. Gang activity is the second most common form of violence on school property, preying on vulnerable youth both as gang members and victims. Violence in this case is often paradoxically caused by perceived threats from rival groups. School shootings are rare occurrences, but the dramatic nature and the simultaneous loss of multiple lives results in large-scale media attention fueling fears and reinforcing the offenders' need for attention. Solutions to school violence are complex and require system-wide interventions that provide mental health and social services to young people in distress, provide support for families who are struggling, address violence attitudes within the culture of the school, and consider societal influences that condone violent actions.

■ Key Terms

Bullying: A form of habitual aggressive behavior that is hurtful and deliberate.

Conditional threat: Warns that a violent act will happen unless certain demands or terms are met.

Direct threat: Identifies a specific act against a specific target.

Indirect threat: Tends to be vague, unclear, and ambiguous.

Personality: Pattern of collective character, behavioral, temperamental, emotional, and mental traits of an individual.

Physical bullying: Pushing, hitting, tripping, spitting at, and physical beating.

School dynamics: Patterns of behavior, thinking, beliefs, customs, traditions, roles, and values that exist in a school's culture.

Social bullying: Rumors and behaviors aimed at deliberate social exclusion.

Threat: Expression of intent to do harm or to act out violently against someone or something.

Veiled threat: Strongly implies but does not explicitly threaten violence.

Verbal bullying: Taunts, threats, name calling, and derogatory comments.

Youth gang: A self-formed association of peers who have in common some sense of identity, some degree of permanence and organization, and an elevated level of involvement in delinquent or criminal activity.

■ Discussion Questions

1. Given the multiple factors that contribute to bullying, what advice would you give a parent who is concerned his or her child might be bullied?

2. What types of legislation and/or school-based policies may more effectively address issues of gang violence in schools?

3. How might teacher training programs more effectively educate teachers to deal with violence in schools?

4. How might the media influence the phenomenon of school shootings and what strategies might be in order?

■ Resources

Bill C-14. (2009). An Act to amend the Criminal Code (organized crime and protection of justice system participants) LS-633E. Retrieved from http://www.parl.gc.ca/About/Parliament/LegislativeSummaries/Bills_ls .asp?lang=E&ls=c14&Parl=40&Ses=2&source=library_prb

BullyingCanada is a national anti-bullying charitable organization http://www.bullyingcanada.ca

National Gang Intelligence Center (FBI) http://www.fbi.gov/about-us/investigate/vc_majorthefts/gangs/ngic

National Youth Gang Center (US Bureau of Justice Assistance) http://www.nationalgangcenter.gov//

RCMP Gang Awareness Quick Facts http://bc.rcmp.ca/ViewPage.action?siteNodeId=453&languageId=1&conte ntId=3871

StopBullying.gov provides information from various government agencies on how kids, teens, young adults, parents, educators and others in the community can prevent or stop bullying http://www.stopbullying.gov/

■ References

Achenbach, J., & Russakoff, D. (1999). Teen shooter's life paints and anti-social portrait. *Washington Post.* April 29, 1999, Page A1.

Arciaga, M., Sakamoto, W., & Jones, E. (2010). *Responding to gangs in school settings.* National Gang Center Bulletin. Washington, DC: U.S. Department of Justice.

Carlie, M.K. (2002). Into the abyss: A personal journey into the world of street gangs (Part 11: How to join a gang). Available from http://faculty .missouristate.edu/M/MichaelCarlie/what_I_learned_about/gangs/join_a_ gang.htm

Casteel, C., Peek-Asa, C., & Limbos, M. (2007). Predictors of non-fatal assault injury to public school teachers in Los Angeles City. *American Journal of Industrial Medicine, 50,* 932–939.

Cathcart, R. (2008, February 23). Boy's killing labeled a hate crime, stuns a town. Retrieved from http://www.nytimes.com/2008/02/23/us/23oxnard .html

Centers for Disease Control and Prevention (CDC). (2011). Bullying among middle school and high school students—Massachusetts, 2009. *Morbidity and Mortality Weekly Report, 60,* 465–471.

Chen, J., & Astor, R. (2008). Students' reports of violence against teachers in Taiwanese schools. *Journal of School Violence, 8*(1), 2–17.

Decker, S., & Curry, D. (2002). Gangs, gang homicides, and gang loyalty: Organized crimes or disorganized criminals? *Journal of Criminal Justice, 30,* 343–352.

Delisi, M., Barnes, J., Beaver, K., & Gibson, C. (2009). Delinquent gangs and adolescent victimization revisited. *Criminal Justice and Behavior, 36*(8), 808–823.

Dzuka, J., & Dalbert, C. (2007). Student violence against teachers. *European Psychologist, 12*(4), 253–260.

Egley, A., & Howell, J. (2011). *Highlights of the 2009 National Youth Gang Survey.* Juvenile Justice Fact Sheet. Washington, DC: U.S. Department of Justice.

Farrington, D., & Ttofi, M. (2009). How to reduce school bullying. *Victims & Offenders, 4*(4), 321–326.

Gendron, B., Williams, K., & Guerra, N. (2011). An analysis of bullying among students within schools: Estimating the effects of individual normative beliefs, self-esteem, and school climate. *Journal of School Violence, 10*(2), 150–164.

Gibbs, N., & Roche, T. (1999). The Columbine Tapes. *Time*. Monday December 20 1999. Retrieved from http://www.time.com/time/magazine /article/0,9171,992873,00.html

Gottfredson, G., & Gottfredson, D. (2001). Gang problems and gang programs in a national sample of schools. Retrieved from www.gottfredson.com /Gang_Problems_%20Programs/report.pdf

Grills-Taquechel, A., Littleton, H., & Axsom, D. (2011). Social support, world assumptions, and exposure as predictors of anxiety and quality of life following mass trauma. *Journal of Anxiety Disorders, 25,* 498–506.

Haravuori, H., Suomalainen, L., Berg, N., Kiviruusu, O., & Marttunen, M. (2011). Effects of media exposure on adolescents traumatized in a school shooting. *Journal of Traumatic Stress, 24*(1), 70–77.

Harrell, E. (2005). *Violence by gang members, 1993–2003*. Washington, DC: Bureau of Justice Statistics.

Hong, J., Cho, H., Allen-Meares, P., & Espelage, D. (2011). The social ecology of the Columbine High School shootings. *Children and Youth Services Review, 33,* 861–868.

Hong, J., Cho, H., & Lee, A. (2010). Revisiting Virginia Tech shootings: An ecological systems analysis. *Journal of Loss and Trauma, 15,* 561–575.

Howell, J., Egley, A., Tita, G., & Griffiths, E. (2011). *US gang problem trends and seriousness, 1996–2009*. National Gang Center Bulletin, no. 6. Washington, DC: U.S. Department of Justice.

Kaminsky, R., Koons-Witt, B., Thompson, N., & Weiss, D. (2010). The impacts of the Virginia Tech and Northern Illinois University shootings on fear of crime on campus. *Journal of Criminal Justice, 38,* 88–98.

Khoury-Kassabri, M., Astor, R., & Benbenishty, R. (2009). Middle Eastern adolescents' perpetration of school violence against peers and teachers. *Journal of Interpersonal Violence, 24*(1), 159–182.

Langton, L. (2010). *Gang units in large local law enforcement agencies, 2007*. Bureau of Justice Statistics Special Report. Washington, DC: U.S. Department of Justice.

Larkin, R. (2007). *Comprehending Columbine*. Philadelphia: Temple University Press.

Lee, C. (2011). An ecological systems approach to bullying behaviours among middle school students in the United States. *Journal of Interpersonal Violence, 26*(8), 1664–1693.

Mishna, F., & Alaggia, R. (2005). Weighing the risks: A child's decision to disclose peer victimization. *Children and Schools, 27*(4), 217–226.

Mishna, F., Pepler, D., & Weiner, J. (2006). Factors associated with perceptions and responses to bullying situations by children, parents, teachers and principals. *Victims and Offenders, 1,* 255–288.

Mishna, F., Wiener, J., & Pepler, D. (2008). Some of my best friends—Experiences of bullying within friendships. *School Psychology International, 29*(5), 549–573.

Moore, J., & Hagedorn, J. (2001). *Female gangs: A focus on research.* Juvenile Justice Bulletin. Washington, DC: U.S. Department of Justice.

Nansel, T., Overpeck, M., Pilla, R., Ruan, W., Simons-Morton, B., & Scheidt, P. (2001). Bullying behaviours among US youth: Prevalence and association with psychological adjustment. *Journal of the American Medical Association, 285,* 2094–2100.

National Youth Gang Center. (2011). Frequently Asked Questions. Retrieved from http://www.nationalgangcenter.gov//

O'Toole, M.E. (1999). *The school shooter: A threat assessment perspective.* Quantico, VA: FBI Critical Incident Response Group, National Center for the Analysis of Violent Crime.

Public Safety Canada. (2008). *Bullying prevention: Nature and extent of bullying in Canada.* Ottawa: National Crime Prevention Centre.

Robers, S., Zhang, J., & Truman, J. (2010). *Indicators of school crime and safety: 2010* (NCES 2011-002/NCJ 230812). National Center for Education Statistics, U.S. Department of Education, and Bureau of Justice Statistics, Office of Justice Programs, Washington: U.S. Department of Justice,

Salzman, A. (2004, May 15). Mother of boy in suicide is spared prison term. *New York Times*, B(6), p. 4.

Santora, M. (2003, September 27). Case tries to link a mother to her boy's suicide. *New York Times*, B(2), p. 1.

Setoodeh, R. (2008, July 19). Young, gay and murdered. Retrieved from http://www.newsweek.com/2008/07/18/young-gay-and-murdered.html

Seymour, A., & Ray, D. (1996). *Victims of Gang Violence: A New Frontier in Victim Services*, special report. Washington, DC: U.S. Department of Justice, Office for Victims of Crime.

Sharkey, J., Shekhtmeyster, Z., Chavez-Lopez, L., Norris, E., & Sass, L. (2011). The protective influence of gangs: Can schools compensate? *Aggression and Violent Behavior, 16,* 45–54.

Society for Adolescent Medicine. (1992). Position paper: Corporal punishment in the schools. *Journal of Adolescent Health, 13,* 240–246.

Stowe, S. (2003, October 7). Boy who sought help was seen as target. *New York Times*, B(1), p. 5.

Thornberg, R., & Knutsen, S. (2011). Teenager's explanations of bullying. *Child and Youth Care Forum, 40*, 177–192.

Thrasher, F. (1927). *The gang: A study of 1,313 gangs in Chicago*. Chicago: University of Chicago Press.

Ttofi, M., & Farrington, D. (2008). Bullying: Short-term and long-term effects, and the importance of defiance theory in explanation and prevention. *Victims and Offenders, 3*, 289–312.

U.S. Department of Health and Human Services. What is Bullying? Retrieved from http://www.stopbullying.gov/what-is-bullying/definition/index.html

Walker, R. (2008). Gangs or us: Gangsta girls. Retrieved from http://www.gangsorus.com/

Wynne, S., & Joo, H. (2011). Predictors of school victimization: Individual, familial and school factors. *Crime and Delinquency, 57*(3), 458–488.

Intimate Partner Violence CHAPTER

9

Objectives

- To identify the scope of intimate partner violence
- To identify legal responses to intimate partner violence
- To identify impacts of intimate partner violence on victims and on children who witness the violence
- To discuss typologies of offenders
- To discuss homicide in the context of intimate partner violence
- To review intervention programs that address intimate partner violence

Key Terms

Battered woman syndrome
Battered woman syndrome defense
Complex posttraumatic stress disorder
Domestic violence
Intimate partner violence (IPV)
Learned helplessness
Posttraumatic stress disorder (PTSD)
Protection orders
Wife battering

CASE

By all accounts R&B singers Rihanna, aged 20, and Chris Brown, aged 19, had it all. (See **Figure 9-1**.) They were frequently pictured together in the press and were referred to as having a fairy-tale romance. Rihanna, a Barbados-born star, had sold nearly 10 million tracks in 2008, the highest number of any singer that year. Brown had made his debut at the age of 16 with a self-titled album that sold over 2 million copies and featured a hit single that topped the Billboard 100 list. His albums continued to roll out and by 2009 his eighth top 20 hit was on the charts. But in February 2009, the night both he and Rihanna were scheduled to appear on the Grammys, Chris Brown surrendered himself to the Los Angeles Police Department and was booked on felony assault of an unidentified female (*LA Times*, 2009; Cruz, 2009). Ten days later a photograph showing Rihanna's bruised and bloodied face, reported to be part of the police investigation, was leaked online (Swash, 2009). Gossip reports suggested that in interviews with the police, Rihanna had indicated this was not the first time Brown had been abusive toward her and that his abuse was becoming more frequent and more violent. That same year Chris Brown pled guilty for the assault and was sentenced to 5 years of probation and 6 months of community service. He was also issued a 5-year restraining order that required him to stay at least 10 yards away from Rihanna at public events. In July 2009 Brown released a YouTube video in which he apologized for his behavior, explaining he would have made an apology earlier but was advised not to by his attorneys (CNN, 2009).

FIGURE 9-1 Rihanna: A victim of intimate partner violence

© LORI SHEPLER/UPI/Landov

■ Introduction

Intimate partner violence (IPV) is any behavior within an intimate relationship that causes physical, psychological, or sexual harm to those in the relationship. It includes acts of physical aggression (slapping, hitting, kicking, or beating), psychological abuse (intimidation, constant belittling), forced sexual intercourse, or any other controlling behavior (isolating a person from family and friends, monitoring a person's movements, and restrictin access to information or assistance). This definition includes current and former spouses and dating partners and people in both heterosexual and same-sex relationships. This is differentiated from the previously used terms **wife battering** and **domestic violence**, which focused on violence between spouses and tended to be used synonymously with woman abuse. These terms reflect the history of study, policy, and interventions in the area of IPV that began with the recognition of assaultive behavior toward women that was perpetrated by their husbands.

Wife battering was an issue for concern in North America from the time the Puritans arrived from England. Family violence was seen to threaten an individual's and the community's standing before God. It threatened the social and political stability of the Puritans' Godly settlement. The wife-beating husband shamed Christianity, dishonored God, and dishonored himself. The Puritan communities dealt with family violence with the combined forces of the church, the state, and the community. Meddling was considered to be a virtue, and consequently neighbors watched, church courts extracted confessions, and civil courts upheld laws and punished wrongdoers. The consequence for wrongdoing was often shame and disgrace before the entire congregation (Pleck, 1987).

However, the goal of this vigor was to restore family order, not to protect individual rights (Pleck, 1987). Abused members were never removed from the home, and despite the reported vigor in exposing and punishing family violence, Pleck (1987), an American historian, could locate only four cases in the Plymouth courts from 1663 to 1682. Yet, although the Puritan laws against family violence were rarely enacted, they did serve as a guide for community moral principles. As the religious community gave way to pluralism, the state relinquished its commitment to enforce morality.

During the 1800s women were viewed as guardians of the domestic fireside. Women had the power to reform the morals of their husbands and sons, but this power was to remain in the home. The temperance movement challenged this, highlighting the plight of abused women and placing women's rights ahead of preservation of the family. Although they originally did not advocate policies to aid victims of wife assault directly, they considered violence to be an evil consequence of alcohol. Therefore, if alcohol was prohibited, violence would end. In the 1840s American women's rights activists joined the temperance movement and called for divorce for drunkards' wives and the right for women to have their own earnings. Nevertheless, divorce was advocated only in the most extreme circumstances (Pleck, 1987).

In 1641, following the British precedent, the Massachusetts Body of Liberties provided that "Everie marryed woeman shall be free from bodile correction or stripes by her husband, unlesse it be in his own defense upon her assault" (as cited in Pleck, 1987). However, divorce on the grounds of severe cruelty was not permitted until 1870. Also in the 1870s, legislation was enacted in America for public flogging at whipping posts for abusive husbands. In three states these laws were not abolished until 1948 to 1952. Although this punishment was infrequently used, many believed the threat to be an effective deterrent.

In 1885 the Chicago Protective Agency for Women and Children was established for the purposes of providing legal aid, court advocacy, and personal assistance to battered women and their children. This is the first recorded women's shelter in North America, and women and their children could stay for up to 4 weeks. Between 1915 and 1920 another 25 cities established protective agencies for women, although most were closed by the 1940s. The next period of interest and assistance for women who were battered did not occur until the 1970s, during which time the feminist rights movement successfully pushed for the opening of assistance programs and shelters in the United States, Canada, and the United Kingdom (Roberts, 2002).

By 1977 there were 89 shelters in the United States for women who were abused, and by 1990 this number had risen to 850. In Canada in 1980 Linda MacLeod made the first attempt to estimate the incidence of wife assault in Canada and suggested that 1 in 10 Canadian women were victims of intimate violence (MacLeod, 1980). As public awareness and outrage over the issue grew, commitment to services for women, public education, and legislative reform increased. By 1987 MacLeod documented significant gains, applauding the progress in bringing the problem of woman abuse from the private sphere into the public domain (MacLeod, 1987).

The number of shelters across Canada increased from 78 to 400 between 1978 and 1989 (Denham & Gillespie, 1998). Funding for woman abuse programs in North America continued to build until the passage of the Violence Against Women Act of 1994 by the U.S. federal government. This legislation included a $1.2 billion appropriation for 1995 to 2000 to improve criminal justice responses, expand community services, improve safety measures, and provide support for education and health-based services.

Although the attention to woman abuse has been critical to improving the lives of women who are affected by violence, more recently views of IPV have expanded to include others who are affected by violence. One focus has been the impact on children as witnesses of parental violence. Another focus has been on men as victims either in heterosexual relationships or in same-sex relationships. A final focus has been on women who are victimized in lesbian relationships. The important focus on women traditionally has left these other victims in the shadows, and their suffering has gone unacknowledged.

■ Scope of the Problem

IPV accounted for 22% of violent crimes against women and 4% of violent crimes against men between 2001 and 2005 in the United States. In 2007 24% of female homicide victims were killed by a spouse or ex-spouse, 21% were killed by a boyfriend or girlfriend, and 19% were killed by another family member. In 2008, 99% of the IPV against women was committed by male offenders and 83% of IPV against men was committed by female partners. Black females were twice as likely as White females to be killed by a spouse and four times more likely to be killed by a boyfriend or girlfriend. Of male homicide victims, 2% were killed by a spouse or ex-spouse and 3% were killed by a girlfriend or boyfriend (Catalano, Smith, Snyder, & Rand, 2009). From 2001 to 2005 women who lived in households with lower annual incomes experienced the highest average annual rates of nonfatal intimate partner victimization; however, women remained at greater risk than men within each income level. On average between 2001 and 2005, children were residents of households in 38% of cases where women were victims of IPV and 21% of the incidents involving men as victims. The presence of alcohol or drugs was reported in 42% of all cases of nonfatal IPV (Catalano, 2007). The National Crime Victimization Survey estimated that more than 50% of homes with calls to law enforcement for severe domestic violence contained children younger than 12 years of age (Catalano, 2007).

According to Statistics Canada (2005), 28% of women and 22% of men in 1999 reported some type of violence (including physical, sexual, and psychological abuse) perpetrated by a former partner, either while living together or after separation. In most cases (63%) violence ended at separation; however, 39% of women and 32% of men indicated they were assaulted after the relationship ended. Of these, 24% indicated the violence became worse, and 39% indicated the violence began after separation. Further, marital separation is a factor that elevates the rate of spousal homicide for women. Ex-spouses are responsible for 38% of all homicides against women and 2% of all homicides against men. Between 1999 and 2004 the 5-year rate of spousal violence has remained unchanged at 7%. In terms of numbers, an estimated 653,000 women and 546,000 men encountered some form of violence. Women who were victims of spousal violence were more than twice as likely to be injured as men. Women were also three times more likely to fear for their life and twice as likely to be the targets of more than 10 violent episodes (Statistics Canada, 2005). In 2002 there were more than 205,000 victims of violent crime reported to a subset of 94 police departments across

Canada (103,001 female victims and 102,447 male victims). Women were much more likely than men to be victims of spousal violence (85% vs. 15%). Common assault was the most frequent offense committed against current spouses (73%), followed by major assault (16%). For ex-spouses common assault (43%), uttering threats (25%), and criminal harassment (20%) were the most frequently reported offenses (Canadian Centre for Justice Statistics, 2004).

On November 24, 2005, the first-ever World Health Organization (WHO) study on domestic violence revealed that IPV is the most common form of violence in women's lives, much more so than assault or rape by strangers or acquaintances. The study reported on the enormous toll that physical and sexual violence by husbands and partners has on the health and well-being of women around the world and the extent to which IPV is still largely hidden. The study was based on interviews with over 24,000 women residing in urban and rural areas in 10 countries, including Brazil, Ethiopia, Japan, Peru, Samoa, Serbia, and Thailand, and the findings indicated that women are at much greater risk from violence in their own homes than on the street (WHO, 2005). One-fourth to one-half of the study's female victims of physical assault by their husbands or partners stated they had sustained physical injuries as a result of the battering, and more than 20% of the women who reported physical violence said they had never told anyone about the abuse before the interview. Despite serious medical consequences, only a very small percentage of victims ever sought help from health care providers or the police; instead, those who sought help tended to reach out to neighbors and extended family members. Also significant was the finding that in most countries studied, 4% to 12% of pregnant women interviewed reported they had been beaten by the unborn child's father during pregnancy, with a disturbing 50% indicating they had been punched or kicked in the abdomen (WHO, 2005). This landmark WHO study concluded that domestic violence by husbands and other intimate partners is still a largely hidden phenomenon around the world. It highlighted the urgent need for policymakers and public health officials to address the health and human costs and for countries to develop policies and programs aimed at preventing and eliminating violence against women and children (WHO, 2005).

Violence does not occur only in marital or common-law relationships but also occurs early in relationships in the context of dating. According to the Centers for Disease Control and Prevention (2006), 1 in 11 adolescents reports being a victim of physical dating violence. One in four adolescents reports verbal, physical, emotional, or sexual violence each year. One in five high school girls has been the victim of physical or

TABLE 9-1 **Intimate Partner Violence Statistics**

- Intimate partner violence accounted for 22% of violent crimes against women and 4% of violent crimes against men between 2001 and 2005 in the United States.
- Children were residents of the households that experienced intimate partner violence in 38% of the incidents involving female victims and 21% of the incidents involving male victims in the United States.
- Thirty-nine percent of women and 32% of men who were victims of IPV in Canada indicated they were assaulted after the relationship ended. Of these, 24% indicated the violence became worse, and 39% indicated the violence began after separation.
- Ex-marital partners are responsible for 38% of all homicides against women and 2% of all homicides against men in Canada.
- In the United States females made up 70% of victims killed by an intimate partner in 2007.
- According to the WHO, in most countries studied 4% to 12% of pregnant women interviewed reported they had been beaten by the unborn child's father during pregnancy, with a disturbing 50% indicating they had been punched or kicked in the abdomen.

Data from Catalano, S. 2007. Intimate partner violence in the United States. Retrieved from http://www.ojp.usdoj.gov/bjs/intimate/ipv.htm; Catalano, S., Smith, E., Snyder, H. & Rand, M. 2009. Female victims of violence. Bureau of Justice Statistics. NCJ 228356. Washington: US Department of Justice; World Health Organization. 2005. Landmark study on domestic violence. Retrieved from http://www.who.int/mediacentre/news/releases/2005/pr62/en/index.html

sexual abuse by a dating partner. Seventy percent of girls and 52% of boys who report abuse in a dating relationship also report they were physically injured, and 8% of boys and 9% of girls have been to an emergency department as a result of an injury sustained from a dating partner. A summary of intimate partner statistics can be found in **Table 9-1**.

Legal Responses to IPV

Despite the history previously described, from a legislative perspective, IPV has been considered a crime in violation of community standards and requiring state intervention for only about 30 years in most parts of the United States and Canada. For example, the right of women to be free of sexual assault committed by their husbands was not acknowledged in the Criminal Code of Canada until the offense of marital rape was formally recognized as a crime in 1983 (MacKinnon, 1987). In the past three decades police and prosecutors have enhanced investigative techniques and the pursuit of charges and convictions. Courts have responded with more severe sentences and mandated interventions for perpetrators (Jaffe, Crooks, & Wolfe, 2003).

A variety of approaches has been attempted over the years to address the issue of IPV from a legal perspective. One approach was the mandatory arrest and charging of perpetrators of IPV that arose because of voiced concerns of victim advocacy groups that due to police discretion and policies of individual police departments male batterers were rarely arrested, prosecuted, or sentenced. Such concerns were substantiated by research on police and prosecutor practices (Fagan, 1996). Most famous among the research studies was the Minneapolis Domestic Violence Experiment, funded by the National Institute of Justice and the first scientifically controlled test of the effects of arrest for any crime (Sherman & Berk, 1984). In the experiment suspects of domestic violence were randomly assigned to three outcomes: (1) arrest, (2) sent away from the scene for 8 hours, or (3) given advice and/or mediation. To be included in the study the police officer needed to have probable cause to believe a misdemeanor domestic assault had occurred within the past 4 hours and both the victim and the offender had to be present. The experiment ran from March 1981 to August 1982 to collect 314 cases.

Outcomes in terms of repeated violence were assessed at 6 months (Sherman & Berk, 1984). The results were presented in three ways: police reports of repeated violence, victim reports of repeated violence, and victim reports of repeated violence when the victim believed the officer had listened to her or his concerns. The results shown in **Table 9-2** are impressive and led to the conclusion of the authors that arrest is the most effective method for reducing domestic violence (Sherman & Berk, 1984).

These impressive results raised hopes that this was a relatively simple solution to a complex problem. However, the legislative changes in many places moved more quickly than the training of police officers who were intended to implement the policies. Later attempts to replicate the findings in five different jurisdictions failed to produce the same results. Methodological problems in the replication studies, which were in large part caused by the attempt to conduct experimental research in naturalized settings, do not allow us to draw the conclusion that mandatory arrests do or do not work (Fagan, 1996). However, they do confirm that mandatory arrest is not the magic bullet for ending IPV. A further set of issues is the unintended side effects of such a policy, such as contempt

TABLE 9-2 **Results of the Minneapolis Domestic Violence Experiment**

	Arrest	**Advice**	**Sent Suspect Away**
Police report	10%	19%	24%
Victim report	19%	37%	33%
Victim report if "police listened"	9%	26%	35%

Data from Sherman, L. & Berk, R. 1984. The Minneapolis Domestic Violence Experiment. Police Foundation Reports. April 1984. Washington: Police Foundation.

of court charges against victim witnesses who refused to testify in court and perjury charges against those who changed their stories (Jaffe et al., 2003). This resulted in a revictimization of those individuals the policy was intended to protect.

Another justice approach to IPV has been the reliance on protection orders or restraining orders to increase the safety of IPV victims. A study of 227,941 restraining orders issued in California revealed that in 72.2% of the cases the order was for a woman to be protected from a male abuser and in 19.3% of the cases the protection was from someone of the same sex (Sorenson & Shen, 2005). As originally envisioned, these orders were viewed as potentially more effective than criminal prosecutions because they could enhance the safety of the victim and could reduce the chances of retaliation from an offender who was angered at criminal charges. Further, protection orders were viewed as possible deterrents because offenders would seek to avoid criminal prosecution. Nevertheless, research suggests that 23% to 50% of victims experience revictimization within a 2- to 4-month follow-up period. Where comparison groups have been used, this has resulted in no differences in victimization rates between victims who did use protection orders and those who did not (Mears, Carlson, Holden, & Harris, 2001). Revictimization rates are higher in those who share biological children, are of lower socioeconomic groups, are of minority status, and when the perpetrator has a history of arrest.

In January 1991 the California State Assembly passed a bill in which it became a public offense for persons subject to domestic violence restraining orders to purchase a firearm. The law also required law enforcement agencies to report domestic violence restraining orders to a central database (Domestic Violence Restraining Order System) to effectively prohibit these individuals from acquiring firearms (Sorenson & Shen, 2005). In 1996 Congress passed the Domestic Violence Misdemeanor Gun Ban, which prohibits anyone convicted of a misdemeanor crime of domestic violence or child abuse from purchasing or possessing a gun. This is an important legislative step because according to U.S. Federal Bureau of Investigation statistics, in homicides during 1995 in which the weapon was known, 50% of domestic violence homicide victims were killed with a firearm (FBI, 1995). Of those female firearm homicides, 75% were killed with a handgun. Canadian statistics reveal that in 1996, 34% of all spousal homicide victims were killed by firearms (RCMP, 2012).

Legislative changes in Canada and the United States resulted in the recognition that the exposure of children to violence between their parents constitutes a form of child abuse. As a result, child protection agencies in Canada experienced a dramatic rise in reports of emotional abuse, the largest proportion of which were children exposed to IPV (Black, Trocmé, Fallon, & MacLaurin, 2008). In 1999 in Minnesota the expanded definition of child abuse to include exposure to IPV resulted in such a substantial increase in reports that child protective services agencies were overwhelmed, and a need for $30 million in additional services was identified. The next year the state repealed the law (Taylor & Sorenson, 2007).

In response to legislative changes and in an attempt to better protect children, child welfare services agencies have developed policies and practices to assess and intervene in cases of child exposure to IPV (Shlonsky & Friend, 2007). However, if child exposure to IPV is equated with child abuse, the abused parent is placed in the position of culpability for failure to protect. That is, an abused parent who chooses not to, or cannot, leave the abusive relationship may be held responsible for exposing the child to violence. Ultimately, this may result in the removal of the child, a double jeopardy for the abused parent. If the abused parent discloses abuse to a health care or social service professional in an effort to obtain assistance, he or she may be penalized with the loss of the child. In a study conducted by Alaggia, Jenney, Mazzuca, and Redmond (2007), this was particularly true for women who were marginalized due to race, sexual orientation, or immigration status. These women found the risks associated with seeking help were simply too high.

This policy was tested by a group of mothers who were victims of domestic violence and had their children removed in a class action lawsuit against New York City's Administration of Children's Services (ACS) (*Nicholson v. Williams*, 2004). The district court concluded that ACS violated the federal constitutional rights of battered mothers and their children. The court concluded that ACS unnecessarily prosecuted mothers for neglect and removed their children when the mothers had been the victims of significant domestic violence and when the mothers themselves had done nothing wrong. The district court issued a preliminary injunction ordering ACS to discontinue its practices and ordered the city and the state to pay assigned counsel for battered women in dependency proceedings. ACS appealed the finding, and in October 2004 the New York Court of Appeals ruled that it was unacceptable to presume a child who witnesses domestic violence is neglected or a child who is exposed to domestic violence should be removed from the family home on this basis alone. Furthermore, the court held that any decision to remove a child must be weighed against the psychological harm to the child that could be created by the removal itself (*Nicholson v. Williams*, 2004).

Effects of IPV on Victims

Lenore Walker first proposed the term battered woman syndrome in 1979 as a means of describing the effects of IPV on the victims. According to Walker (1979), any woman may find herself in an abusive situation once. However, if violence occurs a second time and the woman remains in that situation, she is described as a battered woman. In her extensive studies with battered women, Walker found that battering relationships have a clearly discernible cycle, and she concluded that battered women respond to events in this cycle in a predictable pattern. The battering cycle, according to Walker, has three phases. The first phase is tension reduction, during which a batterer, in an attempt to reduce his own anxiety and tension, begins to inflict his mate with verbal or minor physical abuse. The woman responds with anger reduction techniques, aimed at placating the batterer to avoid a severely abusive episode. As the tension grows the phase is followed by an acute battering episode. At this time the victim is subject to severe physical and verbal abuse, which may include significant injury and threats of death. At the end of the incident there is a sharp, predictable reduction in the tension. The final phase of the cycle is loving attrition, during which the batterer becomes remorseful, apologetic, and loving. At this time he also assures the victim the battering incident will not be repeated. This loving attrition reinforces the woman's commitment to the relationship by making her feel loved and protective of her partner's evident vulnerability. This phase may last for an extended period of time, but invariably it fades as the tension mounts and the cycle begins again. To qualify for battered woman syndrome, according to Walker's criteria, a woman must have gone through this cycle at least twice.

In addition to the battering cycle, a victim of IPV experiences other forms of totalitarian control, often on a daily basis. Psychological abuse can involve the constant undermining of the victim's sense of self, including that she is an inadequate parent, inadequate lover, unable to think clearly, and an unworthy human being. In a study by Regehr and Glancy (1995), one woman who had just been released from the hospital with a colostomy and was told she was smelly and disgusting and was forced to wash the floor with a toothbrush. Another former beauty queen was convinced by her spouse that she had become ugly, and as a consequence, she totally abandoned her self-care in defeat. These constant negative depictions of the victim are unable to be disputed by positive interactions with others outside the relationship because of enforced social isolation. Victims in the Regehr and Glancy study stated their telephones were monitored or disconnected, and they were no longer allowed to interact with friends or family. This isolation was at times overtly enforced or subtly engineered by insulting, demeaning, or sexually harassing the victim's social supports. Financial abuse was also common, where the abuser takes away the victim's paycheck, monitors all grocery and other receipts to ensure no money is saved, and places all jointly owned assets in the abuser's name, denying the victim the right to access them. Finally, physical abuse took many forms, including breaking favorite objects, smashing walls and furniture, threatening harm to children or other family members, sexual assault, kicking, punching, hair pulling, and so on.

Finkelhor and Yllo (1982) were among the first to describe the phenomenon of forced sex in marriage as a form of physical abuse. They include in this definition sexual aggression (including rape) and coercion to engage in forms of sexual activity that the woman did not wish or enjoy (such as oral or anal sex). Women in their study who were victims of forced sex in marriage reported feeling humiliated, angry, and depressed.

The pattern of control and abuse can lead to a state of **learned helplessness**. That is, the victim has learned to accept abuse as a way of life and does not believe she or he has any influence on its occurrence. Thus, with repeated battering and repeated threats of future violence, a victim becomes passive. Furthermore, the victim's cognitive ability to perceive success is altered. The victim does not believe any response will result in a positive outcome. Finally, the victim's sense of emotional well-being becomes precarious, rendering the victim vulnerable to depression and anxiety (Walker, 1979).

Victims of IPV may also experience **posttraumatic stress disorder (PTSD)** (Randle & Graham, 2011). Symptoms of PTSD include a reexperiencing of the assault through dreams, flashbacks and intrusive thoughts, a numbing of responsiveness, and persistent anxiety and arousal. However, in some situations PTSD is inadequate to explain the significant impacts of repeated abuse over long periods of time. Judith Lewis Herman (1992) proposed a new diagnosis to explain the cluster of symptoms experienced by someone who endured a situation of abuse and totalitarian control over a prolonged period of time. Herman argued that survivors of prolonged abuse develop characteristic personality changes that affect both their sense of identity and their ability to form and sustain interpersonal relationships. Elements of this disorder include alterations in self-perception, including shame, guilt, self-blame, and a sense of being completely different from others; alterations in perceptions of the perpetrator, such as ascribing unrealistic power to the perpetrator, idealizing the perpetrator, or rationalizing the abusive behavior; alterations in relations with others, including isolation and withdrawal, distrust or overtrusting behavior, and disruption in relationships; and alterations in systems of meaning, such as loss of faith, hopelessness, and despair (Herman, 1992).

■ Barriers to Disclosing and Ending Abuse

A number of theoretical frameworks have emerged to explain strategies used by women in abusive relationships and their help-seeking actions, obstacles that confront those who attempt to escape partner violence, and decision models for help seeking. Alaggia, Regehr, and Jenny (2011) use ecological theory to describe the multiple factors that influence a victim's decision to disclose abuse and take action to end the abusive relationship. These are summarized in **Table 9-3**.

At the intrapersonal or individual level, current mental health and emotional status are important factors to consider. Women in abusive relationships have been found to suffer from high levels of posttraumatic stress as described above and often find themselves in a perpetual state of fear (Alaggia et al., 2011). This fear is justified as research confirms that leaving an abusive relationship increases the safety risk; in particular,

TABLE 9-3 Why Battered Women Stay

Individual factors	Posttraumatic stress
	Fear
	Love and commitment
	Resilience and ability to self-protect
Family and cultural factors	Bring shame on the family
	Religious and cultural beliefs about the family
	Concern for children
	Beliefs that abuse is normal
Community services	Inadequate social housing
	Limited education, retraining, or employment opportunities
	Insufficient counseling or shelter resources
Social policies	Immigration policies that do not allow sponsored individuals to leave their sponsors
	Social welfare and housing policies that disadvantage single mothers
	Mandatory reporting to child welfare of children witnessing abuse

Data from Alaggia, R., Regehr, C. & Jenny, A. (2011) Risky Business: An Ecological Analysis of Intimate Partner Violence Disclosure. Research on Social Work Practice.

women who leave are more likely to be killed by their abusive husbands than those who stay. In addition, however, somewhat surprisingly perhaps to others, women in abusive relationships describe feelings of love and commitment to their abusive partners. Linda MacLeod (1987), in describing how the shelter system had failed some victims of violence, observed that battered women speak of relationships, of commitment, and of love. The tendency of service providers to push women to leave the relationships is at odds with the goals of some victims and makes them reluctant to seek services. Finally, at the intrapersonal level is the resilience of victims and their ability to self-protect that makes staying in the relationship tolerable.

At a micro-systems level, participants identified family and cultural factors that impacted disclosure and ending the relationship (Alaggia et al., 2011). For instance, victims from some cultural groups were concerned about the way in which their situation and behavior may bring shame on their family. Cultural and religious practices made it impossible for these women to consider divorce or separation. This was particularly true if women perceived their children would be negatively affected by having separated parents. Further, immigrant women in this study identified they came from countries where abuse was considered normal. One woman was quoted as saying, "Being beaten is normal. There are lots of abuses in my country. In my country you call and they never come. They only come if your eye is falling out of its socket, or if you are almost dying, then they come, then they notice. They always come if the woman is dead" (Alaggia et al., 2011).

Exosystems refer to the supports and challenges presented by community services. Ptacek (1999) proposed a *social entrapment* perspective in which women attempting to escape their abusive relationships are often frustrated by inadequate institutional responses. These can include inadequate social housing options, services that do not support the goal of family reunification, inadequate shelters and counseling services, and inability to access education, retraining, or employment. Grauwiler (2008) concluded in her study of women in New York City that women experienced services as being unresponsive to their needs and goals. Of particular concern was the expectation of these services for women to leave their communities and isolate themselves to maintain their safety.

Finally, at the macro-system level, policies and laws limit the choices available to victims. In their study of immigrant women, Alaggia, Regehr, and Rishchynsky (2009) found that immigration laws seriously hampered disclosure, especially when the abusive partners were their sponsors. That is, immigrant women were frequently sponsored by their partners and faced deportation if they were to leave the relationship. Further, as noted earlier, mandatory reporting to child welfare services when children are witnesses to violence can be highly problematic. Finally, social welfare, housing, and education policies can all serve to trap victims. These structural responses can cause women to retreat within themselves and internalize blame, leading them to stay with their abusive partners.

■ IPV in Same-Sex Couples

IPV in same-sex couples has been a relatively unexplored area in both the professional and research literature. Yet studies examining incidence reveal that violence occurs in between 21% and 50% of male same-sex couples (Stanley, Bartholomew, Taylor, Oram, & Landolt, 2006) and between 25% and 50% of female same-sex couples (Hardesty, Oswald, Khaw, & Fonseca, 2011). Women in lesbian relationships are also more likely to come from heterosexual relationships where violence was an issue (Pattavina, Hirshel, Buzawa, Faggiani, & Bentley, 2007). In one study 50% of participants indicated the violence in their same-sex relationship was bidirectional, that is, both partners were physically violent at some point (Stanley et al., 2006).

In many ways violence in same-sex relationships is similar to that in heterosexual relationships. For example, there is often a cycle of violence that involves a building of tension, followed by actual violence, followed by a period of reconciliation and remorse. In addition, the level of violence tends to build over time. Social isolation, minimizing of the abuse, victim blame, and a belief the offender will change are also common features. In addition, the offender typologies are very similar (Brown, 2008). In other ways issues are intensified for people in same-sex relationships who are battered. That is, there is a fear of exposure and possible rejection from family and friends upon reporting based on the victim's sexual orientation. In lesbian relationships victims also confront a political agenda that has identified violence as a male issue (Stanley et al., 2006).

Legal issues can also form an additional barrier for same-sex couples because advances in laws that protect victims from violence in intimate relationships have been primarily directed at heterosexual relationships. Six states (Delaware, Louisiana, Montana, New York, South Carolina, and Virginia) specifically exclude same-sex partners from legal interventions (Hardesty et al., 2011), and only six states specifically provide protection in same-sex couples. Other states use vague terms, such as "partners" and "cohabitants," that leave discretion to individual judges with respect to who qualifies. In addition, three states maintain antisodomy laws, forcing victims to admit to illegal behaviors before they can be protected.

Finally, several studies have provided evidence that police are less likely to intervene, fail to arrest, and ignore standard domestic violence procedures in the case of same-sex IPV (Pattavina et al., 2007).

■ Child Witnesses of IPV

There is a significant overlap between IPV and child abuse. The 2003 Canadian Incidence Study of Reported Child Abuse and Neglect revealed that 34% of all substantiated cases of child abuse in Canada involved some form of children witnessing IPV (Black et al., 2008). Other research has demonstrated that in families reported to child protection where the woman is a victim of IPV, there is a co-occurrence rate of child abuse in 30% to 60% of the cases, with a median rate of 40%. Usually, this abuse is in the form of physical abuse. In community-based studies the co-occurrence rate between IPV and child abuse is 5.6% to 11%. Thus, most studies suggest that the occurrence of IPV in a family increases the risk of physical violence against the child, neglect of the child, sexual abuse of the child, and psychological violence directed at the child (Zolotor, Theodore, Coyne-Beasley, & Runyan, 2007).

Even when children in homes where IPV is present are not victims of direct abuse themselves, there is considerable evidence that these children suffer the aftereffects of violence. Mothers who experience more severe forms of physical abuse are more likely to report that their children are forced to watch the abuse, suggesting this is part of the abusers' strategy for control and intimidation (Mbilinyi, Edleson, Hagemeister, & Beeman, 2007). When compared to children who have not witnessed abuse, children who are exposed to IPV demonstrate increased internalizing behaviors, including depression, anxiety, and social withdrawal; increased externalizing behaviors, including hyperactivity and aggression; more social integration problems; lower self-esteem; and lower school performance (Alaggia et al., 2007; Wolfe, Crooks, Lee, McIntyre-Smith, & Jaffe, 2003). Indeed, in 63% of cases outcomes for children who witness interparental violence are equivalent to children who are physically abused themselves (Kitzmann, Gaylord, Holt, & Kenny, 2003). In large part these childhood effects are the result of severe stress experienced by the abused parent and the affect this stress has on their ability to parent (Huth-Bocks & Hughes, 2008).

A smaller subset of children exposed to interparental violence will develop PTSD. Community-based studies suggest that approximately 13% of these children will develop PTSD and about 50% will have at least one symptom of PTSD, such as intrusive thoughts of the event. Among children who are abused themselves, studies have found that 26% in a clinical sample and 42% in foster care have PTSD. This is considerably higher than those who witness abuse alone (Margolin & Vickerman, 2007). Despite these alarming findings about the impact that witnessing violence has on children, it is important not to conclude that all children who are exposed to IPV will have negative effects. A meta-analysis of 118 studies of children who were exposed to interparental violence demonstrated that 37% showed outcomes that were similar to or better than nonwitnesses (Kitzmann et al., 2003). Thus, as in all cases of victimization, individual resilience can overcome extremely adverse conditions.

Another outcome of child abuse and children witnessing abuse is the possibility of becoming an abuser later in life. In U.S. national surveys 39% of abusive men reported being abused as children, compared to 11% of nonabusive men (Straus & Gelles, 1980). Nevertheless, exposure to domestic violence is a stronger predictor than physical child abuse that a person will become a perpetrator of IPV (Adams, 2009). Straus and Gelles (1980) found that men who were exposed to domestic violence as children were three times more likely to grow up to become perpetrators of IPV. Men who witnessed severe abuse of their mothers by their fathers had rates of IPV that were 100 times greater than men who had not been exposed to spousal abuse. When these two factors—child abuse and witnessing abuse—are combined, the contributions to IPV are intensified (Adams, 2009).

■ Continuum of Intimate Violence

Roberts and Roberts (2005) conducted in-depth interviews with 501 battered women in a variety of settings, deriving an empirically based continuum of IPV based on the common metrics among their responses. Around these metrics the variables clustered into five levels on the battered-woman continuum that progress by duration and severity of abuse: (1) short term, (2) intermediate, (3) intermittent long term, (4) chronic/predictable, and (5) homicidal subtypes. Two variables in the Roberts (2007) study were empirically related to the duration of the battering relationship: (1) a victim's highest level of education completed and (2) relationship status. That is, victims with higher levels of education and lower levels of commitment to the relationship were more likely to leave.

Socioeconomic status appeared to follow an inverse trend in relationship to the duration and intensity of abuse. Thus, victims on the low-risk end of the continuum (short-term battering relationships) were characterized as having high levels of education (88.3% were college students

TABLE 9-4 **Continuum of Intimate Partner Violence**

Level 1 Short term	Level 2 Intermediate	Level 3 Intermittent/ long term	Level 4 Chronic and predictable	Level 5 Homicidal
Less than 1 year duration; usually college or high school students	Several months to 2 years; cohabiting	Long-term committed relationship; maybe has children	Long-term relationship; maybe a religious or cultural element to commitment	Variable but often long term
1–3 incidents	3–15 incidents	4–30 incidents	Several hundred incidents	Numerous violent incidents
Pushing, shoving, sometimes hitting with object	Moderate to severe injuries	Severe and intense episode with no warning; long periods between episodes	Frequent, predictable pattern of abuse, often involving substances	Violence escalates to homicide and life-threatening injuries
Victim leaves after first, second, or third incident Caring support system	Victim leaves due to bruises or injury Caring support system, parents, friends, new partner	Stays until children grow up Stays for status or prestige No other support system	Abuse continues until abuser is arrested, dies, is hospitalized Few financial resources	Victim has limited education or resources Victim suffers from PTSD or complex PTSD

Data from Roberts, A. R. 2002. Duration and severity of woman battering: A conceptual model/continuum. In A. Roberts (Ed.), *Handbook of domestic violence intervention strategies* (pp. 64–79). New York: Oxford University Press.

or graduates), being involved in a dating relationship with their abusive partner (94.7%), and being middle- or upper-middle class (81.5%). In contrast, the vast majority of victims at the high-risk end of the continuum (chronically abusive relationship) were lower or middle class, had low levels of education (88.7% were high school dropouts or graduates), and were either currently or formerly married (70%) or were cohabiting long-term (30%) with their abusive partners (Roberts, 2007) (**Table 9-4**).

■ Batterer Typologies

Typologies of batterers emanate from two different perspectives: (1) clinically and theoretically derived typologies or (2) empirically derived typologies. In general, clinically and theoretically based models are the first to be proposed, and later empirical testing either confirms the clinical models or suggests other forms of grouping. Elbow (1977) described four patterns of behavior in batterers, based on clinical reflections emanating from practice:

(1) the controller, who sees his partner as an object to be controlled; (2) the defender, who expects his wife to love and forgive him no matter how much he abuses her; (3) the approval seeker, who is so insecure he cannot tolerate the rejection implicit in his wife's leaving and often threatens her with death; and (4) the incorporator, who sees his wife as an extension of himself and often threatens violence because her leaving is such a threat to his ego.

As one of the first empirically derived classifications, Gondolf (1988) developed a typology of batterers based on a cluster analysis of batterer abuse and variables drawn from intake interviews with 6,000 battered women. The goal was to identify treatment approaches that reflect different motivations. The typology included three types of batterers: sociopathic, antisocial, and typical. According to Gondolf (1988) the sociopathic batterer engages in high levels of physical abuse and emotional abuse, is likely to be violent outside the home, and is likely to have been arrested for violent and nonviolent crimes. The antisocial batterer is less likely to have been arrested than the sociopathic batterer because this batterer is generally violent and verbally and physically abusive within the intimate relationship. The typical batterer commits less severe verbal and physical abuse than either of the preceding types, is less likely to use a weapon, and is generally less violent outside the home.

Holtzworth-Munroe and Stuart (1994) conducted a comprehensive review of 15 batterer typologies, including both clinically derived (deductive approaches) and empirically derived models (inductive approaches). An analysis of the data across these studies revealed that those who engage in IPV are a heterogeneous group that varies along theoretically important dimensions (**Table 9-5**). Holtzworth-Munroe and Stuart (1994) proposed that batterer subtypes can be classified along three descriptive dimensions: severity and frequency of marital violence, generality of the violence (i.e., family-only or extrafamilial violence), and the batterer's psychopathology or personality disorders. They suggested that using these descriptive dimensions produces three major subtypes: family only, dysphoric–borderline, and generally violent–antisocial. These typologies are useful to predict risk of future violence and to predict treatment success. That is, future violence is most likely to occur with the dysphoric–borderline and generally violent–antisocial abusers. Further, family-only abusers are most likely to benefit from traditional batterer treatment programs. Dysphoric–borderline abusers may be amenable to long-term treatment approaches that focus not only on battering but also on significant difficulties with interpersonal functioning. Finally, generally violent–antisocial abusers are least likely to benefit from any treatment approach.

TABLE 9-5 **Typologies of Batterers**

Family only	Least marital violence
	Lowest levels of psychological and sexual abuse
	Least violence outside the home
	Little or no psychopathology
	Violence resulting from a combination of stress and risk factors (childhood witnessing of IPV, lack of relationship skills)
	Lack of generalized hostility to women
	Remorse leading to lower risk of escalating violence
Dysphoric–borderline	Moderate to severe wife abuse
	Not much violence outside the home
	Most psychologically distressed
	Background of parental abuse and rejection
	Most likely to show borderline characteristics (emotional liability, intense unstable personal relationships, fear of rejection, jealousy)
Generally violent–antisocial	Moderate to severe levels of marital violence
	Highest levels of extrafamilial violence
	Most likely to have antisocial personality disorder (criminal behavior, arrests, substance abuse)
	High levels of family of origin violence
	Associates with deviant peers
	Marital violence is part of general use of aggression

Data from Holtzworth-Munroe, A., & Meehan, J. C. 2004. Typologies of men who are maritally violent: Scientific and clinical implications. *Journal of Interpersonal Violence, 19*(12), 1369–1389.

■ Intersections Between Batterer Typologies and the Continuum of Violence

Bender and Roberts (2007) proposed the batterer typologies intersect with the continuum of violence (**Table 9-6**). That is, Holtzworth-Munroe and Stuart's category of family-only abuser and Gondolf's category of typical batterer will most commonly result in level 1 or short-term violence. These individuals may also present with moderate severity or level 2 violence, depending on the characteristics of the victim and the victim's ability to exit the situation. Dysphoric–borderline abusers in Holtzworth-Munroe and Stuart's typology are likely to be found in level 2 (intermediate violence) or level 3 (intermittent long-term violence), again depending on the victim's characteristics and resources. Finally, the most severe abusers, the generally violent, antisocial, and sociopathic types, are most likely to be found

TABLE 9-6 Intersections Between Batterer Typologies and the Continuum of Violence

Batterer Typologies		Violence Continuum	
Typology	**Description**	**Typology**	**Description**
Low risk			
Family-only (Holtzworth-Munroe & Stuart, 1994)	Low level of severity	Level 1	Mild to moderate intensity of abuse
	Low frequency of violence	Short-term	1–3 incidents
Typical batterer (Gondolf, 1988)		(Roberts & Roberts, 2005)	Less than 1 year dating relationship
	Little or no psychopathology		
	Usually no criminal history		Presence of caring, responsive support system
Moderate risk			
Family-only (Holtzworth-Munroe & Stuart, 1994)	Moderate severity of violence	Level 2	Moderate to severe abuse
		Intermediate	3–15 incidents
Typical batterer (Gondolf, 1988)	Moderate frequency of violence	(Roberts & Roberts, 2005)	Cohabiting or recently married
OR	Moderate to high psychopathology		Presence of caring, responsive support system
Dysphoric–borderline (Holtzworth-Munroe & Stuart, 1994)		Level 3	Severe and intense violent episodes without warning; long periods without violence between violent episodes
		Intermittent long term	
		(Roberts & Roberts, 2005)	
			4–30 incidents
			No alternative support system
High risk			
Generally violent–antisocial (Holtzworth-Munroe & Stuart, 1994)	High severity of violence	Level 4	Severe repeated incidents, frequent, predictable pattern
	High frequency of violence	Chronic and predictable	Violence often precipitated by substance abuse
Antisocial type and sociopathic type (Gondolf, 1988)		(Roberts & Roberts, 2005)	Several hundred violent acts
	High levels of psychopathology		
OR	Usually has a criminal record		
Dysphoric–borderline (Holtzworth-Munroe & Stuart, 1994)		Level 5	Violence escalates to homicide and life-threatening injuries
		Homicidal	
		(Roberts & Roberts, 2005)	

Data from Bender, K. & Roberts, A. 2007. Battered women versus male batterer typologies: Same or different based on evidence-based studies? *Aggression and Violent Behavior.* *12*(5) 519-530.

in the highest risk category of the continuum of abuse, which is chronic and predictable and often leads to significant injury or death. Victims in this category frequently have come to expect battering as a part of life, have histories of violence in their families of origin, and have few person resources or social supports to draw upon. Level 5 violence, homicide, may occur in the context of chronic abuse that continues to escalate, as with the antisocial–sociopathic abuser, or it may occur in the course of an emotional rage, such as in the case of a dysphoric–borderline abuser.

Spousal homicide is an all-too-common occurrence in the context of IPV. As noted earlier, in 2007 intimate partners committed 14% of all homicides in the United States; 70% of those people killed by an intimate partner were women (Catalano et al., 2009). Also, 24% of women who were murdered were killed by a spouse or ex-spouse, 21% were killed by a girlfriend or boyfriend; 2% of male homicide victims were killed by a spouse or ex-spouse and 3% were killed by a girlfriend or boyfriend. Most intimate partner homicides (67–80%) occur in the context of ongoing IPV (Catalano et al., 2009). Research in Canada suggests that spousal homicide is a significant contributor to the overall number of homicides; 17% of Canadians who were accused of murder in 2006 were accused of murdering their current or former spouse. Seventy-two percent of Canadians who were murdered by their spouses in 2006 were female; during the 11 previous years, 82% of spousal homicide victims were women. The youngest person killed by his or her spouse in Ontario between 2003 and 2005 was aged 15 years; the eldest was aged 89 years. The youngest perpetrator was aged 21 years and the eldest, 89 years. Forty-one percent of spousal homicides involved stabbing, 29% were firearms deaths, 9% were due to beating, 6% were due to strangulation, and 3% each were due to poisoning and burns (Selley, 2008).

What differentiates battering spouses who kill from those who do not? Campbell and colleagues (2003) reviewed 220 intimate partner murders in 11 cities and identified both preincident and incident risk factors when compared to a control group of abused women. The strongest demographic risk factor was the abuser's lack of employment, followed by an education level of high school or lower. Individual risk factors included the abuser's access to a firearm and the abuser's use of illicit drugs. Substance abuse of the victim was not a risk factor. The risk was lower for victims who had never lived with the abuser and highest for victims who had separated from the abuser. This increased ninefold if the victim was separated from a highly controlling abuser. Stalking, however, was not a risk factor. A previous arrest for spousal assault reduced the risk of murder. Having a child in the home who was not the biological child of the abuser more than doubled the risk of homicide. **Table 9-7** summarizes risk factors associated with homicide in IPV.

Dixon, Hamilton-Giachristis, and Browne (2008) reviewed the cases of 90 perpetrators of intimate partner homicide and attempted to classify them on the dimensions of psychopathology and criminality. Most intimate partner murderers fell into the category of high criminality and low to moderate psychopathology (49%) or moderate to high criminality and high pathology (36.1%). These offenders had characteristics that corresponded with Holtzworth-Munroe's classifications of general violence–antisocial batterers and dysphoric–borderline batterers. Compared to community sample rates, which indicated the incidence of both these two types of batterers to be 25%, these two groups are represented at a considerably higher rate in IPV offenders who murder their partners. Low criminality and low pathology cases (akin to family-only batterers) represented only 15.3% of the sample, despite the fact that they are the most common type of batterer found in community samples.

Others proposed more dynamic approaches to understanding batterers who kill. Adams (2009), in describing men who murdered their intimate partners, identified five overlapping typologies: jealous, substance abusing, materially motivated, suicidal, and career criminal. Most of the jealous types of killers in Adams's work appeared to have been perpetually vigilant toward their intimate partners, which escalated over the course of their relationships. Adams hypothesized that this distrust had its roots in the offender's family of origin. That is, in many cases adverse childhood events, such as child abuse and exposure to interparental violence, contributed to the development of insecurity and anxiety about intimacy, which led to difficulty establishing meaningful interpersonal relationships. Further, elements of possessive control had

TABLE 9-7 **Risk Factors Associated with Homicide in Intimate Partner Violence**

- Abusers with a lower level of education
- Abusers with access to a firearm
- Use of illicit drugs by abuser
- Abuser separated from victim
- Highly controlling abuser
- No previous abuser arrests for intimate partner violence
- Having a stepchild in the home
- Abuser previously threatened victim with a weapon

Data from Campbell, J., Webster, D., Koziol-McLain, J., Block, C., Campbell, D., et al. 2003. Risk factors for femicide in abusive relationships: Results from a multisite case control study. *American Journal of Public Health, 93*(7), 1089–1097.

their roots in direct paternal modeling of spouse abuse, which was then socially reinforced through peer and cultural supports of male dominance within male–female relationships.

Honor Killings

Honor killings, previously believed to be a phenomenon found only in other places in the world, have recently become an increasing issue in North America. A Canadian report (Papp, 2010) indicates 13 honor-based murders of women in Canada between 2002 and 2010, examples of which can be found in **Table 9-8**. This report sparked considerable attention in the media and government. As a result, Rona Ambrose, the Canadian Minister of Public Works and Government Services, called upon cultural communities, stating "honour crimes and to the subjugation, oppression and repression of women and girls wherever it happens. Repression, oppression and violence to maintain a family's honour may even happen because a girl wants to wear westernized clothing, date a boy who may not

TABLE 9-8 Examples of Honor Killings

Incident	Details of the Case
2003, British Columbia Amandeep Atwal, age 17	Her father was convicted of stabbing her to death because he did not approve of her boyfriend, who was from another ethnic group.
2006, Ottawa, Ontario Khatera Sadiqi, age 20	She and her fiancé were shot to death in a shopping mall parking lot by her brother because he believed his sister was being disrespectful of their father.
2007, Mississauga, Ontario Aqsa Parvez, age 16	Strangled to death by her father and brother. Friends say they were upset she would not wear a hijab.
2011, Vancouver, BC Ravinder Bhangu, age 24	Killed when her estranged husband entered her workplace, a Punjabi-English newspaper, and repeatedly struck her with an axe.
2011, Toronto Shaher Shahdady	Strangled to death by her husband. Friends report her husband was upset she wanted to go to school and get a job. A member of the Canadian Muslim Congress referred to the murder as an honor killing of the worst sort.
2009, Kingston, Ontario Zainab, Sahar, and Geeti Shafia (sisters age 19,17, and 13) and Rona Amir Mohammad (father's first wife age 52)	Drown when their vehicle is submerged in a canal. The sisters' mother, father, and brother were found guilty of murder in 2012. The court heard that the parents refused to let the older daughter attend school because she was dating "unapproved" males. Ms. Amir was seen as supporting the girls' rebellion against their family.

Data from Hopper, T. 2011. Murders spark fears of honor killings. *National Post*. August 3, 2011, p.1; Hildebrandt, A. 2009. Honour killings: domestic abuse by another name. CBC News. July 24, 2009. Retrieved from http://www.cbc.ca/news/canada/story/2009/07/24/f-honour-killings.html.

be from her own religion or culture or simply wanting to wear make-up" (Wilkes, 2010).

Honor killings originated as a patriarchal tribal custom in Muslim, Sikh, and Hindu cultures. These killings involve the murder of a wife or daughter, usually by her father or brother, to restore a family's or community's reputation. Although originally linked to adultery or premarital sex, increasingly they are associated with a woman's push for independence (Hildebrandt, 2009). The idea that honor is a cause for murder stems from the belief that a person's honor or a family's honor depends on the behavior of others. Status and acceptance in some traditional cultures rests on the family honor, which stems from the behavior of family members, including the purity of female family members. Killing of a wayward woman can be seen as an act of purification for the family to restore the respect of the community (Baker, Gregware, & Cassidy, 1999).

Honor killings have distinct characteristics that differentiate them from other forms of IPV. Honor killings are generally planned in advance and often occur after multiple threats have been made. Honor killings frequently involve the complicity of multiple family members. Those who perpetrate honor killings do not necessarily face stigma in their communities (Hopper, 2011).

Battered Woman Syndrome Defense

An alternative area of study and law related to homicide in intimate relationships pertains to women who kill their abusive husbands. Battered woman syndrome testimony began emerging in the United States during the late 1970s and early 1980s to support defense strategies in criminal cases. In 1990, as a result of a decision by the Supreme Court of Canada, **battered woman syndrome defense** became accepted as a legitimate extension of self-defense in Canadian courts (Regehr & Glancy, 1995). Similar developments are noted in the United Kingdom, Australia, and New Zealand. This defense arose out of concerns that the real-life experiences of battered women had not been reflected in the laws of self-defense. Traditional self-defense law is intended to explain the behavior of an individual who responds to a threat of death or bodily harm with lethal force or force that causes bodily harm. The standard example of this was the barroom brawl and an interpretation of how the average man would have behaved if he had been in a similar situation. The law of self-defense carries an assumption that the force used in self-defense would be applied in the course of mutual combat, but many women who kill their abusive husbands do not do so while they are being assaulted. Faced with memories of previous abuses, fears for the safety of their children who may also be present, and the reality of marked physical strength advantage, those women recoil during the assault. It is only later that these traumatized women protect themselves in the only way they can conceive, by killing their husbands as they lie drunk or asleep (Regehr & Glancy, 1995).

A common question asked of battered women is why they did not just leave the threatening situation. In most American jurisdictions, one is not required to retreat from an imminent threat of death or serious bodily injury, even if such retreat can be accomplished with complete safety. This doctrine, called the "true man rule," states, "There is a strong policy against the unnecessary taking of human life but there is also a strong policy against making one act in a cowardly and humiliating role" (Ewing, 1990, p. 81). Nevertheless, whereas a man's right to stand his ground and defend himself, his family, and his property was generally recognized, a woman who did so in the context of IPV had to demonstrate why she did not flee. The battered woman syndrome defense was an attempt to modify gender-biased self-defense laws to allow for the experiences of battered women. Elements of the battered woman syndrome defense include the following: (1) the existence of complex posttraumatic stress disorder; (2) the existence of battered woman syndrome; (3) the uniqueness of events leading to the ultimate offense; (4) elements of the woman's psychological functioning that led to an apprehension that her death was imminent, and she consequently used lethal force; and (5) a description of why the woman remained trapped in the relationship and was unable to leave (Regehr & Glancy, 1995).

The precedent-setting case in the Supreme Court of Canada was *R v. Lavallee*. Ms. Lavallee was a 22-year-old woman who had been living with the victim, Kevin Rust, for 3 to 4 years. After a boisterous party the couple had an argument. Ms. Lavallee had hidden in the closet upstairs and was dragged out by Mr. Rust. He gave her a gun and stated, "Either you kill me or I will kill you," and then "he kind of smiled and turned around." Although she claims to have been aiming over his head, Ms. Lavallee killed Mr. Rust with a single shot to the back of the head with a .303 caliber rifle. A psychiatrist with extensive experience working with battered women testified at the trial that Ms. Lavallee had been terrorized by her husband to the point of feeling worthless, trapped, vulnerable, and unable to escape the relationship despite the violence. In his opinion the shooting was a final desperate act of a woman who sincerely believed she would be killed that night. Ms. Lavallee was acquitted at the original trial but was convicted by the Supreme Court of Manitoba. The defense appealed to the Supreme Court of Canada, who restored the acquittal. The written judgment made it clear that battered woman syndrome defense was now an acceptable extension of self-defense. It was stated that although the Criminal Code of Canada does not stipulate imminence, it is an assumed element of self-defense; however, in the case of battered women, the perception of lethality goes beyond the immediate assaultive situation. "The issue is not what an outsider would have reasonably perceived, but what the accused reasonably perceived given her situation and experience. The question the jury must ask itself is whether, given the history, circumstances and perception of the accused, her belief that she could not preserve herself from being killed by the deceased that night except by killing him first, was reasonable" (*R v. Lavallee*, 1990, S. 51).

Although battered woman syndrome defense in both Canada and the United States was heralded by some as a great victory in light of the historical treatment of women in the courts, others suggest it disadvantaged women as a group. That is, the defense is thought to reinforce negative stereotypes of women as passive and helpless (Ferraro, 2003). Others suggest that those women who received acquittals on this basis are forced to embrace their victimhood as the sole defining characteristic. Further, it is suggested that this defense, which is based on stereotypes, does not necessarily fit all women. For example, research has shown that stereotypes of women of color do not allow for the overlay of another stereotype of being weak, helpless, and passive (Tang, 2003).

The use of the defense has been extended beyond its original intent to include men who killed their spouses and victims of IPV who committed other crimes, such as fraud. This trend has led some to use the term "abuse excuse," whereby guilty people use previous abuse to justify crime. Cited examples of the abuse excuse as a defense include the Menendez brothers, who killed their parents; Lorena Bobbitt, who is accused of hiding behind "the murky battered woman's defense"; and terrorists (Dowd, 1999; Dershowitz, 2006).

■ Intervention Programs in IPV

Intervention programs related to IPV fall into three broad categories: programs for child witnesses of violence, which are aimed at preventing future harm; programs for victims of violence, which are aimed at providing emergency assistance and increasing available choices; and programs for batterers, which are aimed at stopping violent behavior. As noted earlier, the passage of the Violence Against Women Act (1994) by the U.S. federal government signaled a commitment to improve criminal justice responses, expand community services, improve safety measures, and provide support for education- and health-based services. Similar investments in programs have been made in other Western countries.

Interventions for Victims of IPV

The first line of intervention for victims of IPV is ensuring safety. Shelters for victims of violence (which in the vast majority of cases are aimed at abused women and their children) provide shelter and offer anonymity. Shelters have security measures that often involve secret locations, electronic security, and arrangements with local police forces. Other safety programs involve hotlines or provide counselors who work with victims to develop a safety plan that may include removing weapons from the home, confiding in friends or family who could help in an emergency, obtaining a protection order, or relocating. In extreme cases services that are focused on safety can assist victims to relocate to another city and change their identity.

The next level of intervention is programs that provide ongoing treatment and assistance to victims. Many treatment programs, both for victims of IPV and for batterers, use a group work model, which frequently is based on feminist ideology. Even when couples choose to remain together, current clinical wisdom suggests that both victim and offender fare better in gender-specific programs aimed at enhancing self-esteem, recognizing violence, and changing attitudes and behaviors. Groups reduce isolation, normalize the woman's experience, allow for an environment where victims can challenge one another for self-blaming statements or for beliefs that minimize the abuse, and allow victims to support one another in the difficult transition to change. Research evidence for the usefulness of women's support groups demonstrates statistically significant pretest–posttest improvements in areas such as self-esteem, anger, and depression (Tutty, Ogden, & Wyllie, 2006).

Treatment programs for victims of same-sex violence are often far more limited. Traditional feminist-based programs may not provide ideal services for this group of victims because of the basic assumptions about male violence and power that underlie many of the approaches. This may be at odds not only with assumptions about who is the victim and who is the perpetrator but also with issues of mutual violence or alternating violence. Shelters that address personal safety, which is a paramount concern to all victims of IPV, may not be welcoming or available to those who are openly lesbian. Gay men are excluded from these shelters, and the only option is shelters for indigent or substance-abusing men. Yet formal programs that address same-sex violence are available only in large cities that have visible gay and lesbian communities (Gillis & Diamond, 2006). In the end, this population of victims has fewer options and may feel more trapped in relationships than heterosexual victims.

Interventions for Child Witnesses

Interventions for children similarly need to be stratified to address varying needs at different times. Crisis intervention may be necessary at times of acute distress, such as when children enter a shelter. The focus of this intervention is to make the children feel safe, normalize the children's feelings, and develop a plan for when the children feel that either they or their parent are at risk. At the next stage, group therapy can provide support, education, problem-solving skills, and coping skills (Lehmann & Rabenstein, 2002). Many children benefit from the positive, fun atmosphere where they feel validated and appreciated. However, group treatment may be contraindicated for children with particularly poor social skills who are at risk of further rejection (Vickerman & Margolin, 2007). Group treatments are designed to be specific to different developmental stages. Interventions for younger children often incorporate play. Interventions for adolescents draw on adult-oriented treatment models but attend to the unique challenges of adolescents, including peer group pressures and risk taking.

Parents' and children's groups are a newer model of intervention that teaches improved parenting skills and emphasizes discipline techniques that do not involve violence or psychological abuse. The goal is to increase positive and supportive parenting techniques and reduce coercive interactions (Vickerman & Margolin, 2007). These groups also work to improve the relationship between the parent and child. Essentially, the abused parent is encouraged to move beyond his or her own distress to be available to and support the child.

Interventions for Offenders

Glancy and Saini (2005) conducted a meta-analysis of psychological treatments for anger and aggression. Their review concluded that a number of treatment approaches are effective in reducing anger and aggressive behavior in a variety of populations, including both male and female perpetrators of IPV. Programs that used a cognitive-behavioral therapeutic approach were most frequently studied, and all these programs showed at least moderate gains in reducing problematic behavior, often in as few as six to eight sessions. When a follow-up was conducted of male batterers, 85% were still refraining from physical violence 1 year later. Psychoeducational approaches were also effective in reducing aggressive acts of violence in intimate relationships. Although fewer studies exist on psychotherapeutic approaches, comparative studies with cognitive-behavioral therapy demonstrate equal effectiveness, and the effects were sustained at 12 and 24 month follow-ups.

Despite these successes, anger management groups have been criticized for ignoring the context of IPV and merely concentrating on skills. Conceptualizing IPV as simply a problem with anger ignores the basic belief systems that contributed to the abusive treatment of an intimate partner. From a feminist perspective, problematic beliefs include attitudes that view women as chattels of men and as people who can and should be controlled. The concern that arises from this is that although physical aggression may cease, emotional abuse may remain or increase. That is, a controlling abuser may simply learn more sophisticated means of control, such as emotional blackmail, from the group process. As a result, outcome measures to assess group effectiveness must go beyond physical violence alone and also address attitudes and other controlling behaviors (Tutty et al., 2006).

■ Summary

IPV has a long history that begins in ancient society. It continues to pervade our society at an alarming rate, causing profound effects on victims and their children. Early work in the area of IPV focused on woman abuse and addressed issues such as unequal treatment and protection under the law and patriarchal structures that condoned the abuse of women. More recent attention has been paid to male victims of interpersonal violence in both heterosexual and same-sex relationships and to women in same-sex relationships.

The continuum of violence spans from single-incident violence, which often occurs within dating relationships, to chronic ongoing abuse with serious bodily injury and ultimately to homicide. Typologies of abusers similarly span people who commit violence only within the confines of their family as a result of a variety of risk factors, to those with significant personality pathology, to those for whom violence is a way of life and a means for achieving their goals. Treatment approaches for both victims and abusers must consider these varying levels and types of abuse and be tailored to address both immediate needs and to maximize the possibilities of success.

■ Key Terms

Battered woman syndrome: The effects of intimate partner violence on victims.

Battered woman syndrome defense: An extension of self-defense laws that appreciates battered women's perceptions of risk and the possibility of escape.

Complex posttraumatic stress disorder: Reactions experienced by survivors of prolonged abuse, which includes symptoms of posttraumatic stress disorder and personality changes.

Domestic violence: Incidents of interspousal physical or emotional abuse perpetrated by one of the spouses upon the other spouse.

Intimate partner violence (IPV): Any behavior within an intimate relationship that causes physical, psychological, or sexual harm to those in the relationship.

Learned helplessness: A cognitive state in which a victim no longer believes that any action can change an aversive situation.

Posttraumatic stress disorder (PTSD): An anxiety disorder that develops in some individuals who have had major traumatic experiences. PTSD is characterized by intrusive thoughts and images and heightened arousal.

Protection orders: An order made when the court makes a final decision and is satisfied that domestic and family violence has occurred and is likely to occur again.

Wife battering: Assault against a woman by her husband.

■ Discussion Questions

1. Select a legal response to intimate partner violence. What are the pros and cons of the particular approach?

2. What are the long-term effects of intimate partner violence on children who witness abuse?

3. Identify characteristics of various typologies of batterers. What policies and interventions may best address their violence?

4. What intervention strategies can be used for victims at various points along the continuum of violence?

5. In your opinion, is battered woman syndrome defense justifiable homicide? Explain.

■ Resources

Centre for Children and Families in the Justice System, Domestic Violence
http://www.lfcc.on.ca/children_exposed_to_domestic_violence.html

Health Canada, Violence against Women
   http://www.hc-sc.gc.ca/hl-vs/pubs/women-femmes/violence-eng.php
National Clearing House on Family Violence
   http://www.phac-aspc.gc.ca/ncfv-cnivf/index-eng.php
U.S. Department of Justice, Office for Victims of Crime
   http://www.ojp.usdoj.gov/ovc/
Violence Policy Center
   http://www.vpc.org/aboutvpc.htm

■ References

Adams, D. (2009). Predisposing childhood factors for men who kill their intimate partners. *Victims and Offenders, 4*(3), 215–229.

Alaggia, R., Jenney, A., Mazzuca, J., & Redmond, M. (2007). In whose best interest? A Canadian case study of the impact of child welfare policies in cases of domestic violence. *Brief Treatment and Crisis Intervention, 7*(4), 275–290.

Alaggia, R., Regehr, C., & Jenny, A. (2011). Risky business: An ecological analysis of intimate partner violence disclosure. *Research on Social Work Practice.* doi:10.1177/1049731511425503

Alaggia, R., Regehr, C., & Rishchynsky, G. (2009). Intimate partner violence and immigration laws in Canada: How far have we come? *International Journal of Law and Psychiatry, 32*(6), 335–341.

Baker, N., Gregware, P., & Cassidy, M. (1999). Family killing field: Honor rationales in the murder of women. *Violence Against Women, 5*(2), 164–184.

Bender, K., & Roberts, A. (2007). Battered women versus male batterer typologies: Same or different based on evidence-based studies? *Aggression and Violent Behavior, 12*(5), 519–530.

Black, T., Trocmé, N., Fallon, B., & MacLaurin, B. (2008). The Canadian child welfare system response to exposure to domestic violence investigations. *Child Abuse and Neglect, 32*, 393–404.

Brown, C. (2008). Gender-role implications on same-sex intimate partner abuse. *Journal of Family Violence, 23*, 457–462.

Campbell, J., Webster, D., Koziol-McLain, J., Block, C., Campbell, D., Curry M., . . . Laughon, K. (2003). Risk factors for femicide in abusive relationships: Results from a multisite case control study. *American Journal of Public Health, 93*(7), 1089–1097.

Canadian Centre for Justice Statistics. (2004). Family violence in Canada: A statistical profile. Retrieved from http://www.phac-aspc.gc.ca/ncfv-cnivf/familyviolence/pdfs/fv-85-224-XIE2004000_e.pdf

Catalano, S. (2007). Intimate partner violence in the United States. Retrieved from http://www.ojp.usdoj.gov/bjs/intimate/ipv.htm

Catalano, S., Smith, E., Snyder, H., & Rand, M. (2009). Female victims of violence. Bureau of Justice Statistics. NCJ 228356. Washington, DC: U.S. Department of Justice.

Centers for Disease Control and Prevention. (2006). Dating violence fact sheet. Retrieved from http://www.cdc.gov/ncipc/dvp/dating_violence.htm

CNN. (2009). Chris Brown apology video. Retrieved from http://www.cnn.com/video/?/video/showbiz/2009/07/20/dcl.brown.apology.cnn

Cruz, A. (2009, February 9). Chris Brown and Rihanna: A fairy-tale romance gone awry. Retrieved from http://www.people.com/people/article/0,,20257828,00.html

Denham, D., & Gillespie, J. (1998). *Two steps forward . . . one step back: An overview of Canadian initiatives and resources to end wife abuse 1989–1997.* Ottawa, Ontario, Canada: Family Violence Prevention Unit, Health Canada.

Dershowitz, A. (2006, April 20). The abuse excuse. Zacarias Moussaoui's lawyers float the "Impoverished French Muslim Syndrome." Retrieved from http://www.slate.com/id/2140262/

Dixon, L., Hamilton-Giachristis, C., & Browne, K. (2008). Classifying partner femicide. *Journal of Interpersonal Violence, 23*(1), 74–93.

Dowd, M. (1999). Women and the abuse excuse. Retrieved from http://library.findlaw.com/1999/Nov/1/129404.html

Elbow, M. (1977). Theoretical considerations of violent marriages. *Social Casework, 58*(9), 515–526.

Ewing, P. (1990). Psychological self-defense: A proposed justification for battered women who kill. *Law and Human Behavior, 14*(6), 579–594.

Fagan, J. (1996). *The criminalization of domestic violence: Promises and limits.* National Institute of Justice Research Report. Washington, DC: U.S. Department of Justice.

FBI. (1995). The structure of family violence, An analysis of selected incidents. Retrieved from http://www.fbi.gov/about-us/cjis/ucr/nibrs/nibrs_famvio95.pdf

Ferraro, K. (2003). The words change, but the melody lingers: The persistence of battered woman syndrome in criminal cases involving battered women. *Violence Against Women, 9*(1), 110–129.

Finkelhor, D., & Yllo, K. (1982). Forced sex in marriage: A preliminary research report. *Crime and Delinquency, 28*(3), 459–478.

Gillis, R., & Diamond, S. (2006). Same-sex partner abuse: Challenges to the existing paradigms of intimate violence theory. In R. Alaggia & C. Viner (Eds.), *Cruel but not unusual: Violence in Canadian families* (pp. 127–146). Waterloo, Ontario: Wilfrid Laurier University Press.

Glancy, G., & Saini, M. (2005). An evidence-based review of psychological treatments for anger and aggression. *Brief Treatment and Crisis Intervention, 5*(2), 229–248.

Gondolf, E.F. (1988). Who are those guys? Toward a behavioral typology of batterers. *Violence and Victims, 3*, 187–203.

Grauwiler, P. (2008). Voices of women: Perspectives on decision-making and the management of partner violence. *Children and Youth Services Review, 30*, 311–322.

Hardesty, J., Oswald, R., Khaw, L., & Fonseca, C. (2011). Lesbian/bisexual mothers and intimate partner violence: Help seeking in the context of social and legal vulnerability. *Violence Against Women, 17*(1), 28–46.

Herman, J.L. (1992). *Trauma and recovery.* New York: Basic Books.

Hildebrandt, A. (2009, July 24). Honour killings: Domestic abuse by another name. Retrieved from http://www.cbc.ca/news/canada/story/2009/07/24/f-honour-killings.html

Holtzworth-Munroe, A., & Stuart, G.L. (1994). Typologies of male batterers: Three subtypes and the differences among them. *Psychological Bulletin, 116*(3), 476–497.

Hopper, T. (2011, August 3). Murders spark fears of honor killings. *National Post,* p. 1.

Huth-Bocks, A., & Hughes, H. (2008). Parenting stress, parenting behaviour and children's adjustment in families experiencing intimate partner violence. *Journal of Family Violence, 23*, 243–251.

Jaffe, P., Crooks, C., & Wolfe, D. (2003). Legal and policy responses to children exposed to domestic violence: The need to evaluate intended and unintended consequences. *Clinical Child and Family Psychology Review, 6*(3), 205–213.

Kitzmann, K., Gaylord, N., Holt, A., & Kenny, E. (2003). Child witnesses to domestic violence: A meta-analytic review. *Journal of Counselling and Clinical Psychology, 71*(2), 339–353.

LA Times. (2009, February 8). Singer Chris Brown under investigation for alleged assault. Retrieved from http://latimesblogs.latimes.com/lanow/2009/02/chris-brown-boo.html

Lehmann, P., & Rabenstein, S. (2002). Children exposed to domestic violence. In A. Roberts (Ed.), *Handbook of domestic violence intervention strategies* (pp. 343–364). New York: Oxford University Press.

MacKinnon, C. (1987). *Feminism unmodified: Discourses on life and law.* Cambridge, MA: Harvard University Press.

MacLeod, L. (1980). *Wife battering in Canada: The vicious cycle.* Ottawa, Ontario, Canada: Canadian Advisory Council of the Status of Women.

MacLeod, L. (1987). *Battered but not beaten: Preventing wife battering in Canada.* Ottawa, Ontario, Canada: Canadian Advisory Council of the Status of Women.

Margolin, G., & Vickerman, K. (2007). Posttraumatic stress in children and adolescents exposed to family violence: Overview and issues. *Professional Psychology: Research and Practice, 38*(6), 613–619.

Mbilinyi, L., Edleson, J., Hagemeister, A., & Beeman, S. (2007). What happens to children when their mothers are battered? Results from a four city anonymous telephone survey. *Journal of Family Violence, 22,* 309–317.

Mears, D.P., Carlson, M.J., Holden, G.W., & Harris, S.D. (2001). Reducing domestic violence revictimization: The effects of individual and contextual factors. *Journal of Interpersonal Violence, 16,* 1260–1283.

Nicholson v. Williams. (2004). U.S. Court of Appeals, 2nd Cir., No. 2, 171 (amicus).

Papp, A. (2010). Culturally-driven violence against women: A growing problem in Canada's immigrant communities. Frontier Centre for Public Policy. Retrieved from http://www.fcpp.org/publication.php/3351

Pattavina, A., Hirshel, D., Buzawa, E., Faggiani, D., & Bentley, H. (2007). A comparison of the police response to heterosexual versus same-sex intimate partner violence. *Violence Against Women, 13*(4), 374–394.

Pleck, E. (1987). *Domestic tyranny: The making of social policy against family violence from colonial times to present.* New York: Oxford University Press.

Ptacek, J. (1999). *Battered women in the courtroom: The power of judicial certainty.* Boston: North Eastern University Press.

Randle, A., & Graham, C. (2011). A review of the evidence of the effects of intimate partner violence on men. *Psychology of Men and Masculinity, 12*(2), 97–111.

RCMP. (2012). Research summary: Domestic violence involving firearms. *Royal Canadian Mounted Police.* Retrieved from http://www.rcmp-grc.gc.ca /cfp-pcaf/res-rec/violence-eng.htm

Regehr, C., & Glancy, G. (1995). Battered woman syndrome defense in the Canadian courts. *Canadian Journal of Psychiatry, 40*(3), 130–135.

R v. Lavallee. (1990). 55, CCC 3d 97.

Roberts, A.R. (2002). Duration and severity of woman battering: A conceptual model/continuum. In A. Roberts (Ed.), *Handbook of domestic violence intervention strategies* (pp. 64–79). New York: Oxford University Press.

Roberts, A.R. (2007). Domestic violence continuum, forensic assessment, and crisis intervention. *Families in Society: Journal of Contemporary Social Services, 88*(1), 30–43.

Roberts, A.R., & Roberts, B. (2005). *Ending intimate abuse: Practical guidance and survival strategies.* New York: Oxford University Press.

Selley, C. (2008, April 11). Spousal homicide: Just the facts. Retrieved from http://www.macleans.ca/article.jsp?content=20080411_141047_4888

Sherman, L., & Berk, R. (1984). *The Minneapolis Domestic Violence Experiment. Police Foundation Reports.* Washington, DC: Police Foundation.

Shlonsky, A., & Friend, C. (2007). Double jeopardy: Risk assessment in the context of child maltreatment and domestic violence. *Brief Treatment and Crisis Intervention, 7*(4), 253–274.

Sorenson, S., & Shen, H. (2005). Restraining orders in California. *Violence Against Women, 11*(7), 912–933.

Stanley, J., Bartholomew, K., Taylor, T., Oram, D., & Landolt, M. (2006). Intimate violence in male same-sex relationships. *Journal of Family Violence, 21*(1), 31–41.

Statistics Canada. (2005, July 14). Family violence in Canada: A statistical profile. Retrieved from http://www.statcan.ca/Daily/English/050714/d050714a.htm

Straus, M., & Gelles, R. (1980). *Behind closed doors: Violence in the American family.* Garden City, NJ: Anchor/Doubleday.

Swash, R. (2009, February 20). Rihanna assault photo leaked. Retrieved from http://www.guardian.co.uk/music/2009/feb/20/rihanna-alleged-assault-photo-leaked

Tang, K. (2003). Battered woman syndrome testimony in Canada: Its development and lingering issues. *International Journal of Offender Therapy and Comparative Criminology, 47*(6), 618–629.

Taylor, C., & Sorenson, S. (2007). Intervention on behalf of children exposed to intimate partner violence: Assessment of support in a diverse community-based sample. *Child Abuse and Neglect, 31*, 1155–1168.

Tutty, L., Ogden, C., & Wyllie, K. (2006). An evaluation of the Peer Support Services peer model. Final report to Peer Support Services for Abused Women. Calgary Alberta, Canada, RESOLVE Alberta.

Vickerman, K., & Margolin, G. (2007). Posttraumatic stress in children and adolescents exposed to family violence: Treatment. *Professional Psychology: Research and Practice, 38*(6), 620–628.

Walker, L.A. (1979). *Battered women syndrome.* New York: Springer.

Wilkes, J. (2010, July 13). Ottawa condemns honour killings. Retrieved from http://www.thestar.com/news/canada/article/835153--ottawa-condemns-honour-killings

Wolfe, D., Crooks, C., Lee, V., McIntyre-Smith, A., & Jaffe, P. (2003). The effects of children's exposure to domestic violence: A meta-analysis and critique. *Clinical Child and Family Psychology Review, 6*(3), 177–187.

World Health Organization. (2005). *Landmark study on domestic violence.* Retrieved from http://www.who.int/mediacentre/news/releases/2005/pr62/en/index.html

Zolotor, A., Theodore, A., Coyne-Beasley, T., & Runyan, D. (2007). Intimate partner violence and child maltreatment: Overlapping risk. *Brief Treatment and Crisis Intervention, 7*(4), 305–321.

Stalking Victims

CHAPTER
10

◼ Objectives

- To discuss the nature of stalking behaviors
- To identify legal responses to stalking
- To identify a typology of stalkers
- To discuss effects of stalking on victims
- To discuss risk assessment of offenders
- To discuss treatment for offenders

◼ Key Terms

Celebrity stalking
Credible threat
Cyberstalking
de Clérambault's syndrome
Erotomania
Obsessional harassment
Peace bond
Protection order
Psychiatric gating
Restraining order
Sexually violent predator
Stalking

CASE

Catherine Zeta-Jones and Michael Douglas live a life of luxury and have ample resources to ensure their privacy in their several residences around the world. But in March 2004, while staying at a luxury hotel Douglas co-owns in Bermuda, they received a message from a female caller indicating she was going to kill Zeta-Jones. The call was followed by a series of letters sent to others including Zeta-Jones's father-in-law, Kirk Douglas in which 32-year-old Dawnette Knight threatened to slice Zeta-Jones up and feed her to the dogs, chop her into pieces, or shoot her in the head.

In July 2004 Knight issued an apology for her threats toward Zeta-Jones, indicating she was a confused young woman who was infatuated with Michael Douglas. However, later on the witness stand she intimated that she and Douglas had a love affair and that Douglas paid her off to go away. Douglas denied meeting Knight, although he had received a note from her offering to show him a good time. Knight's fiancé in her defense described her as a fun-loving girl who wanted to pursue a career as a child psychologist. Legal proceedings were suspended after Knight took an overdose while in jail awaiting trial; however, a subsequent fitness hearing found her competent to stand trial for 24 felony counts of threatening and stalking. Zeta-Jones testified at trial that she was terrified for the safety of herself and her family. One year after her initial apology, Knight plead no contest to stalking charges and was sentenced to 3 years imprisonment and was ordered to pay $200 in restitution (Rathi, 2005; Taylor, 2004; Telegraph, 2004). See **Figures 10-1a** and **10-1b**.

© Nick Ut/AP Photos   A   © Alastair Grant/AP Photos   B

FIGURE 10-1 Dawnette Knight, celebrity stalker of Michael Douglas and Catherine Zeta-Jones

■ Introduction

Stalking is defined as a pattern of conduct in which one person inflicts on another repeated, unwanted intrusions and communications to the extent the victim fears for his or her own safety (Pathé & Mullen, 1997). In and of themselves, stalking behaviors experienced by the victim can seem benign to the outside observer. Someone leaves repeated phone messages, sends gifts, or shows up in places where the victim habitually goes, all of which in isolation do not appear to be threatening (Purcell, Pathé, & Mullen, 2004). Yet, the context of the relationship sets the stage for what the victim experiences as intimidation. That is, the stalker pursues a relationship the victim does not desire, often because the victim is a former partner of the stalker, the victim is a famous person who has no relationship with the stalker, or the victim is a professional who has no interest in a personal relationship with the victim. What differentiates these behaviors from normal interpersonal interactions and characterizes them as stalking is that they are (1) intentional, (2) repeated, and (3) result in fear (Spitzberg & Cupach, 2007).

Stalking behaviors can cover a wide range of activities. Generally, stalking includes harassing or threatening an individual during his or her repeated activities, such as following the person, appearing at the person's home or place of business, making harassing phone calls, leaving objects or written messages, or vandalizing property. Stalking may or may not involve threatened or actual violence. **Table 10-1** provides a list of common stalking behaviors.

More recently, stalking behaviors have expanded and now include cybermethods of harassment. **Cyberstalking** provides an additional means to harass victims in a manner that is more anonymous and has less chance of detection than other methods of stalking. The advent of virtual social networks, such as Facebook, allows stalkers easy access to information about victims. Pictures posted on multiple sites often reveal friends, common activities, and favorite places to frequent. Messages can be transmitted

TABLE 10-1 Common Stalking Behaviors

- Repeated telephone calls, letters, or e-mails
- Sending unwanted gifts (flowers, candy, etc.)
- Showing up uninvited at work or home
- Intercepting mail or e-mail
- Following, watching, or tracking
- Collecting photos or videos of the person
- Contacting the victim's employer, colleagues, or family
- Threatening harm to the victim
- Threatening the victim's family, friends, or pets
- Vandalizing the victim's car or property
- Assault (physical, sexual, or emotional)
- Kidnapping or holding hostage

to the victim, which can be received anytime or anywhere through e-mail and text messaging. A study conducted by Moriarty and Freiberger (2008) revealed that cyberstalking behaviors were most likely to involve, in order of frequency, (1) threatening, harassing, or obscene e-mails; (2) live chat harassment or online verbal abuse; (3) threatening or obscene calls to a cell phone; (4) improper messages on message boards; and (5) text and instant messaging. Infrequent but highly threatening activities included tracking a person's whereabouts on a GPS system without the person's consent and electronic identity theft. Interestingly, the nature of the stalking differed with cyberstalking when compared to other methods of stalking. In general, stalking is most commonly associated with domestic violence; however, Moriarty and Freiberger (2008) found a full one-third of cyberstalkers were considered to be nuisance stalkers.

One of the troublesome issues in stalking is the degree to which stalking behaviors are an exaggeration of normal courtship behaviors. When someone is infatuated with another person, he or she thinks of them constantly throughout the day. Early in an amorous relationship people call each other frequently and want to spend a great deal of time together, and they might send notes and/or purchase small gifts for each other. Initially, therefore, it can be difficult to differentiate between the behaviors associated with love and those associated with obsessional harassment. Similarly, with a famous person, fans are encouraged to be adoring. Fan mail is rewarded with signed pictures and personalized letters. In fact, the existence of people waiting in areas where the famous person is expected to arrive in the hopes of getting a picture or autograph is a sign of success and celebrity. When does fan behavior become stalking?

A further problem associated with stalking is the victim's lack of authority to end the behavior. Although laws that address stalking have emerged, beginning with California in 1990, a continuing problem is that many strategies used by stalkers, such as calling a victim or being in the same place as the victim, are basic rights and freedoms guaranteed under law. Thus, victims try to use a number of strategies that are generally unsuccessful. First, the victim often tries to ignore or normalize the behavior, trying to assess whether or not it should be regarded as threatening. Next, the victim may try to negotiate, request, or plead with the offender to stop the behavior. When these attempts fail the victim may move to threats, such as calling the police, notifying a superior (such as an employer), or other forms of harm to the stalker. Such strategies, however, can serve to escalate the situation because the threats are often unsuccessful (for example, the police have limited jurisdiction to intervene) and the victim has now demonstrated the impact of the stalker on his or her life. The victim therefore may begin to alter his or her customary patterns and limit his or her activities to avoid contact with the stalker. He or she may change telephone numbers, move to a different residence, restrict excursions, or refrain from going anywhere unless accompanied. Finally, the victim may seek assistance from a shelter or other service or seek legal options. The experience consumes the victim's time and emotional energy and is highly distressing and seemingly without end.

■ Scope of the Problem

A large number of studies have attempted to determine the nature and incidence of stalking. Spitzberg and Cupach (2007) conducted a meta-analysis of 175 studies using unique samples ranging from large-scale population studies to studies of forensic populations, which in total represent 122,207 individuals. From their analysis, they determined that population-based studies report a lifetime prevalence of stalking ranging from 2% to 13% for males and 8% to 32% for females. Across the studies examined, 60% to 80% of the victims were female. Stalking was most likely to emerge from a preexisting relationship; 79% of victims knew their pursuer, and half of all stalking emerged from romantic relationships. Physical violence was reported in 32% of cases, and sexual violence was reported in 12% of cases.

The U.S. National Crime Victimization Survey (U.S. Department of Justice, 1997) found a lifetime prevalence of 8.1% for women and 2.2% for men, which, by extrapolation, translates to 2.04 million women and 820,000 men in the United States who at some time in their lives have been victims of stalking behavior (Douglas & Dutton, 2001). The 2006 Supplemental Victimization Survey estimated that over a 12-month period in the United States, 3.4 million people over age 18 were victims of stalking (Baum, Catalano, Rand, & Rose, 2009). Nearly three-fourths of those reporting stalking knew their attacker. The National Violence Against Women Survey revealed that 87% of stalking victims were women and 87% of stalkers were men. Of all groups in the survey, Native American women were significantly more likely to report being stalked than members of other ethnic and racial groups (Tjaden & Thoennes, 1998).

The General Social Survey in Canada found that 11% of women aged 15 and older (or 1.4 million women) stated they had been stalked in a way that caused them to fear for their safety or the safety of someone close to them (Statistics Canada, 2006). Clearly, stalking is a much more common experience than most of us would expect.

■ Stalking Laws

California passed the first stalking law in the Western world in 1990 as a result of five stalking-related murders that occurred in Orange County over a 1-year period, the most famous of which was the murder of actress Rebecca Schaeffer (California Penal Code, 1990). In 1996 the National Institute of Justice brought a Model Anti-Stalking Code to Congress. This code defines stalking as "repeatedly maintaining visual or physical proximity to a person, repeatedly conveying verbal or written threats or threats implied by conduct" (p. 43). The code was seen as necessary because generally legal remedies for victims were covered under laws addressing harassment, trespassing, or vandalism, which addressed very specific aspects of stalking behavior; were frequently misdemeanors that were not given serious attention; and could not be enacted until the stalker had inflicted physical assault or property damage on the victim (Dennison & Thomson, 2005; Purcell et al., 2004). This was exemplified by Sandra Pollard, the mother of a stalking victim, who testified before the 1992 U.S. Senate Judiciary Committee hearings on antistalking legislation. "Despite threats he has made against our lives, despite repeated violations of restraining orders, despite the professional assessment of him as dangerous, both the District Attorney and our own attorney have said that nothing can be done until he has 'done something.' What is the 'something' they must wait for him to do? Kidnap [my daughter]? Rape her? Kill her?" (Purcell et al., 2004, p. 159).

As a result, public pressure and concern resulted in legislative reform with the goal to better address the needs of stalking victims. Current legislation varies by state but generally covers repeatedly following or harassing an individual where the behavior of the pursuer contains a credible threat of harm. Some states specify which acts are included in the term "conduct," whereas others focus on the criminal outcome of the conduct. All states require the prosecution to demonstrate the stalking was intentional (Tjaden, 2009). Some states classify stalking as a misdemeanor, and others define it as a felony, resulting in wide variation in sanctions. Even where stalking is a felony offense, sentences vary from a maximum of 12 months in West Virginia to 7 years for an equivalent offense in Illinois. Further, some states require prior incidents of stalking or the violation of existing protection orders, and others do not (Dennison & Thomson, 2005).

Stalking (defined as criminal harassment) was introduced into the Criminal Code of Canada in April 1993. The Code stipulates that "No person shall, without lawful authority and knowing that another person is harassed or recklessly as to whether the other person is harassed, engage in conduct referred to in subsection (2) that causes that other person reasonably, in all the circumstances, to fear for their safety or the safety of anyone known to them" (Criminal Code of Canada, 1993, Section 264). Prohibited conduct outlined in the Code includes the following (Criminal Code of Canada, 1993, Section 264):

(a) repeatedly following from place to place the other person or anyone known to them;
(b) repeatedly communicating with, either directly or indirectly, the other person or anyone known to them;
(c) besetting or watching the dwelling-house, or place where the other person, or anyone known to them, resides, works, carries on business or happens to be; or
(d) engaging in threatening conduct directed at the other person or any member of their family.

Criminal conviction of stalking behavior carries a penalty of up to 5 years imprisonment. In England, Wales, and Scotland the legislation similarly takes the form of protection from harassment in which harassment is defined as conduct that causes distress.

Although the stalking laws are, without question, an improvement over the previous laws that address this issue, critics indicate these laws continue to have limitations (Abrams & Robinson, 1998). For example, in some jurisdictions definitions can be problematic, such as when stalking is viewed as limited to situations where the victim and the offender have a previous relationship (Gilligan, 1992; Lingg, 1993). In many states there is a requirement that a "credible threat" of violence is established, which is defined as a threat causing a reasonable person to fear for his or her physical safety (Perez, 1993). This is potentially problematic in all situations but in particular in cases of intimate partner violence where the threat is perceived differently by the victim because of previous experiences of violence with this offender. Thus, the victim's view may not be equivalent to the "reasonable person" defined by law. Indeed, less than half of the stalking victims in a national survey were directly threatened by their stalker, thereby making them ineligible for assistance under statutes that include the requirement of credible threat (Tjaden & Thoennes, 1998).

A separate set of laws related to stalking emanate out of concerns related to stalking among **sexually violent predators**. This is the least common form of stalking; nevertheless, the serial rapist or serial murderer who stalks and then attacks his or her victim is one of the most primal fears in our society. Sexually violent predator laws provide a means to incarcerate sex offenders judged to be mentally disordered and dangerous to others at the end of their court-imposed sentences for crimes already committed. These laws were developed throughout the United States to address public concerns for safety and provide a mechanism for keeping individuals who are dangerous away from the public (Prentky, Janus, Barbaree, Schwartz, & Kafka, 2006). In essence, these laws attempt to curtail future stalking in an individual who has been tried and convicted of this offense in the past.

Canadian legislation and practice uses four procedures for dealing with sexual predators. In 1997 a federal task force, with input from the Canadian Psychiatric Association and the Canadian Academy of Psychiatry and Law, amended sexual predator legislation to create an indeterminate sentence for dangerous offenders and include the new category of long-term offender. Long-term offenders are those sexual offenders who appear to have a reasonable prospect of successful treatment. Further, a new section that amounts to a preventive peace bond has been enacted for situations where there is a reasonable fear of a sexual offense. Finally, an informal mechanism of psychiatric gating exists, where a person is certified under provincial mental health legislation and sent to any hospital (Glancy, Regehr, & Bradford, 2001). There is an increasing use of this dangerous offender legislation in most Canadian jurisdictions.

In summary, legislation enacted since 1990 throughout North America and much of Western Europe has led to considerable improvement in legal options that are available to manage stalking behavior. Nevertheless, these laws do not provide perfect protection, and victims of stalking, to a large extent, are still left to their own devices to ensure their safety.

◼ Typology of Stalking

The term "stalking" is used to describe a pattern of behavior that is intrusive, repeated, and fear provoking. However, the motivations behind this behavior are highly variable. In an example discussed below under Celebrity Stalkers, Robert Bardo, a fan, sought to develop a relationship with Rebecca Schaeffer, a celebrity, based on his idealized fantasies about who she was and how she might change his life. In another example, an abusive husband was rejected by his wife, who sought to secure her safety and improve her life. His motivation was likely a mixture of desire to reconcile and anger at the fact that his wife had left him. These are but two examples of a wide range of motivations for stalking behavior.

Several authors have attempted to develop typologies of stalking based on a number of dimensions, including the psychological characteristics of the stalker and the relationship between the stalker and the victim. Zona, Sharma, and Lane (1993) identified three types of stalkers:

1. The classic erotomania stalker, who is often a woman with a delusional belief that a powerful man is in love with her (for example, her doctor)
2. The love-obsessed stalker, who is delusionally focused on a famous person (for example, an actor or politician)
3. The simple obsessional stalker, who stalks a former partner with intense resentment as a result of perceived rejection

Mullen, Pathé, Purcell, and Stuart (1999) identified five types of stalkers:

1. The rejected stalker, who is motivated by a mixture of revenge and desire for reconciliation after a relationship ends
2. The intimacy-seeking stalker, who often has erotomanic delusions
3. The incompetent stalker, who may be intellectually or socially limited
4. The resentful stalker, who seeks to frighten and distress the victim
5. The predatory stalker, who is preparing for a sexual attack

Dziegielewski and Roberts (1995), in an attempt to better understand and treat victims of stalking, suggested three categories:

1. Domestic violence stalking
2. Erotomania or delusional stalking
3. Nuisance stalking.

Meloy (1998b) focused on relational typologies: intimates, strangers, and acquaintances. Melton (2000) differentiated between delusional and nondelusional stalkers and known and not-known victims. More recently, authors have focused on cyberstalking, although there is no clear consensus whether this represents another typology of stalker or whether this is simply a method of stalking. Glancy (2008) recommended a multiaxial approach that addresses motivation, mental state, method, and victim relationship (**Table 10-2**).

Although all these typologies are useful, for the purposes of this chapter four main categories of stalking are discussed: (1) celebrity stalking, (2) erotomanic stalking, (3) stalking as an extension of intimate partner, and (4) the sexually sadistic stalker.

TABLE 10-2 **Classification Criteria for Stalkers**

Motivation	Mental Status	Method	Relationship
Rejected	Psychotic	Harassment	Known
Intimacy seeking	Nonpsychotic	Threats	Ex-intimate
Incompetent		Assaults	Potential suitor
Resentful			Professional
Predatory			
			Unknown
			Professional
			Potential suitor
			Celebrity
			Head-of-state

Data from Glancy, G., & Saini, M. 2005. An evidence-based review of psychological treatments for anger and aggression. *Brief Treatment and Crisis Intervention, 5*(2), 229–248.

Celebrity Stalkers

In 1989, 21-year-old actress Rebecca Schaeffer was a star on the rise. She had just completed a 3-year run on a CBS situation comedy, was the celebrity spokesperson for a charity for high-risk adolescents, and was preparing for an audition for the movie *The Godfather: Part III*. Although her fan mail was increasing, she continued to try to respond to each letter she received. One of these letters was from 19-year-old Robert John Bardo, a young man who, unknown to Rebecca, had become obsessed with her. He filled his room with photographs and video clips of her, and in 1987 he went twice to the studio where she worked but was turned away. Then, via computer databases, he discovered whom she called, what car she drove, and where she shopped; subsequently, he hired a detective to obtain her address from the Department of Motor Vehicles. Bardo's love turned to rage, however, when he saw a movie scene in which Rebecca was in bed with a man. Bardo then determined to kill her for this perceived relationship breach and documented on a drawing of her body where he intended to shoot her. On July 18 Bardo went to Rebecca's apartment. Expecting a script delivery she opened the door and, surprised to see a fan, quickly sent him away. A few minutes later he returned and shot her to death. Rebecca's fatality provoked legislation prohibiting the release of addresses through the Department of Motor Vehicles, legislation directed at curtailing stalking, and led to the creation of the first Threat Management Unit through the Los Angeles Police Department.

The very nature of the activities in which celebrities engage to enhance their fame and fortunes make them ideal targets for stalkers. Celebrities appear on talk shows and tell their innermost secrets, they appear in music videos and sing songs of love and lust while looking directly into the viewers' eyes, and they have a staff that sends signed photos with intimate messages to eager fans. Given the ever-present availability of TV programming—including music video stations and entertainment news shows—tabloids that track every relationship and every excursion, and Internet video footage posted by anyone with a cell phone, information about celebrities is easily accessible to everyone (Philips, 2008).

Although there are several types of celebrity stalkers, one type has been described as "love obsessed," where the adoration of a fan becomes exaggerated and the stalker believes he or she is in love. At times, the belief systems of celebrity stalkers may be related to a psychotic illness and results in delusional beliefs that they have a special relationship with the famous person. These celebrity stalkers closely resemble erotomanic stalkers (discussed below).

Park Dietz and associates (1991a, 1991b) reviewed thousands of letters, identified as concerning, sent to celebrities and members of Congress. Their study revealed that even though the subjects had no personal relationship with the people to whom they wrote, many believed they did have a relationship, and often an important one. The most common roles individuals believed they had with celebrities were friend or advisor (41%), spouse or would-be spouse (30%), and lover or would-be lover (25%). Twenty-two percent of the letter writers saw themselves as special fans, and only 17% appropriately identified themselves simply as fans or strangers. For those with delusional beliefs, publicity tactics such as encouraging individuals to e-mail the star or offering a phone call from the star only served to intensify their beliefs. When this type of celebrity stalker believes he or she has been rejected, behaviors can be intensified, and the person begins to seek reconciliation and/or revenge. If, as a result of intensified attempts to contact the celebrity, the stalker feels humiliated or mistreated, the motivation for the stalking may change from love to distress or anger. In such a case, for example, that of Rebecca Schaeffer, the outcome may be tragic.

Other celebrity stalkers may engage in stalking behavior out of rage due to a perceived injustice. Robert Philips (2008), in his work as a consulting psychiatrist to the Protective Intelligence Division of the U.S. Secret Service, reviews various motivations of presidential stalkers. One motivation, retribution, occurs when an individual holds a political figure or the government in general responsible for his or her own personal failures. Such was the case of Samuel Byck, who sent many threatening letters to President Nixon and others and eventually moved to execute a plan to hijack a commercial airliner and fly it into the White House. Byck killed himself with his own gun but not before killing a police officer, the pilot, and the copilot of the plane he was attempting to hijack (Philips, 2008). Other motivations for stalking a political figure include erotomania, such as in the case of Jane Doe and President Clinton, or delusional obsessions, such as in the case of John Hinckley, Jr., and President Reagan.

Erotomanic Stalkers

Erotomania, also known as **de Clérambault's syndrome,** is delusional loving. The symptoms of this syndrome were first delineated by French psychiatrist de Clérambault (1942) in his work *Les Psychoses Passionelles*. However, Jordan and Howe (1980) trace the origins of the disorder back to Hippocrates and later to Pardoux's book, *Disease of the Mind*, published in the late 1500s. One who suffers from this syndrome believes a person of higher social stature or professional standing is passionately in love with him or her but that this person is restricted from expressing this love because of external constraints. For instance, if the object of affection is a professional, the stalker may believe it is regulations that forbid relationships between patients and doctors or students and professors that are standing in the way of their happiness together. Alternately, the stalker may attribute blame to the victim's family, believing, for instance, that if the pregnant wife were out of the way the stalker and victim could be together. Thus, the stalker may confront or harass family members, attempting to convince them or scare them into freeing the loved one to be with the stalker. The delusions of love are fixed and constant, and despite repeated confrontations with reality, the person is unable to let go of the belief (Jordan & Howe, 1980). When the love and hope are not realized, however, they may disintegrate to resentment and anger (de Clérambault, 1942). At that time the stalker may become threatening or assaultive.

Of all categories of stalkers, women who stalk are most likely to fall into this category of erotomanic stalkers (Purcell, Pathé, & Mullen, 2001). Erotomanic stalkers are likely to have a diagnosis of personality disorder, paranoid disorder, or psychotic disorder such as schizophrenia. They are more likely than other types of stalkers to have never been married, to misuse substances, to have a history of assault and self-harming, and to have more repeated hospitalizations.

The most common victims of erotomanic stalkers are professionals who have had contact with the stalker and with whom the stalker desires to establish a close and loving relationship. Mental health professionals are at particularly high risk, and a variety of surveys suggest that 8% to 11% of mental health professionals have been stalked at one point in their career by a patient. Men are the more common victims in this category. Psychiatrists and psychologists are at highest risk, with reported stalking as high as 20% to 33% in these professions (McIvor & Petch, 2006).

The high rate of stalking among mental health professionals is not particularly surprising. Mental health professionals frequently work with individuals who have significant difficulties in forming interpersonal relationships and often have histories of abuse or neglect. The warm, supportive, and accepting relationship that a professional forms with a patient as part of the treatment process can easily be misinterpreted as an indication of love or desire in someone who has not experienced such relationships in the past and can become incorporated into a delusional system (Regehr & Glancy, 2011). Further, mental health professionals are more likely to tolerate harassing and other behaviors that are not tolerated in other circumstances as a standard part of the management of behaviors of psychiatric patients (McIvor & Petch, 2006). As with celebrity stalkers, the behaviors at first are not overtly threatening and begin more as a nuisance and then escalate. Whereas others may stop contact at an earlier stage, the mental health professional may persist in the relationship, reinforcing false beliefs about love, until the situation is more difficult to control.

This group of stalkers is least likely to result in threats of violence or actual violent activity (Rosenfeld, 2000). However, the cost of the harassing behavior to the victim in both emotional and professional terms is often very disturbing. Stalkers in this group have been known to send letters to the spouses and children of victims declaring the imaginary relationship and indicating that the victim has been unfaithful to loved ones. Flowers, gifts, and letters are left at professional offices or on personal property. Items such as photographs or signs with the person's name may be stolen and kept as tokens of imagined love. Declarations of the relationship can be made to other colleagues, raising suspicions of sexual impropriety. Finally, complaints of impropriety may be made to professional licensing bodies, resulting in lengthy and embarrassing investigations (Regehr & Glancy, 2011).

Stalking as an Extension of Domestic Violence

Stalking as a form of domestic violence is the most common form of stalking, encompassing an estimated 75% to 80% of all cases (Roberts & Dziegielewski, 2006). Women are twice as likely as men to be stalked by their intimate partner. This is not surprising when considering the incidence of intimate partner violence against men and women. When stalking does occur in intimate relationships, it is likely to coexist with other forms of violence. Eighty-one percent of women in the National Violence

Against Women Survey who reported being stalked by an intimate partner also reported other forms of physical abuse, and 31% had been sexually assaulted (Tjaden & Thoennes, 1998).

There is considerable evidence that victims of spousal violence who attempt to separate from their abusive partner may be at higher risk after the separation than before. According to Statistics Canada (2006), in most cases (63%) where intimate partner violence was reported in a general population survey, violence ended at separation; however, 39% of women and 32% of men who had been in violent relationships indicated they were assaulted after the relationship ended. Of these, 24% indicated the violence became worse, and 39% indicated the violence began only after separation. Further, marital separation is a factor that elevates the rate of spousal homicide for women. Ex-marital partners are responsible for 38% of all homicides against women in Canada and 2% of all homicides against men (Hotton, 2002).

Burgess and colleagues (1997) studied 120 people charged with domestic violence who were attending a treatment program, and 30% admitted to stalking their partners. Those that did stalk a former partner had more serious histories of domestic violence. Similarly, Schwartz-Watts and Morgan (1998), using a clinical sample, reported that 80% of violent stalkers had previous relationships with the victims, compared to 55% of nonviolent stalkers. Palarea, Zona, Lane, and Langhinrichsen-Rohlings (1999), in an analysis of stalking cases from the Los Angeles Threat Management Unit, found that stalkers with previous intimate relationships were significantly more likely to threaten, damage property, and physically harm the victim.

Amrita and Sulay were married shortly after being introduced by family members, and they moved into the home of Sulay and his family. Although initially this went well, family problems in Sulay's home resulted in increased distress for all members. During this time Amrita and Sulay also began to have fights, and on more than one occasion Sulay's mother asked Amrita to leave their home to end the argument. Fights between Amrita and Sulay intensified, at times including physical assaults against Amrita. After 9 months of marriage Amrita elected to leave the marriage and return to the home of her own parents. Sulay began contacting Amrita with increasing intensity, hanging around outside her university classes, parking in front of her home for hours on end, calling her incessantly, and sending cards, flowers, and gifts. In each encounter he insisted that she was mistaken in breaking up with him and was not telling him the truth about the reason for the breakup, which he believed to be another man. Sulay became increasingly tearful, sleepless, angry, and withdrawn. After a few months of harassment Amrita's father attempted to intervene by contacting Sulay's family. Shortly thereafter, Sulay physically assaulted Amrita as she was leaving a university class, resulting in severe bruising. He was arrested and charged with assault. After he was released from jail, Sulay continued to contact and follow Amrita. One month later he approached her at the hospital at which she had a part-time job and stabbed her. Fortunately, Amrita survived the attack.

Stalking behavior in this category is frequently seen to be motivated by the desire for power and control. In this conceptualization the ending of a relationship is a threat to the power and control that an abuser exercised over his or her partner. Stalking then includes a series of behaviors aimed at regaining control and reestablishing the relationship (Burgess et al., 1997; Dziegielewski & Roberts, 1995). One set of strategies can involve limiting social activities of the victim by contacting family and friends, going to places or events the victim is likely to attend, and driving or walking by the victim's residence to limit who might visit (Brewster, 2003). Other strategies involve influencing children, attempting financial control, and physical violence (Brewster, 2003). The intimidation can be extended beyond the victim and include other vulnerable members of the victim's family, such as children, a sister, or an elderly parent. Domestic violence stalking is often open in nature, in part because the stalker believes the behavior is justified and a right. When it leads to violence, the stalker believes the violence was provoked by the victim. However, to an outsider the actual behavior of the victim that may result in an attack is not predictable; rather, the nature of the provocation resides in the fantasy world of the stalker (Burgess et al., 1997).

The need for power and control in domestic violence stalkers is generally fueled by rage at abandonment (Douglas & Dutton, 2001). Mullen and colleagues (1999) thus referred to this group of stalkers as "rejected stalkers." In their study of 145 stalkers, people in this category described a complex mixture of desire for reconciliation and revenge. They experienced a sense of loss, alternately combined with frustration, anger, jealousy, vindictiveness, and sadness. The majority of this group carried a diagnosis of personality disorder, although a smaller percentage of them had delusional disorders. Burgess and colleagues (1997) described a process that occurs in these types of stalking situations based on their research of domestic violence cases in Michigan. First, the stalker is open in his or her attempts to contact the ex-partner. When this fails the stalker begins to contact others and discredit the partner. Next, the positive emotion of love becomes converted to hatred, and the stalker goes underground and clandestine, using tactics such as phoning and hanging up or entering the premises without permission. After this comes a phase of ambivalence, where the stalker may send gifts and flowers. When this attempt at reconciliation is unsuccessful, the stalker may become explosive and violent.

Sexually Sadistic Stalkers

Although sexually violent predators are perhaps the most distressing type of stalker from a public perspective, this type of stalking remains relatively rare. Purcell et al. (2001) suggested that 7% of male stalkers in their studies (and 0% of female stalkers) fall into the designation of sexually motivated predatory stalkers. Nevertheless, this has been a focus of legislative activity in Canada and the United States in recent years. In this situation stalking occurs when a violent and dangerous offender seeks a victim to satisfy his desires. A particular victim is selected because she represents a particular type of person to whom the offender is attracted. This type of stalker may identify a potential victim over a period of time, establish her patterns, and in the end sexually assault or murder her.

Alicia Ross, age 25, was killed by her next door neighbor, Daniel Sylvester, a social recluse who fantasized about raping and killing women and spied on women in his neighborhood. In the 7 years he lived next door to Ross they had never spoken. Then one evening after her boyfriend left, Sylvester approached Alicia on the driveway. When she rejected his advances, he hit her over the head to subdue her, dragged her away, and raped her, killed her, and then hid the body. The court heard that Sylvester had been treated by mental health professionals beginning at the age of 9 years, and from an early age had fantasies about jumping out of the bushes and raping women (Mitchell, 2007). In these situations the victim is often unaware that she is being stalked and can do little to protect herself.

■ Effects of Stalking on Victims

Victims of stalking believe they are under siege. In studies victims report receiving repeated unwanted phone calls where the stalker hangs up immediately, remains silent, declares love, shouts obscenities, or threatens. Calls are usually received at inconvenient times, such as in the early morning or at work, and the victim's voice mail is often filled with the stalker's messages. Letters are frequently sent, or written messages are dropped off. Gifts arrive with some frequency. In the current days of electronic communication, e-mails are frequent forms of communication. The stalker may come to the victim's home or office and refuse to leave. Surveillance is commonly reported by victims in which they are followed or watched. In a study by Pathé and Mullen (1997), 36% of a sample of 100 victims reported property damage. Cars were covered with graffiti, the paint was scratched, and the tires were slashed. Homes were attacked via broken windows and smashed fences. In addition, in more than half the cases, stalkers made threats directly to harm the victims or their families and friends, or they threatened to discredit the victim by spreading malicious gossip. In one-third of cases the victim was assaulted.

In light of these repeated attacks on the privacy, property, and life of the victim, it is not surprising that stalking victims experience a wide range of social and psychological sequelae. Victims who are in a constant state of threat experience feelings of fear, anxiety, and apprehension that sometimes may border on paranoia. Symptoms of depression, anger, and helplessness are also reported, occasionally leading to suicidal ideation (McEwan, Mullen, & Purcell, 2007). The arousal, intrusion, and avoidance symptoms associated with posttraumatic stress disorder are also common (Pathé & Mullen, 1997). Victims are in a constant state of heightened anxiety, are easily startled by any noise (such as the telephone ringing for the 50th time that day), and remain hypervigilant, carefully watching for any sign of the stalker. They check their rearview mirror and drive home by different routes. Thoughts of the stalker begin to intrude throughout the day, and at night they invade the victim's dreams. The victim begins to avoid any possibility of contact, restricting activities such as going outside and answering the telephone, thereby becoming more isolated.

Pathé and Mullen (1997) reported that over half of the victims in their study decreased or ceased work or school attendance. These symptoms are likely to be more pronounced when the stalking involves a former history of violence, because the number of stalking behaviors increases, or when the duration of the stalking is prolonged (Kamphuis & Emmelkamp, 2001; Kamphuis, Emmelkamp, & Bartak, 2003; Pathé & Mullen, 1997). As stalking continues, victims report sleep disturbances, nausea or stomach upset, fatigue, headaches, and exacerbation of pre-existing medical conditions, such as asthma. Consequently, according to the National Violence Against Women Survey, 30% of female victims and 20% of male victims seek psychological counseling as a result of their victimization (Tjaden & Thoennes, 1998).

On a social level, the victim's occupational and educational status is affected if he or she reduces his or her attendance or has frequent interruptions at work. Friends and family are called on to accompany the victim to various places or stay at the victim's home. Family members become distraught and angry, as there seems to be no end in sight, and may alternately express anger toward the justice system for failing to protect the victim or anger at the victim for bringing this into their lives. Social supports can diminish with prolonged stalking as friends seek to have their own lives return to normal (Regehr & Glancy, 2011).

■ Safety Strategies for Victims

Given the highly distressing nature of stalking, victims frequently seek assistance from others, including mental health professionals. It is important to reinforce the victim's perception of being stalked and that he or she is not simply being paranoid or overreacting. Added to this is the provision of education on safety measures. Victims must be made aware that they are primarily responsible for their own safety (Meloy, 1998a). That is, despite even their best efforts, police and others in the justice system will be unable to ensure that no harm comes to the victim.

The victim should first be vigilant about safety risks. Any unusual occurrences or uncomfortable feelings about situations should be addressed. Victims can enlist the assistance of others in this regard by telling neighbors or coworkers about the situation and enlisting their assistance in being alert to dangers. One forensic psychiatrist who was under threat from a previous inmate circulated pictures of the stalker to selected neighbors (in particular, a police officer who lived across the street) and to others in his office building. Security firms can be enlisted to evaluate the safety of the victim's home and install often-inexpensive measures to increase security. The victim should ensure that doors and windows are locked and that outside lights are illuminated. The door should not be answered without verifying the identity of the visitor. Cars should be parked in well-lit areas. Habitual travel patterns should be modified regularly (Dietz, 1989).

Victims should create and maintain documentary evidence of the stalking to assist with apprehension and successful prosecution of the offender. Voice mail messages, although they are upsetting and often abhorrent, should be recorded and stored. All letters, e-mails, notes, and gifts should be retained. Photos should be taken of damage or messages left on property, such as writing on windows. Contemporaneous recording of incidents is an excellent way of demonstrating a pattern of repetition, for example, that the phone rang on 20 separate occasions in one evening, and when the phone was answered by the victim the caller did not respond. Although any single occurrence seems innocuous, pages of notes that record repeated small events leads to a more compelling argument of threat.

The victim should avoid contact with the stalker and never initiate contact. Although at first glance this suggestion may seem obvious, it is not uncommon for victims to attempt to confront the stalker, plead for him or her to stop, or try to negotiate limited contact. These actual contacts can be reinforcing for the stalker, demonstrating that repeated attempts do result in intermittent rewards (Meloy, 1998b). Alternately, these contacts can serve to incite anger and violence if the stalker feels slighted or rebuked.

Victims who are in need of legal protection can obtain a **restraining order** made under civil law, usually in the context of family court. Such orders forbid a person from molesting, annoying, harassing, or communicating with another person except as set out in the order. A **protection order** may give temporary custody of children and the home to the victim and order the abusive person out of the home. It can include conditions such as not allowing any contact (Department of Justice Canada, 2004). To obtain a protection order, a person must make an application to the court, often done with the assistance of a lawyer. A protection order is not dependent on fear of personal safety.

Although in the United States protection orders are made at the state level, the Interstate Stalking Punishment and Prevention Act of 1996 made the orders enforceable across state lines and violation of the order a federal crime. In Canada the police do not enforce civil orders such as a restraining order, and breach of the civil order does not result in criminal charges. If the designated person ignores the order, a civil contempt proceeding must be initiated. At the contempt hearing the judge can order the named person to be fined or to jail until such time as he or she obeys the court order. Another option for victims in Canada therefore is a **peace bond**, which can be initiated by victims, often through the prosecutor's office or the police, who fear they or their family will be harmed by the offender. The standard of proof for the victim's fears is the balance of probabilities, that is, it is more likely to be true than not. If the conditions of a peace bond are broken, the named person can be charged with a criminal offense (Regehr & Kanani, 2010).

In a review of protection orders, Benitez, McNiel, and Binder (2010) concluded there is clear evidence that orders will be violated and the risk of violation is greatest soon after the order is implemented. Further, the risk of violence tends to increase after a protection order violation. Indeed, the National Violence Against Women Survey revealed that 69% of female stalking victims and 81% of male stalking victims who had obtained restraining orders indicated their stalkers had violated the order (Tjaden & Thoennes, 1998).

TABLE 10-3 **Safety Strategies for Victims**

- Accept responsibility for own safety
- Develop surveillance strategies
- Enlist the assistance of others
- Increase security for home, work, and travel
- Document incidents and retain evidence
- Avoid contact and never initiate contact
- Obtain legal orders (peace bonds, restraining orders, protection orders)
- Relocate or stay in a shelter

Storey and Hart (2011) conducted a case analysis of strategies used by victims immediately before the desistance of a stalker. Effective strategies inevitably involved legal interventions. In 90% of these cases legal intervention occurred, including police monitoring, a peace bond, or conviction. Second, in 23% of the cases the police collaborated with mental health professionals to obtain psychiatric intervention and in 16% of cases they collaborated with other policing jurisdictions. Interestingly, in 13% of cases the lead detective developed a relationship with the stalker or a member of the stalker's family, which allowed for monitoring of the stalker. On the other hand, in 25% of cases victim attempts to stop the behavior through direct interactions with the stalker in fact worsened the stalking.

If all else fails, victims may have to consider relocation to another home, by staying with a family member or friend, or by staying in a shelter. In Storey and Hart's analysis, this was the final strategy that ended stalking in 13% of cases. Battered women's shelters are a good option for domestic violence stalking victims, in particular, because they offer immediate assistance and security through established mechanisms. However, this is perhaps the most disruptive option for victims because it feels as though their lives have been placed on hold. **Table 10-3** provides a summary of safety strategies for victims of stalking.

■ Threat Assessment of Stalkers

As discussed earlier, the threat of violence usually implicit in stalking is in and of itself highly distressing. Nevertheless, it is important to have a framework for evaluating the likelihood that the stalker will indeed physically harm the victim. Prediction of dangerousness based solely on clinical assessments for offenders of any kind has proven to be remarkably inaccurate and results in very low rates of interrater reliability among professional assessors (Hilton & Simmons, 2001). Consequently, considerable effort in the past decade has focused on the development of actuarial tools with the aim of improving accuracy in predicting dangerousness. Although developers of the tools have reported favorable results in terms of predictive validity, considerable controversy exists about the role of actuarial testing in the assessment of offenders (Sreenivasan, Kirkish, Garrick, Wineberger, & Phenix, 2000; Zonana, 1999, 2000). Also, most of these tools predict the recidivism of physical or sexual violence and are not useful for understanding the risk in someone who has not offended. Further complicating this is that although stalking carries an implicit threat, there may not be overt indications of aggression or violence. Finally, when predicting recidivism, the assessor generally has access to the offender and can conduct a full clinical interview and make use of a large number of biological, psychological, and actuarial tests to aid in the prediction (Glancy & Regehr, 2002).

Research on correlates of violence in stalkers does, however, lead to some indications that stalkers are at higher risk of committing violent acts against the victim (**Table 10-4**). Research suggests that those who threaten are indeed more violent. For example, in one study 81% of those who did not make threats were, in fact, not violent (Harmon, Rosner, & Owens, 1998). Other factors associated with violence in stalkers are that violent stalkers tend to be young (below age 30 years), have lower levels of education, have made prior threats, and had previous intimate relationships with the victims (Rosenfeld & Harmon, 2002). Violent stalkers have been found to be more likely to have a history of violence and abusing substances (Burgess et al., 1997). Schwartz-Watts and Morgan (1998), using a clinical sample, reported that 80% of violent stalkers had previous relationships with the victims, compared to 55% of nonviolent stalkers; Palarea and colleagues (1999) found similar results.

TABLE 10-4 **Factors Associated with Increased Risk of Violence Among Stalkers**

- History of making threats
- Young age
- Lower level of education
- Previous intimate relationship with the victim
- History of ignoring legal orders to stay away from the victim
- History of violence
- Substance abuse

Data from Burgess, et al. 1997. Schwartz-Watts and Morgan. 1998. Rosenfeld & Harmon. 2002.

Burgess, Harner, Baker, Hartman, and Lole (2001) offered very useful guidelines for assessing dangerousness in stalkers:

- *Reason for contacts:* There is greater concern when a stalker is seeking contact as a result of a need for retaliation or control than when the stalker is trying to reestablish the relationship or deal with practical details. It is important to note, however, that the motivation for contact can shift as the stalker's attempts to establish or reestablish a relationship are repeatedly met with frustration.

- *Emotional response:* Is the stalker expressing anger or frustration, or is there a sense of acceptance or hope?

- *Thought content:* In terms of thought content, it is important to understand what fantasies the stalker may have about the victim's behavior and attitudes. Are the beliefs simply denial of the reality or are they embedded in a delusional system? What are the stalker's fantasies about what he or she would like to do to or with the victim?

- *Contact pattern and predatory behaviors:* The assessor needs to determine the intrusiveness of the contact pattern and the degree to which the stalker is violating laws, such as trespassing, destruction of property, and making threats. Such violations can suggest an escalating pattern of violence.

- *Preoccupation:* Preoccupation can be determined in part by the frequency of contacts and the ability of the stalker to maintain other roles, such as continuing to work or attend school. When the stalker spends every free moment on attempts to be near to, to monitor, or to make contact with the victim, risk increases.

■ Treatment of Stalkers

The treatment of stalkers is highly challenging, and generally there is considerable pessimism about the likelihood of success, although there is a lack of studies in the literature to support this contention. Stalkers, by the very nature of their problem, are not motivated for treatment because they rarely see themselves as having a disorder or problem. Nevertheless, treatment approaches to stalking depend on the nature of the stalking behavior.

Delusional stalkers with erotomania are best treated with psychotropic medications aimed at addressing the psychotic symptoms. Involuntary commitment and treatment may be an option when there is a defined mental illness and a probable risk of harm. Each jurisdiction has different legal language related to the nature of illness and the severity and imminence of danger required for involuntary admission to hospital. Further, the lengths of involuntary stays and the ability to enforce treatment are highly variable, depending on legislation in that jurisdiction. This group of stalkers is largely impervious to judicial sanctions, at times regarding court appearances or jail terms as the price of true love (Mullen et al., 1999).

Domestic violence stalkers who are reacting to rejection can at times be persuaded to desist through fines and incarceration. However, this is by no means universal, and recidivism rates up to 44% have been reported 6 months after sentencing (Koss, 2000); other studies found that for a subgroup of male batterers, arrests tend to actually increase violence (Coker, 2002). Thus, arrest of domestic violence stalkers in no way guarantees the cessation of the behavior or the reduced risk of violence.

The field of batterer intervention has been grappling for over two decades with how to address the seemingly intractable problem of men's violence against their female partners. After a comprehensive review of the literature on psychological treatment for anger and aggression, Glancy and Saini (2005) concluded that there is no consensus among therapists and researchers about the best way to treat and reduce anger and aggression and that little empirical evidence exists to support intervention strategies and guide therapists. Nevertheless, a review of the research on treatment effectiveness reveals two main findings that have important implications for considering the appropriateness of restorative processes. First, it appears that court coercion does not significantly affect whether or not a man will attend treatment. The second major finding is that confrontational treatment approaches that focus on getting men to take responsibility for their abusive behavior have not been very effective. They have failed to promote lasting change in most cases (Babcock & Steiner, 1999; Feder & Dugan, 2002).

Predatory or sexually sadistic stalkers, because of the nature of their planned offense, are generally dealt with only through the justice and correctional systems. When they are incarcerated, the risk of future threat is determined by careful risk assessment, which generally determines long-term disposition. Sexual predator laws in Canada and the United States provide a number of provisions for those at high risk of offending, including indeterminate sentences, mandatory monitoring, and preventive peace bonds (Glancy et al., 2001).

In conclusion, approaches to managing stalking behavior, both from a criminal justice and a mental health treatment perspective, have been met with limited success at best. Clearly, there is little comfort for victims with respect to hope that interventions will stop the behavior.

■ Summary

Stalking is an insidious crime in which victims feel terrorized, isolated, and helpless. Stalking involves a constellation of behaviors that involve repeated and unwanted attempts to contact another person. This behavior can include physical presence at places the victim frequents, telephone calls, e-mail messages, letters and packages, notes and gifts, and, less frequently, identity theft, threats of violence, or actual physical violence. The nature of stalking makes it very difficult for law enforcement personnel to intervene because in many jurisdictions there is a requirement for what is referred to as a "credible threat." Yet the behavior of many stalkers does not include an overt threat; rather, threat is implied through access to the victim and knowledge of the victim's activities.

Victims frequently find it difficult to convey the accumulation of what appears to others to be relatively harmless behaviors constitutes a harassing and fear-inducing situation. Although some legal safeguards exist, such as peace bonds and restraining orders, they are difficult to enforce. Even when the offender is charged and/or is brought into treatment, the nature of the underlying pathology limits the success of available treatment approaches. In the end, stalking is a powerful yet largely invisible crime that impacts victims profoundly. Victims are aware of escalating behaviors and fears, yet they are frequently unable to obtain assistance until after a violent incident has occurred.

■ Key Terms

Celebrity stalking: Harassment of a well-known figure who generally does not know the stalker.

Credible threat: A legal term that indicates a clear threat that, to an outside observer, is a cause for concern for the safety of the victim.

Cyberstalking: Use of the Internet to stalk another person.

de Clérambault's syndrome: A syndrome of delusional loving first described by de Clérambault in 1942.

Erotomania: A syndrome of delusional loving.

Obsessional harassment: Harassment causing fear that originates from the obsession of one individual with another individual who is uninterested in the relationship.

Peace bond: An order from a criminal court that restrains one person from bothering or threatening another.

Protection order: A civil court order that is issued under family violence legislation. It provides various emergency and long-term orders to protect victims of family violence.

Psychiatric gating: Where a sexually violent person is certified under provincial mental health legislation and sent to any hospital.

Restraining order: An order issued after the aggrieved party appears before a judge that tells one person to stop harassing or harming another person.

Sexually violent predator: Any person who has been convicted of or charged with a crime of sexual violence and who suffers from a mental abnormality or personality disorder that makes the person likely to engage in predatory acts of sexual violence if not confined in a secure facility.

Stalking: Any form of harassment that causes the person being harassed to have a reasonable fear for his or her safety.

■ Discussion Questions

1. To outsiders, the behavior of a stalker can appear to be relatively benign. Why?
2. How useful are stalking laws in the protection of victims?
3. What challenges exist in the treatment of offenders?
4. What advice should be given to victims of stalking to protect themselves?

■ Resources

Department of Justice Canada, Criminal Harassment: A Handbook for Police and Crown Prosecutors
http://www.justice.gc.ca/eng/pi/fv-vf/pub/har/part1.html

National Institute of Justice, Stalking in America
http://www.nij.gov/pubs-sum/169592.htm

RCMP, Criminal Harassment: Stalking—It's NOT Love
http://www.rcmp-grc.gc.ca/cp-pc/crimhar-eng.htm

Stalking Resource Center, National Center for Victims of Crime
http://www.ncvc.org/src/main.aspx?dbID=DB_NVAW587

Statistics Canada, Stalking—Criminal Harassment
http://www.statcan.gc.ca/bsolc/olc-cel/olc-cel?lang=eng&catno=85-224-X20050008645

U.S. Department of Justice, Stalking
http://www.ovw.usdoj.gov/aboutstalking.htm

References

Abrams, K., & Robinson, G. (1998). Stalking part II: Victims' problems with the legal system and therapeutic considerations. *Canadian Journal of Psychiatry, 43*, 477–481.

Babcock, J.C., & Steiner, R. (1999). The relationship between treatment, incarceration, and recidivism of battering: A program evaluation of Seattle's coordinated community response to domestic violence. *Journal of Family Psychology, 13*(1), 46–59.

Baum, K., Catalano, S., Rand, M., & Rose, K. (2009). *Stalking victimization in the United States.* NCJ 224527, Washington, DC: Bureau of Justice Statistics.

Benitez, C., McNiel, D., & Binder, R. (2010). Do protection orders protect? *Journal of the American Academy of Psychiatry and the Law, 38*, 376–385.

Brewster, M. (2003). Power and control dynamics in prestalking and stalking situations. *Journal of Family Violence, 18*, 207–217.

Burgess, A., Baker, T., Greening, D., Hartman, C., Burgess, A., Douglas, J., & Halloran, R. (1997). Stalking behaviors within domestic violence. *Journal of Family Violence, 12*, 389–403.

Burgess, A., Harner, J., Baker, T., Hartman, C., & Lole, C. (2001). Batterers stalking patterns. *Journal of Family Violence, 16*, 301–321.

California Penal Code, s. 646.9. (1990).

Coker, D. (2002). Transformative justice: Anti-subordination processes in cases of domestic violence. In H. Strang & J. Braithwaite (Eds.), *Restorative justice and family violence* (pp. 128–152). New York: Cambridge University Press.

Criminal Code of Canada. (1993). R.S., c. C-34, s. 264. Retrieved from http://www.canlii.org/ca/sta/c-46/whole.html

de Clérambault, C. (1942). Les psychoses passionelles. In *Oeuvres psychiatriques* (pp. 315–322). Paris, France: Nationale Universitaires de France.

Dennison, S., & Thomson, D. (2005). Criticisms or plaudits for stalking laws? What psycholegal research tells us about proscribing stalking. *Psychology, Public Policy and Law, 3*, 384–406.

Department of Justice Canada. (2004). Criminal harassment. Retrieved from http://www.justice.gc.ca/eng/pi/fv-vf/pub/har/index.htmlhttp://canada.justice.gc.ca/en/ps/fm/harassment.html#rest

Dietz, P. (1989). Defense against dangerous people when arrest and commitment fail. In R. Simon (Ed.), *American Psychiatric Press review of clinical psychiatry and the law* (pp. 205–219). Washington, DC: American Psychiatric Press.

Dietz, P., Matthews, D., Martell, D., Stewart, T., Hrouda, D., & Warren, J. (1991a). Threatening and otherwise inappropriate letters to Hollywood celebrities. *Journal of Forensic Sciences, 36*, 181–209.

Dietz, P., Matthews, D., Martell, D., Stewart, T., Hrouda, D., & Warren, J. (1991b). Threatening and otherwise inappropriate letters to members of the United States Congress. *Journal of Forensic Sciences, 36*, 1445–1468.

Douglas, K., & Dutton, D. (2001). Assessing the link between stalking and domestic violence. *Aggression and Violent Behavior, 6*, 529–546.

Dziegielewski, S., & Roberts, A. (1995). Stalking victims and survivors: Identification, legal remedies and crisis treatment. In A. Roberts (Ed.), *Crisis intervention and time-limited cognitive treatment* (pp. 73–90). Thousand Oaks, CA: Sage.

Feder, L., & Dugan, L. (2002). A test of the efficacy of court-mandated counseling for domestic violence offenders: The Broward experiment. *Justice Quarterly, 19*(2), 343–375.

Gilligan, M. (1992). Stalking the stalker: Developing new laws to thwart those who terrorize others. *Georgia Law Review, 27*, 285–342.

Glancy, G. (2008). Commentary on attacks on the British Royal Family: The more we know the more we can classify. *Journal of the American Academy of Psychiatry and the Law, 36*, 68–73.

Glancy, G., & Regehr, C. (2002). A step by step guide to assessing sexual predators. In A. Roberts & G. Greene (Eds.), *Social work desk reference* (pp. 702–708). New York: Oxford University Press.

Glancy, G., Regehr, C., & Bradford, J. (2001). Sexual predator laws in Canada. *Journal of the American Academy of Psychiatry and the Law, 29*(2), 232–237.

Glancy, G., & Saini, M. (2005). An evidence-based review of psychological treatments for anger and aggression. *Brief Treatments and Crisis Intervention, 5*, 229–248.

Harmon, R., Rosner, R., & Owens, H. (1998). Sex and violence in a forensic population of obsessional harassers. *Psychology, Public Policy and Law, 4*, 236–249.

Hilton, Z., & Simmons, J. (2001). The influence of actuarial risk assessment in clinical judgements and tribunal decisions about mentally disordered offenders in maximum security. *Law and Human Behaviour, 25*(4), 393–408.

Hotton, T. (2002). *Spousal violence after marital separation.* (Statistics Canada Cat. No. 85-002-XPE, Vol. 21, No. 7) Ottawa, Ontario, Canada: Statistics Canada.

Jordan, H., & Howe, G. (1980). de Clérambault syndrome (erotomania): A review and case presentation. *Journal of the National Medical Association, 72*(10), 979–985.

Kamphuis, J., & Emmelkamp, P. (2001). Traumatic distress among support-seeking female victims of stalking. *American Journal of Psychiatry, 158*, 795–798.

Kamphuis, J., Emmelkamp, P., & Bartak, A. (2003). Individual differences in post-traumatic stress following post-intimate stalking. *British Journal of Clinical Psychology, 42*, 145–156.

Koss, M.P. (2000). Blame, shame, and community: Justice responses to violence against women. *American Psychologist, 11*, 1332–1343.

Lingg, R. (1993). Stopping stalkers: A critical examination of anti-stalking statutes. *St. John's Law Review, 76*, 347–377.

McEwan, T., Mullen, P., & Purcell, R. (2007). Identifying risk factors for stalking: A review of current research. *International Journal of Psychiatry and the Law, 30*, 1–9.

McIvor, R., & Petch, E. (2006). Stalking of mental health professionals: An underrecognized problem. *British Journal of Psychiatry, 188*, 403–404.

Meloy, J. (1998a). The clinical risk management of stalking: "Someone is watching over me. . . ." *American Journal of Psychotherapy, 51*, 174–184.

Meloy, J. (1998b). *The psychology of stalking*. San Diego, CA: Academic Press.

Melton, H. (2000). Stalking: A review of the literature and direction for the future. *Criminal Justice Review, 25*, 246–262.

Mitchell, B. (2007, May 29). Life sentence in Ross murder: Markham man found guilty of second degree murder of young woman. Retrieved from http://www.thestar.com/article/218866

Moriarty, L., & Freiberger, K. (2008). Cyberstalking: Utilizing newspaper accounts to establish victimization patterns. *Victims and Offenders, 3*, 131–141.

Mullen, P., Pathé, M., Purcell, R., & Stuart, G. (1999). Study of stalkers. *American Journal of Psychiatry, 156*, 1244–1249.

National Institute of Justice. (1996). *Domestic violence, stalking and anti-stalking legislation: Annual report to Congress*. Washington, DC: U.S. Department of Justice.

Palarea, R., Zona, M., Lane, J., & Langhinrichsen-Rohlings, J. (1999). The dangerous nature of intimate relationship stalking: Threats, violence and associated risk factors. *Behavioral Science and the Law, 17*, 269–283.

Pathé, M., & Mullen, P. (1997). The impact of stalkers on their victims. *British Journal of Psychiatry, 170*, 12–17.

Perez, C. (1993). Stalking: When does obsession become crime? *American Journal of Criminal Law, 20,* 263–280.

Philips, R. (2008). Celebrity stalkers. In D. Pinals (Ed.), *Stalking: A psychiatric perspective* (pp. 227–250). New York: Oxford University Press.

Prentky, R., Janus, E., Barbaree, H., Schwartz, B., & Kafka, M. (2006). Sexually violent predators in the courtroom: Science on trial. *Psychology, Public Policy and Law, 12,* 357–393.

Purcell, R., Pathé, M., & Mullen, P. (2001). A study of women who stalk. *American Journal of Psychiatry, 158,* 2056–2060.

Purcell, R., Pathé, M., & Mullen, P. (2004). Stalking: Defining and prosecuting a new category of offending. *International Journal of Law and Psychiatry, 27,* 157–169.

Rathi, R. (2005). Zeta-Jones stalking case ends in plea. Retrieved from http:// articles.latimes.com/keyword/dawnette-knight

Regehr, C., & Glancy, G. (2011). When social workers are stalked: Risks, strategies, and legal protections. *Clinical Social Work Journal, 39*(3), 232–242.

Regehr, C., & Kanani, K. (2010). *Essential law for social work practice in Canada* (2nd ed.). Toronto, Ontario, Canada: Oxford University Press.

Roberts, A., & Dziegielewski, S. (2006). Changing stalking patterns and prosecutorial decisions: Bridging the present to the future. *Victims and Offenders, 1,* 47–60.

Rosenfeld, B. (2000). Assessment and treatment of obsessional harassment. *Aggression and Violent Behavior, 5*(6), 529–549.

Rosenfeld, B., & Harmon, R. (2002). Factors associated with violence in stalking and obsessional harassment cases. *Criminal Justice and Behavior, 29,* 671–691.

Schwartz-Watts, D., & Morgan, D. (1998). Violent vs. non-violent stalkers. *Journal of the American Academy of Psychiatry and the Law, 26,* 241–245.

Spitzberg, B., & Cupach, W. (2007). The state of the art of stalking: Taking stock of the emerging literature. *Aggression and Violent Behavior, 12,* 64–86.

Sreenivasan, H., Kirkish, P., Garrick, T., Wineberger, L., & Phenix, A. (2000). Actuarial risk assessment models: A review of critical issues related to violence and sex offender recidivism assessments. *Journal of the American Academy of Psychiatry and the Law, 28,* 438–448.

Statistics Canada. (2006). Violence against women in Canada: By the numbers. Retrieved from http://www42.statcan.ca/smr08/2006/smr08_012_2006-eng.htm

Storey, J., & Hart, S. (2011). How do police respond to stalking? An examination of the risk management strategies and tactics used in a specialized anti-stalking law enforcement unit. *Journal of Police and Criminal Psychology, 26*(2), 128–142.

Taylor, J. (2004, August 19). Alleged stalker found competent. Retrieved from http://articles.latimes.com/keyword/dawnette-knight

Telegraph. (2004, September 14). Woman claims Michael Douglas affair. Retrieved from http://www.telegraph.co.uk/news/1471717/Woman-claims-Michael-Douglas-affair.html

Tjaden, P. (2009). Stalking policies and research in the United States: A twenty year perspective. *European Journal of Criminal Policy Research, 15,* 261–278.

Tjaden, P., & Thoennes, N. (1998). *Stalking in America: Findings from the National Violence Against Women Survey.* (NCJ 169592.U.S.) Washington, DC: U.S. Department of Justice, National Institute of Justice.

U.S. Department of Justice. (1997). *Domestic violence and stalking: The second annual report to Congress under the Violence Against Women Act.* Washington, DC: U.S. Department of Justice, Office of Justice Programs.

Zona, M.A., Sharma, K.K., & Lane, J.C. (1993). A comparative study of erotomanic and obsessional subjects in a forensic sample. *Journal of Forensic Sciences, 38*(4), 894–903.

Zonana, H. (1999). *Dangerous sex offenders. A task force report of the American Psychiatric Association.* Washington, DC: American Psychiatric Association.

Zonana, H. (2000). Sex offender testimony: Junk science of unethical testimony. *Journal of the American Academy of Psychiatry and the Law, 28,* 386–388.

Victims of Rape and Sexual Assault

CHAPTER
11

■ Objectives

- To outline a theoretical framework of rape based on myths about sexual assault
- To outline measurement of rape, rape reform, and legislation
- To describe programs of services for victims
- To outline a typology of sexual trauma
- To describe the dynamics of reporting a rape
- To describe a classification of rapists

■ Key Terms

Anger rapist
Blitz rape
Incest
Marital rape
Rape
Sexual assault
Sexual coercion
Sexual sadist

CASE

The threat of terrorism and biochemical warfare heralded the 21st century, impacting the nation's sense of safety and security. But a February 2006 rape and sadistic murder of a

New York criminology student brought us back to the reality of rape, violence, its aftermath, and the inevitable victim blaming. Imette St. Guillen, a graduate student in criminal justice at John Jay College in New York, was brutally sexually assaulted, stabbed, and bound. A sock had been stuffed into her mouth to suffocate her; her face was wrapped like a mummy in clear plastic packaging tape, suggesting her killer wanted to freeze the pained expression on her face. The killer chopped off her signature long, black hair before disposing of her body. About to turn 25, Imette was reportedly drinking and having a good time when she left a local club alone at 4 a.m., closing time. She never made it home. Her mutilated body was found in an isolated area miles away along a road in Brooklyn on February 25, 2006.

Within a short time investigators linked Darryl Littlejohn to St. Guillen's murder. Police investigated the potential links and similarities to the three previous rapes and that of the rape and murder of Imette St. Guillen:

- Littlejohn had been known to impersonate law enforcement. He had a van.
- In the three attacks the rapist identified himself as an immigration officer before pulling the women into the van and throwing a blanket over their heads so they could not identify him, the sources said. He then drove to an underground garage, where the women were raped and sexually assaulted.
- No DNA evidence was recovered from the three attacks. The victims told investigators their attacker wiped them down after the rape with some sort of disinfectant swabs, the police sources said.
- When police searched Littlejohn's home they recovered alcohol swabs, plastic ties, sections of his carpet, hair samples, and fibers. Police also located his 1992 blue-gray minivan. In another strange coincidence of possible linkage between the crimes, the assaults took place between 4 a.m. and 6 a.m. One of the previous rape victims was Japanese. Sources say a busboy at The Falls, the Soho bar where St. Guillen was last seen alive, told them he heard Littlejohn ask the exotic-looking St. Guillen, "Are you Japanese?," just before he walked her outside.

■ Introduction

Talk shows expressed shock and outrage at the brutality of the rape and murder of Imette St. Guillen, but many suggested Imette was "asking for it" and "inviting" trouble because she stayed out late and had a lot to drink. Women were again reminded to "stay home" and "be safe." Noted Boston attorney Wendy Murphy's editorial in the Boston Globe (Murphy, 2006, p. 6) argued that there is no doubt that if women stayed home, serial killers or evil bouncers at nightclubs might not murder them. Nevertheless, she continued, shouldn't the message be that rapists and murderers, rather than the victim, should be afraid of public shame, humiliation, and punishment? This case highlights the inequity of sexual violence as a form of victimization and the challenges faced by victims and those working with victims.

All states include legislative statutes that define **rape** and **sexual assault**. For this chapter we use a general definition from the World

Health Organization in their "World Report on Violence and Health" in which sexual violence was defined as follows (Krug, Dahlberg, Mercy, Zwi, & Lozano, 2002, p. 149):

> Any sexual act, attempt to obtain a sexual act, unwanted sexual comments or advances, or acts to traffic, or otherwise directed, against a person's sexuality using coercion, by any person, regardless of their relationship to the victim, in any setting, including but not limed to home and work.

Sexual violence may include attempted and/or completed rape, sexual coercion and harassment, sexual contact with force or threat of force, and threat of rape (Fisher, Daigle, Cullen, & Turner, 2000). Rape, on the other hand, has a more specific definition. In December 2011 U.S. Federal Bureau of Investigation (FBI) Director Robert S. Mueller III told Congress that a new definition of rape was approved by the FBI Advisory Board to define rape as "Penetration, no matter how slight, of the vagina or anus with any body part or object, or oral penetration by a sex organ of another person, without the consent of the victim" (Ryan, 2011, p. 1). This revised definition includes both males and females. Although legal definitions of rape and sexual assault vary greatly from state to state, in this chapter the terms are used interchangeably. The terms "rape" and "sexual assault" in this chapter refer to any unwanted contact of the sexual organs of one person, whether male or female, by another person, regardless of gender, with or without penetration and with or without resulting physical injury.

■ Scope of the Problem

Measurement of rape against women began in the 1980s. Estimates were derived from two primary sources, statistics from the Uniform Crime Reporting (UCR) Program and the nationwide crime victimization survey, the National Crime Survey (NCS). Despite these efforts researchers and feminists believed the true incidence of rape was underestimated. The criticism of the NCS was that it used too narrow a definition of rape and poorly designed interview questions. The criticism of the UCR Program was that many rapes were not reported to the police (Fisher, 2004). These criticisms prompted the development of new surveys and the redesign of existing surveys. For instance, Koss, Gidycz, and Wisniewski (1987) developed the Sexual Experiences Survey to address methodological concerns about existing surveys. The survey was designed to use graphic language to describe specific behavioral acts and assessed a wide range of criminal elements of victimization (e.g., unwanted sexual contact, sexual coercion, and attempted and completed rape) (Fisher, 2004). Similarly, in 1992 the NCS was redesigned to address methodological shortcomings inherent in the NCS and was renamed the National Crime Victimization Survey (NCVS). The intent of the NCVS was to expand the definition of rape by adding screen questions to uncover incidents of rape and sexual assault further to make it as "comparable as possible" to annual rape estimates from the National Violence Against Women Survey (NVAWS) (Bachman, 2000, p. 839). Nevertheless, critics continue to argue that their different methodologies are responsible for divergent rape estimates. Despite attempts to improve the NCVS Bachman concluded that "the NVAWS has a greater likelihood of capturing incidents of intimate-perpetrated rape . . . compared to the NCVS" (p. 860). Her conclusion supports the critics who first argued that NCS, the precursor to NCVS, underestimates rape (Fisher, 2004).

Several problems exist in determining the statistics in rape. First, the manner in which rape is defined affects incidence and prevalence rates. *Prevalence* measures how many people have experienced sexual assault during their lifetimes. *Incidence* gives a snapshot of how many people have been sexually assaulted during a particular period of time, often 1 year. The varying definitions of sexual assault and rape result in differing rates of incidence and prevalence. For instance, determining the yearly incidence using the UCR depends on the victim and the police interpretation of what occurred. Victims must (1) perceive a rape has occurred, (2) decide it was an illegal act, and (3) decide whether or not to disclose it and (4) the police (or researcher) must decide whether the act meets the definition of an illegal act. For that act to come before a court of law, the prosecutor must decide if the evidence meets the charge. Only if the authority's classification concurs with that of the victim does the incident become recorded and thus counted in some of the measurement systems.

Second, underreporting makes it difficult to determine the number of sexual assaults. Guilt, fear of retribution, humiliation, lack of knowledge and trust in the legal and medical system, and impaired cognitive processing that occurs after intense trauma are some reasons persons may not report (Burgess, Fehder, & Hartman, 1995). In the original Burgess and Holmstrom study (1974), someone other than the victim was involved in reporting the sexual assault to police in more than half of the cases. According to the U.S. Department of Justice (2002) only 39% of rapes and sexual assault crimes were reported to law enforcement officials. NVAWS found that only one in five adult women (19%) reported their rapes to police (Tjaden & Thoennes, 2006). A study of nonincarcerated sex offenders found that 126 men admitted they had committed a total of 907 rapes involving 882 different women, with the average number of different victims per rapist being 7 (Abel et al., 1987).

Using the findings from the NVAWS, 17.6% of surveyed women and 3% of surveyed men were raped at some time in their lives (Tjaden & Thoennes, 2006). Rape was defined in the study as an act that includes attempted and or completed vaginal, oral, and anal penetration. Thus, in the United States the prevalence of rape is equivalent to 1 of every 6 women and 1 of every 33 men. Because some victims were raped more than once, the NVAWS estimated that 17.7 million women and 2.8 million men were forcibly raped at some time in their lives, with over 300,000 women and over 92,000 men forcibly raped in the year before the survey (Tjaden & Thoennes, 2006). The FBI reports in its "Crime in the United States," or UCR publication, that 88,097 forcible rapes were reported to the police at a rate of 56.6 crimes per 100,000 female residents in 2009 (FBI, 2008). **Table 11-1** shows statistics for rape and sexual assault.

The NCVS (2000) noted that adolescent females aged 16 to 19 are four times more likely than the general population to report sexual assault, rape, and attempted rape. Often, this violence occurs within the context of dating or acquaintance relationships, with the female partner the likely victim of violence and the male partner the likely perpetrator. Thus, rape studies on college students conducted by researcher Mary Koss provided important insights (Koss, 1987). Some of the most

TABLE 11-1 **Rape and Sexual Assault Statistics***

- An estimated 88,097 forcible rapes were reported to law enforcement in 2009. (By comparison, the estimated volume of rapes for 2009 was 2.6% lower than the 2008 estimate, 6.6% lower than the 2005 number, and 2.3% below the 2000 level.)

- The rate of forcible rapes in 2009 was estimated at 56.6 per 100,000 female inhabitants, a 3.4% decrease when compared to the 2008 estimated rate of 58.6.

- Based on rape offenses actually reported to the UCR Program in 2005, rapes by force comprised 91.8% of reported rape offenses, and assaults to rape attempts accounted for 8.2% of reported rape offenses. This equated to 48.4 rapes by force per 100,000 female inhabitants and 4.3 assaults to rape attempts per 100,000 females in 2005.

- Rapes by force comprised 93.0% of reported rape offenses in 2009, and attempts or assaults to commit rape accounted for 7.0% of reported rapes.

- A little over 41% of forcible rapes were cleared by arrest or exceptional means.

* Forcible rape, as defined in the 2011 UCR Program, is the carnal knowledge of a female forcibly and against her will. The new FBI definition of forcible rape is to be operationalized in 2012. On December 21, 2011, FBI Director Robert Mueller approved an expanded definition of rape as penetration no matter how slight, of the vagina or anus with any body part or object, or oral penetration by a sex organ of another person, without the consent of the victim. Data from FBI Uniform Crime Reports. 2010.

TABLE 11-2 **Prevalence and Responses of College Age Women**

Prevalence	• One in four women surveyed was a victim of rape or attempted rape.
	• An additional one in four women surveyed was touched sexually against her will or was a victim of sexual coercion.
	• 84% of those raped knew their attacker.
	• 57% of those rapes happened while on dates.
	• One in 12 male students surveyed had committed acts that met the legal definitions of rape or attempted rape.
	• 84% of those men who committed rape said that what they did was definitely not rape.
	• 16% of the male students who committed rape and 10% of those who attempted a rape took part in episodes involving more than one attacker.
Responses of the victim	• Only 27% of those women whose sexual assault met the legal definition of rape thought of themselves as rape victims.
	• 42% of rape victims did not tell anyone about their assaults.
	• Only 5% of rape victims reported the crime to the police.
	• Only 5% of rape victims sought help at rape crisis centers.
	• Whether they had acknowledged their experience as a rape or not, 30% of the women identified as rape victims contemplated suicide after the incident.
	• 82% of the victims said the experience had permanently changed them.

Data from Koss, M.P. Hidden rape: (1980). Sexual aggression and victimization in the national sample of students in higher education. In M.A. Pirog-Good & J.E. Stets (Eds.). *Violence in dating relationships: Emerging social issues.* (pp. 145–168). New York, NY: Praeger; and Curtis, D. G. 1997. Perspectives on acquaintance rape. The American Academy of Experts in Traumatic Stress, Inc. Retrieved from http://www.aaets.org/article13.htm.

important statistics from Koss's research on prevalence and responses of college-aged women are noted in **Table 11-2**.

■ Legislative Framework

Laws greatly shape public opinion and attitudes. Legislation in the form of law reform can be both instrumental and symbolic. Such was the case with rape-law reform, especially in conveying the concept of rape as an injurious, if not always physically damaging, act. Changes in rape laws helped to influence attitudes within both the criminal justice and general communities, although some would argue that jurors/citizens are still inclined to view rape in morality terms rather than criminal terms.

U.S. criminal rape laws were derived from British common law. Codification of the law against sexual violence began with the Statutes of Westminster in 1275 and 1285 and established rape as a serious crime with the possibility of a death penalty. Three elements needed to be proven: carnal knowledge of a woman by force and against her will. Two influential legal theorists were 17th-century jurist Lord Chief Justice Matthew Hale and the Edwardian-era scholar John Henry Wigmore (1863–1943). Hale's belief that rape is "an accusation easily made, and hard to be proved, and harder to be defended by the party accused, though ever so innocent" (Hale, 1847, p. 634) was reflected in both American jury instructions and standards of proof. Similarly, Wigmore's concern about sexually precocious minors and unchaste women who fantasize about rape gave rise to the corroboration doctrine and influenced such practices as the routine polygraph examination of victims (Wigmore & Chadbourn, 1970). Although neither man's assertions were supported by empirical data, they received widespread endorsement by legal bodies. As a result U.S. law would reflect a concept of rape as a sexual rather than a violent offense and would impose a vast array of safeguards against false accusations by the turn of the 20th century (Largen, 1988).

The need for rape-law reform was clearly noted by women's rights movements, who were encouraging former victims to speak publicly about insensitive and indifferent treatment they had experienced in the criminal justice system. These disclosures fostered recognition for systematic change that women activists believed must begin with the law itself. To this end, movement activists organized to develop a rape-law reform agenda, solicit public support for reform, and present their case to state legislators. Although the political climate was favorable to these citizen-initiated efforts, it was a growing presence of women and sympathetic men within the legal and lawmaking professions that reduced most resistance to change. A review of rape-law reform by Largen (1988) suggested, among other things, that in most states social concepts of sexual assault were changing more rapidly than legal concepts. Again, this was evidence of the radical shift in the concept of unacceptable behavior.

The rape-law reforms implemented in the 1970s and 1980s in the United States were noted to be successful only to the extent that victims increasingly accessed the systems through reporting rape. Bachman and Paternoster (1993) analyzed the NCVS from 1973 to 1990 to examine the extent to which rape reporting changed during those years compared to the change in reporting for robbery and nonsexual assaults. The NCVS data demonstrated that rape victims who reported to police increased by 10% compared to a 4% increase for assault and a 12% decrease for robbery. Based on these findings, Bachman and Paternoster concluded, "rape victims were slightly more likely to report their victimizations after statutory reforms were in place" (1993, p. 566). Data from the NVAWS comparing rape-reporting practices before rape-law reforms (pre-1975) and after rape-law reforms (1980–1996) found a more significant change in reporting. Clay-Warner and Burt (2005) reported the likelihood of women reporting rape to police in the modern reform period (1990–1996) was 88% more likely to be reported than a rape occurring before 1975. A sexual assault that occurred in the middle reform period (1975–1989), however, was no more likely to be reported than one occurring before the enactment of reforms (Clay-Warner & Burt, 2005).

Similarly, a review of rape-law reform in Canada held that the 1983 reform addressed some of the key issues relating to sexual assault but that critical issues still remained. These issues were underreporting of sexual assault; low founding, charging, and conviction rates; the status of rape shield rules; and the defense of honest but mistaken belief of consent. Collective and social actions on the part of women's groups and education are seen as important policy tools to counter sexual assault (Tang, 1998).

Rape Shield Laws

During the 1970s in the United States as the problem of rape came into focus, several groups and organizations joined a movement to reform rape laws with the intention of increasing the reporting of rape victimizations (Torres, 2008). One product of reform was the emergence of rape shield laws to "limit the introduction of sexual history evidence in rape trials" and "challenge the view that women with extensive sexual histories more frequently fabricate charges of rape than other women" (Flowe, Ebbesen, & Putcha-Bhagavatula, 2007, p. 159). Torres (2008) explained that the purposes of rape shield laws vary and suggested that rape shield laws encourage focus on the culpability of the accused rather than on the victim's sexual history. This is supported by the idea that no matter how promiscuous, a victim's sexual history should be irrelevant to the offender's culpability. In addition, Torres claimed that rape shield laws serve to encourage and facilitate victims coming forward to report rape (Torres, 2008).

Because of concerns surrounding false allegations of rape, laws governing rape remained stagnant and unfavorable to victims for many years before the 1970s. There was also significant skepticism toward claims of rape by victims that were met with "cautionary instructions to the jury warning of women's propensity to make false charges of rape" (Flowe et al., 2007, p. 160). In addition, evidence of promiscuity was frequently admitted at trial in an attempt to discredit a complainant and establish the likelihood of consent to sexual intercourse (Flowe et al., 2007). It is evident that false rape allegations may have a drastic impact on a person who is wrongly accused. However, the emotional and physical trauma that rape victims endure must also be considered in decisions made in the courtroom. Flowe et al. (2007) argued that "rape shield provisions attempt to balance protecting the complainant from potentially capricious invasions of privacy, and the defendant's rights to confront and cross-examine witnesses about potentially probative information" (p. 160). This is especially true for cases of "he said, she said" where physical evidence and witnesses are limited or absent.

Rape shield laws are intended to limit the exploration of complainants' sexual psychological history and protect them from "embarrassment and unnecessary publicity by dredging up irrelevant information on their background" (Meadows, 2004, p. 282). Meadows added that probing into a victim's prior sexual history would be humiliating and would discourage victims from reporting rape and pursuing charges (Meadows, 2004).

Anderson (2004) argued that despite the good intentions of rape-law reform, the functionality of rape shield laws was limited in providing protection to complainants. Furthermore, the useful application of these laws was exempted from many cases, especially those involving women who were previously intimate with the defendant, women who were deemed promiscuous, and prostitutes. Anderson (2004) attributed the inefficiency of rape shield laws to "their exceptions [which] routinely gut the protection they purport to offer" (p. 1). The Federal Rule of Evidence 412 states as follows (Anderson, 2004, p. 1):

> Evidence to prove a rape complainant's "other sexual behaviour" or "sexual predisposition" is inadmissible, except: (1) when it is offered "to prove that a person other than the accused was the source of semen, injury or other physical evidence," (2) when it is offered to prove consent and it consists of "specific instances of sexual behaviour by the alleged victim with respect to the person accused," or (3) when the exclusion of the evidence "would violate the constitutional rights of the defendant."

Anderson (2004) further argued that the second exception defeats the purpose of rape shield laws because "62 percent of adult rapes are committed by prior intimates—spouses, ex-spouses, boyfriends, or ex-boyfriends" (p. 1). She also argued that the third exception has the same effect because "courts routinely misinterpret and exaggerate the scope of the defendant's constitutional right to inquire into the complainant's sexual history" (p. 1).

Rape shield laws are also known to be used and applied inconsistently across the United States. Although some states diminish the use of rape shield laws through exceptions defined in state legislatures, other states may permit exceptions based on requirements by the constitution, based on a judge's discretion, or based on the purpose for which the evidence is offered at trial. For example, evidence of sexual history of the accuser may be admitted for the purpose of attacking the credibility of the accuser in one state, whereas the same evidence might be used to prove the accuser had given consent in another state (Torres, 2008). **Table 11-3** provides a more detailed classification of rape shield laws.

TABLE 11-3 **Application of Rape Shield Legislation: Manner and Degree to Which Women's Sexual History Is Admitted as Evidence**

Types of Laws	Description
Legislated exception laws	25 states have enacted legislation that prohibits evidence of the victim's sexual predisposition or history unless • There have been relevant instances of prior consensual sex between the accuser and the defendant • Someone other than the defendant was the source of semen, other bodily fluids, or the cause of injury • There has been a relevant pattern of prior sexual conduct of the complainant • There is bias or bad motive that could cause fabrication of the accusation • There is evidence that shows the accused believed the complainant gave consent • There have been previous instances of false accusations on the part of the accuser
Constitutional catch-all laws	11 states have enacted legislation that resembles the legislated exception laws with an added exception: • Evidence of previous sexual history of the complainant will be admitted if the judge determines that the inadmissibility of such evidence will violate the defendant's constitutional right.
Judicial discretion laws	9 states grant the judge broad discretion to determine whether evidence of the complainant's sexual history should be admitted: • The judge will balance the evidence's relevancy and probative value against its prejudicial effect.
Evidentiary purpose laws	4 states determine admissibility of previous sexual history evidence based on the purpose of doing so in trial. For example, • In California and Delaware sexual history offered to prove consent is prohibited, but using it to attack the complainant's credibility is permissible. • In Nevada and Washington the opposite occurs: evidence for attacking credibility is prohibited, but using it to prove consent is allowed.

Data from Anderson, M.J. 2004. Understanding Rape Shield Laws. The National Alliance to End Sexual Violence. Retrieved from http://naesvorg.ipower.com/Resources/Articles/UnderstandingRapeShieldLaws.pdf

Although inconsistencies in the application of rape shield legislation and exceptions to these laws can give favor to defendants, incorrect application can have damaging implications to defendants as well. In 1998 a case involving the conviction of Oliver Jovanovic for an attack of a 20-year-old student created significant controversy and revealed possible injustices created by rape shield legislation. After having met a woman over the Internet and having explicit conversations with her involving sadomasochistic subject matter, the two met on several occasions where such acts took place. Jovanovic's lawyer attempted to undermine the woman's claims of physical injury by submitting evidence of her consent, which was believed to be apparent in e-mails exchanged between the two. The judge refused the e-mails as evidence, improperly citing the state's rape shield laws. Under a new trial ordered by the appellate court, the following was found: "Jovanovic was precluded not only from bringing out the degree to which the complainant seemed to be inviting sadomasochism but also from exploring whether she was a less reliable narrator of events than she appeared to be at trial" (Meadows, 2004, p. 286). The conviction was eventually overturned on appeal and a new trial ordered on the grounds that Jovanovic was not allowed to present an adequate defense—but not until he had spent 20 months in prison and suffered an assault from another inmate. (The woman was denounced as a habitual liar by some members of her own family.) The New York Supreme Court dismissed all charges after the accuser was no longer willing to testify.

■ Typologies of Rape and Sexual Assault

Incest

Incest is considered sexual activity between close relatives that is illegal in the jurisdiction where it takes place and is conventionally considered a taboo. Incestuous unions have an ancient history in that they were frowned upon and considered a violation of the natural and social order. In current times sexual activity between adults and underage children is illegal and considered one of the most extreme forms of childhood abuse, often resulting in serious and long-term psychological trauma, especially in the case of parental incest.

Statistics on incest are difficult to gather and generalize. The Canadian Incidence Study on Child Abuse and Neglect (Trocmé et al., 2005) reported that in 22% of cases of child sexual abuse, the perpetrator was the father or stepfather of the child; in an additional 40% of cases the perpetrator was another relative, totaling 62% of all child abuse cases. Similarly, the National Incidence Study in the United States revealed that 60% of cases of child sexual abuse are perpetrated by a biological parent or nonbiological parent (U.S. Department of Health and Human Services, 2010).

Statutory Rape

Statutory rape is defined as nonforcible sexual intercourse with a person who is younger than the statutory age of consent. The underlying premise is that young people under a certain age are incapable of fully understanding the nature and consequences of sexual activity and are thus vulnerable to manipulation and exploitation by adults. The actual age of consent across the United States ranges from 13 (in Delaware and Kentucky) to 18 years of age (in California and Arizona). Many of these statutes refer to the offense as unlawful sexual intercourse with a minor or child who is not one's spouse. Penalties can range from 1 year of imprisonment in Nebraska and 2 years in Texas and Tennessee up to the possibility of life imprisonment in several states. In 2000 the U.S. Department of Justice reported one statutory rape for every three forcible rapes of a juvenile (Troupe-Leasure & Snyder, 2005). Ninety-five percent of reported statutory rapes involved female victims, two-thirds of whom were aged 14 or 15. If the victim was a female, the offender was a male in 99% of cases. If the victim was a male, 94% of offenders were female (Troupe-Leasure & Snyder, 2005). In one highly publicized case, Mary Kay Letourneau, a 37-year-old Seattle schoolteacher, was imprisoned from 1997 to 2004 for child rape charges with her 13-year-old student, Vili Fualaau. She gave birth to two of Fualaau's children while on probation. After her release from prison in 2004 Letourneau married Fualaau, and they are raising their two daughters.

Sexual activity between an adult and young person that appears to be "voluntary" is a troubling problem for law and society. Hines and Finkelhor (2007, p. 311) identified the following vulnerability factors and risks for young people involved in sex with adults.

- Youth involved in conflict with their families who may be looking for alliances with adults to help them gain independence more completely than they could through relationships with other youth.
- Youth who are isolated from peers or have other barriers to peer involvement that may orient them more toward adult relationships.
- Youth who have extremely limited career or employment opportunities, for whom relationships with adults may provide a quicker route to motherhood or family formation.
- Youth who are sexually precocious or who may gravitate to adults for sexual opportunities not available among their peers.

- Youth who are gay, confused about sexual orientation, or have other sexual concerns that may make them vulnerable to offers from adults to help mentor them around these concerns by engaging with them sexually.

Adolescents involved in statutory relationships are more likely to have histories of abuse and have troubled or nonexistent relationships with their parents. Statutory relationships are associated with higher rates of teenage pregnancy, single parenthood, and poverty. Indeed, research suggests that in two-thirds of cases of teenage pregnancy the father is an adult male. In the case of younger teenagers who are pregnant, the father of the baby is on average 10 years older. Consequently, several teen advocacy and pregnancy prevention programs have called for increased utilization of existing statutory rape laws to protect young women and reduce teenage pregnancy (Harner, Burgess, & Asher, 2001).

Marital Rape

Marital rape is nonconsensual sex in which the perpetrator is the victim's spouse. On July 5, 1993, marital rape became a crime in all 50 states. In fact, marital rape was once widely condoned or ignored by law, and to this day it is widely tolerated and accepted as a husband's prerogative. This legal attitude was exemplified by Michael Hale, Chief Justice in England in the 17th century, who stated that a husband could not be guilty of the rape of his wife "for by their mutual matrimonial consent and contract the wife hath given up herself in this kind unto the husband which she cannot retract" (Russell, 1990, p. 17). In the late 1970s advocates began efforts to change these laws, and currently the rape of a spouse is a crime in all 50 states and the District of Columbia. The Criminal Code of Canada formally recognized marital rape as a crime in 1983.

Acquaintance Rape

Acquaintance rape, also described as date or hidden rape, is a relatively common problem in American society, especially in the teenage and young adult years. Psychologist Mary Koss (1988) defined rape as being subjected to unwanted sexual intercourse, oral sex, anal sex, or other sexual contact through the use of force or threat of force. Unsuccessful attempts are also subsumed within the term "rape." Sexual coercion is defined as unwanted sexual intercourse or any other sexual contact subsequent to the use of menacing verbal pressure or misuse of authority (Koss, 1988). Acquaintance rape remains a controversial topic, primarily due to the lack of agreement on the definition of consent. Publicized trials indicate an increased awareness of sexual coercion and acquaintance rape has been accompanied by important legal decisions and changes in legal definitions of rape. Views on acquaintance rape also appear quite capable of creating opposing camps. Despite the violent nature of acquaintance rape, the belief that many victims are actually willing, consenting participants is held by both men and women alike. "Blaming the victim" seems to be an all too prevalent reaction to acquaintance rape (Curtis, 1997).

In a 2011 case WikiLeaks founder, Julian Assange, was accused by two women of committing sexual offenses. His defense team countered the women were lying. One woman said she had consensual sex with Assange, but the condom broke and he used his body weight to hold her down, presumably to complete the act. She hosted a party for him the next evening. A few days later Assange had sex with another woman—allegedly while she was asleep—also without wearing a condom. Both women reportedly acknowledged they freely chose to engage in sex acts with Assange—but that some of his conduct was nonconsensual. One woman reported that he engaged in unwanted, unprotected sex while she was asleep, an act considered criminal in Sweden. Assange denied the allegations, suggesting that the women were expressing the anger of jilted lovers. In his defence, Assange's attorneys sought to cast doubt on both the accusers and Swedish prosecutors. To this end, one of the witnesses called to the stand was a former Swedish judge who testified that Marianne Ny, the Swedish prosecutor, was an overzealous women's rights crusader with a bias against men (Faiola & Adam, 2011).

Sexual Homicide

The St. Guillen case reported earlier in this chapter illustrates not only a rape case but also a sexual homicide. So, what are the statistics in this area? Data on murder and murder victims and circumstances are obtained from the annual Supplemental Homicide Reporting program of the FBI (FBI, n.d.). Since the latter half of the 1980s the percentage of all murders with known circumstances in which investigators have identified rape or other sex offenses as the principal circumstance underlying the murder has been declining from about 2% of murders to less than 1%. This is good news that cases are declining. However, the decline is predicated on whether (or not) a homicide victim is examined for sexual assault. A study of sexual homicide (Ressler, Burgess, & Douglas, 1988) determined many rapes were missed because medical examiners did not know the variations of sexual assault in a homicide. Between 1976 and 1994 there were an estimated 405,089 murders in the United States. Of these, the circumstances surrounding the murder are known in 317,925, or 78.5%. Among the cases

TABLE 11-4 Comparing Murders Involving Sexual Assault and Not Involving Sexual Assault

- Known offenders in sexual assault murders were more likely to have been male.
- Sexual assault murders are more likely than all murders to involve a White offender (58% vs. 48%).
- Sexual assault murder offenders are on average about 5 years younger than all murderers.
- Sexual assault murder victims are more likely to be female and White.
- Sexual assault murder victims are both younger and older than the aggregate of all murder victims (25% under age 18 vs. 15% of all murder victims; 1 in 7 sexual assault murder victims are 60 or older vs. 1 in 14 murder victims).
- About 8 of 10 sexual assault murders are intraracial (that is, the offender and victim are of the same race).
- Sexual assault murders are about twice as likely as all murders (39.2% vs. 20.9%) to involve victims and offenders who were strangers.

Data from Ressler, R. K., Burgess, A. W., & Douglas, J. E. (1988). *Sexual homicide: Patterns and motives.* New York: Free Press.

with known circumstances, an estimated 4,807, or 1.5%, were classified as involving rape or another sex offense. Sexual assault murder victims differ markedly from other murders, as indicated in **Table 11-4**.

■ Rape Myths

Among the challenges confronting women who are raped are the myths that surround the issue of rape and the culpability of the victim. Rape myths can be categorized into classic rape myths and contemporary rape myths. The theoretical framework on rape and sexual assault is predicated on a legal and cultural theory of rape that has as a basis classic rape myths. Great efforts are made to encourage women to report a rape immediately; however, societal expectations concerning the reporting of rape are in conflict. One expectation is that if a woman is raped she should be too upset and ashamed to report it, and therefore this crime goes largely unreported. The other is that if a woman is raped she should be so upset she would report it. Both expectations exist simultaneously; it is the latter one, however, that is written into law. This legal principle was researched and reported by Brownmiller (1975) to have been carried since the 13th century, when according to Henry of Bratton (Bracton), who lived and wrote in the 13th century and is considered an authority for the ancient Saxon times, the procedure for a raped virgin went like this:

> She must go at once and when the deed is newly done, with the hue and cry, to the neighboring townships and show the injury done to her to men of good repute, the blood and her clothing

stained with blood and her torn garments (Brownmiller, 1975, p. 17).

The rule then continues that if the accused man protests his innocence, the raped virgin must then have her body examined by four law-abiding women sworn to tell the truth as to whether she was defiled or is still a virgin (Brownmiller, 1975). Thus, in modern language, this is called "making the fresh complaint."

Research on rape myths has been reported in the literature for about three decades, beginning with Burt (1980). Burt (1980) defined a rape myth as "prejudicial, stereotyped or false beliefs about rape, rape victims, and rapists" (p. 217). Lonsway and Fitzgerald (1994) argued for a conceptually grounded definition of the concept of rape myths as "attitudes and beliefs that are generally false yet are widely and persistently held, and that serve to deny and justify male sexual aggression against women" (p. 158). An underlying support for the cultural theory of rape myths is the example of the "just world" concept (e.g., Gilmartin-Zena, 1987). This concept purports that the world is a just place where bad things happen only to those who deserve them. Thus, people will search for evidence that victims provoked or deserve their misfortune (Lerner, 1980). The function of this myth is to explain why a victim "asked for it" by her dress or behavior. The prevailing rape myths include factors around (1) false accusations of rape, (2) only certain women are raped, (3) victim–offender relationship, (4) violence of the assault, (5) resistance of the victim, (6) emotional response of the victim, and (7) sexual history of the victim (Koss, 1987).

The contemporary or newer generation of rape myths derive from the research since the 1980s where studies revealed that most sexual assaults were not committed by strangers but by acquaintances or nonstrangers. Terms such as "date rape" and "acquaintance rape" began to take hold. Victims of date rape were typically viewed as less harmed than those raped by strangers, and date rapists were viewed as less serious offenders and less culpable than stranger rapists. Often, the context of the rape included shared culpability by the two parties because of too much alcohol and too little clear communication regarding consent (Lisak, 2011).

Rape myth acceptance is played out in the courtroom wherein the victim is treated like the offender. Technically, only the man is on trial. But as the drama of the courtroom unfolds it becomes clear in people's minds the victim is as much on trial as the defendant (Holmstrom & Burgess, 1978). Clearly, her character is being judged as much as his. Her statements are viewed with as much suspicion as his. She says he raped her.

He says either in testimony or by pleading not guilty that he did not. The jury or judge must decide which of these contradictory statements to believe. Tomlinson (1999) observed barriers of police reporting "stem directly from rape myths that are deeply embedded in our general culture" (p. 86). The following are common myths: women falsely accuse men of rape, rape is not harmful, risky behavior of women leads to rape, only certain women are raped, women enjoy it, rape is sexually motivated, most rape is committed by strangers, violence characterizes the assault, victims can resist, and sexually "loose" women cannot be raped (Ben-David & Schneider, 2005; Boeschen, Sales, & Koss, 1998; Burt, 1980; Koss, 1987).

■ Dynamics of Reporting Rape

Rape has been termed the "hidden crime" because it occurs at high rates yet frequently goes unreported to police and other authorities (Abbey, Zawacki, & McAuslan, 2000). The NVAWS (Tjaden & Thoennes, 2000) documented that 1 of 6 U.S. women and 1 of 33 U.S. men has experienced an attempted or completed rape as a child and/or adult, indicating how pervasive rape is in our society. However, data have consistently shown that rape and sexual assault victims, more so than victims of other crimes of comparable severity, keep their victimization hidden. According to a report by the Bureau of Justice Statistics (Rennison, 2002), only 31.6% of all rapes and sexual assaults were reported to law enforcement officials in 1998 compared to 62% of all robberies, 57.6% of all aggravated assaults, and 40.3% of all simple assaults. Data from the NCVS for the years 1992 through 1994 found that only 25% of rape and sexual assault victims reported the crime to the police (Bachman, 1998), and when surveying college women, Fisher and associates' (2003b) national-level study found that only 13.3% of rapes and 14.3% of sexual assaults were reported to the police.

There are factors that increase the chances of a rape being reported. Bachman (1998) noted that reporting a rape is strongly related to the perceived seriousness of the offense, indicated by the presence of injuries, if another crime was committed during the rape (i.e., theft), or if the offender used threats and weapons. DuMont, Miller, and Myhr (2003) found that reporting was more likely to occur when the victim was injured. Women who sustained bruises, lacerations, abrasions, bumps, internal injuries, and/or fractures were approximately three and one-half times more likely to contact the police than those who were not clinically injured. The presence of weapons, threats or use of force, completion of rape, and monetary losses were other aspects that influenced the seriousness of the incidents. In a study of 897 women who reported experiencing victimization, Gartner and Macmillan (1995) found that harm, economic loss, and use of a weapon together explained approximately 15% of the variation in reporting to police. Women who were physically coerced (had their clothes torn and/or were slapped, kicked, hit, or choked) were approximately three times more likely to contact the police than those who were not. This finding is consistent with Bachman's (1998) examination of American NCVS data. Her analysis of 235 incidents of rape found that victims were more likely to report if the assailant had used physical force.

The motivation to take corrective action may be stronger because victims believe a serious crime occurred and they deserve justice (Bachman, 1998). Furthermore, the woman may believe the physical injury provides the "physical evidence" she needs for the police to take her complaint more seriously and eliminate any suspicions about false claims. Injuries may function to corroborate the victim's claims of forced sex. Police, prosecutors, and judges were more likely to believe an allegation of rape was false if a woman had not been injured. In Fisher, Daigle, Cullen, and Turner's (2003a; 2003b) study of college women, one-third to 40% of their sample did not report to the police because they believed they lacked proof the incident happened and thought the police would not believe it was serious enough.

Physical injury may also facilitate prosecution by having physical evidence to hold the perpetrator accountable for his criminal behavior. Findings from empirical examinations of police and prosecutorial decisions tend to support this supposition. A review of sexual assaults reported to the police in Canada between 1993 and 1997 found a significant relationship between the presence of mild, moderate, or severe injury and the laying of charges (McGregor, DuMont, & Myhr, 2002). Rape cases with physical evidence of rape are more likely to move forward in the criminal justice system, according to Horney and Spohn's (2001) study of rape case processing in Detroit. In another study, Bouffard (2000) found that the victim agreeing to the forensic exam increased the probability that a case would remain open, suggesting the role that physical evidence and injury play in prosecutors' rape case processing decisions (as cited by Sommers, Fisher, & Karjane, 2005).

It still is a major concern among rape advocates that women and men are not reporting. In addition to national surveys reporting only 3 or 4 of 10 women report rapes to authorities, there are additional facts supporting the low reporting. Clinicians and researchers acknowledge low reporting rates in women they are treating or studying. Third, rape crisis center staff document the numbers of women who do not report under the mechanism of a third-party report. That is, they report the rape to law enforcement but withhold the name and identifying information of the victim. **Table 11-5** illustrates some of the barriers and facilitators of rape reporting.

Nonreporting

Less than half of persons who are raped report to authorities. Reasons for this nonreporting are discussed below.

DENIAL Before a rape is reported, the victim needs to be able to acknowledge the act was a rape. In many cases there is denial that it occurred. In a study of college women Fisher, Daigle, Cullen, and Turner (2003a) noted that although the act met the legal definition of rape, less than half (46.5%) personally defined the experience as rape. Another study using university

TABLE 11-5 Barriers and Facilitators to Reporting Rape

Factors	Characteristics of Reporting
Demographic	Women who are older, more educated, and earn higher incomes are more likely to report sexual assaults (Gartner & Macmillan, 1995; Pino & Meier, 1999).
	Race: There are conflicted findings regarding race and reporting. Bachman (1998) found that African American women are more likely to file a sexual assault police report, whereas other studies found White women are more likely to do so.
Assault characteristics	*Alcohol:* Studies have indicated there is a belief that crimes against intoxicated students who have not reached the legal drinking age should not be reported to the police.
	Relationship to the assailant: Victims are less likely to report an assault to the police of a known offender versus a stranger (Gartner & Macmillan, 1995; Pino & Meier, 1999).
	Seriousness of assault: Victims are more likely to report when they perceive their assault to be a serious one.
	Weapons: Other factors include the presence of weapons, threats or use of force, completion of a rape, and monetary losses (Bachman, 1998; Felson, Messner, & Hoskin, 1999; Gartner & Macmillan, 1995; Pino & Meier, 1999; Williams, 1984).
Personal issues	Personal reasons for not reporting an assault include the following (Tjaden & Thoennes, 2006): • *Fear* of retaliation from the assailant (22.1%) • *Shame* and embarrassment regarding the assault (18.1%) • *Fear of blame:* police would not believe me or would blame me (11.9%)

women as participants conducted by Bondurant (2001) found that 64% of women did not acknowledge their rape experiences.

Women who perceived their rapes as more violent were more likely to acknowledge the rapes (Bondurant 2001), which is consistent with the rape mythologies stating that rapes are seen as violent acts. In a nationwide study of university women, Fisher et al. (2003a) found that incidents were considered rapes three times more often when the offender used physical force than when the offender did not and six times more when a weapon was used. When an injury was sustained, incidents were considered rape almost four times more than when an injury was not sustained (Fisher et al., 2003a). Layman, Gidydz, and Lynn (1996) reported that a significant proportion of the women who were acknowledged, as opposed to unacknowledged, rape victims were threatened with force, had their arms twisted or held down, and were hit or slapped during the rape.

Only one measure of the victim's behavior significantly increased the odds of the incident being considered a rape. The victim's use of forceful verbal resistance increased the odds of the incident being considered a rape almost three times more than when the victim did not vocalize (Fisher et al., 2003a).

Because injuries are commonly viewed as a social criterion of violent crime, they may assist a woman in defining her experience as a sexual assault. This is problematic insofar as the evidence suggests a substantial proportion of sexual assaults do not involve physical violence. Data from the Bureau of Justice Statistics from 1992 to 2000 revealed that less than half (38%) of female rape victims sustained an injury in addition to the rape (Rennison, 2002).

FEAR OF THE LEGAL SYSTEM A common rationale for the underreporting of rape is the treatment that victims receive from societal institutions, especially the legal system. This realization is not a contemporary idea but one that initiated reforms in the 1970s and 1980s to shift the focus from the consent of the victim to the behavior of the offender (Bachman, 1998).

Campbell, Wasco, Ahrens, Sefl, and Barnes (2001) found that only 25% of participants' cases that were reported to the legal system were prosecuted. Of these 25% that were actually prosecuted, 10% of the reported rapes were tried but the rapist was not convicted at trial, 10% were tried and convicted, and 5% were resolved by a guilty plea from the assailant. A study examining legal outcomes of women seeking treatment for sexual assault in an urban emergency room found that of 888 women seeking treatment, only 132 (15%) had charges filed by the prosecutor (Wiley, Sugar, Fine, & Eckert, 2003). Most cases resulted in either a plea before trial (70%) or a guilty verdict by the jury (15%). Another 13% of cases were dismissed or acquitted (Wiley et al., 2003). This is consistent with previous research showing that the most typical disposition for cases accepted for prosecution is not trial but a plea agreement. In response to agreeing to plead guilty and saving the state the expense of a trial, the offender is allowed to admit to a lesser crime (Koss, Bachar, Hopkins, & Carlson, 2004).

Victims who do have their cases prosecuted may find the procedures are traumatizing. Defense attorneys will use rape myths to convince the jury the victim consented to the rape (Koss et al., 2004). Victims can be subjected to probing and embarrassing questioning by the police and prosecutors to verify that a crime has occurred, and the extent to which the victim used (or did not use) physical resistance may be a factor (Pino & Meier, 1999).

FEAR OF RETALIATION Some victims do not report because they fear retaliation by their offender, especially when he is known or is a boyfriend or partner. In Bachman's (1998) analysis of NCVS, more than 1 in 10 victims said they did not report because they were afraid of reprisal by the offender. Among college-aged women, Fisher et al. (2003b) noted that 39.5% of victims cited the fear of reprisal by the assailant or others as factors influencing their decision not to report the crime.

GUILT AND BLAME Prevailing stereotypes of rape depict self-blame and guilt as central issues for victims. Rape myth attitudes, which are commonly held beliefs that shift the blame for a sexual assault from the assailant to the victim, serve to minimize the prevalence and seriousness of rape and may play a major role in why women feel blame. Some of the most pervasive myths include the beliefs that women falsely accuse men of rape, rape is not harmful, women want or enjoy rape, or women cause or deserve rape by inappropriate or risky behavior (Frese, Moya, & Megias, 2004). These underlying assumptions about rape suggest that women are essentially responsible for male sexual behavior.

Wiehe and Richards (1995) found guilt and self-blame to be primary reasons a sample of 236 victims of acquaintance rape did not report their victimizations to the police. They reported that self-blame was a recurring theme in survivors' comments and was reinforced by family or friends who overtly or covertly blamed the victim for what occurred by questioning her behaviors ("Why did you invite him to your apartment?" "Why did you go to his house?" "Were you drinking at the time?"). These and similar questions, although appearing to be asking for information, can be seen as blaming the victim for what happened (as cited by Bachman, 1998).

Self-blame was especially prevalent when victims were under the influence of alcohol at the time of the incidences and when victims perceived their own actions led to their being sexually victimized (Fisher et al., 2003b). In addition, women who had alcohol-related assaults received more negative reactions from formal and informal sources than did women who did not have alcohol-related assaults. Specifically, women who experienced alcohol-related assaults received more blaming and stigmatizing responses than women whose assaults did not involve alcohol (Ullman & Filipias, 2001). Notably, in Fisher et al.'s (2003b) sample of college-aged women, alcohol and/or drugs were present in 7 of 10 incidents.

PERSONAL MATTERS In Bachman's (1998) analysis of NCVS data, victims overwhelmingly said the incident was a "personal matter" and they dealt with it another way. These data are supported by the Bureau of Justice Statistics, from the years 1992 to 2000, in which the most often cited reason for rape, attempted rape, and sexual assault victims not reporting to the police was a personal matter. In addition, 16% of rape victims from the NVAWS reported they were too ashamed or wanted to keep the incident private (Tjaden & Thoennes, 2000). Victims may elect to keep their experiences private for a wide variety of reasons. It could be a feeling of embarrassment at having been victimized, lacking confidence that reporting would lead to arrest, wishing to avoid the stigma associated with being a crime victim, or protecting their families or those close to the perpetrators (Fisher et al., 2003b). Alternatively, it could be fear of making the rape public. If the rape goes to trial, they are expected to testify about the details of sexual assault in an open court and they may fear what their family, friends, and community members may think of them (Koss et al., 2004).

VICTIM–OFFENDER RELATIONSHIP The closer the relationship between victim and offender, the more difficult the road to prosecution. Rapes committed by a stranger are still viewed as more serious and legitimate than rape by acquaintances, romantic partners, or husbands. Studies suggest acquaintance rape victims are less likely to label their assaults as rapes than woman assaulted by strangers (Fisher et al., 2003a). The Bureau of Justice Statistics data from 1992 to 2000 reported that the closer the relationship between the female victim and the offender, the greater the likelihood the police would not be told about the rape or sexual assault (Rennison, 2002). When the offender was a current or former husband or boyfriend, 77% of completed rapes and 75% of sexual assaults were not reported to the police. When the offender was a friend or acquaintance, 61% of completed rapes, 71% of attempted rapes, and 82% of sexual assaults were not reported. When the offender was a stranger, 54% of completed rapes, 44% of attempted rapes, and 34% of sexual assaults were not reported to the police (Rennison, 2002).

Nonstrangers commit approximately 74% of rapes or sexual assaults; thus, if victims are less likely to report such assaults, most offenses will not come to the attention of police (Fisher et al., 2003a). Other studies have replicated these results. Survey data from a community study by Ullman and Filipias (2001) found that more women sexually assaulted by strangers (78%) told formal support sources (including police, physicians, rape crisis counselors) than did women assaulted by known men (57.6%).

Rape treatment outcome research found that 51.6% of victims were raped by strangers (Vickerman & Margolin, 2009). This finding was similar in studies by Frazier (2003) and Resick, Jordan, Girelli, Hutter, and Marhoeder-Dvorak (1988) in which 45% and 54% of victims, respectively, were assaulted by a stranger. In one recent cross-sectional correlational study of 1,172 patients presenting to a local emergency department with a complaint of rape, the relationship between the victim and perpetrator was documented in 88.5% of cases ($n = 1,037$) (Avegno, Mills, & Mills, 2009). Of the total, 550 patients (53.0%) reported knowing their attacker, 437 (42.2%) did not know the perpetrator, and 50 (4.8%) were unsure. Results indicated that victims who were African American as opposed to White (62.6% vs. 43.5%, respectively, $p < 0.0001$) and young (age < 26 years) reported significantly higher rates of known perpetrators than older victims (58.1% vs. 49.2%, respectively, $p < 0.005$). Victims who reported knowing their attacker most often categorized the relationship as "acquaintance" (50.8%) or "friend" (30.8%) (Avegno et al., 2009). Contrary to other studies, categorizing the relationship as a "date" comprised only 9.6% of cases, as spouse or partner 4.0%, and as family member 4.9%.

For rapes reported to the police, the question becomes whether the victim–offender relationship actually influences legal outcomes. Some studies point to the fact that stranger rapes result in more positive legal outcomes. For example, Campbell et al. (2001) found that 80% of the prosecuted cases in their sample involved stranger rapes and 20% were nonstranger rapes. In contrast, Wiley et al.'s (2003) study of legal outcomes in women who presented to the emergency department with a complaint of sexual assault found significantly greater likelihood of a legal outcome if one's partner or spouse was the assailant (60%) compared to 31% in those cases not involving a partner or spouse. A stranger as the assailant did not affect legal outcome, and a friend or acquaintance as the assailant negatively influenced legal outcome (Wiley et al., 2003).

However, partner or spousal sexual assault is more likely to include physical violence and to result in physical injuries to the victim than sexual assault from an acquaintance (Stermac, DelBove, & Addison 2001). An earlier study by Stermac, Dumont, and Dunn (1998) of 1,162 women seeking treatment also found intimate partner sexual assaults were more similar to stranger assaults, as both had greater physical violence and injuries than acquaintance assaults. It is possible that if a woman reports to the emergency department after sexual assault by an intimate partner, she may have experienced a more violent assault with more physical trauma than women assaulted by a stranger. The victim–offender relationship then becomes secondary to the presence of injuries, which validates the crime. It is also possible that assailants who are strangers may not be located, in contrast to a spouse/partner who is an assailant.

In court, crime factors of relationship, reporting, use of force and/or weapon, and forensic findings play a critical role to the jury. **Table 11-6** illustrates some of these factors.

Despite 20 years of public attention to the prevalence of rape and sexual assault in our society, the validity of reports is often questioned and rape victims continue to be blamed. Not reporting rape has negative

TABLE 11-6 **Rape Beliefs and Phase of Rape**

Phase of Rape	Crime Factors	Rape Attitudes and Beliefs
Before the rape	Stranger vs. nonstranger relationship	She is acquainted with the offender
	Time between incident and report	She meets him in a risky setting (e.g., bar)
	Use of force	Her behavior is provocative (drinking, demeanor, clothing)
During the rape	Location of assault	She consents (then changes her mind)
	Weapon shown	She doesn't resist or scream or call for help
After the rape	Weapon used	She doesn't immediately report or tell anyone for a while
	Resistance of victim	She has no bruises or torn clothing
		She doesn't go for a medical exam or the exam has no forensic findings
		She stays with the offender or sees him again or resumes her usual lifestyle

consequences. It reduces the likelihood that an offender will be arrested or convicted by failing to initiate the criminal justice system. If rapists perceive the likelihood of apprehension from authorities is low, this undermines any deterrent value the legal system may have in preventing rape (Bachman, 1998). By not reporting, victims may not have access to victim-assistance services provided by the criminal justice system, such as support programs, or to medical treatment.

◼ Typology of Sexual Trauma

The rape trauma syndrome was one of three typologies identified by Burgess and Holmstrom in 1974 and published in the *American Journal of Psychiatry*. The typologies were the result of personal interviews with 146 people who ranged in age from 3 to 73 years at the time of admission to the Boston City Hospital emergency department. The individuals all were admitted with the complaint of rape. Three types of sexual trauma were conceptualized from the sample of 146 and based on consent (or not) to have sex: rape trauma (no consent), pressured sex (coerced sex), and sex stress (initial consent but then denial of consent). Of the 146 individuals, 92 women ages 18 to 73 were classified as rape trauma victims and their responses to the assaultive experience formed the basis for the rape trauma syndrome.

Rape: Sex Without the Victim's Consent

Control is a key ingredient of a rape. In practical terms the assailant has two goals: physical and sexual control of the victim. In listening to victims describe the assailants' styles of attack, it was clear that some rapists gained control in a direct physical action, such as a sudden surprise attack, whereas others used verbal ploys in an attack with the qualities of a confidence game. In both types the rapist gains sexual control of the victim by force and without her consent.

BLITZ RAPE The blitz rape occurs "out of the blue" and without any prior interaction between assailant and victim. The person is leading a normal everyday life. A split second later that lifestyle is shattered and that individual is a victim. As one 36-year-old victim said, "He just popped out of nowhere. There was no way to get away. It happened so fast—like a shock of lightning go through you. I didn't have time to think of an escape." From the victim's point of view there is no ready explanation for the man's presence. He suddenly appears, his presence is inappropriate, he is uninvited, and he forces himself into the situation. Often, he selects an anonymous victim and tries to remain anonymous himself. He may wear a mask or gloves or cover the victim's face as he attacks.

The "mark," to use the language of the criminal world, is the person destined to become a victim of some form of illegal exploitation. The classic example of the blitz-type rape is a woman walking down the street and who, from the assailant's viewpoint, is the "right mark at the right time." He is looking for someone to capture and attack, she happens on the scene, and she becomes the target. The surprise attack outdoors is a common blitz-type rape. However, it is not unusual for victims to be attacked while they are asleep in their own beds because the assailant has gained entry into the home. The following case illustrates such a rape in which the victim was in her own apartment sleeping.

Lauren, age 22, lived with two roommates in a second-floor apartment. Neither roommate was home when she went to bed around midnight. She awoke about 5:30 a.m. to a man on top of her and wearing a Halloween-type mask and a pair of gloves. Lauren tried to scream, and he put his hands over her mouth and nose and was choking her. He ripped off her nightclothes. She believed he would kill her. He told her to "Shut up" and proceeded to rape her. When he finished, he got up and walked out of the room. Lauren jumped up, locked the door, and looked for her cordless phone. She believed the assailant was in the apartment and that she had to escape. She cut the window screen with a pen, jumped out, and continued running to several doors, pounding on them for someone to help her. At about the third door a man responded and let her use his phone to call 911 and report the rape.

In blitz-type rapes victims describe being jumped on, grabbed, pushed, or shoved when the assailant approached them from behind. Other victims describe being in the process of entering their cars or apartments or stopped at a traffic light when a man opened the unlocked passenger side door. Other victims describe being pulled into cars or grabbed outside and taken to an indoor area such as a hallway, building, or car. One woman had just stepped into her shower when the lights went out and the man grabbed her and took her into a bedroom.

CONFIDENCE RAPE   The confidence rape is a subtler setup than the blitz style and is an attack in which the assailant obtains sex under false pretenses by using deceit, betrayal, and often violence. There is interaction between the assailant and the victim before the assault. He may know the victim from some other time and place and thus already may have developed some kind of relationship with her. Or, he may establish a relationship as a prelude to attack. Often, there is quite a bit of conversation between victim and assailant. Like the confidence man, he encourages the victim to trust him and then betrays this trust as in the following example.

About 6:20 p.m. Sarah, age 23, was on the phone with a friend when a person, known to her as one of the workmen who had been in her apartment once, knocked on her door to tell her he needed to fix a leak for the apartment below hers. She unlocked her door, and he checked under her sink and in the bathroom. As he was leaving the apartment he suddenly locked the door handle. He then said he wanted to date Sarah; she was shocked and said no and asked him to leave several times. He then grabbed her wrists; she fought to get away, and he hit her on the sides of her face and proceeded to rape her.

Pressured Sex: Inability to Consent

In rape, the type of victimization discussed above, the victim, whether adult, adolescent, or child, clearly does not consent to the sexual activity. The sexual acts are against their will and they are forced by the assailant to do them. In pressured sex, the types of victimization discussed in this section, the victims aid or contribute in a secondary manner to the sexual activity. The victims' collaboration comes about because of their inability to consent or not consent due to their stage of personality or cognitive development.

It should be noted that we do not define ability to consent arbitrarily by age. In all these cases the primary person involved, the assailant, stands in a relationship of power over the secondary person, the victim, because he is older, an authority figure, and so on.

The assailant gains access to this victim by three methods: (1) pressures the victim to take material goods, (2) pressures the victim to accept human contact, and (3) pressures the victim to believe the sexual activity is appropriate and enjoyable. In each of these three approaches the assailant makes sure the victim gets something out of the sexual encounter; thus, at the time the encounter is not a totally negative experience for the victim.

Sex Stress Situation: Sex with Initial Consent

The third type of victimization is a sex stress situation rather than forced or pressured sex. They are not cases of the male's gaining access without the female's initial consent. Nor are they cases in which the victim, for personality or cognitive reasons, was incapable of making a decision of consent. Rather, in this type the male and female initially agreed to have sexual relations but then something drastically "went wrong." Usually, what went wrong was the male exploited this agreement in several ways. In some cases what went wrong was that authorities—police or parents—came upon or found out about the consenting couples and then these authorities themselves defined the situation as rape or caused the person to say it was rape as a way out of a dilemma of being caught.

Also, in some of these sex stress cases the person who referred to the problem as rape in reality wanted some service from the hospital and believed she could not directly ask for it. After all, given the prevailing attitudes, a young teenager cannot walk into a hospital and say that she and her boyfriend had sex the evening before, she is scared of getting pregnant, and she needs medication to prevent pregnancy. It should be emphasized that very few of these sex stress victims took the case to court; they did not become "spite cases," that is, cases in which the female sought to "get the guy" on a rape charge simply out of spite.

Workplace Harassment

Confidence rapes also occur in the workplace or school setting where the victim needs to be present, harassment occurs, and authority (school or employer) fails to intervene. Consider the following case.

Michelle was in her senior year of high school when she began to work afternoons at a local fast food restaurant. She soon became upset with the work environment, in particular the sexual language and talk, references to women as "sluts," and unwanted physical contact. One employee in particular, Victor, frightened Michelle. He was over 6' tall and in his 30s. He would tell her she was sexy, pretty, and hot and that he wanted to have sex with her; he would also touch her despite her telling him to stop. Her coworkers or the supervisors took no action. Victor's behavior escalated to attempting to lift her skirt, rub her body, and kiss her. He threatened harm to her if she told anyone. Michelle tried to avoid Victor by procrastinating going to work and trying to work when Victor was not present. The sexual pressuring and harassment continued until Victor forced Michelle into a small, unlocked, unsupervised closet in the restaurant where he forced her to perform oral sex on him. The sexual assaults were reported to Victor's probation supervisor, the police, and Michelle's family.

■ Psychological Impact of Sexual Assault

The study of victim response to short-term crisis intervention revealed a differential response to sexual assault and rape: that symptoms persisted over a long period of time and that some symptoms did not abate despite therapeutic efforts. It was realized that more fundamental changes had occurred as a consequence of the sexual assault. These fundamental changes suggested a type of trauma learning that caused biological shifts.

These assumptions have been bolstered by the rapidly developing areas of neuroscience and biology and have revealed substantive changes and alterations in basic central nervous system functioning.

One of the conclusions reached by Burgess and Holmstrom (1974) as a result of studying 92 adult rape victims was that victims suffer a significant degree of physical and emotional trauma during a rape. This trauma can be noted immediately after the assault and over a considerable time period afterward. Victims consistently described symptoms that included flashbacks, intrusive thoughts of the rape, fear, anxiety, nightmares, daymares, and the development of phobias. A cluster of symptoms was described as the rape trauma syndrome. The rape trauma syndrome has two phases: the immediate or acute phase, in which the victim's lifestyle is completely disrupted by the rape crisis, and the long-term process, in which the victim must reorganize this disrupted lifestyle. The syndrome includes physical, emotional, and behavioral stress reactions that result from the person being faced with a life-threatening event to one's life or integrity.

The Burgess and Holmstrom study had a clinical focus on victim response to rape and an institutional focus. The study made clear that rape does not end with the assailant's departure; rather, the profound suffering of the victim can be diminished or heightened by the response of those who staff the police stations, hospitals, and courthouses. Ironically, the institutions that society has designated to help victims may in fact cause further damage (Holmstrom & Burgess, 1978).

Rape trauma syndrome was accepted as a nursing diagnosis into the North American Nursing Diagnosis Association official nomenclature in 1979. Also included were two variations of rape trauma syndrome: silent response to rape and compounded reaction to rape. The silent response to rape was observed in persons who had never told anyone of a childhood rape experience but later (months or years) the assault was revealed. In the Burgess and Holmstrom study (1974) women talked freely of these early experiences in the context of the new assaultive experience. In the compounded rape trauma the individual had a primary presenting medical or psychological disorder through which the rape trauma symptoms were filtered. Examples include elders with dementia, persons with a psychiatric disorder or physical disorder, and persons with an intellectual disability.

Posttraumatic Stress Disorder

Rape trauma syndrome preceded the term posttraumatic stress disorder by 6 years. When the American Psychological Association's work group on anxiety disorders was considering how to classify a number of traumatic events (e.g., combat stress, natural disasters, and rape trauma), it was decided to make an umbrella term under which the various life-threatening events could fall. The designated term, "posttraumatic stress disorder," came into the official nosology of the American Psychological Association in 1980 with the publication of the third edition of the *Diagnostic and Statistical Manual of Mental Disorders*.

■ Classifying Rapists

To more fully appreciate rape victimization, it is helpful to understand the dynamics of the offender. What prompts men to rape? What are such offenders like? Do they progress from less serious to more aggressive offenses? What determines their choice of victims? What can a potential victim do, when faced with such an assailant, to deter him? Will the offender return? These are some of the questions commonly asked about rapists, and it is difficult to provide simple and unequivocal answers to them.

Early Research

Early research for classifying the underlying motivational intent for sexual assault identified three domains: power, anger, and sexuality (Groth, Burgess, & Holmstrom, 1977). This early classification was taken from the perspective of the rapist and clinical work with him.

Clinical work with offenders and victims in the 1970s through the 1990s revealed that rape was in fact serving primarily nonsexual needs: It was the sexual expression of power and anger. Rape was viewed as motivated more by retaliatory and compensatory motives than sexual ones; it was a pseudo-sexual act, complex and multidetermined but addressing issues of hostility (anger) and control (power) more than desire (sexuality).

The defining issue in rape is the lack of consent on the part of the victim. Sexual relations are achieved through physical force, threat, or intimidation. Rape is therefore first and foremost an aggressive act, and in any given instance of rape, multiple psychological meanings may be expressed in regard to both the sexual and the aggressive components of the act.

The most basic observation one can make regarding rapists is that not all such offenders are alike. They do not do the very same thing in the very same way or for the very same reason. In some cases similar acts occur for different reasons, and in other cases different acts serve similar purposes. Clinical experience both with identified offenders and with victims of reported sexual assault note that in all cases of forcible rape, three basic components are always present: anger, power, and sexuality (Groth et al., 1977). The hierarchy and interrelationships among these three factors, together with the relative intensity with which each is experienced and the variety of ways in which each is expressed, may vary from one offense to another. Yet there is sufficient clustering so that distinguishable patterns of rape become evident: the anger rape, in which sexuality becomes a hostile act; the power rape, in which sexuality becomes an expression of conquest; and the sadistic rape, in which anger and control become eroticized. In every act of rape, then, both aggression and sexuality are involved. However, it is clear that sexuality becomes the means of expressing other, nonsexual needs and feelings that operate in the offender and motivate his assault. Rather than being primarily an expression of sexual desire, rape is, in fact, the use of sexuality to express issues of power and anger. It is a sexual act that is concerned much more with status, aggression, control, and dominance than with sexual pleasure or sexual satisfaction. It is sexual behavior in the service of nonsexual needs, and in this sense, rape is clearly a distortion of human sexuality.

Theory of Interpersonal Aggression

Rape and sexual assault are acts ensuing from interpersonal aggression that result in sexual victimization to person(s) who may or may not be known to the offender. These rape and sexual assaults are not primarily motivated by material gain and are not sanctioned by a group. Rather, an underlying emotional conflict or psychological issue propels the offender to commit rape and sexual assault. Although the case may be legally defined as rape, the term "sexual assault" is used in this classification to encompass a wide range of forced and pressured sexual activities. (Douglas, Burgess, Burgess, & Ressler, 2006; Prentky & Burgess, 2000).

Exploitative Rape

In exploitative rape, sometimes called power reassurance rape, expressed aggression is generally low and does not exceed what was necessary to force victim compliance. Callous indifference to the victim is evident. Issues of power and control are underlying psychological conflict.

Sexualization essentially refers to a high degree of preoccupation with gratifying one's sexual needs. In this type of sexual assault the offender quickly gains control over his victim. The evidence of such power and control is that the victim submits to sexual demands on the part of the offender. The offender places his victim in a situation through verbal threat, intimidation with a weapon, and/or physical force where she cannot refuse or resist him, and this provides the offender with a reassuring sense of power, security, strength, mastery, and control. In this fashion he compensates for underlying feelings of inadequacy, vulnerability, and helplessness.

This type of rapist often shows little skill in negotiating interpersonal relationships and feels inadequate in both sexual and nonsexual areas of his life. Having few other avenues of personal expression, sexuality becomes the core of his self-image and self-esteem. Rape becomes the means by which he reassures himself of his sexual adequacy and identity, of his strength and potency. Usually, the goal of the assault is to effect sexual intercourse as evidence of conquest, and to accomplish this the victim may be kidnapped, tied up, or rendered helpless in some fashion.

Because it becomes a test of his competency, the rape experience for this offender is one of anxiety, excitement, and anticipated pleasure. The assault is premeditated and preceded by an obsessional fantasy in which, although his victim may initially resist him, once overpowered she will submit gratefully to his embrace because she will be so impressed with his sexual abilities. In reality, this offender may often be handicapped by impotency or premature ejaculation. If not, he still tends to find little sexual satisfaction in the rape. The assault is disappointing because it never lives up to his fantasy. The power rapist commits his offense in an effort to resolve disturbing doubts about his sexual adequacy and masculinity. He aims to place a woman in a helpless, controlled position where she cannot refuse him or reject him and thus shore up his failing sense of worth and adequacy.

Often, he must convince himself that his victim became attracted to him, really wanted sex but could not admit it, and clearly consented nonverbally to, and enjoyed, the sexual contact. Yet at some level he realizes that he has not found what he is looking for in the offense; he senses that something he cannot clearly define is lacking. He does not feel reassured by either his own performance or his victim's response to the assault; therefore, he must go out and find another victim—this time the "right one."

The offenses become repetitive and compulsive. The amount of force used in the assault may vary, and there may be an increase in aggression over time as the offender becomes more desperate to achieve that indefinable experience that continues to elude him. Usually, there is no conscious intent on the part of this offender to hurt or degrade his victim; his aim is to have complete control over her so she will have no say in the matter and will be submissive and gratify his sexual demands. Aggression, then, may constitute a show of force or a reaction to resistance on the part of the victim. That is, when the victim resists the advances of her assailant, he retaliates by striking or hitting her. Aggression here usually becomes expressed less as an anger motive and more as a means of dominating, controlling, and being in charge of the situation. Rape becomes an assertion of the offender's virility or a reassurance of his competence—a reflection of the inadequacy he experiences in terms of his sense of identity and effectiveness.

Anger Rape

Sexual assault in this category is characterized by high expressive aggression (unprovoked physical and verbal aggression or physical force in excess of that necessary to gain victim compliance must be present). Rage is evident in this offender. He may have manifested behaviors listed for sadistic sexual assault, but these must appear to be punishing actions done in anger, not to increase sexual arousal. The primary motive for the offense is anger and not sexual gratification. When the offender knows the victim, the assault on that victim appears to be the result of the offender's easy access to that victim. These offenses are predominantly impulse driven (e.g., opportunity alone, possibly coupled with impaired judgment due to drugs/alcohol).

The degree of force used in this type of assault is excessive and gratuitous. The violence is an integrated component of the behavior even when the victim is compliant. Resistance from the victim is likely to increase the aggression, and serious injury or death may occur. The rage is not sexualized, suggesting the assault is not fantasy driven. The violence is a lifestyle characteristic that is directed toward males and females alike. The rape is but one feature in a history of unsocialized aggressive behavior noted across various social settings.

In some cases of sexual assault it is very apparent that sexuality becomes a means of expressing and discharging feelings of intense anger, rage, contempt, hatred, and frustration; the assault is characterized by excessive brutality. Far more physical force is used in the commission of the offense than is required simply to overpower and subdue the victim. Instead, the assault is one of explosive physical violence to all parts of the victim's body. This type of offender approaches his victim by striking and beating her; he tears her clothes, knocks her to the ground, uses abusive and profane language, rapes her, and frequently makes her perform or submit to additional degrading acts.

The **anger rapist** finds it difficult to explain his assault, when he cannot deny it, except to rationalize that he was drunk or on drugs. Often, the specific details are lost to his memory in that he becomes "blind with rage" during the assault. Satisfaction and relief result from the discharge of anger rather than from sexual gratification. Pleasure is derived from degrading and humiliating his victim.

His relationships to important women in his life are fraught with conflict, irritation, and irrational jealousy, and he is often physically assaultive toward them. His sexual offenses tend to be episodic and sporadic, triggered by conflicts in his relationships to these actual women in his life.

Sadistic Rape

In the sadistic rape, aggression itself is eroticized. The offender, referred to as a sexual sadist, derives satisfaction in the sexual abuse of his victim. Sexuality and aggression become intertwined into a single psychological experience: sadism. The assault itself appears ritualistic and usually involves bondage and torture. Sexual areas of the victim's body—her breasts, genitals, and buttocks—become the focus of injury. The rape experience for this type of offender is one of intense and mounting excitement. He finds pleasure in the victim's torment, anguish, distress, and suffering. His assault is deliberate, calculated, and premeditated. The victim is stalked, captured, abused, and, in extreme cases, murdered. The nature of the assault may or may not involve the offender's genitals: The victim may be raped with an instrument or foreign object, such as a spoon or bottle. In some cases sexual penetration may take place after she is dead.

■ Sexual Predators in the Community

Although research on sex offenders has expanded our knowledge of the behavior and characteristics of rapists, their motivation, and their developmental antecedents, the studies have been conducted on incarcerated offenders. However, because many victims do not report their rape, the offenders remain undetected, not subject to prosecution, and therefore in the community. Psychologist David Lisak and colleagues began a series of interviews of undetected rapists primarily in college environments and found similarities to incarcerated offenders in that they shared the same motivational matrix of hostility, anger, dominance, hypermasculinity, impulsiveness, and antisocial attitudes. It was also noted that these men were likely to be serial offenders (Lisak & Miller, 2002).

Lisak characterized the modus operandi of undetected rapists as follows. First, they are adept at identifying possible victims and testing prospective victims' boundaries. Second, these offenders plan and premeditate their attacks using sophisticated strategies to groom the victim and isolate her for an assault. Third, they use only enough aggression to control and coerce the woman into submission. Fourth, they use psychological weapons of power, control, manipulation, and threats rather than weapons of knives or guns. Fifth, they use alcohol deliberately to render victims more vulnerable to attack or sometimes to make them unconscious (Lisak, 2011).

■ False Allegations of Rape and Sexual Assault

On August 23, 2011, a New York judge dropped all criminal sexual assault charges against former International Monetary Fund chief Dominique Strauss-Kahn. The decision ended a case that brought 3 months of sordid headlines about a hotel maid who accused Strauss-Kahn of attempting to rape her in his luxury Manhattan hotel suite ("Strauss-Kahn," 2011).

Prosecutors stated they were not convinced of his culpability beyond a reasonable doubt due to serious issues in the complainant's credibility and inconclusive physical evidence and therefore could not ask a jury to believe it. Prosecutors pointed to a "pattern of untruthfulness" about the 32-year-old woman's past that included a convincingly delivered story of being gang raped by soldiers in her native Guinea; she later admitted to fabricating the story, and prosecutors characterized her ability to recount a fictionalized sexual assault with complete conviction as "fatal" to her credibility. She had also denied an interest in making money from the case, despite a recorded conversation prosecutors said captured her discussing just that with her fiancé, a detainee in an immigration jail in Arizona, shortly after the encounter in the hotel ("Strauss-Kahn," 2011).

The case pitted supporters of Strauss-Kahn, who said he was the victim of an overzealous U.S. criminal justice system, against backers of the woman, Diallo, who complained it was an example of race, class, and gender where sexual assault victims are denied justice ("Strauss-Kahn," 2011).

Potential Consequences of a False Allegation

Imprisonment of men falsely accused of rape has been described since Biblical times. Potiphar, an Egyptian captain of Pharaoh's guard, employed Joseph to watch over his household. Potiphar's wife "cast her eyes upon Joseph . . . caught him by his garment, saying lie with me." Joseph resisted this temptation, but his rejection of her caused her to say that the Hebrew servant came to "mock her," that she lifted up her voice and cried, and that he fled, leaving his garment with her. Potiphar imprisoned Joseph for 2 years (Genesis, 39).

Although not resulting in imprisonment, a more contemporary, and nationally infamous, false allegation case occurred in the 1980s in Duchess County, New York. Tawana Brawley, a 15-year-old Black girl from the quiet little town of Wappingers Falls, New York (population 5,000), was missing for 4 days when she was found on November 28, 1987. She was observed in the backyard of a townhouse, previously occupied by her family, standing in a green garbage bag and literally hopping around the yard before lying down and pulling the bag over her head. Her hair had been cut short, she had feces smeared on her body, and "KKK" and "nigger" had been printed on her body with a soot-like substance. She refused to speak with police but, speaking through her aunt and mother, reported she had been abducted, taken to a wooded area, and repeatedly raped by four to six White men, one of whom had a police-style badge. Reverend Al Sharpton and others became involved, and it was alleged that the county police and prosecutor were involved in a cover-up to protect members of the local police force. Consequently, the national news media became involved, and then-Governor Cuomo asserted state jurisdiction over the investigation that resulted in the formation of a combined state and federal task force. After an intensive and lengthy criminal and state grand jury investigation lasting more than 7 months, it was concluded that Brawley had falsified the story. Additionally, the grand jury found no evidence of a cover-up by law enforcement officials and recommended that their minutes be released to the public.

Another, but equally infamous, incident involved a Black female alleging that several White Duke University lacrosse players had assaulted her. Again, the national news media became involved because of inflammatory statements made by the local prosecutor. This matter collapsed from a preponderance of evidence supporting the defense, a lack of evidence supporting the allegation, and numerous conflicting statements given by the alleged victim. The state attorney general intervened and issued a blistering statement concerning the abilities and motivation of the local prosecutor.

Difficulty of Measuring Rates of False Allegations of Rape

For centuries there has been an assumption that many women allege being raped for purposes of revenge or other motives. In the 17th century the suggestion of rape being an easily made accusation formed the basis of corroboration warnings issued by judges to the jury, cautioning of "women's propensity to make false charges of rape" (Flowe et al., 2007, p. 160). It is unclear whether this skepticism originated from a high frequency of false charges, because research findings on false rape allegations vary considerably from estimates of 1.5% to 90% (Lisak, Gardinier, Nicksa, & Cote, 2010). To obtain an accurate rate the definition of a false allegation of rape must be clearly outlined. The International Chiefs of Police explained this definition as follows (Lisak et al., 2010, p. 1319):

> The determination that a report of sexual assault is false can be made only if the evidence establishes that no crime was committed or attempted. This determination can be made only after

a thorough investigation. This should not be confused with an investigation that fails to prove a sexual assault occurred. In that case the investigation would be labeled unsubstantiated. The determination that a report is false must be supported by evidence that the assault did not happen.

Evidence that the assault did not happen may include physical evidence or credible witnesses who may contradict key aspects of the victim's version of the story. According to the International Chiefs of Police, uncooperative victims, insufficient evidence, inconsistencies in victim statements, lying on behalf of the victim, delayed reporting of a rape incident, or incidents that involved intoxication are all factors that, by themselves, do not make a rape allegation false (Lisak et al., 2010). As mentioned above, false allegations can also be confused or combined with the category of unfounded or unsubstantiated claims that are commonly defined as "lacking a sound base, groundless, unwarranted" (Lisak et al., 2010, p. 1321). Lisak et al. (2010) claim that "both terms are used to code and administratively clear sexual assault cases that are often mislabelled as false allegations" (p. 1321). The UCR, for example, reports 8% of rape allegations are unfounded. Lisak et al. (2010, p. 1321) explain as follows:

> The UCR guidelines also make clear that the category of "unfounded" is broader than the category of false allegation, since "unfounded" includes cases that are determined to be "baseless." A case can be classified as "baseless" if, for example, a victim reports an incident that, while truthfully recounted, does not meet, in the eyes of investigators, the legal definition of a sexual assault. For example, if a victim reports to the police that she was raped while she was intoxicated, and truthfully states that she cannot clearly recall whether there was penetration, investigators might classify such a case as "baseless/unfounded." This classification is clearly distinct from a case in which a victim deliberately fabricates an account of being raped, yet the "unfounded" category is very often equated with the category of "false allegation."

This is further evidence of how variations in the classifications and definitions of false rape allegations and differing methodologies of measuring false rape allegations add to a bank of unreliable data. In fact, Rumney (2006) concluded that the current research literature cannot be used to determine the rate of false rape allegations. Lisak et al. (2010) add that, "There is considerable evidence of widespread misclassification by

TABLE 11-7 Rates of False Allegations of Rape

Study	Sample Size	Rate of False Reports
Toronto (1970)	116	10.3% false
Philadelphia (1972–1975)	709	15% unfounded, 3% false
British Home Office Study (1985)	302	24% no-crime, 8.3% false
British Home Office Study (1996)	483	25.5% no-crime, 10.9% false
British Home Office Study (15-year period)	2,643	8.2% false, 2.5% recalculated false under more stringent criteria
Australian Study (3-year period)	812	2.1% false
Making a Difference Study by End Violence Against Women (18- to 24-month period)	2,059	6.8% false

Data from Lisak, D., Gardinier, L., Nicksa, S.C., & Cote, A.M. 2010. False Allegations of Sexual Assault: An Analysis of Ten Years of Reported Cases. *Violence Against Women, 16*(12); 1324.

police departments and enormous disparities among police agencies in how cases are classified" (p. 1322).

Lisak et al. (2010) developed a list of studies that, according to them, use a clear definition of a false allegation, explain the source of data used, and attempt to evaluate data received from law enforcement agencies. **Table 11-7** provides the studies with most consistent rates of false rape allegations per Lisak et al.

Lisak et al. outlined the importance of providing reliable and accurate data on false rape allegations that contradict widely held stereotypes that false rape allegations are common. Such a stereotype may result in increased underreporting because victims may be under the impression their claims are less likely to be believed. The stereotype may also influence law enforcement agents to handle victims' allegations through hostile interrogation rather than fact finding (Lisak et al., 2010). Furthermore, incorrect assumptions about false rape allegations may inhibit appropriate policy developments surrounding rape reform and legislature (Rumney, 2006).

■ Reasons for False Allegations of Rape

Studies have revealed that some false allegations of rape may be motivated by malicious intent, medical conditions leading to a mistaken account of rape (such as Munchausen's syndrome), or complainants who thought they might have been sexually assaulted while they were highly intoxicated or asleep (Rumney, 2006). In Kanin's study 109 false allegations were revealed as a means for acquiring sympathy or attention, retaliation against a rejecting male, or served as an alibi function to explain a consensual encounter or account for some other event (Kennedy & Witkowski, 2000). Other studies concluded that the most frequent motive for fabricated rape were instances that involved consensual sex that led to some sort of problem for the accuser, such as contracting a sexually transmitted disease or becoming pregnant (Gross, 2009, p. 68).

Emotional Problems in Need of Attention

Frequently, those who make false allegations have legitimate problems worthy of attention in their own right. However, if their complaints are accepted at face value, the underlying problem will go untreated and may surface at a later date. When rape complaints are determined to be false, investigators would be wise to seek the assistance of mental health professionals.

Investigators may suspect a false allegation when the victim repeatedly changes his or her accounts of the assault. This was one of the issues in the Duke lacrosse case. Care must be taken to distinguish a true changing of the story from a legitimate recollection of additional data. In both true and false claims, new information and more detail may be added in subsequent interviews. The false claimant wishes to "shore up" the allegation to make it more believable, whereas the genuine victim (as composure and equilibrium are regained) may remember more detail and descriptive data in the days after the assault.

Related to this same discussion is the distinction one must make between deliberate deceit and an honest mistake. The person making a false allegation may offer data that differ from the original report to further deceive and mislead the authorities. In the initial stages of an investigation a legitimate rape victim, because of stress and psychic pain, may provide incorrect information related to an altered ability to accurately process information.

When a rape, or for that matter any crime, occurs, there must be three elements: perpetrator(s), act(s), and a setting or set of conditions. One can make a false allegation with reference to any or all of these elements.

■ Care for Victims of Sexual Violence

National Sexual Violence Resource Center

The National Sexual Violence Resource Center (NSVRC), founded by the Pennsylvania Coalition Against Rape and funded by the Centers for Disease

Control and Prevention's Division of Violence Prevention, is the nucleus of a national movement to prevent sexual violence and to sustain a national momentum that influences practice, research, policy, and, ultimately, public attitudes and belief. The broad goals of the NSVRC are as follows:

1. To strengthen the support system serving sexual assault survivors by providing competent leadership, resources, and information to develop capacity of national sexual assault organizations, state sexual assault coalitions, community-based programs, and allied professionals

2. To provide accurate and comprehensive information and technical assistance in supporting effective intervention in the prevention of sexual violence

3. To identify emerging policy issues and research needs to support the development of policy and practice leading to the prevention of sexual violence

4. To develop the organizational structure and technological capacity supporting the development and implementation of NSVRC activities.

The NSVRC is housed in Enola, Pennsylvania, and provides information and resources, technical assistance, and access to research through its toll-free number and e-mail address. Organizational partners who collaborate with the NSVRC are the Violence Against Women Prevention Resource Center, the VAWnet/National Resources Center, the National Alliance of Sexual Assault Coalitions, and the National Coalition Against Sexual Assault.

Nationally, the sexual assault nurse examiner (SANE) and/or sexual assault response team model has grown exponentially. Although virtually all these programs were developed to facilitate standard comprehensive and expert care of sexual assault survivors, the literature clearly shows that policies and procedures do vary from program to program (**Table 11-8**).

In addition, SANE programs use specialized forensic equipment, such as a colposcope, which is a noninvasive, lighted, magnifying instrument for examining the perineum and anogenital area for the detection of small lacerations and bruises (Voelker, 1996). Other equipment may include a camera attached to the colposcope, and toluidine blue dye may be used for the detection of micro-lacerations and abrasions. SANEs also document bruises and injuries using photography, usually digital cameras. SANEs are also trained in identifying and documenting patterned injuries, treatment of injuries, maintaining chain of evidence, and providing expert witness testimony (Ledray, 1999).

TABLE 11-8 Evidentiary Care for Victims of Sexual Assault

Type of Care	Description
Initial medical evaluation	This is not a routine physical exam. Vital signs of the victim are taken; however, there is no treatment of injuries until the SANE documents injuries with pictures and collects evidence. The victim is advised of this procedure and must sign a consent form.
Evidentiary exam	The SANE is responsible for conducting the evidentiary exam and ensures the victim's dignity is protected and the victim is not retraumatized by the exam. Victims are a part of the decision process throughout the evidence collection phase. Most protocols suggest the exam be completed within 72 hours after the sexual assault. All evidentiary exams include the following: • Written consent from the victim, documentation of assault history • Forms of violence used and where • Medical information of the victim, including pregnancy status • Physical exam for trauma, genital and nongenital • Collecting the victim's clothing and packaging according to state policy • Specimen collections, including skin, hair, and nails • Body fluid and orifice specimen collection • Blood draw and urine specimen for drug analysis DNA screen • Prophylactic treatment of sexually transmitted infections or culturing
Maintaining chain of evidence and evidence integrity	The SANE is responsible for ensuring complete documentation with signatures and the disposition of evidence. Additionally, the SANE is also responsible for identifying, collecting, and preserving evidence and for securing evidence in an area designated free of contaminants.
Crisis intervention and counseling	This includes a mental health assessment and referral for follow-up counseling. This is usually the primary role of the rape crisis center advocate. However, the SANE also provides crisis intervention and ensures follow-up counseling services are available.

Data from Ledray, L. 1999. Sexual assault nurse examiner (SANE) development & operations guide. Washington, DC: Office for Victims of Crime, US Department of Justice.

■ Summary

Rape and sexual assault are acts of aggression where sexual activity is used to degrade and humiliate the victim. Rape affects the lives of victims and their significant others with various physical and emotional consequences. Great strides have occurred over the past 30 years in terms of reform in the sexual assault law and protection of women. Many of these reforms come from the implementation of sexual assault response teams and of rape crisis centers developing services and programs for victims of rape.

Studying the motivation and characteristics of the sex offender has captured the television scene with interviews with offenders shown to illustrate their plan and how they carried out their crimes. Such information helps for prevention efforts and is used in educational programs. In addition, it is critical for the clinician to understand the factors that have injured the victim in order to assess and provide a treatment protocol. Law enforcement officers and agents benefit from understanding the dynamics that exist for both apprehension and investigative purposes.

■ Key Terms

Anger rapist: Displaces his anger, rage, and hatred onto a victim.

Blitz rape: Sudden, out of the blue, physical attack.

Incest: Sexual activity between close relatives that is illegal in the jurisdiction where it takes place.

Marital rape: Nonconsensual sex in which the perpetrator is the victim's spouse.

Rape: Use of sexuality to express issues of power and anger.

Sexual Assault: Any sexual act, attempt to obtain a sexual act, unwanted sexual comments or advances, or acts to traffic, or otherwise directed, against a person's sexuality using coercion.

Sexual coercion: Unwanted sexual intercourse or any other sexual contact subsequent to the use of menacing verbal pressure or misuse of authority.

Sexual sadist: An offender who finds pleasure and excitement in the suffering of his victim.

■ Discussion Questions

1. Discuss the barriers and facilitators of reporting a sexual assault to law enforcement.

2. Outline the history of rape reform in the United States and Canada, and evaluate rape reform in your jurisdiction.

3. What are the similarities and differences in rape trauma syndrome and posttraumatic stress disorder?

4. What are some dynamics and motivational factors noted in rapists?

5. How can a classification of rape be useful to the criminal justice system?

6. Debate the Strauss-Kahn false allegation case.

7. What might be some solutions to increase reporting of sexual assault in college student populations?

■ Resources

Federal Bureau of Investigation. Crime in the United States 2004. http://www.fbi.gov/ucr/cius_04/

National Center for Victims of Crime http://www.ncvc.org/ncvc/main.aspx?dbName=DocumentViewer&DocumentID=32458

National Clearinghouse on Family Violence http://www.phac-aspc.gc.ca/ncfv-cnivf/familyviolence/

National Sexual Violence Resource Center http://www.nsvrc.org/

■ References

Abbey, A., Zawacki, T., & McAuslan, P. (2000). Alcohol's effects on sexual perception. *Journal of Studies on Alcohol, 61,* 688–697.

Abel, G.G., Becker, J.V., Mittelman, M.S., Cunningham-Rathner, J., Rouleau, J.L., & Murphy, W.D. (1987). Self-reported sex crimes of nonincarcerated paraphilics. *Journal of Interpersonal Violence, 2*(1), 3–25.

Anderson, M.J. (2004). Understanding rape shield laws. The National Alliance to End Sexual Violence. Retrieved from http://naesvorg.ipower.com /Resources/Articles/UnderstandingRapeShieldLaws.pdf

Avegno, J., Mills, T., & Mills, L. (2009). Sexual assault victims in the emergency department: Analysis by demographic and event characteristics. *Journal of Emergency Medicine, 37*(3), 328–334.

Bachman, R. (1998). The factors related to rape reporting behavior and arrest: New evidence from the National Crime Survey. *Criminal Justice and Behavior, 25,* 8–29.

Bachman, R. (2000). A comparison of annual incidence rates and contextual characteristics of intimate-partner violence against women from the National Crime Victimization Survey (NCVS) and the National Violence Against Women Survey (NVAWS). *Violence Against Women, 6*(8), 839–867.

Bachman, R., & Paternoster, R. (1993). A contemporary look at the effects of rape law reform: How far have we really come? *Journal of Criminal Law and Criminology, 84,* 554–574.

Ben-David, S., & Schneider, O. (2005). Rape perceptions, gender role attitudes, and victim-perpetrator acquaintance. *Sex Roles, 53,* 385–399.

Boeschen, L.E., Sales, B.D., & Koss, M.P. (1998). Rape trauma experts in the courtroom. *Psychology, Public Policy, and Law, 4,* 414–432.

Bondurant, B. (2001). University women's acknowledgment of rape: Individual, situational, and social factors. *Violence Against Women, 7,* 294–314.

Bouffard, J.A. (2000). Predicting sexual assault case closure categories from case characteristics. *Journal of Criminal Justice, 28*(6), 527–542.

Brownmiller, S. (1975). *Against our will: Men, women and rape.* New York: Simon & Schuster.

Burgess, A.W., Fehder, W.P., & Hartman, C.R. (1995). Delayed reporting of the rape victim. *Journal of Psychosocial Nursing and Mental Health Services, 33*(9), 21–29.

Burgess, A.W., & Holmstrom, L.L. (1974). Rape trauma syndrome. *American Journal of Psychiatry, 131,* 981–986.

Burt, M.R. (1980). Cultural myths and supports for rape. *Journal of Personality and Social Psychology, 38*(2), 217–230.

Campbell, R., Wasco, S., Ahrens, C., Sefl, T., & Barnes, H. (2001). Preventing the "second rape": Rape survivors' experiences with community service providers. *Journal of Interpersonal Violence, 16,* 1239–1260.

Clay-Warner, J., & Burt, C.H. (2005). Rape reporting after reforms: Have times really changed? *Violence Against Women, 11,* 150–176.

Curtis, D.G. (1997). Perspectives on acquaintance rape. *The American Academy of Experts in Traumatic Stress, Inc.* Retrieved from http://www.aaets.org /article13.htm

Douglas, J.E., Burgess, A.W., Burgess, A.G., & Ressler, R.K. (2006). *Crime classification manual.* San Francisco: Jossey-Bass.

DuMont, J., Miller, K.L., & Myhr, T. (2003). The role of "real rape" and "real victim" stereotypes in the police reporting practices of sexually assaulted women. *Violence Against Women, 9,* 466–487.

Faiola, A., & Adam, K. (2011). Assange sex assault allegations debated for 2nd day. Retrieved from http://www.canada.com/news/Assange+assault+allegations +debated/4244862/story.html#ixzz1V2Nm7unI

Federal Bureau of Investigation. Supplemental reports. Sex and murder statistics. Retrieved from http://www.fbi.gov/about-us/cjis/ucr/nibrs /addendum-for-submitting-cargo-theft-data/shr

Federal Bureau of Investigation. (2008). Crime in the United States, 2007. Retrieved from http://www.fbi.gov/about-us/cjis/ucr/ucr

Felson, R.B., Messner, S.F., & Hoskin, A.W. (1999). The victim-offender relationship and calling the police in assaults. *Criminology, 37,* 931–947.

Fisher, B. (2004). Measuring rape against women: The significance of survey questions. Retrieved from https://www.ncjrs.gov/pdffiles1/nij/199705.pdf

Fisher, B., Daigle, L., Cullen, F., & Turner, M. (2000). *The sexual victimization of college women.* Washington, DC: U.S. Department of Justice, National Institute of Justice, and Bureau of Justice Statistics.

Fisher, B.S., Daigle, L.E., Cullen, F.T., & Turner, M.G. (2003a). Acknowledging sexual victimization as rape: Results from a national-level study. *Justice Quarterly, 20,* 535–574.

Fisher, B.S., Daigle, L.E., Cullen, F.T., & Turner, M. (2003b). Reporting sexual victimization to the police and others: Results from a national-level study of college women. *Criminal Justice and Behavior, 31*(1), 6–38.

Flowe, H.D., Ebbesen, E.B., & Putcha-Bhagavatula, A. (2007). Rape shield laws and sexual behavior evidence: Effects of consent level and women's sexual history on rape allegations. *Law and Human Behavior, 31*(2), 159–175.

Frazier, P. (2003). Perceived control and distress following sexual assault: A longitudinal test of a new model. *Journal of Personality and Social Psychology, 84,* 1257–1260.

Frese, B., Moya, M., & Megías, J.L. (2004). Social perception of rape: How rape myth acceptance modulates the influence of situational factors. *Journal of Interpersonal Violence, 19*(2), 143–161.

Gartner, R., & Macmillan, R. (1995). The effect of victim-offender relationship on reporting crimes of violence against women. *Canadian Journal of Criminology, 37,* 393–429.

Gilmartin-Zena, P. (1987). Attitudes toward rape: Student characteristics as predictors. *Free Inquiry in Creative Sociology, 15,* 175–182.

Gross, B. (2009). False rape allegations: An assault on justice (case study). *Forensic Examiner, 18*(1), 66–70.

Groth, A.N., Burgess, A.W., & Holmstrom, L.L. (1977). Rape: Power, anger, and sexuality. *American Journal of Psychiatry, 134,* 1239–1243.

Hale, M. (1847). *The history of the pleas of the crown* (Vol. 1). Philadelphia: R. H. Small.

Harner, H., Burgess, A.W., & Asher, J. (2001). Caring for pregnant teenagers: Medicolegal issues for nurses. *Journal of Obstetric, Gynecologic & Neonatal Nursing, 30*(2), 139–147.

Hines, D., & Finkelhor, D. (2007). Statutory sex crime relationships between juveniles and adults: A review of social scientific research. *Aggression and Violent Behavior, 12,* 300–314.

Holmstrom, L.L., & Burgess, A.W. (1978). *The victim of rape: Institutional reactions.* New York: Wiley.

Horney, J., & Spohn, C. (2001). The influence of blame and believability factors on processing of simple versus aggravated rape cases. *Criminology, 34*(2), 135–162.

Kennedy, D.B., & Witkowski, M.J. (2000). False allegations of rape revisited: A replication of the Kanin study. *Journal of Security Administration, 23*(1), 41–46.

Koss, M. (1987). The scope of rape. *Journal of Consulting and Clinical Psychology, 55,* 162–170.

Koss, M., Bachar, K., Hopkins, C.Q., & Carlson, C. (2004). Expanding a community's justice response to sex crimes through advocacy, prosecutorial, and public health collaboration: Introducing the RESTORE program. *Journal of Interpersonal Violence, 19,* 1435–1463.

Koss, M.P. (1988). Hidden rape: Sexual aggression and victimization in the national sample of students in higher education. In M.A. Pirog-Good & J.E. Stets (Eds.), *Violence in dating relationships: Emerging social issues* (pp. 145–168). New York: Praeger.

Koss, M.P., Gidycz, C.A., & Wisniewski, N. (1987). The scope of rape: Incidence and prevalence of sexual aggression and victimization in a national sample of higher education students. *Journal of Counseling and Clinical Psychology, 55*(2), 162–170.

Krug, E.G., Dahlberg, L.L., Mercy, J.A., Zwi, A.B., & Lozano, R. (2002). *World report on violence and health.* Retrieved from http://whqlibdoc.who.int /hq/2002/9241545615.pdf

Largen, M.A. (1988). Rape-law reform: An analysis. In A.W. Burgess (Ed.), *Rape and sexual assault II* (pp. 271–292). New York: Garland Press.

Layman, M.J., Gidydz, C.A., & Lynn, J. (1996). Unacknowledged vs acknowledged rape victims: Situational factors and posttraumatic stress. *Journal of Abnormal Psychology, 105,* 124–131.

Ledray, L. (1999). *Sexual assault nurse examiner (SANE) development & operations guide.* Washington, DC: Office for Victims of Crime, U.S. Department of Justice.

Lerner, M.J. (1980). *The belief in a just world: A fundamental delusion.* New York: Plenum Press.

Lisak, D. (2011). *Sexual assault report, 14*(4), 49–50, 56–57. Kingston, NJ: Civic Research Institute, Inc.

Lisak, D., Gardinier, L., Nicksa, S.C., & Cote, A.M. (2010). False allegations of sexual assault: An analysis of ten years of reported cases. *Violence Against Women, 16*(12), 1318–1334.

Lisak, D., & Miller, P.M. (2002). Repeat rape and multiple offending among undetected rapists. *Violence and Victims, 17,* 73–84.

Lonsway, K.A., & Fitzgerald, L.F. (1994). Rape myths in review. *Psychology of Women Quarterly, 18,* 133–164.

McGregor, M., Dumont, J., & Myhr, T. (2002). Sexual assault forensic medical examination: Is evidence related to succesful prosecution? *Annal of Emergency Medicine, 39*(6), 639–647.

Meadows, R. (2004). Rape shield laws: A need for an ethical and legal reexamination? *Criminal Justice Studies, 17*(3), 281–290.

Murphy, W. (2006, March 8). *The murder of Imette St. Guillen.* Boston Globe, p. 6.

National Crime Victimization Survey. (2000). Washington, DC: Bureau of Justice Statistics.

Pino, N., & Meier, R. (1999). Gender differences in rape reporting. *Sex Roles, 40,* 979–990.

Prentky, R.A., & Burgess, A.W. (2000). *Forensic management of the sex offender.* New York: Plenum.

Rennison, C.M. (2002). *Rape and sexual assault: Reporting to police and medical attention, 1992–2000.* Washington, DC: US Government Printing Office.

Resick, P.A., Jordan, C.G., Girelli, S.A., Hutter, C.K., & Marhoeder-Dvorak, S. (1988). A comparative outcome study of behavioral group therapy for sexual assault victims. *Behavior Therapy, 19,* 385–401.

Ressler, R.K., Burgess, A.W., & Douglas, J.E. (1988). *Sexual homicide: Patterns and motives.* New York: Free Press.

Rumney, P. (2006). False allegations of rape. *Cambridge Law Journal, 65*(1), 128–158.

Russell, D.E.H. (1990). *Rape in marriage: Expanded and revised edition with a new introduction.* Bloomington and Indianapolis: Indiana University Press.

Ryan, J. (2011). FBI to change definition of forcible rape. Retrieved from http://abcnews.go.com/blogs/politics/2011/12/fbi-to-change-definition-of-forcible-rape/

Sommers, M.S., Fisher, B., & Karjane, H. (2005). Using colposcopy in the rape exam: Health care, forensic, and criminal justice issues. *Journal of Forensic Nursing, 1,* 28–36.

Stermac, L., del Bove, G., & Addison, M. (2001). Violence, injury and presentation patterns in spousal assault. *Violence against Women, 7*(11), 1218–1230.

Stermac, L., Du Mont, J., & Dunn, S. (1998). Violence in known-assailant sexual assaults. *Journal of Interpersonal Violence, 13,* 398–412.

Strauss-Kahn criminal sexual assault charges dropped. (2011). Retrieved from http://www.reuters.com/article/2011/08/23/us-strausskahn-idUSTRE77J20620110823

Tang, K. (1998). Rape law reform in Canada: The success and limits of legislation. *International Journal of Offender Therapy and Comparative Criminology, 42*(3), 258–270.

Tjaden, P., & Thoennes, N. (2000). *Full report of the prevalence, incidence, and consequences of violence against women: Findings from the National Violence Against Women Survey* (NCJ183781). Washington, DC: National Institute of Justice, Office of Justice Programs, U.S. Department of Justice.

Tjaden, P., & Thoennes, N. (2006). Special report on the extent, nature, and consequences of rape victimization: Findings from the National Violence Against Women Survey. Retrieved from http://www.ncjrs.gov/pdffiles1/nij/210346.pdf

Tomlinson, D. (1999). *Police-reporting Decisions of Sexual Assault Survivors: An Exploration of Influential Factors.* Alberta, Canada: Alberta Law Foundation.

Torres, J. (2008). Rape shield laws and game theory: The psychological effects on complainants who file false rape allegations. *Law & Psychology Review, 32*(1), 135–151.

Trocmé, N., Fallon, B., MacLaurin, B., Daciuk, J., Felstiner, C., Black, T., . . . , Barter, K. (2005). *Canadian incidence study of reported child abuse and neglect—2003: Major findings.* Ottawa, Ontario, Canada: Canadian Child Welfare Research Portal.

Troupe-Leasure, K., & Snyder, H. (2005). Statutory rape known to law enforcement. Juvenile Justice Bulletin. Retrieved from http://www.ojp.usdoj.gov/

Ullman, S., & Filipias, H. (2001). Correlates of formal and informal support seeking in sexual assault victims. *Journal of Interpersonal Violence, 16*(10), 1028–1047.

U.S. Department of Health and Human Services. (2010). Fourth national incidence study on child abuse and neglect. Retrieved from http://www.acf.hhs.gov/programs/opre/abuse_neglect/natl_incid/reports/natl_incid/natl_incid_title.html

U.S. Department of Justice. (2002). *Rape and sexual assault: Reporting to police and medical attention, 1992–2000.* Washington, DC: Government Printing Office.

Vickerman, K.A., & Margolin, G. (2009). Rape treatment outcome research: Empirical findings and state of the literature. *Clinical Psychology Review, 23*, 18–34.

Voelker, R. (1996). Experts hope team approach will improve the quality of rape exams. *Journal of the American Medical Association, 275*, 973–974.

Wiehe, V.R., & Richards, A.L. (1995). *Intimate betrayal: Understanding and responding to the trauma of acquaintance rape.* Thousand Oaks, CA: Sage.

Wigmore, J.H., & Chadbourn, J.H. (1970). *Evidence in trials at common law* (Vol. 3A). Boston: Little, Brown.

Wiley, J., Sugar, N., Fine, D., & Eckert, L. (2003). Legal outcomes of sexual assault. *American Journal of Obstetrics and Gynecology, 188*(6), 1638–1641.

Williams, J.E. (1984). Secondary victimization: Confronting public attitudes about rape. *Victimology, 9*, 66–81.

Elder Abuse Victims

CHAPTER
12

■ Objectives

- To identify the incidence and pervasive nature of abuse against the elderly
- To discuss types of abuse and categories of abusive situations involving the elderly
- To introduce screening tools to assess abuse in the elderly
- To present models of intervention in elder abuse

■ Key Terms

Alzheimer disease
Cognitively impaired
Dementia
Elder abuse
Fiduciary
Medically fragile
Power of attorney
Psychological abuse

CASE

Mickey Rooney, the legendary American actor, appeared in over 200 films and received a Juvenile Oscar in 1939, an honorary Oscar for Lifetime Achievement in 1983, an Emmy Award, and two Golden Globes (Mickey Rooney, 2011). But in March 2011 he made the news for a very different reason. Ninety-year-old Mickey Rooney appeared before a Senate

FIGURE 12-1 Mickey Rooney giving testimony on his abuse before a Senate Special Committee on Capitol Hill in Washington, D.C.
© Jim Young/Thomson Reuters

Special Committee in Washington, DC (**Figure 12-1**), stating he was a victim of elder abuse. Mr. Rooney testified that he was victimized by Chris Alber, the son of his eighth wife ("Mickey Rooney speaks out," 2011). He indicated his stepson withheld food and medication, interfered with his finances, and subjected him to intimidation, bullying, and harassment (Freeman, 2011). Rooney told the Senate committee he suffered in silence for years: "I didn't want to tell anybody. I couldn't muster the courage and you have to have courage. . . . I needed help and I knew I needed it. Even when I tried to speak up, I was told to shut up and be quiet" (Cohen, 2011; "Mickey Rooney claims to be elder abuse victim," 2011). In his statements Mr. Rooney made this impassioned plea: "I'm asking you to stop this elderly abuse. I mean to stop it. Now. Not tomorrow, not next month, but now," he shouted from the witness table. He urged the committee to pass legislation and send it to be signed into law by President Barack Obama so the nation can say "it's a crime and we will not allow it in the United States of America" (Cohen, 2011).

■ Introduction

In 2002 the World Health Organization (WHO) published the *Toronto Declaration on the Global Prevention of Elder Abuse*, which included the following definition: "**Elder abuse** is a single or repeated act, or lack of appropriate action, occurring within any relationship where there is an expectation of trust, which causes harm or distress to an older person. It can be of various forms: physical, psychological/emotional, sexual, financial, or simply reflect intentional or unintentional neglect" (boldface added). Further, the declaration states, "Elder abuse is the violation of human rights and a significant cause of injury, illness, lost productivity, isolation and despair. Confronting and reducing elder abuse requires a multi-disciplinary approach" (WHO, 2002, pp. 3–4). This statement by the WHO underlines that elder abuse is a universal issue and is not limited to any one culture or country. Indeed, a special issue of *Educational Gerontology* in 2006 contained articles highlighting the problem of elder abuse in Israel (Rabi, 2006), Japan (Arai, 2006), Germany (König & Leembruggen-Kallberg, 2006), Brazil (Bezerra-Flanders & Clark, 2006), and African Americans (Tauriac & Scruggs, 2006).

■ Scope of the Problem

The WHO estimates the rate of elder abuse across Canada, the Netherlands, the United States, Finland, and Great Britain is between 4% and 6%. Data from the United States are consistent with these estimates. The 2008 National Social Life, Health and Aging Project was the first U.S. population-based, nationally representative study to ask older adults living in the community about their recent experiences regarding mistreatment by family members. Over 3,000 Americans between the ages of 57 and 85 participated in the survey. Results revealed that 9% of older adults reported verbal mistreatment, 3.5% reported financial mistreatment, and 0.2% reported physical mistreatment in the past year (Laumann, Leitsch, & Waite, 2008).

In this analysis and others, reports of financial mistreatment were significantly higher among older African Americans than among older White adults (Beach, Schulz, Castle, & Rosen, 2010). Older Latinos were less likely than others to report either financial or verbal mistreatment (Beach et al. 2010).

Using a broader definition of perpetrator that was not limited to family members, a recently released U.S. nationally representative sample of 5,777 older adults discovered that 5.1% of adults over the age of 60 reported emotional mistreatment, 5.2% reported financial abuse, 1.6% reported physical mistreatment, and 0.6% reported sexual mistreatment in the past year (Amstadter et al., 2010).

In Canada approximately 7% of 4,000 adults aged 65 years and older who responded to the 1999 General Social Survey on Victimization reported they had experienced some form of emotional abuse by an adult child, spouse, or caregiver in the past 5 years, 1% reported physical abuse, and 1% reported financial abuse (Statistics Canada, 2002). When older adults are victims of family violence, the perpetrator is most likely to be an adult child, followed by a current or ex-spouse (Statistics Canada, 2007). In 2005, 44% of Canadian senior homicide victims were killed by family members and 31% were killed by an acquaintance (**Figure 12-2**). Of older women who are murdered, 37% are killed by a spouse and 37% are killed by an adult son. Older men are killed by their son or stepson in 57% of cases (Statistics Canada, 2007).

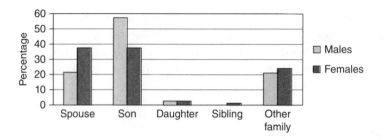

FIGURE 12-2 Relationship Between Older Domestic Homicide Victim and Accused in Canada
Data from Statistics Canada. 2007. Family violence in Canada: A statistical profile. Ottawa, Ontario, Canada: Canada.

Why is elder abuse a growing concern? The population of older adults in the Western world is growing rapidly with improved health care, nutrition, and living conditions. In 2006 in Canada the proportion of older adults was 13.7%, and it is expected to reach 24% by 2031 (Statistics Canada, 2007). In the United States the proportion of older adults hit 13% in 1990 (11 years earlier than Canada), with 31 million Americans at least 65 years of age. By 2030 it is expected that 85 million people will be age 65 years or older, and 8 million will be older than age 85 years. Other countries already have much higher proportions of persons aged 65 years or older than do Canada and the United States. In Japan, Germany, and Italy roughly one person in five is aged 65 years or older. Increasingly, older adults are living with family members and spouses. As people become more medically fragile or cognitively impaired, they place an increased burden on family members physically, emotionally, and financially. Increased family frustration combined with increased vulnerability of the elderly person can create a dangerous environment.

Elder Abuse Legislation

In the United States the issue of elder abuse is addressed in both state and federal law. Combined hearings held by the Senate and House Committees on Aging in 1980 resulted in the proposed Prevention, Identification and Treatment of Adult Abuse Bill. This Bill, which was never enacted, was modeled on child abuse legislation and called for, among other things, mandatory reporting (Dubble, 2006). The federal Older Americans Act was amended in 1987 to provide definitions of elder abuse and direct the use of federal funds for awareness and coordination activities (American Bar

Association Commission on Law and Aging, 2005). Subsequently, the Elder Justice Act, first introduced in 2005, became law in March 2010 as part of the Patient Protection and Affordable Care Act (Elder Justice Coalition, 2011). Under this Act the Elder Justice Coordinating Council is charged with providing reports on activities, accomplishments, and challenges in this area and with making recommendations to congressional committees (Dong & Simon, 2011). The Act further provides states with resources to prevent elder abuse, increase prosecution of those who mistreat the elderly, and provide victim assistance.

A special issue in nursing home care of vulnerable elderly people relates to the care of elderly sexual offenders previously convicted of crimes such as rape. The legislation was championed by Wes Bledsoe, an activist in the rights of elderly nursing home victims after reports that a 43-year-old man accused of killing four people had been ordered by a judge to live in a nursing home (Associated Press, 2008). Further study revealed that 30 registered sexual offenders lived in nursing home facilities in Oklahoma and that more than 500 older sexual offenders were due to be released from prison within the next 10 years in that state, many of whom may have required long-term care. A U.S. Government Accountability Office report further determined that more than half of the registered sexual offenders in nursing homes were younger than age 65 years, compared to only 10% of other residents who were younger than age 65 years (Adams & Calloway, 2009). As a result Governor Brad Henry of Oklahoma signed the first U.S. legislation forbidding registered sexual offenders from being in standard nursing home facilities and requiring the establishment of a separate facility to address their needs (Associated Press, 2008). This represented another important step in the protection of vulnerable elderly individuals.

Laws enacted in all U.S. states establish systems for reporting and investigating abuse through adult protective services. In general, these laws require mandatory reporting of elder abuse requiring certain groups of people (health care providers, bank tellers, police officers, etc.) to report suspected cases of abuse to the appropriate social service (U.S. Government Accountability Office, 2011). The statutes vary widely with respect to types of abuse, definitions of abuse, reporting requirements, investigation procedures, and remedies. For example, although virtually all state legislation covers physical abuse, neglect, and financial abuse, some states exclude psychological abuse, sexual abuse, and abandonment. Some states cover only older adults who live in the community, whereas others also cover abuse that occurs within institutions. Some states cover this abuse as a criminal offense, and others define it as a civil matter (American Bar Association Commission on Law and Aging, 2005).

Financial abuse of elderly individuals is not limited to abuse perpetrated by family members or caregivers but also includes investment fraud schemes that target vulnerable individuals, particularly the elderly. Yet, despite concern about the widespread nature of this type of abuse, few states have enacted legislation that specifically targets this issue. Florida enacted legislation in 2004 that identified civil remedies for fraud committed by a person in a position of trust against a vulnerable adult, defined as someone who lacks the capacity to consent. Nevada similarly enacted a statute in 2003 that stipulated a person who exploits an older or vulnerable adult is liable for two times the actual damages. Illinois, Oregon, and Tennessee, on the other hand, limit liability in these circumstances to cases where there has been a criminal charge or indictment (Catalano & Lazaro, 2008).

The Criminal Code of Canada does not specifically address elder abuse; thus, cases of elder abuse must be addressed through various other provisions. For example, financial abuse may be addressed through provisions related to theft, forgery, criminal breach of trust, or fraud; physical and sexual abuse under provisions such as criminal negligence causing bodily harm, assault, sexual assault, or failure to provide the necessities of life; and psychological abuse under provisions related to intimidation, uttering threats, or criminal harassment (Donovan & Regehr, 2010). Further, the Code does include a provision whereby the court must take into account for the purposes of sentencing whether the offense was motivated by age- or disability-based bias (Department of Justice Canada, 2007). Four Canadian provinces—Nova Scotia, New Brunswick, Prince Edward Island, and Newfoundland—have adult protection laws that cover elderly persons. These laws give specific health or social service departments responsibility to respond to abuse or neglect cases brought to their attention. However, in reviewing the use of these forms of legislation to protect older adults, the courts and policy analysts have expressed concerns that actions taken under the legislation are contrary to individual rights to liberty and self-determination. That is, cases have been reviewed where elderly people have been removed from the living situations determined to be neglectful or abusive and forcibly placed in institutional care (Gordon, 2001).

Therefore, the main controversy in the implementation of legislation to prevent elder abuse is the right of elderly individuals to self-determination and the understandable resistance to treating elderly individuals as essentially equivalent to children in need of protection.

At what point do people no longer have the right to determine how they will live, who they will live with, and how they will use their financial resources? When is a person incapacitated to the point that mandatory reporting of suspected abuse is warranted? As with other forms of court-mandated practice, these issues raise ethical, clinical, and civil liberties concerns for all those attempting to intervene in cases of abuse and neglect of elder people (Regehr & Antle, 1997).

■ Types of Elder Abuse

As with other forms of victimization that target a particular population, there are various types of elder abuse that are categorized based on the nature of the injury. **Table 12-1** describes the types of elder abuse.

Physical Abuse

Physical abuse includes any act of violence or the intentional inflicting of pain whether or not it results in physical injury. Obvious forms of physical abuse include beating, burning or scalding, pushing or shoving, hitting, or rough handling. However, it may also include tying an older person to furniture, misusing physical restraints, excessive restraint through drugs or alcohol, and confining him or her to rooms or spaces. Older adults who are frail may also suffer abuse within the context of the health care system, such as overmedication or performing a medical procedure without consent.

TABLE 12-1 **Types of Elder Abuse**

Type	Description	Examples
Physical	Any act of violence or the intentional inflicting of pain whether or not it results in physical injury	Hitting, misusing physical restraints or medication, forcible confinement
Neglect	Intentional or unintentional failure to care for or meet the needs of a dependent elderly person	Failing to provide adequate food, clothing, or shelter
Sexual	All forms of nonconsensual sexual activity	Rape, coerced nudity, and sexually explicit photography
Psychological	Attempts to dehumanize or intimidate older adults through verbal or nonverbal acts	Threats of violence or abandonment, lying, making insulting derogatory comments
Financial	Financial manipulation, exploitation, or dishonesty by a person in control	Homes sold without consent, checks cashed without authorization or via forged signatures, possessions stolen

Neglect

Neglect is the intentional or unintentional failure to care for or meet the needs of a dependent elderly person. Typically, this involves failing to provide adequate nutrition, clothing, and a safe, clean environment, resulting in dehydration, malnutrition, and poor hygiene. It can also involve the refusal to provide necessary medical care or leaving incapacitated elderly persons alone without proper care or supervision.

Sexual Abuse

Sexual abuse involves all forms of nonconsensual sexual activity. As with other populations, this may involve touching, rape, coerced nudity, and sexually explicit photography. Although this constitutes less than 1% of all elder abuse, it is nevertheless highly disturbing to imagine such abuse could occur. Ramsey-Klawsnik and colleagues (2007) identified five types of perpetrators of sexual abuse against elderly persons: (1) abuse by strangers or acquaintances, (2) abuse by care providers, (3) incestuous abuse, (4) marital or partner sexual abuse, and (5) sexual abuse perpetrated by another resident of a long-term care facility. In their research the vast majority of victims were female and were highly dependent. Almost all offenders were male, 81% were care providers, and 78% were family members, generally husbands or adult sons. About one-fourth of the assaults occurred within an institution.

Impairments, such as dementia, may be one factor that limits the ability of a victim to report and stop the abuse. For those who are in highly dependent situations, there may appear to be no safe way to report the abuse. In addition, like victims of sexual violence of any age, reporting the abuse is frequently experienced as humiliating, and victims fear their claims will not be believed (Ardovini, 2006). The rape or sexual assault of an elder is a felony. In some states the sentence for the crime carries special sanctions because of the victim's advanced age.

In an almost unbelievable case, two teenage female nursing home aides, Ashton Larson and Brianna Broitzman, were sentenced for sexually and psychologically abusing residents suffering from Alzheimer disease and other dementia disorders between January 1 and May 1, 2008 (Collin, 2010; Myfox.com, 2010). Police reports documented the perpetrators shut the residents' doors and pulled the privacy curtain that protected them from being observed and held the residents down, covered residents' mouths, pinched their breasts, applied pressure on their perineal area, and inserted their fingers into the residents' vaginas and/or rectums. Larson wept in court as families of her victims told a judge what her actions had done (Collin, 2010). During the time the abuse was noted to be occurring, the victimized residents had daily episodes of yelling and were rude, critical, verbally aggressive (swearing), and physically aggressive (hitting). However, after the perpetrators were suspended, the residents' mood was reported to dramatically improve.

Psychological Abuse

Psychological abuse is when an individual attempts to dehumanize or intimidate older adults through verbal or nonverbal acts. This can involve threats of violence or abandonment, lying, making insulting derogatory comments, ignoring or excessively criticizing, and treating the elders like servants or children. Other forms of psychological abuse can involve dismissive and isolating behavior where the person is simply treated as though he or she does not exist.

The impact of psychological abuse is more difficult to identify and quantify than abuse that causes physical or financial harm. Each person is affected differently by psychological abuse, with some being highly vulnerable and others being mostly unaffected. In addition, there is a cultural overlay in which behavior in one cultural context that may be viewed as minimally harmful or benign can, in another cultural context, be experienced as highly harmful. Tam and Neysmith (2006) provided an interesting analysis on the cultural basis of psychological abuse. In their study of elderly Chinese Canadians, psychological abuse took the form of disrespect, which violates the basic Chinese cultural norms of values and behaviors. In their study bossy, rude, or dismissive behavior of children or grandchildren and refusal to place the elderly person in a place of honor was considered to be highly damaging abuse that has no equivalent in Western culture.

Financial Abuse

Older adults can be vulnerable to financial manipulation or exploitation in such forms as fraud, theft, or forgery. At times, older adults' property or money is used in a dishonest manner or without consent. For example, homes can be sold without consent, checks can be cashed without authorization or via forged signatures, possessions can be stolen, or deception can be used to have the person sign **power of attorney** forms. Trusted individuals, such as health care providers, visitors to long-term care facilities, other residents, or relatives, may misappropriate funds while promising to act in the person's best interest.

Elderly persons are frequently targets of consumer fraud, telemarketing schemes, and identity theft because their isolation makes them vulnerable to deception (Nerenberg, 2006). A study of consumer fraud in a psychogeriatric population in Canada revealed that all victims were women with an average age of 85 years and all had designated power of attorney to another person who was unaware of the financial abuse (Cohen, 2006). These individuals are ideal victims for many reasons. Older women are of a generation that was not taught money management, and thus they frequently hand over financial issues to men. Older people frequently have significant financial resources and are motivated to donate to charitable causes, which in cases of fraud are not legitimate. Their isolation limits their ability to consult and determine the legitimacy of financial management companies or charitable organizations.

Stopping financial abuse and recovering property is extremely difficult. A possible means for protecting the financial resources of an elderly person is through awarding power of attorney to a trusted individual. A power of attorney is the authority granted by one person to another to act on behalf of the grantor in making personal (or financial) decisions for the grantor. A person may not act as a power of attorney for an individual if he or she is paid to provide health care, residential, social training, or support services to that individual, unless the person is the individual's spouse, partner, or relative. The authority given may be comprehensive or may be restricted to specific acts or types of decisions. The appointed attorney acts as a **fiduciary** and must act in concert with the wishes and best interests of the grantor. A person who is capable of giving a power of attorney may revoke it as long as he or she is still mentally capable (Hiltz & Szigeti, 2004; Regehr & Kanani, 2010). When the grantor has lost capacity, the power of attorney may be terminated if the appointed attorney resigns or by application to the court (Fowler, 2004).

■ Categories of Abusive Situations

Abuse of the elderly occurs both as a result of actions or inactions of family members, intimate partners, institutional caregivers, and, on rarer occasions, strangers to the victim.

Spousal Violence as Elder Abuse

As noted earlier, spouses make up a substantial percentage of elder abusers, and frequently these are within relationships where there is a history of one member exerting control over the other through intimidation and violence. In a stratified random sample of 2,000 community members older than age 65 years, Pillemer and Finkelhor (1988) discovered that 58% of perpetrators of sexual abuse were intimate partners. As indicated earlier,

Statistics Canada (2007) data suggest that older women are almost twice as likely as older men to be killed by their spouses.

Women of the elder generation preceded public awareness and outrage regarding intimate partner violence. By the time the issue of woman abuse was recognized in the late 1970s, these women had raised their children. The emerging shelters aimed at protecting women and their young children were not geared toward them. The empowerment messages of the feminist movement against intimate partner violence were not directed toward them. To many in the youth movement, these women were part of a generation of oppressors. Later, when elder abuse became an issue of concern in the late 1980s, the attention was focused on those who were abused outside of the marital relationship (Fisher & Regan, 2006).

Older women who are victims of intimate partner violence have many experiences that are similar to those of their younger counterparts. However, they additionally face challenges related to isolation, social roles, and income (Desmarais & Reeves, 2007). Older women are less likely to have independent sources of income. They are less likely than younger women to have higher education, were not encouraged to enter the workforce until after the end of World War II, and in fact were encouraged to relinquish jobs they may have had during the war to returning veterans. As a result, they frequently have no pensions beyond that offered through the federal government. Older women were raised in an era where divorce was a source of shame, whereas today, considering the high divorce rates, it has almost become a developmental stage in adulthood. These elder women became wives and mothers in the prefeminist era when gender roles were more strictly defined and marriage and family were the primary, and perhaps only, responsibilities of women. Many have never lived alone. Many have never learned independent skills at managing finances, negotiating contracts (such as leases), or interacting with lawyers. Although many women in abusive relationships experience tremendous obstacles to leaving and ensuring their own safety, older women often feel more trapped and have fewer resources and options on which to rely.

Abuse by Adult Children and Relatives

Motivations to care for an elderly relative are often multifaceted. Some individuals may view the cost of nursing home care to be a waste of the elderly person's assets, which would otherwise be inherited. At times, the elderly person may be able to contribute to the household through housework, cooking, or child care, although in time this may be limited by physical or mental infirmity. Other individuals provide care to their elderly relatives out of a sense of love, duty, or obligation (Fryling, Summers, & Hoffman, 2006). Similarly, elderly persons may elect to live with a relative because they have no alternative and choose not to live in an institution or because they truly desire to live their lives with their children and grandchildren. In situations where a relative (most often a child) cares for an elderly person, often a type of role reversal ensues; the parent becomes the dependent. The caregiver experiences more obligations and less time for other responsibilities or interests. Both the elderly person and his or her caregiver(s) experience less privacy. Regardless of the initial motivations for caring, if the arrangement becomes abusive and violent, the lack of autonomy experienced by the elderly person can make it very difficult to end the abuse.

Research has demonstrated two main types within the category of children as abusers. In the first type, adult child abusers, individuals are dependent on their victims for financial assistance, housing, and other supports. This is frequently because of personal problems, including mental illness, substance abuse, and dysfunctional personality characteristics. As a result, the adult child as caregiver has a decreased ability to tolerate stress and frustration and controls the elderly relative through violence and abuse (Gordon & Brill, 2001). Financial abuse in these cases may result from a need for money to support a drug habit, gambling, or a generally dysfunctional lifestyle. In such situations there may also be a longstanding history of difficult relationships, perhaps involving the parent historically abusing the child. Alternately, the child may have witnessed violence between his or her parents and learned this is the method to deal with stress, anxiety, and frustration (Hightower, Smith, & Hightower, 2006). The adult child abuser has few resources on which to draw, and the abusive behavior is generally consistent with his or her other interactions with the world.

The following clinical case example illustrates this type of abuse. Iris was 80 years of age and continued to live in a relatively spacious apartment above the store in which she worked for 42 years on a main street of a large city. She suffered from diabetes and quite advanced arthritis that limited her ability to walk down the stairs from her second-floor apartment. In her younger years Iris supported both herself and her two sons on her income from her job as a sales clerk. Her husband, an abusive alcoholic, had suffered a brain injury in his early 30s, which Iris believed may have been caused by substance abuse or may have been a stroke. As a result he was significantly disabled. Because of his highly abusive behavior toward her, Iris refused to take him home, and he remained institutionalized for the remainder of his life. Two years earlier Iris's son,

Paul, returned to live with his mother. Paul had a long history of substance abuse like his father and throughout his life worked in a series of jobs, including short order cook, bartender, and waiter. He had a series of short-term relationships, and when he returned to his mother's home at the age of 50 years, he had just separated from his current common-law wife and lost his job. After moving in Paul had his mother's phone number changed so she would not "be bothered by other people who just wanted to use her." He decided to get rid of some of her prized possessions because they "took up too much room in the apartment." Paul intercepted his mother's mail and cashed her checks so he could "buy groceries and her medications," but very scarce amounts of food actually came into the home, and he "forgot" to buy her medication. This left her in significant pain and further limited her mobility and her ability to care for her personal needs. When Iris would protest, Paul would yell at her, demean her, and berate her for "robbing" him of a father when he was growing up. Finally, Iris collapsed due to inadequate control of her diabetes, and Paul phoned an ambulance to take her to the hospital, where she disclosed her situation.

A second type of adult children as abusers can emerge as a result of caregiver stress caused by the demands of caring for an individual who may suffer from dementia or other illnesses that manifest themselves in a high need for physical care or disruptive behaviors. In these situations the caregiver may strike out and assault the person for whom they are caring. A significant degree of caregiver stress has emerged from the results of government policies that focus on deinstitutionalization or the movement of care of elderly and infirm individuals from institutional care to the community. Part of this move has been ideological, that is, it is better for individuals to be in the community. However, part of this move has also been financial in that community-based care is far less expensive than institutional care. The lower cost is in large part due to limited resources flowing to community care and a reliance on family members to take over care responsibilities.

Caregiver burden is the negative impact on one's social, occupational, and personal well-being as a result of caring for an infirm person, usually a relative. The greatest area of research regarding caregiver burden is with caregivers of elderly individuals with dementia. The burden experienced by caregivers of those with Alzheimer disease or other forms of dementia results from functional deficits of the ill person, the degree to which the ill person depends on family members for personal care (such as hygiene), disorientation of the ill person, and difficult behaviors such as wandering and aggression (Sussman, 2006). As a result of this burden, family members often experience depression and a variety of physical health problems related to stress (Gonzalez Salvador, Arango, Lyketsos, & Barba, 1999). In one study of family caregivers for individuals with Alzheimer disease, the most common form of senile dementia, 65% exhibited symptoms of depression (Papastavrou, Kalokerinou, Papacostas, Tsangari, & Sourtizi, 2007). Certainly only a small percentage of those caring for individuals with Alzheimer disease or other forms of dementia abuse their family members, and thus stress cannot be equated with abuse. However, familial caregivers who strike out against those with dementia are more likely to suffer from low self-esteem and clinical depression (McDonald, Collins, & Dergal, 2006).

Institutionally Based Abuse

CBS News reported the tragic case of Mrs. Helen Love, who had been attacked by a staff member in the nursing home in which she resided (CBS News, 2000). On a visit to their mother, her sons Bruce and Gary discovered bruises on her neck, chin, and legs. When they questioned the injuries, they were informed her injuries were caused by her "medical illnesses." Upon examination in a local emergency room, at the insistence of her sons, it was discovered that Mrs. Love had a dislocated neck and a broken wrist in addition to the visible bruises.

In an interview with police, Mrs. Love revealed a nursing home attendant, Tim Saelee, had attacked her in retribution for soiling herself. She reported, "He got real ferocious and started beating me all around the bed," said Helen Love. "He choked me and went and broke my neck . . . and broke my wrist," she said. Mrs. Love believed she survived only by playing dead. Two days after she was interviewed on videotape, Helen Love died. Saelee pled guilty to assault and received 1 year in jail. Although this was his first conviction, it was not his first accusation of abuse. At previous times he was warned and fired for abusive behavior (CBS News, 2000).

Institutional abuse refers to older adults who are abused while they are residents of long-term care facilities. A relatively small percentage of older adults live in institutional environments (7% of older adults in Canada), and this may be one reason institutional abuse has been less a subject of examination than community-based abuse (McDonald, 2007). Nevertheless, by definition these are the most vulnerable elderly individuals because their need to live in institutions demonstrates their need for care and protection.

In a survey of 577 nurses and nurse's aides conducted in the United States, 36% of participants reported having seen at least one incident of physical abuse perpetrated by a staff member of an institution in the past year, most frequently the inappropriate use of restraints. Eighty-one percent reported seeing at least one incident of psychological abuse in the past year, most frequently yelling at the older person (Pillemer & Moore, 1989). Most surprising about this study was that 10% of staff members admitted to having committed physical abuse and 40% admitted to psychological abuse (mostly yelling). A report from the Committee on Government Reform of the U.S. House of Representatives (2001) indicated that over 30% of nursing homes in the United States had been cited for abuse.

The causes of institutional abuse are complex, but McDonald (2007) reported the results of several studies that point to the following factors:

- Lack of comprehensive policies governing care in institutions for the elderly and poor enforcement standards
- The financial structure of institutions for the elderly reward low-cost measures that often result in poor care
- Lack of qualified, well-trained staff in part due to poor wages and stressful working conditions
- Vulnerability of the residents and/or resident aggression toward staff
- Detrimental organizational culture and staff burnout

Flowing from these causes, prevention of abuse and neglect of elderly persons in institutions is relatively straightforward. The National Center on Elder Abuse (2005) recommends coordination between law enforcement and adult protection workers, education and training of nursing home workers on managing behavior and conflict resolution, improved working conditions in long-term care institutions, strict enforcement of mandatory reporting, improved hiring practices and compliance with federal requirements regarding staffing, and the support and strengthening of residents' councils.

Investigations of allegations of institutionally based elder abuse are complex. Nursing homes do not promptly report allegations of sexual or physical abuse, which results in delays in the investigation. Often, evidence has been compromised and investigations delayed, which results in a reduced likelihood of a successful prosecution (Burgess, Prentky, & Dowdell, 2000). Reasons for untimely reporting of allegations are as follows: (1) residents may fear retribution if they report the abuse, (2) family members are troubled with having to find a new place because the nursing home may ask the resident to leave, (3) staff members do not report abuse promptly for fear of losing their jobs and recrimination from coworkers and management, and (4) nursing homes want to avoid negative publicity and sanctions from the state.

Societal Neglect

Although not traditionally viewed as a form of elder abuse, the neglectful practices of a society can also be highly abusive to vulnerable elderly individuals. A striking example occurred in August 2003 when a heat wave swept through southern Europe and temperatures rose to 40°C (104°F). The sweltering temperatures hit those most vulnerable, elderly individuals with health problems and limited mobility. By the end of the heat wave scientists at Inserm (the National Institute for Health and Medical Research), using data supplied by funeral directors, deduced that 14,802 more deaths occurred in that 3-week period than would have been expected in an average year. Almost all who died were elderly individuals who suffered from dehydration and hyperthermia. The heat wave hit when most of France was on annual vacation and large numbers of doctors, nurses, and hospital staff were away. Many bodies were not claimed for several weeks because relatives were on vacation. Others were never claimed, and on September 3, 2003, 57 unclaimed bodies were buried in Paris. In the end the government of France was forced to admit that many of its 4.6 million people aged 75 years and older were ignored and left to fend for themselves or die (CNN, 2003; Crumley, 2003; "France heat wave," 2003).

Sexual Assault

Sexual assault against elderly persons is similar in many ways to sexual violence committed against people at all stages of life. However, the particular nature of the victim often belies general attitudes the public may hold for causes of sexual violence. Frequently, these views include victim-blaming attitudes, which people find more difficult to apply to elderly victims. Burgess, Commons, Safarik, Looper, and Ross (2007) presented a typology of motivations for sexual violence against the elderly based on the typologies for sexual offenders originally proposed by Prentky, Cohen, and Seghorn (1985). In their study they classified 77 convicted sexual offenders of elderly victims.

TYPOLOGIES OF SEXUAL OFFENDERS AGAINST THE ELDERLY   Burgess and colleagues (2007) identified several types of sexual offenders against elders:

- *Opportunistic rapists:* An opportunistic motive pertains to an impulsive rapist type who shows little planning or preparation. The offender usually has a history of unsocialized behavior, and the rape serves as an example of the degree to which the rapist lacks interpersonal awareness. These rapists show no concern for the welfare or comfort of their victims. The rape is for immediate sexual gratification rather than the enactment of a highly developed fantasy or sexualized ritual. The rape is in the service of dominance and power. In the Burgess and colleagues study (2007), 13% of offenders fell into this category. Interestingly, offenders in this classification often claimed not to have penetrated the victim but rather committed acts of fondling, kissing, and molestation. In this way these offenses are similar in nature to the sexual act committed by some child molesters.

- *Pervasive anger rapists:* Pervasive anger is a second typology of elder rape in which the use of force is excessive and gratuitous, represented by 22% of the offenders in the Burgess and colleagues study sample (2007). The violence for this group is an integrated component of the behavior even when the victim is compliant. Resistance from the victim is likely to increase the level of aggression where serious injury or death may occur. The rage is not sexualized, suggesting the assault is not fantasy driven. The violence is a lifestyle characteristic that is directed toward males and females alike. The rape is but one feature in a history of unsocialized aggressive behavior noted across various social settings.

- *Sexual-type rapists:* In sexual-type motivations, there is a high degree of preoccupation with gratifying one's sexual needs. This was represented by 40% of the offenders in the Burgess et al. study (2007). Sexual preoccupation is typically evidenced by highly intrusive, recurrent sexual and rape fantasies, frequent use of pornography, reports of frequent uncontrollable sexual urges, use of a variety of alternative outlets for gratifying sexual needs (e.g., massage parlors, X-rated movies, sex clubs, strip bars), and engaging in other deviant sexual behaviors (paraphilias), such as voyeurism, exhibitionism, or fetishism. The sexual assaults of these offenders are often well planned, as evidenced by a clear, scripted sequence of events, possession of assault-related paraphernalia, and an apparent plan to procure the victim and elude apprehension after the assault. Sexual-type rapists include sexual sadistic rapists and sexual nonsadistic rapists:

  - *Sexual sadistic rapists:* These rapists intend to inflict fear or pain on the victim and manifest a high level of aggression. The cardinal feature is the intertwining or fusing of the two feelings such that an increase in one leads to an increase in the other. There are two subgroups in the sexual sadistic rapist category:
    - *Overtly sadistic rapists:* These rapists appear to be angry, belligerent people who, except for their sadism and the greater planning of their sexual assaults, seem to be very similar to the pervasive anger rapists.

- *Muted sadistic rapists:* For muted sadistic rapists the victim's fear or discomfort, or the fantasy of violence, contributes to the offender's sexual arousal (or does not inhibit such arousal), and the amount of physical force used in the sexual assault does not exceed what is necessary to gain victim compliance. Symbolic expressions of sadistic fantasy characterize these offenders, who may use various forms of bondage or restraint, noninjurious insertion of foreign objects, and other sexual aids, such as a lubricant or shaving cream. What is absent is the high level of expressive aggression that is clearly manifest in the overt sadism type. In general, muted sadistic offenders, except for their sadistic fantasies and their slightly higher lifestyle impulsivity, resemble the highly socially competent, nonsadistic rapists.

- *Sexual nonsadistic rapists:* For these rapists the thoughts and fantasies associated with their sexual assaults are devoid of the synergistic relationship between sex and aggression that characterizes the sadistic types. Indeed, these two rapist types are hypothesized to manifest less aggression than any of the other rapist types. If confronted with victim resistance, sexual nonsadistic rapists may flee rather than force the victim to comply. Their fantasies and behaviors are hypothesized to reflect sexual arousal, distorted male cognitions about women and sexuality, feelings of social and sexual inadequacy, and lack of masculine self-image. Compared to the other rapist types, these offenders have relatively few problems with impulse control in domains outside of sexual aggression.

- *Vindictive-type rapists:* These rapists have a core feature of anger at women. Unlike pervasive anger rapists, women are the central and exclusive focus of vindictive rapists' anger. Their sexual assaults are marked by behaviors that are physically injurious and appear to be intended to degrade, demean, and humiliate their victims. The misogynistic anger evident in these assaults runs the gamut from verbal abuse to brutal murder. As noted, these offenders differ from pervasive anger rapists in that they show little or no evidence of anger toward men (e.g., instigating fights with or assaulting men). This group constituted 21% of the Burgess et al. sample (2007).

■ Assessment of Elder Abuse

Although health care practitioners are most likely to be in a position to identify abuse in an elderly person, everyone has an obligation to ensure vulnerable individuals in our society are safe from harm. This moral

TABLE 12-2 **Factors Associated with Risk of Abuse**

Factor	Description and Examples
Physical impairment	Elderly individuals with poorer health or limited mobility are at higher risk of abuse.
	Physically impaired individuals are less able to defend themselves.
Mental health problems	Clinical depression is associated with financial and psychological abuse.
	Victims of abuse are more likely to suffer from mental health problems.
	Alcohol abuse is associated with aggressive behavior in perpetrators of elder abuse.
Cognitive impairment	Cognitively impaired adults are at greater risk of abuse.
	Cognitively impaired individuals often cannot report abuse.
	Dementia in an elderly person may cause increased caregiver stress.
Lack of social support	Social contact can diffuse tension and allow others to monitor behavior.
	Social dependency on caregivers increases risk of abuse.

Data from GAO. 2011. Elder Justice. Report of the Chairman, Special Committee on Aging, US Senate. GAO-11-208.

obligation is reinforced by legislation enacted in several jurisdictions requiring people in a range of occupations to report suspected elder abuse. Several factors shown in **Table 12-2** are associated with increased risk of abuse and should be considered when abuse is suspected (U.S. Government Accountability Office, 2011).

In addition to general factors that may lead one to suspect abuse, a number of tools exist that assist with identification of abuse; some require training and others are simple to administer without training (Fulmer, Guadagno, Bitondo, & Connolly, 2004). One of the most user-friendly tools is distilled into six short screening questions found in **Table 12-3** (Bomba, 2006; Fulmer et al., 2004). The use of these questions not only

TABLE 12-3 **Elder Abuse Screening Survey**

1. Are you afraid of anyone in your family?
2. Has anyone close to you tried to hurt or harm you recently?
3. Has anyone close to you called you names, put you down, or made you feel bad recently?
4. Does someone in your family make you stay in bed or tell you you're sick when you aren't?
5. Has anyone forced you to do things you did not want to do?
6. Has anyone taken things that belong to you without your permission?

Data from Bomba, P. 2006. Use of a single page elder abuse assessment and management tool: A practical clinician's approach to identifying elder mistreatment. In J. Mellor & P. Brownell (Eds.), *Elder abuse and mistreatment: Policy, practice and research* (pp. 103–122). Birmingham, NY: Haworth Press; and Fulmer, T., Guadagno, L., Bitondo, C., & Connolly, M. 2004. Progress in elder abuse screening and assessment instruments. *Journal of the American Geriatrics Society, 52*(2), 297–304.

identifies abuse but demonstrates an openness to discussing issues of abuse and the desire to offer assistance.

If elder abuse is suspected, there are three issues to consider (Bomba, 2006):

- Is the person safe?
- Will the person accept intervention?
- Does the person have the capacity to refuse intervention?

Not all abuse situations constitute an emergency; thus, if the person is safe, it is possible to develop a longer-term relationship and move toward a plan to end the abuse if the person agrees to intervention. If the person does not agree to allow assistance, intervention can be forced only if the person does not have the capacity to consent to or refuse intervention. That is, people are allowed the self-determination to remain in abusive situations if they fully understand the nature and consequences of their decision. If they are not competent to consent or refuse, other options, such as adult protective services, can be called in to assist.

■ Interventions

Intervention strategies with regard to elder abuse fall into several categories, including prevention programs, adult protection programs, and domestic violence programs. Each intervention strategy is based on a particular view of the causes of elder abuse. For example, domestic violence programs target elder abuse as a form of family violence and focus on intimate partner or spousal violence, and adult protective services focus on vulnerability and often intervene when the abuser is an adult child or community caregiver.

Prevention Programs

One form of prevention attempts to address family stress caused by caregiving. In this approach increased services are offered in the community, such as community nursing day treatment programs for elderly individuals with physical disabilities (for example, caused by stroke) or dementia. The notion is that increased services will result in reduced stress and burden, which in turn will reduce abuse caused by caregiver stress. A study of spousal caregivers of people with dementia, however, suggested that services alone do not provide a simple solution to caregiver stress. Using interviews and surveys, Sussman and Regehr (2009) found that in-home services, such as homemakers, nurses, occupational therapists, and case managers, did little to reduce the burden of spouses who care for their partners with dementia. In fact, the stress of dealing with multiple service delivery people in the home created additional stress for some.

Rather, the only effective service in reducing caregiver stress in this study was the provision of adult day treatment programs (sometimes referred to as day care), which provided not only respite for the spousal caregivers but also opportunities for social interaction for their partners with dementia (Sussman & Regehr, 2009). Thus, investment in day treatment would seem to be an effective means for reducing elder abuse caused by stress.

Another form of prevention focuses more on education. The premise behind this approach is that, as with child abuse and spousal assault, increased knowledge by service providers, community members, and victims themselves will result in early detection, increased reporting, and therefore increased safety. In some jurisdictions specific interventions have been established and have met with success. New York City's Domestic Violence Prevention Project (DVPP) began in 1983 as a joint program of the police and victim services. In this program a police officer and a domestic violence counselor visit homes a few days after the police have responded to a domestic violence emergency call. The counselor meets with the victim to discuss the abuse and establish a safety plan. The police officer meets with the offender, if possible, and informs the offender the police are watching the household. There is evidence that this project is successful in assisting the victim to contact the police, but it does not result in lower levels of violence (Davis & Medina-Ariza, 2001). Although elder abuse cases were theoretically included in the DVPP model, in most situations in which the DVPP intervened, the victims were younger spouses. Subsequently, an elder abuse prevention project was initiated where public education about elder abuse was distributed to 30 of 60 public housing projects in New York City. If cases were reported to police, the DVPP attended and provided service. These interventions saw a significant increase in reports of abuse both to the police and to researchers who asked about the incidence of abuse. Hopefully the increased reporting indicated an increased awareness among elderly persons of their rights and an increased willingness to seek assistance.

Adult Protection Programs

Mandatory reporting laws and adult protective services are integrally linked. That is, as previously stated, most jurisdictions require professionals of varying types to report suspected elder abuse. This report, in turn, triggers an assessment and possible intervention by adult protective services. At this point an adult protective services worker generally investigates the report of abuse and determines the most appropriate course of intervention. When an elderly person is determined to be abused and he or she agrees to the intervention, safety plans and alternate living arrangements can be initiated. The problem arises when the person is unwilling to agree to the intervention. In such cases a determination must be made whether the individual is competent to consent. For a person to have the capacity to consent, the person must be able to understand information that is provided to him or her and how that information applies to his or her specific situation. The Ontario Health Care Consent Act (1996), for example, states that a person is capable of consenting to treatment if "the person is able to understand the information that is relevant to making a decision about the treatment . . . and able to appreciate the reasonably foreseeable consequences of a decision or lack of decision" (s. 4(1)). Capacity is not viewed as a blanket status; it is specific to a particular procedure and particular time frame. Thus, a person may be incapable of consenting to some treatments yet capable of consenting to others. For example, a person may be able to consent to such procedures as blood work but not to major procedures such as cardiac surgery. In addition, consent is fluid. A person may be capable of consenting to a particular procedure at one time but incapable of consenting to the same procedure at another time (Regehr & Kanani, 2010). As a result of the complexities around the issue of consent and the risk of undermining the civil rights and self-determination of elderly individuals, adult protective services as an approach to elder abuse remains highly controversial (Anderson & Mangels, 2006).

Domestic Violence Programs

Domestic violence programs as an approach to elder abuse are modeled on woman abuse intervention programs. They can include telephone hotlines, criminal charges against offenders that are made by police, protection orders, emergency shelters, and counseling services for both victims and offenders (McDonald, 2007). For example, changes in the criminal justice system in the United States include laws to enhance sentences in elder abuse cases, training programs for police and judges, and special units within police departments and prosecutors offices to deal with cases of elder abuse (Anderson & Mangels, 2006). Problems with this approach also mirror those in domestic violence, including the inadequacy of restraining orders, the reluctance of police to criminalize domestic matters, and shortage of resources for intervention and shelter (McDonald, 2007).

A program established in New York City, called Hebrew Home, is an excellent example of a domestic violence model of service. This center uses a multidisciplinary team approach, which includes the district attorneys' offices, adult protective services, a medical center, and an advocacy organization. Services offered by the center include legal advocacy, short-term emergency housing, long-term care planning and possible admission, education and support for caregivers, public education and training, meals-on-wheels, and law enforcement training (Reingold, 2006). This integrated system provides a spectrum of services that address immediate safety needs and long-term needs for ongoing care or intervention.

■ Summary

The abuse and neglect of the elderly—either by a society that fails to adopt health, legal, and social service measures to meet the needs of older people; by staff members in institutions who have a fiduciary responsibility for vulnerable older people; or by relatives who are either stressed by or take advantage of vulnerability—is perhaps one of the saddest secrets of most societies. Our seniors worked to develop our societies into the form they take today, they nurtured and educated our leaders, and they created our economies. Yet aging is a dreaded outcome of living, and the elderly are often relegated to insignificant roles and are viewed as a burden. Added to these prejudices are issues related to vulnerability and autonomy. Although we can all agree the vulnerability of children justifies mandated protection services, as societies we are less clear when an older person loses the right to individual choice and the need for protection takes precedence. In recent years many countries have moved to address these issues, but as yet there is no perfect solution.

■ Key Terms

Alzheimer disease: A slowly progressive disease of the brain characterized by impairment of memory and eventually by disturbances in reasoning, planning, language, and perception.

Cognitively impaired: A brain disorder in which thinking abilities are impaired.

Dementia: A condition in which memory loss has progressed to such a point that normal independent functioning is impossible and affected individuals can no longer successfully manage their finances or provide for their own basic needs.

Elder abuse: Any physical, sexual, verbal, psychological, or financial abuse perpetrated against an older adult.

Fiduciary: A business or person who may act for another with total trust, good faith, and honesty and who has the complete confidence and trust of that person.

Medically fragile: Individuals who have *medically* intensive needs that usually result in chronic health-related dependence.

Power of attorney: Authority granted by one person to another to empower the grantee to make financial and health care decisions on the grantor's behalf.

Psychological abuse: When an individual attempts to dehumanize or intimidate older adults through verbal or nonverbal acts.

■ Discussion Questions

1. What social policies protect older persons from abuse?
2. What challenges are faced when attempting to address allegations of abuse in nursing homes?
3. If an educational program is to be focused on assisting elderly people to find assistance if they are abused, what would be the most effective messages to convey?
4. What factors differentiate the assault and abuse of the elderly from similar assaults and abuse of people in other age groups?

■ Resources

Canadian Network for the Prevention of Elder Abuse
  http://www.cnpea.ca/

National Center on Elder Abuse
  http://www.ncea.aoa.gov/ncearoot/Main_Site/index.aspx

National Committee for the Prevention of Elder Abuse
  http://www.preventelderabuse.org/elderabuse/

World Health Organization, Elder Abuse
  http://www.who.int/ageing/projects/elder_abuse/en/

■ References

Adams, J., & Calloway, M. (2009) Convicted Sex Offenders: New Responsibilities for Long-Term Care Facilities. Virginia Department of Health Office of Licensure and Certification. Retrieved from *www.vhca.org/IlluminAgeApps/whatsnewApp/files/69383C9C6.pdf*

American Bar Association Commission on Law and Aging. (2005). *Information about laws related to elder abuse.* Newark, DE: National Center on Elder Abuse.

Amstadter, A., Cisler, J., McCauley, J., Hernandez, M., Muzzy, W., & Acierno, R. (2010). Do incident and perpetrator characteristics of elder mistreatment differ by gender of the victim? Results from the National Elder Mistreatment Study. *Journal of Elder Abuse & Neglect, 23*(1), 43–57.

Anderson, J., & Mangels, N. (2006). Helping victims: Social services, health care interventions in elder abuse. In R. Summers & A. Hoffman (Eds.), *Elder abuse: A public health perspective* (pp. 139–166). Washington, DC: American Public Health Association.

Arai, M. (2006). Elder abuse in Japan. *Educational Gerontology, 32*(1), 13–23.

Ardovini, J. (2006). Sexual violence against older women. In R. Summers & A. Hoffman (Eds.), *Elder abuse: A public health perspective* (pp. 131–138). Washington, DC: American Public Health Association.

Associated Press. (2008, June 18). Governor signs sexual predator bill. Retrieved from http://www.tulsaworld.com/news/article .aspx?articleID=20080610_12_OKLAH04125

Beach, S., Schultz, R., Castle, N., & Rosen, J. (2010). Financial exploitation and psychological maltreatment among older adults: Differences between African Americans and non-African Americans in a population based survey. *Gerontologist, 50*(6), 744–757.

Bezerra-Flanders, W., & Clark, J. (2006). Perspectives on elder abuse and neglect in Brazil. *Educational Gerontology, 32*(1), 63–72.

Bomba, P. (2006). Use of a single page elder abuse assessment and management tool: A practical clinician's approach to identifying elder mistreatment. In J. Mellor & P. Brownell (Eds.), *Elder abuse and mistreatment: Policy, practice and research* (pp. 103–122). Birmingham, NY: Haworth Press.

Burgess, A., Prentky, R., & Dowdell, E. (2000). Sexual predators in nursing homes. *Journal of Psychosocial Nursing, 38*, 9–17.

Burgess, A.W., Commons, M.L., Safarik, M.E., Looper, R.R., & Ross, S.N. (2007). Sex offenders of the elderly: Typology and predictors of severity of crime. *Aggression and Violent Behavior, 12*, 582–597.

Catalano, L., & Lazaro, C. (2008). Financial abuse of the elderly: Protecting the vulnerable. *PIABA Law Journal,* 1–15.

CBS News. (2000, December 27). Tracking abuse in nursing homes. Retrieved from http://www.cbsnews.com/stories/2002/01/31/health/main327525 .shtml

CNN. (2003, August 29). French heat toll tops 11,000. Retrieved from http:// www.cnn.com/2003/WORLD/europe/08/29/france.heatdeaths/

Cohen, C. (2006). Consumer fraud and the elderly: A review of Canadian challenges and initiatives. In J. Mellor & P. Brownell (Eds.), *Elder abuse and mistreatment: Policy, practice and research* (pp. 137–144). Birmingham, NY: Haworth Press.

Cohen, T. (2011). Mickey Rooney tells Senate panel that he was the victim of elder abuse. Retrieved from http://articles.cnn.com/2011-03-02 /entertainment/rooney.elderly.abuse_1_elder-abuse-marie-therese-connolly-elder-population?_s=PM:SHOWBIZ

Collin, L. (2010). 2nd Nursing home worker sentenced for abuse. Retrieved from http://minnesota.cbslocal.com/2010/12/22/2nd-nursing-home-worker-sentenced-for-abuse/

Committee on Government Reform of the U.S. House of Representatives. (2001). Abuse of residents is a major problem in US nursing homes. Retrieved from http://oversight.house.gov/documents/20040830113750-34049.pdf

Crumley, B. (2003, August 24). Elder careless. Retrieved from http://www.time.com/time/magazine/article/0,9171,901030901-477899,00.html

Davis, R., & Medina-Ariza, J. (2001). *Results from an elder abuse prevention experiment in New York City.* National Institute of Justice: Research in Brief. Washington, DC: U.S. Department of Justice.

Department of Justice Canada. (2007). Abuse of older adults. Retrieved from http://www.justice.gc.ca/en/ps/fm/adultsfs.html

Desmarais, S., & Reeves, K. (2007). Gray, black and blue: The state of research and intervention for intimate partner abuse among elders. *Behavioral Sciences and the Law, 25,* 377–391.

Dong, X., & Simon, M. (2011). Enhancing national policy and programs to address elder abuse. *Journal of the American Medical Association, 305*(23), 2460–2461.

Donovan, K., & Regehr, C. (2010). Elder abuse: Clinical, ethical and legal issues in social work practice. *Clinical Social Work Journal, 38*(2), 174–182.

Dubble, C. (2006). A policy perspective on elder justice through APS and law enforcement collaboration. *Journal of Gerontological Social Work, 46*(3/4), 35–55.

Elder Justice Coalition. (2011). Elder Justice Act. Retrieved from http://elderjusticecoalition.com/legislation.htm

Fisher, B., & Regan, S. (2006). The extent and frequency of abuse in the lives of older women and their relationship with health outcomes. *Gerontologist, 46,* 200–209.

Fowler, L. (2004). *Powers of attorney.* Toronto, Ontario, Canada: Law Society of Upper Canada.

France heat wave death toll set at 14,802. (2003, September 25). Retrieved from http://www.usatoday.com/weather/news/2003-09-25-france-heat_x.htm

Freeman, D. (2011). Mickey Rooney: Elder abuse victim? Retrieved from http://www.cbsnews.com/8301-504763_162-20032211-10391704.html

Fryling, T., Summers, R., & Hoffman, A. (2006). Elder abuse: Definition and scope of the problem. In R. Summers & A. Hoffman (Eds.), *Elder abuse:*

A public health perspective (pp. 5–18). Washington, DC: American Public Health Association.

Fulmer, T., Guadagno, L., Bitondo, C., & Connolly, M. (2004). Progress in elder abuse screening and assessment instruments. *Journal of the American Geriatrics Society, 52*(2), 297–304.

Gonzalez-Salvador, M., Arango, C., Lyketsos, C., & Barba, A. (1999). The stress and psychological morbidity of the Alzheimer patient caregiver. *International Journal of Geriatric Psychiatry, 14*, 701–710.

Gordon, R. (2001). Adult protection legislation in Canada: Models, issues and problems. *International Journal of Law and Psychiatry, 24*, 117–134.

Gordon, R., & Brill, D. (2001). The abuse and neglect of the elderly. *International Journal of Law and Psychiatry, 24*, 183–197.

Health Care Consent Act. (1996). S.O. 1996, C.2.

Hightower, J., Smith, M., & Hightower, H. (2006). Hearing the voices of older abused women. In J. Mellor & P. Brownell (Eds.), *Elder abuse and mistreatment: Policy, practice and research* (pp. 205–227). Birmingham, NY: Haworth Press.

Hiltz, D., & Szigeti, A. (2004). *A guide to consent and capacity law in Ontario.* Toronto, Ontario, Canada: LexisNexis Canada.

König, J., & Leembruggen-Kallberg, E. (2006). Perspectives on elder abuse in Germany. *Educational Gerontology, 32*(1), 25–35.

Laumann, E., Leitsch, S., & Waite, L. (2008). Elder mistreatment in the United States: Prevalence estimates from a nationally representative study. *Journal of Gerontological Behavioral, Psychological Sciences and Social Sciences, 63*(4), S248–S254.

McDonald, L. (2007). Elder abuse and neglect. In E. Birren (Ed.), *The encyclopedia of gerontology* (2nd ed., Vol. 1, pp. 1–10). New York: Academic Press.

McDonald, L., Collins, A., & Dergal, J. (2006). The abuse and neglect of older adults in Canada. In R. Alaggia & C. Vine (Eds.), *Cruel but not unusual: Violence in Canadian families: A sourcebook for educators & practitioners* (pp. 624–688). Waterloo, Ontario, Canada: Wilfrid Laurier University Press.

Mickey Rooney. (2011). Biography. Retrieved from http://www.mickeyrooney.com/biography.html

Mickey Rooney claims to be elder abuse victim. (2011). Retrieved from http://www.thestar.com/entertainment/article/947875--mickey-rooney-claims-to-be-elder-abuse-victim

Mickey Rooney speaks out against elder abuse. (2011). Retrieved from http://www.theglobeandmail.com/news/arts/video/mickey-rooney-speaks-out-against-elder-abuse/article1927308/

Myfox.com. (2010). Sentencing in Alberta Lea nursing home abuse. Retrieved from http://www.myfoxtwincities.com/dpp/news/minnesota/sentencing-in-albert-lea-nursing-home-abuse-oct–22–2010

National Center on Elder Abuse. (2005). *Nursing Home Abuse Risk Prevention Profile and Checklist.* U.S. Administration on Aging. Retrieved from www.ncea.aoa.gov/main_site/pdf/publication/NursingHomeRisk.pdf

Nerenberg, L. (2006). Communities respond to elder abuse. *Journal of Gerontological Social Work, 46*(3/4), 5–33.

Papastavrou, E., Kalokerinou, A., Papacostas, S., Tsangari, H., & Sourtizi, P. (2007). Caring for a relative with dementia: Family caregiver burden. *Journal of Advanced Nursing, 58*(5), 446–457.

Pillemer, K., & Finkelhor, D. (1988). The prevalence of elder abuse: A random sample survey. *Gerontologist, 28*, 51–57.

Pillemer, K., & Moore, D. (1989). Abuse of patients in nursing homes: Findings from a staff survey. *Gerontologist, 29*(3), 321–327.

Prentky, R.A., Cohen, M.L., & Seghorn, T.K. (1985). Development of a rational taxonomy for the classification of sexual offenders: Rapists. *Bulletin of the American Academy of Psychiatry and the Law, 13*, 39–70.

Rabi, K. (2006). Israeli perspectives on elder abuse. *Educational Gerontology, 32*(1), 49–62.

Ramsey-Klawsnik, H., Teaster, P., Mendiondo, M., Abner, E., Cecil, K., & Tooms, M. (2007). Sexual abuse of vulnerable adults in care facilities: Clinical findings and a research initiative. *Journal of the American Psychiatric Nurses Association, 12*(6), 332–339.

Regehr, C., & Antle, B. (1997). Coercive influences: Informed consent in court mandated social work practice. *Social Work, 42*(3), 300–306.

Regehr, C., & Kanani, K. (2010). *Essential law for social work practice in Canada.* Toronto, Ontario, Canada: Oxford University Press.

Reingold, D. (2006). An elder abuse shelter program: Build it and they will come, a long-term care based program to address elder abuse in the community. In J. Mellor & P. Brownell (Eds.), *Elder abuse and mistreatment: Policy, practice and research* (pp. 123–135). Birmingham, NY: Haworth Press.

Statistics Canada. (2002). *Family violence in Canada: A statistical profile.* Ottawa, Ontario, Canada: Author.

Statistics Canada. (2007). *Family violence in Canada: A statistical profile.* Ottawa, Ontario, Canada: Author.

Sussman, T. (2006). Negotiating community care as a stress: The experience of spousal caregivers. Paper presented at the Fourth Annual National Gerontological Social Work Conference, February 16–18, 2006. Chicago, Illinois.

Sussman, T., & Regehr, C. (2009). The influence of community based services on the burden of spouses caring for their partners with dementia. *Social Work in Health Care, 34*(1), 29–39.

Tam, S., & Neysmith, S. (2006). Disrespect and isolation: Elder abuse in Chinese communities. *Canadian Journal on Aging, 25*(2), 141–151.

Tauriac, J., & Scruggs, N. (2006). Elder abuse among African Americans. *Educational Gerontology, 32*(1), 37–48.

U.S. Government Accountability Office. (2011). *Elder justice. Report of the Chairman, Special Committee on Aging, U.S. Senate.* GAO-11-208. Washington, DC: Author.

World Health Organization (WHO). (2002). Toronto declaration on the global prevention of elder abuse. Retrieved from http://www.who.int/ageing /projects/elder_abuse/alc_toronto_declaration_en.pdf

Homicide: Victims, Their Families, and the Community

CHAPTER

13

■ Objectives

- To identify types of homicide by victim and motive and case example
- To outline the statistics of homicides and trends
- To outline the theories of crime and homicide
- To identify victimization concepts related to homicide
- To outline homicide typologies including homicide-suicide
- To describe the grief and trauma response of homicide co-victims

■ Key Terms

Classic mass murder
Co-victim
Homicide
Murder
Recidivism
Serial murder
Spree murder
Traumatic grief
Uniform Crime Reporting (UCR)

Until his double life came to light with his arrest in February 2011, Canadian Air Force officer Russell Williams had a brilliant future, was a man entrusted with flying prime ministers and Queen Elizabeth II, and was the commander of Canada's largest air force base. Colonel David Russell Williams, the former Canadian commander unmasked as a thief and killer, videotaped his extended, brutal assaults on the two women he murdered. The first murder victim was Corporal Marie-France Comeau, an air force flight attendant from Colonel Williams's base. Prosecutors said, after hours of repeatedly being raped and beaten in the head with a large flashlight, she was suffocated by duct tape covering her mouth and nose. After Corporal Comeau's body was discovered, Colonel Williams sent her father a letter of condolence in his capacity as base commander. Jessica Lloyd, the second murder victim, had been spotted by the colonel as he drove on a road near a cottage he owned. Williams had targeted the corporal after meeting her while she worked on a military flight.

FIGURE 13-1 Colonel Russell Williams
© Master Corporal Miranda Langguth/Department of National Defence/Thomson Reuters

Williams pleaded guilty to the murders, two other sexual assaults, and 82 break-ins. The disturbing accounts of the crimes were drawn from Colonel Williams's own meticulous records and videotapes of his 2-year rampage, which began with home break-ins to steal girls' and women's underwear for his sexual arousal and culminated in the murders. Williams took pictures of himself wearing the underwear in the women's bedrooms. He then stored the photographs on a computer hard drive. Williams burgled at least 47 homes, starting in 2007. Many of the targeted homes were in the same street as Williams's cottage in Tweed, Ontario. Other targeted homes were in the vicinity of Williams's main home in Orleans, outside Ottawa (BBC, 2010). Williams was given a life sentence with no chance of parole for 25 years for two murders and sexual assaults (Austen, 2010). See **Figure 13-1**.

■ Introduction

Homicide can be operationally defined as the intentional and sometimes unintentional or accidental killing of another person. It is a tragic phenomenon that has aroused great public and professional concern for decades. Homicide is clearly one of the most violent forms of crime, and it is probably one of the oldest puzzles in criminology and criminal justice (Nash, 1993). Murder is the unlawful taking of human life. It is a behavioral act that terminates life in the context of power, personal gain, brutality, and sometimes sexuality. Murder is a subcategory of homicide, which also includes lawful taking of human life, such as manslaughter, and deaths resulting from criminal and noncriminal negligence, such as unpremeditated vehicular deaths (Megargee,

1966). By definition, a murder is a homicide (the killing of one human being by another) that is committed intentionally or with malice aforethought. Although a distinction is made in the literature among homicide, murder, and killing, for the purpose of this book the terms are used interchangeably.

■ Scope of the Problem

The earliest system for classification of homicide in the United States is the Uniform Crime Reporting (UCR). The U.S. homicide rate steadily decreased throughout the decade of the 1990s. In 1991 the homicide rate was 9.8 per 100,000 inhabitants. In 2000 it was reduced to 5.5 per 100,000 inhabitants (Fox, 2001). However, it began to increase again from the beginning of 2001. In 2001 the nation's homicide rate was 5.6, and it remained at 5.6% in 2005 (Federal Bureau of Investigation [FBI], 2006). Between 2004 and 2005 homicide in the United States increased at a rate of 2.4% (FBI, 2006). The rate of increase, however, was much higher in many states, such as Alabama (+46.0), Rhode Island (+31.2), Delaware (+30.0), Wyoming (+26.6), Wisconsin (+25.2), Utah (+19.3), West Virginia (+17.4), Virginia (+16.9), Pennsylvania (+16.0), Ohio (+15.5), Missouri (+12.8), South Carolina (+8.7), and New Jersey (+6.0). In 2006 there were an estimated 5.7 murders per 100,000 inhabitants. An estimated 17,034 persons were murdered nationwide in 2006, an increase of 1.8% from the 2005 estimate (FBI, 2007).

Weapon use in crime, especially murder, provides a trend for law enforcement and health care personnel. **Figure 13-2** displays the number of murders by type of weapon used, illustrating that almost half (47.32%)

FIGURE 13-2 Number of Murders by Type of Weapon Used

Data from FBI Uniform Crime Report—Crime in the United States. 1977, 1981, 1987, 1989, 2003, 2007. Washington, DC: Department of Justice.

were handguns and 14.14%, unknown firearms. Knives and cutting instruments comprised 13.38%; other weapons, 13.6%; hands, fists, and so on as weapons, 5.87%; shotguns, 3.07%; and rifles, 2.55% (FBI, 2011).

The murder rate in Canada is considerably lower than that in the United States. The number of murders in Canada rose 12% in 2004 after hitting a 36-year low in 2003. This, however, was due to increases in the population, as the rate of 1.9 homicides for every 100,000 population was 5% lower than it was 10 years earlier. In 2006 the number of homicides decreased again, and a total of 606 murders were reported across the country. Numbers have remained relatively stable since then, at 1.8 per 100,000 (Statistics Canada, 2011).

The highest homicide rates are traditionally reported in the northern territories and western Canada, whereas the lowest rates were reported in Atlantic Canada. Nunavut, Canada's region with a very sparse population, has a staggering murder rate of 18.64 per 100,000, whereas the Yukon and the North West Territories have rates of 5.94 and 4.60, respectively. Provincially, Manitoba reported the highest rate in 2009 (4.66), followed by Saskatchewan (3.49). Among the nine largest cities, Winnipeg has the highest homicide rate, followed by Edmonton and Vancouver. The cities of Quebec and Ottawa reported the lowest rates (Statistics Canada, 2011).

■ Legislative Framework

All legal codes classify murder as a crime. Where the element of intent exists and there are no extenuating circumstances, the penalty may be death or life imprisonment.

Penalties for Homicide

Homicide offenders, in comparison to other forms of violent crime, serve longer prison terms. One study by the Bureau of Justice Statistics (1998) on prison sentencing in 1994 showed the average sentencing for homicide offenders in the United States was 266.4 months (slightly over 22 years) compared to 123 months for rape, 88.8 months for robbery, and 47.8 months for assault. After the enactment of the Violent Offenders Incarceration and Truth-in Sentencing Act of 1994, the average length of sentencing given to and average prison time served by homicide offenders further increased in almost all states (Bureau of Justice Statistics, 1995; Illinois Department of Corrections, 2002; Washington Institute for Public Policy, 2004). In Iowa, for example, between 1996 and 2003—after the enactment of new state statutes on Violent Offenders Incarceration and Truth-in Sentencing Act—the average length of stay for second-degree homicide offenders increased from 190 months to 510 months (168%); for attempted homicide, from 85 months to 255 months (200%); and homicide by vehicle Class B, from 85 months to 255 months (200%) (Iowa Legislative Services Agency, 2003). Between 1986 and 2003 the average length of stay in prison by homicide offenders in the state of Washington increased by about 116% (Washington Institute for Public Policy, 2004). These trends of growth in sentencing and time served by homicide offenders in recent years have significantly impacted not just state correctional budgets and populations but also on issues related to their reentry and reintegration to society.

Thirty-six states have capital punishment as a penalty for murder under certain circumstances. In general, these circumstances include first-degree murder, aggravated murder, murder involving sexual assault or kidnapping, or murder involving drug trafficking. The FBI reported that at 2010 year-end, these 36 states and the Federal Bureau of Prisons held 3,158 inmates under sentence of death. More than half of these inmates were being held in four states: Florida, Texas, California, and Pennsylvania (Snell, 2011).

Recidivism

One of the significant challenges for prison reentry is the high rate of recidivism and re-incarceration. Of the more than 650,000 released prisoners from federal and state prisons every year, about 67% (435,500) are rearrested and 50% (325,000) are re-incarcerated within 3 years (National Governors Association Center for Best Practices [NGA], 2004). One of the major studies done on recidivism by the Bureau of Justice Statistics (2002) tracked 272,111 prisoners for 3 years after their release from prisons in 15 states in 1994. The rate of recidivism among homicide offenders was about 40.7%. Of 19,268 homicide offenders released, 3,051 committed homicides again within 3 years. The study also found the released homicide offenders accounted for about 7.7% of other crimes committed between 1994 and 1997. The homicide offenders committed 10% of other crimes within a year after their release (Bureau of Justice Statistics, 2002).

The National Governors Association's Best Practices is currently running seven Prisoner Reentry Academies in six states: Georgia, Idaho, Massachusetts, Michigan, Rhode Island, and Virginia. Predicting recidivism and understanding the social ecology of returning prisoners is one of the major issues being raised and studied in these academies (NGA, 2004). Is homicide typology a good predictor of assessing the risk of repeat offending by homicide offenders? Do we know what configuration of offender characteristics can predict whether a particular homicide offender will reoffend? In other words, do we have a homicide typology that can make reasonably valid predictions about the nature of reoffending by homicide offenders? These and other related questions have been explored and examined on the basis of the study of 336 homicide offenders released from 14 correctional institutions between 1990 and 2000 in New Jersey (Travis, Keegan, & Cadora, 2005). The major objective of this research is to determine which offender characteristics correlate with recidivism versus nonrecidivism among a diverse group of homicide offenders released throughout the state of New Jersey.

Civil Litigation

Civil litigation is one option open to families affected by homicide. Two areas of law can be used: denial of equal protection and failure to act. In denial of equal protection, liability can occur when an agency or organization fails to respond to a crisis. Cases involving 911 calls or victims of spousal abuse cases have attempted to force police departments to arrest the perpetrators of family violence. In some cases local agencies have been held responsible in civil suits for failing to act. These situations can include lack of proper training, lack of proper supervision, or lack of protection on the part of law enforcement.

■ Classification of Homicides

As mentioned above, the UCR is the earliest system for classification of homicide. The UCR, prepared by the FBI in conjunction with the U.S. Department of Justice, presents statistics for crimes committed in the United States within a given year. The current UCR classifies murders as follows:

- Felony murder (occurs during the commission of a felony)
- Suspected felony murder (elements of felony are present)
- Argument-motivated murder (noncriminally motivated)
- Miscellaneous or nonfelony types (any known motivation not included in previous categories)
- Unknown motives (motive fits into none of the above categories)

Percentages for all categories of murder except the unknown motives category have decreased. The number of murders classified in the unknown category, however, has risen dramatically. In 2003 of 14,054 murders, 4,476 murders were categorized in the unknown category (FBI, 2005). This trend is particularly noteworthy in that it suggests both the heterogeneity of motives that give rise to murder and the clear inadequacy of a system that partitions murder essentially into three categories: felony, noncriminal, and miscellaneous. The miscellaneous and unknown motives categories represent wastebasket classifications. A classification system that fails to capture 40% to 50% of the cases (other and unknown) clearly is suboptimal in its ability to explain the universe of behavior. The FBI Academy's Behavioral Science Unit at Quantico, Virginia, began contributing to the literature on the classification of homicide with the Hazelwood and Douglas (1980) publication on typing lust murderers, followed by the classifying of homicides by number of victims, type, and style (Douglas, Burgess, Burgess, & Ressler, 2006).

Single Homicide

A single homicide, as illustrated by the Cosby murder described next, is defined as one victim and one homicidal event. Mikhail Markhasev murdered Ennis Cosby, age 27 and only son of entertainer Bill Cosby, on January 16, 1997, in Los Angeles, California. Cosby had pulled his Mercedes to the side of Interstate 45 to change a flat tire when he was confronted by Markhasev. According to prosecutors, Markhasev demanded money from Cosby and then shot him in the head and fled the scene. Markhasev was convicted after a jury trial and sentenced to life in prison without the possibility of parole. The main evidence used to convict him was that his DNA was found in a cap wrapped around the murder weapon and the testimony of a man to whom he had sent incriminating letters and told of the location of the murder weapon. Markhasev confessed his guilt in 2001 in a letter to the court stating he wished to discontinue his appeals, also stating in the letter that he "wanted to do the right thing.... More than anything, [he] wanted to apologize to the victim's family" (Robinson, 2004, p. 1). Markhasev is serving his sentence in a California prison. Ennis Cosby's family and the larger community felt the tragedy of his death due to his father's high profile reputation as a television star and entertainer.

Double Homicide

A double homicide is defined as two victims who are killed at one time in one location. The January 27, 2001, murder of Dartmouth College Professors Half and Suzanne Zantop by teenage classmates James Parker and Robert Tulloch is an example of a double homicide. The two teenagers posed as students taking a survey as the lure to gain entrance into a home where the motive was robbery. Investigators who traced the knives to Parker, who bought them online, solved this case. They also were identified by fingerprints and boot prints. The pair were located hitchhiking west in Massachusetts and taken into custody (Weber, 2002). Parker testified against Tulloch and pled to second-degree murder. He is eligible for parole in 2026 at age 41. Tulloch is serving a life sentence without parole.

As another example of a double homicide, the bodies of 27-year-old Rachel Entwistle and 9-month-old Lillian were found on January 22, 2006, in the master bedroom of the couple's rented Massachusetts home, where the Entwistles had been living for only 10 days. Autopsy results showed that Rachel died of a gunshot wound to the head and the baby died of a gunshot wound to the stomach. Police located British-born Neil Entwistle at his parents' home in England, where he had fled after discovering the bodies. Entwistle told the police he was so distraught upon seeing the corpses of his wife and daughter he decided to kill himself. However, because he was unable to bring himself to end his life, he decided to fly home to England to see his parents. The defense theory was that Rachel was depressed, killed her baby, and then shot herself in a murder-suicide act (Leonard, 2008).

Entwistle's DNA was found on the handle of the .22 handgun owned by his father-in-law, which he told authorities he'd never touched. Additionally, DNA matching that of his wife Rachel was found on the gun's muzzle. A search of Entwistle's computer also revealed that days before the murders, Entwistle viewed a website that described "how to kill people" and searched for escort services. Entwistle had been unemployed since September 2005 and was essentially penniless at the time of the killings (Leonard, 2008). Authorities suspected a financial motivation for the killings.

After deliberating for 9 hours over 2 days, on June 25, 2008, the jury found Entwistle guilty to the charge of first-degree murder. He was also found guilty of the illegal possession of a firearm and ammunition. He was sentenced to life in prison without the possibility of parole on June 26, 2008, the mandatory sentence for someone convicted of first-degree murder in the state of Massachusetts. Entwistle's appeal for a new trial was heard in court in April 2012 (*Boston Globe*, 2012).

Triple Homicide

A triple homicide is defined as three victims killed at one time in one location. The triple homicide of young college students illustrates the targeting of victims and a hate crime. On August 5, 2007, four young adults in Newark, New Jersey, were shot in the head at close range in a school parking lot, killing all but one (*New York Times*, 2007). One victim was shot in the schoolyard where the four were sitting, and three victims were taken to a secluded area and shot. The shootings happened just a few weeks before these four young college students were to start their fall semester at Delaware State University in Dover, Delaware. The victims were friends from Newark who had gone to the schoolyard to hang out and listen to music; some of the victims' belongings had been stolen.

Newark homicide detectives apprehended four males between the ages of 15 and 28 in the Newark area, and two males were apprehended on August 19, 2007, in Oxen Hill, Maryland, and the Woodbridge section of northern Virginia. The detectives had received a tip that the perpetrators were heading to Mexico and then to El Salvador, the birthplace of the violent MS-13 gang. The suspects were believed to be members of a Central American gang, which has a strong presence in Washington, DC; Prince George's County, Maryland; and Newark, New Jersey. The motives for the shootings have been heavily debated between robbery and a gay hate crime. The victims were believed to have planned to participate in a Black Gay Parade the following day. An adult suspect, Jose Carranza, 28, and a 15-year-old juvenile were apprehended in August 2007 (Scroope, 2007).

Mass Murder

Any single-event, single-location homicide involving four or more victims is classified as mass murder. There are two subcategories of mass murder: classic mass murder and family mass murder. Classic mass murder involves one person operating in one location at one period of time, which could be minutes or hours or even days. The prototype of a classic mass murder is a mentally disordered individual whose problems have increased to the point that he acts out against groups of people who are unrelated to him or his problems, unleashing his hostility through shootings and stabbings. One classic mass murderer was Charles Whitman, who in 1966 armed himself with boxes of ammunition, weapons, ropes, a radio, and food; barricaded himself in a tower at the University of Texas at Austin; and opened fire for 90 minutes. He had committed a double homicide the evening before when he shot and killed his mother and wife. He left a suicide note in which he described himself as appearing as an average intelligent person. He then wrote of his recurring disturbing thoughts that seemed to be taking over his concentration and required significant mental energy to control (Douglas & Olshaker, 1999).

The second type of mass murder is family mass murder. If four or more family members are killed and the perpetrator takes his own life, it is classified as a mass murder-suicide. Without the suicide and with four or more victims, the murder is classified as family mass murder. An example is John List, an insurance salesman who killed his mother, wife, and their three children in 1972. There was a note to his pastor found, along with the bodies, wherein he wrote that there was too much evil in the world and that he had ended the lives of his family to save their souls. List had difficulty holding a job and was taking money from his mother's account to pay the mortgage. List disappeared after the crime, and his car was found at an airport parking lot. He was located 17 years later in Virginia following a television program describing the murders and posting an age-progressed picture of how he might look in 1989. A neighbor recognized him from the horn-rimmed glasses he was wearing in the picture. He died at age 82 from complications of pneumonia (Stout, 2008).

Spree Murder

A spree murder is defined as a single event with two or more locations and no emotional cooling-off period between murders. The single event in a spree murder can be of short or long duration. On September 6, 1949, spree murderer Howard Unruh of Camden, New Jersey, took a loaded German Lugar with extra ammunition and randomly fired the handgun while walking through his neighborhood, killing 13 people and wounding three in about 20 minutes. Although Unruh's killing took a short length of time, it was not classified as a mass murder because he moved to different locations (Douglas et al., 2006). Unruh was diagnosed with paranoid schizophrenia and never stood trial. He was confined for 60 years to the high-security prison for the criminally insane in New Jersey and died at age 88 (Goldstein, 2009).

Andrew Phillip Cunanan was an American spree killer who murdered five people, including fashion designer Gianni Versace, in a cross-country journey during a 3-month period in 1997, ending with Cunanan's suicide at the age of 27.

Serial Murder

Serial murder was initially defined as three or more separate events in three or more separate locations with an emotional cooling-off period between homicides. At a 2005 FBI conference on serial murder (Morton & Hilts, 2005), discussion focused on the number of events needed for classification as serial murder. There was considerable support for reducing the number to two or more events to qualify as serial in nature. The serial murder is hypothesized to be premeditated, involving offense-related fantasy and detailed planning. When the time is right and the serial murderer has cooled off from his or her last homicide, he or she selects the next victim and proceeds with his or her plan. The cooling-off period can last for days, weeks, or months and is the key feature that distinguishes the serial killer from other multiple killers. Ted Bundy is an example of a serial murderer. Bundy killed 30 or more times over a period of many years in at least five different states.

Other differences are hypothesized to distinguish mass, spree, and serial murderers. In addition to the number of events and locations and the presence or absence of a cooling-off period, the classic mass murderer and spree murderer are not concerned with who their victims are; they will kill anyone who comes in contact with them. In contrast, the serial murderer usually selects a type of victim. He thinks he will never be caught, and sometimes he is right. A serial murderer carefully monitors his behavior to avoid detection, whereas a spree murderer, who often has been identified and is being closely pursued by law enforcement, is usually unable to control the course of events. The serial killer, by contrast, plans and chooses victim and location, sometimes stopping the act of murder if it does not meet his requirements. With a sexually motivated murderer, the offense may be classified as any of the aforementioned types.

Canadian serial killers include the child killer, Clifford Olson, who murdered a total of 11 children. He pleaded guilty at his trial in 1982, was sentenced to life in prison, and died of cancer in 2011 at age 71 (Canadian Press Files, 2011). There was also the team of Paul Bernardo and his wife Karla Homolka who killed three teenage girls, including Homolka's sister. Bernardo was sentenced to life for the three murders and Homolka pled guilty to manslaughter, was sentenced to twelve years in prison and was released on parole in July 2005 (Serial Killer Profiles, 2009). Pig farmer Robert Pickton was charged with the first-degree murders of 27 women. Pickton is alleged to have killed and dismembered the bodies of his victims on his farm in Port Coquitlam, British Columbia. He was convicted of second-degree murder in the deaths of 6 women in 2007 and sentenced to life imprisonment. The remaining 20 first-degree murder charges were stayed by Crown prosecutors, noting that there could be no further sentence imposed (Cameron, 2011). See **Figure 13-3**.

FIGURE 13-3 Robert Pickton
© REUTERS/Global TV/Landov

■ Homicide-Suicide

The incident of a homicide followed by suicide is generally defined as a two-stage sequential act in which a person kills one or more individuals and then commits suicide shortly thereafter. Homicide-suicide incidents can have long-term traumatic effects on those closely associated with the incident and frequently have a profound psychological impact on communities. In the following case the impact extended to the wrestling community. On June 25, 2007, professional wrestler Chris Benoit; his wife, Nancy; and their 7-year-old son, Daniel, were found dead in their Fayetteville, Georgia, home at around 2:30 p.m. EDT. Police entered Benoit's home on a "welfare check" after several missed shows (including the "Vengeance" pay-per-view event) and found the three bodies. The Fayette County, Georgia, Sheriff's Department closed their investigation on February 12, 2008, having reached the conclusion that Benoit, over a 3-day period, murdered his wife and son and then committed suicide (ABC News "Nightline," 2007).

Homicide-suicide cases have been difficult to study for several reasons: (1) until recently there has been no centralized database for analysis; (2) because there is no medicolegal distinction of homicide-suicide, cases typically do not result in a criminal charge or trial to provide in-depth analysis of the perpetrator; (3) researchers have had to rely on newspaper accounts of cases and thus cannot report on prevalence or incidence; (4) the research community arrives separately at suicide from a clinical orientation or homicide from a forensic orientation rather than engaging the combination of lethal behaviors; and (5) with the death of the perpetrator, classifying a case based on assumed psychopathology or motive is particularly prone to speculation. As a result there is a missing theoretical foundation to understand motivation in specific subcategories of homicide-suicide that, in turn, can direct prevention strategies.

For example, the psychoanalytical literature has a long history of proposing a link between homicidal and suicidal tendencies, characterized by Freud's notion of the death instinct. This notion was further elaborated on by Menninger (1938), who posited that suicide involved the wish to kill, to be killed, and to die. However, there is minimal evidence to support or refute this link.

Some studies proposed typologies for categorizing these incidents based on the victim–perpetrator relationships and generally include the following, by order of commonality: intimate partner–related homicide-suicide incidents, familicide (killing of all family members in a household) or filicide (killing of children), and extrafamilial homicide (killing of nonfamily members)-suicide incidents. Some incidents are also of mixed type, where there are familial and extrafamilial victims involved. Other studies have evaluated homicide-suicide incidents within selected populations (e.g., among the elderly), in individual states, and across multiple cities and other countries. Few population-based studies on homicide-suicide incidents from multiple states are available in the literature.

The Centers for Disease Control and Prevention established a national surveillance system, the National Violent Death Reporting System, that collects data from selected states on all homicides, suicides, injuries of unknown intent, and firearm accidents (**Table 13-1**). Information is gathered from death certificates with death investigation reports filed by law enforcement and coroner or medical examiner offices. Although the Violence Policy Center (2006) reported U.S. statistics on homicide followed by suicide represents an estimated 5% to 6% of homicides and 2% of suicides, this dual behavior remains a very serious form of interpersonal violence that occurs in families, the workplace, schools, and community settings. Homicide-suicide accounts for 1,000 to 1,500 deaths annually, or 20 to 30 violent deaths weekly (Violence Policy Center, 2006). It can result in dyadic death or multiple victims, as in the 32 deaths at Virginia Tech in 2007.

There have been mixed advances through study results of homicide-suicides. On the positive side both workplace homicide and school shootings as phenomena have inspired successful public health intervention and threat assessment. The U.S. Department of Labor statistics (2010) reported the 2008 numbers represent an 18% drop in workplace homicides from 2007 and a 52% drop from 1994, when 1,080 workplace homicides occurred. However, family annihilation crimes and their prevalence have made minimal progress in preventive strategies.

TABLE 13-1 Surveillance Data for Violent Deaths (CDC)

Sources and Causes	Data
Sources of data	Death certificates
	Coroner/medical examiner reports
	Toxicology results
	Law enforcement reports
	And other reports related to each death
Causes of violent death in 2008	Suicides (58.7%)
	Homicide/legal intervention deaths (26.4%)
	Deaths of undetermined intent (14.5%)

Data from Centers for Disease Control (CDC). 2007. The effectiveness of universal school-based programs for the prevention of violent and aggressive behavior: A report on recommendations of the Task Force on Community Preventive Services. MMWR 2007; 56 (No. RR-7). Centers for Disease Control (CDC). 2002. Atlanta, Georgia.

■ Homicide Victimization Theories

Criminologists develop theories that try to explain why some people murder others. In contrast, victimologists describe theories from the injured parties' perspective. From this perspective the question becomes why the victim was killed (Doerner & Lab, 2008).

One of the earliest theories was social interactionalism, the idea of victim precipitation or the role of the victim in the crime. Drawing on von Hentig's insight that in many violent crimes "the victim shapes and molds the criminal" and "assumes the role of a determinant" (von Hentig, 1948, p. 384), Wolfgang (1958) introduced the concept of victim precipitation into the study of homicide. Wolfgang reviewed Philadelphia police records between 1948 and 1952 and determined that in 26% of the 150 cases reviewed, the victims were the first ones to display a weapon, throw a punch, or use other physical action to escalate the violence to a lethal outcome.

Victim risk by virtue of his or her lifestyle or routine activities is another way to explain homicide events. This theory suggests that individuals may be put at risk by their everyday behavior. Hindelang, Gottfredson, and Garofalo (1978) wrote on the lifestyle of persons influencing their risk for victimization. This view is based on the assumption that some types of interactions between people are nonrandom and their results may, in fact, be predictable.

Social learning theories have also been advanced to explain homicide. Modeling theory suggests that people learn by imitating the behavior of others (Bandura, 1973). Differential association theory suggests that learning comes from interpersonal contacts and individuals will act from input they have from authority figures in their life (Sutherland, 1947). Differential identification argues that personal contact is not necessary for the transmission of behavior but that viewers can model what they see on a media screen.

For nearly 100 years, observed Anderson and Bushman (2002), the effects of exposure to violent media (e.g., comic books, movies, television, and video games) have come under scrutiny by the scientific, political, and public communities. As early as 1910 comic strips published in newspapers were believed (by some) to be a menace to society, to weaken the use of good manners, to teach lawlessness, to cheapen life, and to increase the chance of mental illness (Starker, 1989). By the 1950s there was concern that violence in comic books might increase aggression in children (Wertham, 1954). This concern led to the development of a Comics Code Authority, a self-censoring agency for comic book content developed and enforced by the producers of comic books (Savage, 1990).

In the 1970s the U.S. Surgeon General warned of the potential negative effects of violent television (U.S. Surgeon General's Scientific Advisory Committee, 1972). In 2000 a hearing was held on the effects of violent video games on children and adolescents by the U.S. Senate Commerce, Science, and Transportation Committee (U.S. Senate Commerce, Science, and Transportation Committee, 2003). Research has demonstrated that exposure to violent media appears to increase aggressive behavior, thoughts, and feelings in young people. However, in spite of these findings, Anderson and Bushman (2002) noted the impact of media violence continues to be underreported by news services.

■ Demographic Correlates and Homicide Offending

The demographic variables most consistently examined in homicide research are race, ethnic origin, gender, social class, age, and victim–offender relationship. The FBI's *Supplementary Homicide Reports 1980–2004* show that Blacks represented 48.38% of the homicide offenders in 1980 (FBI, 2005). This high representation of Blacks among homicide offenders remained consistent through the past 24 years. In 2004 Blacks, who constitute about 13% of the U.S. population, represented 49.42% of the homicide offenders (FBI, 2005). Between 1980 and 2004 Blacks committed 50.50% of all total homicides reported to law enforcement compared to 46.29% by Whites, 1.24% by Asians, and less than 1% by Native Americans (FBI, 2005).

Homicide offending also shows a consistent pattern of variations in terms of gender, age, victim–offender relationship, and weapons used in the commission of homicide. Homicide is primarily a male crime. According to the FBI's *Supplementary Homicide Reports 1980–2004*, males in the year 1980 represented 86.10% of the homicide offenders (FBI, 2005). In 2004 males accounted for 90.20% of the homicides, and females accounted for 9.80% of the homicides. Between 1980 and 2004 males accounted for a total of 88.81% of the homicides (FBI, 2005). In terms of age, most homicide offenders are relatively young but are not juveniles. In 2004 juveniles between ages 12 and 17 accounted for only 8.42% of homicides. Adults between 18 and 34 were responsible for 44.44% and those between 25 and 59 accounted for 42.09% of the homicides (FBI, 2005). In most highly populated cities, acquaintance homicide is consistently the most frequent, with stranger homicide a close second, followed by family-related homicides. The FBI's *Supplementary Report* indicates that in 2004, 43.75% were acquaintance homicides, 18.96% were stranger homicides, and 14.89% were family-related homicides

(FBI, 2005). Additionally, the firearm is the weapon used in most homicide cases. In 2004 firearms were used in 62.77% of homicide cases. This has remained consistent since the 1980s. In 1980 firearms were used in 63.62% of cases (FBI, 2005).

Supplemental homicide report data are collected and compiled by the FBI as part of the UCR Program and provide incident-level details on the location, age, sex, and race of the victims and offenders, the victim–offender relationship, weapons used, and the circumstances of the homicide (Fox, 2001). A large amount of literature in recent years has empirically substantiated these variations in homicides in terms of race, gender, age, victim–offender relationship, and the use of weapons. Race combined with social class has a strong correlation to homicide. Disadvantaged minority group members were overrepresented as both perpetrators and victims of homicide. In examining Black–White differentials in adult homicide mortality it was found that Blacks living in the inner city had a higher risk of homicide compared to Whites living in the inner city despite controlling for age and gender. Much of the racial gap seems to be highly correlated with socioeconomic status especially low marriage rates, low educational attainment, and high unemployment rates. Disadvantaged communities with large amounts of social disorganization, economic and social distress, drug use, and street gang membership have a large number of homicides (FBI, 2005, 2007, 2011).

◼ Homicide Offender Typologies

In addition to their efforts to understand the nature of homicide offender characteristics and the sociodemographic contexts of homicide offending, criminologists and criminal justice researchers have also developed a number of homicide typologies or classificatory schemas to profile and explain the personality and the inner motivations of homicide offenders.

Organized and Disorganized Offenders: Typology of Crime Scene Dynamics

One of the oldest and widely known typologies is between organized and disorganized homicides originally described by FBI agents Robert Hazelwood and John Douglas (1980). Megargee (1966) properly described it as a syndrome rather than as a typology and delineated two categories, the organized nonsocial category and the disorganized asocial category, that were not intended to embrace all cases of sexual homicides. These categories were derived from the understanding of crime scene behavior. A brief history of the development of the typology and the dichotomy of organized/disorganized follows (Ressler, Burgess, & Douglas, 1992) (**Table 13-2**).

TABLE 13-2 **Profile Characteristics of Organized and Disorganized Offenders**

	Organized	Disorganized
Offender characteristic	Average to above-average intelligence Socially competent	Below-average intelligence Socially inadequate
Crime characteristics	Skilled work preferred	Unskilled work
	Sexually competent	Sexually incompetent
	High birth order status	Low birth order status
	Father's work stable	Father's work unstable
	Inconsistent childhood discipline	Harsh discipline as child
	Controlled mood during crime	Anxious mood during crime
	Use of alcohol with crime	Minimal use of alcohol
	Precipitating situational stress	Minimal situational stress
	Lives with partner	Living alone
	Mobility with car in good condition	Lives/works near crime scene
	Follows crime in news media	Minimal interest in news media
	May change jobs or leave town	Significant behavior change (drug/alcohol abuse, religiosity, etc.)
	Planned offense	Spontaneous offense
	Victim a targeted stranger	Victim/location known
	Personalizes victim	Depersonalizes victim
	Controlled conversation	Minimal conversation
	Crime scene reflects overall control	Crime scene random and sloppy
	Demands submissive victim	Sudden violence to victim
	Restraints used	Minimal use of restraints
	Aggressive acts before death	Sexual acts after death
	Body hidden	Body left in view
	Weapon/evidence absent	Weapon/evidence often present
	Transports victim or body	Leaves body at death scene

During the 1970s the special agents at the Behavioral Science Unit at the FBI Academy located in Quantico, Virginia, were becoming quite experienced in assessing violent criminality patterns. Police photography departments from around the United States were routinely sending crime scene and investigative reports of unusual murder cases where no suspect had been identified. These crime scenes included grisly murders, mutilations, and bodies thrown into ravines. FBI agents had to communicate back to the police departments, and that required developing a language the detectives could understand. To characterize the types of offenders, a terminology was needed that was not psychiatric in nature, as the typical police officer had no training in psychology. The agents needed to speak to the police in terms they could understand to assist them in their searches for killers, rapists, and other violent criminals. One of the important findings of the Ressler et al. (1992) serial murderer study was the dichotomy of organized and disorganized offenders.

The organized versus disorganized crime scene distinction became the great divide, a fundamental way of separating two very different types of crime scenes and types of personalities who commit multiple murder. The term "organized" was selected to imply a nonpsychotic person who was organized in his criminal behavior patterns and more often than not fit the criteria for a sexual criminal psychopath. The "disorganized" term applied to a person who had mental problems more likely than not as the basis of his criminality either as being a borderline psychotic, having a full-blown mental illness, or being a substance abuser.

Some crime scenes and some murderers displayed organized as well as disorganized characteristics, and those were called "mixed." For instance, Ed Kemper was a highly organized killer, but his mutilation of bodies after death was more typical of a disorganized one. Ed Kemper at age 14 was incarcerated until age 22 for killing his grandparents after being sent to live with them on their farm after his parents divorced. Upon his release he murdered seven coeds from the university where his mother worked. He also killed his mother and her friend. He knew she was planning a trip with an elderly friend and, after killing his mother, telephoned the woman to come over to the house. He then strangled her supposedly to prolong his confrontation with the police (Douglas et al., 2006).

ORGANIZED OFFENDER The key attribute of the organized offender is his planning of the crime. Logic is displayed at the crime scene. Organized crimes are planned, not spontaneous or spur of the moment. The planning derives from the offender's fantasies, which develop (in strength) over time.

John Joubert, an 18-year-old airman in the U.S. Air Force, killed three young males ranging in age from 11 to 14 years. His assaults dated back to age 15 and eventually led to the murder of three young boys. He had assaulted others with a knife, building up to the murder. Bite marks on two of his victims were matched against his teeth marks, providing evidence. John Joubert told of having crimes in mind for years before the opportunity for a slashing murder presented itself and he crossed the line into action. Monte Rissell, too, had violent fantasies for years before a likely victim showed up in the parking lot after the night when, in his mind, his former girlfriend had spurned him.

Most victims of organized offenders are targeted strangers. The offender stakes out or patrols an area, hunting for someone who fits a certain type of victim he has in mind. Age, appearance, occupation, hairstyle, and lifestyle may be elements of choice. David Berkowitz, also known as "Son of Sam," looked for women who were alone or sitting with men in parked cars. Berkowitz was an early serial killer with at least six known victims. His shootings were of opportunity, with some shot while sitting in a car and others while sitting on a porch. He was looking for vulnerable women (Douglas et al., 2006). His crimes were similar to the Washington, DC, beltway sniper shootings by Malvo and Mohammed.

The organized offender often uses a ruse or con to gain control over his victim. This is a man who has good verbal skills and a high degree of intelligence, enough to lure a victim into a vulnerable area. Control is of the essence for an organized offender. An organized offender might offer a prostitute a 50-dollar bill, give a hitchhiker a ride, assist a disabled motorist, and tell a child he is taking him to his mother. Because the crime has been planned, the offender has devoted time to figuring out how to obtain a victim and may have perfected the ruse. John Gacy was known as the "Killer Clown," who murdered 33 young males in the Chicago area in 1970s. He buried 29 of the young men under the floor-boards of his homes in Des Plaines, and the remainder were dumped in a nearby river. John Gacy promised money to young men in a homosexual transient district in Chicago if they would come home and perform sex acts with him (Ressler et al., 1992).

During the criminal act the organized offender adapts his behavior to the exigencies of the situation. After Ed Kemper shot two young women on a college campus, he had the presence of mind to drive past security officers at the gate with two dying women in his car, without alarming the officers. Although admittedly in a state of anxiety, Kemper was not on an hysterical shooting spree. He was able to adapt his behavior to the danger of getting by the checkpoint. Adaptability and mobility are signs of an organized offender. Moreover, organized killers learn as they go on from crime to crime; they get better at what they do, and this shows their degree of organization.

Further evidence of planning that sometimes becomes available to police investigators lies in the organized offender's use of restraints—handcuffs, ropes, and the like. Many murderers take "rape kits" along when they hunt for victims so they do not have any difficulty restraining those whom they wish to assault.

Taking one's own car or a victim's car is part of a conscious attempt to obliterate evidence. Similarly, the organized offender brings his own weapon to the crime and takes it away once he is finished. He knows fingerprints on the weapon or ballistic evidence may connect him to the murder and so he removes it from the crime scene. He may wipe away fingerprints from the entire scene, wash away blood, and do many other things to prevent identification either of the victim or himself. The longer a victim remains unidentified, of course, the greater likelihood the crime will not be traced back to the offender. Usually, the police will find the victim of an organized offender to be nude; without clothing, they are less easily identified. It may seem a large step from wiping fingerprints off a knife to decapitating a body and burying the head in a different place from the torso, but all these actions serve to prevent identification of the victim and of the killer.

The organized offender often takes personal items belonging to his victims as trophies or to deny the police the possibility of identifying the victim. Wallets, jewelry, class rings, articles of clothing, photographs—all these, once belonging to victims, have been found in the dwellings of organized killers after their arrests. Usually, these are not items of intrinsic value, such as expensive jewelry, but rather items used to recall the victim. These trophies are taken for the incorporation of the offender's postcrime fantasies and as acknowledgment of his accomplishments. Many take photographs of their crimes to keep alive the excitement of the crime. Although Monte Rissell stole money from the purses of his victims, he also took jewelry from them and kept them in his apartment. He further extended his fantasy involvement with the victims by driving their cars for hours after he had killed them (Ressler et al., 1992).

These crimes are sexual in nature even if there is no completed sexual act with the victim. The truly organized offender generally completes a sexual act with a living victim, taking full advantage of the situation to rape and torture before murdering the victim. The organized offender seeks to increase his erotic interest through keeping the victim alive and performing perverted and destructive acts on the victims near death several times before the murder so he can enjoy their suffering while he rapes them. During rapes the organized offender demands that the victim display submissive behavior and act fearful and/or passive. If a victim fights back, the organized offender's aggressive behavior usually becomes heightened, sometimes so much that a man who had originally planned on only raping a victim escalates in violence into murder when the victim resists.

The organized offender takes steps to hide the bodies of his victims, or otherwise attempts to conceal their identity, and then keeps track of the investigation. He does so to elongate the time period in which his fantasy seems to be in control of events. In one particularly egregious case of postcrime fantasy, the killer was a hospital ambulance driver. He would kidnap his victims from the parking lot of a restaurant and transport them elsewhere for rape and murder. Unlike many organized offenders, he would leave their bodies in locations that were only partially concealed and then would call the police to report finding a body. As the police rushed to the location of the body, the offender rushed back to the hospital so when the call from the police came to the hospital for an ambulance to be dispatched, he would be in a position to answer that call. He derived special satisfaction from driving the ambulance to the dumpsite, retrieving the body that he himself had killed, and transporting it back to the hospital (Douglas et al., 2006).

Organized offenders generally had a father who had steady employment and who inconsistently disciplined, often leaving the offender with a feeling that he was entitled to everything. The organized offender as a child "acts out" in school, with aggressive and sometimes senseless acts. They externalize their hurt, anger, and fear. Organized offenders feel superior to nearly everyone. Gacy, Bundy, and Kemper all belittled the police who were too stupid, they said, to catch them and the psychiatrists who were too inept to understand them. They overcompensate, often believing themselves to be the smartest and most successful even when they are only moderately so and not particularly distinguished except for the monstrousness of their crimes. After the crime they often follow the progress (or nonprogress) of the investigation in the news media.

Organized offenders also perform well sexually. Often, they have multiple sex partners. As good con artists with excellent verbal skills, they are often able to convince women (and men, in some cases) to have sex with them. They may be superficially attractive and be good amateur psychologists. Their lives are characterized by having many partners, none of whom stick with them very long. An ex-girlfriend of Bundy said he was an unexciting sex partner. Most if not all organized offenders have tremendous anger toward women, often expressed in the belief that a certain woman is not "woman" enough to "turn him on." The ranks of organized offenders contain many rapists who beat up women, they report, because the women did not stimulate them to orgasm.

Organized offenders are angry at their girlfriends, at themselves, at their families and at society in general. They believe they have been mistreated during their entire lives and that everything is stacked against them. In their murders these men strike back not only at individual victims but at society as a whole.

DISORGANIZED OFFENDER   Whereby the organized offender displays planning and logic in every aspect of his crime, the disorganized offender's actions are devoid of normal logic. Until he is caught and can tell his version of the crimes, chances are no one can follow the twisted reasoning he uses to pick his victims or to commit his crimes. Many times the disorganized offender is too mentally ill to drive a vehicle and control his victims, so he will have walked to the scene or taken public transportation. If the disorganized offender owns a car, it will often appear unkempt and in poor condition; so too will his dwelling.

The disorganized offender may pick up a steak knife in the victim's home, plunge it into her chest, and leave it sticking there. Such a disorganized mind does not care about fingerprints or other evidence. If police find a body rather readily, that is a clue the crime was done by a disorganized offender.

A disorganized crime scene displays the confusion of the killer's mind and his spontaneous and symbolic qualities that are commensurate with his delusions. If the victim is found, as is often the case, he or she will likely have horrendous wounds. Sometimes the depersonalization of the victim by the attacker manifests itself in an attempt to obliterate the victim's face or in mutilation after death. Often, the death scene and the crime scene are the same for the disorganized offender; he does not possess the mental clarity of mind to move the body or conceal it.

The disorganized offender does not take symbolic trophies; rather in his confused mental state he takes an obscure item such as a body part, a lock of hair, or an article of clothing as a souvenir whose value cannot be discerned.

These crimes all have a sexual component whether or not there is a completed sexual act with the victim. The disorganized offender often does not complete the sex act or, if he does, completes it only with a dead or entirely inanimate victim. The disorganized killer kills quickly, with a blitz style of attack.

Organized and disorganized killers have very different personalities. The ways in which the personalities develop, and the behavioral consequences of these developmental patterns, are often important to unraveling a crime. The disorganized offender grows up in a household where the father's work is often unstable, where childhood discipline is harsh, and where the family is subject to serious strain brought on by alcohol, mental illness, and the like.

The disorganized offender grows up to internalize hurt, anger, and fear. Although normal people also internalize these emotions to some degree—that's necessary to live together in our society—the disorganized offender goes way beyond the norm in his internalization. He is unable to let off steam and lacks the verbal and physical skills for expressing these emotions in the proper arenas. He cannot be easily counseled because he cannot tell the therapist very much about the emotional turmoil inside him.

Part of the reason for the unexpressed anger within disorganized offenders is that they are not necessarily handsome people. They do not appear attractive, as measured by others, and they have a very poor self-image. They may have physical ailments or disabilities that make them different, and they are not comfortable being different. Rather than accepting their disabilities, they believe themselves to be inadequate, and they act in an inadequate manner, thus reinforcing their hurt, anger, and isolation. Disorganized offenders tend to withdraw from society almost completely, to become loners. Whereas many organized killers tend to be reasonably attractive, outgoing, and gregarious, disorganized killers are incapable of relating to other people at all. Therefore, disorganized offenders most likely do not live with a member of the opposite sex, probably not even with a roommate. If they live with anyone else, chances are it will be with a parent and probably a single parent. No one else will be able to tolerate their strange ways, so disorganized offenders are alone, possibly recluses. Such offenders actively reject the society that has rejected them.

Commensurate with these disorganized offenders' poor self-image is that they are underachievers. In general, they are less intelligent than are organized offenders, but most are not seriously deficient. However, they never live up to their potential either in school or in the workplace. If they work at all, it will be at a menial job, and they are habitually disruptive because of their inability to get along with other people. They also accept that they underachieve. When police questioned one killer, he said he was an unemployed actor. That was wishful thinking. Actually, he was an unemployed stagehand—certainly by his own admission, an underachiever in the theatrical profession.

Other Typologies Based on Crime Scene Dynamics

Under the leadership of Unit Chief John Douglas, FBI agents Robert Ressler and others associated with the FBI's National Center for the

Analysis of Violent Crime, which is part of the FBI's Behavioral Science Unit at Quantico, Virginia, expanded the twofold typology into a fourfold typology of homicide motivations. These typologies are also primarily based on crime scene indicators. The four types are (1) criminal enterprise homicides (contract murders, gang-motivated murders, insurance/inheritance–related killings, and felony murders); (2) personal cause homicides (domestic violence–related murders, political and religious murders, or mercy killings); (3) sexual homicide (rape and murder, child rape and child serial killings); and (4) group cause homicides (cult-related homicides and homicides related to extremism and terrorism).

Later, Holmes and Holmes (1998, 2001) classified homicide offenders, particularly serial killers, in terms of four categories: visionary killer, mission killer, hedonistic killer, and power or control killer. Visionary killers kill in the name of God, a devil, or an angel. They believe they are commanded from some supernatural powers to kill. Mission killers are driven by earthly missions to establish a just regime or a group. They are driven by their own constructed rationality of removing the ills of society. Hedonistic killers, on the other hand, kill for thrills, lust, and pleasure. Killing for them is the expression of their pleasure principle. Power killers kill to symbolize their power over and control of the victims. Killing for them is a way of regaining the control of their fractured minds and personalities.

A considerable number of homicide studies have been generated in recent years on the basis of a model developed by C. Gabrielle Salfati of the Center for Investigating Psychology of the University of Liverpool, England. Salfati (2011) and Salfati and Grey (2002) classified homicides into two categories on the basis of 36 crime scene indicators: expressive homicide and instrumental homicide. Expressive homicides are anger induced and linked to rape, arson, or physical attack. Extreme violence, multiple wounds, and the use of multiple weapons, suffocation, and dismemberment of the bodies of the victims characterize expressive crime scenes. Instrumental homicides are linked to violence, theft, robbery, and burglary, where the offenders are motivated by some ulterior aims for money or sex. In instrumental crime scenes, bodies are not hidden and the offenders leave traces of weapons, blood, clothes, semen, and shame and guilt.

Fox and Levin (1996, 2005, 2006) have studied the issue of homicide typology for several decades. They divided homicide into three main categories: serial murders, mass murders, and spree killing. On the basis of these three categories they developed a fivefold motivational typology: power-based homicides, revenge-based homicides, loyalty-based homicides, profit-based homicides, and terror-based homicides.

These typologies, used as tools in much empirical analysis, have considerably improved our knowledge of the nature of homicide offending and homicide offenders (**Table 13-3**). What is missing in most of these typologies, however, is an analysis of how and whether they can predict homicide recidivism. The core concern in most of these typologies is to be able to comprehend the inner mind of the homicide offenders—the complex trajectories of motivations for homicide. The search for homicide motivation is a genuine intellectual challenge in criminology and criminal justice. But the extent to which motivational understanding can help us develop an understanding of the social trajectory where the offenders live and commit the crime and the degree to which the complex nature of homicide motivations are amenable to empirical analysis are open to questions (Canter & Wentink, 2004; Goodwin, 1998, 2002).

Most typologies based on motivational understanding are drawn from the Freudian theory of psychodynamics, the theory that is based on assumptions that most homicide offenders are driven by the unconscious and their psychopathic personalities are the byproducts of childhood trauma and victimization. It seems that to use homicide typology as predictors of recidivism and to develop evidence-based reentry policies, we need a typology that is based on a more structural (Sampson & Wilson, 1995) understanding of the social ecology within which the offenders live and where offenders will return after they are released. Roberts, Zgoba, & Shahidullah (2007) suggest that a typology is needed that can provide a more empirically grounded analysis of offender characteristics and their complex relations with homicide offending and recidivism. Their empirical analysis of 336 homicide offenders drawn from New Jersey aims to contribute to this end through the development of a new typology and an analysis of its application and relevance to homicide reentry and recidivism (Roberts, Zgoba, & Shahidullah, 2007).

Underclass Homicide Typology

Criminal profiling and typifying criminal personalities is one of the enduring scientific passions in criminology and criminal justice, a passion that goes back to the study of Italian criminologist Cesare Lombroso's *Criminal Man*, originally published in 1876. Lombroso's theory of anthrological criminology essentially stated that criminality was inherited and that someone "born criminal" could be identified by physical defects. These defects were identified as large jaws, forward projection of jaw, low sloping foreheads, high cheekbones, flattened or upturned nose, handle-shaped ears, large chins, very prominent in appearance hawk-like noses or fleshy lips, hard shifty eyes, scanty beard or baldness, insensitivity to pain, and long

TABLE 13-3 Typologies of Homicides

Source	Nature	Homicide Categories	Core Focus
Hazelwood & Douglas, 1980	Twofold typology	Disorganized homicides Organized homicides	Crime scene analysis as to evidence or clues for determining a suspect
Douglas, Burgess, Burgess, & Ressler, 2006	Fourfold typology	Criminal enterprise Personal cause homicides Sexual homicides Group cause homicides	Material gain Narcissistic gain Sexual intent Ideology of group
Holmes & Holmes, 1998, 2001	Fourfold typology	Visionary killers Mission killers Hedonistic killers Power killers	Motivations of the killer
Salfati, 2001	Twofold typology	Expressive homicides Instrumental homicides	Homicide motivations
Fox & Levin, 2005	Fivefold typology	Power-based homicides Revenge-based homicides Loyalty-based homicides Profit-based homicides Terror-based homicides	Homicide intent by ideology of murderer
Roberts, Zgoba, & Shahidullah, 2007	Fourfold typology based on underclass homicides analyzed data from New Jersey Department of Corrections	Altercation/argument– precipitated homicides	Magnified perception of money or property loss; dispute escalates into fight, stabbing, or shooting
		Felony homicides	Robbery, burglary, grand theft, kidnapping, and other felony crimes induce homicides
		Intimate partner violence	Homicides precipitated because of complexities involving sex, love, and emotion
		Accident homicides	Victims killed by vehicular accidents where driver under the influence of alcohol or drugs

arms. Very few criminologists today lend scientific credence to Lombroso's physiognomic approach to the understanding of criminality, but the search for a typology of criminal offenders, particularly homicide offenders, has remained as a genuine curiosity (Lombroso-Ferrero, 1972).

Homicide research is disproportionately dominated by intellectual passion and scientific curiosity to understand the mind of the serial and brutal killers—the high class of the murderers—who make headlines, create terror, and generate a collective sense of national traumas (Fox & Levin, 2005). Many even believe the classification of serial killers is a misleading venture (Hickey, 2002). There are hundreds of thousands of homicide offenders who do not make headlines and who do not raise any collective sense of terror and tragedies. They commit the crime, serve the time, and get back to the community only to return to prison committing new crimes. The understanding of the nature and peculiarities of this "underclass" of homicide offenders is far more significant from the point of view of increased stress and strains on criminal justice. They commit violence and kill people for few dollars and over few stretches of arguments. They come from a fragile social ecology, fragmented families, and failed communities. They come from communities where some even glorify and justify a culture of violence (Sampson, Raudenbush, & Earls 1997; Sampson & Wilson, 1995).

Toward a New Homicide Typology

We have come a long way since Marvin Wolfgang's doctoral dissertation and book was completed at the University of Pennsylvania in the 1950s. For those criminologists like the authors studying offender typologies based on the victim–offender relationship, we owe a great debt to Wolfgang's classic study. Dr. Wolfgang provided the first sociological and statistical analysis of 588 homicide victims and 621 homicide offenders in the city of Philadelphia between 1948 and 1952 (Wolfgang, 1958). The Roberts et al. (2007) typology of homicide offenders and recidivism builds on the early classification of homicide by Wolfgang. Wolfgang conceptualized the term "victim-precipitated homicide" because most homicide offenders in his study were acquaintances or close relatives of the victims.

The Roberts, Zgoba, and Shahidullah (2007) typology emphasized that although there is no excuse or rational reason for almost all homicides, the interaction and distorted perceptions of many homicide offenders do result in lethal outcomes. Despite the unique characteristics, circumstances, and criminal history of each of the 336 homicide offenders, as a result of longitudinal analysis four patterns and types of homicide were documented: stranger to stranger/felony homicide, domestic violence, accidental (usually drunk driving–related), and altercation/argument precipitated.

Despite a great deal of information on various types of offenders, there is only limited longitudinal research on the offending patterns, typologies, and recidivism of different types of homicide perpetrators. There is also limited knowledge of the underclass and lower socioeconomic class type of homicide offender included in the Roberts et al. study compared to notorious middle-class serial killers. A random sample of 336 homicide offenders who were released between the years 1990 and 2000 from the New Jersey Department of Corrections were identified and followed for a minimum of 5 years. These offenders were tracked to determine whether incarcerated homicide offenders who have no criminal histories before their current homicide conviction recidivated less and which specific variables correlated with recidivism. As a result of the Roberts et al. analysis, the researchers conceptualized were able to conceptualize a new fourfold typology of homicide offenders: (1) offenders who committed a homicide that was precipitated by a general altercation or argument, (2) offenders who committed a homicide during the commission of a felony, (3) offenders who committed a domestic violence–related homicide, and (4) offenders who were charged with a degree of homicide after an accident. Statistical analysis was completed to determine which variables correlated with the different types of recidivism and which of the four types of homicide offenders recidivated. In conclusion, none of the 336 homicide offenders committed another murder. However, the Roberts et al. found the highest risk of recidivism for new violent or drug crimes were the felony homicide group (slightly over one-third), followed by the altercation-precipitated homicide offenders (27%), which was in sharp contrast to the domestic violence homicide offenders with less than 10% recidivism due to a new violent or drug offense and the accidental homicides with 17% recidivism due to a new violent or drug offense. This exploratory study shows a homicide typology can be a good indicator of homicide offender recidivism if it is structurally grounded to examine the complex articulation of relations between offender characteristics and their post-incarceration behavior (Roberts, Zgoba, & Shahidullah, 2007).

During the past decades, particularly after the formation of the Homicide Research Working Group in 1991, a considerable amount of literature has emerged on issues of understanding the social and demographic characteristics of homicide offenders and their behavioral peculiarities, motivational contexts, crime scene behavior, and typology (Canter, 2004; Fox & Levin, 2005; Hickey, 2002; Holmes & Holmes, 2002; Petherick, 2005; Ressler et al., 1992; Salfati, 2001). See **Table 13-4**.

TABLE 13-4 A Fourfold Typology of Homicides

Homicide Types	Nature and Characteristics	Case-Based Data and Homicide Circumstances
Altercation- or argument-precipated homicides	Magnified perception of money or property loss; argument over money or property; dispute over relatively small amount of money or possessions; verbal dispute escalates into fight and fight into stabbing and shooting. In this category, homicides are driven by what Salfati (2001) called instrumental expressions.	Argument and fight over $4.00. Victim died from beating. Defendant hit victim in the head with a 2×4 because they were fighting over a bike. Shot victim over argument about dog. Victim was shot after argument over money. Beat victim with a bat and dumped his body in the woods over argument about drugs.
Felony homicides	Perpetrators kill their victims during the commission of a felony crime. Homicides are committed as a means to commit other crimes. Most felony offenders have records of past criminal histories.	Robbery, burglary, grand theft, kidnapping, and other felony crimes induce homicides.
Domestic violence or intimate partner violence–induced homicides	Perpetrators are family members, current or ex-spouses, cohabitating intimate partners, or girlfriends or boyfriends. This category of homicides is mostly precipitated not because of intentions to commit a felony crime or achieve any instrumental goals but because of complexities and fragilities in relations involving sex, love, and emotion.	Shot victim. He believed she was unfaithful. Shot wife after she left him. Defendant used car to run over and kill husband who had beaten her badly in the car. Shot and killed victim after years of emotional abuse. Defendant stabbed boyfriend in chest with kitchen knife after argument.
Accident homicides	Perpetrators cause death of victims usually by automobiles	Driving under the influence of alcohol or drugs. Driving after binge drinking.

■ Co-Victims of Homicide

The term "co-victim" is used synonymously with "survivor" and emphasizes the depth of the trauma of a homicide. In the aftermath of the murder it is the co-victim who deals with the medical examiner, the criminal or juvenile justice system, and the media. The term "co-victim" may be expanded to any group or community that is touched by the murder: a classroom, a dormitory, a school, an office, or a neighborhood. Most of the individuals who make up these communities are wounded emotionally, spiritually, and psychologically by a murder, some more deeply than others. Common problems that confront co-victims are outlined in **Table 13-5**.

TABLE 13-5 **Issues Confronting Co-Victims**

Issue	Examples
Financial considerations	Co-victims are faced with unplanned expenses related to funeral, burial, medical treatment, mental health care for family members, and other costs. These unexpected issues contribute to the continuing distress experienced.
Criminal or juvenile justice system	Co-victims of homicide will be asked to participate in and understand the complex issues of a cumbersome legal system.
Employment	A co-victim's mental and cognitive ability to function, be motivated, and to perform on the job is diminished. They experience emotional mood swings and can be impatient with trivia. Some co-victims use work as a way to manage their grief.
Marriages	Marital partners may have difficulty relating, and they may even separate after a death due to homicide. Partners tend to grieve differently. They may blame each other for the loss, may each wish to turn away from the memories that the other partner evokes, and sometimes are unable to help each other because they cannot help themselves.
Children	Parents may ignore or fail to communicate with their children when they are preoccupied with their own issues. The children, in turn, fear adding to their parents' pain and simply withdraw. Children who witness the murder can experience significant emotional trauma, including posttraumatic stress disorder, and need a referral for intervention.
Religious faith	Questions for, anger at, and challenges to religious beliefs and faith can occur. Oversimplistic comments and responses to questions about God by clergy and church members sometimes create more problems for co-victims who are questioning the "why" of the murder.
Media	Homicide co-victims are subjected to the intrusion of an insensitive media. Reporters may override the co-victim's need for privacy and reminders of the violence associated with the homicide.
Dealing with professionals	Co-victims report that often professionals (police, court personnel, hospital personnel, funeral directors, clergy, school personnel, psychologists, and psychiatrists) demonstrate by their comments and actions that they do not fully understand the impact of death by homicide on the remaining family members.
Substance use and abuse	Co-victims may seek to self-medicate the traumatic memories with alcohol and/or drugs after the homicide. Careful attention to this potential problem is required.

Data from 1999 National Victim Assistance Academy Text, Chapter 11: Homicide. Authors: Carroll Ann Ellis and Janice Lord, editors: Grace Coleman, Mario Gaboury, Morna Murray, and Anne Seymour.

Co-Victim Response to Family Member Homicide

Darlene R., age 53, began working at Food King in 1975 and married Bill Bowen, owner of the store, in 1978. She started as an office manager and eventually became a vice president working in all parts of the store including public relations and customer relations. Darlene and Bill raised three children. In the fall of 1996 Darlene was recuperating from neck surgery. In part to celebrate their wedding anniversary and to visit their daughter Terry, who was enlisted in the military at Kessler Air Force Base, the Bowens decided to travel to Gulfport over the weekend of October 25, 1996. The couple checked into a local inn on Thursday, October 24, 1996. Their daughter joined them for dinner and then left to return to her quarters to study. Darlene and Bill went sightseeing, ending up visiting a food store and then a casino. They returned later that evening to the inn. After several loud knocks to the door, the door burst open, a man dragged Bill out of the room, and gunshots were heard. A gun was placed to Darlene's head with the threat of death if she didn't stop screaming. She turned around and was hit over the top of her head. More shots were fired and the gunmen left. Darlene screamed for help, called on the room telephone, and eventually the police arrived. Bill was pronounced dead at the scene.

Darlene, a witness to the murder of her husband and a victim of a head and neck assault, suffered traumatic bereavement and symptoms of chronic posttraumatic stress. Immediately after the murder Darlene's daughter and sister arrived to help. She was taken to the military base and provided room in the officer's quarters. Armed guards were placed outside her room to make her feel safe. Darlene stayed in a state of shock for months. She described how she lost time and had no memory of those months. Her friends became so concerned about her they made arrangements for her to see a doctor. However, she had problems remembering appointments and would just stay at home. She developed severe headaches and neck pain from the assault to her head. She sought help with pain management and medication. She had injections into her neck. Nothing relieved the headaches and the pain. Darlene had continual flashbacks to the murder and recurring nightmares. She needed sleeping medication but then would be exhausted all day. She believed she was losing her mind. She refused to see her friends or be with people she knew. She felt paranoid. She didn't want to talk with anyone. She was irritable and cried constantly. She missed her husband. She could not take care of the business and had to sell it. This made her feel like a failure, saying not only had she lost her husband but also the stores. She did not feel she could manage without him. She would not answer the telephone because she did not want to talk to people.

Two years after the murder, Darlene believed she was making some progress but had a setback after her deposition for a civil suit. All the traumatic memories came back. She withdrew by sleeping. She believed she lost several years. When reminded of something she said, she said her mind was a blank. She used to be very social, managing public relations for the store. After the murder she could hardly get through a dinner with friends. She hyperventilated in social settings. She became suspicious of people, a new behavior. She could not stay in a hotel. She was chronically fatigued and had little interest in current events. She watched reruns of television shows from the 1970s and 1980s. On the radio she listened to oldies but goodies music. She would read but stopped if there was any violence. She went to a movie with her sister, became ill while watching a scene where someone was shot, vomited, and had to leave the movie. Then she felt guilty. She had mood dysregulation and many crying spells. Her weight fluctuated.

Darlene's experience is not uncommon, as the murder of a family member leaves more than just bodies behind. Murder leaves survivors to struggle and cope with sudden and violent loss of life. The impact of violence on families is a complex issue (Buka, Stichnick, Birdthistle, & Earls, 2001). Parents, spouses, siblings, and children are forever marred by the horrific event. From media coverage and those speaking out against the horrors of murder, the focus is usually on adults, often the parents or spouses of the deceased. In addition, however, children are profoundly affected by the experience of loss yet may think about the victim, feel about the murder, and express their grief in ways that are significantly different from adults.

Forensic Issues

A number of agencies swing into action when a homicide is reported. There is a flurry of media coverage and a police investigation ensues at the crime scene. Emotions run high with fear and disbelief, with the focus usually on the deceased and the assailant. Families search desperately for answers and, if a body has not yet been found, live in hope for a happy ending that over time seems more and more remote.

Law enforcement usually has the responsibility of ringing the doorbell and announcing to the family that one of their members has been murdered. News of a homicide is inherently sudden and traumatic in nature and raises many questions. What happened? Who is the murderer? Why did it happen? Death notification requires families to face a horrifying reality and then immediately move to complete a number of activities including identifying the victim, making funeral arrangements, and notifying friends and family while at the same time juggle investigative demands with daily life activities, such as caring for children.

The medical examiner's office plays a critical role in the aftermath of a homicide. The medical examiner's office is the final voice of the victim in that he or she makes a final determination of the cause and manner of death from the information gleaned from the forensic autopsy. In the search for answers, however, family members can become obsessed with the details of death. Some family members insist on seeing pictures of the deceased or crime scene; others want details regarding the physical state of the body from autopsy and other reports. One study of parents who lost a child to violent death reported an unending quest for information, for instance, seeking to find out how much water was in the lungs in the case of a drowning murder (Janzen, Cadell, & Westhues, 2004). All these questions seem to be part of the search to find answers and create meaning out of the unthinkable.

Funeral Activities and the Immediate Aftermath

One of the duties that occupies the family's time in the first week after a homicide is attending to the funeral details and arrangements. Such decisions as to whether to have an open casket must be made. This may depend on the physical appearance of the body and can be a difficult decision for the family. In the case of a child murder, families often express an interest in being a part of the process of preparing and bathing the child, seeking to care for their child one last time (Janzen et al., 2004). While planning the funeral, families must also take into account how newspaper reporting has handled the situation in terms of what peoples' fantasies might be of the injuries to the deceased. Murder is newsworthy and as a crime it becomes an act against the community. There is no confidentiality. Murder victims are named and family members are thrown into the public's view. Privacy for grief and stabilization of the family system is lost.

Post-Funeral Life

After the crisis of the death notification and funeral activities, friends and relatives typically must return to the daily routines from which they came before the death. The house, which may have been burgeoning with love, support, and numerous shoulders to cry on, may now seem like an empty shell, filled with haunting reminders and echoes of the person who is now dead. Returning to work, school, or church can be quite ominous. The immediate time period after the death notification and funeral is one of shock and disbelief for the family and the children. Families are numb and confused and generally have a number of physical concerns. Insomnia, sleep pattern disturbance, headaches, and gastrointestinal upsets are common.

Because the return to work or school may occur within a time frame of less than a week after the murder, the reentry into this subcommunity has been described as pivotal in dealing with trauma. It can be distressing in this phase. Family members may feel misunderstood by coworkers, teachers, and peers. There may be little validation of the homicide of the family member. People may not know what to say. Children may be unable to concentrate and to complete certain school tasks. They can become defiant, verbally aggressive, and, in some cases, physically violent. They may skip class, refuse to do their work, and succeed in being sent home.

Intersections Between Grief and Trauma

The horror of murder and the events that lead to it cannot be overstated with respect to the grieving process of those left behind. Kristen French was kidnapped, tortured, sexually assaulted, and murdered by Paul Bernardo and his wife, Karla Homolka, in what became known as the Ken and Barbie murders due to the good looks of the two serial murderers. Donna French, mother of Kristen, became a well-known figure after the deaths, championing the cause for those who are co-victims of murder. Donna French stated at a 2010 conference, "The details of Kristen's captivity wiped me out. I had no idea such evil existed. Each detail [of the trial] seemed to physically assault me. Day after day, I would listen to graphic details and try to avoid looking at explicit pictures." Eight years after the murders she still indicated, "Not a day goes by I'm not filled with thoughts of Kristen. The emptiness is all encompassing," French said (Edwards, 2010, pp. 1–2).

Family members are hit with a sudden death and are aware of the violence and horror experienced by their loved one, but they are also faced with the context in which it occurs, be it during a sexual assault or argument, as an act of arson, or as the result of torture, drunk driving, or a "romantic triangle" (Gross, 2007). Grief and mourning are part of the bereavement process. Grief is a subjective experience and behavior noted after a significant loss, whereas mourning refers to the process of the attenuation of grief as an adaptation to loss (Horowitz, Krupnick, Kaltreider, Leong, & Marmar, 1981). Family members feel sad, depressed, guilty, preoccupied, lonely, and angry and struggle to adjust to their environment, including home, school, and peers. Unlike other losses, however, when family members are faced with murder, their grief is intertwined with trauma. Trauma-related responses include avoiding reminders of the deceased; feeling purposeless and futile about the future; sensing numbness or detachment resulting from the loss; feeling shocked, stunned, or dazed by the loss; denying the reality of the death; feeling that life is empty and unfulfilling without the deceased; feeling a fragmented sense of trust, security, and control and anger over the death (Regehr & Sussman, 2004) as well as intense and often paralyzing fear, and thinking near-consuming thoughts of revenge (Gross, 2007).

Such experiences have led to a new conceptual framework called **traumatic grief** (Regehr & Sussman, 2004). Several factors differentiate traumatic grief from "normal" grief. These factors include the *closeness of the relationship* with the deceased (Gleser, Green, & Winget, 1981), the *violence* associated with the death (Kaltman & Bonanno, 2003; Thompson, Norris, & Ruback, 1998), and the sense of *injustice* (Armour, 2002; Rock, 1998). In addition to the cause of death, factors related to perceptions of justice include the age of the deceased, whether the death was expected, and the co-occurrence of other losses or stressors. The magnitude of traumatic grief can easily develop into a diagnosable depressive disorder or posttraumatic stress disorder (Gross, 2007).

Guilt and Blame

Murder undermines one's faith in the world as an ordered and secure place. Studies show that untimely natural deaths shake confidence in this sense of security. Blaming someone for a tragedy is a less disturbing alternative than facing the fact that life is uncertain. It allows people control by putting the responsibility onto another person. Not to be able to explain a situation makes people feel helpless. People look for a target to project their feelings. A main target, of course, is the assailant. Families want justice and the assailant prosecuted. Another target is the criminal justice system. Families can become angry with the police for being unsuccessful in finding the assailant. And not infrequently the victim may be blamed. This concept holds that no victim is entirely innocent but rather participates to some degree in the crime. Family members may have thoughts of how he or she could have prevented the death. This phenomenon is known as survivor's guilt, is not uncommon, and is extremely disturbing.

Stigma

Homicides are often sensationalized in the media, and thus, violent death can damage the victim's family and social network. There are cases where people deliberately avoid the family and consequently are not supportive. Such cases may involve drugs in which the victim "squealed" to federal agents. Thus, the victim was not seen as worthy of grieving and the family member receives no support. And there are situations where people unwittingly avoid the family and thus no support is offered. Such cases usually involve horrific situations that overwhelm the social network to the point they do not know what to say to the family. Family members may feel "different" and embarrassed especially if the death evolved around a crime such as drug trafficking and this was on the news.

Fears and Phobias

As with crime victims, fears and phobic reactions are common and develop according to the specific circumstances surrounding the events of the crime. Families become very aware of the potential for a crime occurring and cope by adding protective measures. Adults will obtain permits to carry guns or will put burglar alarms in their homes.

Supporting the Co-Victim

Several points are helpful to review in providing support to homicide co-victims. It is critical to learn the details of the case before speaking to the co-victim or family for determining their wishes for talking to the media, assistance with funeral details, and needs for contact and information as the investigation progresses. Staff needs to understand the stages of bereavement and grief as they meet with co-victims, have available the names of support groups, and provide court services that are available to family members and witnesses. Staff need to alert the prosecutor of co-victims' concern for safety and inform co-victims of their rights to file civil suits if applicable. Staff need to be prepared to provide long-term victim assistance in cases involving the death penalty as well as to provide information on their rights and services available in the post-sentencing phases of their cases, including victim protection, notification of offender status and location, restitution, victim input, and parole release hearings (Tennessee Victim Assistance Academy Participant Manual, 2008).

In death penalty cases co-victims have the right to witness the execution. Depending on the state, co-victims may also have a face-to-face meeting with the criminal. For those co-victims who have restructured their lives after a homicide, they can be asked whether they wish to participate in victim impact panels, where they can provide firsthand knowledge of victim trauma and the injustices victims endure (Ellis & Lord, 1999).

Grief work is the psychological process that moves the person from being preoccupied with thoughts of the lost person, through painful recollections of the loss experience, to the final step of settling the loss as an integrative experience (Parkes, 1972). Successful mourning allows for the slow withdrawal of the attachment to the deceased and the increased availability of psychic energy to forge new or stronger relationships. In addition, however, those experiencing traumatic grief may need interventions that focus on managing the trauma-related symptoms such as the fears, nightmares, and physiological arousal (Regehr & Sussman, 2004).

■ Summary

In summary, this chapter has examined homicide and how victimology concepts of victim–offender relationship and victim risk information provide important directions for understanding the criminal and his victim. Based on research and crime trends the important conclusions are as follows. First, the United States has a high crime and homicide rate when compared to other industrialized nations. Second, homicide is an interactional crime whereby victim risk and offender risk result in a lethal outcome affecting not only the victim but also the victim's family members and the community. Third, a large number of characteristics of victims, offenders, and situations can increase the risk of a violent outcome. Homicides can be decreased or prevented as people are educated and resources are available to persons before they become victims. Fourth, case illustrations are presented to sensitize the student to the vicissitudes of victimization and to increase compassion for the family members.

■ Key Terms

Classic mass murder: One person operating in one location at one period of time, which could be minutes or hours or even days.

Co-victim: Immediate family, significant others, work associates, and close personal friends who had dealings with the deceased.

Homicide: The intentional and sometimes unintentional or accidental killing of another person.

Murder: A subcategory of homicide, which also includes lawful taking of human life.

Recidivism: The repeating of crimes by the offender.

Serial murder: Two or more separate events in three or more separate locations with an emotional cooling-off period between homicides.

Spree murder: A single event with two or more locations and no emotional cooling-off period between murders.

Traumatic grief: Grief associated with traumatic loss, such as murder.

Uniform Crime Reporting (UCR): The earliest reporting system of homicide.

■ Discussion Questions

1. Compare and contrast the type of homicide by motive in the single, double, and triple homicide cases cited in this chapter and the dynamics of homicide-suicide.

2. What homicide theory best describes your perception of victimization by homicide?

3. Which of the various homicide typologies best explains the hotel murder of Bill (last case in the chapter)?

4. What treatment intervention would you recommend for Darlene?

5. Discuss the type of homicide, victim risk, crime scene, and motive in the following case:

   A 41-year-old separated woman was found dead in her home, clad in a short nightgown covering to the waist. There was no sign of forced entry. The assault began at the entry (kitchen) door, with the assailant stabbing and slashing at the victim, pursuing her from the kitchen area back to the victim's daughter's bedroom and back to the hallway where she died. The victim put up a fight and suffered numerous defensive wounds along with indications that she did grab the blade of the knife at some point with both hands. Her hands were severely cut. The throat slashing was postmortem. There was no evidence of sexual assault. Victimology noted the victim maintained a low social profile, was employed as a telephone sales representative, and lived in a single-family house on a rural farm with her teenage daughter.

■ Resources

Compassionate Friends
   www.compassionatefriends.org
Mothers Against Drunk Driving
   www.madd.org
National Center for Victims of Crime
   http://www.ncvc.org/ncvc/Main.aspx
National Organization for Victim Assistance (NOVA)
   http://www.trynova.org
Parents of Murdered Children (POMC)
   www.pomc.com

■ References

ABC News "Nightline." (2007). Chris Benoit's murder, suicide: Was brain damage to blame? Retrieved from http://abcnews.go.com/Nightline /chris-benoits-dad-son-suffered-severe-brain-damage/story?id=11471875

Anderson, C.A., & Bushman, B.J. (2002). Human aggression. *Annual Review of Psychology, 53*, 27–51.

Armour, M. (2002). Experiences of covictims of homicide. *Trauma, Abuse and Violence, 3*, 109–124.

Austen, I. (2010, October 19). Canadian commander videotaped murders. Retrieved from http://www.nytimes.com/2010/10/20/world/americas /20canada.html

Bandura, A. (1973). *Aggression: A social learning analysis.* Englewood Cliffs: NJ: Prentice Hall.

Boston Globe. (2012). *Neil Entwistle's attorney argues before SJC that searches in murder case were illegal.* Metro D, p. 1. Retrieved from http://www.boston .com/Boston/metrodesk/2012/04/neil-entwistle-attorney-argues-before- sjc-that-searches-murder-case-were-illegal/2cQ8nIqjf94ZmmbysDToAO /index.html

British Broadcasting Corporation (BBC). (2010). Full horror of Canda's pilot murders revealed. Retrieved from http://www.bbc.co.uk/news/world-us- canada-11577048

Buka, S.L., Stichnick, T.L., Birdthistle, I., & Earls, F.J. (2001). Youth exposure to violence: Prevalence, risks and consequences. *American Journal of Orthopsychiatry, 71*(3), 298–310.

Bureau of Justice Statistics. (1995). *Violent offenders in state prison: Sentences and time served.* Washington, DC: Department of Justice, Office of Justice Programs.

Bureau of Justice Statistics. (1998). *Justice in the United States and in England and Wales.* Washington, DC: Department of Justice, Office of Justice Programs.

Bureau of Justice Statistics. (2002). *Recidivism of prisoners released in 1994* (Special Report by P.A. Langan & D.J. Levin). Washington, DC: Department of Justice, Office of Justice Programs.

Cameron, S. (2011). *On the farm: Robert William Pickton and the tragic story of Vancouver's missing women.* New York, NY: Random House Digital, Inc.

Canadian Press Files. (2011). Serial killer Kenneth Olsen dies. Retrieved from http://www.cbc.ca/news/canada/story/2011/09/30/clifford-olson-death .html

Canter, D. (2004). Offender profiling and investigative psychology. *Journal of Investigative Psychology and Offenders Profiling, 1,* 1–15.

Canter, D.V., & Wentink, N. (2004). An empirical test of Holmes and Holmes' serial murder typology. *Criminal Justice and Behavior, 3*(4), 488–515.

Doerner, W.G., & Lab, S.P. (2008). *Victimology.* Cincinnatti, OH: Anderson Publishing.

Douglas, J., Burgess, A.W., Burgess, A., & Ressler, R. (2006). *Crime classification manual* (2nd ed.). San Francisco: Jossey-Bass.

Douglas, J., & Olshaker, M. (1999). *The anatomy of motive.* New York: Scribner.

Edwards, J. (2010). A victim speaks. Canada: Simcoe.com. Retrieved from http://www.simcoe.com/news/article/835045--a-victim-s-story

Ellis, C.A., & Lord, J. (1999). Homicide. In G. Coleman, M. Gaboury, M. Murray, and A. Seymour (Eds.), *National victim assistance academy text.* Retrieved from http://www.crimevictimservices.org/page/victimtypes/81

Federal Bureau of Investigation (FBI). (2005). *Supplementary homicide reports 1980–2004.* Washington, DC: Department of Justice.

Federal Bureau of Investigation (FBI). (2006). *Uniform crime report—Crime in the United States.* Washington, DC: Department of Justice.

Federal Bureau of Investigation (FBI). (2007). *Uniform crime report—Crime in the United States.* Washington, DC: Department of Justice.

Federal Bureau of Investigation (FBI). (2011). *Uniform crime report—Crime in the United States.* Washington, DC: Department of Justice.

Fox, James Alan. 2001. Uniform Crime Reports [United States]: Supplementary Homicide Reports, 1976–1999. ICPSR 3180.

Fox, J.A., & Levin, J. (1996). *Over kill: Mass murder and serial killing exposed.* New York: Bantam Books.

Fox, J.A., & Levin, J. (2005). *Extreme killing: Understanding serial murder.* Thousand Oaks, CA: Sage.

Fox, J. A., & Levin, J. (2006). *Will to kill: Explaining senseless murder.* Boston: Allyn Bacon.

Goodwin, M. (1998). Reliability, validity and utility of extant serial murder classifications. *The Criminologist, 22,* 194–210.

Goodwin, M. (2002). Reliability, validity, and utility of criminal profiling typologies. *Journal of Police and Criminal Psychology, 17,* 1–18.

Gleser, G., Green, B., & Winget, C. (1981). *Prolonged psychosocial effects of disaster: A study of Buffalo Creek.* New York: Academic Press.

Goldstein, R. (2009). Howard Unruh dies at 88; Killed 13 people in Camden in 1949. *New York Times,* NY Region. Retrieved from http://www.nytimes.com/2009/10/20/nyregion/20unruh.html?_r=1&pagewanted=all

Gross, B. (2007). Life sentence: Co-victims of homicide. *Annals of the American Psychotherapy Association*. Retrieved from http://www.annalsofpsychotherapy.com/articles/fall07.php?topic=article10.

Hazelwood, R., & Douglas, J. (1980). The lust murderer. *FBI Law Enforcement Bulletin, 49*(3), 18–22.

Hickey, E. (2002). *Serial murderers and their victims* (3rd ed.). Belmont, CA: Wadsworth.

Hindelang, M.J., Gottfredson, M.R., & Garofalo, J. (1978). *Victims of personal crime: An empirical foundation for a theory of personal victimization.* Cambridge, MA: Ballinger.

Holmes, R.M., & Holmes, S.T. (1998). *Serial murder* (2nd ed.). Thousand Oaks, CA: Sage.

Holmes, R.M., & Holmes, S.T. (2001). *Mass murder in the United States.* Upper Saddle River, NJ: Prentice Hall.

Holmes, R.M., & Holmes, S.T. (2002). *Profiling violent crime: An investigative tool* (3rd ed.). Thousand Oaks, CA: Sage.

Horowitz, M.J., Krupnick, J., Kaltreider, N., Leong, A., & Marmar, C. (1981). Initial psychological response to parental death. *Archives of General Psychiatry, 137,* 316–323.

Illinois Department of Corrections. (2002). *Statistical presentation, 2001: Part II: Length of stay.* Springfield, IL: State of Illinois.

Iowa Legislative Services Agency. (2003). *Review of Iowa's 85.0% sentencing laws.* Des Moines, IA: State Capital.

Janzen, L.M, Cadell, S., & Westhues, A. (2004). Dealing with the sudden death of a child: Advice to professionals from parents. *Omega: Journal of Death and Dying, 48*(2), 175–190.

Kaltman, S., & Bonanno, G. (2003). Trauma and bereavement: Examining the impact of sudden and violent deaths. *Anxiety Disorders, 17,* 131–147.

Leonard, T. (2008, June 6). "Neil Entwistle lived a double life, US court told". *The Daily Telegraph* (London). Retrieved from http://www.telegraph.co.uk/news/worldnews/northamerica/usa/2085878/Neil-Entwistle-lived-a-double-life,-US-court-told.html

Lombroso-Ferrero, G. (1972, c1911). *Lombroso's criminal man.* Montclaire, NJ: Patterson Smith.

Megargee, E. (1966). Undercontrolled and overcontrolled personality types in extreme antisocial aggression. *Psychological Monographs, General and Applied, 80,* 1–29.

Menninger, K. (1938). *Man against himself.* New York: Harcourt, Brace.

Morton, R.J., & Hilts, M.A. (2005). Serial Murder. Retrieved from http://www.fbi.gov/stats-services/publications/serial-murder

Nash, J.R. (1993). *World encyclopedia of the 20th century murder.* New York: Marlowe & Company.

National Governors Association Center for Best Practices (NGA). (2004). *The challenges and impacts of prison reentry.* Washington, DC: National Governors Association.

New York Times (NYT). (2007). Shooting of 4 college friends baffles Newark. Retrieved from http://www.nytimes.com/2007/08/06/nyregion/06newark.html?_r=1

Parkes, C.M. (1972). *Bereavement: Studies of grief in adult life.* New York: International Universities Press.

Petherick, W. (2005). *The science of criminal profiling.* New York: Barnes and Noble.

Regehr, C., & Sussman, T. (2004). Intersections between grief and trauma: Towards an empirically based model for treating traumatic grief. *Journal of Brief Treatment and Crisis Intervention, 4*(3), 289–309.

Ressler, R., Burgess, A., & Douglas, J.E. (1992). *Sexual homicide.* New York: Free Press.

Robinson, B. (2004). *Convicted killer of Ennis Cosby confesses.* ABC News, February 9, 2004, p. 1.

Roberts, A.R, Zgoba, K., & Shahidullah, S.M. (2007). Recidivism among found types of homicide offenders: An exploratory analysis of 336 homicide offenders in New Jersey. *Aggression and Violent Behavior, 12*(5), 493–507.

Rock, P. (1998). *After homicide: Practical and political responses to bereavement.* Oxford, UK: Oxford University Press.

Salfati, C.G. (2001). A European perspective on the study of homicide. *Homicide Studies, 5*(4), 286–291.

Salfati, C.G. (2011, November). Behavioral & Victim Consistency Patterns by Serial Sexual Homicide Offenders First Annual International Multidisciplinary Collaborative Conference on Violence Research & Evidence-Based Practice: Sexual Homicide, Binghamton, NY: University of Binghamton.

Salfati, C.G., & Grey, J. (2002). Profiling U.S. homicide. Paper presented at the Annual Meeting of the American Society of Criminology, November 2002, Chicago, Il.

Sampson, R.J., Raudenbush, S.W., & Earls, F. (1997). Neighborhoods and violent crime: A multilevel study of collective efficacy. *Science, 277*, 918–924.

Sampson, R.J., & Wilson, W.J. (1995). Towards a theory of race, crime and urban inequality. In J. Hagan & R.D. Peterson (Eds.), *Crime and inequality* (pp. 37–52). Stanford, CA: Stanford University Press.

Savage, W.W. (1990). *Comic books and America, 1945–1954.* Norman, OK: University of Oklahoma Press.

Scroope, H. (2007). Suspect pleads not guilty in New Jersey students' execution-style deaths. Retrieved from http://www.foxnews.com/story/0,2933,292717,00.html

Serial Killer Profiles. (2009). Famous Serial Killers. Retrieved from http://www.serialkillers.ca/paul-bernardo-and-karla-homolka/

Snell, T. (2011). *Capital punishment, 2010 statistical tables.* U.S. Department of Justice. NCJ 236510. Washington, DC: Government Printing Office.

Starker, S. (1989). *Evil influences: Crusades against the mass media.* New Brunswick, NJ: Transaction Publishers.

Statistics Canada. (2011). Homicide offences, number and rate, by province and territory. Retrieved from http://www40.statcan.gc.ca/l01/cst01/Legal12b-eng.htm

Stout, D. (2008). *John E. List, 82, Killer of 5 family members, dies. New York Times.* Retrieved from http://www.nytimes.com/2008/03/25/nyregion/25list1.html

Sutherland, E.H. (1947). *Principles of criminology.* Philadelphia: J.B. Lippincott.

Tennessee Victim Assistance Academy Participant Manual. (2008). Retrieved from http://www.utc.edu/Academic/CriminalJustice/documents/Chapter15-Homicide_000.doc

Thompson, M., Norris, F., & Rubach, R. (1998). Comparative distress levels of inner-city family members of homicide victims. *Journal of Traumatic Stress, 11*(2), 223–242.

Travis, J., Keegan, S., & Cadora, E. (2005). A portrait of prisoner reentry in New Jersey. Retrieved from http://www.njisj.org/reports/portrait_report.html

U.S. Department of Labor. (2010). Workplace shootings fact sheet. Retrieved from http://www.bls.gov/iif/oshwc/cfoi/osar0014.htm

U.S. Senate Commerce, Science, and Transportation Committee. (2003). Hearing on The Impact of Interactive Violence on Children on April 14, 2000. Washington, DC: Government Printing Office.

U.S. Surgeon General's Scientific Advisory Committee on Television and Social Behavior. (1972). *Television and growing up: The impact of televised violence.* DHEW Publication No. HSM 72–9086. Washington, DC: U.S. Government Printing Office.

Violence Policy Center. (2006). American roulette: Murder-suicide in the United States. Retrieved from http://www.vpc.org/studies/amroul2006.pdf

Von Hentig, H. (1948). *The criminal and his victim.* New Haven, CT: Yale University Press.

Washington Institute for Public Policy. (2004). *Sentencing for adult felons in Washington. Part 1. Historical Trends.* Olympia, WA. Retrieved from http://www.scribd.com/doc/11202120/Sentences-for-Adult-Felons-in-Washington-Options-to-Address-Prison-Overcrowding-Part-II-Recidivism-Analyses http://www.scribd.com/doc/11202120/Sentences-for-Adult-Felons-in-Washington-Options-to-Address-Prison-Overcrowding-Part-II-Recidivism-Analyses

Weber, H.R., & Associated Press. (2002, June 28). "False leads in Dartmouth murder case took investigators elsewhere." *Boston Globe.* Retrieved from http://www.boston.com/news/daily/28/tulloch_leads.htm

Wertham, F. (1954). *Seduction of the innocent.* New York: Holt, Rinehart & Winston.

Wolfgang, M.E. (1958). *Patterns of homicide.* Philadelphia: University of Pennsylvania Press.

Hate Crimes

CHAPTER
14

■ Objectives

- To discuss the nature and sources of hate crimes
- To discuss legal controversies related to hate crimes
- To identify types of hate crimes
- To identify typologies of hate crime offenders
- To identify the impact of hate crimes on victims

■ Key Terms

Anti-Semitism
Genocide
Hate crime
Hate speech
Islamophobia
Suicide bomber
White supremacist
Xenophobia

CASE

On January 24, 2011, two young men from Shenandoah, Pennsylvania, Derrick Donchak, age 20, and Brandon Piekarsky, age 19, (see **Figure 14-1**) were sentenced to 9 years in prison for the beating death of 25-year-old Luis Ramirez, an undocumented Mexican immigrant (CNN, 2011). During the trial witnesses provided evidence the accused had repeatedly warned Ramirez to leave their neighborhood (which is 97% White) because they did not like immigrants. It was stated they made racial slurs before and during an attack in which they threw Mr. Ramirez to the ground and repeatedly kicked him in the head. Three Pennsylvania police officers, Chief Matthew Nestor, Officer William Moyer, and Officer Jason Hayes, were acquitted of charges of conspiracy to obstruct a federal investigation. It was alleged they attempted to cover up the 2008 murder. In summarizing the entire case, U.S. Department of Justice prosecutor Myesha K. Braden stated, "Because of Mr. Ramirez's race, he was somehow worthy of being beaten like a dog. Mr. Ramirez's race is the reason that he died," Braden said. "Every Hispanic member of the community was victimized. What happened to Luis Ramirez was no different than what happened in the 1940s, 1950s and 1960s" (Bortner, 2010).

■ Introduction

A hate crime is criminal conduct motivated in whole or in part by a pre-formed negative opinion or attitude toward a group based on race, ethnicity, religion, gender, sexual orientation, or disability. The perpetrator views the victim as lacking in full human worth based on those characteristics (California Department of Justice, 2000). Victims of hate crimes include members of racial, ethnic, and religious minority groups; people with disabilities; and people who are not heterosexual. Hate speech is defined as words used as weapons to ambush, terrorize, wound, humiliate, and degrade (Lawrence, Matsuda, Delgado, & Crenshaw, 1993). These messages threaten the individual's freedom and dignity in addition to his or her psychological and emotional state. These messages also continue the oppression and subordination of groups whose history has included discrimination. Lawrence and colleagues (1993) argued that by protecting hate speech we support those who hate in further subjugating oppressed groups. Conversely, others suggested that hate legislation and suppression of free speech can equally be used against oppressed and minority groups, restricting their ability to express views that contradict majority opinion (Cowan, Resendez, Marshall, & Quist, 2002). As American jurisprudence leans heavily on free speech as opposed to speech regulation, many challenges exist in attempting to address hate speech. Therefore, "hateful and offensive online speech enjoys the same robust First Amendment protections as any other form of speech" (Henry, 2009, p. 236).

A prime example of the conflict between the right to freedom of expression and the right to be protected from hate is the case of the Jones family in St. Paul, Minnesota. In the spring of 1990 an African American family, the Joneses, moved into a predominantly White neighborhood where within a few months they were subject to slashed tires, racial slurs, and finally a burning cross on the front lawn. A young man known to be a skinhead was convicted on trespassing and vandalism (Cowan et al., 2002). A St. Paul city ordinance allowed for legal prosecution of hate crimes, and thus the offender was charged. However, on appeal in 1992 the St. Paul ordinance was overturned by the Supreme Court of the United States on the basis that the ordinance violated the U.S. Constitution, specifically the right to free speech under the First Amendment. This Supreme Court ruling jeopardized all city and state laws throughout the United States regarding hate crimes. Hate crime debates therefore focus on what is the most fundamental right: the right to be protected from hatred or the right to free expression of one's views.

■ Scope of the Problem

Estimates of the incidence of hate crimes are variable and are also fraught with controversy. In the United States hate crime data come from two main sources: the Federal Bureau of Investigation (FBI) Uniform Crime Reporting Program and the Bureau of Justice Statistics. As a result of Congress passing the Hate Crime Statistics Act of 1992, the FBI has been reporting hate crime numbers conveyed by law enforcement agencies since 1994. The FBI's *Hate Crime Statistics 2009* identifies 6,604 incidents and includes information on 7,789 offenses, 8,322 victims, and 6,219 known offenders (FBI, 2009) (**Figure 14-2**). Some critics have suggested these numbers are extremely low for the entire population of the United States and suggest that such low numbers confirm that hate crimes are not as serious a problem as the media and society believe (Jacobs & Henry, 1996; Morgan, 2002). Consequently, these critics suggest that hate crime laws should be abandoned. Others suggest these numbers reflect significant underreporting of hate-related offenses to police. They argue that low numbers represent fear on the part of victims who choose not to self-identify through police reports and bias on the part of law enforcement who are reluctant to classify crimes as motivated by hate. Perhaps confirming that suspicion, the Bureau of Justice Statistics reports considerably higher numbers than those of the FBI. Using interview data and extrapolating to the population base, they estimated an annual average of 191,000 incidents in the United States between 2000 and 2003, affecting 210,000 victims (Shively & Mulford, 2007).

In 2006, using the 12 major police forces in Canada, a total of 892 hate-motivated crimes were reported (Dauvergne, Scrim, & Brennan,

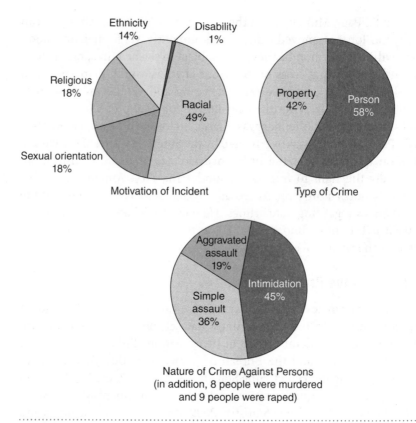

Motivation of Incident

Type of Crime

Nature of Crime Against Persons
(in addition, 8 people were murdered
and 9 people were raped)

FIGURE 14-2 FBI Hate Crime Statistics

Data from Federal Bureau of Investigation. Hate crime statistics 2009. Retrieved from http://www2.fbi.gov/ucr/hc2009
/incidents.html.

2006). Overall, 61% of the hate crimes were motivated by race or ethnicity, 27% were motivated by religion, and 10% were motivated by sexual orientation. Half of all racially motivated hate crimes were directed toward Black people, and two-thirds of religiously motivated crimes were directed toward Jewish people. Half of all hate crimes involved property, 23% involved assault, and almost 15% involved threats or harassment. One hate crime resulted in murder, and one involved sexual assault. Hate crimes were more likely to involve young people, victims were most likely to be between the ages of 12 and 24, and the perpetrators of hate crimes were most likely to be between the ages of 12 and 17. In most cases (77%) the perpetrator was a stranger to the victim. The offender was identified in approximately one-half of the incidents. Men constituted 90%

of the known offenders. Only 10% of the offenders had previously been involved with criminal activity (Dauvergne et al., 2006).

A newer venue for hate crimes is the Internet. In March 1995 former Klansman Don Black created the first neo-Nazi website, which featured links, essays, and graphics promoting White supremacy, Nazism, and guerrilla warfare and attesting to Jewish conspiracies and Black inferiority. By March 1998, 163 active sites in North America publicized racial hatred. Of these, 29 were based on Klan beliefs, 27 were founded by skinheads, and 25 were focused on anti-Semitism (Southern Poverty Law Center, 1998).

With the explosion of information on the Internet since that time, current estimates of websites that promote hate are not available. However, in 2010 the Southern Poverty Law Center identified 1,002 hate groups using a variety of sources, a 7.5% increase from the year before (Southern Poverty Law Center, 2010). The popularity of the Internet for extremists is due in part to low cost, the ease of global distribution, and the anonymity with which someone can access and contribute to the discourse without ever self-identifying or attending a meeting (Levin, 2002a). These sites can provide tools for extremists; for example, a prominent animal liberation site offers do-it-yourself instructions for creating basic incendiaries from easily acquired materials. They also provide lists of possible victims, for example, a radical antiabortion site lists the names of physicians who perform abortions, complete with their driver's license information, home addresses, and images. Names of those who have been murdered feature slash marks. Hate on the Internet is especially hard to regulate due to the unlimited number of access points, the lack of legal precedence and mechanisms for defining Internet-based activity, and the tremendous flexibility and technology growth of the medium (Levin, 2002a).

■ Hate Crime Legislation

Although violence on the basis of hate has a long history, its legislative history is very short. As stated earlier, in the United States this was in large part due to the difficulties in prohibiting hate speech and subsequent actions due to the emphasis on freedom of speech in the U.S. Constitution (Morgan, 2002). The first attempts to address hate crimes in the United States occurred from the 1920s to the 1940s when attempts were made to enact statutes to deter the incitement of hatred and the lynching of African Americans. However, although there were a few successes in creating state legislation to address this terrifying issue, most early efforts failed to find a means to prohibit hate-based crime. In the 1950s seven U.S. states and several large cities adopted group libel statutes that addressed hate speech, and in 1952 the Supreme Court upheld the constitutionality of these statutes (Dixon & Ray, 2007).

During the 1980s and 1990s most U.S. states, beginning with California in 1978, moved to criminalize actions against persons or property motivated by hate. In 1981 the Anti-Defamation League drafted model legislation that served as a template for similar legislation in other states (McPhail, 2000). By 1999, 43 U.S. states had developed statutes that targeted the intent of the crime as being motivated by hate or bias. Most of these states also delineated particular groups as being specific targets of hate crimes. For example, 41 states have identified racially motivated hate, 40 have identified hatred related to religious affiliation, 22 have identified hatred of sexual orientation, 22 have identified hatred of gender, and 19 have identified hatred of persons with a disability (Morgan, 2002). In addition, 25 states determined that hate crimes are deserving of greater punishment than crimes motivated by other causes. The state-based legislation was enhanced by federal legislation, including the Hate Crimes Prevention Act of 2000, the 1990 Hate Crime Statistics Act, and the 1994 Hate Crime Sentencing Act (Jenness, 1999). In the Hate Crime Sentencing Act, enhanced penalties are allowed if a victim or property was selected by the offender because of the actual or perceived race, color, religion, national origin, ethnicity, gender, disability, or sexual orientation.

Despite the aim of these statutes to both symbolically and practically deal with the special harms created by crimes motivated by hate, it is suggested that prosecutions are rare, and when they are attempted they often fail due to practical and legal difficulties (Franklin, 2002). To begin with, initial decisions about whether to charge someone with a hate crime are made by frontline police officers, who are influenced not only by their own beliefs but also by the belief systems within their communities and organizations. Variations between policing divisions in laying charges related to hate crimes are quite striking particularly when the offenses are committed by youth (Franklin, 2002). When a decision to lay a charge related to hate is made, the next challenge is to prove the motivation behind the crime, and the final decision on the guilt of an offender rests with a judge and/or jury, who bring their own biases to the table.

In Canada, hate crimes are addressed under three sections of the national Criminal Code. Section 318, Advocating Genocide, is defined as supporting or arguing for the killing of members of an identifiable group. Advocating genocide is an indictable offense and can result in a prison term of up to 5 years. Section 319 of the Code, Public Incitement of Hatred, occurs when a person (1) communicates statements (2) in a public place (3) that incite hatred against an identifiable group (4) in such a way that there will likely be a breach of the people. Conviction can result in a sentence of up to 2 years. Finally, under Section 320, physical hate propaganda material kept on any property for distribution can be seized (Criminal Code of Canada, 2004). Although originally the "identifiable groups" in these provisions were defined by color, race, religion, and ethnic origin, Bill 59-11, which was passed in 2004, extended the definition to include sexual orientation.

The most famous case related to hate crime legislation in Canada is that of Ernst Zündel, who was jailed several times in Canada for publishing literature that claimed the Holocaust was a hoax and incited hatred against Jews. Zündel immigrated to Canada in 1958 from West Germany. In the 1970s he established a publishing company, which by the early 1980s had become a major worldwide distributor of Nazi memorabilia, books, and pamphlets denying the Holocaust and books denouncing Zionism. His mailing list in the United States alone included 29,000 addresses, and in 1978 to 1979 the West German government seized over 200 shipments of material bound for distribution there. Zündel was criminally tried and convicted in 1985 and 1988 for hate crimes, but this was overturned on appeal to the Supreme Court of Canada in 1992 on the grounds the conviction violated the right to free speech under the Canadian Charter of Rights and Freedoms. Having been denied citizenship in Canada, his permanent residency status in Canada expired, and he went to the United States, where he was arrested and deported in 2003 for overstaying a visa. Upon his return to Canada a national security certificate was issued and deportation to Germany was sought. After 2 years of court battles and appeals during which Zündel was held in solitary confinement, he was extradited to Germany in 2005, where he was to face 14 charges of inciting racial hatred. Finally, in February 2007 he was convicted in a German court and sentenced to 5 years in prison, the maximum allowed for such an offense under German law (CBC News, 2007). This case is perhaps the most telling example of the difficulty that various Western legal systems have in dealing with activities that incite racial and other forms of hatred.

In 2004 the Council of Europe, the United States, Canada, South Africa, and Japan entered into the Cybercrime Convention and in 2010 were joined by 30 additional countries. This convention mandates countries to have unified legislation for international crime prevention to address cross-jurisdictional issues related to cybercrime. The convention is supplemented by a Protocol on Xenophobia and Racism, encompassing xenophobia and racism committed on the Internet. This protocol prohibits "any written material, any image or other representation of ideas or theories, which advocates, promotes or incites hatred, discrimination or violence, against any individual or group of individuals, based on race, color, descent or national or ethnic origin, as well as religion if used as pretext for any of these factors" (Council of Europe, 2006, Ch1, A.1). It also prohibits Internet sites that deny or minimize crimes against humanity, including the Holocaust. The United States, while signing the Cybercrime Convention, did not sign the protocol on racism due to concerns that it conflicted with the First Amendment. Thus, any hate-related website originating in the United States is safe from recrimination under the treaty (Henry, 2009).

■ Typology of Hate Crimes

Hate crimes are motivated by extremist views related to the characteristics of a particular individual or group. In this chapter we highlight hate crimes motivated by discrimination based on race, religion, gender, sexual orientation, and disability. In addition, although all hate crimes may have an underlying political motivation, some are committed specifically for the purposes of effecting political responses.

Racial

As indicated in **Figure 14-2**, although hate crimes based on race can be directed at many different racial groups, both historically in North America and to the present day, the majority of racially motivated hate crimes are directed toward individuals who are Black. As Levin (2002b) pointed out, "The text of the Declaration of Independence leaves the impression that the notion of harmful status-based deprivations did not exist at America's founding: 'We hold these truths to be self evident, that all men are created equal.' Yet status-based violence and deprivations are old as the nation itself" (p. 228). Slavery, and the concomitant violence committed against slaves, would easily fit under current definitions of hate crimes. Nevertheless, courts were clear that slaves were not to be afforded basic rights of safety. In an 1829 North Carolina case in which a slave master shot an escaping female slave, the judge declared the power of the master and the submission of slaves were absolute regardless of the resultant harm (*State v. Mann*, 1829). Decisions of this sort were upheld by the Supreme Court, which in 1857 found that Blacks, due to their inferior nature, were incapable of being citizens of the United States and thus were not subject to the rights of citizenship (*Scott v. Sandford*, 1857). Seven years later the Civil Rights

Act of 1866 extended citizenship and other rights to Blacks, and in 1871 legislation was enacted banning the activities of the Ku Klux Klan.

Despite protective legislation the 1870s saw a rise in hate crimes against Blacks in America, with lynching one of the major forms of violence where victims were mutilated, burned, or hung in public arenas. By 1915 the Ku Klux Klan reemerged, and by the mid-1920s it had 4.5 million members. Klan members held influential roles in state and national assemblies (Levin, 2002b). Legislation in the late 1920s placed restrictions on membership in these groups, so they largely went underground, reemerging in the 1960s. Thus, hate crimes committed against Blacks in North America have a long tradition, initially sanctioned by law and only very recently condemned by law.

James Byrd, Jr., was a 49-year-old African American man living on disability income in a subsidized apartment in Jasper, Texas. In June 1998 he accepted a ride from three young White men, Shawn Allen Berry, Lawrence Russell Brewer, and John William King. Instead of driving him home, however, they beat him and chained him by his ankles to the back of a pickup truck. At the trial a pathologist testified that Mr. Byrd was alive through much of the dragging, and it appeared that he attempted to keep his head off the ground. However, about one-half of the way through the 3-mile drag he hit a culvert and was decapitated. His body was then dumped in a cemetery. It was determined that two of the defendants, King and Brewer, were members of a white supremacist group. King's body was covered in tattoos that depicted, among other things, a Black man hanging from a tree, Nazi symbols, and the words "Aryan Pride." All three defendants were found guilty of capital murder, two were sentenced to death, and the third, Berry, was sentenced to life in prison (CNN, 1999; "Third defendant is convicted," 1999). Lawrence Russell Brewer was executed in Texas on September 21, 2011. In 2004, several years after Byrd's murder, two White teenagers were charged with desecrating his grave ("Teenagers charged," 2004).

The horrific death of James Byrd, Jr., is not an isolated incident and merely serves as an example of many tragic crimes committed against people. Racially based crimes often occur in waves, whereby a single incident emotionally incites a community and causes a ripple effect of retaliation and further offending. The police in the United Kingdom, in awareness of this tendency, work to identify critical incidents and critical periods of time and then attempt to engage with the community to ward off further attacks (Dixon & Ray, 2007). Offending against a socially excluded group becomes justified by community prejudice, and victims become dehumanized.

In the 1940s scholars advanced a theory that hate crimes are associated with economic conditions. That is, aggression toward a particular group stems from frustration associated with economic downturns even when these groups have no real responsibility for the economic decline. Early studies in the 1940s identified the correlation between lynching of Blacks in the American South and economic conditions as measured by cotton prices and economic growth between 1882 and 1930. More recent research has challenged these analyses and has suggested that the roots of racially motivated hate crimes are far more complicated than by economic conditions alone (Espiritu, 2004; Green, Glaser, & Rich, 1998).

Another analysis of racially motivated hate crimes relates to the conception that they are caused by xenophobia (Perry, 2002). In recent times groups such as the American-Arab Anti Discrimination Committee and the National Asian Pacific American Legal Consortium have raised concerns about an increase in violence against members of their communities. There is a belief that such an increase in hate attacks emanate from fear. Post-9/11, some have suggested that the Patriot Act has legitimized prejudicial treatment against Arab and Asian Americans (Akiyama, 2008). The Patriot Act expands law enforcement to allow for the conduct of searches, phone and Internet surveillance, and access to personal medical, financial, student, and mental health records. It also requires foreign-born immigrants from certain countries to register under the National Security Entry/Exit Registration System with U.S. Immigration and Customs Enforcement (Akiyama, 2008). Concerns are that such government policies will also be reflected in public attitudes of Islamophobia and ultimately in the commission of hate crimes. A recent Gallup Poll of Americans indicated that 39% were in favor of Muslims carrying special identification, and 25% said they would not want to live next door to a Muslim (Akiyama, 2008).

Religion

On the night of April 5, 2004, the library of United Talmud Torah, a Jewish elementary school in Montreal, Canada, erupted in flames after a kerosene bomb crashed through the window. Although no one was injured in the nighttime attack, it caused $500,000 in damage and destroyed 10,000 books. A note discovered on the scene indicated the attack was in retaliation for Israel's assassination of Hamas leader Sheikh Ahmed Yassin. The note indicated Jews should be punished for Israeli actions and promised to strike again if Israeli policy did not change. It read, "Here is the consequence of your crimes and your occupation. Here is the riposte of your assassinations. Here is where terrorist Ariel Sharon has led you" (Center for Policing

Terrorism, 2007, p. 2). The following year, 19-year-old Sleiman Elmerhebi was sentenced to 40 months in jail (CBC News, 2005; Peritz, 2005). This attack against a Jewish institution in Montreal was not an isolated occurrence. In 2006 a firebombing occurred at a Jewish boys' school, and in 2007 the Jewish Community Centre was firebombed. A report of B'nai Brith's League for Human Rights identified Montreal as a hotbed of anti-Jewish activity in 2006, identifying 215 separate occurrences, including desecration of synagogues, destruction of property, and assaults. Property crime, particularly vandalism, is the most common type of religiously motivated hate crime and includes burning of religious institutions and painting of swastikas on buildings.

In both Canada and the United States most religiously motivated hate crime is directed against people who are Jewish. As indicated earlier, Jewish people are the most common victims of all hate crimes in Canada. According to the FBI's *Hate Crime Statistics 2009*, 70.1% of all religiously motivated hate crimes in the United States were anti-Semitic in nature, down from 86% in 1996 (FBI, 2009). A 2004 report by the U.S. Department of State said, "The increasing frequency and severity of anti-Semitic incidents since the start of the 21st century, particularly in Europe, has compelled the international community to focus on anti-Semitism with renewed vigor" (U.S. Department of State, 2005, p. 1). According to this report the European Union Monitoring Center for Racism and Xenophobia identified France, Germany, the United Kingdom, Belgium, and the Netherlands as the countries with the most significant increases in anti-Semitic incidents. As a result governments in France, Germany, and Belgium are providing enhanced protection to members of the Jewish community and Jewish properties.

It has been suggested that this type of hate crime is frequently based on normative beliefs about acceptable violence toward a particular group. Amjad and Wood (2009) conducted two studies examining whether normative beliefs about aggression predicted whether youth in Pakistan would join an extremist anti-Semitic organization. In this study university students completed a questionnaire eliciting their beliefs and then were approached by a confederate and asked to join a specific organization. Beliefs about normative aggression toward Jews were strongly associated with willingness to join the organization.

Despite the preponderance of religious bias hate crimes being anti-Semitic, other groups are also targeted, as previously noted regarding race. During 2001 after the attack on the World Trade Center, the FBI reported a 17-fold increase in anti-Muslim hate crimes, and in 2004 13% of religiously motivated hate crimes were against Islamic individuals;

however, by 2009 this was reduced to 8.4%. Other discriminatory activities directed toward Muslims post-9/11 included "airport screenings, search and surveillance powers without sufficient review, guilt by association, investigations and deportations, and special alien registration" (Abu-Raz & Suarez, 2009, p. 50).

Disability

The pervasive stigma that people apply to both mental and physical illness is expressed in many forms of discriminatory behaviors against those with disabilities, including placing disabled persons at increased risk of physical and sexual abuse (American Psychological Association, 1998). Research confirms that people with disabilities experience heightened risk of sexual, physical, and emotional abuse (McMahon, West, Lewis, Armstrong, & Conway, 2004). Where disability and gender discrimination intersect, the incidence of violence is alarming. For example, the risk of physical and sexual assault is 4 to 10 times higher for adults with developmental disabilities than for other adults (Sobsey, 1994). Sobsey found that 84% of disabled people who were victims of sexual violence were female, and 93% of offenders were male. Further, studies repeatedly demonstrate high rates of victimization among people suffering from mental illness (Clement, Brohan, Sayce, Pool, & Thornicroft, 2011). Nevertheless, tremendous barriers exist to reporting these crimes and to prosecuting them, including myths in the criminal justice system that women with intellectual disabilities who are victims of sexual violence will not be credible witnesses due to their intellectual or speech limitations and that women with disabilities are promiscuous (Keilty & Connelly, 2001).

The fact that people with disabilities experience discrimination was acknowledged by the U.S. federal government in the Americans with Disabilities Act of 1990. This act proclaimed "that disabled persons have been subjected to a history of purposeful unequal treatment" (42 USC 12101, SEC. 2(7)). It is perhaps the seemingly incomprehensible act of attacking someone who is rendered vulnerable by disability that disability was not added to the Hate Crime Statistics Act until 1994. One of the issues in defining crimes against those with a disability as hate crimes is the individualized nature of these crimes. In hate crimes against those with disabilities, there are no crosses burning on lawns and no swastikas painted on walls; rather, individual vulnerability is exploited.

Waxman (1991) chronicled the history of treatment of those with disabilities and indicated the abuse and murder of children with disabilities were commonplace in traditional societies. This was as a result of several factors: utilitarianism (the greatest good for the greatest number of people); value systems that emphasized strength, beauty, and intelligence; and shame related to beliefs that disability was punishment for sin or disobedience of God. In more recent times forced institutionalization may have somewhat different, yet somewhat similar, motivations (Waxman, 1991). These biases against those with disabilities result in loss of control, loss of worth, social isolation, and ultimately increased vulnerability. Further, individuals with disabilities are more likely to live in poverty, are less likely to be employed on a full-time basis, are more likely to be reliant on public transit, and are more likely to be reliant on others for personal care (McMahon et al., 2004). On a social level, disabled persons are less likely than others in society to have learned social skills to protect themselves against crime.

Gender

Twenty-five-year-old Marc Lépine (born Gamil Gharbi) walked into the École Polytechnique de Montréal on December 6, 1989, carrying a Ruger Mini-14 semiautomatic rifle. He entered a second-floor classroom, separated the men from the women, and then ordered the approximately 50 men to leave. Claiming he was fighting feminism, he shot the nine women who remained, killing six and injuring the rest. He is reported to have screamed "I hate women." After this, Lépine moved to other areas of the building, killing a total of 14 women and four men and injuring 10 additional women. The incident ended when Lépine turned the gun on himself. In a letter found in his jacket, Lépine indicated the attack was politically motivated. That is, he wished to kill feminists for ruining his life. The letter contained the names of 19 other women he wished to kill. The Montreal Massacre became a galvanizing moment in which mourning turned into outrage about all violence against women (CBC Digital Archives, 1989). The date is remembered by a walk and vigil in cities across Canada.

The pervasive nature of violence against women in our society has led many to advocate for this violence to be considered a hate crime. Portraying violence against women as hate based underscores the public and societal nature of the crime and moves the focus away from the individual victim, thereby reducing the possibility of victim blaming. During a congressional hearing on the Hate Crime Statistics Act, the president of the National Organization for Women presented feminist research and theory to argue that women were a group targeted for violence due to hate. Nevertheless, gender was not included (McPhail & DiNitto, 2005). More recently, it has been added to federal legislation, to the legislation of 20 states, and to the model hate crime statute prepared by the Anti-Defamation League. However, gender has rarely been used in hate crime prosecutions, and by 2005 McPhail and DiNitto reported only two successful prosecutions of gender-related hate bias crimes. Their study of prosecutors' attitudes supports the notions that those in the justice system find it difficult to fit violence against women into the hate crime model. Thus, although legislation supports gender as a basis for hate crime, there is no evidence that practice will change in the near future.

Sexual Orientation

On a cold October night in 1998 in Laramie, Wyoming, Matthew Shepard, a 21-year-old gay college student, was robbed, savagely beaten, tied to a fence in a remote rural area, and left to die. Eighteen hours later he was found alive but unconscious. He died of head injuries 5 days later in a Colorado hospital. The high-profile murder galvanized gay rights activists but also fueled antigay opponents. Tensions were so high Matthew Shepard's father wore a bulletproof vest under his suit when he spoke at his son's funeral (ABC News, 2004). The public response to the attack was instantaneous. Thousands of people staged candlelight vigils, prominent figures issued statements condemning the attack, and Matthew Shepard became a symbol of antigay hate crimes (Hoffman, 2011).

Local residents Aaron McKinney and Russell Henderson were both convicted of kidnapping and murder and sentenced to two consecutive life terms in prison. However, because there was no statute for hate crimes in Wyoming, subsequently a bill was introduced into the Wyoming legislature that defined attacks motivated by hate. The bill was voted down in the Wyoming House of Representatives. On May 3, 2007, the Matthew Shepard Act (HR 1592) passed the U.S. House of Representatives, and on September 27, 2007, it passed the Senate. However, the hate crimes provision was not included in the final version of the bill. The Act that sought to extend federal hate crime legislation to include individuals who are victims of hate as a result of gender, sexual orientation, or disability fell victim to House opponents of hate crimes (Human Rights Campaign, 2008).

In 1984 the National Gay and Lesbian Task Force collected data in eight cities and found that 19% of gay men and lesbian women had experienced physical assault because of their sexual orientation, 44% had been threatened with violence, 83% lived in fear of being victimized, and 45% had changed their behavior to avoid violent attacks (Noelle, 2002). There is evidence that the nature of violent attacks against gay males is particularly brutal. Research refers to excessive brutality, mutilation, and aggravated assault inflicted with a wide variety of weapons, such as guns, baseball bats, clubs, chains, and ropes (Willis, 2004). The majority of hate crimes based on sexual orientation are committed by young males (Espiritu, 2004).

Many writers suggest that hate crimes against gays and lesbians stem largely from general societal attitudes toward homosexuality (Herek, Gillis, & Cogan, 1999; Noelle, 2002; Willis, 2004). The 2001 General Social Survey on Victimization in the United States, for example, found that 59% of respondents endorsed the sentiment that homosexuality is always wrong. Thus, it is not surprising that hate crime legislation, which includes sexual orientation as a justification for protection, is not generally supported (Johnson & Byers, 2003). It is suggested that these attitudes also extend to law enforcement related to hate crimes against gays and lesbians. In 1999, of the total number of incidents of hate crimes against gays, lesbians, bisexuals, and transgender people, law enforcement personnel refused to take a report in 10% of the cases, took a report but made no arrest in 73% of the cases, and made arrests in 17% of the cases (Espiritu, 2004).

Political

Politically motivated hate crimes are often based on conspiratory beliefs of the offender or deep-seated religious beliefs. As indicated above regarding Internet crimes, the identification and killing of physicians who perform abortions is an example of a politically motivated hate crime. Prolife movement members, frustrated by increasing moves to legalize abortion, begin to resort to extremist methods. Born in 1923, Henry Morgentaler studied gynecology upon his release from Auschwitz and went to Canada where, in 1969, he gave up his family practice and began to perform illegal abortions in Montreal. By the time Morgentaler opened his Toronto clinic in 1983, abortion was the most controversial issue in Canada. In the decade that followed, attempts were made on the life of Morgentaler and other physicians; the clinic was bombed, shot at, and desecrated on numerous occasions; and women who entered the clinic were harassed and assaulted. Although abortion was legalized in the United States in 1973 by the Supreme Court ruling in *Roe v. Wade*, statutory restrictions to abortions in Canada were not overturned until 1988 in the Supreme Court case of *Morgentaler v. Her Majesty the Queen*. Despite the Supreme Court ruling, or perhaps fueled by it, attacks on Morgentaler and his clinics continued well into the 1990s. To this day, he lives behind bulletproof glass.

Conspiracy beliefs are another motivation for political bias hate crimes. Timothy McVeigh's bombing of the government building in Oklahoma City, which killed 168 people and injured 850 more, is the deadliest case of domestic terrorism in the United States. McVeigh was a former member of the U.S. Army who specialized in explosives and demolition. Upon his release he lived a transient life, acting as a vendor in gun shows and visiting Waco, Texas, at the time of the Waco Siege. McVeigh claimed the bombing was in response to the government crimes at Waco and instructed his lawyers to use a necessity defense and to argue that his bombing of the federal building was justifiable. Nevertheless, McVeigh was sentenced to death by lethal injection.

■ Typology of Offender Motivation

McDevitt, Levin, & Bennett (2002) developed a typology of hate crime offenders based on an examination of 169 cases of the Boston Police Department. These four types (thrill seeking, defensive, retaliatory, and mission) are widely accepted and taught in law enforcement training and have been corroborated in other research (Franklin, 2000). A summary of these typologies can be found in **Table 14-1**.

Thrill-seeking offenders are motivated by a desire for excitement and constituted 66% of the cases in McDevitt and colleagues' study. This category consists mainly of youths who act in groups. When perpetrating these crimes, youths have frequently been out drinking together and when caught they frequently explain to police they were bored and looking for some fun. Groups of youths engaged in thrill-seeking hate crimes generally leave their own neighborhoods and seek a target such as a gay bar, synagogue, or minority neighborhood where they inflict violence against persons or property and in doing so make slurs or leave graffiti that is indicative of hate. These offenders have no previous relationship with the victim. Their weapons tend to be hands, feet, and rocks or other easily accessible items because the premeditation and consideration of consequences are limited. Their behavior is often not consistent with

TABLE 14-1 Typology of Offenders of Hate Crime Motivation

Type	Description
Thrill seeking	Desire for excitement
	Youths acting in groups
Defensive	Seen as necessary from offender's prejudiced point of view
	Committed near victim's home, school, or business
Retaliatory	In response to real or believed incident committed by someone in the targeted group
	Seen as avenging the death of someone
Mission	Attempt to rid the world of perceived evil
	Usually a member of an organized group

Data from McDevitt, J., Levin, J., & Bennett, S. 2002. Hate crime offenders: An expanded typology. *Journal of Social Issues, 58*(2), 303–317.

the typical behaviors of these youths. Further, their general attitudes are often not of deep-seated hate; rather, they may have been swept up in the moment. Because the commitment to the bias of these groups is frequently limited, there is a strong possibility of deterrence from further criminal activities of this type simply by police intervention. Parents are frequently stunned this has occurred when they are notified by police, and they act as a further force for deterrence.

Defensive offenders constituted 25% of the hate crimes examined. These attacks are committed, from the offenders' prejudiced point of view, because they are necessary to protect their neighborhood from others who are considered to be outsiders. These offenders report to police that members of a minority group had moved into a previously all-White neighborhood, school, or workplace and introduced the risk that more of their group would follow, resulting in lower property values, heightened crime, more drugs, and so on. Because such defensive crimes are based on firmly held beliefs that the minority group represents a danger, offenders in this category tend to have limited worldviews, have not been exposed to people in the "other category," and due to their fears and prejudices are unlikely to allow themselves to have sufficient exposure to those in the feared group to develop relationships and quell fears. As a result of their belief systems, deterrence through individual criminal charges or therapeutic interventions is unlikely. Externally imposed strategies, such as the forced integration of schools in the southern states, coupled with security for those in the minority group, eventually lead to change. These crimes tend to be perpetrated by groups of young people and occur near the home, school, or business of the offenders. There are often previous acts of intimidation by the offenders in which threatening messages are spray painted on homes, racist comments are made directly to individuals, physical intimidation is used, or actual physical assaults are perpetrated.

Retaliatory hate crimes occur after a real or believed incident was committed by someone within the group that is now targeted. For example, after the attack and shooting death of a 16-year-old Black adolescent, Yusuf Hawkins, in a White working class neighborhood of Brooklyn in August 1989, violence erupted throughout New York City. Hawkins and three friends were confronted by a crowd of 10 to 30 White youths, some of whom had baseball bats and one had a handgun. The youths mistakenly believed Hawkins was dating a local girl. Although the original attack on Hawkins could be viewed as falling into the defensive category of hate crimes, what followed was a number of retaliatory attacks resulting in the month with the largest number of hate crimes in New York

City's history (McDevitt et al., 2002; Pinderhughes, 1993). Thus, retaliatory hate crime offenders act on the belief that they are avenging the death or violation of someone who is like them. The attack frequently follows merely the rumor that a crime was committed against someone in the offender's own group and rarely is any effort put into verifying the rumor. The actual target of the attack needs only to be someone in the targeted group and is not the actual perpetrator of the original crime. The attack is likely to be on the turf of the victim and can involve lethal weapons as a result of premeditation.

Mission is the final category of hate crime offender motivations. In this category offenders are totally committed to bigotry, and this becomes the focus of their life. In mission hate crimes the perpetrator seeks to rid the world of perceived evil. A mission offender is usually a member of an organized group, such as the Ku Klux Klan, although the offender may operate alone, as in the case of Timothy McVeigh, who bombed the federal building in Oklahoma City. Commitment to the belief system is complete, and the methods of attack are premeditated and often lethal. This type of offender will not be deterred by reason or legal intervention. In McDevitt and colleagues' study (2002), deterrence occurred in less than 1% of cases. The ultimate example of the mission-motivated hate crime is the suicide bomber.

■ Suicide Bombers as Perpetrators of Hate Crimes

Suicide bombing, as a form of terrorism, is the targeted use of self-destructing human beings against civilian populations to effect political change. It serves as a weapon of psychological warfare intended to affect a large population. The primary targets are not those killed in the attack but those who witness it (Atran, 2003). This type of activity can best be viewed as theater for the media (Hutchinson, 2007). What separates suicide bombings from other forms of hate crimes is they are rarely conducted independently by one individual, but rather the individual is executing an organizationally planned attack. Suicide bombings are, however, consistent with other hate crimes in that they are random attacks based on hatred toward a particular group of people. The outcomes of such terror are often highly successful, and governments frequently capitulate to the demands of the terror group in fear of further widespread death and destruction.

Classical literature describes suicides where there is clearly declared hostile and aggressive intent toward an enemy. These include suicide out of revenge in Greek writings and suicide by devotion by Roman soldiers. Although the history of suicide attacks is long, in modern times the first noted examples were the Japanese kamikazes, who used aircraft as flying bombs to destroy Allied ships. It has been suggested that in the Battle of Okinawa, all requests for volunteers met with unanimous acceptance although no shame was to be associated with refusal (Atran, 2003). However, in a study of the diaries of the pilots, Ohnuki-Tierney (2004) disputed this contention and concluded that most of these pilots did not die for the emperor, and they did not fully embrace the military ideology. They did not volunteer but were coerced through social forces in a totalitarian regime.

Modern suicide bombing started in the Middle East during the 1980 Iran–Iraq War. This was punctuated in December 1981 when the Iraqi embassy in Beirut was destroyed, leaving 27 dead and 100 wounded (Hutchinson, 2007). Then, in April 1993 the first of 20 suicide attacks between 1993 and 1997 occurred in Israel. These 20 attacks killed 175 people and injured 928. The second, more lethal wave began in 2000, and by 2005 suicide bombers had killed 657 people in Israel and injured 3,682 others (Brym & Araj, 2006). Finally, on September 11, 2001, suicide attackers crashed commercial aircraft into the World Trade Center in New York City and the Pentagon in Arlington, Virginia. A third plane failed to meet its target and crashed in Somerset County, Pennsylvania. In all, 2,986 people were recorded dead after the attacks on that single morning.

Earlier theories regarding the nature of suicide bombers have been disputed by research. One such theory is that suicide bombers are unstable individuals, plagued with psychopathology and harboring a death wish. However, interviews with prospective suicide bombers and reconstructions of biographies indicate there is no greater incidence of psychopathology in this group than in the general population and that the incidence may indeed be lower (Brym & Araj, 2006). A second explanation focuses on deprivation and the motivation for suicide bombing as being to act out against those in positions of power who withhold resources. However, studies of Arab suicide bombers indicate they have higher levels of education and are from higher socioeconomic classes than others in their society (Brym & Araj, 2006). Scholars have begun to consider suicide bombing in terms of strategically rational political action—a means of coercing a foreign state. Within this framework, specific motivations are revenge against a state for their actions against the group to which the suicide bomber belongs, the desire to achieve a strategic gain (for example, the withdrawal of Israel from occupied territories), or the desire to achieve a religious goal (such as the defense or spread of Islam). Studies of Palestinian suicide bombers, for example, suggest they are motivated by the effectiveness of the attacks as a means to revenge national and personal humiliation and hatred of Israel and America (Grimland, Apter, & Kerkhof, 2006).

For the individual suicide bomber the process begins with indoctrination, where leaders of the organization embrace the bomber and reinforce his or her preexisting beliefs and motivations. The second stage is to obtain commitment to the group and its goals. Group dynamics then serve to solidify motives and create social pressure to act. Finally, the suicide bomber is asked to make a personal pledge committing to the act. This pledge is frequently videotaped, making it extremely difficult to change one's mind (Hutchinson, 2007).

◼ Impact of Hate Crimes on Victims

Violent attacks against one's person, loved ones, or property have well-known psychological effects. When the cause of the crime is hate, however, some research suggests these effects can be more severe. Hate crime victims have reported trying to be less visible and relocating to attempt to reduce the possibility of further attacks on their emotional or physical selves. Victims of hate-based assaults report higher symptoms of intrusive thoughts and higher levels of anxiety and anger than victims whose assaults were not hate based (Sullaway, 2004). One reason is that when hate-based crimes involve physical assault, the severity of the assaults is significantly higher than that of other assaults, and people are more likely to require hospitalization. From a psychological perspective, the lack of control a victim of a hate-based crime experiences is another possible factor. Unlike other victims who may believe they can reduce the risk of further assaults by changing their behavior (for example, not going to dangerous areas), victims of hate-based crimes cannot change many of the factors that make them identifiable targets. For example, people obviously cannot change the color of their skin, and the only option may be to move to another area.

Herek, Gillis, & Cogan (1999) hypothesized that lesbian, gay, and bisexual people might be particularly vulnerable to hate crimes for two main reasons: (1) sexual prejudice is still acceptable in many segments of society, and thus the crime may reinforce internalized negative views, and (2) the development of sexual identity often occurs in opposition to family and community, thereby reducing resources and support. Their research about the victimization experiences of 2,259 Sacramento-area lesbians, gays, and bisexuals confirmed that gay and lesbian victims of hate crimes manifested significantly more symptoms of depression, anger, anxiety, and posttraumatic stress than those who were victims of violent crimes not associated with hate. Hate crime victims also displayed significantly more crime-related fears than victims of violent crimes that were not motivated by bias and those who were not crime victims. Comparable differences were not found among bisexuals, perhaps indicating differing identity and support issues among bisexuals than among gays and lesbians.

Hate crimes affect not only individuals but also communities. The fact that a member of a group has been targeted simply because of his or her skin color, religion, or sexual orientation sends shock waves throughout the group. All members become acutely aware of the risk they face, and their sense of safety and security is severely undermined. The response of police and the justice system can serve to allay fears or intensify the sense of vulnerability depending on whether the crime is taken seriously and whether offenders are apprehended, charged, and convicted. In the absence of this, a fear develops that it is open season on violence. The increased fear in the gay and lesbian community that was documented by researchers is an excellent example of this point (Noelle, 2002). Indeed, there does appear to be escalations in violence toward a group after a highly publicized hate crime. For example, there was a two-fold increase in hate crimes after the mob attack of a young Black man in New York in 1986 (Craig, 1999). Further, a group's historical experiences of oppression, denial of rights, and violence are resurrected in the aftermath of hate-based crimes, and fears of a return to earlier days emerge.

■ Summary

Hate against one group by members of another group is a pervasive aspect of human history. Hate crimes and hate speech are direct attempts to degrade, oppress, and control members of certain groups. Victims tend to be innocent members of the targeted group and generally have no previous relationship with the offenders. Unpredictability and the fact that the behavior is unprovoked serve to keep not only the victims but all members of that group in a state of anxiety or even fear. Despite the highly destructive qualities of hate crimes, Western societies have found it tremendously difficult to define and control them in a legal context. What constitutes statements of hate and what constitutes valid opinion continues to be a point of debate that does not appear will be settled anytime soon.

■ Key Terms

Anti-Semitism: Hostility toward or prejudice against Jews or Judaism.

Genocide: Systematic murder of an entire political, cultural, or religious group.

Hate crime: Criminal conduct motivated in whole or in part by a preformed negative opinion or attitude toward a group based on race, ethnicity, religion, gender, sexual orientation, or disability.

Hate speech: Words used as weapons to ambush, terrorize, wound, humiliate, and degrade members of an identified group.

Islamophobia: Hostility toward or prejudice against Muslims.

Suicide bomber: The targeted use of self-destructing human beings against civilians.

White supremacist: A person who believes White people are racially superior to others and should therefore dominate society.

Xenophobia: Fear and hatred of strangers or foreigners or of anything that is strange or foreign.

■ Discussion Questions

1. Some would suggest there is a fine line between hate speech and freedom of speech. Discuss.
2. How do hate crimes affect a community, and how do they differ from other forms of crime?
3. Discuss possible intervention strategies for hate crime offenders based on offender typologies.
4. What is the intersection between suicide bombing and hate crimes?

■ Resources

FBI, Hate Crimes
   http://www.fbi.gov/about-us/investigate/civilrights/hate_crimes/hate_crimes

National Criminal Justice Association, A Policymaker's Guide to Hate Crimes
   www.ncjrs.gov/pdffiles1/bja/162304.pdf

Reading Hate, Hate Crime Research and Scholarship in Canada
   http://www.criminologyandjustice.uoit.ca/hatecrime/index.html

Southern Poverty Law Center
   http://splcenter.org/

U.S. Department of Justice, Hate Crime
   http://www.fbi.gov/news/stories/2011/november/hatecrimes_111411/hatecrimes_111411

References

ABC News. (2004, November 26). New details emerge in Matthew Shepard murder. Retrieved from http://abcnews.go.com/2020/story?id =277685&page=1

Abu-Raz, W., & Suarez, Z. (2009). Muslim men and women's perception of discrimination, hate crimes, and PTSD symptoms post 9/11. *Traumatology, 15*(3), 48–63.

Akiyama, C. (2008). When you look like the enemy. *Journal of Brief Treatment and Crisis Intervention, 8*(2), 209–213.

American Psychological Association. (1998). Hate crimes today. Retrieved from http://www.apa.org/releases/hate.html

Americans with Disabilities Act. (1990). Including changes made by the ADA Amendments Act of 2008 (P.L. 110-325). Retrieved from http://www.ada .gov/pubs/adastatute08.htm

Amjad, N., & Wood, A. (2009). Identifying and changing the normative beliefs about aggression which lead young Muslim adults to join extremist anti-Semitic groups in Pakistan. *Aggressive Behavior, 35,* 514–519.

Atran, S. (2003). Genesis of suicide terrorism. *Science, 299,* 1534–1539.

Bortner, P. (2010, October 20). Donchak, Piekarsky in Pike County Correctional Facility. Retrieved from http://newsitem.com/news/donchak-piekarsky-in-pike-county-correctional-facility–1.1051243#axzz1RKn0b1o4

Brym, R., & Araj, B. (2006). Suicide bombing as strategy and interaction: The case of the second intifada. *Social Forces, 84*(4), 1969–1986.

California Department of Justice. (2000). Hate crime in California 2000. Retrieved from http://ag.ca.gov/cjsc/publications/hatecrimes/hc2000 /preface.pdf

CBC Digital Archives. (1989, December 6). The Montreal massacre. Retrieved from http://archives.radio-canada.ca/IDD–1-70-398/disasters_tragedies /montreal_massacre/

CBC News. (2005, January 18). Man given 2 years for firebombing Montreal Jewish school. Retrieved from http://www.cbc.ca/canada/story/2005/01 /18/firebombsentence-jewishschool0118.html

CBC News. (2007, February 15). Ernst Zundel sentenced to 5 years for Holocaust denial. Retrieved from http://www.cbc.ca/world/story/2007 /02/15/zundel-germany.html

Center for Policing Terrorism. (2007). Analysis: Firebombing of Jewish elementary school in Montreal in 2004. Retrieved from http://www.cpt-mi.org /pdf/jewishschool1.pdf

Clement, S., Brohan, E., Sayce, L., Pool, J., & Thornicroft, G. (2011). Disability hate crime and targeted violence and hostility: A mental health and discrimination perspective. *Journal of Mental Health, 20*(3), 219–225.

CNN. (1999, February 22). Closing arguments today in Texas dragging-death trial. Retrieved from http://www.cnn.com/US/9902/22/dragging.death.03/

CNN. (2011, February 23). Men convicted of hate crime sentenced to 9 years in prison. Retrieved from http://articles.cnn.com/2011-02-23/justice /pennsylvania.hate.crime_1_derrick-donchak-brandon-piekarsky-federal-court?_s=PM:CRIME

Council of Europe. (2006). Additional Protocol to the Convention on cybercrime, concerning the criminalisation of acts of a racist and xenophobic nature committed through computer systems. Retrieved from http://www .coe.int/t/dghl/cooperation/economiccrime/cybercrime/Default_en.asp

Cowan, G., Resendez, M., Marshall, E., & Quist, R. (2002). Hate speech and constitutional protection: Priming values of equality and freedom. *Journal of Social Issues, 58*(2), 247–263.

Craig, K. (1999). Retaliation, fear and rage: An investigation of African American and white reactions to racist hate crimes. *Journal of Interpersonal Violence, 14*(2), 138–151.

Criminal Code of Canada. (2004). R.S., c. C-46, s. 318–319.

Dauvergne, M., Scrim, K., & Brennan, S. (2006). *Hate crime in Canada.* Canadian Centre for Justice Statistics Profile Series. Ottawa: Statistics Canada.

Dixon, L., & Ray, L. (2007). Current issues and developments in race hate crime. *Journal of Community and Criminal Justice, 54*(2), 109–124.

Espiritu, A. (2004). Racial diversity and hate crime incidents. *Social Science Journal, 41,* 197–208.

Federal Bureau of Investigation (FBI). (2009). Hate crime statistics 2009. Retrieved from http://www2.fbi.gov/ucr/hc2009/incidents.html

Franklin, K. (2000). Antigay behaviours among young adults: Prevalence, patterns and motivations in a noncriminal population. *Journal of Interpersonal Violence, 15*(4), 339–362.

Franklin, K. (2002). Good intentions. *American Behavioral Scientist, 46*(1), 154–172.

Green, D., Glaser, J., & Rich, A. (1998). From lynching to gay bashing: The elusive connection between economic conditions and hate crime. *Journal of Personality and Social Psychology, 75*(1), 82–92.

Grimland, M., Apter, A., & Kerkhof, A. (2006). The phenomenon of suicide bombing. *Crisis, 27*(3), 107–118.

Henry, J. (2009). Beyond free speech: Novel approaches to hate on the Internet in the United States. *Information and Communications Technology Law, 18*(2), 235–251.

Herek, G., Gillis, R., & Cogan, J. (1999). Psychological sequelae of hate-crime victimization among lesbian, gay and bisexual adults. *Journal of Consulting and Clinical Psychology, 67*(6), 945–951.

Hoffman, S. (2011). "Last night, I prayed to Matthew": Matthew Shepard, homosexuality, and popular martyrdom in contemporary America. *Religion and American Culture: A Journal of Interpretation, 21*(1), 121–164.

Human Rights Campaign. (2008). The local law enforcement hate crimes prevention act/Matthew Shepard act. Retrieved from http://www.hrc .org/5660.htm

Hutchinson, W. (2007). The systemic roots of suicide bombing. *Systems Research and Behavioral Science, 24*, 191–200.

Jacobs, J., & Henry, J. (1996). The social construction of a hate crime epidemic. *Journal of Criminal Law, 86*(2), 366–391.

Jenness, V. (1999). Managing differences and making legislation: Social movements and the racialization, sexualization, and gendering of federal hate crimes law in the US 1985–1998. *Social Problems, 46*(4), 548–571.

Johnson, S., & Byers, B. (2003). Attitudes toward hate crime laws. *Journal of Criminal Justice, 31*, 227–235.

Keilty, J., & Connelly, G. (2001). Making a statement: An exploratory study of barriers facing women with an intellectual disability when making a statement about sexual assault to police. *Disability and Society, 16*(2), 273–291.

Lawrence, C., Matsuda, M., Delgado, R., & Crenshaw, K. (1993). Introduction. In M. Matsuda, C. Lawrence, R. Delgado, & K. Crenshaw (Eds.), *Words that wound: Critical race theory, assaultive speech and the First Amendment* (pp. 1–15). Boulder, CO: Westview Press.

Levin, B. (2002a). Cyberhate. *American Behavioral Scientist, 45*(6), 958–988.

Levin, B. (2002b). From slavery to hate crime laws: The emergence of race and status-based protection in American criminal law. *Journal of Social Issues, 58*(2), 227–245.

McDevitt, J., Levin, J., & Bennett, S. (2002). Hate crime offenders: An expanded typology. *Journal of Social Issues, 58*(2), 303–317.

McMahon, B., West, S., Lewis, A., Armstrong, A., & Conway, J. (2004). Hate crimes and disability in America. *Rehabilitation Counselling Bulletin, 47*(2), 66–75.

McPhail, B. (2000). Hating hate: Policy implications of hate crime legislation. *Social Science Review, 74*(4), 635–653.

McPhail, B., & DiNitto, D. (2005). Prosecutorial perspectives on gender-bias hate crimes. *Violence Against Women, 11*(9), 1162–1185.

Morgan, J. (2002). US hate crime legislation: A legal model to avoid in Australia. *Journal of Sociology, 38*(1), 25–48.

Noelle, M. (2002). The ripple effect of the Matthew Shepard murder. *American Behavioral Scientist, 46*(1), 27–50.

Ohnuki-Tierney, E. (2004). Betrayal by idealism and aesthetics. *Anthropology Today, 20*(2), 15–21.

Peritz, I. (2005, January 19). Library bomber jailed two years. Retrieved from http://www.theglobeandmail.com/servlet/story/RTGAM.20050119 .wbomber19/BNStory/National/

Perry, B. (2002). Defending the color line: Racially and ethnically motivated hate crime. *American Behavioral Scientist, 46*(1), 72–92.

Pinderhughes, H. (1993). The anatomy of racially motivated violence in New York City: A case study of youth in southern Brooklyn. *Social Problems, 40*(4), 478–492.

Scott v. Sandford. (1857). 19 How. 393.

Shively, M., & Mulford, C. (2007). Hate crime in America: The debate continues. *National Institute of Justice Journal, 257*, 1–13.

Sobsey, D. (1994). *Violence and abuse in the lives of people with disabilities: The end of silent acceptance?* Baltimore, MD: Brookes.

Southern Poverty Law Center. (1998). Intelligence project. Monitoring hate and extremist activity. Retrieved from http://www.splcenter.org/intel/intpro.jsp

Southern Poverty Law Center. (2010). Hate map. Retrieved from http://www .splcenter.org/get-informed/hate-map

State v. Mann. (1829). 13 NC (2 Dev) 263.

Statistics Canada. (2004, June 1). Pilot survey of hate crime. Retrieved from http://www.statcan.ca/Daily/English/040601/d040601a.htm

Sullaway, M. (2004). Psychological perspectives on hate crime laws. *Psychology, Public Policy, and Law, 10*, 250–292.

Teenagers charged in grave desecration. (2004, May 12). Retrieved from http://www.nytimes.com/2004/05/12/us/national-briefing-southwest-texas-teenagers-charged-in-grave-desecration.html?n =Top%2FReference%2FTimes%20Topics%2FSubjects%2FC%2FCemeteries

Third defendant is convicted in dragging death in Texas. (1999, November 19). *The New York Times*, p. A33.

U.S. Department of State. (2005). Report on global anti-Semitism. Retrieved from http://www.state.gov/g/drl/rls/40258.htm

Waxman, B. (1991). Hatred: The unacknowledged dimension against disabled people. *Sexuality and Disability, 9*(3), 185–199.

Willis, D. (2004). Hate crimes against gay males: An overview. *Issues in Mental Health Nursing, 25*, 115–132.

Victims of Cybercrime

CHAPTER
15

■ Objectives

- To identify types of computer- and Internet-based crimes
- To identify the incidence and costs of cybercrime
- To discuss legal approaches to cybercrime
- To discuss the impact on victims and means for protecting one-self from cybercrime

■ Key Terms

Child sexual exploitation on the Internet
Computer hacking
Copyright piracy
Cyberbullying
Cybercrime
Cyberstalking
Cyberterrorism
Identity theft
Internet fraud
Mail fraud
Telemarketing fraud
Telephone hacking

CASE

"Rupert Murdoch acted with characteristic ruthlessness by closing the *News of the World*, Britain's best-selling Sunday newspaper, in a desperate attempt to limit the political and commercial fallout from the phone-hacking affair engulfing his media empire" (Robinson, 2011). In early July 2011 media throughout the world ran similar articles confirming early suspicions that the 168-year-old tabloid, which sold 2.6 million copies per week in the United Kingdom, illegally obtained information via telephone hacking. Targets included messages left on the mobile phone of murdered teenager Milly Dowler in 2002; family members of British servicemen killed in Afghanistan and Iraq; family members of people killed in the London bombings of 2005; British Prime Minister Tony Blair; and members of the Royal Family, including Prince William, Prince Harry, (**Figure 15-1**) and Prince William's new wife, Catherine, Duchess of Cambridge. Evidence of the hacking of the royal family occurred in 2005 when it became evident that telephone messages left by Prince William and Prince Harry were finding their way into the tabloids (Ginsberg, 2011; Prodhan, 2011; Robinson, 2011). Two hundred *News of the World* employees lost their jobs, as senior officials of the media empire were arrested on suspicion of conspiring to intercept communications, contrary to the Criminal Law Act of 1977, and on corruption allegations, contrary to the Prevention of Corruption Act of 1906 related to telephone hacking and police bribes.

FIGURE 15-1 Prince William and Prince Harry, among the victims of telephone hacking by *News of the World*

© TIM OCKENDEN/PA Photos/Landov

■ Introduction

Broadly speaking, **cybercrime** is any illegal activity conducted through a computer. Most frequently, these crimes occur through global Internet networks. The Internet is the largest single component of cyberspace. Present in over 200 countries, it has over 2 billion users worldwide (Internet World Stats, 2011). The countries with the highest percentage of the population with Internet access are Greenland at 90.2%, Canada at 79.2%, Bermuda at 78.6%, and the United States with 78.2% (**Figure 15-2**). However, when actual numbers of people with Internet access are considered, people in Asia represent 44% of world Internet users (**Figure 15-3**).

In addition to computer use, Internet use through mobile devices is dramatically on the rise. During 2008 Americans sent and received approximately twice as many text messages as phone calls, 2.5 billion per day across the country. The 2008 numbers represented a 160% increase over the year before. The surge is driven by 13- to 18-year-olds who on average received 1,742 text messages per month in 2008 (Reardon, 2008). Worldwide, over 5 billion people had mobile phone connections in 2010 (Hunton, 2011).

Internet crime takes many forms. Telephone hacking is the art and science of cracking into a telephone network. Originally, this was primarily done to make free long-distance phone calls, but now, as noted above, it involves seeking private information on individuals. Computer hacking refers to unauthorized access to a computer or network, which may be motivated to publicize beliefs or protest against a certain cause or simply for personal gain. Hacking may be simply annoying or may turn to cyber-terrorism in which essential services, such as medical systems or banking systems, can be disrupted (Chung, Chen, Chang, & Chou, 2004). Internet fraud is deception conducted through the Internet for the purpose of

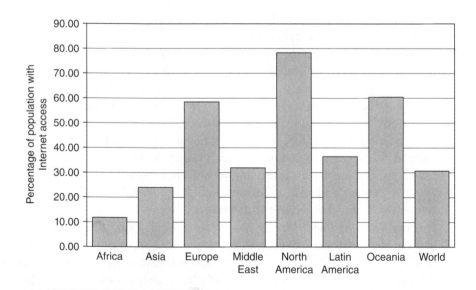

FIGURE 15-2 World Internet Penetration

Data from Internet World Stats. 2011. Usage and Population Statistics. http://www.internetworldstats.com/stats.htm.

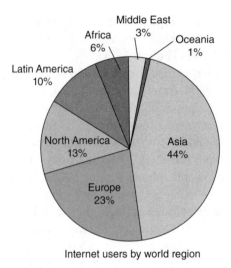

Internet users by world region

FIGURE 15-3 International distribution of Internet users

Data from Internet World Stats. 2011. Usage and Population Statistics. http://www.internetworldstats.com/stats.htm.

financial gain. Copyright piracy, although not necessarily viewed as a serious crime by the general public, is receiving a great deal of attention by law enforcement officials. Growing concerns are child pornography and child sexual exploitation on the Internet and victimization among young people in the form of cyberbullying.

In addition, the Internet can be used as a mechanism to lure people into other forms of victimization. Famously, the murders of two women were attributed to the use of Craigslist. In the first, Katherine Ann Olson, a 24-year-old Minnesota woman, was found dead after responding to a phony ad for a babysitter. The killer, Michael John Anderson, 19, posed as a married woman named "Amy" who was looking for nanny services. Anderson exchanged e-mails with Olson, and when she arrived at his parents' house for an interview, he shot her (*New York Daily News,* 2009). In the second case a Boston medical student, Phillip Markham, was arrested and charged in the death of a 25-year-old masseuse, Julissa Brisman, who he had allegedly contacted through Craigslist. Markham had contacted women advertising erotic services on Craigslist to set up meetings in their hotel rooms. He brought a gun with him to gain control over victims and used duct tape and plastic restraints to tie them up. He then stole cash, credit cards, and gift cards from victims. It is believed that Brisman is the only victim murdered (Ford & Kennedy, 2009).

Scope of the Problem

Cybercrime statistics are not collected in the same uniform manner as are other crimes in part because they fall into the jurisdiction of many different agencies (**Table 15-1**). Although the scope of cybercrime is difficult to measure, there are some indicators of the widespread nature of the problem:

- In 2009, 18,146 Canadians claimed to be victims of identity theft resulting in economic losses of $9.4 million (Canadian Anti-Fraud Centre, 2010).
- An estimated 11.7 million persons, representing 5% of all persons age 16 or older in the United States, experienced at least one type of identity theft in a 2-year period. The total financial cost of identity theft in the United States was nearly $17.3 billion over a 2-year period (Langton & Planty, 2010).
- In 2011, 13,603 Canadians reported being victims of mass media fraud (Canadian Anti-Fraud Centre, 2010).
- One in four victims of stalking in the United States reports some form of cyberstalking (Baum, Catalano, Rand, & Rose, 2009).

TABLE 15-1 **Agencies Responsible for Internet Crime in the United States**

Type of Crime	Responsible Agency in the US
Hacking	• FBI Local Office • US Secret Service
Child Pornography and Child Exploitation	• FBI Local Office • US Customs and Immigration Enforcement
Internet Fraud	• FBI Local Office • US Secret Service (Financial Crimes Division) • Federal Trade Commission • Securities and Exchange Commission
Internet Harassment	• FBI Local Office
Internet Bomb Threats or Trafficking in Firearms	• FBI Local Office • Bureau of Alcohol, Tobacco and Firearms
Copyright Piracy	• FBI Local Office • US Customs and Immigration Enforcement

Data from US Department of Justice. 2011. Reporting computer, internet related or intellectual property crime. Computer Crime and Intellectual Property Section. Retrieved from http://www.cybercrime.gov/reporting.htm#cc.

- In a study of 2,100 school children in Toronto, researchers found that almost half (49.5%) reported being bullied online (Mishna, Cook, Gadalla, Daciuk, & Solomon 2010).
- The Federal Bureau of Investigation's (FBI's) National Infrastructure Protection Center identified the vulnerability of the United States to cyberterrorism, noting it is 100% dependent on information systems and computer systems to run the nation (Goodman, Kirk, & Kirk, 2007).
- A 2004 survey of 494 U.S. corporations found that 20% had been subject to attempts of computer sabotage or extortion (Computer Security Institute, 2002).
- A total of 3,672 individuals were arrested in the United States in 2006 for possession of child pornography (Wolak, Finkelhor, & Mitchell, 2011).
- In 2005 it was estimated that there were approximately 14 million pornographic websites, with some posting approximately 1 million child abuse images (Sinclair & Sugar, 2005).

◾ Legal Context

The vast expansion of cybercrime and the human suffering and huge financial losses resulting from cybercrime have resulted in a variety of attempts to fight it, including legal, organizational, and technological approaches. Many countries have instituted legislative approaches; however, the transnational nature of the crime requires international cooperation and coordination (Kierkegaard, 2006). For example, in 1997 the G8 developed an action plan that required members to criminalize cybercrime and to protect the integrity and confidentiality of data systems (Chung et al., 2004). In 2001 the Council of Europe, the United States, Canada, South Africa, and Japan passed the Cybercrime Convention, which mandates countries to have unified legislation for international crime prevention. The Convention was entered into force in 2004, and in October 2010, 30 countries had signed and ratified the agreement. This agreement attempts to deal with the problem that Internet crime often originates in a jurisdiction that may be halfway around the world from the jurisdiction in which the victim lives. Law enforcement then is hampered by cross-jurisdictional issues, including differing laws, definitions, and standards for Internet use, as well as crime descriptions, evidence collection, and offender detention. The convention is supplemented by a Protocol on Xenophobia and Racism, encompassing xenophobia and racism committed on the Internet.

National approaches to Internet crime prevention, detection, and prosecution are complicated by the vast array of types of Internet crime. As a result, legislation that addressed Internet crime is not unified in any way. In the United States the range of legislation that addresses cybercrime is very broad, including the Cyber Security Enhancement Act of 2002, which modified the Homeland Security Act; amendments to the Patriot Act related to computer crime and electronic evidence; amendments to the federal Criminal Code that address, among other things, fraud-related activity pertaining to computer, wire, and electronic communications interceptions and recording of dialing, routing, addressing, and signaling information; and new sentencing guidelines related to cybercrime. These legislative amendments are all recently enacted, demonstrating the developing and changing world of cybercrime and the challenges in addressing it. To ensure future success in combating Internet crime, the U.S. Cyber Security Research and Development Act (2002) authorized an expenditure of $903 million for research in this area.

Specific legislation also exists for particular types of cybercrime. For example, in the fall of 1998 the U.S. Congress passed the Identity Theft and Assumption Deterrence Act. This legislation created a new offense of identity theft, which prohibits knowingly transferring or using, without lawful authority, a means of identification of another person with the intent to commit, or to aid or abet, any unlawful activity that constitutes a violation of federal law or that constitutes a felony under any applicable state or local law (18 U.S.C. § 1028(a)(7)). This offense, in most circumstances, carries a maximum term of 15 years imprisonment, a fine, and criminal forfeiture of any personal property used or intended to be used to commit the offense. Schemes to commit identity theft or fraud may also involve violations of other statutes, such as identification fraud (18 U.S.C. § 1028), credit card fraud (18 U.S.C. § 1029), computer fraud (18 U.S.C. § 1030), mail fraud (18 U.S.C. § 1341), wire fraud (18 U.S.C. § 1343), or financial institution fraud (18 U.S.C. § 1344). Each of these federal offenses is a felony that carries substantial penalties—in some cases as high as 30 years imprisonment, fines, and criminal forfeiture. In January 2010 Canada revised the Criminal Code to more effectively target identity theft. Three new offenses carry a maximum 5-year sentence: obtaining and possessing identity information, trafficking identity information, and unlawfully possessing or trafficking government issued identity information.

Despite these laws, however, the ability of law enforcement agencies to address Internet crime is often hampered by the fundamental right for privacy. The FBI, for example, has reported their investigations are strictly limited by the Fourth Amendment of the U.S. Constitution, which guarantees the right of the people to be secure in their persons, houses, papers, and effects against unreasonable searches and seizure. The European Cybercrime Convention calls for member states to ensure a proper balance between the interests of law enforcement and respect for fundamental human rights (Armstrong & Forde, 2003).

Child pornography is a good example of efforts to deal with serious Internet crime. Child pornography is a category of expression that is not protected by the First Amendment of the Constitution, and until recently it was covered by the 1996 Child Pornography Prevention Act. In 2003 President Bush signed the Protect Act, which redefined child pornography to include not only images of real children engaging in sexually explicit conduct but also computer-generated depictions that were indistinguishable from real children.

The Canadian government enacted an amendment to the Criminal Code in 2002 that addressed child pornography on the Internet and using the Internet to lure children (Schell, Martin, Hung, & Rueda, 2007). In November 2007 Manitoba became the first province to introduce legislation that made failure to report suspected cases of child pornography possession a crime (Welch, 2007). Failure to alert authorities about someone who possesses videos, photographs, or online material can result in a maximum 2-year jail term and a fine of up to $50,000. More recently, in November 2010, the Government of Canada introduced the Investigative Powers for the 21st Century Act (Valiquet & Simonds, 2011), which was intended to "provide law enforcement agencies with new, specialized investigative powers to help them take action against Internet child sexual exploitation, disrupt on-line organized crime activity and prevent terrorism" (Public Safety Canada, 2010). However, this act was not passed and did not become law.

As crime spreads across the Internet, law enforcement has begun to catch up with those using the Web for illicit purposes. Hunton (2011) outlined the specific and unique investigative procedures required to address Internet crime. In the United States the Computer Crime and Intellectual Property Section of the U.S. Department of Justice created the Infotech Training Working Group to investigate online violations of the law. This office evolved into the National Cybercrime Training Partnership that worked with all levels of law enforcement to develop long-range strategies, raise public awareness, and build momentum to combat this problem on many different fronts. The National White Collar Crime Center, based in Richmond, Virginia, offered operational support to the National Cybercrime Training Partnership and functioned as an information clearinghouse for cybercrime. The complexity of these crimes and the fact that they cross many traditional boundaries mean that for any given crime, several law enforcement agencies are responsible for each type in the United States alone (**Table 15-1**). These agencies worked together to generate more funding to help law enforcement keep up with the ever-changing computer world. All cybercrime in the United States can be reported to the Internet Crime Complaint Center (http://www.ic3.gov/default.aspx).

■ Types of Internet Crime

Internet crime comes in many different forms. Some of these forms are directed at particular individuals or groups, and some are not specifically targeted but rather seek general disruption.

Hacking

Hacking (sometimes called network intrusion) refers to unauthorized access of a computer or network. Hackers are individuals or groups who use the Internet to attack computer systems on a global scale. Phone hacking refers to intercepting phone calls or voicemail messages of users without their knowledge. Software for hacking is readily available and easily downloadable at little or no cost. Hackers share and barter their tools and information and mentor those who share their values. For instance, a simple Internet search using the term "phone hacking" reveals how-to videos and free software for casual hackers. Motivation for hacking can come from a number of factors including the thrill and excitement of illegal activity, the challenge of outsmarting corporations and professional computer security experts, recognition of their activities through media attention, and the power of being able to affect many people and bring down powerful organizations (Armstrong & Forde, 2003). Hackers may also be motivated by profit, vengeance, or political aims. Hackers use various types of encryption methods to hide their activities. They retain anonymity by using pseudo-names, remailers, and anonymous servers.

The Computer Security Institute, in cooperation with the FBI, conducted a research study in 2002 with 503 computer security practitioners in U.S. corporations, financial institutions, government offices, medical institutions, and universities (Computer Security Institute, 2002). Ninety percent of the respondents had detected computer security breaches in the past 12 months. Eighty percent acknowledged losses as a result of these breaches. Of those who could quantify the losses, 233 respondents collectively reported $456 million in financial losses. In

80% of the cases independent hackers were the culprit. Over 20 years ago, the Confederation of British Industry estimated the cost of hacking to British companies is £400 million per year (Tan & Newman, 1991). Beyond financial losses, however, hacking leads to damaging of data files and programs, disruption of work in progress, and undermining of public and consumer confidence.

Although the first computer viruses that appeared in the 1980s were unsophisticated codes written by hackers primarily in search of glory, new viruses are highly sophisticated and lucrative for the designers. In 2003 the first of these viruses, called SoBig.A, allowed the designer to monitor commands and control the host computer after a computer was infected (Bradbury, 2007). Since that time the ability to control computers through network servers has intensified, and now hackers are able to use a host to send spam messages throughout the world and even control online gambling and commerce sites. Groups of coders are creating networks that sell software intended for criminal use of another computer and even offer software support for the criminal who is using it.

A report by the U.S. Department of Justice identified the challenges faced by prosecutors and investigators in identifying computer hackers (Morris, 2005). First, hackers may hide or "spoof" their Internet provider address or bounce their messages through intermediary computers. Second, victims often do not discover the hacker's activities until it is too late and all traces of the hacker's identity are gone. In addition, some Internet service providers do not keep records that would allow hackers' identities to be disclosed with a subpoena. Some hackers alter Internet service provider records, thereby obscuring their identities. Finally, some leads may go through foreign countries where hacking is not considered to be a crime. For example, earlier in the history of cybercrime in the United Kingdom, several arguments were put forth both to support the criminalization of hacking and against the criminalization of hacking. Under British law there was no general right to privacy; thus, the interference with privacy involved in hacking was more analogous to trespass and did not constitute criminal activity (Tan & Newman, 1991). The new European-wide agreements have shifted this legislative framework.

Despite problems with apprehension, there is ample evidence that courts in some countries are taking a very serious approach to hacking when offenders are apprehended. One example is Simon Vallor, a 22-year-old Welshman who was sentenced to 2 years in prison after pleading guilty to creating three computer viruses. The judge noted that virus writers are not merely computer buffs or nerds but rather are criminals whose activities cause destruction, disruption, and financial loss

(Barton, Nissanka, & Waterhouse, 2003). Further, in March 2002 a U.S. federal court sentenced Timothy Lloyd to 3.5 years imprisonment and $2 million in restitution for computer hacking, stating the government wished to punish the offender severely to deter others in this increasingly computerized world (Barton et al., 2003). Jeanson James Ancheta of California was sentenced to 5 years in jail after pleading guilty to the use of "botnets" through which he illegally controlled 400,000 computers (U.S. Department of Justice, 2005). However, other countries, such as the Netherlands, took a very lenient approach, sentencing the author of the Anna Kournikova worm to just 150 hours of community service in 2001.

Cyberterrorism

The most dangerous form of hacking is cyberterrorism. Terrorists are individuals or groups of people who attempt to induce fear through threats and apparently random acts of violence that inflict mass casualty or considerable economic loss for the purposes of calling attention to a particular political viewpoint. Cyberterrorism is the convergence of terrorism and cyberspace (Stohl, 2006). It is the use of computers and networks to intimidate or coerce governments, organizations, or individuals for a particular political motivation. Whereas in the past terrorism relied on deadly explosive materials to launch devastating attacks, cyberterrorism creates unprecedented opportunities for committing acts of terror through ubiquitous multimedia communication tools (Chu, Deng, & Chao, 2011). Cyberterrorism can lead to deaths through explosions, plane crashes, water contamination, or the disruption of medical or emergency response systems.

Since the 9/11 attack on the World Trade Center, the Western world has been aware of the threat of terrorism like never before. Ron Dick, former director of the FBI's National Infrastructure Protection Center, highlighted the modern vulnerability to cyberterrorism and noted the United States is 100% dependent on information systems and computer systems to run the nation (Goodman et al., 2007). Critical infrastructures that depend on the Internet include transportation, banking and finance, energy distribution, emergency preparedness and response, public health, water, and others. In 2011 the Pentagon concluded that cybersabotage originating from another country could be considered an act of war. Should such an attack result in death, destruction, or high-level disruption that a military attack may cause, use of force could be involved in the retaliation (Gorman & Barnes, 2011).

In cyberterrorism extremist groups merely exploit modern tools to attain the same goals they have in the past. Chu and colleagues (2011), for instance, described the use of a multimedia smartphone using Web

2.0 and publicly accessible Wi-Fi to perform an act of terrorism. They further identified that digital forensics of mobile phones lag considerably behind computer forensics and that as this becomes a growing mode for terrorist activities, forensic analysis approaches must be developed.

Cyberspace is attractive to terrorist groups for a number of reasons. First, the anonymity of cyberspace allows people to gather information, create communication networks, and collaborate without detection. Innovative social media allows for nimble and vigorous revolutionary movements that can serve to attack existing social and political structures (Deibert & Rohozinski, 2010). Those engaging in this activity are difficult to track down to a particular location or identity in part because of their ability to move information in multiple formats and reroute it through multiple locations and in part because of the easy access to encryption software. Further, the Internet is increasingly accessible to people in all parts of the world, essentially flattening the traditional hierarchy of information access. Information (or propaganda) can be spread to large numbers of people with relative ease.

As an example of cyberterrorism, it is reported that Al-Qaeda used the Internet to coordinate operations, solicit donations via Internet transfers, and recruit volunteers through invitation-only chat rooms in preparation for the 9/11 attack (Goodman et al., 2007). The Internet therefore provides a means for distributing horrifying messages to vast populations, instilling fear and helplessness. One stunning example of this was the beheading of *Wall Street Journal* reporter Daniel Pearl in February 2002, which was broadcast via videos posted on Islamic websites (Stohl, 2006). This was then picked up by the mainstream press, and the propaganda messages and subsequent fear spread further. More recently, the Daniel Pearl story was made into a major motion picture starring Angelina Jolie. By focusing on these horrifying acts, singular acts of violence and terror become international symbols with tremendous power. In 2001 the U.S. Department of State provided a report to Congress on terrorism and terrorist activities, stating as follows (U.S. Department of State, 2001, para. 2):

> [T]errorism cast its lethal shadow across the globe—yet the world's resolve to defeat it has never been greater. . . . This chilling report details the very clear and present danger that terrorism poses to the world and the efforts that the United States and our partners in the international community are making to defeat it. The cold, hard facts presented here compel the world's continued vigilance and concerted action.

Cyberbullying

Traditionally, bullying has occurred most frequently on or around school property. However, the current generation of children have been raised on electronic media. This relatively new medium for communication and information sharing changed individuals' social interactions, learning strategies, and choice of entertainment. Young people use e-mail, MSN, Facebook, webcams, and text messaging to communicate with one another. The well-worn joke of the teenager's excessive use of the family phone no longer applies. The dramatic change in the activities of youth related to the Internet is evidenced by the fact that the Internet is now a preferred pastime over watching television for young people (Mishna, Cook, Saini, Wu, & MacFadden, 2009). This virtual world and easy access to communication has opened up a whole new area in terms of young people's ability to victimize one another. This is not to say that young people are meaner than they used to be or that the Internet has created bullies. Rather, a study by Raskauskas and Stoltz (2007) revealed that almost all youth who admitted to being cyberbullies also admitted to other more traditional forms of bullying. This suggests that those who are prone to bullying merely have more effective and efficient means of hurting other children.

Although the literature on Internet-based bullying is still limited, some incidence data are emerging. Finkelhor, Mitchell, and Wolak (2000) completed a national survey of 1,500 youth and found that 6% of those who used the Internet reported being harassed in the past year. The forms of harassment included instant messages (33%), chat room exchanges (32%), and e-mails (19%). More than 63% of the perpetrators attended the same school as the victims. A study conducted by Berson, Berson, and Ferron (2002) found that 15% of respondents reported receiving threatening e-mails. A more recent study of 177 grade seven students revealed that 54% had been bullied in the traditional manner and over one-fourth had been cyberbullied (Li, 2007). In a 2010 Canadian study of 2,186 middle school and high school students, half indicated they had been bullied online and a third indicated they had bullied others online (Mishna et al., 2010). The majority of cyberbullying victims in their study did not report their experiences to adults.

Typical Internet bullying includes rumors being spread about someone through the use of e-mails or website postings; embarrassing or compromising pictures of a young person, sometimes taken in places like locker rooms; or modified pictures in which the young person's face is attached to a pornographic picture. When these messages are unleashed on the Internet, they are impossible to stop, as was a situation in which a movie taken of a teenage boy was distributed worldwide. The most famous cyberbullying case began on November 4, 2002, when a 15-year-old teenager in Trois-Rivières, Quebec, filmed himself acting out scenes from the movie *Star Wars* using a golf ball retriever as a light saber. The film was discovered by classmates and was loaded onto Kazaa, a global file-sharing network. Subsequently, adapted versions were created with added music and special effects, and the original video was merged with other movies. The clumsy young man became world famous under the name "Star Wars Kid," and by 2006 his video had been viewed 900 million times. Television spoofs of the video appeared on major network shows such as "American Dad!" and "Arrested Development." As a result of this worldwide attention students in the young man's school leaped on tables whenever he entered the room yelling "Star Wars Kid, Star Wars Kid." They harassed him verbally and poked him to get a reaction. As a result of this unbearable attention the teenager became depressed and dropped out of school. Three years later the teenager and his family reached an out-of-court settlement with the families of three former schoolmates who initiated the bullying (Ha, 2006).

Cyberbullying can also include threatening e-mails, text messages, and other messages sent anonymously. In other instances insulting or damning messages are sent to others under the guise of being sent by the bullying victim. In such cases the young person suddenly discovers that he or she is ostracized by others and is unaware of what the cause may be. Bullying is extremely challenging to deal with in any situation; however, as with other cybercrimes, the inability to identify an offender makes addressing cyberbullying, a seriously damaging problem, next to impossible.

The outcomes of cyberbullying parallel those of traditional bullying. Beran and Li (2005) administered a survey asking students about their reactions to cyberbullying. Most students reported feelings of sadness, anxiety, and fear and stated it affected their ability to concentrate on their schoolwork and to attain good marks. Nevertheless, research in this area is still in its infancy.

Child Sexual Exploitation on the Internet

Sexual exploitation of children on the Internet takes many forms. Definitive data on the extent to which Internet child pornography exists are impossible to obtain. However, it has been estimated that there are approximately 14 million pornographic websites, with some posting approximately 1 million child abuse images. In addition, somewhere between 23,000 and 40,000 websites advertise chat rooms that defend adult–child sexual relations (Sinclair & Sugar, 2005).

One indication of the extent of online child pornography is through police arrests and seizures. For instance, the Child Exploitation and Online Protection Centre has a database of 877,000 unique images seized during police investigations in the United Kingdom alone (Quayle & Jones, 2011). As of 1999 the FBI had opened 1,500 new cases of child pornography in America, and many experts contended this was the fastest growing criminal frontier in cyberspace. By 2000 the number of child porn websites had grown to 23,000, and the next year it climbed to 100,000 (Taylor & Quayle, 2003). The U.S. National Juvenile Online Victimization Study revealed that arrests in the United States for possession of child pornography rose from 1,713 in 2000 to 3,672 in 2006 (Wolak et al., 2011).

The child pornography industry yields billions in profits. An FBI investigation into one child pornography website operated by Landslide Productions revealed this one site grossed $1.4 million in 1 month and had 35,000 individual subscribers (Taylor & Quayle, 2003). The images posted on the Internet of child sexual abuse are used by offenders for sexual gratification, to support beliefs about the acceptability of adult–child relations, to lower inhibitions of victims, and to entrap and control victims.

Although in the past obtaining child pornography was difficult because it required a degree of exposure through visiting a specialized store that distributed the material or providing an address where material could be delivered, the Internet has made child pornography not only accessible but its acquisition private. Thus, fears of exposure and humiliation no longer serve as barriers to those individuals seeking child pornography. Many people who are eventually apprehended and charged have huge collections of images—up to 40,000 pictures (Taylor & Quayle, 2003). Increasingly, it appears individuals are obtaining child pornography through peer-to-peer networks that bypass central networks (Wolak et al., 2011). This makes it more difficult both to discover perpetrators and to track the incidence of this activity. Worryingly, purchasers of child pornography do not appear to limit themselves to fantasy alone (Seto, Cantor, & Blanchard, 2006). One report suggested that 80% of these individuals are active child molesters (Schell et al., 2007). Child pornography is viewed as both addictive and progressive. Individuals who view the images become desensitized and seek out more and more violent and shocking material (Schell et al., 2007).

The range of people involved in child pornography crosses boundaries of class, income, and profession. The National Online Juvenile Victimization Survey found that among a sample of 605 people arrested for child porn, perpetrators were overwhelmingly single (61%), White (80%), males (99%) in all age and income groups. However, 31% were married or living common law and lived with children under the age of 18 (Wolak et al., 2011). A convenience sample of 225 cases published in the news media was examined to identify types of people who engage in Internet child pornography (Alexy, Burgess, & Baker, 2005a). More than one-fifth of the offenders lived outside the United States. The largest occupational category of Internet offenders was professional (64%) and included persons in the fields of education, computers, medicine, and law. Other occupational categories included laborer (11.2%), unemployed (8.8%), military (5.6%), student (7.2%), and clergy (3.2%). These findings fly in the face of stereotypes about those who purchase and use child pornography and demonstrate the manner in which this offense infiltrates society. Parents who warn their children of the dangers associated with strangers rarely instruct them that child molesters may also be people they have come to know either in person or online.

The cases identified by Alexy et al. (2005a) were classified using law enforcement terminology to describe Internet offenders as "traders," "travelers," or "combination traders/travelers." Traders are Internet offenders who trade and/or collect child pornography online. They may be involved with any or a combination of the following: production, possession, and distribution of child pornography online. More than half of the cases in this sample involved traders (59.1%). Descriptions of the Internet traders noted they could be charged with child pornography, be interested in a wide variety of sexual acts with children, produce Internet child pornography, distribute child pornography, amass a very large collection of child pornography, operate as partners, and/or operate for profit. Travelers seek to meet a child in person after communicating through e-mail or in a chat room. Characteristics of travelers include offenders with a wide range of sexual interests involving children, including sadistic and homicidal acts. Combination traders/travelers are individuals who participate in trading child pornography as well as traveling across state and/or national boundaries to engage in sexual interactions with a child. Slightly more than 19% of the analyzed cases involved offenders who engaged in a combination of trader and traveler activities.

As noted in the category of travelers, the Internet is also used to contact children. One example of this is the use of Internet advertising for access to child prostitutes in other countries, allowing child sexual tourism to flourish in countries where poverty contributes to an active sex trade industry and poor policing enforcement to limit sexual relations with minors (Sinclair & Sugar, 2005). In Honduras and Costa Rica, for example, pedophilic tourism increased 60% in 1999 as a result of a website that offered children for prostitution.

Another example is child luring through the Internet (Taylor & Quayle, 2003). Finkelhor and colleagues in 2000 estimated that approximately one in five youths receives sexual approaches from people they encounter online each year. Some of these approaches are from others in their own peer group, but some are from adults seeking illegal contact with teens. In a follow-up study it was determined that most Internet-initiated sex crimes involve an adult male who meets and seduces an underage adolescent into sex. Of these cases only 5% of the perpetrators pretended to be younger than their actual age (Wolack, Finkelhor, Mitchell, & Ybarra, 2008). Wolack and colleagues (2008) suggested that these type of Internet sexual offenses fall into the legal category of statutory rape (that is, the youth agrees to meet and have sex with the perpetrator, but the victim is under the legal age of consent) and that crimes involving Internet luring account for approximately 7% of all statutory rapes in the United States.

In these situations an offender enters chat rooms that are frequented by children and poses as someone younger or perhaps of the other gender. Relationships are then established with vulnerable children by the offender becoming a confidant who understands and empathizes with the child's fears and struggles. Eventually, trust is established, and the offender suggests a meeting where they can cement their friendship. The child or youth may agree to the meeting, believing he or she is about to see someone approximately his or her own age with similar hopes, fears, and dreams. In extreme cases the outcome is kidnapping, assault, or murder.

Preventative education of young people is vital. Mishna and colleagues (2009) conducted a review for The Campbell Collaboration to summarize the best available knowledge on school-based intervention programs to help protect children from cyberabuse. They concluded that participation in psychoeducational programs focusing on Internet safety does increase the safety knowledge of children; however, very discouragingly, such interventions do not change risky online behavior.

A key component of Internet sexual abuse investigations is identifying victims and tracking offenders. Images can be reproduced indefinitely with no loss of quality, and they can originate from anywhere in the world and be sent anywhere in a fraction of a second. In 2006, 55% of child pornography sites originated in the United States, 28% in Russia, 8% in Europe, and 7% in Asia (Humphreys, 2007). This has presented tremendous challenges for law enforcement professionals in their aims to apprehend offenders and rescue children.

As a result of frustration caused by technological limitations, in January 2003 the Toronto Police Service contacted Microsoft Corporation to ask for assistance in dealing with online sexual exploitation of children. Their message was simple: "the bad guys are winning." A collaborative effort between Toronto Police and Microsoft emerged, which included a $2.5 million investment by Microsoft Canada that resulted in a software package titled the Child Exploitation Tracking System. In December 2004, after consultations were held with police specialists in North America, the United Kingdom, and Interpol, the product was ready for international deployment (National Child Exploitation Coordination Centre, 2008; Sher, 2007). Groups that came together for the development of this tracking system later formed the Innocent Images International Task force, which includes law enforcement officers from the following countries: United Kingdom, Norway, Finland, Ukraine, Belarus, Australia, Thailand, the Philippines, Croatia, Latvia, Germany, the Netherlands, New Zealand, Canada, Sweden, Fiji, Cyprus, Iceland, Denmark, and Panama.

Undercover investigations to catch child sexual predators on the Internet are conducted in a variety of ways including having investigators pose as minors, having investigators pose as mothers who want to teach their children about sex, or having investigators pose as child pornography traders or sellers. However, research conducted by Mitchell, Wolak, and Finkelhor (2005) revealed that most investigators who used this method posed as female adolescents younger than the age of 12 years. All 124 offenders who were apprehended were male, most were White (91%), and most were employed full time (91%). A substantial proportion of these offenders (37.7%) had annual incomes greater than $50,000. When charges were laid, 91% pleaded guilty. As with other types of undercover work, the investigator falsifies his or her true identity and develops a sense of trust and acceptance by the targeted person(s). These officers are specially trained and work with national and international networks aimed at child exploitation.

In a study of 51 people convicted of offenses involving enticing children over the Internet, 90% were apprehended as a result of an Internet sex sting (Briggs, Simon, & Simonsen, 2011). Nevertheless, concerns have been raised about the ability to successfully prosecute cases involving undercover operations and deception. Courts have been concerned about entrapment, specifically whether undercover officers manufacture crimes or simply give offenders an opportunity to commit them (Mitchell et al., 2005).

Cyberstalking

Gary Dellapenta was a 50-year-old security guard who met 28-year-old Randi Barber at church. When she rejected his romantic approaches, Dellapenta became obsessed with Barber and placed advertisements on the Internet under the names of "playfulkitty4U" and "kinkygal30." Impersonating his victim, he posted her address and phone number along with a message that she fantasized about being raped on Internet bulletin boards and in chat rooms. He answered e-mail inquiries about the ads and invited the potential attackers to come to her home and even offered suggestions about how to get past her security locks. As a result, six different men appeared at the victim's door and indicated they wanted to rape her. Dellapenta had online accounts with four out-of-state companies, which required considerable policing resources to track down and acquire search warrants necessary to collect evidence. As the first person prosecuted under the California law on cyberstalking, Dellapenta pleaded guilty in April 1999 to one count of stalking and three counts of solicitation of sexual assault. In the end, he received a 6-year sentence (Simpson, 2000).

Janet Reno, then attorney general of the United States, delivered the first **cyberstalking** report to the vice president of the United States in September 1999. In it she stated, "As we travel the information superhighway into the next millennium, we must do all we can to ensure the safety of computer users. We must also ensure that our federal and local laws can effectively deal with the threats present in the new electronic age" (U.S. Department of Justice, 1999). The attorney general's report included the following recommendations: (1) states should review their laws to determine whether they address cyberstalking, and, if not, they should promptly expand laws to address cyberstalking; (2) federal laws should be amended to prohibit the transmission of any communication in interstate or foreign commerce with intent to threaten or harass another person where such communication places that person in reasonable fear of death or bodily injury; (3) law enforcement agencies should acquire training on the extent of cyberstalking and appropriate investigative techniques; and (4) the Internet industry should create an industry-supported website containing information about cyberstalking and what to do if a person is confronted with the problem.

The 1999 Reno report suggested that 475,000 people may be victims of cyberstalking each year in the United States, and quoting police figures she estimated that 20% of all stalking cases involved cyberstalking. Reno's estimate was not far off. The 2006 Supplementary Crime Victimization Survey revealed that 1 in 4 victims of stalking identified some form of cyberharassment and 1 in 13 reported being victims of electronic monitoring, including GPS monitoring, listening devices, or bugs (Baum et al., 2009).

In a study conducted on records from the Computer Investigations and Technology Unit of the New York Police Department, approximately 43% of the cases were cyberstalking. In this study approximately 80% of the perpetrators were male. The average age was 24 years; however, 26% of the perpetrators were younger than the age of 16 years. Over half of the victims were female, 35% were male, and the remaining targets were institutions (D'Oivido & Doyle, 2003).

In samples of college students, 3.2% to 3.75% reported being stalked, and of those being stalked, 24.7% to 31.5% reported being victims of cyberstalking (Alexy, Burgess, Baker, & Smoyak, 2005b; Fisher, Cullen, & Turner, 2000). An interesting finding in the study of Alexy and colleagues (2005b) was that although females were significantly more likely than males to be stalked, males were significantly more likely to be cyberstalked. Those who were cyberstalked were significantly more likely to be stalked by a former intimate partner.

Despite the dramatic example of Gary Dellapenta above, the most common methods of cyberstalking involve harassing or threatening e-mail messages, inappropriate e-greeting cards, and digitally altered pornographic photos that lead to harassment of the victim (Glancy, Newman, Potash, & Tennison, 2007). More sophisticated means of cyberstalking may involve the use of spyware to track the victim's activities and communications. Although the impact of stalking on victims has been studied, the impact of cyberstalking has not been investigated. However, Glancy and colleagues (2007), who are forensic psychiatrists, postulated that cyberstalking may be somewhat different in that it involves a pervasive, sometimes anonymous form of stalking that is uncontrollable and leads to a fear of the unknown. Indeed, the 2006 National Crime Victimization Survey revealed the worst fears of stalking victims in general are not knowing what will happen next (46.1%) and believing the behavior will not stop (29.1%) (Baum et al., 2009). Cyberstalking makes it easier to harass the victim at work and at home without any inconvenience to the stalker. Nevertheless, individuals can take steps to prevent and manage cyberstalking (**Table 15-2**).

Internet Fraud

On November 25, 2002, the United States charged Philip Cummings with wire fraud and conspiracy in connection with his participation in a massive identity theft scheme that spanned nearly 3 years and involved more

TABLE 15-2 Preventing and Managing Cyberstalking

Preventing cyberstalking	• Keep your primary e-mail address private.
	• Do not assume that any transaction on the Internet is confidential.
	• Choose online names with care; avoid seductive nicknames.
	• Do not fill out online profiles.
	• Watch what you say online.
	• Avoid chat rooms.
	• Use firewalls and antivirus protection.
Managing cyberstalking	• Notify the Internet provider from which the harassing e-mail originates.
	• Save all harassing communications.
	• In a neutral manner, inform the harasser that the communication is unwanted.
	• Do not have further contact with the harasser.
	• Contact the police.

Data from Glancy, G., Newman, A., Potash, M., & Tennison, J. 2007. Cyberstalking. In D. Pinals (Ed.), *Stalking: Psychiatric perspectives and practical approaches.* pp. 212-226. New York: Oxford University Press; and Pathé, M. 2002. *Surviving stalking.* New York: Cambridge University Press.

than 30,000 victims. Cummings worked at Teledata Communications Inc. (TCI), a company in Long Island that provided the computerized means for banks and other entities to obtain consumer credit information from the three commercial credit history bureaus: Equifax, Experian, and TransUnion. TCI provided software and other computerized devices to its client companies that enabled these companies, through the use of confidential computer passwords and subscriber codes, to access and download credit reports of consumers for legitimate business purposes. Cummings worked at TCI from about mid-1999 through about March 2000 as a help desk employee and was responsible for helping TCI's clients. As such, he had access to these companies' confidential passwords and codes. With these codes he had the ability to access and download credit reports.

Starting in early 2000 Cummings agreed to provide credit reports to a coconspirator (CW) in return for money. He also taught CW how to access the credit bureaus and download the reports. Ford Motor Credit Company was one entity whose confidential TCI password and subscriber code were misappropriated for 10 months to download approximately 15,000 credit reports. Ford discovered the scheme after reviewing bills for those credit histories and receiving numerous complaints from consumers who had been the subject of identity theft and fraud. After searching its databases of passwords and subscriber codes of its various corporate customers, Experian discovered the number of victims of compromised credit reports exceeded 30,000. Consumers whose credit reports had been stolen in this scheme reported many forms of identity fraud. Bank accounts holding tens of thousands of dollars in savings were depleted; credit cards were used to the tune of thousands of dollars without authorization; address changes were made to accounts at various financial institutions; checks, debit cards, ATM cards, and credit cards were sent to unauthorized locations; and identities of victims had been assumed by others. This resulted in $2.7 million in financial losses that have been confirmed to date (U.S. Department of Justice, 2002).

Fraud is defined as the purposeful, unlawful act to deceive, manipulate, or provide false statements to damage others, often in a material sense. Schemes to defraud involve intentionally depriving victims of something of value, generally money or property (Neese, Ferrell, & Ferrell, 2003). As a whole, fraud is estimated to cost U.S. corporations in excess of $600 billion annually or about 6% of the average company's total annual revenue. Fraud is by no means a new concept, with the first recorded laws relating to fraud dating back to the fourth century BC in Greece (Burns, Whitworth, & Thompson, 2004). In the United States the first mail fraud statute was enacted in 1872 in an effort to protect the integrity of the U.S. postal service. In more recent years it has been expanded to include other forms of delivery, including courier services (Neese et al., 2003). Wire fraud legislation followed, which, over time, included wire, radio or television writings, signals, pictures, or sounds.

Telemarketing fraud is the third type of legislation in this area. According to Department of Justice Canada (2008), "Telemarketing fraud has become one of the most pervasive forms of white-collar crime in Canada and the United States, with annual losses in both countries in the billions of dollars. In recent years, authorities have observed concentrations of offenders in metropolitan areas including Las Vegas, Los Angeles-Orange County, Miami-Fort Lauderdale, Montreal, Toronto and Vancouver" (para. 2). As a result of this type of cross-border crime, a special Canada–U.S. working group was set up to address the issue (Department of Justice Canada, 2008).

As with other forms of cybercrime, the Internet merely provides a new mechanism for engaging in deception and theft. Internet fraud refers to any scheme involving the Internet, such as chat rooms, e-mail, message boards, or websites that are used to conduct fraudulent transactions or solicit individuals for fraudulent purposes. The Internet Fraud Complaint Center reports common attempts to scam the public, which are found in **Table 15-3**.

TABLE 15-3 **Types of Internet Fraud**

Type	Description
Auction fraud	Misrepresentation of product for sale
	Nondelivery of a product sold on an auction site
	Frequently originating in Romania
	May also result in courier fraud where apparently legitimate courier e-mails for payment of transportation costs
Credit card fraud	Unauthorized use of credit card
	Often stolen from unsecured websites
Debt elimination	Advertises legal ways to eliminate mortgage or debts
	Pay fee of $1,500 to $2,000
	Sign power of attorney for scammer to manage funds
Employment/business opportunity schemes	Offer the opportunity to "work at home"
	Often involve reselling or shipping merchandise
	Asked to provide personal information to be "hired"
	Asked to make an investment in the enterprise
Lottery fraud	Notification that person has won a lottery
	Request for fee to obtain
Nigerian letter, or "419"	Named for violation 419 in the Nigerian criminal code
	E-mail representing self as government official or royalty
	Need to get money out of the country
	Person is asked to send banking information for money transfer
Phishing or spoofing	E-mail sent from an apparent legitimate business
	Recipient instructed to sign in via a provided link
	Asked to provide password that is then used fraudulently

Data from Federal Bureau of Investigation. 2011. Internet Crime Schemes. Internet Fraud Complaint Center. Retrieved from http://www.ic3.gov/crimeschemes .aspx#item-.1.

What is surprising with respect to Internet fraud is how vulnerable even seemingly savvy consumers may be. Grazioli (2004) conducted a study with 80 MBA students, exposing them to fraudulent and legitimate marketing websites. Only 15% of the students correctly identified fraudulent sites. The authors concluded that the lack of widespread consumer awareness and training on Internet commerce is a significant obstacle to limiting Internet fraud. Internet fraud is not limited to individual victims, however. In a survey of online marketers, 83% indicated fraud was a problem, and 63% indicated they were taking measures to limit fraud caused by customers (Neese et al., 2003). When the target of Internet fraud is a corporation or organization, upward of 70% of the perpetrators are insiders or employees of the organization (Nykodym, Taylor, & Vilela, 2005). The position of the offender within the company has a significant impact on cybercrime. When the perpetrator is a manager, the incidence of crime is lower but the losses are significantly higher due to increased access to secure and confidential data and due to increased ability to hide his or her activities.

Laws related to Internet fraud in the United States are adaptations of mail fraud acts. Although fraud is an age-old problem, the Internet makes the identities of the people in communication difficult to verify, increases the deceiver's reach, makes deception less costly and time consuming, and makes legal prosecution more difficult. It has been suggested that law enforcement agencies are underresourced and undertrained to deal with Internet fraud. The skills of personnel with years of street experience are not useful in this context, and agencies must therefore rely on young techies to deal with the issue (Burns et al., 2004). To adequately address these challenges, enforcement agencies are training staff, developing new competencies, and developing new procedures of operation.

Burns and colleagues (2004), in a nationwide survey of police forces, found that only 7% had an electronic crime division that had existed for more than 5 years and 46.7% did not have an electronic crime division as late as 2004. Of those with a computer crime division, 93.3% had five or fewer staff members in the division. These findings are particularly interesting considering that 76.5% of respondents believed Internet fraud was a significant problem in their jurisdiction. What was less clear among respondents is what level of policing should be responsible for addressing Internet fraud, with slightly more than half believing it was a local responsibility and 93% believing it was a federal responsibility (Burns et al., 2004). New initiatives by the U.S. Department of Justice are addressing these concerns.

Identity Theft

Identity theft occurs when someone uses the information of another, such as name, Social Security number, or credit card number to commit fraud. The 2008 Supplement to the National Crime and Victimization Survey reported that 11.7 million people, or 5% of all people in the United States, had discovered a member of the household had been a victim of identity theft in the past 2 years (Langton & Planty, 2010). These crimes included unauthorized use of credit cards (53%), unauthorized use of other bank accounts, and misuse of personal information. Households more likely to experience identity theft had incomes of $75,000 or higher and lived in urban or suburban areas. These statistics are relatively unchanged from the 2004 survey (Baum, 2006). Rebovich, Layne, Jiandani, and Hage (2000) reported that the National White Collar Crime Center's project, which measured public attitudes regarding identity theft crimes, found one in three households was victimized by white-collar crime in 1999. Although 60% of the respondents thought those most victimized were older than age 60 years, the study indicated that 18- to 34-year-olds with some college education were high-risk targets. The reporting of identity theft was low, with less than 1 in 10 reporting.

Stolen identities can be used in a large number of fraudulent ways, as indicated in **Table 15-4**. Benner, Givens, and Mierzwinski (2000) noted that 76% of the identity theft cases they studied involved "true name fraud" whereby the victims' names were used to commit crimes. Thieves opened an average of 6 new accounts for each person whose identity they stole, ranging from 1 to 30 new accounts. The average charge made using the false identity was $18,000, ranging from $250 to $200,000. The most common amount was $5,000. The crime was discovered when the victim was denied credit or a loan or was contacted by a collection agency, with

TABLE 15-4 Uses of Stolen Identities

Type of Fraud	Uses
Credit card fraud	Opening new credit card accounts
	Cloning and using existing credit cards to run up charges
Phone or utilities fraud	Opening new accounts
	Renting property or other items in the victim's name
Banking fraud	Creating counterfeit cheques
	Opening a new account
	Cloning ATM card and emptying the account
	Taking out a loan in the victim's name
Government document fraud	Getting a driver's license or official identification
	Using the victim's social insurance number to obtain benefits
	Filing a fraudulent tax return
Other	Obtaining employment with the victim's Social Security number
	Obtaining medical care
	Giving false information at the time of arrest; if the offender does not appear in court, a warrant is issued under the victim's name

32% having no idea the theft had occurred. The victim learned about it an average of 14 months after it occurred. In 17% of the cases the victim knew the perpetrator, and 45% of the cases involved a driver's license.

Information that allows others to falsely assume an identity is acquired in a wide variety of ways: dumpster diving (rummaging through trash), skimming (storing credit card information when the victim makes a purchase and his or her card is swiped), phishing (sending spam messages from financial institutions that ask for personal data), changing the victim's address (redirecting mail to the offender), and simply stealing the victim's wallet.

Identifying the victim is a major question in identity theft crime: Is it the individual whose identity is stolen or is it the business, company, or agency upon whom the fraud is perpetrated? Watkins (2000) argued that most police departments considered the business or company to be the victim and the individual who had his or her identity stolen to be a witness. The Privacy Rights Clearinghouse (2000) argued that victims often got little or no help from authorities because the crimes did not get investigated. A report by the Privacy Rights Clearinghouse (2000) on 66 identity theft complaints found the burden of cleaning up the mess fell to victims to repair both their credit rating and their emotional well-being (National Victim Assistance Academy, 2000). The Financial Crimes Division of the U.S. Secret Service (Leas & Burke, 2000), the Los Angeles Police Department (n.d.b), and Tworkowski and Madge (1999) concluded that victims needed months or years to restore their credit and reputations. More recently, information provided in the Crime Victimization Survey revealed that although the total financial cost of identity theft was nearly $17.3 billion over a 2-year period, less than a fourth (23%) of identity theft victims suffered an out-of-pocket financial loss from the victimization (Langton & Planty, 2010). Further, 43% of victims reported spending less than one day resolving the resulting problems although 3% noted that it took months to resolve.

In addition to financial and identity harm, victims of financial crimes can suffer psychological and physical effects and can require assistance and intervention (Alexander & Seymour, 1998; National Victim Assistance Academy, 2000). In the Crime Victimization Survey, for instance, 20% of victims reported the experience was severely distressing (Langton & Planty, 2010). However, victims do not necessarily have the same rights as violent crime victims, and they do not have an organized constituency group. Victims of financial crime often blame themselves, feel embarrassed and betrayed, describe a violation of their personal integrity and sense of trust, and are reluctant to discuss their victimization with others. They can feel isolated and find the criminal justice process unsympathetic, intimidating, and stressful. Identity theft cases can become very complex because multiple jurisdictions may be involved. There may be numerous instances of unauthorized and fraudulent use of an individual's identity. To become an effective, strong advocate for one's own case, it is vital to impose a form of organization on an identity theft case from the first day. **Table 15-5** provides suggestions on protections against identity fraud.

Law enforcement responses to identity fraud have been hampered by both technological and legislative barriers. A Montreal case of a man who acquired a criminal record as a result of having his identity stolen added to the impetus to create a new method of tracking identity theft in Canada using the nationwide Canadian Police Information Centre, which includes the names and descriptions of not only criminals but also victims who have had their identification stolen. In attempting to protect consumers, the California legislature enacted a statute in 2002 that requires all agencies, businesses, or individuals who are conducting a business in which personal data are collected to notify their customers of any security breaches. Also of note was the passage of the federal Identity Theft and Assumption Deterrence Act in 1998. In 2000 the Office for Victims of Crime designed a new curriculum module on financial crime for the National Victim Assistance Academy. In one of the units on identity theft, the crime is defined as occurring when one individual misappropriates another person's identification information and uses it to take over existing credit card or bank accounts, apply for a mortgage or car loan, make large purchases, and/or apply for insurance. Further, in 2000 the FBI in cooperation with the National White Collar Crime Center established the Internet Crime Complaints Center, which focuses

TABLE 15-5 Responding to Identity Theft

Remember: documentation and evidence are key to legally reclaiming your identity.

- Because all documents can be evidence, they should be kept in a safe place for future use.
- Keep a record of all conversations related to your case, including names and contact information of persons with whom you have spoken.
- Request written confirmation of all discussions; e-mail follow-up of discussions can be a very useful tool for creating a paper trail.
- Write summaries of your case every month or so to keep dates and progress clear so you can describe what has transpired.

Data from Privacy Rights Clearinghouse. 2009a. Fact sheet 17: Reducing the risk of identity theft. Retrieved from http://www.privacyrights.org/fs/fs17-it.htm; and Privacy Rights Clearinghouse. 2009b. Fact sheet 17(a): Identity theft victims guide. Retrieved from http://www.privacyrights.org/fs/fs17a.htm.

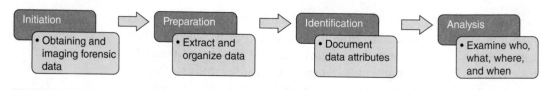

FIGURE 15-4 Process of Digital Forensic Analysis

on public education and responding to complaints of Internet fraud and identity theft. The process of investigation can be found in **Figure 15-4**.

Internet Copyright Piracy

In 2004, in response to increasing concerns regarding intellectual property crime, the U.S. Department of Justice introduced the Task Force on Intellectual Property. This task force is charged with addressing crime related to copyrights, trademarks, trade secrets, and patents. Perhaps of greatest interest to most people is the issue of copyright that includes music, movies, books, and artwork. Copyright law grants the exclusive right to authors and developers for distribution, recording, displaying, and performing their work. Although copyright laws have been in effect since 1909, the Internet provides new opportunities and challenges for distribution of materials. This is of particular concern to legislators given the vast contribution the sale and distribution of copyrighted materials adds to the national economy.

A report of the Task Force on Intellectual Property indicated that "Copyright industries in the United States sold and exported an estimated $89.26 billion in 2002 to foreign nations. Copyright industries exceeded other major industries including the chemical, food and live animal, motor vehicle, and aircraft sectors" (U.S. Department of Justice, 2004, p. 7). Thus, itemized in the report are numerous cases of individuals who were prosecuted for counterfeit DVDs, stolen satellite signals, and illegal movie distribution. In 2010 Immigration and Customs Enforcement made 365 arrests for intellectual property crimes, up 37% from the year earlier and resulting in 170 convictions. That same year the FBI had 95 convictions for intellectual property crime (U.S. Department of Justice, 2011).

Perhaps the most famous case of Internet copyright infringement is the case of the online music downloading service, Napster. Napster allowed individuals to exchange songs by trading computer files in MP3 format. Beginning with a suit launched by Metallica and Dr. Dre, the music industry sought to shut down Napster in 2000 on the basis that it violated copyright law. In a counterargument, Napster claimed that Record Industry Association of America was trying to suppress technology to maintain its dominance in the $39 billion global music business. In 2001 Napster settled with Metallica and Dr. Dre and moved to transition from free file sharing to digital music sales (CNN, 2001).

Summary

Computer crime is a relatively new and growing area where individuals and organizations can become victimized. Computer-based crimes span a wide range of activities including child pornography, cyberstalking and cyberbullying, computer and telephone hacking, cyberterrorism, copyright theft, and fraud and identity theft. Offenders in this category are perhaps the most diverse of any crime category, spanning all nationalities, all ages, and all socioeconomic groups. However, with the possible exception of hacking for the purposes of vandalism, the Internet has not created new categories of crime; rather, it has created new opportunities for criminals to use technology for their own personal ends. Nevertheless, it has created many new challenges for legislators, prosecutors, and law enforcement agencies who work in systems that have been unprepared to deal with this new wave of victimizing activity. In this area of crime, perhaps more than any others, individuals and organizations must actively work to protect themselves on a daily basis through cautious sharing of information and general suspicion regarding the identity and motives of those they cannot see or hear in person.

Key Terms

Child sexual exploitation on the Internet: Use of the Internet to distribute or view child pornography. Use of the Internet to contact children for the purposes of sexual abuse or exploitation.

Computer hacking: Unauthorized use of an information system or network by circumventing or bypassing the security mechanisms. Illegally accessing other people's computer systems for destroying, disrupting, or carrying out illegal activities on the network or in computer systems.

Copyright piracy: Unauthorized use or sale of copyrighted material.

Cyberbullying: Bullying through means of e-mail, instant messages, text messages, blogs, cell phones, pagers, and websites with the goal of tormenting, threatening, harassing, humiliating, or embarrassing a person.

Cybercrime: Crime committed using the Internet. This broad term includes attacks causing electronic commerce sites to lose money, stealing a person's identity, selling contraband, stalking victims, or disrupting operations using malevolent programs.

Cyberstalking: Use of the Internet to stalk another person.

Cyberterrorism: Any premeditated, politically motivated attack against electronic information or systems. The unauthorized use of computers and information technology to cause physical, real-world harm or severe disruption.

Identity theft: Use of a person's identifying information, including name, Social Security number, or credit card number, without permission, to commit fraud or other crimes.

Internet fraud: Deception conducted through the Internet for the purpose of financial gain.

Mail fraud: Willful use of the national mail service to defraud or obtain money or property by means of false pretenses, representations, or promises.

Telemarketing fraud: Fraudulent selling conducted over the phone. It most often targets the poor and elderly.

Telephone hacking: Illegal access to a telephone network for free phone calls or to obtain personal information.

■ Discussion Questions

1. Despite new international agreements, what international challenges continue to exist in combating cybercrime?

2. If you were working with a telecommunications company to develop safeguards for Internet bullying, what elements of the issue would you consider?

3. Describe aspects of an education campaign for college- and university-aged people to protect themselves from cyberstalking.

4. If a new assistance service were to be developed for victims of identity theft, what should the program address?

■ Resources

Canadian Anti-Fraud Centre
   http://www.antifraudcentre-centreantifraude.ca/english/home-eng.html
FBI, Internet Fraud Complaint Center
   http://www.ic3.gov/default.aspx

RCMP, National Child Exploitation Coordination Centre
http://www.rcmp-grc.gc.ca/ncecc-cncee/index-accueil-eng.htm

RCMP, Scams and Fraud
http://www.rcmp-grc.gc.ca/scams-fraudes/index-eng.htm

StopBullying.gov
http://www.stopbullying.gov/

U.S. Department of Justice, Office for Victims of Crime
https://www.ovcttac.gov/nvaa/

■ References

Alexander, E., & Seymour, A. (1998). *Roles, rights and responsibilities: A handbook for fraud victims participating in the federal criminal justice system.* Washington, DC: Police Executive Forum.

Alexy, E., Burgess, A., Baker, T., & Smoyak, S. (2005b). Perceptions of cyberstalking among college students. *Brief Treatment and Crisis Intervention, 5*(3), 279–289.

Alexy, E.M., Burgess, A.W., & Baker, T. (2005a). Internet offenders: Traders, travelers and combination trader-travelers. *Journal of Interpersonal Violence, 20*(7), 804–812.

Armstrong, H., & Forde, P. (2003). Internet anonymity practices in computer crime. *Information Management & Computer Security, 11*(5), 209–215.

Barton, P., Nissanka, V., & Waterhouse, F. (2003). Cyber-crime—Criminal offense or civil wrong? *Computer and Security Report, 19*(5), 401–405.

Baum, K. (2006). Identity theft, 2004. Bureau of Justice Statistics bulletin. Retrieved from http://www.ojp.usdoj.gov/bjs/pub/pdf/it04.pdf

Baum, K., Catalano, S., Rand, M., & Rose, K. (2009). *Stalking victimization in the United States.* Bureau of Justice Statistics Special Report. Washington: Department of Justice.

Benner, J., Givens, B., & Mierzwinski, E. (2000). *Nowhere to turn: Victims speak out on identity theft.* Sacramento, CA: CALPIRG's Consumer Program.

Beran, T., & Li, Q. (2005). Cyber-harassment: A study of a new method for an old behavior. *Journal of Educational Computing Research, 32*(3), 265–277.

Berson, I.R., Berson, M.J., & Ferron, J.M. (2002). Emerging risks of violence in the digital age: Lessons for educators from an online study of adolescent girls in the United States. *Meridian: A Middle School Technologies Journal, 5*(2), 1–32.

Bradbury, D. (2007, December 6). Technique is new, crime is not. *National Post,* SR4.

Briggs, P., Simon, W., & Simonsen, S. (2011). An exploratory study of Internet-initiated sexual offenses and the chat room sex offender: Has the Internet enabled a new typology of sex offender? *Sexual Abuse: A Journal of Research and Treatment, 23*(1), 72–91.

Burns, R., Whitworth, K., & Thompson, C. (2004). Assessing law enforcement preparedness to address Internet fraud. *Journal of Criminal Justice, 32*(5), 477–493.

Canadian Anti-Fraud Centre. (2010). Annual statistical report on mass media fraud and identity theft activities. Retrieved from http://www.antifraudcentre-centreantifraude.ca/english/statistics_statistics.html

Chu, H., Deng, D., & Chao, H. (2011). Potential cyberterrorism via a multimedia smart phone based on a web 2.0 application via ubiquitous Wi-Fi access points and corresponding digital forensics. *Multimedia Systems, 17*(4), 341–349.

Chung, W., Chen, J., Chang, W., & Chou, S. (2004). Fighting cyber-crime: A review and the Taiwan experience. *Decision Support Systems, 41*(3), 669–682.

Computer Security Institute. (2002). Cyber crime bleeds US corporations, survey shows; financial losses from attacks climb for third year in a row. Retrieved from http://www.gocsi.com/press/20020407.jhtml

CNN. (2001, July 12). Napster settles suit. Retrieved from http://money.cnn.com/2001/07/12/news/napster/

Deibert, R., & Rohozinski, R. (2010). Risking security: Policies and paradoxes of cyberspace security. *International Political Sociology, 4,* 15–32.

Department of Justice Canada. (2008). Report of the Canada–United States working group on telemarketing fraud. Retrieved from http://www.justice.gc.ca/eng/dept-min/pub/tf/sum-som.html

D'Oivido, R., & Doyle, J. (2003). A study on cyberstalking: Understanding investigative hurdles. *FBI Law Enforcement Bulletin, 72*(3), 10–17.

Finkelhor, D., Mitchell, K., & Wolak, J. (2000). *Online victimization: A report on the nation's youth*. Alexandria, VA: National Center for Missing and Exploited Children.

Fisher, B., Cullen, F., & Turner, M. (2000). *The sexual victimization of young women*. Washington, DC: U.S. Department of Justice.

Ford, B., & Kennedy, H. (2009). Suspected "Craigslist Killer" Phillip Markoff charged with assault of stripper in Rhode Island. Retrieved from http://www.nydailynews.com/news/2009/05/04/2009-05-04_suspected_craigslist_killer_phillip_markoff_charged_with_assault_of_stripper_in_.html

Ginsberg, J. (2011, July 6). U.K. Prime Minister calls for official inquiry into phone hacking scandal. Retrieved from http://news.nationalpost .com/2011/07/06/u-k-pm-calls-for-official-inquiry-into-phone-hacking-scandal/

Glancy, G., Newman, A., Potash, M., & Tennison, J. (2007). Cyberstalking. In D. Pinals (Ed.), *Stalking: Psychiatric perspectives and practical approaches* (pp. 212–226). New York: Oxford University Press.

Goodman, S., Kirk, J., & Kirk, M. (2007). Cyberspace as a medium for terrorists. *Technology Forecasting and Social Change, 74*(2), 193–210.

Gorman, S., & Barnes, J. (2011, May 31). Cyber combat: Act of War. Retrieved from http://online.wsj.com/article/SB10001424052702304563104576355562 3135782718.html

Grazioli, S. (2004). Where did they go wrong? An analysis of the failure of knowledgeable Internet consumers to detect deception over the Internet. *Group Decision and Negotiation, 13*, 149–172.

Ha, T. (2006, April 7). "Star Wars Kid" cuts a deal with tormenters. Retrieved from from http://www.theglobeandmail.com/servlet/story/RTGAM .20060407.wxstarwars07/BNStory/National/home

Humphreys, A. (2007, December 8). For the sake of the children: Canadian police help lead the fight against child abuse on the Internet. *National Post,* p. A14.

Hunton, P. (2011). The stages of cybercrime investigations: Bridging the gap between technology examination and law enforcement investigation. *Computer Law and Security Review, 27*(1), 61–67.

Internet World Stats. (2011). Usage and population statistics. Retrieved from http://www.internetworldstats.com/

Kierkegaard, S. (2006). EU framework decision on cyber attacks. *Computer Law and Security Report, 22*, 381–391.

Langton, L., & Planty, M. (2010). Victims of identity theft 2010. Retrieved from http://bjs.ojp.usdoj.gov/index.cfm?ty=pbdetail&iid=2222

Leas, M., & Burke, T. (2000). Identity theft: A fast-growing crime. *FBI Law Enforcement Bulletin, 69*(8), 8–13.

Li, Q. (2007). New bottle but old wine: A research of cyberbullying in schools. *Computers in Human Behavior, 23*, 1777–1791.

Los Angeles Police Department. (n.d.b). Identity theft. Retrieved from http:// www.lapdonline.org/search_results/content_basic_view/1364

Mishna, F., Cook, C., Gadalla, T., Daciuk, J., & Solomon, S. (2010). Cyber bullying behaviors among middle and high school students. *American Journal of Orthopsychiatry, 80*(3), 362–374.

Mishna, F., Cook, C., Saini, M., Wu, M., & MacFadden, R. (2009). Interventions for children, youth and parents to prevent and reduce cyber abuse. Campbell Collaboration Review. Retrieved from http://www .campbellcollaboration.org/news_/Preventionf_cyber_abuse.php

Mitchell, K., Wolak, J., & Finkelhor, D. (2005). Police posing as juveniles online to catch sex offenders: Is it working? *Sexual Abuse: A Journal of Research and Treatment, 17*(3), 241–267.

Morris, D. (2005). Tracking a computer hacker. Retrieved from http://www .usdoj.gov/criminal/cybercrime/usamay2001_2.htm

National Child Exploitation Coordination Centre. (2008). Child exploitation tracking system. Retrieved from http://www.rcmp-grc.gc.ca/ncecc-cncee /cets-eng.htm

National Victim Assistance Academy. (2000). Financial crime. Washington, DC: Office of Victims of Crime.

Neese, W., Ferrell, L., & Ferrell, O. (2003). An analysis of federal mail and wire fraud cases related to marketing. *Journal of Business Research, 58*, 910–918.

New York Daily News. (2009). Craigslist killer Michael John Anderson gets life in murder of Katherine Olson. *Retrieved from http://www.nydailynews .com/news/us_world/2009/04/02/2009-04-02_craigslist_killer_michael_ john_anderson_.html*

Nykodym, N., Taylor, R., & Vilela, J. (2005). Criminal profiling and insider cyber crime. *Computer Law and Security Report, 21*, 408–414.

Privacy Rights Clearinghouse. (2000). Identity theft: How it happens, its impact on victims, and legislative solutions. Retrieved from http://www .privacyrights.org/ar/id_theft.htm

Privacy Rights Clearinghouse. (2009a). Fact sheet 17: Reducing the risk of identity theft. Retrieved from http://www.privacyrights.org/fs/fs17-it.htm

Privacy Rights Clearinghouse. (2009b). Fact sheet 17(a): Identity theft victims' guide. Retrieved from http://www.privacyrights.org/fs/fs17a.htm

Prodhan, G. (2011, July 5). Backlash mounts over New Corp's alleged phone-hacking. Retrieved from http://news.nationalpost.com/2011/07/05/backlash-mounts-over-news-corps-alleged-phone-hacking/

Public Safety Canada. (2010). Government of Canada introduces legislation to fight crime in today's high-tech world. Retrieved from http://www .publicsafety.gc.ca/media/nr/2010/nr20101101-eng.aspx

Qualye, E., & Jones, T. (2011). Sexualized images of children on the internet. *Sexual Abuse: A Journal of Research and Treatment, 23*(1), 7–21.

Raskauskas, J., & Stoltz, A. (2007). Involvement in traditional and electronic bullying among adolescents. *Developmental Psychology, 43*(3), 564–575.

Reardon, M. (2008, September 22). Americans text more than they talk. Retrieved from http://news.cnet.com/8301-1035_3-10048257-94.html

Rebovich, D.J., Layne, J., Jiandani, J., & Hage, S. (2000). *The national public surveys on white collar crime.* Morgantown, WV: National White Collar Crime Center.

Robinson, J. (2011, July 7). Murdoch acts to limit fallout. Retrieved from http://www.guardian.co.uk/media/2011/jul/07/news-of-the-world-rupert-murdoch

Schell, B., Martin, M., Hung, P., & Rueda, L. (2007). Cyber child pornography: A review paper of the social and legal issues and remedies—and a proposed technological solution. *Aggression and Violent Behavior, 12,* 45–63.

Seto, M., Cantor, J., & Blanchard, R. (2006). Child pornography offenses are a valid diagnostic indicator of pedophilia. *Journal of Abnormal Psychology, 115,* 610–615.

Sher, J. (2007). *One child at a time: The global fight to rescue children from online predators.* Toronto, Ontario, Canada: Random House.

Simpson, D. (2000). Feds find dangerous cyberstalking hard to prevent. Retrieved from http://archives.cnn.com/2000/TECH/computing/06/12/cyberstalkers.idg.index.html

Sinclair, R., & Sugar, D. (2005). Internet based sexual exploitation of children and youth environmental scan. Retrieved from http://www.rcmp-grc.gc.ca/ncecc-cncee/factsheets-fichesdocu/enviroscan-analyseenviro-eng.htm

Stohl, M. (2006). Cyber terrorism: A clear and present danger, the sum of all fears, breaking point, or patriot games? *Crime, Law and Social Change, 46,* 223–238.

Tan, L.-M., & Newman, M. (1991). Computer misuse and the law. *International Journal of Information Management, 11,* 282–291.

Taylor, M., & Quayle, E. (2003). *Child pornography: An Internet crime.* New York: Routledge.

Tworkowski, N., & Madge, B.E. (1999). Identity crisis survival: Learning the scams of identity theft. *The White Paper, 13*(4), 18–21, 40, 48–49.

U.S. Department of Justice. (1999). Attorney general Janet Reno delivers cyberstalking report to the vice president. Retrieved from http://www.usdoj.gov/opa/pr/1999/September/421ag.htm

U.S. Department of Justice. (2002). US announces what is believed the largest identity theft case in American history; losses are in the millions. Retrieved from http://www.usdoj.gov/criminal/cybercrime/cummingsIndict.htm

U.S. Department of Justice. (2004). *Report of the Department of Justice's Task Force on Intellectual Property.* Retrieved from http://www.justice.gov/opa/documents/ipreport61906.pdf

U.S. Department of Justice. (2005). Computer virus broker arrested for selling armies of infected computers to hackers and spammers. Retrieved from http://www.justice.gov/criminal/cybercrime/anchetaArrest.htm

U.S. Department of Justice. (2011). Reporting computer, internet related or intellectual property crime. Computer Crime and Intellectual Property Section. Retrieved from http://www.cybercrime.gov/reporting.htm#cc

U.S. Department of State. (2001). Patterns of global terrorism. Retrieved from http://www.state.gov/s/ct/rls/pgtrpt/

Valiquet, D., & Simonds, K. (2011). Legislative Summary of Bill C-51: Investigative Powers for the 21st Century Act. Parliament of Canada Publication No. 40-3-C51E. Retrieved from http://www.parl.gc.ca/About /Parliament/LegislativeSummaries/bills_ls.asp?Language=E&ls= c51&source=library_prb&Parl=40&Ses=3

Watkins, M. (2000). Identity theft a nightmare, not impostor in Internet age. *Police, 24*(7), 26–29.

Welch, M. (2007, November 29). Child porn law to be toughened in Manitoba. *National Post,* p. A12.

Wolak, J., Finkelhor, D., & Mitchell, K. (2011). Child pornography possessors: Trends in offender and case characteristics. *Sexual Abuse: A Journal of Research and Treatment, 23*(1), 22–42.

Wolak, J., Finkelhor, D., Mitchell, K., & Ybarra, M. (2008). Online "predators" and their victims: Myths, realities, and implications for prevention and treatment. *American Psychologist, 63*(2), 111–128.

Other Forms of Victimization

CHAPTER
16

■ Objectives

- To discuss property-related crime and its victims
- To discuss victims of workplace violence
- To discuss the effects of terrorism
- To expose the harms caused by major forms of white-collar and corporate crime
- To identify issues related to the accused as victims, including wrongful convictions and racial profiling

■ Key Terms

Burglary
Corporate victimization
Home invasion
Larceny (or theft)
Racial profiling
Robbery
Terrorism
Theft

CASES

Home Invasion and Carjacking

On Monday, July 18, 2011, a federal jury in Greenbelt, Maryland, convicted Jason Thomas Scott for a series of violent home invasions, carjackings, firearms offenses, and the molestation of a teenage girl. The 3-week trial portrayed Jason Scott as a professional, methodical, dangerous criminal as he escalated his activities from committing burglaries and demanding PIN numbers from the victims' bank accounts, to armed home invasion robberies. Scott admitted to 28 burglaries, nine armed home invasions, and sexually assaulting and photographing the teenage girl (Castaneda, 2011). These convictions were added to recent homicide convictions. On January 26, 2009, he entered the home of Karen Lofton, a 45-year-old nurse, and fatally shot both her and her 16-year-old daughter, Karissa. Three months later the bodies of Delores Dewitt, a 42-year-old nurse, and her 20-year-old daughter, Ebony, were found in a burning car less than a mile away from the Lofton's home after what was believed to be a carjacking. Police believe Scott might also have committed murders in Washington, DC; Texas; and Florida; which remain unsolved (Thomas, 2011). Scott, who had a degree in computer science from the University of Maryland and worked for a courier company, researched police forensic tactics and may have used his employer's database to research potential victims (Castaneda, 2011; Thomas, 2010). Scott faces a mandatory minimum sentence of 97 years in prison for the federal offenses.

Wrongful Conviction

Dr. Smith (**Figure 16-1**), a renowned forensic pathologist in Toronto, conducted over 1,000 autopsies of children over a 24-year period, many of which involved suspicious deaths. Many of these cases involved "shaken baby syndrome," a condition often leading to death where a child incurs brain injury due to intentional shaking. However, over the course of the 1990s he was subject to an increasing amount of criticism by the judicial system regarding his methods, competence, and, in particular, his testimony at trial. In 2005 the Chief Coroner for Ontario instituted a review into 45 cases of homicide about which Dr. Smith had expressed

FIGURE 16-1 Dr. Charles Smith
© Adrian Wyld/The Canadian Press/AP Photos

professional opinions that the death was either homicide or criminally suspicious. The coroner's review determined that Smith made questionable conclusions of foul play in 20 cases, 13 of which resulted in criminal convictions. Subsequently, a commission was established in which Justice Stephen Goudge was charged with examining 20 cases identified in the earlier chief coroner's review (Glancy & Regehr, 2012). In one of these cases William Mullins-Johnson was convicted of murder in the 1994 death of his niece. After 10 years in jail, Mullins-Johnson was released on bail pending review of his conviction. In 2007 he was acquitted of the murder.

In the opening pages of the Goudge inquiry report, the costs of misleading expert testimony are underlined. The attorney for Mullins-Johnson asked Dr. Smith to apologize to his client who was in the audience at the inquiry. The emotionally charged exchange follows (Goudge, 2008, p. 5):

> *Dr. Charles Smith:* Could you stand, sir? [brief pause] Sir, I don't expect that you would forgive me, but I do want to make it-I'm sorry. I do want to make it very clear to you that I am profoundly sorry for the role that I played in the ultimate decision that affected you. I am sorry.
>
> *Mr. William Mullins-Johnson:* For my healing, I'll forgive you but I'll never forget what you did to me. You put me in an environment where I could have been killed any day for something that never happened. You destroyed my family, my brother's relationship with me and my niece that's still left and my nephew that's still living. They hate me because of what you did to me. I'll never forget that, but for my own healing I must forgive you.

■ Introduction

This text has provided an overview of issues related to people who become victims of a wide variety of crimes. At times these crimes are specific to particular populations, such as children, the elderly, women, or individuals and groups of a specific race or religion. At times these crimes are more general in who is targeted, such as in the case of Internet and white-collar crime. The incidence of each type of victimization, the impact of the crime on victims, strategies for intervention, and laws that define the nature of the crime and legal attempts to punish offenders and protect victims and society at large are covered extensively elsewhere in this text. This chapter focuses on other forms of victimization including (1) victims of property-related crime, (2) victims of terrorism, (3) victims of violence in the workplace, (4) corporate and white-collar victimizations, and (5) victims of the justice system.

■ Victims of Property-Related Crime

In this section we focus on criminal activity related to property. These crimes can involve the loss of property alone or they can also include sexual violence, other forms of physical assault, or murder. Further, the level of threat to the victim differs in these crimes; whereas theft involves minimal personal threat and robbery, home invasion and carjacking can involve lethal threat.

Robbery

The Federal Bureau of Investigation (FBI), in its Uniform Crime Report, defines robbery as the "taking or attempting to take anything of value from the care, custody, or control of a person or persons by force, or threat of force or violence and/or by putting the victim in fear" (U.S. Department of Justice, 2010). Larceny (or theft), on the other hand, concerns the taking of a person's property without the permission of the property owner or possessor of that property but does not involve threat, intimidation, or violence to the individual in possession of the property. The charge applied in any particular case depends on the value of the merchandise stolen or the amount of money stolen (Basics of a Burglary Case, 2011). Legislation in various jurisdictions differentiates between petty larceny and grand larceny based on a particular value (for instance, over $1,000). Grand larceny is a felony offense. Personal larceny involves the theft or attempted theft of property or cash directly from the victim by stealth but without force or threat of force, such as in the case of pick-pocketing.

Robbery is different from theft in that it involves the use of force, the threat of force, the use of violence, or the threat of violence to intimidate the victim or put the victim in fear for his or her safety. If there is a struggle between the victim and the offender during a theft, it will more likely be classified as a crime of robbery (National Center for Victims of Crime, 2011). Robbery may be further classified according to the *degree of force used or threatened*; thus, a jurisdiction might consider armed robbery a more serious crime than robbery without a weapon. The FBI Uniform Crime Reports estimate the rate of victimization by robbery was 119.1 per 100,000 people in 2010 (U.S. Department of Justice, 2010). This represented a 10.5% decrease over the year before. The most common place to be robbed is on the street (43.2% of all robberies) with an average loss of $908 per offense. However, 17.3% of people were robbed in their own homes and 22.9% are robbed in a workplace such as a gas station or convenience store. Although banks are the least likely place for a robbery to occur (2.2% of all robberies), they result in the highest average loss ($4,410). Firearms were used in 41.4% of all robberies reported to police (U.S. Department of Justice, 2010).

Robbery is a feared crime as it not only entails loss of property but also the threat or actual use of violence. The upfront confrontation with a threatening offender strips victims of their sense of control, leaving them feeling both helpless to protect themselves and self-blaming for not resisting. When a weapon is involved, the loss of control is even more acutely experienced, often resulting in both short-term crisis reactions and long-term distress (Bard & Sangrey, 1986). Frighteningly, this crime often occurs in the victim's home, place of work, or on the street in his or her local neighborhood. This undermines the person's general sense of safety and can often lead to restricting activities to avoid further risk, inability to work, and excessive fear at home. Studies of bank tellers, shop owners, and others who experience armed robbery at work demonstrate trauma profiles very similar to that of other violent crimes. This has led the banking industry to invest in crisis counseling services to assist those affected by robbery.

Most property lost in robberies is never recovered. When stolen property is recovered by a police department, it is kept in the police property room until it is known whether it will be needed as evidence at trial. If the defendant pleads guilty, the property is not needed as evidence, and efforts are made to release the property to its legal owner. The police agency first is required to photograph the item and identify it on a printed form prepared by the prosecuting attorney's office. The victim is required as the true owner of the possessions to sign a statement indicating ownership of the items recovered. In those instances in which the property is needed as evidence at trial, it cannot be released until completion of the trial and appeal process, which may take years (Hancock County, 2011).

Burglary

Under U.S. law, burglary is the uninvited and illegal entry into a person's property, cargo container, or any vehicle or vessel. In Canada the equivalent term *break and enter* refers to the entrance into a building for the purpose of committing an indictable offense or the unlawful entrance into a home, house, or abode. In both countries the entry may involve force, such as breaking a lock or window, or may involve entry through an unlocked door. Approximately 60% of burglaries in homes occur during the daytime. Between 2003 and 2007 household members were not present in 72.4% of

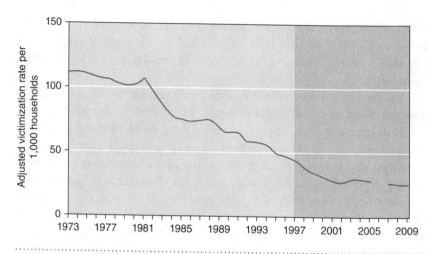

FIGURE 16-2 U.S. Burglary Rates

Data from Bureau of Justice Statistics. http://bjs.ojp.usdoj.gov/content/glance/burg.cfm.

cases. Yet despite increased availability of empty homes, burglary rates have decreased over the past three decades, as depicted in **Figure 16-2**.

Although definitions and penalties for burglary differ across the various states in America, the severity of the crime is influenced by certain common factors:

- Type of property (residential or commercial property, cargo container, or type of vehicle or vessel)
- Whether there are people in the property at the time
- Possession of a weapon while committing the burglary
- If the burglar is under the influence or in possession of illegal drugs
- Intent to commit a crime and the severity of that crime

Burglary is frequently a secondary crime or byproduct of the intention to commit another crime, typically a more serious crime such as arson, murder, kidnapping, identity theft, sexual assault, destruction of property, and violation of civil rights (Basics of a Burglary Case, 2011).

Although victims of burglary usually do not encounter the burglar, they nevertheless express considerable fear and often report a feeling of personal violation. Further, the fear of home burglaries makes people anxious about leaving their homes unattended even to go away for a weekend or to go to work.

Home Invasion

Home invasion is a situation in which one or more perpetrators force entry into a home where inhabitants are present for the purposes of robbery, rape, or other criminal activity. Also known as "push-in robberies," home invasions frequently involve highly violent activities. For example, Maxwell Bogel, aged 38 years, was a drug gang enforcer who was on the U.S. Marshal's most wanted list for many months. In 1998 he was sentenced in absentia to 68 years for kidnapping, rape, and robbery. His criminal activity involved forcing his way into the homes of people who owed the gang money, often keeping family members captive for more than a day. He would then repeatedly rape and sodomize the girls in the families until the money was paid (Cardwell, 2001).

Other reports from Florida describe home invasions of elderly people, the perpetrators severely beating the inhabitants and then ransacking their homes (Hurley, 1995). Home invasion robberies can be distinguished from other types of robberies because in most commonplace robberies, the perpetrator avoids contact with the home owner. Such burglars tend to enter the house covertly through a back entrance. Their entire operation is based on stealth. In contrast, confrontation is often the key element of home invasion robberies (Hurley, 1995). These robbers carry weapons of control such as firearms, handcuffs, masks, and tape. Victims are forced to open safes and reveal their valuables. Although several theories attempt to explain the rise in home invasions, the answers are often tied to the drug trade for one category of offender, and in other cases the advanced technology that prevents robbery of institutions, such as banks, may have pushed armed robbers to an easier target. Not only is security much lower in residential properties, but alarms are generally off when the property is occupied.

Legislators and law enforcement personnel have attempted to manage this relatively new threat. In Florida a law was passed in 1993 that makes home invasion robbery a first-degree felony even when no weapon is used. This law provided for stiff penalties (Hurley, 1995). In January 2008, after a burglary where a woman and her two daughters were murdered, the state senate in Connecticut similarly passed a law moving home invasion robbery to a first-degree offense. Sentences were made stiffer, and the requirement that the offender knew the home was occupied was dropped. The bill further requires global positioning monitoring of an additional 300 parolees. One senator was reported as saying, "The people in my district have had it. If you don't feel safe in your own home what else do you have?" ("Senate OKs new home invasion law," 2008).

Carjacking

On January 28, 1993, Ellis McHenry approached someone at a gas station in Cleveland, Ohio, asked if he needed drugs, and then asked to rent his car. When the patron refused, McHenry revealed a gun with which he struck the victim and then stole his car. Over the subsequent week McHenry committed two additional carjackings. One involved two women and the 2-year-old daughter of one of the victims. In the end, he robbed them at gunpoint and ordered them from the car, which he stole. The final carjacking involved a woman who was transporting two emotionally disturbed students, whom he held at gunpoint. McHenry was found guilty of three counts of carjacking, three counts of using a firearm in the commission of a crime of violence, and one count of receiving a firearm from an illegal alien (Blatt, 1998).

In 1992 a federal statute came into effect in the United States that criminalized carjacking. In 1994 the statute was amended, and carjacking was defined as follows:

"Whoever, *with intent to cause death or serious bodily harm* takes a motor vehicle that has been transported, shipped, or received in interstate or foreign commerce from the person or presence of another by force and violence or by intimidation, or attempts to do so, shall (1) be fined under this title or imprisoned not more than 15 years or both, (2) if serious bodily injury results, be fined under this title or imprisoned not more than 25 years, or both, and (3) if death results, be fined under this title or imprisoned for any number of years up to life, or both *or sentenced to death*" (18 U.S.C. § 2119; italics added).

Carjacking in the United States has increased dramatically in recent years—a 40% increase per year between 1987 and 1992—and in 2003 it was estimated to average 49,000 per year (Jacobs, Topalli, & Wright, 2003). Concern about this crime has led to an extension of provisions related to home invasion to carjacking in some jurisdictions. For example, in 1998 Louisiana passed a "Shoot the Carjacker" law, which extended the defense of habitation law. This law makes justifiable a homicide committed by a person who is lawfully inside a motor vehicle against someone who is unlawfully attempting to enter the vehicle if the person believes that deadly force is necessary to prevent the entry or to compel the intruder to leave (Green, 1999).

■ Victims of Workplace Violence

During the past decade newspapers rarely have missed an opportunity to report the latest murder, robbery, physical or sexual assault, or stalking incident occurring in the workplace. Factories, offices, criminal courts, public schools, and hospitals are no longer the safe places they once were for employees. Other victimization in institutions can occur by peers, customers, and authority persons, as well as by strangers. The most high profile of these was a series of incidents between 1986 and 2006 in which current or former workers in the U.S. postal service committed mass murders in their places of work. Indeed, the term "going postal" has become a slang term for extreme and uncontrollable rage in the workplace. Examples of shootings in the postal service include the 1986 murder of 14 employees in Oklahoma by Patrick Sherrill, who then shot himself to death; two separate shootings on May 6 in Michigan and California that resulted in five dead and three wounded; and the mass murder of 6 postal employees in California in 2006.

According to the National Institute for Occupational Safety and Health (2012), those workplaces with the highest death-by-homicide rates in the United States are taxicab establishments, liquor stores and local bars, gas stations, and hotels/motels, whereas the job categories with the highest risk are police officers and sheriffs, security guards, and jewelry storeowners.

Violence in the workplace is a serious safety and health issue. Its most extreme form, homicide or suicide, is one of the causes of fatal occupational injuries in the United States. According to the Bureau of Labor Statistics Census of Fatal Occupational Injuries, there were 506 workplace homicides in 2010 in the United States, out of a total of 4,547 fatal work injuries. For the same year there were 258 workplace suicides (U.S. Department of Labor, 2011). Given the rates of death in the workplace, American companies have identified workplace violence as one of the most serious threats they must manage. Beyond the human costs, workplace violence results in tangible costs such as damage, sick time, and health and life insurance costs and also adversely affects the ability to attract and maintain high-quality employees, undermines morale, and decreases productivity (Hunt & Hughey, 2010).

Environmental conditions associated with workplace violence and fatalities have been identified and control strategies implemented in a number of work settings. For instance, handling money while in contact with the public increases the risk of being victimized at work during a robbery. Workplace strategies implemented include installing locked drop safes, limiting the cash on site through the use of credit and debit cards, and creating physical barriers between the worker and the public. Other environmental strategies involve use of closed-circuit cameras, alarm doors, and improved lighting (Loomis, Marshall, Wolf, Runyan, & Butts, 2002).

Individuals in health and social services are also at high risk of violence, in this case from patients or consumers of services. In one study 82%

of emergency department nurses had been assaulted in the previous year (Gacki-Smith et al., 2009). In a Canadian study almost 70% of paramedics reported being assaulted and 56% reported being in situations where they believed their lives were at risk (Regehr & Bober, 2005). Environmental strategies in such settings involve reducing overcrowding and wait times that increase patient frustration, ensuring that health care workers operate in teams, and developing violence management skills in workers.

Despite the fact that victimization by the public is the more likely risk, media and other attention has focused on violence committed by employees of the organization, most specifically homicides. In these cases, typically a distressed employee perceives that he or she has been unfairly treated in the workplace and as a result threatens a coworker or supervisor. Such situations are more difficult to predict and guard against than robbery or patient violence in large part due to the rare nature of these events (they account for only about 7% of all workplace homicides). Nevertheless, Park Dietz, a psychiatrist specializing in threat assessment, suggested that all threats must be reported to those who are responsible for managing them. The company may have in-house specialists to assess the risk of each individual threat, may seek the assistance of external consulting firms that specialize in risk assessment, or may seek the assistance of FBI threat assessment specialists. Dietz (2009) suggested that threat assessment should be part of a comprehensive program of risk management that includes the following:

- Policies regarding violence, threats, misconduct, weapons, intimate partner violence, and bomb threats
- A system for reporting, investigating, assessing, and managing all threats, misconduct, and inappropriate behavior
- Access controls
- A security plan and procedures
- Preemployment screening procedures
- A drug-free workplace program
- An employee assistance program
- Critical incident response procedures
- Training of all employees in their roles in each of the above

■ Victims of Terrorism

Disasters involving large numbers of people are all too common events. In March 2011, a tidal wave hit the coast of Japan destroying towns and killings thousands. Dramatic video footage demonstrates the overwhelming

power of nature and human vulnerability (see for instance http://www
.dailymail.co.uk/news/article-1366000/Japan-tsunami-video-shows-
tidal-wave-destroying-path.html). Closer to home, hurricane Katrina hit
Louisiana on August 29, 2005. The collapse of two levees resulted in 80%
of the city of New Orleans being submerged in up to 6 feet of water (CBC,
2005). While disasters resulting in devastation and loss take a huge toll on
people involved (Norris et al., 2002), the effect of disaster caused by human
action is all the more disturbing (North & Pfefferbaum, 2002; Weisaeth
& Tonnessen, 2003). In 2001 the U.S. Department of State (2001, para. 2)
provided a report to Congress on terrorism and terrorist activities:

> [T]errorism cast its lethal shadow across the globe—yet the
> world's resolve to defeat it has never been greater. . . . This chill-
> ing report details the very clear and present danger that terror-
> ism poses to the world and the efforts that the United States
> and our partners in the international community are making to
> defeat it. The cold, hard facts presented here compel the world's
> continued vigilance and concerted action.

The RAND Corporation, after the Oklahoma City bombing, developed a worldwide database on terrorist incidents between 1968 and 2004.
The database identified a total of 19,828 events and 86,568 casualties, of
which 25,408 were fatal. Most terror-related events involved bombs and
guns (Bogen & Jones, 2006).

In the face of disaster, the immediate response of people is often
adaptive. Media coverage of 100th anniversary of the Titanic has highlighted stories of bravery and chivalry. Following the directive of Captain
Edward Smith "Women and children first!" 72% of women survived the
disaster while only 19% of men arrived safely on shore (Boesveld, 2012).
Similarly in interviews held with survivors of the 9/11 terrorist attack
on the World Trade Center, the vast majority of people did not report
becoming immobilized or incapacitated by their feelings or the circumstances. Rather, people described their actions as adaptive, looking for
exits, joining coworkers and strangers in finding a way out of the damaged office floor, and moving in a deliberate and cooperative manner
(Perry & Lindell, 2003; Regehr & Bober, 2005).

In the aftermath, however, victims of terrorist violence have a wide
variety of responses. A nationally representative study of 512 Israelis who
had been directly exposed to a terrorist attack and 191 who had family members exposed demonstrated that 76.7% had at least one symptom of traumatic stress and 9.4% met the criteria for posttraumatic stress
disorder (PTSD) (Bleich, Gelkopf, & Solomon, 2003). Seven weeks after

9/11, the New York City health department and the Centers for Disease Control and Prevention conducted a door-to-door survey of those living in the neighborhood of the World Trade Center, which revealed that 40% of people reported having symptoms of PTSD (Galea et al., 2002). A national survey conducted 3 to 5 days after the attack revealed that 44% of the respondents reported one or more substantial symptoms (Schlenger et al., 2002). A similar survey conducted months later revealed that 17% of the population across the United States had 9/11-related symptoms at 2 months after the attack, and 5.8% had symptoms at 6 months after the attack (Ai, Evans-Campbell, Santangelo, & Cascio, 2006).

The widespread impact of terrorism reflected in these studies echo the impact of hate crimes. That is, these crimes affect not only individuals but also communities. The fact that a member of a group has been targeted simply because of his or her skin color, religion, or sexual orientation sends shock waves throughout the group. All members become acutely aware of the risk they face, and their sense of safety and security is severely undermined.

At an individual level, those directly affected by the event understandably have higher levels of response. In a study conducted by Stellman and colleagues with over 11,000 World Trade Center employees 10 to 61 months after the 9/11 attack, 11.1% of workers met criteria for probable PTSD, 8.8% met criteria for probable depression, 5.0% met criteria for probable panic disorder, and 62.0% met criteria for substantial stress reaction. The PTSD prevalence of workers in this study was comparable with that seen in returning Afghanistan war veterans and was much higher than in the U.S. general population. The point prevalence of mental health concerns declined from 13.5% to 9.7% over the 5 years of the study. Comorbidity was extensive and included extremely high risks for impairment of social function. PTSD was significantly associated with loss of family members and friends; disruption of family, work, and social life; and higher rates of behavioral symptoms in their children (Stellman et al., 2008). A study of 777 people who were affected by 9/11 because they lived or worked near the site, witnessed the attack, knew a victim, or knew a recovery worker who revealed specific symptoms including somatic responses, such as stomach pain, back pain, headaches, chest pain, dizziness, or heart rate increases; depressive symptoms; and anxiety symptoms, including concentration difficulties and arousal (Colarossi, Heyman, & Phillips, 2005).

■ Corporate Victimization

Corporate victimization has received far less attention from criminologists, victimologists, and law enforcement alike than many other forms of victimization. Croall (2001) identified that positivist victimologists have traditionally focused on conventional definitions of crime and when measuring crimes against organizations have limited their scope to such crimes as robbery or burglary. Similarly, she contends that while radical victimologists have been interested in the structural forces that underpin crime and victimization, they have nevertheless focused on street crime and interpersonal violence. Croall (2001, 2007) suggests that this lack of attention in part may stem from the sense that victims are invisible for instance in the case of environmental crimes, crimes against the government, or crimes against corporations. It may also stem from notions that victims of corporate crimes may be undeserving. That is, investors can be blamed for engaging in risky investments solely for the purpose of becoming wealthier. The absence of corporate crime in most crime analyses is particularly interesting given the long-standing awareness of these issues and the devastating consequences this type of crime holds for large numbers of people.

Heralded as the pioneer in the area of corporate crime is Edwin Sutherland, who in a presidential address to a joint meeting of the American Economic Society and the American Sociological Society in 1939, raised the issue that he published 10 years later in his groundbreaking book "White Collar Crime" (Sutherland, 1949). Sutherland defined white collar crime as "crime committed by a person of respectability and high social status in the course of their occupation" (p. 9). Braithwaite modified this definition and suggested that corporate crime is "the conduct of a corporation, or employees acting on behalf of the corporation, which is proscribed and punishable by law" (Braithwaite, 1984, p. 6).

More recently white collar crime has been front and center in public awareness as a result of a series of high profile cases reported in the media and popular novels and movies based on real cases. In 2009, Bernie Madoff was sentenced to a jail term of 150 years by a New York federal court judge for swindling investors out of $65 billion (Moyer, 2009). Hollywood film *Erin Brockovich* focused on the battle led by the legal clerk against Pacific Gas and Electric for allegedly poisoning the drinking water of a small town in Hinkley, California, resulting in a $333 million dollar settlement. Twenty years later in 2011, Brockovich returned to Hinkley due to concerns that the problem of contamination had returned (Schwartz, 2011). February 2012 marked the 40th anniversary of a flood in Buffalo Creek, West Virginia, caused by the bursting of a dam designed to hold back coal wastewater, four days after it was declared safe by a federal mine inspector. The resulting rush of 130 million gallons of sludge water killed 125 people, injured 1,100, and left 4,000 homeless (Herald-Dispatch, 2012). Organizations are also the victims of corporate crime.

The 2010 Annual Report of the Certified Fraud Examiners revealed that the typical organization loses 5% of its annual revenue to fraud resulting in an estimated total cost of $2.9 trillion worldwide. Most costly frauds were those caused by the most senior people in the organization including both owners and executives (Association of Certified Fraud Examiners, 2010). Thus, corporate crime can take many forms ranging from defrauding people out of money to negligent practices causing injury and death. Croall (2007, 2011) provides an overview of corporate crimes and their victims (see **Table 16-1**).

Legislative and law enforcement attempts to deal with corporate crime have varied according to the nature of the activity and are primarily divided into three categories: environmental, consumer protection, and corporate securities and commodities fraud. Price and Norris (2009) provide an excellent summary of U.S. legislation and law enforcement efforts to combat corporate crime related to securities and commodities fraud. In 2001 the FBI established the Corporate Fraud Initiative, which focused on three categories of corporate fraud: falsification of financial information; self-dealing by corporate traders; and obstruction of justice,

TABLE 16-1 **Victims of Corporate Crimes**

Victim	Examples
Government	Tax evasion by corporations
	Fraudulent billing for services (such as by consultants or construction firms)
Organizations	Embezzlement
	Employee theft
	(Association of Certified Fraud Examiners, 2010)
Investors and savers	Cheating of investors through bogus trades, insider trading, kickbacks, and falsified records (FBI, 2008)
Consumers	Deceptive advertising
	Deceptive mortgage and lending practices
	Internet, telecommunications, and mail fraud
	(Federal Trade Commission, 2012)
Employees	Refusal to pay fair wages and benefits (for instance to foreign workers)
	Neglect of health and safety regulations
	(U.S. Department of Labor, 2011)
The public	Environmental contamination including illegal emissions from industry, farming, and transport; littering; waste dumping; the pollution of land, water, and rivers; and noise pollution (EPA, 2012)

Data from Croall, H. 2011. Victims of white colar and corporate crime. Retrieved from http://www.uk.sagepub.com/stout/croall_white_collar%20-%20vics_crim_soc .pdf.

specifically to conceal criminal conduct. Investigations continue to focus on market manipulation, high-yield investment fraud, hedge-fund fraud, foreign exchange fraud, and broker embezzlement. The establishment of the FBI unit was followed one year later by the Sarbanes-Oxley Bill, which incorporated both corporate governance and criminal law and established provisions for increasing maximum sentences for corporate crimes (Moohr, 2007) and allowed for fines of up to $5 million for perpetrators who falsified company records. These changes reflected changing public attitudes toward the perpetrators of such crime (Price & Norris, 2009) but also arose from a need for government to appear to be addressing the economic crisis in which the United States and other nations found themselves (Simpson, 2002).

The Environmental Protection Agency (EPA) was established in 1970 and is the lead agency for developing and enforcing environmental regulations passed through the U.S. congress (Gibbs & Simpson, 2009). Topics of legislation covered by the EPA include air pollution, water contamination, waste disposal, pesticides use, and toxic substances (EPA, 2012). One of the mechanisms for addressing environmental concerns is through the Comprehensive Environmental Response, Compensation, and Liability Act, which (1) taxes chemical and petroleum industries and (2) provides authority to respond to actual or threatened releases of toxic agents that may threaten public health or the environment (EPA, 2012). The EPA can also make recommendations to the Department of Justice that criminal charges be filed. In addition, as noted earlier, compensation for damages can be acquired through civil action as occurred in the case of Pacific Gas and Electric described previously.

The Federal Trade Commission Bureau of Consumer Protection is responsible for conducting investigations and initiating action in the case of consumer fraud. It coordinates with criminal investigation agencies, litigates civil actions, and enforces consumer protection laws (Federal Trade Commission, 2012).

■ Victims of the Justice System

Although much research has focused on individuals who were victimized primarily by those engaged in crime, victimization can also occur at a systemic level.

Victims of Wrongful Convictions

Sometimes the accused also becomes a victim by way of wrongful conviction. Wrongful convictions are of grave concern to society and to the administration of justice. As stated by U.S. Senator Patrick Leahy, "These mistakes in our system of justice carry a high personal and social price. They undermine the public's confidence in our judicial system, they produce unbearable anguish for innocent people and their families and for the victims of these crimes, and they compromise public safety because for every wrongly convicted person, there is a real criminal who may still be roaming the streets" (2003, para. 3).

Concern about not only the incarceration but also the possible execution of innocent people led to the passing of the Justice for All Act in 2004. This Act provides for the development of effective systems within states that have the death penalty for monitoring prosecutions and funding for obtaining DNA evidence. In addition, advocacy comes from the legal community and other parts of society to ensure those who are wrongfully convicted are freed, the most famous initiative being the Innocence Project. According to its website, "The Innocence Project is a national litigation and public policy organization dedicated to exonerating wrongfully convicted people through DNA testing and reforming the criminal justice system to prevent future injustice" (Innocence Project, 2008, para. 1). At the time of this writing, the Innocence Project had helped to exonerate 210 people who were wrongly convicted.

There are several causes of wrongful convictions in the cases of people who have been assisted by the Innocence Project (**Table 16-2**). In about 75% of convictions that are overturned, the issue has been eyewitness misidentification. At times these misidentifications are a result of variables outside the control of the criminal justice system, such as poor lighting, great distances, and stress experienced by the witness. They also may be the result of factors within the criminal justice system, such as the use of lineups or photo arrays that bias the witness in a particular direction. Perhaps the most striking case of injustice caused by eye witness testimony was early in the 19th century when seven men

TABLE 16-2 **Causes of Wrongful Convictions**

- Eyewitness misidentification
- Faulty or inexact science
- False or bad scientific testimony
- False confessions
- Misconduct in the criminal justice system
- Paid informants or witnesses
- Bad legal representation

Data from Innocence Project. 2008. The Innocence Project. Retrieved from http://www.innocenceproject.org/.

were executed for a robbery committed by five men (Sporer, Koehnken, & Malpass, 1996). A large body of psychology literature focuses on the fallibility of eye witness testimony, which, in general, concludes that such testimony is frequently highly unreliable and very amenable to manipulation (Malpass, 2006). As the Innocence Project and others weighed into the discussion of problems with eyewitness testimony with dramatic examples of wrongful convictions, the U.S. Department of Justice initiated a Technical Working Group for Eyewitness Evidence (n.d.b) that produced a report aimed at creating changes in the way that this testimony is acquired.

Another cause of wrongful conviction relates to scientific evidence. Despite what the public has been led to believe with television shows such as *CSI: Crime Scene Investigation*, the science on which criminal investigation and prosecution relies is highly inexact. All tests, including blood tests and DNA tests, have a margin of error and often rely on professional judgment in the interpretation of results. This is evident in the case of Dr. Charles Smith, discussed previously. Among his areas of expertise was shaken baby syndrome, a form of head trauma that often leads to death, in which an infant is vigorously shaken. The shaking can lead to hemorrhages in the retinas of the eyes, skull fractures, swelling of the brain, subdural hematomas (blood collections pressing on the surface of the brain), rib and long bone (bones in the arms and legs) fractures, and bruises around the head, neck, or chest. On the basis of Dr. Smith's testimony in 20 cases where he proclaimed that shaken baby syndrome had occurred, 13 individuals, primarily parents, were criminally convicted of murder for allegedly shaking a small infant to such an extent that brain damage and death resulted (CBC News, 2008). In 2010, the Province of Ontario announced a fund to pay compensation to 19 people who were directly impacted by the flawed testimony of Dr. Smith (Boyle, 2010).

Approximately 25% of cases of wrongful conviction involve false confessions of guilt. False confessions can occur as a result of many factors, including duress or coercion, intoxication, diminished capacity, and mental disorder. The Innocence Project (2008) suggests, for example, that juveniles in particular may be convinced that if they confess, they can go home. People of all ages may become exhausted under the scrutiny of interrogation and may believe they will have the opportunity to prove innocence at a later time. Of greatest concern, however, are individuals with mental impairments, who are disproportionately represented among those who give false confessions. An example is Eddie Joe Lloyd, a man with schizophrenia who was convicted in 1984 of the rape and murder of a 16-year-old girl. Mr. Lloyd wrote to the police on numerous occasions with suggestions on how to solve crimes. On this occasion the police interrogated Mr. Lloyd and in doing so provided him with information about the crime. Mr. Lloyd confessed to the crime with the belief that he would assist the police in smoking out the real killer. After spending 17 years in prison for the crime, Mr. Lloyd was exonerated by DNA evidence (Innocence Project, 2008).

Clearly, there is much attention at this time to ensuring that wrongful convictions do not occur. Nevertheless, we continue to have many wrongfully accused individuals in our jail systems, and even with improved measures, there is no fail-safe way to ensure innocent persons are not found guilty of crimes they have not committed. In our efforts to help victims, we must remain diligent that we do not create new victims through wrongful convictions.

Victims of Racial Profiling and Disproportionate Penalties

Racial profiling, according to the Ontario Human Rights Commission (2003), is any action undertaken for reasons of safety, security, or public protection that relies on stereotypes about race, color, ethnicity, ancestry, religion, or place of origin (or a combination of these) rather than on reasonable suspicion to single out an individual for greater scrutiny or different treatment. A large body of evidence supports the view that there are biases in the criminal justice system against members of minority groups. To begin with, the use of race as a criterion for discretionary traffic and field stops is well documented and has long been a hotly debated topic (Birzer & Birzer, 2006; Parker, MacDonald, Alpert, Smith, & Piquero, 2004; Wilson, Dunham, & Alpert, 2004). Such a practice is related to the Fourth Amendment right of the police to exercise discretion, and this discretion, when applied to racial profiling, leads to increased danger of convicting an innocent minority (Georgakopoulos, 2004).

The setting of bail and the imposition of the death penalty are disproportionately applied to members of different races. For example, of persons under sentence and awaiting death in 2006, 1,802 were White, 1,352 were Black, 28 were Native American, 35 were Asian, and 11 were of unknown race (U.S. Department of Justice, n.d.a). This is staggering considering that in the 2005 census, 80.2% of the population was White, 12.8% was Black, 1% was Native American, and 4.3% was Asian (U.S. Census Bureau, 2006).

Aboriginal people in Canada comprised 3.3% of the nation's population (Statistics Canada, 2001), yet in 1997 they account for approximately 12% of Canada's federal offender population (Canadian Criminal Justice

Association, 1997). For example, in the Canadian province of Manitoba, aboriginal people constituted approximately 12% of the population, yet aboriginal people accounted for over one-half of the 1,600 people who were incarcerated on any given day of the year in Manitoba's correctional institutions in 2004 (Aboriginal Justice Implementation Commission, 2004). Facts and figures of this kind have led to the conclusion that discrimination against aboriginal people pervades the operations of the justice system of Canada and that aboriginal people are significantly disadvantaged as a result (Dylan, Regehr, & Alaggia, 2008). Some contend this increased risk of apprehension and conviction is due to preexisting views of criminality, which can lead to unintentional racial profiling and prejudicial sentencing (Georgakopoulos, 2004). This is problematic because one of the issues in dealing with discriminatory practices is that the legal apparatus for antidiscrimination law is based on intentional discrimination. Others suggest that practices leading to increased apprehensions and convictions are clearly intentional and based on racist beliefs (Parker et al., 2004; Wilson et al., 2004).

These issues of overrepresentation of minority group members at all levels of the justice system have profound effects not only for those who are accused and convicted but also for the victims of crime. Victims from racialized communities, knowing that members of their community are unfairly treated under the law, may feel both personal pressure and community pressure to not report crimes committed against them or testify in court. The Ontario Human Rights Commission (2003) reported that racial profiling seriously erodes public confidence in public institutions. As a result, people are mistrustful of the criminal justice system, law enforcement, customs and border control, and the education system. In a study conducted by the Commission, people of aboriginal ancestry reported significant alienation from the criminal justice system. Many communities expressed a lack of faith and sense of uselessness of registering complaints with police, human rights commissions, or other complaint bodies because they believed they would not be taken seriously or, worse yet, would be treated like suspects. The Commission was also told that negative treatment received from various service providers discouraged many racialized individuals from taking advantage of services that are taken for granted by mainstream communities. This conclusion was reinforced by research conducted by Dylan and colleagues (2008) in which aboriginal women reported reluctance to report crimes of violence committed against them as a result of previous experiences of being discounted, disbelieved, and accused of precipitating the violence.

■ Summary

A great deal of effort has been directed toward research in the area of victimology, legal policy analysis, and reform to improve protections for people to avoid victimization. Efforts are also needed to assist in obtaining justice for individuals and groups who have been victimized and in developing social service interventions to assist those suffering from victimization. For example, many forms of white-collar and corporate victimization reflect wider patterns of social and economic inequality and indicate a need for victim-centered initiatives to include these forms of crime. Added to these efforts are new innovations to further ensure safety and reduce harm caused by victimization. Nevertheless, victimization has a history as old as humankind, and the mechanisms to address the problem will continue to need refinement and creative new thinking.

■ Key Terms

Burglary: Unlawful entry of a residence, industry, or business, with or without force, with the intent to commit a larceny.

Corporate victimization: Classic white-collar crime involves personal gain at the expense of employers, the government, or clients (which can also be described as occupational crime).

Home invasion: Burglary of a dwelling while the residents are at home.

Larceny (or theft): Unlawful taking (or attempted taking) of property other than a motor vehicle from the possession of another by stealth with intent to permanently deprive the owner of the property.

Racial profiling: Any action undertaken for reasons of safety, security, or public protection that relies on stereotypes about race, color, ethnicity, ancestry, religion, or place of origin (or a combination of these) rather than on reasonable suspicion to single out an individual for greater scrutiny or different treatment.

Robbery: Unlawful taking or attempted taking of property that is in the immediate possession of another by force or threat of force.

Terrorism: Systematic use of terror especially as a means of coercion.

Theft: Taking of a person's property without the permission of the property owner or possessor of that property.

■ Discussion Questions

1. Discuss why home invasions are increasing.

2. Give a case of someone who has been victimized by a corporate crime.

3. What are the problems associated with documenting and measuring victimization from white-collar and corporate crime?

4. How might society deal with the fact that a person has been imprisoned for a crime for which is it later determined they did not commit?

5. How does racial profiling harm victims of crime?

■ Resources

Environmental Protection Agency
    http://www.epa.gov/

Innocence Project
    http://www.innocenceproject.org/

National Crime Prevention Council
    www.ncpc.org

National Institute for Occupational Safety and Health
    http://www.cdc.gov/niosh/

Office for Victims of Crime
    www.ojp.usdoj.gov/ovc

Office for Victims of Crime Resource Center
    www.ojp.usdoj.gov/ovc

■ References

Aboriginal Justice Implementation Commission. (2004). The justice system and aboriginal people. Retrieved from http://www.ajic.mb.ca/volumel/toc.html http://www.ajic.mb.ca/volume1

Ai, A., Evans-Campbell, T., Santangelo, L., & Cascio, T. (2006). The traumatic impact of the September 11, 2001, terrorist attacks and the potential protection of optimism. *Journal of Interpersonal Violence, 21*(5), 689–700.

Association of Certified Fraud Examiners. (2010). Report to the Nations on Occupational Fraud and Abuse. Retrieved from http://www.acfe.com/rttn-highlights.aspx

Bard, M., & Sangrey, D. (1986). *The crime victim's book*. (2d ed.). Secaucus, NJ: Citadel Press.

Basics of a Burglary Case. (2011). Retrieved from http://www.lawfirms.com/resources/criminal-defense/the-basics-a-burglary-case.htm

Birzer, M., & Birzer, G. (2006). Race matters: A critical look at racial profiling, it's a matter for the courts. *Journal of Criminal Justice, 34*(6) 643–651.

Blatt, D. (1998). The federal carjacking statute under commercial clause scrutiny after Lopez: *United States v. McHenry. University of Cincinnati Law Review, 66,* 747–774.

Bleich, A., Gelkopf, M., & Solomon, Z. (2003). Exposure to terrorism, stress-related mental health symptoms, and coping behaviors among a nationally representative sample in Israel. *Journal of the American Medical Association, 290*(5), 612–620.

Boesveld, T. (2012). Was chivalry's finest hour its last? *National Post.* April 14, 2012, A1.

Bogen, K., & Jones, E. (2006). Risks of mortality and morbidity from worldwide terrorism: 1968–2004. *Risk Analysis, 26*(1), 45–59.

Boyle, T. (2010). Province to compensate victims of Dr. Charles Smith. *Toronto Star,* August 10, A1.

Braithwaite, J. (1984). *Corporate crime in the pharmaceutical industry.* London: Routledge and Kegan Paul.

Canadian Criminal Justice Association. (1997). *Aboriginal peoples and the criminal justice system.* Retrieved from http://www.ccja-acjp.ca/en/abori2.html

Cardwell, D. (2001). Fugitive gang enforcer arrested in push-in robberies in the Bronx. *New York Times.* March 2, 2001. Retrieved from http://www.nytimes.com/2001/03/02/nyregion/fugitive-gang-enforcer-arrested-in-push-in-robberies-in-bronx.html

Castaneda, R. (2011). Man convicted in federal carjacking, home invasion case. Retrieved from http://www.washingtonpost.com/blogs/crime-scene/post/man-convicted-in-federal-carjacking-home-invasion-case/2011/07/18/gIQAgOxNMI_blog.html

CBC News. (2005, September 4). Hurricane Katrina Timeline. Retrieved from http://www.cbc.ca/news/background/katrina/katrina_timeline.html

CBC News. (2008, October 1). Dr. Charles Smith: The man behind the public inquiry. Retrieved from http://www.cbc.ca/news/background/crime/smith-charles.html

Colarossi, L., Heyman, J., & Phillips, M. (2005). Social workers' experiences of the World Trade Center disaster: Stressors and their relationship to symptom types. *Community Mental Health Journal, 41*(2), 185–198.

Cone, D.C., Weir, S.D., & Bogucki, S. (2003). Convergent volunteerism. *Annals of Emergency Medicine, 41*(4), 457–462.

Croall, H. (2001). The victims of white collar crime. In Lindgren, S. (Ed.), *White collar crime research. Old views and future potentials.* Sweden: National Council for Crime Prevention.

Croall, H. (2007). White collar crime, consumers and victimization. In G. Geis & H. Pontell (Eds.), *International handbook of white collar crime*. New York: Springer.

Dietz, P. (2009). Threat assessment: Workplace. *Wiley Encyclopedia of Forensic Science*.

Dylan, A., Regehr, C., & Alaggia, R. (2008). And justice for all? Aboriginal victims of sexual violence. *Violence Against Women, 14*(6), 678–696.

Environmental Protection Agency. (2012). Regulatory topics. Retrieved from http://www.epa.gov/lawsregs/topics/#air

FBI. (2008). Financial Crimes Report to the Public: Fiscal Year 2008. Retrieved from http://www.fbi.gov/stats-services/publications/fcs_report2008/financial-crimes-report-to-the-public#corporate

Federal Trade Commission. (2012). About the Bureau of Consumer Protection. Retrieved from http://www.ftc.gov/bcp/about.shtm

Gacki-Smith, J., Juarez, A., Boyett, L., Homeyer, C., Robinson, L., & MacLean, S. (2009). Violence against nurses working in US emergency departments. *Journal of Nursing Administration, 39*(7/8), 340–349.

Galea, S., Resnick, H., Ahern, J., Gold, J., Bucuvalas, M., Kilpatrick, D., . . . Vlahov, D. (2002). Posttraumatic stress disorder in Manhattan, New York City, after the September 11th terrorist attacks. *Journal of Urban Health: Bulletin of the New York Academy of Medicine, 79*(3), 340–353.

Georgakopoulos, N. (2004). Self-fulfilling impressions of criminality: Unintentional racial profiling. *International Review of Law and Economics, 24*, 169–190.

Gibbs, C., & Simpson, S. (2011). Measuring corporate environmental crime rates: Progress and problems. *Crime, Law and Social Change, 51*(1), 87–107.

Glancy, G., & Regehr, C. (2012). From schadenfreude to contemplation: Lessons for forensic experts. *Journal of the American Academy of Psychiatry and the Law, 40*(1), 81–88.

Goudge, S. (2008). *Inquiry into pediatric forensic pathology in Ontario report*. Toronto: Ministry of the Attorney General.

Green, S. (1999). Castles and carjackers: Proportionality and the use of deadly force in defense of dwellings and vehicles. *University of Illinois Law Review, 1*, 1–42.

Hancock County. (2011). Information for victims of property crime. Hancock County, Indiana. Retrieved from http://www.hancockcoingov.org/property-crimes.html

Herald-Dispatch. (2012). Gallery: The Buffalo Creek Flood. Feb. 26, 2012. Retrieved from http://www.herald-dispatch.com/specialsections/100years/x1107815709/Gallery-The-Buffalo-Creek-Flood

Hunt, M., & Hughey, A. (2010). Workplace violence: Impact and prevention. *KCA Journal, 29*(1), 39–43.

Hurley, J. (1995). Violent crime hits home: Home invasion robbery. FBI Law Enforcement Bulletin. Retrieved from http://findarticles.com/p/articles/mi_m2194/is_n6_v64/ai_17312586

Innocence Project. (2008). The Innocence Project. Retrieved from http://www.innocenceproject.org/

Jacobs, B., Topalli, V., & Wright, R. (2003). Carjacking, streetlife, and offender motivation. *British Journal of Criminology, 43*, 673–688.

Leahy, P. (2003). Leahy urges Senate to vote on DNA bill. Retrieved from http://leahy.senate.gov/press/200410/100704B.html

Loomis, D., Marshall, S., Wolf, S., Runyan, C., & Butts, J. (2002). Effectiveness of safety measures recommended for prevention of workplace homicide. *Journal of the American Medical Association, 287*(8), 1011–1017.

Malpass, R. (2006). A policy evaluation of simultaneous and sequential lineups. *Psychology, Public Policy and Law, 12*(4), 394–418.

Moohr, G. (2007). On the prospects of deterring corporate crime. *Journal of Business and Technology Law, 2*(1), 25–41.

Moyer, L. (2009). It could have been worse. *Forbes.* June 29, 2009. Retrieved from http://www.forbes.com/2009/06/24/bernie-madoff-prison-sentence-business-beltway-madoff.html

National Center for Victims of Crime. (2011). Robbery. Retrieved from http://www.ncvc.org/ncvc/main.aspx?dbName=DocumentViewer&DocumentID=32367

National Institute for Occupational Safety and Health. (2012). Diseases and Injuries. Retrieved from http://www.cdc.gov/niosh/

Norris, F.H., Friedman, M.J., Watson, P.J., Byrnie, C.M., Diaz, E., & Kaniasty, K. (2002). 60,000 disaster victims speak, part 1: An empirical review of the empirical literature, 1981–2001. *Psychiatry: Interpersonal and Biological Process, 65*(3), 207–239.

North, C.S., & Pfefferbaum, B. (2002). Research on the mental health effects of terrorism. *Journal of the American Medical Association, 288*(5), 633–636.

Ontario Human Rights Commission. (2003). Paying the price: The human cost of racial profiling. Retrieved from http://ohrc.yy.net/en/resources/news/NewsRelease.2006-05-17.8048765200

Parker, K., MacDonald, J., Alpert, F., Smith, M., & Piquero, A. (2004). A contextual study of racial profiling. *American Behavioral Scientist, 47*(7), 943–962.

Perry, R.W., & Lindell, M.K. (2003). Understanding citizen response to disasters with implications for terrorism. *Journal of Contingencies and Crisis Management, 11*(2), 49–60.

Price, M., & Norris, D. (2009). White collar crime: Corporate and securities and commodities fraud. *Journal of the American Academy of Psychiatry and the Law,* 37, 538–544.

Regehr, C., & Bober, T. (2005). *In the line of fire: Trauma in the emergency services.* New York: Oxford University Press.

Schlenger, W., Caddell, J., Ebert, L., Jordan, K., Rourke, K., & Wilson, D. (2002). Psychological reactions to terrorist attacks: Findings from a national survey of American's reactions to September 11, 2001, terrorist attacks. *New England Journal of Medicine,* 345, 1507–1512.

Schwartz, N. (2011). Erin Brockovich Returns To Hinkley Testing Chromium-Polluted Water. *Huffington Post.* 03/09/2011. Retrieved from http://www.huffingtonpost.com/2011/03/09/erin-brockovich-returns-to-hinkley_n_833423.html

Senate OKs new home invasion law. (2008). Retrieved from http://www.newstimes.com/latestnews/ci_8048791

Simpson, S. (2002). *Corporate crime, law and social control.* Cambridge: Cambridge University Press.

Sporer, S., Koehnken, G., & Malpass, R. (1996). Introduction: 200 years of identification. In S. Sporer, R. Malpass, & G. Koehnken (Eds.), *Psychological issues in eyewitness identification* (pp. 1–6). Hillsdale, NJ: Erlbaum.

Statistics Canada. (2001). Aboriginal peoples of Canada. Retrieved from http://www12.statcan.ca/english/census01/Products/Analytic/companion/abor/canada.cfm#1

Stellman, J., Smith, R., Katz, C., Sharma, V., Charney, D., Herbert, R.,…, Southwick, S. (2008). Enduring mental health morbidity and social function impairment in World Trade Center rescue, recovery and cleanup workers: The psychological dimension of an environmental health disaster. *Environmental Health Perspectives, 116*(9), 1248–1253.

Sutherland, E. (1949). *White-collar crime.* New York: The Dryden Press.

Thomas, P. (2011). Maryland serial-killer suspect Jason Thomas Scott "evil," victim's mom says. Retrieved from http://abcnews.go.com/GMA/jason-thomas-scott-suspected-maryland-serial-killer-evil/story?id=11266673

U.S. Census Bureau. (2006). National population estimates. Retrieved from http://www.census.gov/popest/national/

U.S. Department of Justice. (n.d.a). Capital punishment statistics. Retrieved from http://www.ojp.usdoj.gov/bjs/cp.htm

U.S. Department of Justice. (n.d.b). Technical working group for eyewitness evidence. Retrieved from http://www.ncjrs.gov/nij/eyewitness /tech_working_group.html

U.S. Department of Justice. (2010). Crime in the United States: Robbery. Retrieved from http://www.fbi.gov/about-us/cjis/ucr/crime-in-the-u.s/2010/crime-in-the-u.s.-2010/violent-crime/robberymain

U.S. Department of Labor. (2011). Injuries, illnesses and fatalities. Retrieved from http://www.bls.gov/iif/oshcfoi1.htm

U.S. Department of State. (2001). Patterns of global terrorism. Retrieved from www.state.gov/s/ct/rls/pgtrpt

Weisaeth, L., & Tonnessen, A. (2003). Responses of individuals and groups to consequences of technological disasters and radiation exposure. In R. Ursano (Ed.), *Terrorism and disaster: Individual and community interventions* (pp. 209–235). New York: Cambridge University Press.

Wilson, G., Dunham, R., & Alpert, G. (2004). Prejudice in police profiling. *American Behavioral Scientist, 47*(7), 896–909.

Name Index

This index contains proper names. For subject references, please see the separately presented Subject Index.

Subject Index

Tables, figures and boxes are indicated by an italic *t*, *f*, or *b*, respectively. Please see the separately presented Name Index for references to proper names.

battered woman syndrome defense,
313–315, 319
batterers
intervention programs for, 317–318
risk of violence with, 308–312,
309t, 311t
typologies of, 306–308, 308t
battery, civil action in, 179t
Bay Area Women Against Rape, 117
BCS. *see* British Crime Survey
Beck Depression Inventory, 131
*Behavior of Organisms: An Experimental
Analysis* (Skinner), 132
Behavioral Science Unit (FBI), 451–452,
457–458
Beirut embassy attack (1981), 497
beltway snipers, 453
bench trial, 164
Beyond the Pleasure Principle (Freud), 128
bias, in victim surveys, 60–61
Bill of Rights, 164, 166, 172, 175,
511–512, 558
biological theories, 74
BJS. *see* Bureau of Justice Statistics
blame, by co-victims, 469
"blaming the victim," 370
blitz rape, 381–382, 398
"Bloody Code," 175
*Blueprint for the Future of the Uniform Crime
Reporting Program* (FBI), 38
body location scene, 25
bombings
evidence collection at, 22t
FBI victim assistance for, 111–112, 112t
Booth v. Maryland (1987), 173
"botnets," 515
break and enter, 545
Briquet's syndrome, 127
British Crime Survey (BCS), 34t, 57
bullying. *see also* school violence
defined, 283
effects of, 268–270, 271t
factors contributing to, 266–268
incidence of, 266
prevention of, 270–271
toleration of, 262–263
types of, 266
Bully-Proofing Your School, 270
burden of proof, 166, 180
Bureau of Justice Statistics (BJS), 44, 52, 481
burglary, 12, 545–546, 546f, 560

C

Canada
battered woman syndrome defense in,
313–315
central statistical office, 15
child labor in, 244
child pornography legislation in, 512
costs of victimization in, 16
court system in, 156
crime databases for, 34t
decrease in crime in, 15
estimate of wife assault, 292
ethics in victim services, 126
hate crimes in, 481–482, 484–485
homicide rates in, 438
honor killings, 312, 312t
intimate partner violence in, 293,
297–298, 340
lack of elder abuse laws, 410
legislation against exploitation, 235–236
legislation against gangs, 265
missing children program, 231–232, 232t
rape-law reform in, 364
recognition of marital rape, 295
serial murder in, 445
spousal homicide in, 310
stalking in, 331, 332–333, 334
victim impact statements, 114
victims' rights legislation in, 104–106,
109, 112–113
youthful offenders legislation in, 143
Canada Border Services Agency, 231–232
Canadian Centre for Justice Statistics, 40, 44
Canadian Charter of Rights and Freedoms, 485
Canadian Constitution, 149, 153
Canadian Department of Justice, 126
Canadian General Social Survey, 56
Canadian Police Information Centre, 531
cao gio, 201
capital punishment, 174–177, 439, 558
capitalism, 88
caregiver stress/burden, 416, 417, 424–425
carjacking, 548
Casey Anthony case, 6, 141–142, 163–164,
168–171, 173
CBT. *see* cognitive-behavioral therapy
celebrity stalking, 335, 336–338, 350
Cell 2455, Death Row (Chessman), 176
cesarean section murder, 236
change of plea hearings, 164
charges, pressing, 160–161